BERT GREENE'S *Kitchen*

A COOKBOOK CELEBRATION OF

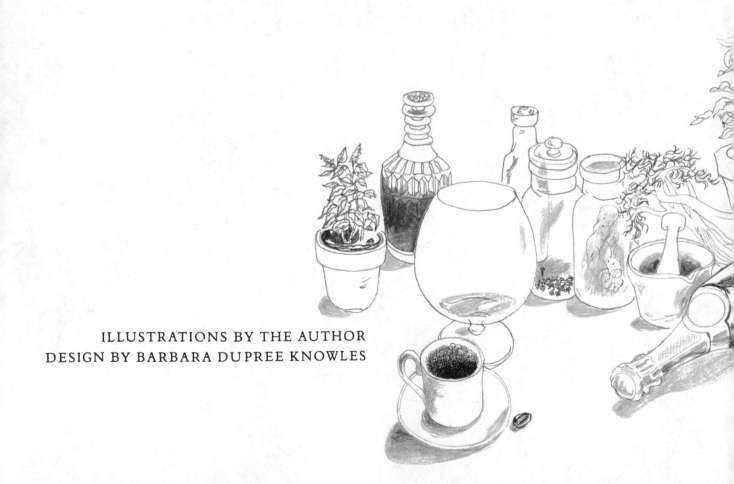

ILLUSTRATIONS BY THE AUTHOR
DESIGN BY BARBARA DUPREE KNOWLES

Bouquets

AROMAS AND FLAVORS

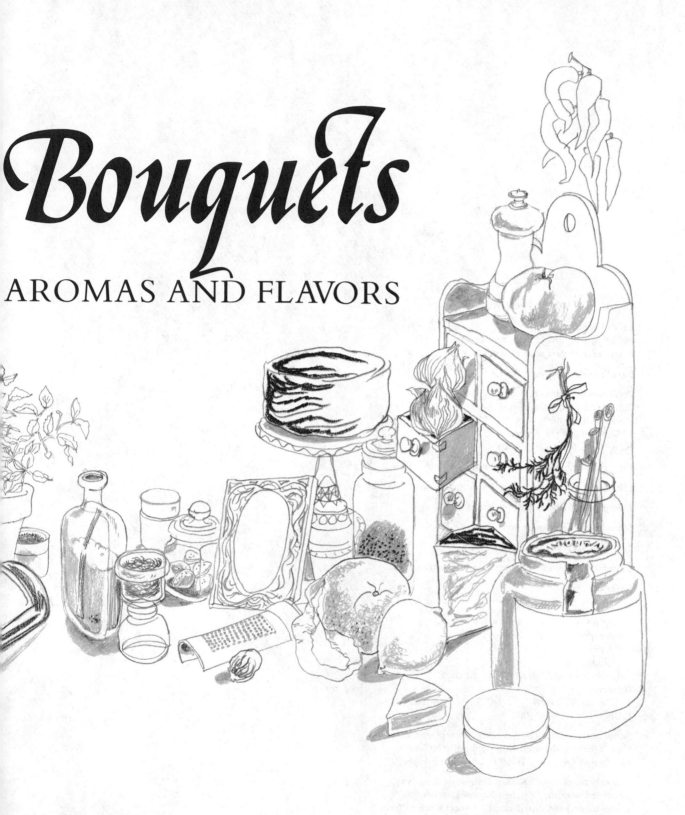

A FIRESIDE BOOK
Published by Simon & Schuster, Inc.
NEW YORK

First Fireside Edition, 1986

Published by Simon & Schuster, Inc.
Simon & Schuster Building
Rockefeller Center
1230 Avenue of the Americas
New York, New York 10020

Originally published by Contemporary Books, Inc.

FIRESIDE and colophon are registered trademarks of Simon & Schuster, Inc.

Designed by Barbara DuPree Knowles

Manufactured in the United States of America

10 9 8 7 6 5 4 3 2 1 Pbk.

Library of Congress Cataloging in Publication Data

Greene, Bert.
    Bert Greene's kitchen bouquets.

    Reprint. Originally published: Chicago:
Contemporary Books, 1979.
    "A Fireside book."
    Includes index.
    1. Cookery. I. Title. II. Title: Kitchen
bouquets.
TX715.G8119   1986   641.5   86-13835
ISBN 0-671-62793-7 Pbk.

Some of the material in this book has appeared in rather
altered form in the following publications: *Cuisine,
Gentlemen's Quarterly, Travel & Leisure,* and *Vogue.*

The title *Bert Greene's Kitchen Bouquets* is in no way
associated with the "Kitchen Bouquet" products
manufactured and distributed by Grocery Store Products
Company, Westchester, Pa.

This book is lovingly dedicated
to the memory of

Margo Henderson

She never lived to see it in print,
but her boundless enthusiasm and overwhelming
support (moral and otherwise)
helped make it possible

Contents

BERT
GREENE'S *Kitchen Bouquets*

Introduction

TO THE 1986 EDITION

If books are a writer's children (and make no mistake, they are) the favored progeny never diminishes in the parental eye—no matter what torturous upheaval it may have wreaked during the birthing process.

Kitchen Bouquets was written in the darkest period of my life. My best friend and ardent supporter—to whom the book is dedicated—was inexplicably dying at age thirty-four, and in and out of hospitals constantly. Time spent at her bedside was literally stolen from its pages. Never facing the reality of her day-to-day life, we would fitfully talk about "the book" instead. Contemplation of its future seemed to give sustenance and a curious opiate to deal with pain. An unfulfilled though extraordinarily talented singer, she believed this book would break the barrier for me, at least. And that knowledge nourished her. I must confess I was not so confident. So broke (financially) during the book's long gestation, at one point I could not afford to pay the gas and electric bill to finish testing its recipes. The final version may never have seen light (or hard cold print) if the original publisher had not sent me a highly unorthodox advance on as yet unearned royalties—to turn the power back on!

However, each successive chapter became more potent in spite of every new adversity.

More than anything I have written, this book gave me the instinct to know *exactly* who I am—and the fortitude to write (and cook) as I please without giving a damn about passing fancies or prandial fads. It also made me very many warm good friends all over the world.

When *Kitchen Bouquets* was first printed, some wag said: "Greene writes novels with recipes on the side." No compliment pleased me more—at least until the following quote appeared in the New York *Daily News,* two months after the book's publication.

"This volume is . . . a true cookbook, filled with 350 recipes; an explicit and eclectic collection of extraordinarily good food, lusty and seductive food that makes you want to eat. On the other hand . . . it is also an autobiography, a rambling, warm, anecdotal and sometimes sad account of a life that, from the beginning, has been full of close person-to-person encounters. *Kitchen Bouquets* reads like a split screen—food on one side, life on the other. The result is an extremely odd cookbook; unexpected and much too big to be taken at one sitting."

What more can one say about a pet child—out of six, so far? It is my hope that this collection of bouquets will perfume your life half as much as it has mine.

Bert Greene
April 1986

BERT GREENE'S *Kitchen Bouquets*

Author's Note

Scent of scents? Flavor of flavors? For me there is no talisman aroma that summons the dim luster of my past with one sudden rush of authority. My nose, I am afraid, has been far and away too spoiled by the giant banquet of a good life. Monsieur Proust's slender beak was more fortunate in confronting only the single bouquet of a madeleine crumbled in his tea cup!

The essences I mean to extol in print are those favored in my kitchen. This collection is a testament to the culinary versatility of a whole garland of flavors—with the cookery compounded by a little lore and legend and great deal more personal feeling and prejudice.

Recipes are clustered in these bouquets of aromatics according to the flavorings that give them unusual zest. So do not be too irritated with the author when you discover that the formula for Garlic Almonds is not included in the section on "Almonds" at all. Instead, you'll find this piquant hors d'oeuvre under "Garlic," because the pungent herb is the key to its character.

Similarly, there are four or five remarkable chocolate cakes included in this collection but the cookbook writer has excercised the option of tucking them away under "Orange," "Tomato," "Rum," or "Almond," as the case may be, because it is these flavorings that distinguish their chocolate-ness.

This book was an olfactory joy to produce. I know that the dishes will please because I have inhaled the wonderful and myriad aromas of each from cookpot to fork-end. I can only wish you the same delectable experience!

There is no way possibly to thank all the many friends whose time and labor helped cull and arrange this kitchen bouquet. Phillip Schulz's efforts are lauded elsewhere in the text, but it must also be noted that without his demanding palate and diligent testing of recipes (over and over again until they were deemed worthy of inclusion), there would not have been a book at all. Other kitchens across the country were pressed into service as testing grounds as well: to Betsy Cooper, Pati Scott, and Mildred Schulz—a very special debt of author's gratitude.

To Myra Greene, who typed most of this manuscript and corrected a vast amount of questionable spelling and worse grammar—another kudo.

There are three others who deserve encomiums. Nao Hauser brilliantly edited this book against almost insuperable odds, including long distance, while Barbara Knowles designed it with elegance and logic and I am eternally grateful for their twin efforts. My last acknowledgment is to my publisher, Harvey Plotnick, who contracted for a slim volume and received this mammoth enterprise instead—without any demurral whatsoever.

Bless them all.

Introduction

The kitchens in which I have been happiest have not been miracles of modern enterprise.

I don't know why, but the mystique of the microwave, the Garland range, and those islands of tile and burled butcher block have always eluded me. When I had money to afford such utility, I frankly hadn't the heart. Instead, I bought my kitchen a grandmotherly rocking chair—with hand-carved applewood scrolls. And a spatterware bowl or two. Appropriately, blue.

My rationalization for not renovating was quite lame. I claimed an unwillingness to disinter the happy shades that had carved and chopped there ages before me. Actually, I mistrusted the spic and the span of the new-fledged.

Sensuality is what I love best about cooking. It is the frizzle of bacon on the back burner and the froth of scalded cream whisked into vanilla and sugar until the pans, sink, cook, and even the walls are pale, polka-spotted that make a kitchen kitchenly. Remove the mess and, for me, you dispel a measure of the magic.

I grew up during the Depression of the 1930s. Our family larder, however, although not as full as it once had been, was never empty. We were impoverished but, as my sister and I were constantly reminded, others were poorer—they did not *eat* as we did.

Yet there was no savor to our kitchen. My mother was a perfunctory cook whose pride kept a taut galley. There were no home-worked fragrances of bubbling stews and soups on her stove because they would have taken both time and love to create and she had neither of these to expend. My mother went to work early on and considered her timecard an emancipation from the chores she never had enjoyed in the first place.

I inherited the chef's mantle in our household, not through any initiative on my part but merely because I had the most freedom to essay the role.

My first encounters with *cuisine de la faire* began drearily. I peeled and put the potatoes on a gas jet at five o'clock each night. Later, I learned to mash them. Later still, I added chopped parsley and turned them green or grated American cheese into them and turned them orange—both less than tonic results. But somehow I did develop a solid repertoire of potato cookery.

Meat preparation followed potatoes in my realm of experimentation. And I quickly discovered the animate tang that a dash of garlic, clove, orange peel, or red pepper can add to even the simplest of fare.

Like all innocents in love, of course, I overdid. Some of my early attempts at seasoning were so dreadful (really inedible!) that my working parents hinted at banishment from my kingdom of pots and pans. Alas, they couldn't exercise the option. I was there at the stove—and they were not. I continued to cook and reason came to prevail. In time, my *plats du jour* even gave relish to their diet.

I inherit my celebration of aroma from my grandmother. She was a lady who lived for house and garden. Whatever her matriarchal frailties, she erred only on the side of homely pleasures. She cooked like an angel—and her thumb was solid jade!

My grandmother's house was modest but her garden was an embarrassment of riches; the trees and flowers were the showiest in the neighborhood. Her azalea bush, a minimal Easter Sunday variety, grew to staggering proportions—ten or twelve feet in diameter, spring after spring. And why not, when she poured the very best of her gravies and soup stocks on its roots all winter long!

My grandmother lived near the old Durkee factory (not far from where the Long Island Railroad bisects the narrowest section of Queens on its trek eastward), the spices of which always perfumed her garden as heavily as the attar of pot herbs suffused her kitchen stove. When it was going to rain, one always knew it in advance because the street outside was fragrant with the musk of Durkee cinnamon; when the weather was stable, Durkee's allspice hung in the still air!

When I turned ten or eleven, we lost our big house and moved to a small apartment several miles away. The rupture caused by the loss was stunning. The grammar school where I was transferred was old and fusty but my mother liked it, precisely because it seemed so venerable. I would develop standards there, she predicted. I did. I also contracted innumerable colds, traveling back and forth the twenty or so blocks in rain and snow.

I hated the brown lunch bag with a passion but I hated school lunchrooms more. Instead of eating with my schoolmates, who were all relative strangers then, I chose to eat my cold sandwich on the streets, wandering about in the vacant lots and back alleys and throwing most of my lunch to the pigeons, who were happier there than I.

It was my grandmother who excised the brown lunch bag from my life. She, who lived closer to my school than we, observed me climbing the railroad sidings alone one midday and allowed as how it might be better if I partook of a hot meal with her and my maiden aunt (who never worked or cooked or even washed a dish in that house as long as my grandmother was well and strong).

I cannot know if the invitation was generously advanced—or if my mother conspired for the overture. But the bid was made and, being by nature greedy, I acceded. And it was in my grandmother's kitchen, redolent with bouquets always, that I learned to temper my seasoning spoon.

My grandmother cooked quickly. She made an omelet in one motion, using a fork to beat the eggs (no wire whisk for her) and then the same fork to scramble the golden froth in a buttery pan. She would fill the runny center with perhaps a mince of leftover asparagus tips and chives and turn the whole delectable dish onto a warmed plate with the very same fork. All in less than five minutes.

We developed a curious rapport, my grandmother and I, over our mutual menus. She, the master, and I, the acolyte. Many days I would be late for my first afternoon class because I lingered too long while she advanced her theory as to why my souffle had fallen the night before. Or, having listened thoughtfully to my recipe for chicken salad with fresh peas added for crunchiness, she would suggest that nuts would be crunchier (almonds, if one toasted them first) and that the peas might be nicer on the side, served warm with just a little mint, which she would then proceed to pick for me from her herb garden.

Yes, I learned the pungence of aromatic cookery at my grandmother's elbow—and I never forgot the lessons.

The quest for tincture and spice sent me roaming through the kitchens of the Old World (reversing Columbus's order of things) but it all began in a little frame kitchen in Queens, where a tiny, energetic woman instructed me about the first rules of cooking. "Does it smell good?" she would question as I entered her kitchen. "If it smells good, it will taste good!"

This book is a compendium of the experience with aromatics that I have acquired since I left the world of my grandmother.

Years after my grandmother, Minna, died, I read about Colette's mother, Sido, and I recognized the common blood the two women shared. When I adapted Colette's stories about her childhood into a play, *My Mother's House,* which was later televised, a phrase of the original text clung to the dialogue like perfume.

What Colette said of her mother, I quote about my mother's mother: "Both the house and the garden are living still, I know; but what of that, if the magic has deserted them? If the secret is lost that opened to me a whole world—lights, scents, birds, and trees in perfect harmony, the murmur of human voices now silent forever—a world of which I have ceased to be worthy?"

BERT GREENE'S KITCHEN BOUQUETS

Almond

The smell of almonds toasting in a metal pan, their papery skins turning rusty as the kernels scorch, is the most agreeable incense I know.

I can still remember my vigorous grandmother snatching up a handful of these blazing nuts from the top of her coal stove just before they burned. Having greased her worn hands with butter, she would press the almonds between her palms and—in an action so swift one hardly had time to observe it—rub them together to peel them. Coincidentally, she filled her kitchen with a scent more redolent than any perfume I have ever sniffed before or after.

My mother went to Paris for the very first time when she was seventy. Although she was impressed with the wonders of the city—the Eiffel Tower, the Louvre, the Tuilleries—by far her most indelible perception was of those ancient ladies, the nut sellers, who preside over small charcoal stands along the corners of chic boulevards, raking almonds and sugar together so that Parisians may nibble sweetmeats as they stroll.

"It was a smell I recognized at once," my mother confided to me later. "Mama's kitchen before the holidays!"

Like my parent, I, too, recognized the scent. Almonds and sugar meant Passover *seders* spent in the matriarchal bosom when I was a very small boy.

As the youngest male at the family table at that time, I was the one designated by tradition to ask the four *kashes*. These are the mysterious questions, chanted during the long ritual dinner, that prompt the retelling of Jewish history. They begin, "Why is this night different from all other nights?'' But I was much too shy and diffidently gentile in my upbringing ever to attempt such a query. The questions were spoken by my elders instead, while I, only mildly censured for my defection, shrank from the responsibility year after year.

My grandmother's enclave, the kitchen, became my refuge from the torment of the limelight. There I would sniff the rich food in various stages of deliverance from oven to table and watch with unabashed admiration as the masterful cook went about her appointed tasks.

Having toasted and peeled the almonds for her unleavened Passover specialty, she would pound them with sugar and matzo flour to produce a golden nut sponge. As light as air but drier than an August dust storm to the tongue, the cake was inevitably served with slender, crystal stemware filled to brimming with the watery liqueurs that my grandfather made in his basement still. Slivowitz, kümmel, and kirschwasser (all as colorless as high octane and twice as fiery) would be drunk, pleasurelessly it seemed, in the living room. All my male relatives would tilt their throats backward before they imbibed; each murmured ''L'chaim'' silently to the others before the liquid touched their lips. Although, in truth, they knew nothing of the life to which they toasted.

There is something else I remember about almonds and the *seders* at my grandmother's house. A bowl of unshelled nuts was always brought to the table after the main course but before coffee and tea were served. They were offered as an extra course—to be consumed while the wine stains were being sponged off the damask tablecloth. Year after year, the almonds came to the table in the very same manner: piled high in a heavy, cut-glass bowl of unusual design. A crystal porringer on legs, it was etched with a faint tracery of roses and its prisms scattered the light over the pale, golden nuts.

I have good reason to know the bowl well, for this crystal remnant of all my grandmother's prized table possessions was finally passed down to me when my own mother died. I loved it dearly but must confess it sat unused on a coffee table in my dining room in Amagansett. Austere and empty, except for occasional arrangements of dried flowers, it endured until the night my ever-inquisitive kitten, Dinah, swatted it (and its contents of scarlet rose hips) to the slate floor while the household slept.

Had it been omened?

Shortly before, I had visited a medium for the first (and only) time in my life. I made this sortie with some trepidation, but the spiritualist turned out to be notably commonplace. He resembled nothing so much as a young businessman and lived in a typical studio apartment on New York's chic East Side. And, far from extolling any cabal or forensic prowess, he merely explained that his psychic gift permitted him to receive missives from beyond "like telephone calls."

The séance was conducted in broad daylight and I was told to relax completely but, if possible, to note all messages on the pad of lined yellow paper provided—"for future reference," the seer said. While I held my ball-point at the ready, he closed his eyes and promptly went into a trance.

After delivering some canon from persons positively unknown to me, the medium finally opened his eyes and announced a communication from my Uncle Benjy. As I had no relative by that name, I dismissed this relay as well—until suddenly it came upon me that my mother had indeed had a brother (probably ten or twelve years older than she) who died when she was an infant. A sibling named Ben.

In a flurry of metaphysics, I commanded the seer to bypass Benjy (after all, what had this kid to say to me?) and allow some tidings from my grandmother instead. I had recently praised her talents in a cookbook that had just been published.

The medium tried. He tried very hard, actually, but could find no dispatch to satisfy my request.

"It's very strange. I only get an image now," he reported flatly after some while. "It is a crystal receptacle, like a cut-glass football sliced at the midsection and standing on three short glass legs. And this is very strange—the bowl is filled with almonds."

Not strange to me. They belonged there. What he didn't foretell, however, is how short-lived the bowl would be without them! Meanwhile, Dinah flourishes!

Unlike my grandparent, I never serve almonds after a meal. My recipe file does include spectacular Garlic Almonds (see Index), which I usually pass around with drinks. And another almond formulation, Snow Almonds, sometimes makes an hors d'oeuvre appearance at my dinner parties as well. I borrowed the idea from a wonderful book, *The Art of Turkish Cooking,* by Neset Eren. And although I amended Ms. Eren's original dictum with a grain or two of salt, the dish is otherwise traditionally Ottoman. The nuts are not roasted but rather pickled in ice water and served on a frosty bed of ice. If that sounds a bit disconcerting, be assured that these almonds are most salubrious to the palate even with the frostiest martini a host can provide.

SNOW ALMONDS

1 pound shelled almonds
2 tablespoons kosher salt

Serves 10.

1 Place almonds in a plastic container or a bowl. Add salt and cold water to cover. Refrigerate tightly covered 4 to 5 days.

2 One day before serving, drain almonds. Rub off and discard skins. Return almonds to container; cover with cold water. Refrigerate tightly covered until just before serving time.

3 Several hours before serving, fill a glass bowl or serving dish with 2 to 3 inches of water; place in freezer until solidly frozen. At serving time, drain almonds thoroughly; spread over the top of ice.

Note: You can, if you wish, dust the Snow Almonds lightly with additional kosher salt before serving.

According to the Book of Numbers, Moses's brother Aaron placed his rod into the ground at Mount Ararat and the stick instantly blossomed into an almond tree. Samson is said to have courted Delilah with offerings of almond branches (though lemons probably would have been more appropriate). Esau sold his birthright for a mess of pottage, which was almost certain to have been a lentil stew mixed with crushed almonds, since the ancient Mesopotamians always used these nuts for thickeners.

For an example of the last-named biblical tradition, consider a tasty bowl of Cream of Almond Soup. This excellent dish (a rich relation of Vichyssoise) calls for flavorsome, pulverized almonds as a lacing for chicken broth enriched with cream and egg yolks. Try it hot or cold—it is excellent in either guise.

CREAM OF ALMOND SOUP

2 cups blanched almonds
4 cups strong chicken stock
1 small onion
1 cup whipping cream
½ teaspoon ground coriander
4 egg yolks
Dash of hot pepper sauce
Chopped chives
Grated orange peel

Serves 6 to 8.

1 Chop the almonds; then pound them to a paste in a mortar or grind in a food processor until the texture of smooth peanut butter.

2 Bring the chicken stock to a boil in a large saucepan; stir in the almond paste until thoroughly blended. Add onion; reduce heat. Simmer 30 minutes; discard onion. Stir in the cream and coriander; simmer 5 minutes.

3 Lightly beat the egg yolks; stir ½ cup hot soup into egg yolks. Gradually stir egg yolk mixture into the soup. Add hot pepper sauce. Cook over low heat, stirring constantly, until thickened; do not boil.

4 Serve hot or well-chilled. Garnish with chopped chives and orange peel.

Note: I find Tabasco brand hot pepper sauce to be less watery than others and preferable for all cooking.

For toasted (or roasted) almonds, I usually blanch the nuts in a small amount of boiling water and then peel them and allow them to dry in a low (200°) oven for about 45 minutes. When they are crisp, I place about 1½ cups of almonds in a heavy skillet with about 2 tablespoons of butter and toss the mixture over moderately low heat until the nuts turn a deep ivory color.

Like my mother and grandmother, I am decidedly addicted to the perfume of these nuts browning atop the stove. However, I add my own touch as well, having discovered that a final splash of about 1 tablespoon of good dry sherry makes the bouquet of the sizzling nuts absolutely irresistible. Seasoned with a measure of salt and pepper, these almonds make an excellent cocktail snack but are even more roborant in conjunction with cooked dishes.

Please note that toasted almonds wilt when soaked in liquids too long. So the following Shrimp Quiche with Almonds must be made just before it goes into the oven—and eaten as soon as it cools. This is one quiche, moreover, that definitely *should not be frozen* prior to baking!

SHRIMP QUICHE WITH ALMONDS

1 To prepare the pastry: Combine flour, salt, sugar, butter, and shortening. Blend with a pastry blender or two forks until the texture of coarse crumbs. Gradually add enough water to form a dough. Knead briefly; refrigerate 1 hour.

2 Heat oven to 325°. Butter a 9- to 10-inch quiche pan. Roll out dough; line pan with pastry. Line pastry with aluminum foil; fill with dried rice or beans. Bake 20 minutes. Remove foil and rice or beans.

3 Increase oven heat to 400°. Combine all ingredients for the filling. Pour into the pastry. Bake until light brown, 25 to 30 minutes. Let stand at least 5 minutes at room temperature before serving.

For the pastry:
1½ cups all-purpose flour
¼ teaspoon salt
Pinch of granulated sugar
6 tablespoons cold butter
2¼ tablespoons cold shortening
3¾ to 4½ tablespoons cold water

For the filling:
½ pound uncooked shrimp, shelled, deveined, coarsely chopped
¼ cup chopped toasted almonds
1 cup whipping cream
2 tablespoons clam juice
2 eggs plus 1 egg yolk, lightly beaten
⅛ teaspoon grated nutmeg
Salt to taste

Serves 6 to 8.

Almonds are a crunchy bite of history from Hammurabi to Hershey bars. Historians note their appearance in a kitchen in 400 B.C., when some Anatolian first combined the nuts with cooking meat. Four of the most tonic recipes I know are similar inspirations.

Lamb Pilau Faisal is an authentic Iranian stew stirred up a bit on home shores. The fresh mint and gingerroot are definitely prerequisites for its unique savor and it loses much without the crunch of almonds, too. I know—I've made it both ways!

2 pounds boneless lamb, cut in 1-inch cubes
Flour
Salt and freshly ground pepper
⅓ cup vegetable or olive oil
4 tablespoons butter
2 large onions, chopped
1 clove garlic, minced
1 green pepper, cut into thin, 2-inch-long strips
1 teaspoon chopped fresh mint
½ teaspoon chopped gingerroot
½ cinnamon stick
2 cardamom pods
4 cloves
1¼ cups chicken broth (approximately)
Juice of 1 lemon
2 tomatoes, chopped
¾ cup unflavored yogurt
⅓ cup white raisins
Dry sherry
⅓ cup toasted sliced almonds
Chopped parsley for garnish
4 to 6 cups cooked rice

Serves 4 to 6.

LAMB PILAU FAISAL

1 Pat meat dry with paper toweling. Season the flour with salt and pepper; coat meat with flour mixture. Heat oil and butter in a heavy skillet; saute meat until golden brown on all sides. Remove meat with a slotted spoon; place in a Dutch oven.

2 Add onions and garlic to skillet; saute 3 minutes. Add green pepper and mint; cook 3 minutes. Add onion mixture, ginger, cinnamon, cardamom, cloves, and chicken broth to meat (use more broth if needed to cover meat).

3 Simmer meat, stirring frequently, 15 minutes. Add lemon juice, tomatoes, yogurt, and salt and pepper to taste; simmer partially covered until meat is tender, about 2½ hours.

4 Meanwhile, soak raisins in sherry to cover 15 minutes. Drain; reserve raisins.

5 Add raisins to meat; simmer 5 minutes. Add the almonds; sprinkle with parsley. Serve with rice.

Almonds were first cultivated in Europe at the beginning of the seventeenth century—just about the same time that a canny French palace chef named François Pierre de la Varenne discovered that less than prime cuts of meat could (with some imagination) be coaxed into kitchen delicacies. Thus the founder of classical French cuisine happened upon the combination of almonds and tongue. This dish is only slightly abridged from La Varenne's cookbook, *le Cuisinier français,* published in 1651.

SMOKED TONGUE WITH ALMONDS

1 Place tongue in a large bowl. Add water salted with 1 tablespoon salt per quart of water to cover. Let stand 1 hour.

2 Remove tongue from brine; place in a large heavy kettle. Add sliced onion, onion stuck with cloves, the carrot, celery, bay leaves, 1 large clove garlic, the parsley, port, and enough water to cover. Simmer until tender, about 3 hours. Remove skin from tongue; return tongue to cooking liquid. Keep warm.

3 To make the sauce, saute the almonds in the oil in a saucepan until brown. Remove with a slotted spoon; drain on paper toweling. Add chopped onion and the bruised clove garlic to saucepan; saute until onion is tender. Stir in the consomme and tomato paste; cook over low heat 10 minutes. Mix the cornstarch with ¼ cup Madeira in a small bowl; stir until smooth. Stir cornstarch mixture into saucepan with the sugar, spices, salt, pepper, and vinegar. Cook until thick, about 5 minutes; strain. Return sauce to saucepan over low heat; stir in remaining Madeira. Cook 3 minutes. Stir in the almonds.

4 Place tongue on a serving platter. Spoon sauce over. (Serve with a spinach souffle and a green salad, if desired.)

Note: Tongue may be prepared in advance through Step 2. Cool. Reheat in cooking liquid over low heat.

1 smoked beef tongue (3½ to 4 pounds)
Salt
½ onion, sliced
½ onion stuck with 3 cloves
1 carrot, chopped
2 ribs celery with leaves, coarsely chopped
2 bay leaves
1 large clove garlic
2 sprigs parsley
1 cup port wine
1 cup slivered almonds
3 tablespoons vegetable or olive oil
1 onion, finely chopped
1 clove garlic, bruised
1 cup beef consommé
2 teaspoons tomato paste
2 tablespoons cornstarch
⅔ cup Madeira
2 teaspoons granulated sugar
Pinch each of allspice, cloves, and cinnamon
Salt and pepper to taste
2 tablespoons tarragon vinegar

Serves 6 to 8.

Almonds grow on trees. A member of the rose family (of the order *Rosaceae*), the flowering almond is a distant cousin of the apricot, cherry, peach, raspberry, sloe, plum, and you name it—everything in the garden, including the red rose. Historically, almonds were constantly in demand as a food and medicine, as well as in the more frivolous role of a cosmetic. Crushed into a perfumed unguent, the little nut found itself anointing some of the better busts and butts this side of Babylon. Then as now, almonds were definitely versatile—in the kitchen and out!

Chicken Pizzuta is Roman in origin—or so I was told by a completely irresponsible English chef (with divine kitchen capabilities) who pressed her recipe into my hot hand after a stunning lunch on her terrace facing the cool Mediterranean. Pizzuta is certainly one of the most fertile almond-producing regions of Italy; so the story should have washed. But the touch of mayonnaise left me with decided misgivings. Italian derivation seemed doubtful; French seemed possible. Shortly afterward, however, I came upon a similar Mexican formula that substituted roasted pumpkin seeds for almonds. When challenged, milady merely smiled.

"*Tant pis,*" she murmured sweetly. And the subject was closed forever.

CHICKEN PIZZUTA

1 chicken (2½ to 3 pounds), cut into serving pieces
Salt and freshly ground black pepper
2 thick slices French bread
1 tablespoon red wine vinegar
3 tablespoons olive oil (approximately)
25 shelled, unblanched almonds
3 cloves garlic
½ bay leaf
1 cup hot chicken broth
3 tablespoons mayonnaise
2 teaspoons fresh lemon juice

Serves 3 to 4.

1 Sprinkle the chicken with salt and pepper. Trim crusts from bread; sprinkle bread with vinegar.

2 Heat 3 tablespoons oil in a heavy skillet. Add the bread, almonds, garlic, and bay leaf. Saute over medium heat until bread is golden. Transfer mixture with a slotted spoon to a blender container or food processor; blend until smooth. Scrape into a bowl. Add the hot chicken broth; mix well.

3 Add chicken to skillet. Saute until golden brown on all sides, about 15 to 20 minutes, adding more oil if necessary. Pour off fat. Add the almond mixture. Cook covered over medium heat until tender, about 20 minutes.

4 Combine the mayonnaise and lemon juice. Gradually stir into skillet over medium heat. Do not allow mixture to boil. Stir in additional salt and pepper, if necessary.

Country Captain is a Creole dish (out of an old New Orleans cookbook) that has been amended—and abetted—by the crunch of the essential nut.

COUNTRY CAPTAIN

1 Season the flour with seasoned salt and pepper; coat chicken with mixture. Melt 4 tablespoons butter in a large heavy skillet or Dutch oven. Saute the chicken until crisp and golden brown, about 10 minutes on each side, adding more butter if necessary.

2 Remove chicken and all but 2 tablespoons butter from the skillet. Add the onion, bell pepper, and garlic; cook, stirring frequently, 5 minutes. Stir in the fresh tomatoes, canned tomatoes, sugar, curry powder, and ground thyme. Return chicken to skillet, pressing pieces into the sauce. Spoon some of the sauce over chicken. Cook covered over medium heat until tender, 30 to 40 minutes.

3 Meanwhile, add beans to large pot of boiling salted water; return to boil. Immediately rinse under cold running water and drain.

4 Heat oven to 400°. Spread almonds on a baking sheet; toast in oven until light brown, about 10 minutes.

5 Melt 3 tablespoons butter in a skillet over medium-high heat. Add shallot and green beans; cook and stir just until warmed through, about 5 minutes. Stir the currants into the chicken; then stir in the green bean mixture and the almonds. Garnish with fresh thyme. Serve with chutney.

Flour
Seasoned salt and freshly ground pepper
1 chicken (3½ to 4 pounds), cut into serving pieces
7 tablespoons butter (approximately)
1 yellow onion, chopped
1 red bell pepper, chopped
1 large clove garlic, mashed
2 ripe tomatoes, peeled, seeded, chopped
1 can (8 ounces) Italian tomatoes
1 teaspoon granulated sugar
1½ teaspoons curry powder
½ teaspoon ground thyme
½ pound green beans, French cut
½ cup slivered almonds
1 large shallot, finely chopped
⅓ cup dried currants
Fresh thyme for garnish
Chutney

Serves 4.

The ancient Persians perfumed almonds before using them in desserts by adding the blanched nuts to jars filled with flower petals. Roman legions carried such sweetmeats from Persia to Rome, and Jordan almonds (coated with hard sugar) first appeared in the Italian diet back in 177 B.C. They are still around, too—though never to my taste, thank you all the same. I lost a tooth on a Jordan almond when I was ten years old and never forgave the confection.

Almond 9

Equally jaw-breaking, but much more salubrious, is the French notion of combining almonds and sugar into a shattering caramel candy called praline. From that remarkable alloy come the following ambrosial desserts in my own repertoire.

PRALINE ICE CREAM

¾ cup Praline Powder (recipe follows)
1¼ cups granulated sugar
4 teaspoons vanilla
¾ cup water
¼ cup Amaretto liqueur
4 egg yolks
3 cups whipping cream, lightly beaten
1 cup milk
1 tablespoon dark rum

Makes about 2 quarts.

1 Make praline powder.

2 Place the sugar, vanilla, and water in a saucepan; bring to a boil. Boil over medium heat 5 minutes. Add the Amaretto; boil 2 minutes.

3 Beat the egg yolks until light and lemon-colored. Gradually beat the syrup into the egg yolks; continue beating until cool to the touch. Beat in the cream, milk, and rum. Pour mixture into the canister of an ice cream maker. Freeze according to manufacturer's directions.

4 When ice cream is set, remove the dasher. Stir in the praline powder, mixing thoroughly. Cover the canister tightly; surround with ice. Place a rug or heavy blanket over canister and ice. Allow to "bloom" for at least an hour. Store in airtight plastic containers in freezer.

PRALINE POWDER

¾ cup shelled, unblanched almonds
1½ cups granulated sugar
½ teaspoon cream of tartar

1 Place all ingredients in a heavy saucepan; cook over medium heat, stirring occasionally, until mixture caramelizes and turns a dark golden color.

2 Pour mixture onto a lightly oiled jelly roll pan; let stand until cool. Break praline into chunks. Place in a blender container or food processor; blend until pulverized. Store in a glass container in a cool place.

Note: For ice cream making, I always reserve about ¼ cup of the praline, chop it coarsely and add it to the ice cream with the praline powder. It gives a nice "crunch" to the ice cream. Praline powder is also great to have on hand as a flavoring for souffles, mousses, and frostings, or as a dessert topping.

Praline combined with melted bittersweet chocolate is a prerequisite for the most heavenly almond dessert, which was invented in Paris (where else?) during the roaring '20s to honor the publication of Ernest Hemingway's brilliant novella, *The Snows of Kilimanjaro*. According to literary lore, the well-appetited Mr. H. consumed three portions of this cake at one sitting. It's still a best-seller at my table too, for the subtle crunch of nut with silky chocolate summons up memories of the candy bars that served as palliatives to the sorrows of my youth.

MOUNT KILIMANJARO

1 Heat oven to 350°. Butter and flour a 9-inch round cake pan.

2 Place the chocolate and coffee in the top of a double boiler; cook over hot water until chocolate melts. Remove from heat; let cool.

3 Cream the butter and ⅔ cup sugar in a large bowl until light and fluffy. Add the egg yolks, one at a time, beating well after each addition.

4 Sprinkle egg whites with pinch of salt; beat in a bowl until soft peaks form. Sprinkle with 1 tablespoon sugar; beat until stiff.

5 Blend the chocolate into the butter mixture with a rubber spatula. Stir in the almonds. Immediately stir in half the egg whites; fold in remaining egg whites in three parts, alternating with thirds of the flour.

6 Spread batter evenly in pan. Place in oven on middle rack. Bake until toothpick inserted in center of cake comes out clean, about 30 minutes. Cool completely in pan on a wire rack. Invert cake onto wire rack; let stand at least 1 hour.

For the cake:
4 ounces semisweet chocolate
2 tablespoons strong coffee
½ cup unsalted butter
⅔ cup plus 1 tablespoon granulated sugar
4 egg yolks
4 egg whites
Pinch of salt
⅓ cup ground almonds
¾ cup sifted cake flour

---

1 Spread almonds evenly on a lightly greased cookie sheet. Place the sugar in a heavy saucepan; cook over medium-low heat, stirring constantly, 5 minutes. Heat to boiling. Boil, without stirring, until syrup begins to caramelize; then stir constantly, until mixture turns a dark golden color. Immediately pour over almonds. Let stand to cool completely. Break praline into small chunks. Place in a blender container or food processor; blend until pulverized.

For the chocolate praline leaves:
1 cup toasted blanched almonds
1 cup granulated sugar
8 ounces semisweet chocolate

2 Place the chocolate in the top of a double boiler; melt over hot water. Stir praline powder into chocolate until thoroughly mixed.

3 Cut eight 12-inch squares of waxed paper. Quickly place chocolate mixture in equal amounts on four squares of paper; cover with remaining four squares. Flatten the chocolate mixture and spread it evenly between the squares of paper with a rolling pin. Without unwrapping them, place the "leaves" on a platter; refrigerate or freeze until firm, at least 1 hour.

For the chocolate butter icing:
6 ounces German sweet chocolate
¾ cup butter, softened
1 can (14 ounces) condensed milk
1 egg, lightly beaten
1 tablespoon Grand Marnier liqueur

1 Melt chocolate in the top of a double boiler over hot water. Remove from heat; allow to cool.

2 Beat butter in a medium bowl until light and fluffy. Gradually beat in milk, egg, Grand Marnier, and cooled chocolate; beat until smooth. Set aside until ready to use.

For the chocolate and vanilla whipped cream toppings:
1 cup whipping cream
2 tablespoons sweetened cocoa
1 tablespoon vanilla
1 tablespoon confectioners' sugar

1 Beat ½ cup cream with the sweetened cocoa until stiff. Cover and refrigerate until ready to use.

2 Beat ½ cup cream with the vanilla and confectioners' sugar until stiff. Cover and refrigerate until ready to use.

For the final assembly:
Cake
Chocolate butter icing
Chocolate whipped cream topping
Vanilla whipped cream topping
Chocolate praline leaves
Confectioners' sugar

Serves 12.

1 Place the cake on a flat serving plate. Using a very sharp knife, cut horizontally into two halves; remove top half. Spread bottom half with ⅓ of the chocolate butter icing; replace top half. Spread remaining icing on side and top of cake. Place cake in freezer until frosting sets, about 15 minutes.

2 Spread chocolate whipped cream topping over top of cake with a spatula, mounding it higher in center. Place in freezer for 30 minutes.

3 Remove cake from freezer and immediately spread vanilla whipped cream topping over chocolate topping, mounding it into a peak. (Cake should double in height with the addition of the two toppings.) Place in freezer until second topping is slightly firm, about 30 minutes.

BERT GREENE'S *Kitchen Bouquets*

4 Remove chocolate praline leaves from the refrigerator. Remove top layers of waxed paper; loosen bottom papers slightly but do not remove. Let stand 1 to 2 minutes at room temperature. Praline leaves will soften enough to be molded into shape.

5 Remove cake from freezer. Holding 1 praline leaf by bottom sheet of waxed paper, mold it around one side of cake and over whipped cream toppings. Remove waxed paper. Repeat with remaining praline leaves, overlapping leaves slightly until entire surface of cake is covered. If leaves become too soft, place in freezer for a few minutes before continuing. (Cake will resemble a mountain peak—or the upper half of a large onion. Do not worry if peak of whipped cream topping is not completely covered; top will be dusted with confectioners' sugar before serving.)

6 Refrigerate or freeze cake.* Remove from refrigerator 15 minutes before serving (45 minutes, if frozen); let stand at room temperature. Just before serving, sprinkle the "peak" with confectioners' sugar. Cut with a sharp knife and don't be upset if the mountain crumbles— it's delicious eating anyway.

*Note: Mount Kilimanjaro may be prepared to this point and kept frozen in an airtight plastic bag up to 6 weeks before the night of its fabulous appearance. Don't sugar the top until just before serving.

Have you ever seen an almond tree in bloom? I did, one April morning by detour and default. Tooling through a side road in Normandy after a heavy rainfall, I got my rented car stuck in a mud bank and had to wait three long hours until a very young boy and a very old ox managed to extricate the wheels.

The stay in the ditch was illuminating, for it gave me a chance to observe all manner of trees flowering on the French slopes, including apple, peach, and almond. I only recognized the latter from prints of its tiny, shell-pink petals and long serrated leaves but I think I might have known from other signs as well, for bees avoid the almond's blossom assiduously.

Why? The bitter almond fruit contains a measure of prussic acid and canny bees obviously take no chances about where they alight. Almond and peach are kissing cousins in an orchard, and, truth to tell, the bitter almond flavoring that is extracted from a peach pit seems to bring out a measure of sweetness in the rosy fruit's flavor. I have never made peach ice cream, for instance, without adding a few drops of almond essence to make the concoction "peachy" enough for my tongue. Ponder on the homely joys of Peach and Almond Upside Down Cake for a truer demonstration of this saporous proclivity.

PEACH AND ALMOND UPSIDE DOWN CAKE

4 fresh peaches
½ cup sliced almonds
1 cup unsalted butter
1 cup dark brown sugar
½ cup granulated sugar
2 eggs
½ teaspoon vanilla
1½ cups all-purpose flour
1½ teaspoons baking powder
½ teaspoon salt
¼ cup whipping cream
¼ cup orange juice
Whipped cream or sour cream

Serves 8.

1 Heat oven to 350°. Place the peaches in boiling water for 1 to 2 minutes to loosen skins; remove skins and discard. Cut peaches lengthwise into ¼-inch slices.

2 Spread the almonds on a baking sheet. Toast in oven until brown, about 10 minutes.

3 Melt 4 tablespoons butter; pour into a 9- × 2-inch round (preferably Teflon) pan and swirl to coat bottom and sides. Sprinkle bottom and sides of pan with ¾ cup brown sugar. Spread half the almonds in bottom of pan. Arrange peach slices in bottom and around sides of pan in a decorative pattern. Sprinkle with remaining brown sugar and almonds. Let stand in a cool place.

4 Cream remaining butter with the granulated sugar; beat in the eggs and vanilla. Sift the flour, baking powder, and salt together. Combine the cream and orange juice in a small bowl. Add the flour mixture to the butter mixture in three parts, alternating with the liquid. Spoon batter carefully over the peaches in the cake pan. Bake until toothpick inserted in center comes out clean, 35 to 40 minutes. Cool cake on a wire rack 1½ hours. Invert onto a serving platter. Serve slightly warm with the whipped cream.

Deipnosophistai (variously translated as *A Banquet of The Learned* or *Specialists in Dining*) is a book that was compiled around 230 A.D. by Athenaeus, one of the first food critics around. Cheesecake was by far the author's favorite dessert and a whole section of his work is devoted to the culinary affinity of sweet cream, honey, and almonds, which usually were baked in the shape of a woman's breast. I cannot offer you the design secret, for it is lost to the ages. But the Greek writer's recipe for Almond Cheesecake holds up remarkably—after a bit of fiddling here and there!

¼ cup butter
⅞ cup granulated sugar
1 pound cream cheese, room temperature
½ cup whipping cream
5 egg yolks
¼ cup sifted all-purpose flour

ALMOND CHEESECAKE

1 Heat oven to 325°. Cream the butter with the sugar in a large bowl; beat in the cream cheese and cream until well mixed. Add the egg yolks, one at a time, beating well after each addition. Beat in the flour, honey, almond extract, and vanilla. Fold in the egg whites; fold in the ground almonds.

2 Butter a 9-inch spring-form pan; pour batter into pan. Combine the brown sugar, cinnamon, and almonds; sprinkle over batter.

3 Place in oven on bottom rack. Bake 1 hour. Turn oven off; let cake stand in oven 1 hour without opening oven door.

4 Remove cake from oven; cool completely on wire rack. Remove sides of pan. Combine the sour cream, confectioners' sugar, and Amaretto in a small serving dish; serve as an optional topping for cake.

Note: Almond Cheesecake is of a curiously frangible texture; sudden temperature change can affect the outcome irremediably. I have baked this cake as stately and upstanding as *la belle poitrine* itself—but I have also made it only to see it sag terribly. Not to worry! The taste is an anodyne to any kitchen labor pains, I assure you.

2 tablespoons honey
¼ teaspoon almond extract
1 teaspoon vanilla
5 egg whites, beaten until stiff but not dry
½ cup finely ground blanched almonds
¼ cup light brown sugar
1 teaspoon ground cinnamon
¼ cup chopped almonds
1 cup sour cream
1 heaping tablespoon confectioners' sugar
⅓ cup Amaretto liqueur

Serves 8 to 10.

The next two recipes in this chapter are from time-honored cooking mentors. The Almond Sponge is remarkably like one my grandmother wrought, though perhaps a mite less dry for a shower of almond liqueur after baking. The Tender Tart began as one of Alice B. Toklas's contributions to my culinary store-house; originally its main ingredient was crushed filberts. She will forgive me, I know, my inconstancy since almonds lend inexplicable relish to her invention.

ALMOND SPONGE CAKE

1 Heat oven to 350°. Butter the bottom and sides of a 9-inch spring-form pan. Cut a circle of parchment paper or a brown paper bag to fit bottom of pan. Place circle in pan and butter it. Dust paper and sides of pan lightly with flour.

2 Beat egg whites in a large bowl until fluffy; add the salt and beat until stiff. Add egg yolks, one at a time, beating well after each addition.

3 Combine the ground almonds, sugar, 1 tablespoon flour, and the baking powder. Gradually add to the eggs. Add the brandy and 2 tablespoons Amaretto. Pour batter into pan. Place in oven on middle rack; bake 1¼ hours. Cool completely in pan on a wire rack. Remove sides of pan. Sprinkle cake with remaining Amaretto and dust with confectioners' sugar.

Unsalted butter
Flour
5 eggs, separated
Pinch of salt
½ pound blanched almonds, ground
1 cup granulated sugar
1 tablespoon all-purpose flour
¼ teaspoon baking powder
2 tablespoons brandy
6 tablespoons Amaretto liqueur
Confectioners' sugar

Serves 8 to 10.

A TENDER TART À LA ALICE B. TOKLAS

9 tablespoons unsalted butter
1 cup plus 2 tablespoons all-purpose flour
1 egg yolk
1½ tablespoons cold water (approximately)
2 eggs
1 cup plus 2 tablespoons granulated sugar
1 teaspoon vanilla
1 cup finely chopped blanched almonds
½ teaspoon grated orange peel

Serves 10.

1 Blend the butter, flour, and egg yolk with a pastry blender until the texture of coarse crumbs. Add just enough water to form a dough. Knead briefly. Refrigerate.

2 Heat oven to 350°. Stir eggs and sugar together in a medium bowl for 20 minutes; do not beat (you may use an electric mixer only if it has a *very low* speed). Add the vanilla, almonds, and orange peel.

3 Lightly grease a 9-inch quiche pan. Roll out a little more than half the dough. Line bottom and sides of pan; trim edge. Fill with the almond mixture. Roll out remaining dough; place over filling. Press edge into sides of pan. Cut small hole in center of tart. Bake 30 minutes.

Rose Schweitzer, who presented me with a treasured family recipe for Almond Squares, is a new friend but an old hand in the kitchen. She used to co-own the raffish Five Oaks restaurant in Greenwich Village.

"But I never could afford to make a dessert like this *there*," Rose explained as she passed a plate of Almond Squares around for the third time. "These are special. And special things should only be made for someone you love!"

So said Rose, and I agree. Now *you* get the almonds and take it from there!

ROSE SCHWEITZER'S ALMOND SQUARES

1 cup all-purpose flour
2 tablespoons confectioners' sugar
½ cup unsalted butter, cut into small pieces
1½ cups brown sugar
2 tablespoons all-purpose flour
2 eggs, beaten
1 teaspoon almond extract
½ cup shredded coconut
¾ cup chopped almonds
Confectioners' sugar

Serves 12.

1 Heat oven to 400°. Place 1 cup flour, 2 tablespoons confectioners' sugar, and the butter in a bowl; blend well with a pastry blender. Grease a cookie sheet with sides (no larger than 14 × 9 inches). Pat flour mixture evenly over bottom. Bake 10 minutes.

2 Combine the brown sugar, 2 tablespoons flour, the eggs, almond extract, coconut, and almonds in a bowl; mix well with your hands. Spread over pre-baked crust; bake until toothpick inserted comes out clean, 15 to 20 minutes. Sprinkle with confectioners' sugar. Let stand to cool; cut into squares.

Anise

Licorice was a childhood addiction of mine. And the staple of my early diet was Black Jack chewing gum. I think I must have chewed six packs a day—sometimes in tandem—during my formative years. Black Crows were another secret vice; they still are, but expensive dental bridgework discourages any youthful six-pack orgies. One box at a time nowadays, and then only if those inky candies have been placed in a freezer to develop the degree of hard-rubber elasticity that once made them so irresistible to me.

In maturity I still love the flavor but, sad to report, my tastes have swung violently from licorice whips and tar-babies to *fenouil braisé* and Pernod on the rocks. I will admit, however, that I was fully forty years old before I learned the differences among licorice, anise, and fennel.

Licorice is the dried root of the *Glycyrrhiza glabra* shrub, which is native to the Caucasus but grown in all the shore-line countries of the Mediterranean. The leafy, umbrellalike anise plant, *Pimpinella anisum,* grows wild over the very same territory. Its leaves are pale green and as feathery as wild parsley and, like that herb, they are most felicitous when chopped and sprinkled over low-caste vegetables like turnips, carrot, and rutabaga. Fresh anise, however, is very rarely seen on our shores. Fennel (*Foeniculum vulgare*) has moved from its native Florence into kitchens all over Europe. The bulb and leaf stalk are eaten just like celery and the leaves are minced judiciously over fish and fowl. Oddly enough, Italians dote on *finocchio,* as they call it, but apply the same term to an effeminate male, much as we would refer to a like type as a "fruit."

The use of licorice, anise, and fennel in cooking was first noted in Asia Minor around the sixth century. In early Arabian kitchens, licorice bark was employed to preserve dried meats, fresh fennel was served as a vegetable, and dried fennel weed was added to soups and stews to fortify their flavors. Aniseed, considered the most potent of all the aromatics, was distilled with fermented fruits to produce medicinal liqueurs. When the Arabs invaded Europe, they brought the trio of distinctive seasonings (along with rye, sesame, and mustard) with them as part of the mess-hall chef's spice shelf.

The Arabian culinary regimen obviously took hold in the mistral country around the Mediterranean; today, most of southern France and northwestern Italy are distinctly anise-oriented.

I stayed near Nice for a while in the early 1970s and the bouquet of licorice—always in the air—is printed forever on my memory of that time. Once a fishing port of some magnitude (before pollution sullied the brine), Nice is still peopled with sea folk and the heart of the city is, and always will be, the gray-stone wharf area, with its open-air cafes that face the sea. Strongholds of past glory, these waterfront establishments become crowded each morning with fishermen and traders who drink a *pastis* as a preamble to the serious business of hammering out the day's price for sardines or anchovies. The cloudy aroma of the sticky anise liqueur, mixed with the more redolent smell of the morning's catch, hangs high over the entire breakwater until the hot midday sun burns it off. And I still cannot summon up a geography of the city without an involuntary quiver of the nostrils.

My passion for all things licorice once prompted me to waste a perfect August (sequestered alone in a beach house with a new ice cream freezer) trying to devise a sherbet flavored with anisette and Pernod. The results were so dismal that I had to slurp them down alone. Even my dog of the time, named Folly, turned his nose away from the greenish-puce blend with absolute disdain.

A decade later, when Baskin and Robbins announced that their thirty-one ice cream flavors would be expanded by one—a licorice confection—I was first in line to try the stuff. A brackish sweetmeat it turned out to be! It looked (in the ice cream case) like a bucket of battleship-gray paint that had fallen in mortal combat with a freezer. The taste was too dreadful even for my anise-oriented buds, the aroma worse. Like the late, great Folly, I merely turned away my nose—and found a nearby trash can.

Anise does far better in unsweetened combinations. One of the best breads in the world, I think, is the anise-seeded Kisra baked in Morocco. Coarse textured, yet curiously light to the tongue, it is one of the easiest recipes in the world for a neophyte bread-maker. I consider it a splendid supplement, well-slathered with butter, to the western diet, and I never serve up a pot of ratatouille without a loaf on the table. However, Kisra forms a perfect amalgam when served (without butter) with native North African fare like spicy couscous.

KISRA

1 Dissolve the yeast with the sugar in ¼ cup lukewarm water. Let stand 10 minutes.

2 Combine the flours, salt, and pepper in a large bowl. Add the yeast, milk, and enough lukewarm water (about 1 cup) to form a dough. Knead 15 minutes on a floured board (or about 8 minutes with a mixer equipped with a dough hook). Knead in the seeds. Divide dough into two balls; let stand 5 minutes.

3 Sprinkle a baking sheet with cornmeal. Rub your hands with butter and form each ball of dough into a cone about 7½ inches long. Flatten each cone, point down on the baking sheet, into a disc about 5 inches in diameter and slightly raised in the center. Cover with a damp towel; let stand 2 hours.

4 Heat oven to 400°. Bake bread 12 minutes. Reduce heat to 300°; bake 35 minutes.

Note: See Yeast Chapter for more detailed bread-making instructions.

1 package dry yeast
1 teaspoon light brown sugar
1¼ cups lukewarm water (approximately)
3 cups unbleached all-purpose flour
1½ cups stone-ground whole wheat flour
2 teaspoons salt
⅛ teaspoon cayenne pepper
½ cup lukewarm milk
1 teaspoon sesame seeds
1 teaspoon fennel seeds
2 teaspoons aniseed
Cornmeal
Butter

Makes 2 loaves.

Fennel is apparently an anomaly among agriculturists. According to the *Dictionary of Food,* it is considered a symbol of heroism in a vegetable garden. Yet in *Larousse Gastronomique,* the same plant is described as growing wild mostly and as being the accursed emblem of falsity. Heaven alone knows why!

In Scandinavian countries, dieters consider a brew of two tablespoons fennel seeds in a cup of boiling water (or half that amount in strong tea) to be an appetite depressant. It has never worked for me, however. And in Brazil, smokers chew dried fennel root to break the habit. But as a confirmed non-smoker, I can't verify the cure.

One sure curative (for whatever ails you!) is the delicate Fennel–Pernod Bisque that follows.

FENNEL-PERNOD BISQUE

¾ pound fresh fennel
2 tablespoons vegetable or olive oil
1 large onion, sliced
1 pound ripe tomatoes, seeded, chopped
6 cups strong chicken stock
Bouquet garni composed of 1 sprig parsley, pinch of thyme, pinch of savory, ½ small bay leaf
Salt and freshly ground pepper
2½ to 3 tablespoons tapioca
1 tablespoon Pernod
½ cup whipping cream

Serves 4 to 6.

1 Remove fronds from fennel; chop and reserve 2 tablespoons for garnish. Trim rough outer stalks from fennel; save for use in stocks or discard. Coarsely chop fennel. Cook in boiling water 3 minutes; drain.

2 Heat the oil in a saucepan. Saute the onion over low heat until soft but not browned. Add the fennel; cook over medium heat until fennel is lightly browned. Add the tomatoes and stock; cook 20 minutes. Transfer mixture, 3 cups at a time, to a blender container; blend until smooth.

3 Return soup to saucepan; add the bouquet garni and salt and pepper to taste. Cook over medium heat until soup is reduced to about 4½ cups, 10 to 15 minutes. Gradually stir in tapioca and Pernod; cook until thickened. Remove from heat; stir in cream. Refrigerate until cold. Serve garnished with chopped fennel fronds.

The Mediterranean is mightily renowned for (among other things) the potency of its anise-inspired liquors. Catalonians produce a spectacularly rousing drink they call *anis del mono,* which, curiously, I have never been able to find outside Spanish borders. The cannier French, however, export their *pastis* all over the world; both Pernod and Ricard are familiar bar-man's staples everywhere. Rumored to be distantly related to absinthe, which (before it was prohibited) supposedly drove men mad after sufficient consumption, these licoricey drinks only induce a very slight glow in me!

My sole experimentation with absinthe, I might add, was a Sazerac cocktail in New Orleans that also left me unruffled. Greek *ouzo* and Turkish *rakı* are slightly more maddening, particularly as they are served on their home territories with endless varieties of hors d'oeuvre to blur the appetite. Like *pastis,* both are colorless liquids that turn milky once diluted with water and, like the rest of the vocabulary of anise potions, both should be imbibed slowly, in small quaffs. I recommend you use them extravagantly as kitchen adjuncts for seafood, however; you will notice elsewhere in this book that my *paella* is generously sauced with Pernod.

Consider the following Mediterranean fare as well. For the palate not addicted to anise, the subtle flavor of these dishes will prove surprising.

SHRIMP WITH PERNOD

1 Place shrimp in a shallow bowl; sprinkle with lime juice. Let stand at room temperature ½ hour. Drain well.

2 Heat the butter in a heavy skillet; add the shrimp and shallots. Cook and stir over medium heat until shrimp turn pink, 4 to 5 minutes. Stir in the Pernod. Remove shrimp with a slotted spoon; reserve.

3 Add the cream to the skillet; cook over high heat 2 minutes. Reduce heat; add the hot pepper sauce, salt, pepper, and reserved shrimp. Stir over medium heat until warmed through. Serve with rice.

1½ pounds uncooked shrimp, shelled, deveined
Juice of 1 lime
3 tablespoons butter
2 tablespoons finely chopped shallots
2 tablespoons Pernod
¾ cup whipping cream
⅛ teaspoon hot pepper sauce
Salt and freshly ground pepper to taste
4 cups cooked rice

Serves 4.

FILLETS OF SOLE
SUR LA MER

1 Place the fillets in a bowl with the juice of 1 lemon and the water. Let stand 5 minutes; drain. Cut the fillets in half lengthwise. Reserve 2 tablespoons crabmeat for garnish; divide remainder among fillets. Roll each fillet around crabmeat; secure with toothpicks.

2 Place rolled fillets in a large saucepan; pour in wine to ½ depth of fillets. Add the onion, 4 lemon slices, and the bouquet garni. Cover pan with heavily buttered wax paper. Cook over low heat until fish flakes easily when pierced with a fork, 4 to 5 minutes. Remove fillets with a slotted spoon to a heated ovenproof serving dish. Remove toothpicks.

3 Heat oven broiling unit. Boil cooking liquid until reduced by half. Strain; return to saucepan. Add the juice of ½ lemon, the cream, butter, fennel seeds, salt, and pepper. Heat to boiling; remove from heat. Stir ¼ cup sauce into egg yolks; gradually stir egg yolks into saucepan. Cook over low heat, stirring constantly, until thick. Do not boil!

4 Pour sauce over rolled fillets. Place under broiler to glaze, 1 to 2 minutes. Garnish with reserved crab, remaining lemon slices, and chopped fennel fronds, if desired. Serve immediately.

6 large sole or flounder fillets
Juice of 1½ lemons
3 cups water
1½ cups cooked crabmeat or lobster
½ bottle dry white wine (approximately)
1 onion stuck with 2 cloves
1 lemon, thinly sliced
Bouquet garni composed of 1 sprig parsley, 1 bay leaf, and 1 sprig fresh thyme or a pinch of dried
1 cup whipping cream
2½ tablespoons butter
⅛ teaspoon fennel seeds
Pinch of salt
Pinch of freshly ground pepper
2 egg yolks, lightly beaten
Chopped fennel fronds for garnish

Serves 6 to 8.

The recipe for Pain de Poisson Provençale that follows actually produces a sensuous fish mousse. So do not be put off by its earthy cognomen!

PAIN DE POISSON PROVENÇALE

Homemade tomato sauce (see Index)

1¾ pounds white fish fillets (such as flounder, fluke, or sole)

2 egg yolks

Salt and fresh pepper to taste

2 pinches freshly grated nutmeg

⅛ teaspoon hot pepper sauce

2 tablespoons Pernod

1½ cups whipping cream

3 medium shallots

2 small green peppers, seeded, cut into 1-inch pieces

4 medium carrots, cut into 1-inch pieces

Dash of Pernod

Serves 8 to 10.

1 Make tomato sauce.

2 Cut fish into cubes, removing any bones. Place half the fish in the bowl of a food processor. Add 1 egg yolk and half of the salt, pepper, nutmeg, hot pepper sauce, and 1 tablespoon Pernod to bowl. With machine running, gradually add half the cream. Process until smooth; scrape into a large mixing bowl. Repeat with remaining fish.

3 Wash food processor bowl; add the shallots. Process until finely chopped. Add the peppers and carrots; process just until chopped. Add to fish; mix thoroughly. Add more salt and hot pepper sauce, if necessary.

4 Heat oven to 400°. Spoon fish mixture into a greased 9-inch tube pan or mold. Cut a ring of waxed paper to fit top of pan; press over fish mixture. Place tube pan in a roasting pan; pour boiling water into roasting pan to half depth of tube pan. Bake until set, about 35 minutes.

5 Remove tube pan from the oven; let stand 5 minutes. Place a wire rack over pan; invert over sink, as some hot liquid will spill out. Drain thoroughly; invert back into pan. Remove waxed paper; unmold onto a serving plate. (Sop up any remaining juice that may spill onto plate with paper toweling.)

6 Stir dash of Pernod into tomato sauce; serve with fish. (Fish may also be served cold with mayonnaise seasoned with Pernod.)

There are probably more recipes for ratatouille floating around this world than there are veal concoctions. Both are kitchen favorites of mine; so I keep collecting them—compulsively. Fennel Ratatouille is a wonderful, sexy vegetable stew; it can be made with celery when the other stalk is scarce, but be aware that some sensuality will be lost in translation. Fennel alone has the robust flavor to keep garlic, onion, and even anchovy at bay.

FENNEL OR CELERY RATATOUILLE

1 Cut eggplant in half lengthwise; pierce cut surfaces all over with a fork. Sprinkle with salt. Place cut sides down on paper toweling; let stand 30 minutes.

2 Add the fennel and Pernod to a large pot of boiling salted water; boil 10 minutes. Rinse under cold water and drain.

3 Melt 3 tablespoons butter with 2 tablespoons oil in a skillet. Saute the onion slices, half at a time, until golden on both sides. Remove from skillet.

4 Wipe salt off eggplant; cut eggplant into ¾-inch-wide strips. Add to skillet; saute until golden, adding more butter as needed. Drain on paper toweling.

5 Add garlic and ⅓ of tomatoes to skillet. Cook over medium heat until tender. Raise heat; stir in ⅓ of the anchovy paste and ½ teaspoon vinegar; remove from skillet. Repeat with remaining tomatoes, anchovy paste, and vinegar.

6 Add green peppers to skillet; sprinkle with crushed hot pepper. Cook over medium heat 5 minutes; remove from skillet. Add zucchini slices to skillet with remaining oil, if necessary; saute until tender.

7 Heat oven to 350°. Butter a casserole dish. Spread ⅓ of the fennel in dish; sprinkle with ½ teaspoon fennel seeds. Top with thirds of the zucchini, onions, eggplant, peppers, and tomatoes; sprinkle salt, pepper, and chopped parsley among layers. Repeat layers twice. Sprinkle with olives. Bake 20 minutes. Serve hot or well chilled, garnished with additional chopped parsley.

1 large eggplant
Salt
1 large stalk fennel or celery, cut into strips 2-inches long × ¼-inch wide
1 jigger Pernod
6 tablespoons butter (approximately)
4 tablespoons olive or vegetable oil (approximately)
1 large yellow onion, cut into ½-inch slices
2 cloves garlic, minced
3 large ripe tomatoes, seeded, cut into ½-inch wedges
1 teaspoon anchovy paste
1½ teaspoons red wine vinegar
2 green peppers, cut into thin strips
1 dried hot red pepper, crushed
2 medium zucchini, cut into ½-inch slices
1½ teaspoons fennel seeds
Freshly ground pepper
½ cup chopped parsley
6 or 7 pitted black olives, cut into slivers

Serves 6.

Unlike the ratatouille, the next recipe, Bracioline Con Anice, requires only seeds!

BRACIOLINE CON ANICE

3 cups Homemade Tomato Sauce
  (see Index)
¼ cup cubed salt pork
2 shallots, chopped
8 slices prosciutto
¼ cup chopped parsley
1 teaspoon crushed fennel seeds
2 tablespoons freshly grated
  Parmesan cheese
8 veal scallops, pounded thin
3 tablespoons butter
1 tablespoon olive or vegetable oil
Dash of Pernod
4 cups hot, buttered green noodles
Freshly grated Parmesan cheese

Serves 4.

1 Make tomato sauce.

2 Place salt pork, shallots, prosciutto, parsley, fennel seeds, and 2 tablespoons Parmesan cheese in the bowl of a food processor; process into a paste. Spread mixture in equal amounts over veal scallops. Roll scallops tightly; tie with string in two or three places to secure.

3 Heat the butter and oil in a Dutch oven; brown veal rolls on all sides. Remove excess fat. Add the tomato sauce and Pernod. Cook covered over medium heat 30 minutes. Serve with noodles and Parmesan cheese.

Lamb is one viand that doesn't please every palate. Why, I cannot rightly judge, since I am so addicted to its savor—especially when the meat is highly seasoned and redolent of herbs. The following is a splendid lamb improvisation straight from a Nice kitchen, where the chef shook a bottle of Pernod directly into her roasting pan before she flambéed the meat. Her thumb, held over the bottle top, did all the measuring—and fended off conflagration of the total contents. Rest assured, I am more cautious!

GIGOT AU PASTIS NIÇOISE

1 leg of lamb (about 4½ pounds)
1 clove garlic, cut into slivers
3 sprigs rosemary, finely chopped
1 sprig thyme, finely chopped
2 tablespoons olive oil
Homemade Tomato Sauce (see
  Index)
Salt and freshly ground pepper
½ cup plus 2 tablespoons Pernod

Serves 4 to 5.

1 Four hours before roasting, make shallow incisions in the lamb with a sharp knife; insert garlic slivers in incisions. Combine the herbs and olive oil; rub over the lamb.

2 Make tomato sauce.

3 Heat oven to 350°. Place the lamb on a rack in a roasting pan; sprinkle with salt and pepper. Roast 15 minutes per pound for rare, or longer if desired. Let stand 10 minutes at room temperature.

4 Heat the tomato sauce; stir in 2 tablespoons Pernod. Place lamb on heatproof serving platter. Heat ½ cup Pernod in a small saucepan; pour over lamb and ignite immediately with a long match. Serve lamb with tomato sauce on the side.

The flavor of anise sweetens desserts the world over. A German favorite is a version of the dry Christmas cookie called *springerle*. Another wintery sweet is a hot milk punch admired by devotées of Italian cappuccino. The latter is Dutch, and in Holland skaters drink this *anÿs melk* from Delft mugs in little huts set directly on the frozen canals. The milk simmers all afternoon on a small stove within the wooden hut and is usually dispensed by a very old man wrapped in many, many layers of shawls and tippets. If it all sounds like Hans Brinker revisited, you're not far off target. The milk is delicious too—and not harmed a whit by a jigger of anisette!

ANISE MILK

1 Scald the milk with the aniseed; add the sugar. Cook over low heat, stirring occasionally, 5 minutes.

2 Combine the cornstarch and water; stir until smooth. Add to milk. Cook over low heat, stirring constantly, 5 minutes. Strain.

4 cups milk
1 tablespoon crushed aniseed
½ cup granulated sugar
2 tablespoons cornstarch
2 tablespoons water

Serves 4.

ANISE COOKIES

1 Beat the eggs until light and fluffy; add the sugar. Beat at medium speed 30 minutes. Add the remaining ingredients. Beat 5 minutes.

2 Grease and flour three cookie sheets. Drop the batter onto sheets by teaspoonful about 1 inch apart. Let stand at room temperature at least 10 hours or overnight.

3 Heat oven to 375°. Bake cookies until they spring back when touched, 10 to 12 minutes. Remove from sheets and cool on wire racks. Store in an airtight container in the refrigerator.

Note: This recipe may be halved easily.

3 eggs
1 cup sugar
1¾ to 2 cups all-purpose flour
½ teaspoon baking powder
1 tablespoon aniseed, crushed

Makes 50 to 60 cookies.

Éclairs are a galvanic dessert (when they are made from scratch by an industrious loved one). Although not at all difficult to produce, they are elegant beyond belief when the tender custard is lightened to a froth with anise-flavored whipped cream and the fondant topping is similarly tinctured with coffee and more anisette. Add a final measure of chopped almonds and the result is a sweet to kill for!

ANISETTE ÉCLAIRS

For the pâte à choux:
1 cup water
6 tablespoons butter
1 teaspoon granulated sugar
Pinch of salt
1 cup sifted all-purpose flour
4 eggs
1 egg, beaten with ½ teaspoon water

For the crème pâtissière:
3 egg yolks
¼ cup granulated sugar
1 tablespoon anisette liqueur
1½ tablespoons cornstarch
¾ cup milk, scalded
1 cup whipping cream

For the glaze:
½ cup confectioners' sugar
1 teaspoon anisette
2½ tablespoons whipping cream
½ teaspoon instant espresso
1¼ teaspoons hot water
¼ cup chopped toasted almonds (optional)

Makes about 2 dozen.

1 To make the pate a choux, bring the water, butter, sugar, and salt to a boil in a heavy saucepan. Remove from heat; beat in all the flour at once with a wooden spoon. Place over low heat; beat until the mixture leaves the bottom and sides of the pan and forms a ball. Remove from heat; beat in 4 eggs, 1 at a time, beating thoroughly after each addition. Beat 1 minute longer.

2 Heat oven to 400°. Lightly butter a baking sheet. Fill a pastry bag fitted with a large tube with the dough; pipe 3- to 4-inch-long strips onto baking sheet, 2 inches apart, cutting off each strip with a scissors or sharp knife. (You should have about 2 dozen 3-inch strips.) Brush tops of strips with the egg beaten with ½ teaspoon water; be very careful not to allow eggwash to drip down sides onto baking sheet, as this will impede puffing.

3 Bake until golden and puffy, about 35 minutes. Open oven door; place baking sheet on door. Slit side of each eclair with a sharp knife. Return baking sheet to oven rack; turn off heat. Let stand with oven door ajar 15 minutes.

4 Remove the baking sheet from oven. Carefully cut sides of eclairs enough so that you can scrape out doughy centers with a small spoon. Set baking sheet in a warm dry place; allow eclairs to dry out completely.

5 Meanwhile, make the creme patissiere. Beat egg yolks with the sugar, anisette, and cornstarch until smooth; beat in the scalded milk. Place in the top of a double boiler over hot water; cook, stirring constantly, until *very* thick. Remove from heat; let stand to cool. Refrigerate until cold.

6 Whip the cream until *very* stiff; gently fold into cold creme patissiere. Using a spoon or a pastry bag, fill eclairs with mixture. Place on a large plate; refrigerate 30 minutes.

7 To make the glaze, combine the sugar, anisette, and cream. Dissolve the espresso in the hot water; stir into the sugar mixture. Place eclairs on a wire rack; spoon some of glaze over each one. Sprinkle with almonds, if desired. Refrigerate until serving time.

Basil

What the Greeks call *basileus* is my most treasured pot herb. When I ran The Store in Amagansett, I used to grow yards and yards of it in a brick-bordered kitchen garden behind my house. Bees grew drunk on the perfume every summer but I never quite managed to end a September with a clump hardy enough for transplant. Too many bowls of string beans vinaigrette spent the tender leaves; too many salvers of glistening tomatoes provençale thinned the second blooming; and too many pints of jade-green pesto left the pickings far too slim for any real harvest.

Now I am content to cultivate a half dozen pots on my apartment window sill. Fortunes change in life but basil remains sempiternal.

My gardening thumb begins to itch about mid-April. It is then that I start searching about for seed packets to fill my clay. Tarragon, thyme, marjoram, mint, rosemary, and even oregano are all perennials; so it is only basil that I nurture from scratch in my window-box herbiary. If the seedlings perish in a sudden northeast temperature drop, I mourn the loss no less than if it had been an acre of corn. When the tender shoots thicken at the stem at last and the first tentative, curly green leaves appear in June, I rejoice and, like the Persians, say a silent prayer:

> *However ye are . . . wherever ye be planted,*
> *the true God will bring you back green*
> *for the resurrection.*

Or so it says in the Koran. In India, where the plant first bloomed, they call basil, *tulasi*. The flowers of the fragrant *tulasi* shrub were said to have been torn apart and shredded over the grave of Mohammed and the searching wind, according to legend, blew the pollen across three seas and five continents to rebloom year after year and proclaim the greatness of Allah forevermore.

Basil lore is as persistent as the herb's peppery savor on the tongue. After her infamous *danse du ventre,* Salome hid the head of John the Baptist in a pot of flowering basil, where it embalmed itself. Not surprising, I guess, when one considers that ancient Egyptians always included basil roots in the preparation of a sarcophagus for royal entombment.

In ancient Greece, sweet-scented, green basil was held to be the only antidote to the venom of the basilisk, a fabulous reptile whose very breath was rumored to be fatal. Perhaps that's where the herb got its name; history is a bit fuzzy on that detail. Archestraetus called the herb *basilikon* in his early food philosophies but never mentioned it in connection with any dish; instead, he reported that wise farmers always planted a row of the greens alongside their crops to insure a banner harvest. Even today in Greece, basil rarely is included in the stewpot but bright blue pots of it sit on every citizen's sun-drenched doorstep to ward off the evil eye.

Legends die hard it seems. They still claim, in certain primitive African countries, that the leaf of the basil plant relieves the pain of a scorpion's bite. But scorpions are rare and I, luckily, hold out no assurance for that claim.

In Iran, however, basil is said to be the only preventative against malaria and the houses of the rich are filled with its green leaves, which, unfortunately, never make their way to the saute pan or the chopping board.

In other Middle Eastern countries, branches of basil hung over a connubial bed are said to bring fertility to a marriage. Moroccan women still wear necklaces of dried basil roots during pregnancy to lessen the travail of childbirth. Hindu males consider the plant a potent aphrodisiac because, they say, the liplike leaves resemble the female organ. And a man of enormous sexual capacity will prove it to his *compères* by parting the leaves of the basil plant with the tip of his tongue—before presenting it as an offering to Vishnu.

All such Kama Sutra funny-business aside, I prefer my basil leaves snipped over fresh tomatoes or chopped into garlic-scented eggplant that has been roasted a ductile gold, but other cooks have other ideas on the subject. In the wine country of Provence they slip twigs of basil into casks of certain dry wines "to calm them." As a variation on that theme, you might consider floating a basil leaf on a *spritzer* of white wine and soda sometime.

Since I love the garden second best to the kitchen in any house I occupy, I'll offer a mite of wisdom about growing basil here.

Sweet basil, as I have said, is native to the warm climes of India, so any hint of frost in the air nips the bud in mid-bloom. Starting the seeds indoors, in peat containers or even clay pots, makes for less perilous gardening in the long run. Besides, a window ledge of basil is rumored to have the added virtue of keeping houseflies away from the kitchen. *Rumored,* I say, because I have never noticed that felicitous gift among my greens. Basil does, however, have an unusual attraction for aphids and white flies and nothing rids a clump of those terrible pests except transplantation outdoors.

The best time to transplant seedlings is late spring, after they are fully four or five inches tall. Set them out about eight inches apart, if you have the growing space. If not, don't worry about it. All my green life I have heard the old adage that "crowded gardens are poor gardens" but I say ho-hum to that. My finest herb crop came from an absolute hedge of spicy basil plants blooming furiously cheek by jowl. It was, however, a very hot and well-rained summer, as I recall.

Basil needs lots of water or it wilts, especially on scorching August afternoons (although a generous watering always seems to revive it, too). For a truly lush blossoming, the soil must be dark and rich, with a mite of manure added at the gardener's discretion from time to time.

Choose two types of basil for a kitchen garden. Large-leafed, curly basil holds its flavor best in cooking, while lemon basil, as its name implies, has a pungent, lemony fragrance that is absolutely delicious in salads. Purple basil certainly makes a decorative herbal adjunct, but it has little flavor and will *not* do in your *pot au feu!*

I discovered a while back that adding a pinch or two of rough salt to basil leaves before they are chopped will keep the color a bright, garden green.

A fine way to test that tip is the following receipt, a tonic first course or luncheon dish composed of chilled, cooked zucchini laced with a nippy Italianate dressing of uncooked basil, parsley, onions, garlic, capers, and anchovies.

This basil formula came from a genuine fan of mine who inadvertently threw out a clutch of meat loaf recipes I did for *Family Circle* magazine a year or so ago. In return for a missing spinach meat loaf that I supplied her, Mrs. Cooper kindly sent me Cold Zucchini Salsa Verde. A fair exchange, I think.

BETSY COOPER'S
COLD ZUCCHINI
SALSA VERDE

8 to 10 small zucchini
1 small onion, chopped
1 shallot, chopped
2 cloves garlic, chopped
3 teaspoons capers
4 anchovy fillets
1 cup vegetable or olive oil
½ cup lemon juice
1 teaspoon seasoned salt
Seasoned pepper to taste
1 cup coarsely chopped parsley
1 cup finely chopped parsley
½ cup finely chopped fresh basil
  leaves

Serves 8 to 10.

1 Wash, trim, and cut the zucchini in half lengthwise. Drop into boiling salted water and cook exactly 4 minutes. Rinse immediately under cold running water until cool. Drain on paper toweling and chill.

2 Place the onion, shallot, garlic, capers, anchovies, oil, lemon juice, salt, pepper, and coarsely chopped parsley into a blender container. Blend until smooth. Add the finely chopped parsley and basil and chill until ready to serve.

3 Just before serving, arrange the zucchini on a platter and spoon the sauce over it.

Note: Recipe can be cut in half. I usually cook with Olio Sasso, a mildly fragrant olive oil produced by Sasso and Figli in Oneglia, Italy. This product is packaged in pint-, quart- and gallon-sized tins that I decant into *green* glass wine bottles to protect the precious elixir from the sun. I dilute stronger olive oils (like Olivieri or Plagniol) with equal amounts of Wesson vegetable oil for my saute pan. But I am predisposed to sweet-scented cooking ingredients; a more temperate blending would be one part olive oil to two parts vegetable oil. Wesson has been a family friend since I started cooking—and a bottle has been close at hand in every kitchen I have made my own. I must confess, however, to a recently acquired addiction (for health's sake) to poly-unsaturated sunflower oil. Hain brand (pure cold-pressed) is my hands-down preference in that department!

Remarkably bracing to the tongue, Betsy Cooper's Salsa Verde, sans zucchini, makes a saucy emollient for shellfish or cold mussels—like the ones left over from the creamy soup next on my agenda. The velvety elixir, Billi Bi, was invented by Pierre Franey, one of our nation's great chefs (albeit a French import) when he ruled the kitchen at Le Pavillion a couple of decades ago. I learned the formula during my own stint as chief cook and bottlewasher at The Store in Amagansett, some while back. The recipe was pressed into my hand by a blue-haired East Hampton matron who swore she had slept with Henri Soule

(Pavillion's late owner) just to secure the treasure. Whether truth or fiction I never discovered, but the soup is virtue's own reward. The prescription came to me written in a bad scrawl, almost totally illegible and hopelessly stained. I must confess that I misread basil for parsley and made the soup with that herbal increment instead—a happy accident I have never bothered to repair.

BASIL BILLI BI

1 Scrub mussels, removing "beards" and any sand. Place in a large pot, cover with water, and stir in the cornstarch. Let stand 20 minutes, rinse under cold running water, and drain.

2 In a large kettle, combine mussels with all ingredients except whipping cream, egg yolk, and ¼ cup basil. Cover and bring to a boil. Reduce heat; simmer until mussels open, 5 to 10 minutes. Remove mussels.

3 Strain the cooking liquid through a fine sieve and bring to a boil. Add the cream, return to boiling, and remove from heat. Whisk in the egg yolk and cook over low heat until slightly thickened; do not boil. Serve hot or cold sprinkled with basil.

2 pounds mussels
2 teaspoons cornstarch
2 shallots, coarsely chopped
2 small onions, cut into quarters
2 sprigs parsley
4 leaves fresh basil or ½ teaspoon dried
½ teaspoon salt
Pinch of freshly ground black pepper
Pinch of ground cayenne pepper
1 cup dry white wine
2 tablespoons butter
½ bay leaf
½ teaspoon fresh thyme
2 cups whipping cream
1 egg yolk, lightly beaten
¼ cup finely chopped fresh basil leaves, or 1 teaspoon dried chopped with ¼ cup parsley

Serves 4.

Basil and shrimp are old friends. I like them best in a salad partnership with myriad other flavors and textures—like rice and peas. The secret of a wonderful cold Venetian lunch dish, Risi e Bisi con Scampi, is the mayonnaise sauce, which must be very light and lemony. I usually mix the ingredients together at the very last moment, so that the rice does not get sodden. And I make sure the peas are almost raw—each nubbin almost as crisp and green as it was in the pod!

1½ cups Homemade Mayonnaise
   (recipe follows)
1 cup dry white wine
1 cup clam juice
½ lemon, sliced
3 sprigs parsley
2 ribs celery, with leaves, cut in
   half
1 large onion studded with 3
   cloves
1 bay leaf
1½ cups water
1 pound small shrimp
1 cup uncooked rice
1 teaspoon salt
1 cup fresh or frozen peas
2 shallots, minced
1 rib celery, minced
1 small pimiento, cut into strips
3 tablespoons minced fresh basil
   leaves or 1 tablespoon dried
2 tablespoons chopped parsley
Salt and ground white pepper
Lettuce leaves

Serves 4.

2 egg yolks, at room temperature
1 tablespoon wine vinegar
Juice of ½ lemon
¼ teaspoon salt
Pinch of ground white pepper
1 packet chicken bouillon powder
1 teaspoon Dijon mustard
2 cups vegetable oil, or a mixture
   of 1⅓ cups vegetable oil and ⅔
   cup olive oil
Dash of hot pepper sauce
2 tablespoons boiling water

Makes about 1½ cups.

RISI E BISI CON SCAMPI

1 Make mayonnaise.

2 Place wine, clam juice, lemon, parsley sprigs, 2 ribs celery, the onion, bay leaf, and water in a large saucepan and bring to a boil; add shrimp. Cook 3 minutes. Allow shrimp to cool slightly in the broth. Remove shrimp with a slotted spoon; peel, devein, and reserve shrimp. Return the shells to the broth; boil 3 minutes. Strain broth and return to saucepan.

3 Bring the broth to a boil; add the rice and salt. Cook until rice is barely done, 12 to 15 minutes. Drain rice in a colander. Set the colander over a large pot of boiling water, being careful that bottom of colander does not touch water. Cover colander with paper toweling. Steam the rice over boiling water 15 minutes. Cool.

4 Meanwhile, allow the peas to defrost if using frozen; do not cook them. If using fresh, cook in boiling salted water for 1 minute; immediately rinse under cold running water and drain.

5 Add reserved shrimp, shallots, 1 rib celery, and the peas to the rice. Stir in 1½ cups mayonnaise. Stir in pimiento strips, basil, parsley, and salt and pepper to taste. Serve on lettuce leaves.

HOMEMADE MAYONNAISE

Combine all ingredients except oil, hot pepper sauce, and water. Slowly beat in the oil, a few drops at a time, until mixture begins to thicken; then beat in the remainder of the oil 1 tablespoonful at a time. Add the hot pepper sauce; beat in the boiling water.

Note: A rule of thumb for flawless mayonnaise making: Be sure that all ingredients, as well as the bowl the stuff is beaten in, are at room temperature. Actually, a slightly warmer bowl will hasten the procedure.

Basil and tomato are *more* than just friends. I have noticed that tomatoes ripen redder in the garden when the herb is planted nearby. Now that must mean that something's up! Yet another

Italian leaf from my basil salad collection, Cold Zucchini and Tomato Salad, was a Store standby for eleven years. The secret of its goodness is a tart, mustardy vinaigrette sauce for bindery.

Cold Zucchini and Tomato Salad is, of course, best made in August when the basil grows knee-high, but in a pinch I have turned out an equally green version during a February blizzard. The trick is a *homemade herbal extract* substituted for the ordinary dried herb. It's easy pharmacy: simply transfer the contents of a jar of dried basil leaves to a slightly larger glass container, add an ounce or so of Galliano liqueur and allow the leaves to steep. Cover the jar and keep at room temperature (out of the sunlight) until needed. When a recipe calls for chopped fresh basil, use half the specified quantity of damp, liqueur-preserved basil and chop it with an equal amount of fresh parsley. You will be astounded at how reinvigorated a salad will taste with the addition of this blend.

COLD ZUCCHINI AND TOMATO SALAD

Mix vegetables, basil, and parsley in a large bowl. Season with salt and pepper to taste. Just before serving, add Vinaigrette Dressing and toss well.

Note: For picnic fare, carry the mixed, chilled salad and the Vinaigrette Dressing separately. Toss salad with dressing just before serving.

3 to 4 zucchini, cut into ⅛-inch slices (about 3 cups)
2 cups cherry tomatoes, cut in half
½ cup minced shallots
½ cup chopped fresh basil leaves or 2 teaspoons dried chopped with the parsley
¼ cup chopped parsley
Salt and freshly ground pepper
¾ cup Vinaigrette Dressing (see Index)

Serves 6 to 8.

Another basil exercise, a Northern Italian ratatouille intersticed with potatoes and cheese, was found jotted among Jean Jacques Rousseau's papers—and how it came into his repertoire is any philosopher's guess! This dish (heavy on the basil) makes a very satisfying lunch or supper main course. For brunch, try it with poached eggs on top. I also happen to like it stone cold, drizzled with olive oil and a bit of vinegar. A cooking acquaintance of mine claims she tosses anchovies on top of that—but you mix or match it at your own discretion.

3 tablespoons unsalted butter
1 medium eggplant, thinly sliced, slices cut in half
Salt
¼ cup plus 2 tablespoons olive oil
1 red onion, thinly sliced
1 yellow onion, thinly sliced
4 medium potatoes, peeled, thinly sliced
1 large clove garlic, mashed
3 to 4 small zucchini, thinly sliced
4 tomatoes, seeded, cut into strips
2 green or red peppers, seeded, cut into strips
3 tablespoons chopped fresh basil leaves or 1½ tablespoons dried
½ cup pitted black olives, sliced
Coarse salt and freshly ground pepper
1 cup grated Parmesan cheese
¼ cup chopped fresh parsley

Serves 6.

VERDURA GENOVESE AL FORNO

1 Heat oven to 375°. Butter a gratin dish or 2-quart casserole with 1 tablespoon butter. Sprinkle the eggplant with salt and let stand ½ hour. Saute eggplant in 2 tablespoons butter and 2 tablespoons oil.

2 Layer the vegetables in the gratin dish as follows: half the onions, half the potatoes, half the garlic, half the eggplant, half the zucchini, half the tomatoes, half the peppers, half the basil, half the olives, and 2 tablespoons of the oil. Sprinkle with coarse salt, pepper, and half the cheese. Repeat the layers, omitting cheese.

3 Bake 35 minutes. Sprinkle remaining cheese over the top; bake 15 minutes. Garnish with chopped parsley and serve with additional grated Parmesan cheese.

Everybody has a deviled-egg fetish, I have discovered (except those unlucky folk who are allergic to the egg in any guise). My favored hard-cooked coup combines the lissome yolks with sour cream-cum-mayo and snippings of basil leaves and tops them with a dab of red caviar. Only fresh basil will do in this French interpolation.

PUFF-OF-SILK EGGS

9 hard-cooked eggs
¼ cup mayonnaise
¼ cup sour cream
Juice of ½ lemon
1 teaspoon finely grated lemon peel
3 large shallots, very finely minced
Salt to taste
¼ cup chopped fresh basil leaves
Freshly ground pepper
1 jar (4 ounces) red caviar

Serves 6 to 9.

1 Cut the eggs in half lengthwise and remove the yolks to a bowl. Mash well with a fork; stir in the mayonnaise, sour cream, lemon juice, lemon peel, shallots, salt, and basil. (The mixture should be the consistency of mashed potatoes—not too runny!)

2 Fill the egg whites. Dust with freshly ground pepper and top each with about ½ teaspoon caviar. Chill well.

Note: I let the eggs stand at room temperature for a day before boiling them to assure easy peeling—very fresh eggs are impossible to shell. Eggs are less likely to crack during cooking if you make a small hole in one end of each with a push-pin or a darning needle before bringing them to a boil. Boil 10 minutes; then plunge them into icy water.

You will hardly ever find fresh basil on a supermarket's vegetable shelf because the herb is fragile and has little staying power. However, persistent culinary detectives will discover basil in profusion at most Italian green-grocers from July through Labor Day.

The best way to prolong the freshness of basil is to keep the leaves in a container in the refrigerator. Merely wash the leaves, pat them dry, and pack them loosely into a wide-mouthed jar. Well-covered, the cold cache will keep a week and a half (and sometimes longer) without taint.

Who was Ilena, for whom the next dish is named? I do not truthfully know but the lady certainly knew her onions (or shallots, if you can get them). Anyone who conceived of the combination of sauteed fish—golden beneath its blanket of white wine, cream, and egg sauce—and chopped fresh basil was someone I'd have liked to have had around the house!

FLOUNDER ILENA

1 Heat oven to 275°. Sprinkle the fish with salt and pepper; dust with flour.

2 Melt 3 tablespoons butter in a large skillet and cook the onions until transparent but not browned. Transfer the onions to an ungreased baking dish.

3 Saute the fish until golden, about 2 minutes per side, adding more butter to the skillet if necessary. Arrange fish on top of the onions and keep warm in the oven.

4 Add the wine to the skillet. Cook over high heat, scraping bottom and sides of pan, 3 minutes. Remove from heat. Beat the egg with the cream; whisk into skillet. Add the basil and cook over very low heat until thickened, about 3 minutes. Stir in the lemon juice and pour over the fish. Place under the broiler for a few minutes to brown.

8 small flounder or sole fillets
   (about 1½ pounds)
Salt and freshly ground pepper
Flour
5 to 6 tablespoons unsalted butter
½ cup finely chopped white onions
   or shallots
⅓ cup dry white wine or vermouth
1 egg
½ cup whipping cream
2 tablespoons chopped fresh basil
   or 1 teaspoon dried chopped with
   1½ tablespoons parsley
1 tablespoon lemon juice

Serves 4.

Basil and fruit is not just, as the French say, a marriage of convenience. The mutual dependence of apple and herb gives a fairly standard meat loaf receipt (born during the 1960s era of communal cuisine) a distinctive, winy lacing.

BRATTLEBORO "COMMUNE-STYLE" LOAF

2 slices whole-wheat bread,
   crumbled
½ cup milk
1 egg, lightly beaten
½ cup finely diced apples
½ cup finely diced celery
¼ cup wheat germ
1½ pounds lean ground pork
½ pound spicy pork sausage
½ teaspoon salt
⅛ teaspoon freshly ground pepper
2 tablespoons chopped parsley
1 teaspoon chopped fresh basil
Pinch of thyme leaves
Pinch of ground nutmeg

Serves 4 to 6.

1 Heat oven to 350°. Place the bread in a large mixing bowl and pour the milk over; mix well. Add remaining ingredients, mixing well after each addition.

2 Shape mixture into a loaf in a shallow baking dish. Bake 1 hour and 15 minutes.

More garden-to-stove cookery—Italian fried romaine lettuce pancakes. Need I say they are best when the romaine is picked fresh, at the green of perfection? Basil gives each bite an indefinable zest you will hunger after for days. I speak (as always) from my own experience!

FRITTELLA

1 medium head of romaine lettuce
Kosher salt
1 medium onion, minced
2 eggs, well beaten
1 cup soft bread crumbs
1 tablespoon coarsely chopped
   fresh basil leaves or 1 teaspoon
   dried
½ packet chicken bouillon powder
¼ cup grated Parmesan cheese
Salt and freshly ground pepper
1 tablespoon unsalted butter
Vegetable oil

Serves 6.

1 Cut off the bottom of the lettuce; discard. Wash the leaves, dry, and chop coarsely. Place in a colander and sprinkle with kosher salt. Let stand at least ½ hour. Squeeze dry in a dish towel.

2 Combine the minced onion, eggs, bread crumbs, basil, and bouillon powder in a large bowl. Stir in the lettuce and cheese. Mix well and season to taste with salt and pepper.

3 Melt the butter in a heavy skillet; add oil to depth of ¼ inch. Heat over medium heat.

4 Using a wooden spoon, shape the batter into small cakes and add to the skillet a few at a time. Fry until golden, about 5 minutes per side. Remove with a slotted spoon to several layers of paper toweling; drain well. Keep warm on a serving platter while frying remainder.

Note: Fritella may be reheated by placing them in a 350° oven for about 10 minutes, but they are best served up freshly made. They are delicious as a first course, simple luncheon entrée, or a companion to a roast when you wish to skip potatoes.

At last, the paradigmatic employment of basil in a kitchen— Pesto alla Genovese, the version of the garlicky, green pasta sauce I first concocted when I ran The Store in Amagansett's galley as well as its garden. Nowadays, pesto is converted to many odd uses (I have even seen a salad dressing recipe spiked with it) but its prime utility is as a sauce for newly cooked strands of tender pasta.

Having had my say on that subject, however, I will admit to being an ambivalent Libran, as you can tell by sneaking a glance at the Roast Chicken with Pesto Rice recipe that follows the sauce formula.

First, however, one caveat about pesto making: I have not discovered a way to prepare this illustrious sauce without fresh basil. A sunny window sill in my apartment houses half a dozen plants every summer but despite assiduous pinchings and trimmings, the crop usually dwindles to one sad straggler (entirely encased in a plastic baggie to keep the cold at bay) by Christmas. I have found freezing basil for later use to be an utter waste of time, for the soggy mess is simply too unappetizing for any cook with true mettle to deal with. The best preservation method I have ever come upon is the following:

Remove the largest leaves from a basil plant in early fall and loosely pack them in a large glass jar, covering the layers with olive oil. If the container is airtight, the oil will become flavored with the basil and turn a rich greenish hue; the leaves will retain their true character and taste for several months at least.

PESTO ALLA GENOVESE

2 cups coarsely chopped fresh basil leaves
½ cup chopped parsley
1½ teaspoons kosher salt
1½ teaspoons freshly ground pepper
2 large cloves garlic, chopped
¾ cup olive oil
¼ cup pine nuts
½ cup freshly grated Romano cheese

1 Place all ingredients except the cheese into a blender container. Blend until smooth, about 5 minutes. (You might have to start and stop the blender several times in the beginning.)

2 Transfer the basil mixture to a bowl and stir in the cheese. Serve over pasta with additional grated cheese on the side.

Note: Pesto can be kept refrigerated in a tightly covered jar for several months. It can also be frozen, but then it is best to stir in the cheese upon defrosting.

Makes about 1½ cups or enough for 6 servings.

And now, bring on the chicken! *Molto buono*—I promise you—even in its damned-with-faint-praise lack of orthodoxy.

ROAST CHICKEN WITH PESTO RICE

½ cup Pesto alla Genovese (see previous recipe)
2 small roasting chickens (about 3½ pounds each)
1 clove garlic, bruised
3 cups cooked rice
¼ cup pine nuts
2 tablespoons butter, softened
Salt and freshly ground pepper
½ cup water
1 tablespoon flour
1 tablespoon water
¼ cup whipping cream
1 egg yolk, lightly beaten
1 tablespoon chopped fresh basil

Serves 4 to 6.

1 Make Pesto alla Genovese.

2 Heat oven to 450°. Rub the chickens all over with the garlic. Combine the rice, ½ cup pesto, and the pine nuts. Stuff each chicken with half the mixture; truss.

3 Place the chickens in a roasting pan and rub each with 1 tablespoon butter. Sprinkle generously with salt and pepper. Roast 30 minutes.

4 Pour ½ cup water around the chickens and reduce heat to 350°. Roast the chickens 1¼ hours longer, basting with pan juices every 10 minutes.

5 Place the chickens on a serving platter; remove trussing. Keep warm while making the sauce.

6 Skim fat from pan juices. Place ½ cup juices in a heavy saucepan; heat over medium heat. Mix the flour with 1 tablespoon water; stir into saucepan. Heat to boiling; reduce heat. Simmer 5 minutes. Add the cream; simmer a few minutes longer, until slightly thickened. Remove from heat.

7 Mix 1 tablespoon of the sauce into the egg yolk; stir the egg yolk mixture back into the sauce. Cook over low heat, without boiling, 2 minutes. Add the basil. Pour sauce over chickens.

Brandy

Perhaps because there is the teeniest bit of pyromania in my nature, I never shirk from the prospect of a flambé! But I have seen other cooks demonstrate, in various ways, man's natural reluctance to face instant immolation. Craig Claiborne, for example, inhales very sharply before he sets his pans afire, while Robert Carrier stands at arm's length from his chafing dish target and uses an excessively long matchstick.

The first famous chef I ever watched was Michael Field and he (bless him) always closed his eyes when the time came to ignite a crêpe suzette. Setting the world on fire with a Fieldian version of some terribly complicated recipe like *bisteeya* was child's play to Michael—but face him in the direction of a chafing dish and he acted as if Joan of Arc herself was at the other end of his taper.

"The deed is done," Michael would murmur to his cooking classes as the heavenly scent of cognac drifted over the kitchen. And his loving students would then relax, safe in the knowledge that their *maître* had escaped conflagration once again.

Roy Andries de Groot, another eminent gourmet and foodophile, unfortunately is blind, having sustained injuries during the London blitz of World War II. But no infirmity could ever hamper this man's cooking style. Baron de Groot (and he is truly of a noble Dutch line) is one of the most original and well-informed kitchen savants alive—and he dearly loves to whoosh a brandy bottle aloft as he cooks.

There is a wonderful tale told about the time, some while back, when the baron came to chat and chef on "The Mike

Douglas Show." Being a very independent man, de Groot appeared at the TV studios with only his seeing-eye dog for assistance. All culinary aid proferred by host Douglas and guest-star Sammy Davis Jr. was rejected as the baron prepared to flame a duck *à l'orange* on camera. As the lenses zoomed in for a close-up, the baron confidently tossed back his hair and wielded the Armagnac—but, completely missing his *plat du jour*, he hit the Sterno can below it. And promptly set fire to the tablecloth, the overhead drapes, and very nearly Mr. Davis too.

A fortuitous commercial break saved the day. Sammy D. suffered only a bruised ego while the baron, in the best show-biz tradition, segued into a frozen dessert—proving the indestructibility of television as a medium for the misbegotten. Happily for his fans, de Groot still cooks on TV—but his dishes are restricted to non-flammable recipes only!

If you are asking why this culinary urgency to go to blazes, the answer is—a matter of taste. The addition of spirits (in moderation) gives a dish a particular savor and a rewarding aroma that cannot be achieved by any other flavoring. And the act of igniting the booze (so that the alcohol evaporates) makes the significant difference between Alice B. Toklas's remarkable recipe for Boeuf à la Bourguignonne and anybody else's beef stew.

2 pounds ½-inch-thick boneless beef steak, cut into 3-inch squares
½ cup cognac
8 tablespoons butter
1 cup diced salt pork
12 small white onions, peeled, with a cross cut in each root end
1 tablespoon plus 1 teaspoon all-purpose flour
3 cups red Burgundy wine, warmed
1 cup hot water
½ teaspoon salt
½ teaspoon freshly ground pepper
Bouquet garni composed of 1 sprig thyme, 3 sprigs parsley, 1 bay leaf, pinch of ground nutmeg, and 1 crushed clove garlic
2 cups small mushrooms
2 tablespoons chopped parsley

Serves 4.

MISS TOKLAS'S BOEUF À LA BOURGUIGNONNE

1 Place meat in a bowl; pour ⅓ cup cognac over. Refrigerate at least 6 hours, turning frequently. Drain meat; reserve cognac marinade.

2 Melt 4 tablespoons butter in a Dutch oven. Add meat and brown well on all sides; remove from pan. Saute salt pork until brown; remove from pan. Saute onions until brown; remove from pan.

3 Remove two thirds of the fat from Dutch oven. Add flour; cook over low heat, stirring constantly with a wooden spoon, 10 minutes. Add the meat; pour wine and water over. Add the salt, pepper, salt pork, bouquet garni, and the reserved cognac marinade.

4 Heat remaining cognac in a small saucepan. Ignite and pour over meat. Cover meat; bring to a boil. Reduce heat; simmer until tender, 2½ to 3 hours.

5 Add onions; simmer ½ hour. Saute mushrooms in remaining 4 tablespoons butter in a skillet over medium heat until browned, about

10 minutes. Remove bouquet garni from Dutch oven; skim fat, if necessary. Add mushrooms; simmer 5 minutes. Place stew in a deep serving dish; garnish with parsley.

When I taught cooking, invariably someone at each session would raise a hand to ask a question as I flambéed the beef or chicken.

"Aren't cognac and brandy the same thing?" they always queried.

"Well," I learned to posit amid the flames, "all cognac is certainly brandy. But not all brandy is cognac!"

As that usually made matters more confusing, I would put out the fire and pull out a pocket map of France—to illustrate my point that only those brandies distilled in the Cognac region (roughly the lower left-hand corner of the country) can be legally termed cognac.

Cognac, like wine, originates with grapes, but unlike the vintner's typical harvest of *vin supèrieur et ordinaire,* the wine for cognac is taken one step further and distilled. Happily for genteel imbibers everywhere, that wondrous distillation is unflagging in quality—and still France's second largest export!

Brandy (derived from the German *brantwein* meaning "burnt wine") can be made from practically anything—wood pulp, rosebuds, pine cones, fruit pits, berries, or apples. The trick of turning this oddment into decent liquor lies in the aging process. The oak casks within which the best brandy ages are all made from trees that grow in the forests of Limousin (which also happens to be sensational cherry country, I might add). The barrels are always made by hand to ensure that they are airtight. Brandy makers are so finicky, in fact, that they claim the best Limousin oak must come from the Troncais woods (and only from the right edge, at that).

Brandy is the most commonly used spirit in the kitchen because of its high alcoholic content. However, less is often more than enough when one considers the prospect of setting a dish aflame. Too much brandy tends to toughen meats (like beef, game, or even chicken); so the wise chef is prudent with his pouring arm.

A chicken dish I would hate for you to spoil with overindulgence comes from the hills of Normandy (between Avranches and Alençon). The flaming essential is Calvados, a glowing apple brandy distilled from the fruit that blooms in the Auge Valley.

CHICKEN VALLÉE D'AUGE
WITH SAUTEED APPLES

1 chicken (about 3 pounds), cut up
 for frying
Salt and freshly ground pepper
10 tablespoons butter
2 tablespoons vegetable oil
¼ cup Calvados or applejack
 brandy
½ cup chicken broth or stock
2 tablespoons finely chopped
 shallots
¼ cup finely chopped celery
2 small tart apples, peeled, cored,
 coarsely chopped
½ teaspoon chopped fresh thyme or
 ¼ teaspoon dried
3 large, firm apples, cored, cut
 into ½-inch-thick rings
2 to 4 tablespoons granulated sugar
2 egg yolks
½ cup whipping cream
Cayenne pepper to taste
½ teaspoon lemon juice
2 tablespoons finely chopped
 parsley
Watercress sprigs for garnish
4 cups buttered cooked rice

Serves 4.

1 Wipe chicken with a damp towel; dry thoroughly with paper toweling. Sprinkle with salt and pepper.

2 Heat 4 tablespoons butter with the oil in a large heavy skillet until hot. Brown the chicken, skin side down, over high heat until deep golden. Remove all but 1 tablespoon fat from skillet.

3 Heat the brandy in a small saucepan; ignite and pour over chicken. Shake skillet gently until the flames subside. Pour the stock over the chicken.

4 Melt 2 tablespoons butter in a small saucepan. Add the shallots, celery, chopped apples, and thyme; cook over low heat until vegetables are soft but not brown. Spoon mixture over chicken; cover skillet and heat to boiling. Reduce heat to medium-low; cook until chicken is tender, about 30 minutes, basting every 10 minutes.

5 Heat oven to 250°. Sprinkle apple rings with sugar on both sides. Heat 4 tablespoons butter in a large skillet; add the apples. Saute over high heat until light brown and glazed, being careful not to over-cook. Keep warm in oven until serving time.

6 Remove chicken from skillet; place on serving platter. Keep warm in oven. Press apple mixture from skillet through a sieve into a small saucepan; discard pulp. Let stand several minutes; then skim fat. (There should be about 1 cup of liquid in pan.) Heat to boiling; boil until reduced to ½ cup.

7 Whisk egg yolks with ½ cup cream in a small bowl. Whisk in the reduced liquid, 1 tablespoon at a time. Return mixture to saucepan; cook over low heat, stirring constantly and scraping bottom and sides of the pan, until mixture begins to thicken (Do not boil!). Remove pan from heat; stir vigorously 10 seconds. Return to heat; cook, stirring constantly, until the sauce coats spoon. Continue to stir while adding the cayenne pepper and lemon juice.

8 Spoon sauce over chicken, coating each piece. Sprinkle with parsley; surround chicken with apple rings. Garnish chicken with watercress. Serve with rice.

Note: Chicken and sauce may be prepared in advance and refrigerated separately, tightly covered. Reheat chicken 20 minutes before serving in a covered casserole with 2 tablespoons chicken stock. Reheat sauce in the top of a double boiler over hot water; if it is too thick, thin with stock or cream. A teaspoon of chopped fresh tarragon added to the sauce gives it a good flavor.

Nobody who has shared my dining table with any regularity questions why I cook with spirits—for a splash of cognac seething in a saute pan invokes a perfume too seductive to challenge. I have also found that a marinade of brandy (or Calvados) not only enhances the flavor of the final dish but actually tenderizes the meat and increases its juiciness.

The aforementioned Calvados is a strong drink on its own merits and, I warrant, an acquired taste. I grew to like it when I spent a November in an unheated house at the beach—with a bottle as my only bed-warmer! Though not everyone's cup of cheer, the brew provides a seminal lacing for many a flamed entrée. You can substitute applejack, but let me point out that Calvados has a much more assuasive flavor—for all the fusillade it occasions on the tongue. One of my prime formulas for spicy roasted pork calls for the meat to be marinated overnight in this appley-elixir prior to the fireworks.

ROAST PORK WITH CALVADOS

1 Place pork in a glass or ceramic baking dish; pour brandy over. Refrigerate at least 4 hours or overnight.

2 Heat oven to 325°. Remove pork from marinade; reserve marinade. Rub pork all over with salt, pepper, nutmeg, cloves, and allspice. Place on a rack in a roasting pan. Roast 2½ hours.

3 Peel potatoes. Cook in boiling salted water 5 minutes. Drain; cut into quarters and pat dry with paper toweling. Pour off fat from pork into a shallow baking dish. Add potatoes; toss to coat. Bake at 325° for 1 hour, turning potatoes over after 30 minutes. (Raise heat to 375° for last 10 minutes of baking if potatoes are not crisp.)

4 Remove pork from roasting pan; remove rack. Line bottom of pan with apples; sprinkle with brown sugar and cinnamon. Heat reserved marinade in a small saucepan; pour over apples. Ignite; let flame subside. Place pork over apples; roast 45 minutes. (Cover pan with aluminum foil if pork begins to look dry.) Serve pork surrounded by apples and potatoes.

1 pork loin (about 5 pounds), ribs cracked
¾ cup Calvados or applejack brandy
1 tablespoon coarse salt
Freshly ground black pepper to taste
¼ teaspoon freshly grated nutmeg
¼ teaspoon ground cloves
2 or 3 allspice berries, crushed
6 medium potatoes
6 large, tart apples, peeled, cored, sliced
½ cup brown sugar
¼ teaspoon ground cinnamon

Serves 6 to 8.

Cognac and chicken have a curious flavor affinity. I usually add some spirits to roast chicken pan juices, ignite them, and snuff out the flame with a slurp of heavy cream, which also serves to thicken the sauce.

A parenthetical note, however: as the burned-off cognac leaves only its flavor behind, the spirits must be of a high grade. Three tablespoons of an aged Courvoisier or Martell V. S. P. is my rule of thumb, since quality, not quantity, makes the ineluctable difference between a good and a great chicken dish—like the one limned below.

Two tips for Chicken with Avocado and Mushrooms: Make sure the avocado is really ripe before you marinate it; tough fruit will spoil the silken combination of textures. And serve lots of freshly cooked rice, unbuttered, alongside.

CHICKEN WITH AVOCADO AND MUSHROOMS

1 small avocado (preferably the dark-skinned, California variety)
1 tablespoon lemon juice
2 chickens (2½ pounds each), cut into serving pieces
Salt and freshly ground pepper
6 tablespoons butter (approximately)
3 shallots, finely chopped
3 tablespoons good cognac
⅓ cup dry white wine
1 cup whipping cream
2 cups sliced fresh mushrooms
1 cup chicken stock or enriched chicken broth
Chopped parsley for garnish

Serves 4 to 6.

1 Peel and cube the avocado; sprinkle with lemon juice. Cover and refrigerate.

2 Heat oven to 300°. Sprinkle the chicken with salt and pepper; saute in 3 tablespoons butter in large skillet over low heat until the juices run yellow when chicken is pricked with a fork, about 35 to 40 minutes. (Add more butter during cooking, if needed.) Transfer to a serving dish; cover loosely with aluminum foil. Keep warm in oven 15 minutes while preparing sauce.

3 Add shallots to skillet; cook over medium heat, stirring and scraping sides and bottom of pan with a wooden spoon. Add 2 tablespoons cognac; ignite and let flame subside. Add wine and bring to a boil; boil until mixture has almost evaporated. Add cream; boil 5 minutes.

4 Saute mushrooms in 3 tablespoons butter in a saucepan over high heat until golden.

5 Add chicken stock to cream mixture; cook over medium heat, stirring constantly, until thick. Add the mushrooms, remaining cognac, and avocado cubes; stir until well blended. Pour over chicken. Sprinkle with parsley.

The following device is a bit of culinary fraud or legerdermain, depending upon your point of view. Breast of turkey masquerades as fillet of veal; seasoned with garlic and thyme and aromatically sealed with brandied bread crumbs that also soften the bird's texture immeasurably. An original precept (from Vienna) called for a veal loin, rolled and tied, but I amended the ingredient list recently—out of prudence—when veal prices began to soar skyward. During the Depression, when I was a kid, nobody except Italians ever cooked veal—because it was considered a cheap cut of meat! Chicken was king in those days. And I remember well my mother's penny-pinching trick of roasting a small leg of veal just so she could cut up the leftovers to extend a chicken salad. Tempus definitely has fidgeted since!

BROASTED BRANDIED TURKEY BREAST

1 Place the turkey breast on a rack in a roasting pan and rub well with 2 tablespoons of the cognac. Let stand 1 hour.

2 Heat oven to 425°. Mash the garlic with the butter. Stir in bread crumbs and thyme until smooth. Slowly stir in 2 tablespoons cognac. Spread mixture evenly over top and sides of the turkey breast, making sure it is well coated.

3 Roast turkey breast in oven 15 minutes. Reduce heat to 350°. Film the bottom of the pan with about 1 cup water. Continue to roast until the juices run yellow when breast is pricked with a fork, about 1 hour and 15 minutes longer. Add the chicken stock to the pan about 15 minutes before breast is done.

4 Transfer turkey to a platter; let stand 10 minutes. Strain pan juices, enrich with remaining tablespoon of cognac and serve with turkey.

1 whole turkey breast (about 5 pounds), bone in
5 tablespoons cognac
1 clove garlic, crushed
6 tablespoons butter, softened
1/4 cup fresh bread crumbs
1/4 teaspoon chopped fresh thyme, or a pinch of dried
1 cup chicken stock

Serves 4 to 6.

Cognac and brandy are interchangeable in the next recipes. It is the addition of either essence in tiny dosage, however, that turns the drabbest vegetable trio (peas and carrots plus lettuce) into something sublime. Credit the French with that inspiration, please! And make a mental memorandum: spirits need not always be inflamed in order to vitalize a dish. Sometimes a mere dash of aromatic tincture will add a piquancy and savor to a dish that no other seasoning or spice will afford. My grandmother always kept a small bottle of schnapps in her kitchen cabinet— not for any secret nips, for she was quite teetotal, but for serious recipe resuscitations.

CARROTS AND PEAS NIVERNAISE

6 tablespoons unsalted butter
8 to 10 medium carrots, cut into
  1½-inch-long strips
½ cup strong chicken broth
1 teaspoon granulated sugar
1 package frozen peas
1 small head Boston or Romaine
  lettuce, shredded
Salt and freshly ground pepper
2 tablespoons cognac
3 to 4 tablespoons whipping cream

Serves 4 to 6.

1 Heat 4 tablespoons butter in a saucepan until golden in color. Add carrots and chicken broth; cook covered over medium heat 8 minutes. Sprinkle with sugar.

2 Add peas and lettuce; cook and stir with a fork over high heat until vegetables are crisp-tender and all liquid is absorbed. Stir in 2 tablespoons butter; season to taste with salt and pepper. Remove from heat. Stir in cognac and cream. Serve at once.

The following French formula for Chou Chou stands the old green vegetable in good stead; yet it has nothing at all to do with Chow-Chow, the mustard pickle you grew up on. You didn't? Well, I did!

CHOU CHOU

1 small head cabbage
4 tablespoons butter
3 to 4 slices Canadian Bacon, cut
  into thin strips
½ teaspoon Dijon mustard
2½ tablespoons brandy
1 large yellow onion, finely
  chopped
1 package (3 ounces) cream cheese
1 tablespoon whipping cream
1½ tablespoons chopped fresh dill
Salt and freshly ground pepper to
  taste

Serves 4 to 6.

1 Remove tough outer leaves from cabbage. Cut cabbage into quarters; remove core. Grate cabbage or chop to texture of fine shreds. Add cabbage to large pot of boiling salted water; boil 5 minutes. Drain.

2 Melt 1 tablespoon butter in a small saucepan. Add bacon; cook and stir over medium-high heat just until strips begin to brown. Reduce heat; stir in mustard and brandy. Cook over low heat 3 minutes.

3 Melt remaining butter in a large saucepan. Add onion and saute over medium heat until translucent but not brown. Stir in the cream cheese and cream until cheese melts. Reduce heat; add cabbage. Cook over low heat 3 minutes. Add bacon mixture; cook until cabbage is tender, 4 to 5 minutes. Add dill and salt and pepper to taste. Serve hot or at room temperature. (Consider Chou Chou as a lower-calorie alternative to potato salad at a cookout or barbecue.)

A dram of good cognac is a local addition to an otherwise authentic *Sudamericano* Cream of Pumpkin Soup. I first tasted this velvety bisque at the La Fonda del Sol restaurant on the Avenue of the Americas in New York. The restaurant is long gone, but this wonderful anodyne remains. I like this soup best served very, very cold on a warm summer's afternoon when more normal types drink iced tea or gin.

CREAM OF PUMPKIN SOUP

1 Combine pumpkin, chicken stock, onion, and green onion bulbs in a large saucepan; bring to a boil. Reduce heat; simmer over low heat until pumpkin is soft. Place mixture, 3 cups at a time, in a blender container; puree until smooth.

2 Return puree to saucepan. Bring to a boil; reduce heat. Mash the flour with the butter; stir into puree. Add the brandy; simmer 10 minutes. Let stand to cool; refrigerate until cold.

3 Just before serving, stir in the light cream and salt and cayenne pepper to taste. Ladle into chilled bouillon cups; float a slice of tomato in each. Garnish with a rosette of whipped cream and a sprinkling of chopped green onion tops.

1 medium pumpkin (about 2½ pounds), seeds and membranes removed, flesh cut into 1-inch cubes
6 cups chicken stock
1 small onion, sliced
6 green onions, bulbs sliced, green tops chopped for garnish
2 teaspoons all-purpose flour
2 teaspoons butter
2 tablespoons brandy
1 cup light cream
Salt
Cayenne pepper
8 thin slices very ripe tomato
½ cup whipping cream, whipped

Serves 8.

"Old-time" is a term that would apply to the clutch of brandied desserts on my roster. A pale, vanilla-scented bread pudding, well-laced with Calvados, sweet apples, and raisins, is something a French *grandmère* might have concocted for her family a hundred years ago. Might have, indeed! She did—and this heirloom is part of her legacy.

OLD-FASHIONED APPLE BREAD PUDDING

3 tablespoons butter
1 pound sweet apples, pared,
   cored, thinly sliced
1⅓ cups granulated sugar
⅓ cup seedless raisins
¼ cup Calvados
10 slices French bread, cut ½-inch
   thick
6 eggs
1 teaspoon vanilla
1 cup whipping cream
3 cups milk
Confectioners' sugar

Serves 10.

1 Heat oven to 400°. Melt butter in a heavy skillet. Add the apple slices; stir until well coated. Sprinkle with ⅓ cup granulated sugar, the raisins, and Calvados; cook until heated. Ignite; let flame subside.

2 Arrange bread slices, overlapping slightly, in a buttered, approximately 8- × 14-inch baking dish. Spoon apple mixture over bread.

3 Whisk together the eggs, vanilla, cream, and remaining 1 cup granulated sugar; stir in milk. Pour over apple mixture, being careful to cover entire surface.

4 Place the baking dish in a large roasting pan; pour boiling water into roasting pan to depth of 1 inch. Bake until set, about 40 minutes.

5 Remove pudding from roasting pan; let cool 20 minutes. Sprinkle top heavily with confectioners' sugar. Place under broiler 2 to 3 minutes to glaze top.

Zabaglione (sometimes spelled "zabaione" by culinary pundits) is a showy dessert that may be frothed up in minutes by any chef with a firm backstroke. The trick is: Do not stop whisking until it foams! You may ask what zabaglione has to do with brandy, since it is usually made with Marsala. But mine is a different devise—laced with kirschwasser (colorless cherry brandy)—and it is a smash!

CHERRY ZABAGLIONE

5 egg yolks
5 tablespoons sugar
½ cup kirschwasser (cherry brandy)

Serves 4.

1 Beat the yolks with the sugar until light and fluffy. Whisk in the kirschwasser and transfer to the top of a large double boiler.

2 Continue to beat over hot, but not boiling, water until thick and creamy, 8 to 10 minutes. The mixture will swell and almost fill the double boiler top.

3 Spoon zabaglione into goblets or tulip glasses. Serve immediately.

Brandy (or cognac) and peaches are more culinary antiquarianism. These golden peaches are filled to a gluttonous profusion with cinnamony, nutty sweet meats and then baked. They make a perfect hot dessert for a cold supper of meat and salad and are equally prime served cold with a pitcher of cream after a hearty bowl of soup. I usually compromise and eat the peaches lukewarm—while the kitchen is still bathed in a spirituous scent that's strong enough to intoxicate everyone at the table.

PÊCHE D'OR

1 Place peaches in boiling water for 1 to 2 minutes to loosen skins. Peel, cut in half, and remove the pits. Deepen the hollow in each peach half by pressing with a spoon. Place cut sides up in a buttered baking dish.

2 Heat oven to 375°. Place walnuts and macaroons in a blender container; grind until crumbly. Place in a bowl; stir in ¼ cup cream, the butter, egg yolk, granulated sugar, cinnamon, vanilla, and 2 tablespoons cognac. Mix thoroughly.

3 Spoon walnut mixture into peach halves, mounding tops. Bake 20 minutes.

4 Beat ½ cup cream with the confectioners' sugar and 1 teaspoon cognac. Serve the peaches slightly warm with a good dollop of cream on each. (Baked peaches also may be refrigerated and served cold with cream.)

Note: Number of servings depends on the size of the peaches.

8 firm ripe peaches
½ cup walnut halves
6 macaroons (or 9 amaretti)
¼ cup whipping cream
1 tablespoon butter, melted
1 egg yolk, beaten
2 tablespoons granulated sugar
¼ teaspoon ground cinnamon
½ teaspoon vanilla
2 tablespoons plus 1 teaspoon cognac
½ cup whipping cream
2 tablespoons confectioners' sugar

Serves 6 to 8.

Not truly old-fashioned desserts you were thinking? Bite your tongue. This next devise for Black Bottom Pie was the very rage from the Gay Nineties to the Roaring Twenties. Why did it ever lose culinary favor? Not because of Weight Watchers, I'll warrant—a few slices of this confection and the whole organization would just as soon go out of business.

Be sure you use a really *good* cognac for the flavoring when you make up your pie, even if you have to buy one of those sampler bottles. Quality really tells in this dessert!

BLACK BOTTOM PIE

For the crust:
1½ cups chocolate wafer crumbs
  (the better the wafer, the better
  the crust!)
¼ cup sifted confectioners' sugar
6 tablespoons butter, melted
1 teaspoon ground cinnamon
1 teaspoon instant coffee powder

For the filling:
1 envelope unflavored gelatin
½ cup cold water
⅔ cup granulated sugar
⅛ teaspoon salt
3 eggs, separated
¼ cup cognac
¼ cup crème de cacao
2 cups whipping cream, whipped
Chocolate curls for garnish

Serves 6 to 8.

1 Heat oven to 300°. Combine wafer crumbs, sugar, butter, cinnamon, and coffee; mix thoroughly. Butter a 9-inch pie plate; press crumb mixture over bottom and sides. Bake 15 minutes. Cool thoroughly.

2 Sprinkle gelatin over cold water in a saucepan. Add the granulated sugar, the salt, and the egg yolks. Cook over low heat, stirring constantly, until mixture thickens slightly; do not boil.

3 Remove from heat; stir in cognac and creme de cacao. Refrigerate until mixture is partially set, about 30 minutes.

4 Beat the egg whites until stiff but not dry. Whisk chilled egg yolk mixture to remove any lumps (if mixture is too thick, add a few drops of boiling water and whisk smooth); fold in the egg whites. Fold in 1 cup whipped cream; spread mixture in crust. Refrigerate 3 hours.

5 Before serving, garnish with remaining whipped cream and the chocolate curls. (Make chocolate curls by scraping a piece of chocolate with a vegetable peeler.)

Cheese

At an earlier age than most, I discovered that the fumes of
melting cheese can whet man's appetite—but only under the
right set of circumstances.

When I was about ten, I think, my sister (five years worldlier
than I in the ways of gracious living) decided it was time to
upgrade my untried palate by exposing it to the savor of *haute
cuisine*. This, mind you, in the dead center of the Depression,
when epicurean ingredients were simply out of the question in
our household.

My sister Myra was, however, an intrepid believer in making
do. When a recipe she had discovered called for alligator pears
stuffed with a mixture of Roquefort and black walnuts, she
reasoned that canned Bartlett pears filled with cream cheese and
run-of-the-mill walnuts could not be too disastrous a substitution.

It was. Neither of us ate much of the pretty luncheon she
arranged on hearts of lettuce but, what-the-hell, we probably
would not have downed the mint-original formula with much
relish either.

My sister Myra's plan always called for elegant surroundings
for each food tasting. And, as she was strongly influenced by the
high life we vicariously enjoyed at the movies (as well as the
effulgent color photographs purloined from the women's magazines on my mother's night table), we inevitably ate our
gourmet repasts in the dining room, on damask, while regular
family meals were taken in the kitchen.

These collations of ours always took place on Saturdays, while the rest of the family were at their various employments. My undaunted mother had recently secured a position as a beauty demonstrator—carrying her wares from door to door in a handsome, murrey-colored leather case—and no preparation would begin until she was out the door and safely arrived at the corner bus stand. Our parent, you see, consistently maintained a low threshold for folly, and this sense of righteousness became truly deep-dyed after my father lost his fortune in what she considered to have been foolhardy business deals. So only after we had seen her off on her appointed rounds would my sister bid me bring out the Haviland china, crystal goblets, and sterling to set the table.

Since Myra was really very young and knew little of the luxe life we attempted to emulate (other than what *Photoplay* and *Silver Screen* reported), we drank ginger ale in lieu of champagne at our weekly feast. But the bottle was discreetly wrapped in a towel and placed in a bucket of ice and the stemware was chilled before we toasted each other—in exactly the same manner that William Powell saluted Kay Francis in *One Way Passage*. For it was the magic personae of the silver screen (Carole Lombard, Claudette Colbert, and Joan Crawford), rather than Escoffier or Carême, who influenced our early quest for style.

My sister usually found the original recipes for our luncheons and made up the menus, but we put the formulas to the kitchen test together. All of the food, as I recall, was dreadful, but we pressed on gamely week after week, hoping for better luck next time. One of these culinary forays, however, was such a bona fide disaster that it ended our quest for *haute cuisine* forevermore.

Having stumbled upon the conceit of a Welsh rarebit (in which cheese is melted to a runny compound with an iota of some alcoholic beverage), Myra set about acquiring the components for our next refection. My mother, however, cavalierly ignored the requested Cheddar penciled onto her grocery list. "Because it makes a change to eat something different once in a while," she chose Muenster cheese instead.

Little did she know.

It was not an auspicious beginning for our Saturday concoction. Bravely we set the ocherous half loaf of Muenster in a saute pan and watched as it refused to become liquid. No amount of beer sprinkled into the pan—or the added inducements of cream, mustard, and various seasonings—would set it flowing. Each new ingredient was merely absorbed into the quivering mass and, while the cheese eventually did melt to some minor degree, a rarebit it certainly was not.

What we realized instead for all our efforts was a kind of mucilaginous spaghetti—long rubbery strands of cheese—that we hastily scraped onto "toast fingers" in the kitchen, knowing full well that the dish would never make a transition to the warm plates awaiting it on the dining room table.

"It's interesting," we pronounced over our ginger ales. But weakly—for the substance had become so congealed on the fork that it no longer could be chewed and had to be swallowed whole.

The true death knell for our gourmetry came afterward. For no matter how much Old Dutch cleanser we sprinkled on its surface nor how many Brillo pads we applied, neither my sister nor I could pry the hardened evidence of Muenster cheese turned into solid latex from my mother's favorite saucepan.

Eventually the conceit of those epicurean Saturdays passed into family lore—and the chronicle of Myra's first attempt to produce a Welsh rarebit became an often repeated story. But the intensity of my mother's anger when she discovered the evidence of our defection was so monumental that I can remember the sound of her shrieking still.

I have never quizzed my sister on the matter, but to this day I cannot sniff the scent of scorched cheese without summoning feelings of ill-defined guilt.

The important thing for a cook to remember is that time is of the essence when cheese is a prime ingredient in a dish. Prolonged cookery tends to transform the product into indigestible strands—as my sister and I discovered to our mutual distress. The experienced kitchen hand always shreds or finely grates cheese before attempting to melt it! Combining the cheese with Bechamel sauce or whipping cream will lessen the possibility of a kitchen disaster, but anyone who is not a daredevil chef is advised to use a double boiler rather than try to fuse cheese into a sauce over direct heat. And all cheese will take less time (and trouble) to melt if it is brought 'round to room temperature beforehand.

In my opinion, the best cooking cheeses are Swiss Gruyère and Emmenthal, Norwegian Jarlsberg and Italian Parmesan. Aside from their admirable melting qualities, the Swiss cheeses have a soothing nutty flavor. I am much addicted to Norway's Jarlsberg as well and often combine its mild flavor with the piquant bite of Parmesan (just as the French do) for light souffles, omelets, and even as a topping for crusty onion soup. Parmesan has a remarkable ability to accent and pull diverse kitchen bouquets into line—and where, oh where, would pasta be without it! The best Parmesan cheese, Parmigiano-Reggiano, must be aged at least two years before it may be sold. The very best is over twenty years old and though it costs a king's ransom, it is the most tonic cheese flavoring in the world. Second-best Parmesan is still pretty tasty, however; so if you buy a Grana Padano, you won't go wrong. When selecting Parmesan, always remember that the well-aged cheese should be pale yellow; younger cheeses are whitish-gray and will not taste half as good.

The flavor of a Swiss Emmenthal cheese is usually sweet, with the aftertaste of walnuts. A wheel of Gruyère is much smaller than a whole Emmenthal and its holes are about the size of ripe currants. Both cheeses are best when the color is ivory-yellow. But while the rind of an Emmenthal is smooth and ambery, Gruyère's casing is brown and as wrinkled as a nut. Jarlsberg is a wide-holed, well-textured buttery cheese available packaged in most supermarkets these days. But Jarlsberg is best when cut fresh from a huge wheel because its texture stays moister when it is allowed to breathe.

The following formula for Welsh rarebit (or rabbit, if purists abound) is my adult revenge on the world of gourmet food that my sister once hankered after. It was given to me by an honest-to-gosh Welshman, who insists that a dram of Scotch whiskey is a secret weapon that no self-respecting cheese can stand firm against!

One last shopping tip for the cheese lover who also cooks: Remember that four ounces of any cheese will fill one standard measuring cup when grated; so the ten ounces in the following recipe equals 2½ cups.

WELSH RAREBIT

2 tablespoons unsalted butter
3 egg yolks
1 teaspoon Dijon mustard
½ teaspoon beef bouillon powder
1 teaspoon soy sauce
Dash of hot pepper sauce
Pinch of ground allspice
¾ cup light beer
10 ounces sharp Cheddar, grated
1 tablespoon whipping cream
1 teaspoon Scotch whiskey
4 slices hot buttered toast

Serves 4.

1 Melt butter in the top of a double boiler.

2 Beat the egg yolks with the Dijon mustard, bouillon powder, soy sauce, hot pepper sauce, and allspice. Stir in the beer.

3 Add the beer mixture to the melted butter; place over simmering water. Stir until hot. Add the grated cheese, ¼ cup at a time, stirring constantly in one direction with a wooden spoon until mixture is smooth.

4 Stir in the cream and Scotch. Do not let mixture stand more than 5 minutes before serving over hot, buttered toast.

Note: I get best results with Kikkoman brand soy sauce.

BERT GREENE'S *Kitchen Bouquets*

Among the many marriages of cheese and varied ingredients in my store of recipes, I would unquestionably give priority to vegetable dishes—beginning, alphabetically, with carrots:

CARROT GNOCCI

1 Combine all ingredients through hot pepper sauce in a large bowl; mix thoroughly. Work in flour, starting with 1 cup, until a soft dough is formed. (Do not exceed 1½ cups, however.)

2 Heat oven to 325°. Bring a large pot of salted water to a boil. Roll dough into long ropes; cut into 1½-inch-long pieces. (If dough is too sticky, place in a large pastry bag, pipe out 1½-inch-long pieces and cut off with a scissors directly into the boiling water.) Cook pieces, 5 at a time, in the boiling water until they float to the top but no longer than 5 minutes. Drain well in a colander or on paper toweling; place on a well-buttered, heatproof serving dish.

3 Drizzle melted butter over gnocci. Place in oven until warmed through, 15 to 20 minutes. Sprinkle with Parmesan cheese; serve with additional cheese on the side.

1 cup cold mashed potatoes
1 medium carrot, grated
1 medium shallot, grated
2 eggs
½ cup finely grated Jarlsberg cheese
¼ teaspoon grated nutmeg
¼ teaspoon ground allspice
½ teaspoon salt
⅛ teaspoon white pepper
Dash of hot pepper sauce
1 to 1½ cups all-purpose flour
3 tablespoons butter, melted
Freshly grated Parmesan cheese

Serves 4 to 6.

Cauliflower comes next. My recipe for *chou-fleur à la polonaise* is obviously a "pop" version. The Laughing Cow cheese is a French variety of processed Gruyère and I make no apology for its appearance in this dish—because it tastes just right here!

LAUGHING COW CAULIFLOWER

1 Cook cauliflower in boiling salted water 3 minutes. Rinse under cold running water until cool and drain.

2 Heat oven to 350°. Melt butter in a heavy saucepan; stir in the flour. Whisk over low heat 2 minutes; whisk in the cream. Add the Laughing Cow cheese; stir until smooth and thick. Stir in the bouillon powder, salt, and pepper.

3 Add cauliflower to saucepan; stir to coat with sauce. Spoon into a buttered casserole. Sprinkle with grated cheese; top with bread crumbs. Bake until top is light brown, about 25 minutes.

1 head cauliflower, cut into flowerets
2 tablespoons butter
1 tablespoon all-purpose flour
¾ cup whipping cream
3 wedges Laughing Cow (*La vache qui rit*) cheese
½ teaspoon beef bouillon powder
½ teaspoon salt
¼ teaspoon freshly ground pepper
¼ cup grated Jarlsberg or Parmesan cheese
3 tablespoons buttered bread crumbs

Serves 4.

Kale is baked and crumbed like the cauliflower above but sauced with genuine Gruyère. I play no favorites here—it's just that the cheese enrichment gives unexpected life to a vegetable I once considered putting on a "public enemy" list.

BAKED KALE

2½ pounds kale or spinach
2½ tablespoons butter
2½ tablespoons all-purpose flour
1 cup milk, scalded
½ cup grated Gruyère or Jarlsberg cheese
½ teaspoon salt
½ teaspoon freshly ground pepper
¼ teaspoon nutmeg
Dash of hot pepper sauce
½ cup buttered bread crumbs

Serves 4 to 6 as a luncheon entrée, more as a first course.

1 Heat oven to 425°. Wash kale several times under cold water. Discard faded leaves; remove tough center ribs. Cook covered in a large pot of boiling salted water 20 minutes. Rinse under cold running water and drain, pressing out all liquid. Chop fine.

2 Melt butter in a heavy saucepan over low heat; whisk in flour. Cook and stir 2 minutes; whisk in milk. Add ¼ cup grated cheese, the salt, pepper, nutmeg, and hot pepper sauce. Cook, stirring constantly, until very thick; add the chopped kale.

3 Transfer mixture to a buttered baking dish; sprinkle with bread crumbs and remaining cheese. Bake until golden brown and bubbly, 15 to 20 minutes.

You consider potatoes and cheese old hat? Well, consider again. For my money, this *gratin dauphinoise,* or dish of Cold Scalloped Potatoes, is the perfect amalgam. Served at room temperature or even colder, it is like the most palate-satisfying potato salad in the world and quite bracing with the spinach-stuffed ham that follows.

COLD SCALLOPED POTATOES

2 pounds potatoes
2 cups milk
1½ cups whipping cream
1 large clove garlic, mashed
¾ teaspoon salt
½ teaspoon white pepper
1 tablespoon butter
½ cup grated Gruyère cheese

Serves 6 to 8.

1 Heat oven to 400°. Peel potatoes and slice them ⅛-inch thick. Place in a large saucepan. Add the milk, cream, garlic, salt, and pepper; bring to a boil, stirring constantly.

2 Butter a gratin dish or shallow baking dish with 1 tablespoon butter. Spoon in the potato mixture; sprinkle with cheese. Bake 1 hour. Reduce heat slightly if potatoes brown too much. Serve cold or hot from the oven.

Lay in a store of Swiss and Parmesan for the two zesty dishes to come! One features spinach and cheese in conjunction with a lush baked ham. The other places the same combo in a remarkable mélange that is half meatloaf and half pâté.

JAMBON FLORENTINE

1 Combine the garlic, cloves, lemon juice, and soy sauce. Rub well over top, bottom, and sides of ham. Using a sharp carving knife, slice ¾ of the way into the ham at ½-inch intervals.

2 Add the rice to a pot of boiling salted water; boil 5 minutes. Drain.

3 Melt 4 tablespoons butter in a heavy saucepan; add the onions and stir until well coated. Add the rice; cook and stir over medium heat until the rice turns milky in color, 5 to 6 minutes. Add the spinach; cook covered over medium heat, stirring occasionally, 30 minutes. (The rice should absorb most of the liquid; if it is too wet after 30 minutes, remove cover, raise heat, and cook until liquid evaporates.) Drain mixture in a strainer, pressing to remove excess liquid. Place in a blender container or food processor; blend until smooth.

4 Heat oven to 350°. Melt 6 tablespoons butter in a heavy saucepan; stir in the flour. Cook over low heat, stirring constantly, 2 minutes. Remove from heat. Whisk in the hot chicken broth; return to heat. Add the nutmeg, salt, and white pepper; cook until mixture begins to thicken. Stir in the cream. Cook sauce (which is a veloute) until thick. Remove from heat; remove ¼ cup from saucepan and reserve. Stir pureed spinach mixture into saucepan.

5 Spread creamed spinach mixture between slices in ham. Tie ham with string to hold shape.

6 Combine reserved ¼ cup sauce with mustard; spread over surface of ham. Combine the cheeses; pat evenly over top. Sprinkle with pepper.

7 Bake until golden, 50 to 60 minutes. Cool slightly before serving. Ideally, the ham is carved crosswise on the diagonal, so that each serving contains a cross section of ham and spinach.

Note: I prefer Dubuque Fleur de Lis brand ham.

2 cloves garlic, mashed
½ teaspoon ground cloves
2 teaspoons lemon juice
2 teaspoons soy sauce
1 boneless smoked ham (10 pounds)
½ cup rice
10 tablespoons butter
2 cups coarsely chopped onions
2 packages (10 ounces each) frozen chopped spinach
7 tablespoons all-purpose flour
3 cups strong chicken broth, hot
⅛ teaspoon freshly grated nutmeg
½ teaspoon salt
½ teaspoon white pepper
½ cup whipping cream
¼ cup Dijon mustard
1½ cups grated Swiss cheese
¾ cup grated Parmesan cheese
Freshly ground black pepper

Serves 16 to 20.

Homemade Tomato Sauce (see
Index)
1 package (10 ounces) frozen
chopped spinach, thawed
1½ tablespoons butter
1 teaspoon vegetable or olive oil
⅓ cup finely chopped onion
1 large shallot, minced
1 clove garlic, minced
1 pound ground beef
½ pound ground veal
¼ pound pork sausage
¼ teaspoon ground allspice
¼ teaspoon ground mace
¼ teaspoon freshly grated nutmeg
½ teaspoon salt
¼ teaspoon freshly ground pepper
1 tablespoon Madeira
2 eggs, beaten
Dash of hot pepper sauce
¾ cup bread crumbs
⅓ cup grated Parmesan cheese
2 teaspoons Dijon mustard
1 teaspoon chili sauce
¼ teaspoon dried oregano leaves
¼ cup grated Parmesan cheese

Serves 6 to 8.

SPINACH LOAF

1 Make tomato sauce.

2 Heat oven to 375°. Cook spinach in boiling salted water 1 minute. Drain well in a sieve, pressing out all liquid.

3 Melt the butter with the oil in a saucepan over medium-high heat. Add onion, shallot, and garlic; cook, stirring constantly, until soft. Add the spinach; raise heat and stir until all moisture has evaporated.

4 Combine the beef, veal, and sausage in a large bowl; add allspice, mace, nutmeg, salt, and pepper. Mix well; sprinkle with Madeira. Add eggs, hot pepper sauce, bread crumbs, ⅓ cup Parmesan cheese, and the spinach mixture. Mix thoroughly.

5 Shape meat mixture into a loaf in a shallow baking dish. Mix mustard and chili sauce; spread over loaf. Sprinkle with oregano.

6 Bake 1 hour. Sprinkle top with ¼ cup Parmesan cheese; bake until golden, 15 to 20 minutes. Serve with tomato sauce.

French-cut stringbeans in a spicy, bubbling cheese fondue (of sorts) make a novel dinner first course or a splendid accompaniment for red meats like *à point* leg of lamb or an unfussy steak without any sauce. It's an interesting way to serve the common garden variety of legume, I think you'll agree.

1 pound green beans, French cut
4 tablespoons butter
2 shallots, minced
2 tablespoons all-purpose flour
1½ cups milk, hot
Dash of hot pepper sauce
⅛ teaspoon ground allspice
Salt to taste
⅛ teaspoon white pepper
½ cup finely grated Jarlsberg cheese
¼ cup coarsely grated Jarlsberg cheese

Serves 4 to 6.

HARICOTS VERTS AU FROMAGE

1 Heat oven to 375°. Cook beans in boiling salted water 1 minute. Drain and rinse under cold water until cool; drain thoroughly.

2 Melt 2 tablespoons butter in a heavy skillet. Add shallots; cook over medium heat until soft. Stir in the flour; cook 2 minutes. Whisk in the hot milk; cook until smooth and slightly thickened, about 8 minutes. Stir in hot pepper sauce, allspice, salt, pepper, and the finely grated cheese; cook until thick.

3 Butter a shallow baking dish. Spread half the sauce in dish; cover with beans and top with remaining sauce. Sprinkle with coarsely grated cheese; dot with remaining 2 tablespoons butter. Bake until heated through and bubbly, 10 to 15 minutes.

Tomato and cheese baked together: It's not pizza, my friend, but it's damn good anyway! Try this dish for a dinner first course. Or make it for lunch early in the day, allow it to cool, and serve it with oil and vinegar.

BAKED TOMATOES À LA NIÇOISE

1 Heat oven to 400°. Cut tops off tomatoes; discard. Turn tomatoes upside down and gently squeeze out seeds and pulp (scoop out pulp with a spoon, if necessary). Sprinkle well with salt; turn upside down on a plate. Let stand 10 minutes.

2 Combine shallot, basil, bread crumbs, thyme, anchovy paste, and oil. Mix until the crumbs are well coated. Stir in parsley.

3 Stuff tomatoes with bread crumb mixture. Sprinkle with pepper; cover tops with grated Parmesan cheese.

4 Place tomatoes in a shallow baking dish. Bake until tender but not mushy, 10 to 15 minutes. If tops are not brown, place under broiler 2 to 3 minutes.

4 large ripe tomatoes
Salt
1 large shallot, minced
1 tablespoon fresh basil leaves or 1 teaspoon dried
1½ cups fresh bread crumbs
½ teaspoon fresh thyme leaves or ¼ teaspoon dried
½ teaspoon anchovy paste
3 tablespoons olive oil
2 tablespoons chopped parsley
⅛ teaspoon freshly ground pepper
¾ cup grated Parmesan cheese

Serves 4.

One tale (highly unreliable, I am certain) about the origins of cheese concerns an Arab merchant—thousands and thousands of years ago—who stopped for lunch while wandering the Sahara. Pouring out some cow's milk he had stashed in a sheep's belly flask, he discovered, to history's favor, that the contents had turned to an odd but not unattractive mess known as curds and whey.

Archaeologists have established that cheese in some form or other was well-known to the Sumerians (4000 B.C.), whose cuneiform tablets contain unmistakable references to the zesty food as a staple on their grocery lists. We know from their artifacts that Egyptians and Chaldeans cooked with cheese as well. According to cloudy soothsayers, Queen Semiramis was raised on a diet of unleavened bread and hard Cheddar (crackers and cheese, to you) fed to her by a flock of trained birds. The Bible reports that David was delivering ten cases of cheese to Saul's camp when he encountered the mighty Goliath on the way. "Thou has poured me out as milk," said the latter, later, in some distress, "and curdled me as a cheese." On second thought, perhaps it was Job who made that remark. Regardless, we do know that through the years cheese combined with flour and butter resulted in some ploys seductive enough to win over even a confirmed atheist's appetite.

Consider Dumas the elder's version of a native Burgundian luncheon dish that's more likely to appear as an hors d'oeuvre at my table—tangy, puffy Gougère.

GOUGÈRE

3 tablespoons chopped ham
1 tablespoon Madeira
1 teaspoon butter
1 cup milk, scalded and cooled
4 tablespoons unsalted butter, cut into small pieces
1 teaspoon salt
⅛ teaspoon freshly ground black pepper
1 cup all-purpose flour, sifted
4 large eggs
¾ cup diced Swiss cheese
2 tablespoons cold milk

Serves 6.

1 Sprinkle ham with Madeira in a small skillet; saute in 1 teaspoon butter over low heat until all liquid is evaporated. Reserve.

2 Strain the scalded milk into a large saucepan; add 4 tablespoons butter, the salt, and pepper. Bring to a boil; reduce heat. Add the flour; cook over low heat, beating briskly with a wooden spoon, until mixture forms a ball and cleans sides of pan.

3 Remove pan from heat. Beat in the eggs, one at a time, with a wooden spoon or heavy wire whisk, making sure that each egg is well blended into mixture. When paste is shiny and smooth, stir in ½ cup Swiss cheese. Let dough stand to cool.

4 Heat oven to 375°. Generously butter a baking sheet. Using a knife or your finger, trace a 9-inch circle on the buttered surface.

5 Divide dough in half. Shape ovals of dough with a large serving spoon and arrange on circle traced on baking sheet, using a rubber spatula to scrape dough from spoon. Smooth tops of ovals with back of spoon to connect them into a ring. Shape small ovals from second half of dough with a teaspoon and arrange over top of ring. (Dough should resemble a bumpy coffee-ring.)

6 Brush dough with cold milk; sprinkle reserved ham and remaining Swiss cheese over top.

7 Bake until the Gougere is puffed and golden brown, 45 to 50 minutes. Cut into wedges to serve.

Note: Gougere can be prepared through Step 6 and frozen. Cover and place in freezer on baking sheet until frozen. Remove frozen dough from sheet, wrap in aluminum foil and place in freezer in a plastic bag. Bake frozen Gougere without thawing; allow an additional 20 minutes baking time. This recipe also can be doubled.

Cheese and everything good that grows in the garden! Potatoes, tomatoes, scallions, peppers, string beans, and garlic, too, come together in one amazing dish from Colombia. The cheese, Italian mozzarella, melts all over everything else entrancingly. *Papas Chorreadas* makes a fine luncheon or supper dish. Think about adding a half cup of ham strips before the cheese embellishment to produce a party casserole spectacular.

PAPAS CHORREADAS

1 Cook potatoes in boiling water 20 minutes. Rinse under cold running water and drain. (Potatoes should not be tender.) Cut into ½-inch slices. Cook green beans in boiling water 1 minute. Rinse under cold running water and drain.

2 Melt butter in a large, heavy ovenproof skillet. Add garlic, green onions, and onion; saute until tender but not brown.

3 Add potatoes to skillet; stir over medium heat until slices are coated with butter mixture on both sides. Add tomatoes, red pepper, salt, coriander, cumin, and oregano; cook until mixture begins to thicken. Stir in cream; reduce heat. Add green beans; cook 6 to 7 minutes. Sprinkle with cheese; cook until cheese melts. (Skillet may be placed under broiler 2 to 3 minutes to brown top, if desired.) Sprinkle with chopped parsley and black pepper.

4 medium baking potatoes, pared
¼ pound green beans
3 tablespoons unsalted butter
1 clove garlic, minced
4 green onions with tops, finely chopped
1 medium onion, finely chopped
1 can (8 ounces) Italian plum tomatoes, well-drained, chopped
¼ teaspoon dried hot red pepper
½ teaspoon salt
½ teaspoon dried coriander leaves
Pinch of ground cumin
Pinch of oregano
½ cup whipping cream
½ cup grated mozzarella cheese
2 teaspoons chopped Italian (flat-leaf) parsley
Freshly ground black pepper

Serves 4.

The next is a highly prized formula for Russian cheese tarts that I happily serve with an equally Soviet fruit soup, Chernichny Soop (see Index), on picnic occasions. These excellent Piroshky are fortuitous adjuncts to a cocktail table as well, when strong liquors are flowing. I freely adapted the recipe, I must admit, from a remarkable book on Russian cookery by an even more remarkable young woman named Jane Blanksteen. Her tome is called *Nothing Beets Borscht* and it's a winner!

TREVGOLNICK PIROSHKY

For the pastry:
1¾ cups sifted all-purpose flour
½ teaspoon baking powder
½ teaspoon salt
½ cup unsalted butter, cut into
  small pieces
1 egg
½ cup sour cream

For the filling:
1 package (7½ ounces) farmer's
  cheese, softened
4 ounces cream cheese, softened
½ cup finely grated Jarlsberg cheese
2 eggs
1 egg, beaten, for pastry wash

Makes about 40.

1 Combine flour, baking powder, and salt in a bowl. Add butter; blend with a pastry blender or your fingers until texture resembles coarse crumbs.

2 Beat 1 egg in a small bowl; beat in the sour cream. Work egg mixture into flour mixture with a fork or your fingers. Knead briefly on a lightly floured surface. Refrigerate dough ½ hour.

3 Heat oven to 400°. Beat cheeses together with an electric mixer until light and smooth. Add 2 eggs, one at a time, beating well after each addition.

4 Roll out ⅓ of dough into a large rectangle, ⅛-inch thick. Cut into 2-inch squares. Brush edges of squares with beaten egg; place heaping tablespoon of cheese mixture in center of each. Fold squares in half diagonally to form triangles; press edges with a fork to seal. Repeat with remaining dough and filling. Place triangles on greased and floured baking sheets; brush tops with beaten egg. Bake 15 minutes.

Note: For a sweeter filling, omit the Jarlsberg cheese and add 4 tablespoons sugar.

Cheese played such an important role in the ancient Roman diet that rich landowners had special kitchens in their homes just for cheesemaking. These were similar to the "cold kitchens" devoted to the business of cream-and-buttery by American farmers a hundred or so years ago.

The next recipe is for an authentic Roman tart. It was originally meant to be served with game, but I admire it particularly on Thanksgiving, carved up along with the turkey.

CHESTNUT TORTA

1 Make Pate Brisee and refrigerate 1 hour. Roll out to a 10-inch circle. Line 8-inch pie pan; trim edges and flute. Line pastry with aluminum foil; fill with dried beans or rice. Heat oven to 400°. Bake 5 minutes. Remove foil and beans; let stand to cool.

2 Reduce oven heat to 375°. Cut a cross in flat side of each chestnut. Place chestnuts in a saucepan; cover with water. Bring to a boil; boil 20 minutes. Drain; cover with cold water. Shell chestnuts and peel off skins. (Skins are most easily removed while chestnuts are still warm.) Drain well on paper toweling. Chop chestnuts in a food processor until ground to texture of cornmeal.

3 Combine 1 cup ground chestnuts with cottage cheese, butter, cream, bouillon powder, eggs, green onions, salt, and pepper. Mix thoroughly.

4 Pour mixture into pre-baked pie shell; sprinkle with Parmesan cheese. Bake until set, 25 to 30 minutes. (Serve with roast turkey or chicken.)

Pâte Brisée (recipe follows)
10 to 12 chestnuts
¾ cup cottage cheese
2 tablespoons butter, melted
½ cup whipping cream
1 packet beef bouillon powder
2 eggs, lightly beaten
2 green onion bulbs, minced
¼ teaspoon salt
⅛ teaspoon white pepper
3 tablespoons grated Parmesan cheese

Serves 6 to 8.

PÂTE BRISÉE

Combine flour, salt, and sugar in a bowl. Add butter and shortening; blend with a pastry blender until the texture of coarse crumbs. Add water, 1 tablespoon at a time, and blend with a fork until a smooth dough is formed. Knead briefly. Refrigerate 1 hour before using.

1½ cups all-purpose flour
¼ teaspoon salt
Pinch of sugar
6 tablespoons cold butter
2¼ tablespoons vegetable shortening
¼ cup cold water (approximately)

Makes one 8- to 9-inch pie shell.

My absolutely favorite recipe in this collection, a Viennese veal cutlet upholstered with grated cheese, depends upon Parma's chief culinary export for a very special savor in the saute pan!

WIENERKÄSESCHNITZEL

1 Heat oven to 275°. Sprinkle veal with salt on both sides. Place flour on a flat plate. Beat eggs with water in a wide shallow bowl. Combine 1 cup Parmesan cheese with the bread crumbs on a flat plate. Coat cutlets lightly with flour. Dip into eggs; shake off excess egg mixture. Coat with bread crumbs. Stack cutlets on a plate between sheets of waxed paper. Let stand 20 minutes.

2 Melt the butter with the oil in a heavy skillet. Fry cutlets, 2 or 3 at a time, until golden and crisp, about 4 to 6 minutes on each side. (Turn cutlets with tongs; do not use a fork.) Add more butter to skillet as needed. Transfer cutlets to a serving platter; keep warm in oven. Serve with Parmesan cheese on the side.

8 veal cutlets, pounded thin
Salt
¾ cup all-purpose flour (approximately)
2 eggs
2 tablespoons water
1 cup freshly grated Parmesan cheese
1 cup fine bread crumbs
4 tablespoons butter (approximately)
1 tablespoon vegetable oil
Freshly grated Parmesan cheese

Serves 4.

Another *plat du jour,* of an entirely different ethnic stripe (a hearty beef stew with Spanish overtones), is likewise assured a place of honor in my kitchen by its amendment of grated cheese—added, in this case, just before the dish comes to the table.

MEDITERRANEAN BEEF STEW

¼ pound diced salt pork

2 teaspoons olive or vegetable oil

2½ to 3 pounds beef chuck, cut into 1½-inch cubes

⅓ cup all-purpose flour, seasoned with salt and pepper

2 tablespoons butter

1¼ cups thinly sliced onions

1 cup rice

1 cup white wine

2 cups beef stock or broth

½ teaspoon salt

½ teaspoon freshly ground pepper

2 cloves garlic, crushed

2 tablespoons chopped parsley

½ teaspoon chopped fresh thyme leaves or ¼ teaspoon dried

1 bay leaf, crumbled

Pinch of saffron

1½ cups chopped, seeded tomatoes

1 cup freshly grated Parmesan cheese

Chopped parsley

Serves 4 to 6.

1 Heat oven to 350°. Add salt pork to pot of boiling water; reduce heat. Simmer 10 minutes. Drain well on paper toweling.

2 Heat oil in a heavy skillet. Add salt pork; saute until golden. Remove to a Dutch oven with a slotted spoon.

3 Lightly coat meat with seasoned flour. Add butter to skillet. Add meat, a few pieces at a time; brown well on all sides and transfer to Dutch oven. Add onions to skillet; saute until tender. Transfer to Dutch oven with a slotted spoon. Add rice to skillet; cook and stir over medium heat until milky in color, 2 to 3 minutes. Remove from skillet; reserve. Remove any fat from skillet. Add wine; cook over high heat 3 minutes, scraping bottom and sides of pan. Pour into Dutch oven. Add beef stock, salt, pepper, garlic, parsley, thyme, bay leaf, saffron, and tomatoes to Dutch oven. Bake covered until the meat is almost tender, 1½ to 2 hours. Remove from oven and skim off fat.* There should be about 2 cups liquid in pot; remove any additional and reserve.

4 Raise oven heat to 375°. Stir reserved rice into hot stew. Bake covered until all liquid is absorbed and the rice is tender, about 15 to 20 minutes. (If the rice is dry but not tender, add some of reserved liquid or additional beef stock and bake covered until tender. If too wet, bake uncovered about 5 minutes.) Just before serving, stir in Parmesan cheese; sprinkle with parsley.

*Note: Beef stew may be prepared to this point several hours in advance. Refrigerate covered; heat over low heat before proceeding with recipe.

I cannot claim the next formula as my own, since Alice B. Toklas invented chicken with noodles long before I ever tangled

with a cheese grater. But placing the bird to roost (oops! *roast*) in a hot oven is wholly my idea.

ROAST CHICKEN STUFFED WITH FETTUCINI

1 Bring 3 quarts water to a boil. Stir in the oil and noodles. Cook noodles until barely tender and rinse under cold running water. Drain well and place in a large bowl. Mixing gently with a fork, add ½ cup Parmesan cheese, the Jarlsberg cheese, ½ cup whipping cream, the mushroom caps, 1 teaspoon salt, and ½ teaspoon pepper.

2 Wipe the chicken dry with paper toweling and rub it well, inside and out, with garlic. Stuff with the noodle mixture. Sew and truss.

3 Heat oven to 450°. Place the chicken in a roasting pan and dot with the butter. Lay the bacon across the breast. Pour ⅓ cup water around the chicken.

4 Roast the chicken 30 minutes. Reduce heat to 400° and roast 1¼ hours longer, basting every 20 minutes with pan juices. Remove trussing and transfer chicken to a heatproof platter. Reduce oven heat to low and keep chicken warm in oven.

5 Skim excess fat from pan juices. Add ⅓ cup water to juices and heat to simmering. Whisk the flour with 4 tablespoons hot pan juices until smooth; add remaining ¾ cup cream. Stir into sauce and cook until fairly thick, about 5 minutes.

6 Slowly beat ¼ cup hot sauce into the egg yolks. Remove sauce from heat; whisk egg yolk mixture into sauce. Return sauce to low heat; cook until warmed through but do not boil. Add salt to taste. Pour ½ cup sauce over chicken and sprinkle with remaining ¼ cup Parmesan cheese. Place under the broiler until glazed, 2 to 3 minutes. Dust with parsley and serve with remaining sauce.

1½ tablespoons olive or vegetable oil
1 to 1½ cups fettucini noodles
¾ cup grated Parmesan cheese
½ cup grated Jarlsberg cheese
1¼ cups whipping cream
¾ cup small mushroom caps
1 teaspoon salt
½ teaspoon freshly ground pepper
1 roasting chicken (about 3½ pounds)
1 clove garlic, bruised
1½ tablespoons butter
2 strips bacon
⅔ cup water
1½ tablespoons all-purpose flour
2 egg yolks, beaten
Salt
1 tablespoon chopped parsley

Serves 2 to 4.

The last cheese recipe is for an orange-scented cake my grandmother made when I was very, very young. I never forgot its flavor and, long after my grandmother was dead, I tried to reconstruct it. Feeding experimental slices to my grandfather

(who survived her by almost twenty years), however, I invariably got a negative reaction.

"Minna's was better," he would say.

"Why? More lemon peel . . . more vanilla maybe?"

"I don't know from whys. Just better."

"But do you think that's all she really put into the cake, Grandpa?" I quizzed him further.

"Ah well, who knows?" he finally replied, laying down his fork. "That woman cooked with a secret ingredient. Love!"

For the pastry:
1 cup sifted all-purpose flour
¼ cup granulated sugar
1 teaspoon grated lemon peel
1 teaspoon grated orange peel
Seeds scraped from 1-inch piece
    vanilla bean
½ cup unsalted butter, cut into
    pieces
1 egg yolk

For the filling:
2½ pounds cream cheese
1¾ cups granulated sugar
3 tablespoons all-purpose flour
1½ teaspoons grated lemon peel
1½ teaspoons grated orange peel
Seeds scraped from 1-inch piece
    vanilla bean or ¼ teaspoon
    extract
5 eggs plus 2 egg yolks
¼ cup whipping cream

Serves 8 to 10.

GRANDMOTHER'S CHEESECAKE

1 To prepare the pastry: Combine flour, sugar, lemon peel, orange peel, and vanilla seeds in a large bowl. Add butter; blend with a pastry blender until texture of coarse crumbs. Stir in egg yolk until all flour is moistened. Chill at least 1 hour.

2 Heat oven to 400°. Roll out pastry ⅛-inch thick. Cut 9-inch circle; refrigerate trimmings. Place circle over bottom of a greased 9-inch springform pan. (If pastry is too soft to roll, refrigerate longer or pat half over bottom of pan with your fingers.) Bake pastry until golden, about 20 minutes. Cool on wire rack.

3 To prepare the filling: Beat cream cheese, sugar, flour, lemon peel, orange peel, and vanilla together in a large bowl. Beat in the eggs and egg yolks, 1 at a time, beating well after each addition. Stir in cream.

4 Increase oven heat to 550°. Butter the sides of the springform pan. Roll out reserved pastry trimmings; cut into 2-inch-wide strips. Pat strips into place against sides of pan, pressing edge into bottom crust. Fill immediately with cream cheese mixture. Bake 12 minutes. Reduce oven temperature to 200°; bake 1 hour. Cool cake on wire rack. Refrigerate at least 2 hours before serving.

Chocolate

Chocolate is, I truly believe, the universal flavor of childhood. Young people everywhere react to its blandishment with such bliss and open-mouthed sensuality that watching a small child consume a chocolate bar could tempt even a rational man like me to consider the notion that the delectable stuff has a narcotic potency.

I have been a devoted chocolate fan all my life. Yet I never heard anyone self-incriminated as a "chocoholic" until I came face to face with the legendary Mary Margaret McBride a few years ago.

"That's what I am. Truly . . . ," the lovely lady sighed helplessly over her confession. "I try to control the habit best as I know how but it really is no use at all. I dearly love chocolatey things to distraction—and I guess I always have!"

Mary Margaret's eyes were soft chocolate brown (the color of mocha truffles, actually). And, though she was well past seventy at the time of this admission, they shone with a childlike lack of rectitude. "It's just a cross I bear," they seemed to imply at the revelation of her secret sin, ". . . but such a delicious vice—why try and fight it?"

This lady was hardly a stranger to me, even half a dozen years ago when I came the long route to West Shokan, New York, to be interviewed on her radio show.

Most of my adolescence was spent in an etiolated cocoon

made bearable only by her presence. Listlessly I went to school and did my assigned house chores afterward but I had no real friends and, between bouts at the movies and aching fantasies, I lived my life as if it were the waiting room of a great empty terminal. Mary Margaret McBride, however, provided me with a ticket to the future—awakening (across the air waves) my burgeoning senses to a world of books, theatre, and art that was far, far beyond the kitchen table where I did my Latin verbs and the sink full of vegetables waiting to be scraped for supper.

In a sleepy, Missouri drawl (completely out of joint with any accent in my circle), this lady interviewed the most brilliant and weighty personages of our time. Thornton Wilder, Eleanor Roosevelt, Helen Keller, Jimmy Durante, and Arthur Rubenstein all came before her microphone at one time or another, and totally disarmed by their interlocutor's candor and absence of guile, they revealed themselves to several million listeners simply as other people.

I became such an affixed auditor to Mary Margaret McBride's radio program (which lasted about an hour and a half daily, five days a week) that our family table conversation at the evening meal would invariably begin with my mother's query:

"Well, what did Mary Margaret have to say for herself today?"

For she was always known as Mary Margaret in our house. And, though we were a disparate menage at best, the family banded together belligerently against any radio listener of our mutual acquaintance who shunned Mary Margaret's slightly skittish effervescence in favor of, say, soap operas.

Only my father was a holdout. But once, when he had a false appendicitis scare, I came into the bedroom with a cup of tea and discovered him nodding blissfully as Miss M. extolled the virtues of Dolly Madison ice cream.

"She makes it sound good, doesn't she?" was his only admission of any allegiance. But the rest of us more than made up for his lack of thrall.

"I don't trust people who won't listen to Mary Margaret," my working mother announced on a weekday holiday, after the radio show had ended. "I don't know why, exactly—but if people can't recognize an *honest* human being when they hear one, that's a good reason to be leery of them!"

I told Mary Margaret that story on the air myself, thirty years after the fact, and it still delighted her.

"Oh me," she sighed. "I'm sorry I never met your mother. True fans are hard to find."

But not in our household. When I was growing tall, Mary Margaret's philosophy about success became a watchword. And my slogan.

"If you want a thing badly enough," she always stated on the air, "and you are really willing to work hard to get it, there's nothing in this wide world that can stop you! But, you have to *know* what it is you want.''

All my life I knew that I wanted to write a book and be a guest on Mary Margaret McBride's radio program. But when it finally happened, I found myself curiously unequal to facing the reality of that fantasy. Denis Vaughan, my longtime friend and co-author of *The Store Cookbook,* chafed at my qualms.

''I'll never understand you,'' he said, tapping his forehead meaningfully. ''Going on and on about that woman's radio program for a whole lifetime—and now cold feet when the curtain is about to go up!''

Frankly, I was afraid I would be disappointed but could not bear to state the apprehension. So many other long-awaited tastes had flattened on the tongue by that time. Denis had been a fan too when he was growing up in Chicago, but bravado and black Irish blasphemy overlaid any of his misgivings.

We had to drive a hundred miles to be guests on this program. The taping was called for early morning; so we made our way from the city practically at dawn, without even breakfast tea to settle my *angst.* Moreover, we became lost twice on our way— never a good augury in my book. But the fears were groundless. On first sight Mary Margaret was my past recaptured and, if anything, twice as tonic.

She had, by this time in her life, retired from the fray of a demanding national radio show but she still broadcast daily to the upper localities of New York State. Her studio was the sunny converted barn she lived in, directly facing the serene Ashokan Dam and silvery Catskill mountains; her announcer, a neighboring lady from down the road.

A big strapping woman in her youth, Mary Margaret had grown frail and much smaller than I recalled from having seen her once in the days when she was lionized in New York City and I was a very young man. A series of broken limbs had left her almost beached in a wheel chair—but not quite. She still ran up and down her hallway fifty times each morning, to keep the circulation flowing she said. Demonstrating the feat for us, she hobbled somewhat, it is true, but each jog seemed to produce a new spurt of energy.

Obviously it kept her young. Her skin was miraculously unlined still and soft as a school girl's. And though her hair was now snowy white, she flirtatiously bundled it into an organdy Shaker bonnet, the ribbons of which flew down her shoulders.

I, of course, loved her on the spot, and the emotion, I can truly state, seemed reciprocal. On the air we were like old friends—talking of country things like cured hams, fried chicken, and piccalilli, as well as the chic people who populated The Store in Amagansett.

Amazingly, she seemed to have memorized our book. Picking the plum anecdotes from the dud avocados, and with the same skill that endeared her to my childhood, she maneuvered both Denis and me into telling only the ripest tales on the air.

After the program had been taped, the amenities said, and the coffee finally served, she opened those velvet brown eyes and looked straight into my face.

"Bert Greene," she said, "do you love me?"

"I really do, Mary Margaret," I assured her.

"Well," she suspired softly, "I'll know if that is so if you promise to come back here again and bring one of those Store hams we were talking about with you. I guess there is nothing in this world I'd rather chew on than a piece of real, down-home ham. Yours is not from Missouri (she pronounced it 'Missorah') a'course, but it sure does sound like it might taste like the *real* thing!"

And it did, I am happy to be able to report.

For in due time we did make one more trip to West Shokan with a prize baked ham, still warm from the oven, in the trunk of my Volkswagen.

It could not be tasted (nor the brimming pot of ziti salad we brought as a fitting embellishment), however, until yet another radio program had been taped. But I sensed Mary Margaret's mouth watering throughout the long preamble.

That she seemed to love that ham dearly only made me appreciate her more.

It was on this second radio appearance that she confessed her chocolate addiction to me. So I made a mental note that the next time I trekked up to that territory a luscious devil's food cake would accompany me. But alas, I must confess to never having made that trip. Instead, at the year's end, a bulky parcel arrived for me—from a company in Chicago that I had never heard of before. World's Finest Chocolate was its name and, for once, the cognomen truly fit. Every Christmas Mary Margaret sent her friends (and herself too, I hope) goodly portions of this weakness of hers. Great boxes of succulent confections like cocoa-dipped almonds huge as plum tomatoes and monstrous loaves of rich, velvety milk chocolate engorged with crunchy nut meats. Candy bars to die over!

In retaliation, I sent her brownies by the yard and a pan of (non-chocolate) sour cream coffee cake.

By the next Christmas, Mary Margaret was gone but the candies still arrived from Chicago for me. A last missive from my dear friend was enclosed, with a color photograph of herself—a tiny stalwart figure, dwarfed by a massive red maple tree in flaming fall regalia.

"Item of cheer," read her last Christmas card—in the uncertain scrawl I had come to know well. "This gallant old tree has said goodbye to summer but is confidently awaiting spring. Mary Margaret."

I ate my chocolate but I think I cried over it too.

I have never been to Vienna or Switzerland but I do plan to visit those chocolate centers of the world—preferably in my senility when the battle of the waistline has been long conceded and I can eat myself sick on such indulgent fantasies as Schokolade Pfannkuchen (chocolate pancakes) the way I did in my first childhood!

SCHOKOLADE PFANNKUCHEN

1 Place the eggs, milk, creme de cacao, salt, sugar, and flour, in that order, in a blender container. Blend at high speed until smooth; refrigerate at least 2 hours.

2 Place 1 teaspoon butter in a hot omelet or crepe pan over moderate heat; swirl pan to coat bottom. Pour in a scant ¼ cup of batter, tilting the pan back and forth to spread over the entire bottom. Cook 1 minute. Loosen pancake with a spatula; flip over and lightly brown other side. Transfer to a warm platter; cover with a paper towel and keep warm in oven. Continue until all batter is used.

3 Coat each pancake with chocolate sauce and roll up. Serve immediately with vanilla-flavored whipped cream.

Note: Schokolade Pfannkuchen can be made in advance and reheated in a 300° oven for 10 minutes or served at room temperature.

3 eggs
1½ cups milk
3 tablespoons brown crème de cacao
Pinch of salt
1½ tablespoons sugar
⅔ cup sifted all-purpose flour
Unsalted butter
Chocolate Sauce (recipe follows)
Vanilla-flavored whipped cream

Serves 8 to 10.

CHOCOLATE SAUCE

Melt the chocolate in the top of a double boiler over hot water. Stir in the milk, butter, and creme de cacao. (Mixture will be quite thick.) Thin with coffee. Cool slightly before spreading over pancakes.

4 ounces semisweet chocolate
1 can (14 ounces) condensed milk
4 tablespoons unsalted butter
2 tablespoons brown crème de cacao
2 tablespoons strong hot coffee with ½ teaspoon cream

Makes about 2 cups.

A note on buying chocolate: I was raised on desserts made of Baker's Chocolate (unsweetened and semisweet) and I still buy that brand most frequently because it is both dependable and readily available. On the occasions when I splurge on expensive European chocolates, Maillards, Zaanland, Lanvin, Tobler, and Lindt are my first options. Sweet-dark, semisweet, and bittersweet chocolate are practically interchangeable flavoring agents with a lustrous rich taste. Milk chocolate, while more subtle to the tongue, is rarely melted because its high butterfat content makes it hard to work with. Unsweetened, also called bitter or baking chocolate, is entirely sugarless and can never be used in desserts without the addition of some sweetener as it is very bitter.

Chocolate is a contradiction of flavors: bitter/sweet, for one thing! But even the name is deceiving. If you assume the noun *chocolate* to be synonymous with soothing mellifluence, you're dead wrong. The word comes from the Aztec language *cacahoatl* (or *xocatl*), meaning "very bitter water." And the first drink made from the roasted cacao beans (ground into powder and mixed with water) was probably drunk as medicine. A thousand years ago, the wandering tribes of Central America had but two cures for any illness—chocolate and pepper.

It was the Aztecs, a more sophisticated people, who flavored cocoa powder with vanilla beans and pepper and churned it into a drink. Aztecs took this cocktail neat but cold, chilled by snow brought down from the Sierras. They also considered the drink to be highly aphrodisiac—so stimulating, in fact, that cocoa was forbidden to Aztec women for almost two hundred years.

Although we expect our chocolate to be a sweet for all seasons, those early Mexicans did not. When they weren't quaffing a cup for immoral purposes, they used the cocoa powder exclusively as a preservative. Most meat and seafood in their diet was seasoned highly to prevent the stuff from going rancid. Thus, the following recipe, Chicken Mole, Pueblo Style, was born. A classic of sorts, it is definitely not—being a hot and exotic exercise—for every man's palate. If you are of the mind to be experimental, however, you'll find my rendition, culled from over half a dozen Mexican sources, to be quite tasty. I insist that the sole accompaniment be strong beer—and a plate of a bean and rice dish that I invented to undo the damage!

CHICKEN MOLE, PUEBLO STYLE

For the poaching:
1 stewing chicken (about 4 pounds)
1 small carrot
½ onion studded with 2 cloves
2 sprigs parsley
1 rib celery
½ lemon
1 large clove garlic

1 Cover the chicken with cold water. Add the carrot, onion studded with cloves, 2 parsley sprigs, celery, lemon, and 1 garlic clove. Bring to a boil and simmer until chicken is tender but not falling apart, 45 to 50 minutes. Remove chicken; reserve.

2 Heat oven to 275°. Saute the chopped onions and minced garlic in 4 tablespoons of the butter in a large saucepan or Dutch oven until

golden. Place the chicken in the center of the pan. Cook chicken over high heat, turning it frequently with two wooden spoons, until it becomes nicely browned. Remove chicken to a shallow baking dish and cut into serving pieces. Keep warm in the oven.

3 Add bouillon, chili powder, cloves, cinnamon, sesame seeds, and chili peppers to the saucepan. Cook uncovered over high heat until the mixture begins to thicken. Stir in the coriander and remaining butter.

4 Reduce heat. Stir in the raisins; cook until soft, about 3 minutes. Add the chocolate; cook until melted. Stir in the ground almonds, bread crumbs, and chicken stock. Season to taste with salt and pepper.

5 Pour the sauce over the chicken. Raise oven to 350°. Bake 10 minutes. Sprinkle chicken with the parsley-shallot mixture. Serve with Beans and Rice (recipe follows).

For the mole:
2 onions, finely chopped
3 cloves garlic, minced
6 tablespoons butter
1 beef bouillon cube or packet
1 tablespoon chili powder
¼ teaspoon ground cloves
¼ teaspoon ground cinnamon
1 teaspoon sesame seeds
1 can (4 ounces) green chili peppers
1½ teaspoons chopped fresh coriander or 1 teaspoon ground
½ cup raisins
1 ounce unsweetened chocolate
¼ cup ground blanched almonds
¼ cup toasted dry bread crumbs
1½ cups chicken stock
Salt and freshly ground pepper
¼ cup parsley chopped with 1 small shallot

Serves 4 to 6.

BEANS AND RICE

1 Add the rice to a large pot of boiling salted water. Stir once, bring to a boil, and simmer for 15 minutes. Drain in a colander. Place colander over boiling water; cover with one layer of paper toweling. Steam rice 15 minutes.

2 Meanwhile, cook the bacon and Canadian bacon in a large skillet over high heat until crisp. Add 1 tablespoon butter and the onions; cook over medium heat until the onions are soft.

3 Add the frozen black-eyed peas. Stir in the chicken stock. Cook over high heat 20 minutes. (The peas should have some bite to them.)

4 Stir in the rice; mix until combined. Season to taste with salt and pepper. Cook over high heat 5 minutes. (The rice should absorb any liquid in the pan.) Sprinkle with vinegar and stir in the remaining butter. Serve with the chicken mole or any spicy meat dish.

Note: Beans and Rice is delicious hot, but it is equally tasty served at room temperature with cold broiled chicken or, surprisingly, even cold herbed omelets.

½ cup rice
1 strip bacon, chopped
3 slices Canadian bacon, cut into thin strips
3 tablespoons butter
½ cup finely chopped green onions with tops
1 package (10 ounces) frozen black-eyed peas
1½ cups strong chicken stock
Salt and freshly ground pepper
1½ teaspoons tarragon vinegar

Serves 4 to 6.

Chocolate ___ 73

In its long kitchen history, chocolate has gotten mixed up with a lot of odd fellow flavors. There is a spectacular chocolate tomato cake in a later chapter of this book, for one thing. And another pungent and thoroughly fudgy concoction I think you will admire is Chocolate Beet Root Cake, which is served at Ford's Cafe in Sonoma, California. Jackie Cook, who, with Jane Hyde, runs this popular restaurant, advises that the recipe was given her by the granddaughter of a woman who brought it (by covered wagon) across the Oregon Trail. The red beets preserve and keep the chocolate cake remarkably moist, you'll find.

FORD'S CAFE CHOCOLATE BEET ROOT CAKE

3 ounces semisweet chocolate
1 cup vegetable oil
1¾ cups sugar
3 eggs
2 cups pureed cooked or canned
   beets
2 cups sifted all-purpose flour
2 teaspoons baking soda
¼ teaspoon salt
1 teaspoon vanilla
Confectioners' sugar, optional

Serves 8.

1 Heat oven to 375°. Melt the chocolate with ¼ cup oil in the top of a double boiler over hot water. Cool slightly.

2 Beat the sugar and eggs together until light and fluffy. Stir in remaining oil, the beets, and the melted chocolate mixture. Beat thoroughly.

3 Sift the flour with the baking soda and salt; add to the batter. Stir in the vanilla.

4 Pour into a greased and floured Bundt pan and bake until a toothpick inserted comes out clean, 60 to 65 minutes. Cool on wire rack. Remove from pan. Sprinkle with confectioners' sugar. (Cake may also be frosted with chocolate icing.) Cake will keep, covered tightly, for days—and the flavor seems to improve daily.

Note: Melting chocolate in a double boiler may seem like a chore, but you should never attempt to melt it over direct heat for it burns easily. The top of the double boiler should be placed over hot (not boiling) water. Most recipes in this book combine the chocolate to be melted with butter, oil, or some liquid. When recipe specifies that you melt chocolate alone, make sure that the top of the double boiler is free of all moisture, because even one stray drop of water has been known to "tighten" the chocolate and cause lumps. Chocolate may also be melted in a very low (200°) oven.

My mother was a lackluster cook but a dandy baker. The following recipe is one of the best things she ever taught me!

MY MOTHER'S CHOCOLATE ICING

1 Melt the chocolate in the top of a double boiler. Stir in the condensed milk. Beat until smooth.

2 Stir in the butter, one piece at a time, stirring after each addition. Stir in the egg yolk and vanilla. Beat until smooth and thick. (If the icing becomes too thick, thin with a little hot water.)

3 squares unsweetened chocolate
1 can (14 ounces) condensed milk
½ cup butter, cut in 8 pieces
1 egg yolk, beaten
1½ teaspoons vanilla

Frosts a 2-layer cake.

There are countless formulas in this world for fudge (I have twelve such interpretations logged) but very few instructions for whipping up a fail-safe brownie. The ultimate cake so named should be dense as Mississippi mud and yet chewy as a pan of underbeaten fudge. The recipe I include makes a wonderful contender for the honor. It is named for everyone's Grandma— except mine, who wouldn't consider the preparation of a chocolate dessert. "It's not my flavor," she would shrug, and I guess that's as good a rationale as any.

GRANDMA'S BROWNIES

1 Heat oven to 325°. Melt the butter with the chocolate in the top of a double boiler over hot water.

2 Beat the sugar into the eggs. Slowly beat in the melted chocolate mixture. Stir in the vanilla. Sift in the flour 2 tablespoons at a time, mixing well after each addition. Stir in the salt, sour cream, and walnuts.

3 Pour into a greased 8-inch square pan. Bake 30 minutes. (Be careful not to overcook; brownies should be moist.) Cool and cut into squares.

½ cup butter
2 ounces unsweetened chocolate
1 cup sugar
2 eggs, slightly beaten
1 teaspoon vanilla
½ cup all-purpose flour
Pinch of salt
¼ cup sour cream
⅔ cup chopped walnuts

Makes about 20 brownies.

Speaking of grandmothers brings to mind my pet dessert cookbook. It is *Grandma Rose's Book of SINFULLY DELICIOUS Cakes, Cookies, Pies, Cheese Cakes, Cake Rolls and Pastries*. Grandma Rose (Naftalin) is an ex-baker and restaurant owner from Portland,

Oregon. Her *oeuvre* deserves a place of honor in every cook's bookshelf!

The following luscious chocolate cosset is only slightly altered from the way Grandma Rose ordained it. I like more whipped cream than she prescribed.

SUPER CHOCOLATE PIE

For the meringue shell:
3 large egg whites
Pinch of salt
¼ teaspoon cream of tartar
⅔ cup sifted sugar
½ teaspoon vanilla
⅓ cup finely chopped walnuts or
   pecans

1 Heat oven to 275°. Beat the egg whites, salt, and cream of tartar together until soft peaks form. Gradually beat in the sugar until a very stiff meringue is formed. Beat in the vanilla.

2 Grease the bottom and sides of a 9-inch glass pie plate. Spread the meringue over the bottom and sides, building up the sides as high as possible. Sprinkle the nuts over the bottom. Bake 1 hour. (If after 10 minutes the sides start to sag, gently push them back into place.) Turn off the oven and allow the shell to cool in the oven ½ hour. Remove from oven and cool completely.

3 Melt the chocolate in the top of a double boiler over hot water. Add the milk, vanilla, and salt. Stir until smooth. Cool.

For the filling:
5 ounces semisweet chocolate
¼ cup hot milk
1 teaspoon vanilla
Pinch of salt
1¾ cups whipping cream
2 tablespoons confectioners' sugar
Chocolate curls

Serves 6 to 8.

4 Whip 1 cup of cream until stiff and fold into the cooled chocolate. Spread in cooled meringue shell. Refrigerate 4 hours.

5 No more than 1½ hours prior to serving, whip the remaining cream with the confectioners' sugar; spread over top of pie. Decorate with chocolate curls. Refrigerate until serving time.

Note: To make chocolate curls, scrape a bar of chocolate with a vegetable peeler.

A jewel among chocolate desserts is devil's food cake. The recipe that follows was passed from family to family; I received it from a wonderful black lady who came from Alexandria, Virginia. She mothered me for years—and made the cake whenever she got bored with cleaning. Her Bourbon Velvet Icing is tricky. It must be beaten over hot water for a while, which may seem intimidating to a baker who wants to get on with the business of frosting. But it's worth every moment of bother!

I also recommend My Mother's Chocolate Icing as a wonderful annotation to this cake. It serves as an alternative to the bourbon if you desire a really rich, twin-chocolate taste.

ALEXANDRIA DEVIL'S FOOD CAKE

1 Heat oven to 350°. Sift the flour, soda, and salt together three times.

2 Cream the butter with the sugar. Add the egg and egg yolks, one at a time, beating until fluffy after each addition.

3 Melt the chocolate in the top of a double boiler over hot water; stir into batter. Stir in the vanilla. Add the flour in three parts, alternating with thirds of the milk; beat well after each addition.

4 Pour into two greased and floured 9-inch cake pans. Bake until toothpick inserted comes out clean, 40 to 45 minutes. Cool 5 minutes in pans; turn out onto a wire rack. Cool completely. Frost with Bourbon Velvet Icing (recipe follows) or My Mother's Chocolate Icing (recipe on page 75).

2½ cups sifted cake flour
1½ teaspoons baking soda
½ teaspoon salt
¾ cup unsalted butter, softened
2 cups dark brown sugar
1 whole egg
3 egg yolks
3 ounces unsweetened chocolate
1½ teaspoons vanilla
1½ cups milk

Serves 8.

BOURBON VELVET ICING

1 Combine all ingredients except vanilla in the top of a double boiler. Place over hot water over medium heat. Beat until soft peaks form, about 5 minutes.

2 Immediately transfer mixture to a large electric mixer bowl. Add the vanilla; beat until stiff. (Frosted cake may be garnished with chocolate curls made by scraping a bar of chocolate with a vegetable peeler.)

4 egg whites
1½ cups light brown sugar
2 tablespoons bourbon
3 tablespoons water
1 teaspoon cream of tartar
Pinch of salt
1½ teaspoons vanilla

Frosts a 2-layer cake.

Chocolate as a tonic beverage preceded chocolate as a flavoring agent by a century and a half. Hannah Glasse, who wrote the most successful cookbook of the eighteenth century (*The Art of Cooking Made Plain and Easy*), heralded chocolate as a true aromatic with her recipe for chocolate cream:
 ''Take a quart of cream,'' she advised, ''and a pint of white wine and a little juice of lemon. Sweeten it very well with sugar. Add a sprig of rosemary; then grate some chocolate into it until the color turns muddy and stir all the ingredients over the fire until it is thick. Strain well and then pour it into your cups and cool.''
 I like my version of cocoa better!

COCOA IN A POT

2 tablespoons imported Dutch
  cocoa
¼ cup sugar
Pinch of salt
⅛ teaspoon cinnamon
4 cups scalded milk
¼ teaspoon vanilla
Whipped cream for garnish
  (optional)

Serves 4.

1 Combine the cocoa, sugar, salt, and cinnamon in the top of a double boiler; place over hot water. Add ¼ cup milk; stir until a smooth paste is formed.

2 Whisk in the remaining milk and vanilla; whisk until frothy. Serve topped with whipped cream, if desired.

Note: If using domestic cocoa like Hershey's, which has a slightly acrid flavor, add more sugar and substitute 1 cup cream for 1 cup of the milk. Most cocoa made in America is bitter; it is worth spending a little extra for a Dutch import (such as Droste's) because the cocoa is treated in Holland with an alkali to neutralize the acids.

No one knows exactly when chocolate desserts came into favor. Nor do we know who invented them. Possibly it was the Italian *cioccolatieri* who mixed grated cocoa with sugar, vanilla, and cream and pressed the mixture into little crescents that were sold at fairs in the late 1600s. Certainly Bavarian cream must have been an early formulation, because by 1704 that dessert was so popular that Frederick I of Prussia imposed a tax on it.

CHOCOLATE BAVARIAN CREAM

1 cup milk
3 ounces semisweet chocolate,
  broken into pieces
1 ounce unsweetened chocolate
1 envelope unflavored gelatin
1 tablespoon cold water
5 egg yolks
½ cup sugar
1 cup whipping cream, whipped
  until stiff
Whipped cream for garnish

Serves 8.

1 Heat the milk in a heavy saucepan over low heat. Add the chocolate; stir until smooth.

2 Soften the gelatin in 1 tablespoon cold water. Add to the chocolate mixture. Cook and stir over low heat until dissolved. Remove from heat.

3 Beat the egg yolks and sugar together in a medium bowl until light and fluffy. Gradually stir in the chocolate mixture.

4 Place the bowl in ice-cold water. Stir mixture with a wooden spoon until it begins to thicken. Fold in the 1 cup whipping cream. Pour mixture into a 6-cup mold. Chill until set, about 3 hours.

5 To unmold, fill a large skillet with water to a depth of 1 inch; bring to a boil. Turn off the heat and dip a knife into the water. Run the knife around the edge of the mold; then dip the bottom of the mold into the water for 4 to 5 seconds. Cover with a serving platter and invert. Chill for ½ hour. To garnish, fill a pastry bag with whipped cream and pipe a decorative pattern over top.

Bavaria's cream is only a stone's throw from mightier mousse on my street. I hardly ever make a mousse of chocolate that has gelatin in its devise because I like the emollient of egg and chocolate so much. However, it seems that all rules are made to be broken. The version of chocolate mousse I include here is very classy (whitened with whipped cream and tranquilized with tender bits of almonds)—almost like a chocolate bar on the run.

CHOCOLATE-ALMOND MOUSSE

1 Melt 6 ounces chocolate with the milk in the top of a double boiler over hot water.

2 Soften the gelatin in the water.

3 Lightly beat the egg yolks. Gradually stir in 2 tablespoons of the melted chocolate mixture. Gradually stir the egg yolk mixture into the rest of the chocolate. Stir over low heat until slightly thickened. Add the softened gelatin; stir until dissolved. Cool to room temperature.

4 Beat the egg whites with the salt and cream of tartar until stiff peaks form. Gradually beat in the sugar.

5 Stir the cognac into the cooled chocolate. Fold in the beaten egg whites, 1 cup of the whipped cream, and the chopped nuts. Transfer to a serving dish; chill for at least 6 hours or overnight.

6 Melt the remaining 1 ounce of chocolate in the top of a double boiler over hot water. Stir in the coffee; cool. Stir chocolate mixture into the remaining whipped cream. Using a pastry bag, pipe cream in rosettes around the top of the mousse. Garnish with slivered almonds.

7 ounces semisweet chocolate
½ cup milk
2 teaspoons unflavored gelatin
2 tablespoons cold water
2 eggs, separated
⅛ teaspoon salt
⅛ teaspoon cream of tartar
3 tablespoons sugar
¼ cup cognac
1½ cups whipping cream, whipped
½ cup toasted almonds or walnuts, chopped
½ teaspoon instant coffee powder
Toasted slivered almonds or walnut halves for garnish

Serves 6 to 8.

A recent tome, *The Chocolate Bible,* by Adrianne Marcus (G. P. Putnam 1979), is the second best way—after actual caloric consumption—to sample all the chocolate confections the world has to offer. Ms. Marcus is prejudiced about her light-dark-milk-and-bittersweet compulsions but she makes a perfect tour guide for chocoholics of every stripe. Her favorite candymakers? Too numerous for mention here, but Aldo Pasticerri and Confetteria in Alba, Italy (for chocolate truffles), is very high on her list.

Italians have a wonderful sense of fitness about cuisine. Meals usually end with fruit and cheese. They eat ice cream (called *gelati*) at midafternoon or at night as a special sensuous treat. Their ice cream, while nowhere as rich as ours, is intensely flavored. My sister lived for some while in Rome and returned with tales of a dark and unforgettable sweet chocolate cream that seemed to be sanded with grains of bitterest cocoa—its sensation remained upon the tongue for hours. This is my version of her Italian taste thrill. And I confess that when I finally got to Italy (in 1970) and tried the original, I still preferred my own!

SUPERB ITALIAN CHOCOLATE ICE CREAM

6 ounces unsweetened chocolate, broken into pieces
2 cans (14 ounces each) condensed milk
1 tablespoon vanilla
½ cup unsalted butter, cut into 8 pieces
6 egg yolks
4 ounces semisweet chocolate
1 cup strong black coffee
1½ cups sugar
1 cup light cream
¼ cup dark rum
¼ cup white crème de cacao
4 cups whipping cream
2 ounces unsweetened chocolate, finely grated
½ teaspoon salt

Makes 3½ to 4 quarts.

1 Melt 6 ounces unsweetened chocolate in the top of a double boiler over hot water. Add the milk, stirring until smooth. Stir in the vanilla. Remove from heat. Add the butter, one piece at a time, stirring until all butter has been absorbed.

2 Beat the yolks in a medium bowl until light and lemony colored. Gradually stir in the chocolate mixture; stir until smooth and creamy.

3 Heat the semisweet chocolate, coffee, sugar, and light cream in the top of a double boiler over hot water, stirring constantly, until chocolate and sugar melt. Stir in the rum and creme de cacao. Cool to room temperature.

4 Combine the two chocolate mixtures, the whipping cream, the finely grated unsweetened chocolate, and the salt. Pour into the canister of an ice cream maker; freeze according to manufacturer's directions.

These last two chocolate confections (although you will find countless others, flavored with coffee, almond, orange, and rum, sprinkled throughout the book) are foreign bestowals. Chocolate Cut Velvet, from Vevey, Switzerland, is less a cake than an intense flavor experience. Serve only tiny, tiny pieces. And make sure the chocolate you use is top-notch!

The other prize is a Bavarian Black Forest Torte. I translated this model from a complicated German prescription but it was worth all the labor. It is the best dessert I know of—but I must confess that a guest at my dinner table fainted away after consuming a healthy wedge! So let your portions be more prudent.

CHOCOLATE CUT VELVET

1 Heat oven to 425°. Heat the chocolate, water, and vanilla in the top of a 2-quart double boiler over hot water over low heat. Allow chocolate to melt very slowly. (It should take at least 10 minutes. Melting the chocolate too fast will turn it into a grainy lump.) Remove from heat. Stir in the flour, sugar, and butter.

2 Beat the egg yolks lightly. Whisk into the chocolate mixture.

3 Beat the egg whites just until stiff but not dry peaks form. (Do not overbeat.) Fold gently into the chocolate mixture.

4 Line a buttered 8-inch springform pan with wax paper; butter the paper. Pour in the batter. Bake exactly 15 minutes. Turn off the heat and leave oven door ajar. Cool completely in the oven.

5 Carefully remove the outer rim of the cake pan. Place serving plate over cake and invert. Remove the wax paper (patience is a *must* here).

6 Whip the cream with the Grand Marnier until stiff. Using a pastry bag, pipe the cream over the top of the cake in a lattice pattern. Pipe stars around the base of the cake with the remaining cream. Refrigerate.

7 Remove cake from refrigerator ½ hour before serving. Cut into small pieces, as it is rich.

Note: Do not use domestic chocolate; it just won't do!

1 **pound imported European sweet chocolate**
1 **tablespoon water**
1 **teaspoon vanilla**
1 **tablespoon all-purpose flour**
1 **tablespoon sugar**
10 **tablespoons butter, softened**
4 **eggs, separated**
1 **cup whipping cream**
1 **teaspoon Grand Marnier liqueur**

Serves 8 or more.

BLACK FOREST TORTE

For the cake:
¾ cup all-purpose flour, sifted
1¾ cups sugar
1¼ teaspoons baking soda
1 teaspoon salt
¼ teaspoon baking powder
⅔ cup butter
4 ounces unsweetened chocolate, melted and cooled
1¼ cups water
1 teaspoon vanilla
3 eggs

For the chocolate filling:
6 ounces German sweet chocolate
¾ cup butter, cut into 12 pieces
¾ can (14-ounce size) condensed milk
½ cup chopped toasted almonds

For the cream filling:
2 cups whipping cream
1 tablespoon confectioners' sugar
1 teaspoon vanilla

For the decoration:
Chocolate curls
1 cup fresh pitted sweet cherries or 1 can (8 ounces) pitted dark sweet cherries, well drained

Serves 8 to 10.

1 Heat oven to 350°. Sift together the flour, sugar, baking soda, salt, and baking powder.

2 Cream the butter in a large electric mixer bowl. Stir in the chocolate. Stir in the flour mixture in three parts, alternately with thirds of the water. Beat until smooth. Stir in the vanilla. Beat in the eggs, one at a time. Beat 2 minutes.

3 Butter and flour four 9-inch round cake pans. Pour ¼ of the batter into each pan. (Layers will be thin.) Bake until a toothpick inserted comes out clean, 15 to 18 minutes. Cool 10 minutes in pans. Remove from pans; cool thoroughly on wire racks.

4 To make chocolate filling: Melt the German sweet chocolate in the top of a double boiler over hot water. Remove from heat; allow to cool slightly. Stir in ¾ cup butter and the condensed milk, stirring until blended and smooth. Stir in the almonds.

5 To make cream filling: Whip the cream with the sugar and vanilla until stiff.

6 Place one cake layer on a serving platter. Spread with half of the chocolate filling. Top with second layer. Spread with half of the cream filling. Repeat layers, ending with cream on top. (Do not frost sides.)

7 Decorate top with chocolate curls. (See note for Super Chocolate Pie.) Refrigerate until ready to serve. Just before serving, arrange the black cherries over top.

Cinnamon

It has taken me a long time to recover from certain childhood prejudices.

As a young boy, I detested liver, for example, with such a remarkable passion that I couldn't sit at the same table when it was being served. I remember the liver my mother prepared as being fully two inches thick and battleship gray—it looked not unlike an ink eraser hiding under a wreath of limply fried onions and I hated its texture even more than its taste. It's only forty years later that I'm able to admit to myself that the flesh of an invertebrate organ actually can be quite tasty if it is prepared with some dispatch (sliced paper thin and cooked in a very hot pan) and seasoned judiciously. Still and all, liver is not one of my prized flavors.

My feelings about cinnamon were similarly blighted by one bad experience early in life, but my aversion to the spice is far less pronounced. Matter of fact, the scent of cinnamon in the air (marvelous and heady with augury) has always been so tantalizing to me as a cook that I never could equate that aroma with the artificial *red* taste that my fledgling tongue rejected.

My initial resistance to the trenchant bite of the synthetic flavoring came about when I was barely past the toddling stage. My mother and father were both dedicated movie buffs and long before Garbo talked they trundled me along with them "to the show," hoping vainly that the darkness of the hall and the great black and white images on the silver screen would hypnotize me into a state of co-equal silence. But that was a faulty surmise on their part. I had an inquiring bent to my nature even then and, being quite incapable of reading the subtitles myself, I would turn first to one parent and then the other and whine loudly, "Read to me!" at the absolutely most dramatic moments.

I well remember the end of *Laugh, Clown, Laugh!* when a dying Lon Chaney lay on the sawdust of the circus rings and, still in his clown-face, murmured some last words to a grief-stricken Loretta Young.

"What is he saying?" I cried impatiently to my mother, who was dissolved in tears at my side.

"He is saying . . . that children should be seen and not heard!" she replied from the depths of her handkerchief.

The next time we entered the theater, and thereafter, I was permitted to indulge in those sweet delights of the candy butcher, such as gum drops, jujubes, and jellied fruits, that would clamp my jaws securely shut during most of the picture.

On one such occasion, at an afternoon movie with my sister, I became so surfeit with the taste of cinnamon *Red Dots* (a peculiarly loathsome candy that stung both tongue and tearducts at the same time) that I threw up—right in the middle of *Rosemarie,* starring a silent Joan Crawford. And, for a decade thereafter, I wouldn't allow anything even remotely cinnamon-flavored to pass my lips.

Apple pie, the one truly majestic dish my mother knew how to prepare, won me back into the fold. For what is a gorgeous buttery crust, filled to the brim with tart fruit slices and laved with ample portions of crusty sugar and sweet butter, if the whole is not gently perfumed by cinnamon as well?

Cinnamon, as we know it (most often out of a dust-top can), is the ground-up bark of the Asian Cinnamomum tree. A laurel evergreen, this cinnamon tree grows rather like a birch, with shards of loose bark that can be peeled off and dried. Curiously, the spicy flavor seems to increase as the bark loses its moisture and turns a sun-burnt color.

I like cinnamon sticks—the peeled bark rolled into narrow quills—best of all in my kitchen. They can be used whole or grated (with a grater) for a most tonic addition to practically everything that is stove-worthy.

The seasoning has a long historical frame of reference. In 1500 B.C., the Egyptian Queen Hatshepsut used cinnamon leaves to perfume her body after a bath. And Moses, according to the Talmud, was instructed by the Lord to mix crushed cinnamon with oil to anoint the sacred lambs. Cinnamon was also the attar called *cinname* that, we are told in the Song of Songs, the Queen of Sheba used to captivate the wise King Solomon.

As an incense, cinnamon was burned in the world of antiquity for thousands of years. The Greeks considered the shavings of the bark a sacred powder that they dusted on all their ritual offerings to the gods. And the Persians fed their oil lamps with cinnamon tapers to clear their minds on the nights before battles. The greatest scent of cinnamon in ancient times, however, was probably achieved in Rome near the end of Nero's infamous reign. After he purportedly murdered his second wife, Poppaea, Nero thought it necessary to make some symbolic gesture of his grief. So he had Rome's entire supply of cinnamon bark set afire. The blaze lasted three days, scented the city nicely, and exhausted a year's reserve of the spice.

Some historians believe Nero's pyre of cinnamon was such a stunning gesture that the only way he could top it was to burn the entire city down. Which, in time, he did.

I think cinnamon deserves a revival of showy ritual. But the most conspicuous example I can offer you at the moment is Tori Keema, an absolutely splendid Indian concoction of lamb and slivered zucchini tossed in yogurt and perfumed with cinnamon.

TORI KEEMA

1 Make tomato sauce.

2 Drop the zucchini into boiling salted water. Return to a rolling boil over high heat and cook 1 minute. Rinse under cold running water; drain.

3 Melt the butter in a small skillet, and cook the onion and garlic until soft, but not brown.

4 Brown the lamb in a wok or large skillet over high heat, breaking up the lumps with a wooden spoon. Drain the lamb and return to wok. Stir in the onion, garlic, cumin, ginger, cinnamon, ⅓ cup tomato sauce, red pepper, salt, black pepper, and the cooked zucchini; mix thoroughly. Stir in the yogurt and cook over medium heat 7 minutes. Add more yogurt if mixture seems dry. Stir in the coriander. Serve with rice. Pass the chutney.

⅓ cup Homemade Tomato Sauce (see Index)
4 small zucchini, cut into ¼-inch slices
3 tablespoons butter
1 large yellow onion, finely chopped
2 large cloves garlic, minced
2 pounds ground lamb
1 teaspoon ground cumin
1 teaspoon ground ginger
1½ teaspoons ground cinnamon
1 small dried hot red pepper, crushed
Salt and freshly ground black pepper to taste
1¼ cups unflavored yogurt (approximately)
1 tablespoon chopped fresh coriander (Chinese parsley)
4 cups cooked rice
Chutney

Serves 4.

Cinnamon is one aromatic seasoning that never suffered the slings and arrows of outrageous fortune. In continuous culinary favor since its discovery (at least 2,000 years before the birth of Christ), it is a curio on a kitchen spice shelf precisely because it is as popular today as it was during the Renaissance.

A Florentine soup noted in sixteenth-century cookbooks is called Ginestrata. Named for the *ginestre* flowers (a kind of yellow broom) that cover the Tuscan hills in spring, it is pale golden in color and dependent upon the flavor of cinnamon, chicken broth, and beaten egg yolks for its remarkable flavor and texture.

The secret of this soup is a lacing of Marsala wine—which makes it a probable distant cousin of another Florence-born dish, *zabaglione*, though it's much less sweet, of course. Try it—and not just because it's 500 years old, either!

GINESTRATA

5 egg yolks
2 teaspoons ground cinnamon
¾ cup dry Marsala
1 quart cold chicken stock, all fat removed
Salt to taste
6 tablespoons butter
3 teaspoons granulated sugar
Freshly grated nutmeg

Serves 6.

1 Whisk the egg yolks in a bowl and beat in the cinnamon and Marsala. Strain through several layers of cheesecloth. Beat in the chicken stock. Add the salt and butter.

2 Gradually heat soup in a heavy saucepan over very low heat (or in the top of a double boiler over hot, but not simmering, water), stirring constantly. Do not allow soup to boil. When slightly thickened and hot, pour into soup bowls and sprinkle each with ½ teaspoon sugar and freshly grated nutmeg.

Another historical cinnamon-flavored bisque is Russian Chernichny Soop, made with blueberries and a whole lemon. This elegant indigo dish, it is reported, was devised by Potemkin's chef when the General was trying to woo Catherine the Great back to his bed. History reports the soup a success but his suit "in the soup." And so it goes. This is a perfect brunch starter, what with its dram of vodka added just before serving!

CHERNICHNY SOOP

1 Place the blueberries, sugar, cinnamon, and water in a large saucepan. Scrape the pits from the lemon. Squeeze the lemon quarters into the pot before adding them. Bring to a boil and simmer 15 minutes. Cool.

2 Transfer soup (including cinnamon stick and lemon wedges) to a blender container; blend until smooth. Chill thoroughly. Just before serving, stir in the vodka. Ladle soup into serving bowls; garnish each with a heaping tablespoon of sour cream.

1 pint blueberries
1 cup granulated sugar
½ cinnamon stick
2 cups water
1 lemon, cut into quarters
¼ cup vodka
Sour cream

Serves 6.

To change the culinary geography once more, I offer Smothered Beef, a dish from Provence—the recipe stolen by me from Diable Vert in Arles!

SMOTHERED BEEF

1 Heat oven to 250°. Brown the bacon in oil in a Dutch oven. Add the meat, a third at a time, and brown over high heat on all sides.

2 Add the quartered onions, the carrots, and whole onion. Cook and stir over medium heat 5 minutes. Add remaining ingredients except noodles, butter, and cheese. Bring to a boil, cover and bake 5 hours. Toss noodles with butter and Parmesan cheese. Serve Smothered Beef over noodles.

⅓ cup diced slab bacon
1 tablespoon vegetable oil
4 pounds stewing beef, cut into 2-inch cubes
4 medium onions, cut into quarters
4 small carrots, cut into quarters
1 small whole onion stuck with 2 cloves
3 large tomatoes, chopped
4 large shallots, chopped
2 cloves garlic, minced
3 sprigs parsley, chopped
6 celery leaves, chopped
1 large bay leaf, crumbled
¼ teaspoon ground cinnamon
Pinch each of savory, thyme, and ground ginger
Salt and freshly ground pepper to taste
½ teaspoon finely slivered orange peel
1 cup dry red wine
½ cup beef stock or broth
8 cups cooked noodles or macaroni
Butter
¼ cup grated Parmesan cheese

Serves 6 to 8.

Flavoring fish and seafood with cinnamon is a Greek kitchen specialty. Of course Greek cooks sprinkle everything with cinnamon; so the seafood trick is not unusual—but this bluefish recipe is!

BLUEFISH FILLET

3 tablespoons butter
1½ to 2 pounds bluefish fillet
1 clove garlic, minced
¼ teaspoon ground cinnamon
½ teaspoon lemon juice
Lemon wedges
Chopped parsley

Serves 3 to 4.

1 Heat oven to 400°. Rub a shallow baking dish with 1 tablespoon butter and add the fish.

2 Mash the garlic, cinnamon, lemon juice, and remaining butter together into a paste and spread over the fish. Bake on the bottom rack of the oven 5 minutes; then place under the broiler until fish is golden and flakes when pierced with a fork, about 5 minutes. Garnish with lemon wedges and chopped parsley.

Picadillo is a Mexican peasant's meal—spicy, dark, and as salutary as a distant cousin of chili con carne might be expected to taste.

The odd thing about this recipe is that it is curiously like "Russian Hamburger," a standard Sunday night supper a friend of mine remembers with fond affection from his Colorado childhood. His mother, however, always made the dish with peas—never, never olives! So you've got that option. If you are a pea lover, put them in (raw or defrosted) fifteen minutes before you serve up the glop!

PICADILLO

1 Cover the currants with warm water and let stand for at least 20 minutes. Drain.

2 Heat the butter in a heavy skillet and brown the meat over high heat, breaking up lumps with a wooden spoon. Reserve.

3 Heat the oil in a Dutch oven and cook the onions, garlic, and peppers over medium heat 5 to 6 minutes. Do not brown. Add the olives, capers, vinegar, salt and pepper to taste, cinnamon, cloves, chili powder, bay leaf, and hot pepper sauce. Mix well and cook over low heat 10 minutes.

4 Using a slotted spoon, transfer the meat to the Dutch oven. Add the canned tomatoes, the fresh tomato, and the drained currants. Cook uncovered over medium heat 1 hour, stirring frequently. Serve over rice.

Note: Recipe may be doubled.

I don't rightly know the origin of the next recipe. Perhaps it came full-blown from the fertile brain of Ntozake Shange, the remarkably talented poet and playwright who wrote *For Colored Girls Who Consider Suicide When the Rainbow is Enuf.* She gave me her formula for the dish at lunch a season or so ago when I interviewed her for *Viva* magazine (shortly after her play opened on Broadway and some time before the magazine folded). Although the story was duly paid for, it was never published: "Too outspoken" was the editorial verdict.

So that the long afternoon we spent together should not be written off as a complete loss to either of us, do have the outspoken lady's sweet prescription for Cinnamon Chicken!

⅓ cup dried currants or raisins
1 tablespoon butter
1 pound ground round steak
1 tablespoon vegetable oil
1 cup finely chopped onions
2 tablespoons minced garlic
¾ cup chopped green peppers
⅓ cup pitted green Spanish olives, drained
1 tablespoon capers
2 tablespoons tarragon vinegar
Salt and freshly ground pepper to taste
½ teaspoon ground cinnamon
¼ teaspoon ground cloves
¼ teaspoon chili powder
½ bay leaf, crushed
Dash of hot pepper sauce
1 can (17 ounces) Italian plum tomatoes with juice
1 medium fresh tomato, seeded, chopped
4 cups cooked rice

Serves 4.

NTOZAKE SHANGE'S CINNAMON CHICKEN

1 Heat oven to 400°. Rub the chicken well with garlic. Pour the melted butter into a baking dish. Roll the chicken in the butter to coat each piece; turn skin side up. Dust each piece with cinnamon and sprinkle with soy sauce. Bake ½ hour.

2 Reduce heat to 350°. Sprinkle the chicken with the wine and sugar. Bake until the juices run yellow when pricked with a fork, about ½ hour.

1 chicken (about 3½ pounds), cut into serving pieces
1 clove garlic, bruised
4 tablespoons butter, melted
1 teaspoon ground cinnamon
1 tablespoon soy sauce
¼ cup chablis wine
1 teaspoon granulated sugar

Serves 4.

The notion of string beans cooked until they wilt and turn brown at the edges seems appalling (in print, at least). Not like any other bean dish you will ever dip into, however, this slightly pungent mess of pottage is Turkish delight to my palate.

I came by the recipe at lunch one day with a beautiful young girl whose husband (or lover—I can't remember which) came from Istanbul and was teaching her his native cuisine. This was the first dish she learned and she knew it by heart. I memorized her canon the same way—so I could hie it away the moment the check was paid!

TURKISH GREEN BEANS

1 pound green beans
4 to 6 tablespoons olive oil
1 can (6 ounces) tomato paste
1 large onion, finely chopped
2 cloves garlic, minced
1 teaspoon granulated sugar
1 teaspoon ground cinnamon
1 tablespoon unsalted butter
Salt and freshly ground pepper

Serves 4.

1 Heat oven to 300°. Trim the beans and slice in the French manner. Grease a baking dish with 1 tablespoon oil. Spread beans in dish.

2 Combine the tomato paste, 3 to 5 tablespoons oil, the onion, garlic, sugar, and cinnamon; pour over beans.

3 Dot with butter and sprinkle with salt and pepper. Cover with aluminum foil; bake 1 hour. Remove the foil; bake 2 hours longer. The string beans will become soft and spaghettilike. If they begin to turn too dark, replace the foil. Serve hot or at room temperature.

Come September, you will usually find me knee-deep in peach pits, skimming the sweet aromatic fuzz from a gallon pot of nectarous fruit as it stews with sugar and orange juice. When the yellow gold has thickened sufficiently, it is strained and bottled into Bert Greene's Peach Butter, which is, if I may say so immodestly, one of the few heavenly elixirs known to man.

Peaches and cinnamon are born flavor-mates in a pot of jam or preserves, and I like the combination so much that I often add a speck of cinnamon to peach pie or shortcake, too. Think about that when the fruit hangs heavy on the vine!

PEACH BUTTER

1 Drop peaches into boiling water for several minutes to loosen the skins. Remove skins and reserve. Discard the pits and cut the peaches into ½-inch slices. Place in a colander over a bowl and let stand at least 20 minutes.

2 Using a vegetable peeler, remove the rind of half the orange. Add rind to the reserved peach skins. Remove remaining peel, seed the orange, and chop the pulp. Place the peach skins and the orange pulp in a large heavy pot and add any juice from the sliced peaches. Cook over low heat until the peach skins are tender, about 15 minutes. Place in a blender container, 3 cups at a time; blend until smooth. (Be careful; hot liquids often are volatile in a blender!)

3 Return peach skin puree to pot. Add the sliced peaches, 3 pounds sugar, and the cinnamon stick. Boil 30 minutes. Skim the froth off the top of the liquid as it boils.

4 Remove cinnamon stick. Place peach mixture in a blender container, 3 cups at a time; puree until smooth. Stir in the almond extract. Return peach mixture to pot. Bring to a boil; remove from heat.

5 Taste for sweetness; stir in additional sugar, if desired. Pour into hot, sterilized jars, leaving ½-inch headspace, and seal at once. Process jars 20 minutes in boiling water bath.

13 pounds peaches
1 large orange
3 pounds granulated sugar
    (approximately)
1 cinnamon stick
¼ teaspoon almond extract

Makes about 10 pints.

I have a house at the very end of Long Island where every year I watch the ducklings leave for warmer climes on the very last day of September. One month, to the day, after that, the pumpkins vanish as well. The last of the summer people usually take them back to the city and I, for one, never blame them—for these golden squash are lusher than any other grown in this world, I'll warrant.

   This pumpkin pie recipe is authentically New England, you'll note, in the maple syrup of its devise. Cinnamon gives it a very special (most unpuritan) sensuality, I think. I like to add a speck more cinnamon and a smidge of instant coffee to the sweet cream as I whip it—for a slightly different zing.

NEW ENGLAND PUMPKIN PIE

½ recipe Darlene Schulz's Pie
  Pastry (see Index)
1½ cups pureed fresh pumpkin
3 tablespoons butter, melted
½ cup granulated sugar
¼ cup maple syrup
1 teaspoon ground cinnamon
½ teaspoon ground nutmeg
¼ teaspoon ground cloves
3 eggs, separated
½ cup milk
¼ cup whipping cream
Sweetened whipped cream

Serves 6 to 8.

1 Make pie pastry. Roll out to 12-inch circle. Line 10-inch pie pan. Trim edges and flute. (Excess pastry may be refrigerated for future use.)

2 Heat oven to 350°. Combine all ingredients except the egg whites and whipped cream. Mix thoroughly.

3 Beat the egg whites until stiff but not dry. Fold into the pumpkin mixture. Pour into the pie shell and bake until a toothpick inserted halfway between the center and edge of pie comes out clean, about 50 minutes. Cool. Serve with sweetened whipped cream.

Note: To bake a pumpkin, wash it and cut it in half crosswise. Scrape out the seeds and strings. Place the pumpkin halves in a pan, shell sides up, and bake at 325° for an hour or more until the shell begins to fall in and the pulp is tender. Scrape out the pulp and puree in a blender until smooth. A medium-sized pumpkin will yield enough pulp for one pie.

The following Pumpkin Cake recipe comes from another denizen of East Hampton. But the lady, whose great grandmother made it first, doesn't want any publicity. So here is her family heirloom, anonymously authored.

SOUTH FORK PUMPKIN CAKE

For the cake:
1½ cups pureed pumpkin
1¼ cups vegetable oil
2 cups granulated sugar
4 eggs
2 tablespoons dark rum
3 cups sifted all-purpose flour
2 teaspoons baking powder
2 teaspoons baking soda
1 teaspoon salt
2 tablespoons ground cinnamon
½ cup chopped dried prunes
½ cup golden raisins
1 cup chopped walnuts

For the icing:
1 cup confectioners' sugar
1 teaspoon ground cinnamon
2 tablespoons orange juice
1 teaspoon whipping cream

Serves 8 to 10.

1 Heat oven to 350°. Place the pumpkin, oil, and sugar in a large electric mixer bowl; beat until well mixed. Beat in the eggs, one at a time. Beat in the rum.

2 Sift the flour, baking powder, baking soda, salt, and cinnamon together. Gradually beat the flour mixture into the pumpkin mixture on low speed.

3 Stir in the prunes, raisins, and walnuts. Pour into a greased and floured 10-inch tube pan. Bake until a toothpick inserted in cake comes out clean, 1 hour and 25 to 30 minutes. Cool on a wire rack. Unmold onto plate.

4 Combine all the ingredients for the icing; beat until smooth. Drizzle over cake.

Two other cinnamon-inspired cakes are among the best confections ever logged by a cookbook writer.

The Carrot Pineapple Bundt is a towering golden triumph. I have seen and tasted similar sweet cakes from the South from time to time (carrot cake is usually Gullah in antecedence) but none as tender, nutty, or fruity as this. An irresistible dessert, this cake also keeps remarkably well—if you can restrain your loved ones from demolishing it at the first sitting. I can't!

CARROT PINEAPPLE BUNDT

1 Heat oven to 325°. Sift the flour, sugar, baking soda, salt, baking powder, and cinnamon together and place in a large electric mixer bowl.

2 Drain the pineapple and combine the liquid with the eggs, oil, and vanilla. Beat the egg mixture into the flour mixture, on low speed, until well mixed; beat at medium speed 3 minutes.

3 Stir in the pineapple, walnuts, and carrots. Pour into a greased and floured Bundt pan and bake until toothpick inserted in cake comes out clean, about 1½ hours. Cool completely on a wire rack; unmold onto plate.

4 To make the icing, cream the butter until light and fluffy. Beat in the cream cheese, orange juice, vanilla, and cinnamon. Continue beating while adding enough confectioners' sugar for spreadable consistency. Stir in the walnuts. Spread over cake.

For the cake:
3 cups sifted cake flour
2 cups granulated sugar
2 teaspoons baking soda
1½ teaspoons salt
1 teaspoon baking powder
2 teaspoons ground cinnamon
1 can (8¾ ounces) crushed pineapple with liquid
3 eggs, lightly beaten
1½ cups vegetable oil
2 teaspoons vanilla
1½ cups finely chopped walnuts
2 cups loosely packed, grated raw carrots

For the icing:
¼ cup unsalted butter, softened
2 packages (3 ounces each) cream cheese, softened
1 teaspoon orange juice
2 tablespoons vanilla
Pinch of ground cinnamon
2½ cups confectioners' sugar (approximately)
¼ cup chopped walnuts

Serves 8.

A Rhubarb Cake will perfume your kitchen for a week after it is baked! Moreover, the scent of the spicy fresh fruit oozing cinnamon is so intoxicating that you should be advised to keep your windows shut—so the bees won't alight!

RHUBARB CAKE

½ cup unsalted butter
1¼ cups light brown sugar
2 eggs
1 teaspoon vanilla
2 teaspoons ground cinnamon
1½ cups sifted cake flour
1 teaspoon baking soda
¼ teaspoon salt
⅔ cup sour milk or buttermilk
1½ cups fresh rhubarb, cut into 1-
  inch pieces
¼ cup granulated sugar
Sweetened whipped cream
  (optional)

1 Heat oven to 375°. Cream the butter with the light brown sugar in a large electric mixer bowl until light and fluffy. Add the eggs, one at a time, beating well after each addition. Beat in the vanilla and 1 teaspoon cinnamon.

2 Sift the flour with the baking soda and salt. Beat the flour mixture into the butter mixture in three parts, alternating with thirds of the sour milk. Beat 1 minute longer. Fold in the rhubarb.

3 Pour the batter into a buttered 8×8×2-inch glass baking dish. Combine the remaining 1 teaspoon cinnamon with the granulated sugar and spoon evenly over the batter. Bake until a toothpick inserted in cake comes out clean, about 45 minutes. Serve with sweetened whipped cream, if desired.

Clove

From the day The Store in Amagansett opened its saffron-colored door back in 1966 until the day it was sold, eleven years later, the mainstay of the establishment was unquestionably its ambrosial baked ham.

I suppose it was the amalgam of garlic and orange that gave the meat both its rosy color and remarkable tang. But I would on this occasion write of one underestimated ingredient, which never received equal publicity in all the hoo-har written about The Store Ham—the lowly clove. It always took me about a hundred cloves to stud a ham to my satisfaction but erstwhile partners were more cavalier about this culinary chore and often made do with only sixty.

I never before actively calculated The Store's clove consumption, but from Memorial through Labor Day (our very brief business tenure) we produced a glistening clove-heavy ham daily. That figure increasing upward to five or six additional hams on Saturdays in July and double that figure in August. All in all, a tidy bite of immortality—about a hundred and fifty hams per season and almost fifteen thousand cloves—no matter how you slice it!

During the third year of The Store's operation, a terrible thought occurred to me one stultifying August morning. I was in the middle of studding my hundredth ham of the season when my life seemed to flash before my eyes.

Originally, I had come to Amagansett (practically the little toe of Long Island) to escape a hectic urban life I detested. The

Store had been conceived merely as a means to perpetuate my existence in Arcadia. Yet it seemed that with every serving of our ham more and more city folk were crowding the dappled seascape.

Within three short years, the parade of automobiles parked outside our emporium was causing traffic burdens halfway to Montauk Point. And the once vast and barren beaches I had opted for were becoming so densely populated that the town fathers were forced to deploy litter cans, which filled daily with detritus of ziti salad and string beans vinaigrette in containers all emblazoned with The Store's jaunty label.

I couldn't stop progress, of course, but I committed the only rational act an ecologically minded man could, under the circumstances: I revolted—in mid-ham! Absolutely balked at the idea of ever studding another!

The late 1960s was a period of revolution all over America and though I was fully twenty years past the age of most other radical activists, I felt aligned with their cause at last. Pot had always made me choke and the wondrous decibels of Woodstock irremediably shattered my eardrums; so cloves were the only issue I could—and did—come to grips with!

I wish I could report that I altered the course of ham consumption in Amagansett by this resolve (and saved the Hamptons forever) but that would be sheer fiction. I merely moved up the kitchen ladder to mousse and souffle, while a pretty young Bennington girl (with no apparent scruples) inherited my mantle as ham upholsterer. And thus it always happens.

The recipe for the seminal hock has been printed far and wide and with such notable plaudits for its inventors that I think that I may safely skip its inclusion here.

No? Well, then here it is again.

THE STORE HAM

10 to 12 pound boneless smoked ham (I still prefer the Dubuque Fleur De Lis brand.)
Whole cloves
4 tablespoons Dijon mustard
1 clove garlic, mashed
¼ cup Chinese duck sauce
Dash of orange juice
½ cup brown sugar

Serves about 20.

1 Heat oven to 400°.

2 With a sharp knife, score the top of the entire ham. Stud with cloves at every intersection.

3 Combine the mustard, garlic, and duck sauce with enough orange juice to make a syrupy mixture. Spread evenly over the top and sides of ham.

4 Sprinkle the surface with brown sugar and bake 1½ hours. Serve hot or at room temperature.

About the ubiquitous clove: It is the dried flowering bud of an
Asian evergreen *Eugenia aromatica*. Now grown with some success all over the South Pacific, it was once native to the Moluc-
can Islands. The name *clove* actually is a French derivation—
from *clou*, meaning nail or spike. By the very nature of its
physiology this tiny jib has always been considered an aphrodisiac for males! Ancient oriental cooks concocted a brew of its
attar that was rumored to turn even an impotent oldster into a
rampant stud after a single draught. The clove, naturally
enough, is a masculine-gendered flower of the pink family, but
it is picked long before any of its petals unfold and allow it to
germinate its better half. Pinks are distantly related to carna-
tions, and if you think about their communal scent you will
readily make the association in your nose.

The clove evergreen bears its fruit all year round and the
female blossoms are considered a symbol of money and long life
all over Asia. As a matter of fact, when a male child is born in
Indonesian households, the parents inevitably plant a clove tree,
hoping that both their heir and the stripling will prosper at a
coeval rate. With care, a clove tree usually lives longer than its
human birthmate. The shrub will keep growing, bearing abun-
dantly, for over a hundred years; then it suddenly becomes
barren and withers.

Even today, the spice buds must be picked by hand, one at a
time and with great care, for the tree is curiously fragile about
its gifts and if a clove tree is stripped ruthlessly it will die. That
must suggest some analogy dear to naturalists and old wives
alike.

Clove was precious to me at an early age as an anesthetic for
the pain of toothache. (I suffered this indignity well into my
majority and chewed hundreds of cloves from time to time.)
Aromatic oil of clove also acts as an anti-opthalmic (an eye-
muscle relaxant) but I never had eye problems, so I cannot
personally endorse this cure.

I love clove because it is a thrifty spice—less is usually more
in the kitchen. If you are studding an onion with cloves for a
court bouillon (the aromatic liquid used to poach fish), never use
more than three unless you want an over-clovey broth. The
pungency of the flavoring is released in quantity during the heat
of cooking.

But I would advise even a chary cook to add two cloves to a
béchamel sauce (being careful to remove them from the cream
before serving) to add a piquant flavor to any chicken or fish
dish. And a clove (ground) into browned onions makes them
decidedly more zesty, I think. Clove also makes a wonderful

adjunct to a slice of lemon stirred into a cup of espresso. And a single bud slipped into the milk pan will provide a stimulating fillip to your next cup of hot chocolate. A pinch of powdered clove won't harm your chocolate mousse, either!

Indian food, like this typically hot Lamb Korma, has a healthy respect for the flavor of clove. This is an easy dish to prepare but one that will be long remembered after the party! Serve it over rice or, for a difference, consider steamed buttered barley. Very Indian, that combination!

HOT LAMB KORMA

2½ pounds lamb, cut into 1-inch cubes
4 large cloves garlic, minced
3 tablespoons all-purpose flour
1 1-inch slice fresh ginger, pared, minced
2½ cups strong chicken broth
2 large onions, finely chopped
½ cup butter
3 whole cloves
2 cardamom seeds
1 small cinnamon stick, broken in half
1 cup plain yogurt
3 tablespoons tomato paste
1 tablespoon ground coriander
1 teaspoon ground turmeric
1 teaspoon ground cumin
½ teaspoon ground cloves
1½ tablespoons chili powder
Salt and freshly ground pepper to taste
Pinch of crushed hot red pepper
6 cups cooked rice

Serves 6.

1 Sprinkle the lamb with 2 cloves minced garlic and the flour. Toss lightly and let stand 10 minutes.

2 Combine the remaining garlic and the ginger in a small saucepan; add the chicken broth. Let stand 10 minutes.

3 Saute the onions in half the butter in a large saucepan until transparent. Tie the whole cloves, the cardamom, and the cinnamon stick in cheesecloth. Add them to the onions with the yogurt, tomato paste, coriander, turmeric, cumin, ground cloves, chili powder, salt, and pepper. Cook over low heat 5 minutes.

4 Saute the lamb in the remaining butter in a skillet until the cubes are brown and crusty on all sides.

5 Bring the chicken broth, garlic, and ginger to a boil; remove from heat.

6 Add the browned lamb to the yogurt mixture. Dilute with a little of the chicken broth and simmer until the lamb is tender, about 1½ hours. Add more broth as necessary to make a fairly thick sauce. (Yogurt has a tendency to curdle slightly as it cooks. Stir it with a wooden spoon or add 1 tablespoon whipping cream if the texture offends you. But the dish traditionally is served in India with a streaky-type sauce.)

7 When the meat is fork tender, taste for seasoning and sprinkle with a pinch of crushed hot red pepper. Serve over rice.

I richly like the taste of clove when it combines with oily fish. A sensational first course (or hors d'oeuvre, if you will) from Brittany, Brandade de Saumon, can be prepared in steps well before serving and heated in a chafing dish or even a double boiler at the party hour. Notice the clove tang too. It's very subtle but it's there!

BRANDADE DE SAUMON

1 Place the water, wine, onion, celery, bay leaf, lemon, peppercorns, and 1 teaspoon salt in a large saucepan. Heat to boiling; reduce heat. Simmer 5 minutes. (This court bouillon is suitable for poaching other fish as well and may be stored tightly covered in the refrigerator for several weeks.)

2 Tie the salmon in cheesecloth. Add to saucepan; poach over low heat 7 to 8 minutes, or until fish flakes easily when pierced with a fork. Drain fish and cool slightly; remove skin and bones. Flake the fish with a fork.

3 Place fish, garlic, potato, cream, olive oil, lemon juice, cloves, ½ teaspoon salt, and the pepper in a blender container; blend until smooth and creamy. (This may require a few stops and starts.)

4 Just before serving, heat salmon mixture in the top of a double boiler over simmering water. Serve with buttered toast triangles.

4 cups water
1 cup white wine
1 small onion stuck with 1 clove
½ rib celery with leaves
1 small bay leaf
½ lemon
6 peppercorns
1 teaspoon salt
1½ pounds fresh salmon
1 clove garlic, crushed
1 large baking potato, boiled, pared, cut into 1-inch cubes
1 cup whipping cream
1 cup olive oil
Juice of ½ lemon
¼ teaspoon ground cloves
½ teaspoon salt
⅛ teaspoon freshly ground pepper
Buttered toast triangles

Serves 10 to 12.

Pollo Frito is a Mexican version of fried chicken laden with goodies like Spanish sausage and chili peppers. The dish comes from Aguascalientes and I must admit to having swiped it some while back from a wonderful book called *Mexican Cooking* by Elizabeth Lambert Ortiz. Since I once spent a very pleasant evening in Liz Ortiz's company (as table companion at a dinner party) long, long before either of us were writing cookbooks, I think familiarity gives me some priority in the matter. The recipe is splendid and only slightly different from Mrs. Ortiz's mint formula—cooks being cooks, after all!

POLLO FRITO

2 small chickens (2½ to 3 pounds each), cut into serving pieces
2 cups strong chicken stock
4 large potatoes
3 large tomatoes, peeled, seeded, chopped
1 teaspoon granulated sugar
1 yellow onion, chopped
1 clove garlic, crushed
¼ teaspoon ground cinnamon
½ teaspoon ground cloves
½ teaspoon chopped fresh oregano or a pinch of dried oregano
Salt and freshly ground pepper to taste
Juice of ½ lemon
4 tablespoons butter (approximately)
3 tablespoons olive oil (approximately)
3 hot chorizo sausages
Canned serrano chilies

Serves 4 to 6.

1 Heat oven to 300°. Place the chickens in the stock and simmer slowly until almost tender, about 30 to 35 minutes.

2 Peel the potatoes and cut in half lengthwise; cut halves into ¼-inch slices. Drop into boiling salted water and cook over high heat 5 minutes. Rinse immediately under cold water; drain on paper toweling. (Potatoes should be slightly crunchy.)

3 Remove cooked chicken from the stock; reserve. Add the tomatoes to the stock, sprinkle with sugar and add the onion, garlic, cinnamon, cloves, oregano, salt, and freshly ground pepper. Boil for 5 minutes; reduce heat. Simmer until stock is reduced to a thick sauce, about 30 minutes. Stir in the lemon juice and keep hot.

4 Melt the butter with the oil in a large, heavy skillet. Dip the chicken in the sauce and saute in the skillet until golden brown on all sides. Transfer to a heatproof serving dish and keep warm in the oven.

5 Add the potatoes to the skillet and quickly brown on both sides, adding more butter and oil if necessary. Remove the potatoes and place around the chicken on the serving dish.

6 Cut the sausage into ½-inch pieces and saute in the skillet until brown. Drain on paper toweling and place around the chicken with the potatoes. Pour remaining sauce over the chicken and serve with a bowl of the serrano chilies—a must!

Note: Chorizo sausage and canned serrano chilies are available at Spanish food stores and many supermarkets.

Surprisingly enough, all manner of fowl takes well to the seasoning of cloves. Duck loses its gamey flavor when a pinch is rubbed across its plump breast and Cornish hens, pomaded and massaged with garlic, butter, and a touch of clove, make a particularly tasty *plat du jour*. A small onion impressed with twin nubbins of the spice and added to the lentil dressing points up the unique savor of the hens.

CORNISH HENS WITH LENTILS

1 Heat oven to 400°. Mix 2 tablespoons of the butter with the crushed garlic and the ground cloves. Combine the carrots, the minced onion, and the chopped parsley.

2 Stuff the hens with the carrot mixture, reserving any extra; truss and place in baking pan. Rub hens well with the butter mixture and cover each with 2 half slices of bacon. Pour wine and stock over the hens and sprinkle well with salt and pepper. Bake ½ hour, basting with pan juices every 10 minutes. Reduce heat to 350°; bake 40 minutes longer, continuing to baste.

3 Wash and sort through the lentils to remove any gravel and shriveled lentils. Cover lentils with water and add the onion stuck with cloves. Tie 1 clove garlic and the thyme and parsley sprigs in cheesecloth and add to the lentils. Cook 50 to 60 minutes, until almost tender. Do not allow lentils to get mushy. Remove onion and herbs; discard. Rinse lentils under cold water; drain well.

4 Mix any reserved carrot mixture into the lentils. Remove ¼ cup pan drippings from the hens; stir into the lentils with remaining 1 tablespoon butter.

5 Place lentils in a deep heatproof serving dish. Remove trussing from hens; reserve pan juices. Place hens on top of the lentils. Place in 350° oven for 20 minutes.

6 To serve, moisten lentils with reserved pan juices if lentils seem dry. Garnish with lemon slices.

3 tablespoons butter, softened
1 clove garlic, minced
¼ teaspoon ground cloves
2 carrots, diced
1 onion, minced
¼ cup chopped parsley
2 Cornish hens
2 slices bacon, cut in half
¼ cup white wine
¼ cup chicken broth or stock
Salt and freshly ground pepper
1 cup dry lentils
1 onion stuck with 2 cloves
1 clove garlic
1 sprig thyme
1 sprig parsley
Lemon slices for garnish

Serves 2.

Next comes a veal dish from Auvergne, France. It is made from leftovers only; so file the recipe away for the rainy day after you splurge on a veal roast.

I am very partial to this golden, gooey concoction because of the oddment of flavors: mustard, clove, and zesty Gruyère cheese. If you are like me, and dread eating the same dish two days in a row, you'll doubly appreciate the French mastery of food disguise. Serve your "Avesnoise" with homemade bread and butter and a salad. Oh, and a glass of wine, of course!

VEAL AVESNOISE

6 to 8 slices leftover roast veal, about ¼-inch thick
Freshly ground pepper
1¼ cups grated Gruyère cheese
1 to 2 teaspoons Dijon mustard
¼ teaspoon ground cloves
⅔ cup whipping cream

Serves 3 to 4.

1 Heat oven to 400°. Place veal slices in a buttered baking dish. Sprinkle with freshly ground pepper.

2 Make a paste of the cheese, mustard, cloves, and cream. Spread over each slice of meat and bake until warm, about 5 to 6 minutes. Place under the broiler until golden, about 1 minute.

Russian cuisine makes authoritative use of the pungency and twang of clove. This sublime rendering, borrowed from Jane Blanksteen, of pork and prunes accented with lemon and clove, explains more eloquently than I can how spice can be the variety of life!

RUSSIAN-STYLE PORK CHOPS

For the prune sauce:
1 pound pitted prunes
1 piece lemon peel, 2 inches long
1 stick cinnamon
Grated peel of ½ orange
¼ teaspoon ground cloves
½ cup port wine

4 loin pork chops, each 1½ inches thick
Flour
2 beaten eggs
Bread crumbs
4 tablespoons butter
⅔ cup sour cream

Serves 4.

1 Place the prunes in a heavy saucepan and add enough water to cover by about 1 inch. Bring to a boil and add the lemon peel and cinnamon stick. Reduce heat; simmer 25 minutes. Cool slightly.

2 Remove the prunes and the lemon peel to a blender container with a slotted spoon. Add ½ cooking liquid; blend into a slightly thick puree, adding more liquid if necessary. Transfer puree to a saucepan and add the orange peel, cloves, and port. Cook over medium heat 10 minutes. (The sauce should be the texture of applesauce. If it is too thick, stir in more of the cooking liquid from the prunes.) Reserve.

3 Dust the chops lightly with flour, dip into beaten eggs, and roll in bread crumbs. Melt the butter in a heavy skillet and brown the chops over high heat on both sides. Remove the chops and pour off the fat; add the sour cream, stirring until smooth. Replace the chops; simmer covered over medium heat 40 minutes. Heat the prune sauce and serve with the chops.

Note: For hearty appetites, allow 2 chops per person. Use 3 beaten eggs and 1 cup sour cream.

Italians use clove infrequently in their cooking. Why, I shall never understand, for it is a wonderful friend to both garlic and

tomato in a saucepan. But, no matter. The following baked zucchini devise was definitely born high on the boot—in Parma, where the good cheeses grow!

SPICY BAKED ZUCCHINI

1 Heat oven to 375°. Cut the zucchini into ½-inch slices. Melt 3 tablespoons butter with ¼ cup water in a heavy saucepan. Add the zucchini. Cook covered over medium heat 4 minutes, stirring occasionally. Drain. Sprinkle with salt.

2 Combine the sour cream, ½ cup Parmesan cheese, the cloves, allspice, and pepper in a large saucepan. Cook over low heat, stirring constantly, until cheese melts. Stir in 2 tablespoons butter. Combine the egg yolk and whipping cream; stir into the cheese mixture. Add the zucchini and transfer to a buttered casserole.

3 Sprinkle the bread crumbs over the zucchini mixture. Dot with remaining 1 tablespoon butter. Sprinkle with 2 tablespoons Parmesan cheese; bake 20 minutes. Place under the broiler to brown top.

2 pounds medium zucchini
6 tablespoons butter
¼ cup water
Salt
½ cup sour cream
½ cup grated Parmesan cheese
⅛ teaspoon ground cloves
¼ teaspoon ground allspice
¼ teaspoon freshly ground pepper
1 egg yolk
2 tablespoons whipping cream
¼ cup bread crumbs
2 tablespoons grated Parmesan cheese

Serves 4.

Pliny called a cold North African salad he presumably had enjoyed *carophyllum* for the touch of clove in its composition. Two thousand years later, an Oriental version named *Karumfel,* also named after the spice, is still eaten in Arabia. This Moroccan variation adds mint to the clove for self-assertion.

COLD MOROCCAN CARROT SALAD

1 Drop the carrots into boiling salted water and cook 1 minute. Rinse under cold running water and drain.

2 Place the butter, oil, and garlic in a saucepan over medium heat. When the butter foams, add the carrots, and cook, stirring constantly, until crisp-tender, 5 to 6 minutes. Remove the garlic.

3 Add the shallots, vinegar, cloves, cumin, and paprika. Mix well and transfer to a bowl. Stir in the parsley. Refrigerate 1½ hours. Sprinkle with salt and pepper to taste. Garnish with mint.

1 pound carrots, pared, cut into thin strips
4 tablespoons butter
4 tablespoons olive oil
2 cloves garlic, bruised
2 tablespoons minced shallots
2 tablespoons wine vinegar
½ teaspoon ground cloves
¼ teaspoon ground cumin
Dash of paprika
½ cup finely chopped parsley
Salt and pepper to taste
1 tablespoon chopped fresh mint

Serves 6 to 8.

Cloves in dessert? Of course the spice is used by the French to make a faintly overbearing cherry dumpling called *clafouti*. And our English cousins sprinkle grated cloves on ripe fruit for a tart they call plum duff. Germans savor the combination of sugar, butter, and powdered clove so much that they invented forty different kinds of Christmas cookies out of that essential conjunction. But it is in the American composition, Apple Fritters, I think, that the flavor is most reassuring. Try a batch of these feathery-light cakes from the recipe I include. Of old Vermont extraction, they have achieved perfection with the substitution of orange juice for the apple cider in the original receipt. Thus, they are an unabashed salute to the might of the lowly clove in cookery both past and present.

APPLE FRITTERS

4 red apples
¾ cup granulated sugar
½ teaspoon ground cloves
½ cup orange juice
1 cup all-purpose flour
Pinch of salt
1 cup warm milk
1 tablespoon butter, melted
3 eggs, separated
Vegetable oil
⅛ teaspoon ground cloves
Confectioners' sugar

Serves 4 to 6.

1 Pare, core, and cut the apples into ¼-inch slices. Sprinkle the apples with ½ cup sugar, the cloves, and the orange juice; toss to combine. Let stand ½ hour.

2 Combine the flour, salt, and milk; beat until smooth. Stir in the butter and egg yolks. Beat the egg whites until stiff but not dry; fold into the flour mixture. Fold in the apples with 1 tablespoon of the juices.

3 Heat 1 inch of oil in a heavy skillet. Drop batter by tablespoonfuls, a few at a time, into the oil. Fry until golden on both sides.

4 Drain fritters on paper toweling and sprinkle with ¼ cup sugar mixed with ⅛ teaspoon cloves.

5 Heat oven to 450°. Place fritters on a metal cake rack placed on a cookie sheet. Bake 7 minutes. Sprinkle with confectioners' sugar. (If desired, serve fritters with whipped cream or sour cream flavored with grated orange rind and a splash of Grand Marnier.)

Note: Fritters can be prepared in advance through Step 4 and left standing at room temperature for up to 3 hours.

Coffee

I have never been able to understand all the hue and cry of the anti-caffeine brigade, since I was virtually weaned on Maxwell House.

That's a bit of an exaggeration, I suppose, but my mother always claimed that she bottle-fed me a formula that was judiciously spiked with sweetened coffee because I was a colicky baby and that palliative alone seemed to soothe my ruffled innards.

Truth to tell, it may have started a lifelong addiction, for I began to crave honest-to-goodness cups of the dark and aromatic brew for breakfast at an extremely tender age. Though my maternal parent was duly warned by her friends and relatives that such a heady beverage could stunt my growth, her own good sense, mixed with a like predilection for a steaming cup of mocha-java in the morning, cancelled out the dark auguries.

When I grew to my full height (six feet plus three and a half inches) at age twelve, there didn't seem to be much reason for further concern.

When I was a boy, our closest neighbors were Swedish. A big, brawling family of blondes, they kept the coffee pot on the stove from morn till midnight—with a fresh batch sometimes percolated well after that late hour.

Mrs. Johnson, the matron of this crew, was a no-nonsense lady from Stockholm with a quick hand for administering order. She believed in a slap to quell rebellion among her brood—along with a font of palliation on the back burner, ready to be dispensed whenever there was *real* trouble in her house.

If son Johnny fell off the front stoop and broke his tooth or his sisters Edith and Helen had a hair-pulling match, coffee was always Mrs. Johnson's first prescription. When Marie stayed out too late with a boyfriend or Gertrude talked fresh, they knew that coffee usually came before punishment. Even when the baby of the family, spoiled little Joyce, flushed her new doll down the toilet to see if it could swim, the reaction was the same—anger first, accompanied by a terrible stream of Swedish curses at God for plaguing her with such children, and then coffee, with sugar and sympathy spooned out in equal doses.

When her children and I fought, as we very often did, she defended them like a she-tiger but her rage was always short-lived. "Yees-sus Christ!" she would cry. "I yust don't understand why you damn kids can't play together nice and yentle once in a while!"

Between our separate lawns there grew an enormous shade tree, a catalpa that my father claimed he had planted himself the day our house was completed. This tree, wide-branched and leafy from spring to fall, was the basis of most of our disputes. Often climbed by the six Johnsons—and more often fallen out of by the two Greenes—it was automatically claimed by both sets of progeny whenever there was a fracas brewing between homesteads.

"Get offa my property," my neighbor Johnny would scream from his side of the branches.

"You get off! It's my tree, isn't it?" I would rebut just as belligerently from the ground.

"Maybe it is . . . maybe it isn't. But it's on *our* property—so you can't climb it!"

"Try and stop me. I double dare you to." I was certainly no fighter when I was young and less of a tree climber, but I had the advantage of being at least two years older and a head taller than Johnny; so I could afford this bravado. "I triple . . . no! I *quadruple* dare you."

Sometimes this verbal abuse would continue between us—with nary a blow passed—for hours on end. Until poor Mrs. Johnson could stand it no longer.

"*Hol shefton!*" she would cry, rapping at her window for our attention. "Shut up both you kids! Cut it out you hear me! Yonny! Go upstairs. And you (to me) go home! And if you can't act like a yentleman over here, don't come back neither." Then she would lapse into Swedish—to her children's utter chagrin.

"Mama! Everyone can hear you!"

"Who the hell cares? They certainly heard those two, didn't they? Crazy kids. Fighting like that over a tree for sweet Yees-sus sakes! Come into the house *skynda på!* Coffee's almost up anyway!"

Coffee's up! That was the magical phrase that commanded an instant truce.

"Can't he come too, Ma?" good-natured Johnny Johnson would appeal, pointing from the tree at his tormentor. "See! We're friends again now."

"Sure. Sure. Friends! Till the next time, I betcha. Come on . . . come on. Even though the coffee's all perked out already."

Together Johnny and I would climb up the dark, ammonia-smelling stairs to their apartment, poking each other and giggling all the way. The Johnsons had a two-family house and they always rented out the lower floor to other Scandinavians.

"Don't make such a racket in the hall, neither. Neighbors got a right to peace and quiet around here too! Bert-rum! You sit there and everyone else stop standing around. Sit down for Chrissakes while I pour. Edie, you pass the yelly doughnuts!"

Coffee was an all-day affair at the Johnsons—not merely a breakfast or after-dinner potable, as it was in my own home. Six or seven pots were freshly brewed daily—each one heralding a more delicious accompanying snack than the last. Often there were crumb buns from the corner bakery to go with the cups of fragrant liquid. Or apple cakes smothered in vanilla whipped cream. Or piles of doughnuts, silvery with crystallized sugar and oozing streams of golden custard or dark purply jam.

Mrs. Johnson drank her coffee *Svenska*-style, from a saucer. She would take a lump of sugar between her teeth and, having added milk, drink the coffee through it. Then she would pour another saucer full . . . and yet another.

"Ja. Ja. One of these days," she would say to me between sips, blowing at the hot drink before her, "I'm gonna tell your father to chop that damn tree down once and for all. Everybody be a damn sight happier I bet."

She never carried out her threat.

And when I was a grown man—long, long after we had moved far away from the house next door—I found the tree still standing.

Making my way home from Long Island late one Sunday night in 1969 and feeling that I could not face the traffic one single moment longer, I swerved off the expressway onto a dark, unknown back road.

It did not seem familiar at all. The names on the street signs were foreign to my eye; yet the route was somehow *known* territory. Déjà vu? I first turned right and then left, as if by instinct, and while nothing looked familiar, I knew in my heart that I was driving on the street where I had been raised. No landmark remained. Our house was altered beyond recognition and the Johnsons' white frame home was gone entirely, obviously leveled to make way for an apartment building. Only strangers and their dogs walked the warm, late-night street; everyone I had known had long since moved away or died.

One thing alone was recognizable—the Catalpa tree. Now so lofty that it dwarfed the garage below it and its roots cracked shards in the surrounding island of pavement, it stood like a silent reminder of all those wondrous days of youth and coffee afternoons.

The important thing for a cook to remember when a spot of coffee is called for in a recipe is that the mystic brew is rich in aromatic oils and must be used absolutely fresh. A sensible rule of thumb for coffee cookery is to select the richest, most full-bodied varieties one can find. A few tablespoons of steaming Colombian, Costa Rican, or Jamaican Blue Mountain can add remarkable savor to gravies and stews. Although to be perfectly honest, I sometimes substitute instant coffee powder in my galley. It works admirably in the cookpot, though Lord knows I thoroughly dread it in a cup of hot water!

ESPRESSO FETTUCINI

4 tablespoons unsalted butter
1 large shallot, minced
1 small clove garlic, minced
1 large ripe tomato, seeded, diced
3 tablespoons very strong beef stock or ½ packet beef bouillon powder
Scant teaspoon granulated sugar
¼ teaspoon ground allspice
⅔ cup whipping cream
1 teaspoon instant espresso powder
½ pound fettucini noodles
1 egg yolk
⅓ cup sliced mushrooms
Pinch of finely grated lemon peel
Freshly grated Parmesan cheese

Serves 4 to 6 as a first course.

1 Melt 2 tablespoons butter in a heavy skillet; add the shallot, garlic, and tomato. Sprinkle with beef stock or bouillon powder, sugar, and allspice; cook over medium heat until reduced by one third.

2 Combine cream and espresso in a small saucepan; heat to boiling. Stir into tomato mixture; cook over medium heat, stirring occasionally, until fairly thick.

3 Meanwhile, cook noodles in a large pot of boiling salted water until just barely tender, 3 to 5 minutes. Drain. Add remaining 2 tablespoons butter to pot; return noodles to pot. Cook over low heat, stirring constantly, until butter has melted and noodles are well coated.

4 Beat the egg yolk in a small bowl; stir in ¼ cup of the tomato sauce. Stir mixture back into tomato sauce. Cook over very low heat 3 minutes; do not boil.

5 Add mushrooms and lemon peel to sauce. Pour sauce over noodles; toss well. Serve with grated Parmesan cheese.

Espresso Fettucini is a fairly recent invention—created by an imaginative chef in Rome, as you have no doubt surmised. The next recipe, Ham with Red-Eye Gravy, is far removed from it in geography and sophistication—but it is no less intoxicating. Over a hundred years old, this dish originated in the Klondike, where miners, living in lean-tos or tents without kitchens or plumbing, survived on a diet of smoked meat (the only kind that wouldn't spoil).

A most enterprising gold digger, it is recorded, threw a spot of bourbon into his fry pan one morning. And when it caught fire—as it is guaranteed to do—he put out the flames with a cup of coffee. Thus, one of the best ham recipes I have ever tasted was born.

HAM WITH RED-EYE GRAVY

1 Melt butter in a heavy skillet. Saute ham steaks on both sides over high heat until light brown.

2 Combine coffee, sugar, cream, and bourbon; pour over ham. Cook over medium-high heat 4 to 5 minutes, turning ham once.

3 Remove ham from skillet; keep warm on serving platter. Heat gravy to boiling; boil, stirring constantly, until thick. Pour over ham. (It's traditional to serve homemade biscuits on the side.)

Note: When coffee is called for in a recipe that is already on the fire, I usually expect the coffee to be hot because cold liquid would reduce the temperature. Cold coffee is usually specified for making desserts or softening gelatin.

1 **tablespoon butter**
2 **ham steaks (each ½-inch thick)**
⅔ **cup hot coffee**
1 **teaspoon granulated sugar**
2 **tablespoons cream**
1½ **tablespoons bourbon**

Serves 2 to 4.

Food snoops claim that coffee first grew wild in the Tigris and Euphrates valleys. The first people known to have drunk the stuff were Arabs. And a curious myth persists about a goatherd who noticed his billies acting in a particularly frisky manner after having eaten the scarlet berries of an evergreen bush that grew along a mountainside. After trying a few berries himself, the goatherd felt such a sudden rush of exhilaration that he began to sing. Chewing more, he pirouetted all the way home.

A passing dignitary is said to have observed this phenomenon and become much troubled by the sight. So, having blessed himself and asking Allah's forgiveness, he questioned the goatherd and then timorously tasted the berry himself. Then he tried it again.

"But this is wine," he is said to have declared after the second bite. Actually the word he used was *kahwah,* which has several meanings in Arabic, wine being just one of them. But from *kahwah* came coffee in time.

The following veal dish from Normandy is an elevated offering that has little in common with the mythical goatherd. But its flavoring of coffee and cream, well laced with apple brandy (rather than wine), gives it a celestial taste that you will never forget. Veal is expensive but this recipe is worth the ransom.

VEAU À LA NORMANDE

1 boneless veal roast (3 to 3½ pounds)
1 clove garlic, bruised
Salt and freshly ground pepper
6 tablespoons butter
1 cup strong coffee
2 teaspoons granulated sugar
¼ cup whipping cream
¾ cup Calvados
12 to 16 small new potatoes
6 small tart apples (preferably lady or crab apples)
2 cinnamon sticks, each broken into 3 pieces
6 curls of lemon peel
⅔ cup seedless raisins
1½ tablespoons brown sugar
2 teaspoons cornstarch
1 tablespoon cold water

Serves 6.

1 Heat oven to 375°. Rub veal lightly with garlic; discard garlic. Sprinkle veal with salt and pepper. Place on a rack in a roasting pan; dot with 4 tablespoons butter. Roast 30 minutes.

2 Reduce oven heat to 350°. Mix coffee, sugar, cream, and ¼ cup Calvados; pour over veal. Roast 2 hours, basting every 10 minutes.

3 Meanwhile, cook potatoes in boiling water 10 minutes; drain and reserve. Cut a thin slice from the bottom of each apple; core apples. Divide cinnamon sticks, lemon curls, and raisins among centers of apples; dot with butter and brown sugar. Place in a shallow baking pan; spoon ½ cup Calvados over.

4 Forty-five minutes before veal is done, place apples in oven. Add potatoes to veal, surrounding meat; continue roasting, basting potatoes and veal every 10 minutes.

5 Reduce oven heat to 200°. Remove veal, potatoes, and apples to a serving platter; keep warm in oven. Add enough water to veal pan juices to measure 1½ cups; heat in a small saucepan. Mix the cornstarch with the cold water; stir into the pan juices. Cook over medium heat, stirring constantly, until slightly thickened. Add salt and pepper, if necessary. Serve gravy with veal.

My late, good friend Aaron Fine, the writer and artist whom I have chronicled elsewhere in this book, loved to cook and to eat (to extremes, I am afraid), but he was a very erratic chef. No recipe seemed to satisfy him unless its ingredients were malleable enough to be frozen between stove firings. Why?

"Because the sequence of first a *hot* and then a *cold* environment forces the flavors of a dish to come together, to coalesce," was his ready reply. Aaron loved that word, *coalesce,* and he used it often. He was erratic, as I have said, but this dish is a testament to his genius.

SHORT RIBS AARON

1 Coat meat with flour. Heat butter and oil in a Dutch oven. Add meat and brown well over medium-high heat; remove from pan. Add onions; saute until tender. Return meat to pan; add tomato sauce, tomatoes, wine, coffee, sugar, cream, salt, and pepper. Simmer covered 1½ hours, turning meat every 30 minutes.

2 Transfer meat with sauce to a large bowl; place in freezer 30 minutes.

3 Meanwhile, cook carrots in boiling salted water 4 minutes. Rinse under cold running water and drain. Place potatoes in a saucepan and cover with cold salted water; cook over high heat 20 minutes. Rinse immediately under cold running water and drain.

4 Heat oven to 350°. Remove meat from freezer; remove fat that will have collected on top. Return meat to Dutch oven; heat over medium heat. (If sauce is too thin, remove 4 tablespoons sauce and mix with 1 tablespoon flour; stir into Dutch oven.) Stir in the cognac, carrots, and potatoes. Bake uncovered 30 minutes. Garnish with parsley.

2½ to 3 pounds beef short ribs
Flour
½ cup butter
1 tablespoon vegetable oil
2 onions, chopped
1 can (8 ounces) tomato sauce
1 can (8 ounces) imported Italian tomatoes
1 cup dry red wine
2 teaspoons instant coffee powder
1 teaspoon granulated sugar
3 tablespoons whipping cream
1 teaspoon salt
½ teaspoon freshly ground pepper
4 large carrots, cut into 2-inch-long sticks
4 medium potatoes, pared, cut into quarters
1 tablespoon cognac
Freshly chopped parsley

Serves 4.

We know that Arabs, historically, certainly enjoyed their coffee, because for centuries they would not allow the seeds of the coffee bush to be exported—fearing that the coffee habit, once it caught on in the Western world, would deplete their small resources. The first coffee beans smuggled out of Arabia were said to have been secreted in the breast-cups of an Indian maharani, who carried them back to her country as a patriotic gesture.

Roulage Mocha is a dervish of a dessert—chocolate sponge cake whirled around a bolster of coffee-flavored whipped cream. It's heavenly food—as opposed to devil's food, you understand—but very sexy for all of that. It became part of my repertoire after I had studied with Dionne Lucas in the late 1940s. Ms. Lucas was both an admirable instructor and a great pragmatist. She considered no recipe inviolable—even though she had taught it many times before. "I feel this wants beefing up!" she would announce to her class—with one hand already on the peppermill. After years of making her famous chocolate roll I felt it *wanted* coffee in its devise; so, as Dionne would have, I amended it!

ROULAGE MOCHA

6 ounces semisweet chocolate
⅓ cup cold water
2 teaspoons instant coffee powder
8 eggs, separated
1 cup superfine sugar
2 tablespoons unsweetened imported cocoa (approximately)
1½ cups whipping cream
¼ cup confectioners' sugar
½ teaspoon vanilla
Toasted slivered almonds

Serves 8 to 10.

1 Melt chocolate with water and 1 teaspoon coffee powder in the top of a double boiler over hot water. Stir until smooth. Remove from heat; cool slightly.

2 Heat oven to 350°. Beat egg yolks with the superfine sugar in a large bowl until light and fluffy. Stir in the cooled chocolate; mix thoroughly. Beat egg whites in a medium bowl until stiff but not dry; gently fold into the chocolate mixture.

3 Grease a jelly roll pan with vegetable oil; cover with a sheet of waxed paper extending 1 inch beyond ends of pan. Spread batter evenly over paper. Bake 17 to 18 minutes; cake will puff up and surface will have a dull finish when done. Do not overbake.

4 Soak a layer of paper toweling in water and wring dry; place over top of cake. Cover with a layer of dry paper toweling. Let stand 20 minutes.

5 Remove paper toweling. Loosen edges of cake. Sprinkle top of cake with about 1½ tablespoons cocoa. Soak a dish towel in water and wring dry; stretch taut over cake and invert. Lift off pan and carefully peel off the waxed paper. Roll up towel with cake inside it, beginning with long edge. Let stand 5 minutes.

6 Pour cream into a medium bowl; sift remaining 1 teaspoon coffee powder over it. Add confectioners' sugar and vanilla. Beat until stiff.

7 Unroll cake and spread cream mixture evenly over surface. Re-roll cake without towel; place seam-side-down on a long, flat platter or a jelly roll board. (Don't worry if cake cracks a bit.) Refrigerate until well chilled, at least 3 hours.

8 Just before serving, dust cake with more cocoa (covering any cracks) and sprinkle with toasted almonds.

Note: I use Droste's cocoa in this recipe—and whenever else cocoa is required, as well.

According to Muslim legend, coffee was served to a sleepy Mohammed by the archangel Gabriel. So sixth-century prohibitionists, seeking to rid Islam of alcohol, dubbed coffee "Islam's wine"!

  Arabs do not dilute their beverage with anything but sugar. Coffee with cream is purely a Teutonic conceit and it has spawned a wealth of coffee cream tortes in Germanic countries. The following recipe for thin walnut-crumb layers paved with coffee-flavored whipped cream hails from the American Deep South, however. It is from an old family recipe book—and it certainly wears well.

COFFEE-WALNUT-CRUMB CAKE

1 Heat oven to 400°. Cream ½ cup butter and 2 cups granulated sugar together in a large bowl until light and fluffy. Add the egg yolks, one at a time, beating well after each addition. Add the dissolved coffee, the walnuts, 2 cups bread crumbs, the baking powder, melted butter, and vanilla. Mix well. Beat the egg whites until stiff but not dry; fold into the egg yolk mixture.

2 Grease four 9-inch round cake pans; sprinkle each with 1 table-spoon bread crumbs. Divide the batter among pans. Bake until toothpick inserted in center comes out clean, 15 to 20 minutes. (Layers can be baked two at a time, if desired. They are quite thin.) Cool completely in pans on wire racks.

3 Pour cream into a medium bowl; sift 2 teaspoons instant coffee over. Beat in the confectioners' sugar; beat until stiff.

4 Turn out one cake layer onto a serving dish or cake stand; spread with whipped cream. Turn out each remaining layer onto a sheet of lightly buttered waxed paper. Hold second layer under waxed paper and invert over first layer; remove waxed paper. Spread layer with whipped cream. Repeat with remaining layers and cream. Garnish with chocolate curls made by scraping a bar of chocolate with a vegetable peeler. Refrigerate until serving time.

½ cup unsalted butter, softened
2 cups granulated sugar
6 eggs, separated
½ teaspoon instant coffee powder dissolved in 6 tablespoons hot water
1½ cups chopped walnuts
2 cups plus 4 tablespoons soft bread crumbs
4 teaspoons baking powder
2 tablespoons butter, melted
2 teaspoons vanilla
2 cups whipping cream
2 teaspoons instant coffee powder
½ cup confectioners' sugar
Chocolate curls

Serves 8 to 10.

Coffee and fruit is a post-prandial tradition. But the notion of serving pears with a coffee liqueur-caramel glaze is so fantastic that only the French would have imagined it. Here's the conceit in toto. It's easy to prepare in advance and fairly light on calories if you can resist the cream—which I cannot.

PEARS IN CARAMEL SYRUP

4 firm, unblemished Anjou pears
Juice of 1 lemon
1½ cups water
1 cup granulated sugar
3 tablespoons coffee liqueur
Whipped cream or Crème
   Pâtissière (see Index), optional

Serves 4.

1 Pare the pears, one at a time; cut in half lengthwise and remove seeds and tough fibers. Place in bowl of water with the juice of 1 lemon to prevent discoloration.

2 Place 1½ cups water in a large saucepan; add ½ cup sugar. Bring to a boil. Add pears; cook over medium heat, turning once, until tender, about 5 minutes on each side. Remove pears with a slotted spoon; arrange in a serving dish.

3 Pour half of syrup into a heavy saucepan; add remaining ½ cup sugar. Boil until syrup begins to caramelize, 5 to 10 minutes. Remove from heat; carefully add remaining syrup. Return to heat; add the liqueur and bring to a boil. Pour over pears. Cool at room temperature; refrigerate until cold. Serve with whipped cream or Creme Patissiere.

Italians have a few whims about coffee that I feel are worth borrowing. For one thing, they steam their brew and make it very strong; for another, they take it neat, seasoned only with lemon peel. In a distinctive version, this national drink appears as an icy dessert appropriately named Espresso Gelido, or frozen espresso. Short and sweet, it's the most tonic ending to a rich meal that I have ever tasted. Be warned, however—it's for coffee-lovers only!

ESPRESSO GELIDO

1 Stir the espresso powder into the brewed espresso in a medium bowl. Cool to room temperature.

2 Combine the sugar and water in a saucepan; bring to a boil. Boil 5 minutes; immediately remove from heat. Cool to room temperature.

3 Stir sugar mixture into espresso. Place in freezer until mixture is partially frozen, 2 to 3 hours. Remove from freezer; stir in cream, lemon peel, and coffee liqueur.

4 Pour mixture into the canister of an ice cream maker. Freeze according to manufacturer's directions.

Note: To make very strong espresso, brew 2 cups of espresso or dark-roast coffee with 5 cups of water.

3 **tablespoons freeze-dried or instant espresso powder**
4½ **cups hot, very strong espresso coffee**
2½ **cups granulated sugar**
1 **cup water**
1½ **cups whipping cream**
2 **teaspoons finely grated lemon peel**
½ **cup coffee liqueur**

Makes 3 to 3½ quarts.

Jean Baptiste de Belloy is generally acknowledged to have invented the percolator in 1800. Jabez Burns is credited with having perfected the first coffee-roasting machine in 1900. And in the late 1960s, my good friend Gail Firestone created Chocolate Pecan Pie, which is heavily dependent upon a swig or two of strong coffee—and which should bring its inventor a fame greater than that of the other guys!

CHOCOLATE PECAN PIE

1 Make Pate Brisee and refrigerate. Roll out to an 11-inch circle. Line a 9-inch pie plate; trim edges and flute. Refrigerate until ready to use.

2 Heat oven to 425°. Melt chocolate with coffee in a heavy saucepan over low heat; stir until smooth. Remove from heat; stir in butter. Let stand to cool.

3 Beat eggs with sugar and corn syrup in a medium bowl until light and fluffy. Stir in the chocolate mixture; mix well. Stir in the chopped pecans.

4 Pour mixture into pastry shell. Arrange pecan halves in a circle around edge of pie. Bake 10 minutes. Reduce oven heat to 375°; bake until toothpick inserted in center comes out clean, 20 to 30 minutes. Serve with unsweetened whipped cream.

Pâte Brisée (see Index)
2 **ounces semisweet chocolate**
¼ **cup very strong coffee or espresso**
2 **tablespoons unsalted butter, room temperature**
4 **eggs**
½ **cup granulated sugar**
1 **cup light corn syrup**
1 **cup coarsely chopped pecans**
¼ **pound pecan halves for garnish**
Unsweetened whipped cream

A souffle is as natural a vehicle for coffee flavoring as ice cream, in my opinion. Both make delicate finales to a meal. The following recipe is practically perfect as limned but even more sensational when garnished with fresh raspberries over the whipped cream!

COFFEE SOUFFLE

5 eggs, separated
½ cup plus 1 teaspoon granulated sugar
½ teaspoon cornstarch
⅓ cup whipping cream, warmed
1½ tablespoons strong coffee, cooled
1 tablespoon coffee liqueur
½ teaspoon vanilla
3 tablespoons confectioners' sugar
½ teaspoon instant coffee powder
Whipped cream

Serves 4.

1 Beat 1 egg yolk, 1 teaspoon granulated sugar, and the cornstarch in small saucepan. Whisk in warmed cream; cook over low heat, stirring constantly, until thickened, 2 to 3 minutes. Remove from heat; cool.

2 Heat oven to 400°. Beat 4 egg yolks and ¼ cup granulated sugar in a large electric mixer bowl until thick and lemon colored, about 5 minutes. Fold in cooled custard with a rubber spatula. Combine coffee, liqueur, and vanilla; add to egg mixture.

3 Beat the egg whites in a bowl until soft peaks form; slowly add ¼ cup granulated sugar and beat until stiff. Stir ¼ of the egg whites into the egg yolk mixture; fold in the remainder. Spoon into a buttered and sugared 1-quart souffle dish. Bake until puffed and golden, about 25 minutes. Combine confectioners' sugar and instant coffee; sprinkle over souffle. Serve immediately with whipped cream.

Note: Many adroit cooks of my acquaintance skip souffle-making for dinner parties because it is such a last minute operation and can cause havoc for the already over-worked host or hostess. The aforegoing failproof souffle base may be prepared through Step 2 and refrigerated covered. Merely remove the bowl from the refrigerator half an hour before proceeding with the recipe. I always use Royal Irish coffee liqueur in this souffle.

Are you ready for more instant celebrity?
   The following Coffee Refrigerator Cake recipe was either invented, discovered, or adapted (he refuses to divulge which) by Norman Giguere, who also happens to be an able writer and the only man I have ever met who can sneer and leer at the same time. We worked together for quite a number of years and I purloined this recipe from his file. The cake is the kind of party dessert that reputations are made from.

NORMAN GIGUERE'S COFFEE REFRIGERATOR CAKE

1 Make ladyfingers.

2 Soften gelatin in cold coffee. Combine with hot coffee and sugar in a saucepan. Cook over low heat, stirring constantly, until gelatin is dissolved. Transfer to large bowl. Refrigerate just until mixture *begins* to set, about 30 minutes.

3 Place enough split ladyfingers to line the sides of a 9-inch springform pan on a waxed paper lined plate. Spoon melted chocolate over one end of each. Refrigerate until chocolate hardens.

4 Whip 2 cups of cream; stir in vanilla. Fold into gelatin mixture. (If gelatin mixture is lumpy, first beat it with a drop or two of boiling water.)

5 Spread 1 inch of cream mixture in a 9-inch springform pan. Arrange chocolate-tipped ladyfingers vertically around edge with chocolate tips up. Add ⅓ of remaining cream mixture; cover with a layer of ladyfingers. Repeat layers; spread with cream. Refrigerate until firm, about 6 hours.

6 Place pan on a serving plate; remove sides. Whip remaining ½ cup cream; spread on top of cake. Sprinkle with chopped nuts.

24 ladyfingers (see Index), split
2 envelopes unflavored gelatin
½ cup cold strong coffee
1½ cups hot strong coffee
1 cup granulated sugar
6 ounces semisweet chocolate, melted
2½ cups whipping cream
1 tablespoon vanilla
Chopped nuts

Serves 10 to 12.

I invariably save the best for last and have done so ever since I was a kid eating jelly doughnuts in my Swedish friend's kitchen. Then, I saved the largest blob of jam and usually spilled most of it down my shirt front. Today, I am more circumspect.

The genealogy of this fragile chocolate cake is French, naturally; it was invented by a turn-of-the-century pastry chef for a beautiful circus performer he loved from afar. Oddly, the lady refused his tribute—because she claimed it was too fattening. But everyone else in Paris adored it. Things have a way of working out!

If you are feeling querulous about the inclusion of this chocolate prodigy in a chapter dependent on the savor of coffee, I suggest you try making the cake without it.

On second thought, leave well enough alone!

LA MAXINE

For the cake:
1 cup granulated sugar
¼ cup water
1 teaspoon instant espresso powder
6 ounces semisweet chocolate, broken into squares
1 teaspoon vanilla
6 tablespoons unsalted butter, at room temperature
8 eggs, separated
8 ounces walnuts, coarsely ground
2 tablespoons white bread crumbs
Pinch of salt

For the icing:
6 ounces semisweet chocolate, broken into squares
⅓ cup water
2 teaspoons instant espresso powder
1 cup plus 2 tablespoons unsalted butter, at room temperature
3 egg yolks
⅔ cup confectioners' sugar
½ cup ground walnuts

Serves 8 to 10.

1 Heat oven to 350°. Butter two 9-inch round cake pans. Line bottoms with paper; butter paper. Flour the pans, shaking out any excess.

2 To make the cake: Combine the sugar, water, and espresso powder in a saucepan. Cook over medium heat, stirring constantly, 5 minutes. Add the chocolate and vanilla; stir until smooth. Remove from heat; let stand 10 minutes.

3 Cream the butter in a large bowl until light; add the egg yolks, one at a time, beating well after each addition. Gradually stir in the chocolate mixture, walnuts, and bread crumbs. Mix thoroughly. Beat the egg whites with a pinch of salt in a medium bowl until stiff but not dry. Fold into egg yolk mixture.

4 Pour batter into prepared pans. Place in oven on middle rack; bake 30 minutes. (Centers will be a bit spongy.) Cool in pans on a wire rack ½ hour. Remove from pans; cool on rack at least 2 hours.

5 To make the icing: Place the chocolate, water, and espresso powder in a saucepan. Cook over low heat, stirring constantly, until smooth. Remove from heat; let stand to cool. Refrigerate until cold.

6 Cream butter until light and lemony in color; add egg yolks, one at a time, beating well after each addition. Gradually stir in cold chocolate. Beat in confectioners' sugar.

7 Place one cake layer on serving plate; spread with icing. Place second layer on top; spread icing over top and sides of cake. Press walnuts evenly onto sides of cake. Keep in a cool place until ready to serve.

Curry

Earning my bread as a restaurant reviewer for several national magazines has caused me lately to ponder the proliferation of Indian restaurants on my home turf. I cannot testify about the rest of the country, but I can aver with authority that there are more Indian dining places in New York City at the present moment than there are in New Delhi! A fact which leads directly to my praise for the esoteric cuisine and, particularly, for curry as a seasoning!

When I was a stripling, the only restaurant in New York that served Indian food was a rather small and dark establishment situated in the upper regions of a building on West Forty-ninth Street.

Pressed cheek-by-jowl in a row of much more heavily traveled eateries (of every other possible ethnic persuasion), The Ceylon Inn was only habituated—as far as my untried eye could see—by Hindus. Through its portals passed a sparse parade of dark-skinned men and women, the latter often mysteriously wrapped in saris and inscrutably stamped with caste marks on their foreheads.

Although I didn't enter this restaurant until I was well over forty, I longed to eat there throughout my childhood and adolescence. It wasn't only the aromas that floated down the stairway that intrigued me—although they were disturbingly pungent—it was also the pervading tone of foreignness. It seemed a yellow brick road for a novitiate with a pith-helmet (bred on a diet of endless movies and the novels of Louis Bromfield) and one available for instant flight.

The Ceylon Inn bore two hallmarks of distinction for me. A legend above its narrow cornice proclaimed it to be "America's Oldest Indian Restaurant. Established in 1913." And that motto, even in 1935, proved orthodoxy beyond question in my mind. But the entrance to the edifice compounded this canon twice over, for it was adorned with two massive elephant head carvings—only slightly less than life-size, it seemed to me then, and magnificently crusted with gold leaf and brilliants.

My family never for a moment considered setting foot inside this restaurant. My father was a man with extreme dietary prejudices—he wouldn't even eat hash when it was served at his own table—and was often given to dire pronouncements about the fate of diners who partook of foreign cuisine, because "you never know what *they* put into the food at those places!"

But the gorgeous twin elephant heads suffused my dreams of living an exotic life for years to come.

Thirty years later, when I passed between those paired mammoths for the first time, they were over-painted a drab gray color and seemed remarkably shrunken from my childhood vision. The food, however, was excellent and authentic—and Hindus still dined there.

Curry is one of my most treasured seasonings, although I am discriminating about its usage. Not for me the little dab of curry in scrambled eggs or the sprinkling on grapefruit (heaven forfend!) for I like my native substances unadulterated in the main. I will admit, however, to rubbing a bit of the unctuous powder (along with garlic) on a lamb chop from time to time; but then, lamb and curry, like peaches and cream, are notorious go-togethers.

The funny thing about curry (as probably the whole wide world knows by this time) is that it is not a single spice at all but rather a blend of many Oriental seasonings and herbs. Consequently, no two curry powders are exactly alike in taste or texture. Indian girls learn how to make curry powder from their mothers and the formulas they follow to blend the spices are often a very personal matter; there is no official recipe.

Curry powder is generally acknowledged to have been invented in Bombay, although Madras makes the same claim. The flavoring differs according to region. Here is the composition of a very honest, slightly mild curry powder, gleaned from the confidences of a gourmet from Pondicherry:

AUTHENTIC
INDIAN CURRY POWDER

1 In a large mortar and pestle (or a blender set at high speed), crush all of the ingredients in the order in which they are listed.

2 Strain the mixture through a sieve twice (or reblend it), adding a pinch of cornstarch, until a fine powder is achieved.

3 Store powder in an airtight jar in a dark place until ready to use. (Light dissipates the flavor.)

5 teaspoons turmeric
4 teaspoons dried coriander
2 teaspoons red cumin seeds
2 teaspoons Nepalese pepper
1 teaspoon whole cloves
1 teaspoon cardamom
1 teaspoon white ginger
1 teaspoon ground cayenne pepper
1 teaspoon ground mace
1 teaspoon areca
3 teaspoons fennel seeds, caraway, mustard seeds, and ginseng root (mixed together)
Cornstarch

Makes about 1 cup.

I must confess I rarely make my own curry powders but I have been known to liven up some infirm brands upon occasion.

Two curry mixtures (hot and mild) that I buy are imported by a small shop in Greenwich Village (Aphrodisia, 28 Carmine Street, New York City) that is within easy walking distance of my stove. However, several other robust varieties have crossed my kitchen shelf from outlying areas. Here is a preferred list:

Sun Brand Madras curry powder; from Merwanjee Poonjiajee & Sons; imported by Edward Benneche, Inc., New York City
Javin Brand curry powder; Java-India Condiment Co., New York City
Crosse and Blackwell curry powder
Spice Island curry powder

The last two named are available in most supermarkets across the country. To buttress the piquancy of commercially packaged curry powder, I have learned to spike it as follows: To 2 ounces (¼ cup) curry powder, add 1 teaspoon caraway seeds, 1 teaspoon hot dried chili peppers, 1 teaspoon ground turmeric, 1 medium clove garlic, ½ teaspoon grated lemon peel, and ½ teaspoon ground ginger. Place all ingredients in a blender container and blend until smooth. This mixture may be stored in a tightly covered jar in your refrigerator for several weeks.

There is a wonderful cookbook of curries entitled *The Indian Domestic Economy and Receipt Book* and published in 1853 by the

Christian Knowledge Society in Madras. All of the recipes are highly unusual and authentic and I recommend them to aficionados of unadulterated ethnic cuisines. Neither of the following soup recipes comes with that pedigree—but both are conspicuous additions to any curry lover's repertoire.

GAIL FIRESTONE'S CRÈME PRIMAVERA

1 pound peas, shelled
1 medium onion, sliced
1 small carrot, sliced
1 small potato, pared, sliced
1 rib celery with leaves, broken
  into pieces
1 clove garlic
Salt to taste
1 teaspoon curry powder
2 cups chicken stock
1 cup milk
½ to ¾ cup whipping cream

Serves 4 to 6.

1 Combine peas, onion, carrot, potato, celery, garlic, salt, curry, and 1 cup stock in a saucepan. Bring to a boil; reduce heat. Simmer 15 minutes. Cool slightly.

2 Transfer mixture to a blender container; blend at high speed 15 seconds, being very careful as hot food will expand in the blender. Gradually stir in remaining 1 cup stock and milk; blend 15 seconds. Remove to a large bowl; thin with cream to desired texture. Refrigerate until cold. Taste before serving; add a pinch more curry, if necessary.

CURRIED FISH SOUP

3 cups hot fish stock
2 tablespoons unsalted butter
⅓ cup finely chopped onion
1 small clove garlic, minced
1 tablespoon curry powder
½ teaspoon ground turmeric
Pinch of ground allspice
2 tablespoons all-purpose flour
1 can (8 ounces) imported Italian
  tomatoes
¼ cup rice
¾ pound non-oily, white fish
  fillets, cut into 1-inch pieces
½ cup whipping cream
Salt and freshly ground pepper
Finely chopped parsley for garnish

Serves 4 to 5 as a soup course; double recipe to serve as a main course.

1 Make fish stock (see *Note*); keep hot.

2 Melt 2 tablespoons butter in a large heavy saucepan; add onion and garlic. Cook over low heat until soft but not browned, about 5 minutes. Sprinkle curry powder, turmeric, and allspice over onions; mix well. Stir in flour; cook over low heat 2 minutes.

3 Whisk hot fish stock into saucepan; stir in tomatoes. Heat to boiling; add rice. Boil 12 minutes. Reduce heat. Add fish; simmer 5 minutes. Stir in cream. Heat to boiling; remove from heat. Add salt and pepper to taste. Serve sprinkled with parsley.

Note: To make fish stock, place 1 pound fish bones, including heads, in a large pot; add 1½ cups water, 1 cup white wine, 1½ cups clam juice, 1 onion stuck with 2 cloves, 1 bay leaf, 3 sprigs parsley, ½ rib celery, 10 peppercorns, 1 teaspoon salt, and ½ lemon. Bring to a boil; reduce heat. Simmer 15 minutes. Strain.

Ninety percent of all Indians are vegetarians, in accordance with their belief in non-violence. A meatless curry, devised of eggplant, onion, seasonings, and vinegar, was given to me by a lovely lady from Ceylon, who is affiliated with the United Nations. A stipulation of employment with that prestigious organization forbids any personal notoriety; so her authority must go unheralded here. I can't imagine that a recipe like Eggplant Curry could stir up a brouhaha in the General Assembly—but you never know!

CEYLONESE EGGPLANT CURRY

1 Cut eggplants in half lengthwise; cut halves into ¼-inch-thick slices. Sprinkle with 1 tablespoon salt and the turmeric. Rub slices together; place in colander and let stand 1 hour. Then squeeze to remove as much liquid as possible.

2 Heat 3 tablespoons oil in a large, heavy skillet. Fry eggplant slices, 5 or 6 at a time, over medium heat until crisp. (Use more oil, if needed.) Drain on paper toweling.

3 Add 1 tablespoon oil to skillet; saute onion over medium heat until golden. Stir in curry powder; reduce heat. Return eggplant to skillet; add salt and pepper to taste. Sprinkle with vinegar; simmer 10 minutes.

2 medium eggplants
1 tablespoon salt
½ teaspoon ground turmeric
¼ cup vegetable oil
 (approximately)
1 onion, finely chopped
1 tablespoon curry powder
Salt and freshly ground pepper
1 tablespoon red wine vinegar

Serves 3 to 4.

Curry has a long, long lifeline. Traces of a currylike powder have been discovered in the excavations of Mohenjo-Daro, which flourished in 4000 B.C., a thousand years before the rise of Babylon. The Indus valley inhabitants invented the mortar and pestle—and probably ground up everything in sight once they got the knack of it.

The earliest curry powder on record used the seeds of mustard, fennel, and cumin as well as tamarind rind, which probably gave it a rosier hue than any I've ever tasted.

Arab merchants brought the secret of curry with them when they came to Spain. The Spanish traded it to the Italians during the fifth century and traces of the seasoning blend still cling to a few great Italian vegetable dishes. Here, for example, is a

Milanese formula for stuffed peppers that is *superbo!* These peppers make a memorable meal but the cold leftovers, splashed with freshets of oil and vinegar, are even better!

STUFFED GREEN PEPPERS

½ cup rice
6 green bell peppers
8 mild Italian sausages
1 medium yellow onion, finely chopped
1 clove garlic, minced
1 tablespoon curry powder
¼ teaspoon salt
½ teaspoon freshly ground pepper
1 egg, beaten
¼ cup strong chicken broth
3 tablespoons bread crumbs
2 tablespoons freshly grated Parmesan cheese
2 tablespoons olive oil

Serves 4 to 6.

1 Add the rice to a pot of boiling salted water; stir. Boil rapidly 15 minutes; drain in a colander. Place colander over a pot of boiling water; steam rice, covered with one layer of paper toweling, 15 minutes.

2 Heat oven to 375°. Cut tops off peppers; remove seeds. Cook peppers in boiling water 1 minute; drain.

3 Remove sausage from casings; place in a large, heavy skillet. Cook over medium heat, stirring with a wooden spoon to break up lumps, 5 minutes. Add onion, garlic, curry powder, salt, and pepper. Cook, stirring frequently, 10 minutes. Drain mixture in a sieve.

4 Transfer mixture to a large bowl. Stir in egg, chicken broth, and rice. Stuff peppers with mixture; sprinkle with bread crumbs, Parmesan cheese, and oil. Bake 50 minutes.

I love Mrs. Beeton dearly, but she certainly had some odd kitchen wisdom. In *The Book of Household Management,* published in London, 1859, the preeminent lady prescribed a formula for curry made of coriander, turmeric, cinnamon, and a quarter pound of every other spice in the pantry. She bade her readers place a generous amount of these ingredients " . . . in a cool oven where they should rest over night; then pound them together . . . and keep the powder in a bottle from which all air should be excluded." But in an afterthought, Mrs. Beeton's true feelings surface:

"We have given this recipe," she states, "as some persons prefer to make it at home but [curry] purchased at any respectable shop is, generally speaking, far superior, and taking things into consideration, more economical."

From the Indian word *tucarri,* meaning "sauce," came the English name for Mrs. Beeton's blend. The French (being rather bizarre linguistically) translate the word curry to mean "courage." Hence, two French dishes in the courageous manner.

Neither will test your kitchen mettle beyond the sticking point—a claim not to be made by Mrs. Beeton's *oeuvre*.

BEEF MADRAS

1 Saute the mushrooms in 2 tablespoons butter and 1 tablespoon oil in a large, heavy saucepan over medium heat until light brown. Add shallot; cook 2 minutes. Transfer mixture to a bowl; reserve.

2 Add 2 tablespoons butter and remaining oil to saucepan. Saute meat over high heat on both sides. Transfer to a bowl.

3 Remove excess fat from pan. Add beef stock; heat to boiling. Boil rapidly, scraping sides and bottom of pan, until reduced by two-thirds.

4 Combine cornstarch with 2 tablespoons cream; stir until smooth. Stir into saucepan with remaining cream, the curry powder, turmeric, salt, and pepper. Simmer 5 minutes. Taste for seasoning; add additional curry powder, salt, and pepper, if desired.

5 Add reserved mushrooms and the meat along with any juices to saucepan; baste with sauce. Simmer until hot, about 5 minutes. Stir 1 tablespoon butter, a bit at a time, into sauce. Garnish with parsley.

½ pound mushrooms, sliced
5 tablespoons butter
2 tablespoons vegetable oil
1 large shallot, finely chopped
2½ pounds beef fillet, cut into 2-inch-long strips
1 cup strong beef stock
2 teaspoons cornstarch
1 cup whipping cream
1 tablespoon curry powder, or to taste
Pinch of ground turmeric
1 teaspoon salt
½ teaspoon freshly ground pepper
Chopped parsley for garnish

Serves 4 to 6.

VEAU BRAISÉ AU COURAGE

1 Sprinkle meat with salt and pepper. Coat lightly with flour; shake off excess flour.

2 Melt butter in a Dutch oven. Saute meat over medium-high heat until light brown on all sides. Add onion, garlic, celery, and curry powder; cook, stirring constantly, 5 minutes.

3 Combine chicken stock and tomato paste; stir into Dutch oven. Bring to a boil; reduce heat. Simmer covered until meat is tender, about 1½ hours.

4 Add apple and banana. Cook uncovered over medium heat, stirring constantly, until sauce is quite thick. Stir in cream and allspice; cook 3 minutes. Taste for seasoning; add salt and pepper, if necessary. Sprinkle with parsley. Serve over rice.

2½ pounds boneless veal shoulder, cut into 1-inch cubes
Salt and freshly ground pepper
Flour
3 tablespoons butter
1 medium onion, finely chopped
1 clove garlic, minced
⅓ cup chopped celery
2 tablespoons curry powder
1 cup hot chicken stock
1 teaspoon tomato paste
1 small apple, pared, cored, diced
½ cup chopped ripe banana
2 tablespoons whipping cream
⅛ teaspoon ground allspice
1 tablespoon chopped parsley
6 cups cooked rice

Serves 4 to 6.

There is no single Indian curry tradition. The *korma* curries of the north are rich and brown in color; white poppy seeds and coconut often enliven their seasoning. In contrast, the *vindaloo* curries of the south are lighter, of thinner consistency, and yellow in color, but much hotter to the tongue. Curries from Ceylon are quite different from either of these. Always made of coconut milk and cream, they are very velvety but hardly mild. Here, by way of an example, I offer a chicken dish from my Ceylonese friend, who shall remain nameless here—to save the honor of her delegation and the world organization too, if necessary.

CEYLONESE CHICKEN CURRY

1 large onion, finely chopped
3 tablespoons vegetable oil
1 tablespoon curry powder
1 large clove garlic, minced
1 to 1½ pounds boneless chicken, cut into 2-inch × ½-inch strips
2 or 3 whole cloves
2 or 3 cardamom seeds
1 small cinnamon stick
Salt and freshly ground pepper to taste
Juice of ½ lemon
¼ to ½ cup milk

Serves 2 to 3.

1   Saute onion in oil in a large, heavy saucepan until golden. Stir in curry powder; cook over medium heat 3 minutes. Add garlic and chicken; saute until chicken is brown on all sides. (Lower heat, if necessary, to prevent burning.)

2   Tie cloves, cardamom, and cinnamon stick in cheesecloth; place in center of chicken. Sprinkle chicken with salt and pepper; cook covered over medium-low heat 15 minutes. Add lemon juice; cook covered until tender, 30 to 45 minutes (cook shorter amount of time if using all white meat).

3   Discard cheesecloth-wrapped spices. Add only enough milk to pan to make a fairly thick gravy; heat through.

Rather a traditionalist, in spite of the fact that she has been in New York for a long while, my friend from Ceylon was very amused by the curries I printed in *The Store Cookbook.*

"Not curry. No—this is not curry at all!" she laughed as she read the recipes.

To confound her, I borrowed the best of her native prescriptions for this book—and changed them not a whit. Now, however, let me add one of the most popular curry dishes I ever created for The Store. (But I must note, parenthetically, that the true versions are a heck of a lot shorter and sweeter for the cook.

Fake chicken curry requires about three times the text length of the ancestral recipe!)

CHICKEN AND PRUNE CURRY

1 Place chicken in a large pot with next six ingredients (through 1 rib celery); add equal parts of chicken broth and water to cover. Heat to boiling; reduce heat. Simmer 45 minutes. Let chicken cool in broth.

2 Remove chicken from pot; drain. Remove skin and meat from bones; cut meat into large bite-sized pieces. Reserve meat. Return skin and bones to pot; heat to boiling. Boil until reduced by half. Strain broth; reserve.

3 Melt butter in a large, heavy saucepan. Saute mushroom caps over medium heat 2 minutes; remove from pan. Add minced onions and garlic to pan; saute until tender but not brown. Add apple and curry powder; cook over medium heat, stirring constantly, 3 minutes.

4 Combine cornstarch and cream; gradually whisk into saucepan. Cook over low heat until thick. Add ginger, cardamom, turmeric, cayenne pepper, and salt; stir in coconut milk and 1 cup reserved chicken broth. Heat to boiling, stirring constantly; reduce heat. Simmer 15 to 20 minutes, stirring occasionally.

5 Add reserved chicken, chopped celery, green pepper, lemon peel, and prunes. Simmer 8 minutes, adding 1 cup reserved chicken broth as curry thickens.

6 Heat oven to 300°. Transfer curry to an ovenproof casserole or serving dish; sprinkle with candied ginger and currants; decorate top with reserved mushroom caps.

7 Place in oven for 15 to 20 minutes before serving. Garnish with chopped parsley. (Serve curry with rice and assorted condiments, such as chutney, pickled watermelon rind, diced green pepper, diced cucumber mixed with yogurt, diced avocado sprinkled with lime juice, crumbled bacon, chopped cashews, sliced green grapes, Indian relish, and dried Bombay duck.)

Note: To make coconut milk, combine 1 can of unsweetened shredded coconut with an equal amount of milk in a blender container; blend at high speed for a second or two. Strain. Reserve the coconut for a condiment.

1 **stewing chicken (about 3 pounds)**
1 **large yellow onion stuck with 2 whole cloves**
Bouquet garni composed of 1 bay leaf, 1 parsley sprig, and 1 dill sprig
1 **small clove garlic**
½ **lemon, sliced**
Salt and pepper
1 **rib celery**
Chicken broth
3 **tablespoons unsalted butter**
12 to 16 **medium mushroom caps**
1 **cup minced onions**
2 **cloves garlic, minced**
1 **apple, pared, diced**
4 **tablespoons curry powder (preferably hot)**
4 **tablespoons sifted cornstarch**
½ **cup whipping cream**
¼ **teaspoon ground ginger**
¼ **teaspoon ground cardamom**
1 **tablespoon ground turmeric**
¼ **teaspoon cayenne pepper**
1 **teaspoon salt**
½ **cup coconut milk (see *Note*)**
1½ **cups chopped celery**
½ **cup chopped green pepper**
2 **teaspoons thinly slivered lemon peel**
½ **cup pitted prunes, cut into thin strips**
¼ **cup slivered candied ginger**
½ **cup dried black currants**
¼ **cup chopped parsley**

Serves 6.

Curried Pot Roast comes from the mid-western part of the country (Chicago, not Jaipur). It may seem to you every bit as unorthodox as the chicken and prune dish that preceded it—but give your taste buds a fighting chance before you pass it by!

The curry pomade seems to tenderize as well as flavor the meat. And the sauce, spooned over buttered, parslied potatoes or tiny Spätzle (see Index)—for utter ethnic caprice—adds salubrious relish for the lucky diner.

CURRIED POT ROAST

1 top round beef roast (about 4 pounds)
Salt and freshly ground pepper
1 teaspoon curry powder
1 teaspoon ground turmeric
1 teaspoon ground ginger
3 tablespoons vegetable oil
4 tablespoons butter
2 cups chopped onions
2 cloves garlic, minced
1 cup strong beef broth
1 cup peeled, chopped tomatoes
1 bay leaf, crumbled
3 sprigs fresh thyme, chopped, or ¼ teaspoon dried thyme
1 tablespoon all-purpose flour
1 tablespoon whipping cream
Chopped parsley for garnish

Serves 6 to 8.

1 Rub meat thoroughly with salt, pepper, curry powder, turmeric, and ginger. Let stand 1 hour.

2 Heat oil and butter in a Dutch oven. Saute onions and garlic over medium heat until tender but not brown; remove with a slotted spoon. Raise heat; brown meat well on all sides. Remove from pan.

3 Pour beef broth into the Dutch oven; cook over high heat, scraping bottom and sides of pan until smooth. Return meat to pan. Spoon onions, garlic, and tomatoes around meat; add bay leaf and thyme. Heat to boiling; reduce heat. Simmer covered until meat is tender, 3 to 3½ hours. Heat oven to 300°.

4 Remove meat to a serving platter; keep warm in oven. Combine flour and cream; stir into Dutch oven. Cook over medium heat until slightly thickened, 6 or 7 minutes. Spoon some of the sauce over the meat; sprinkle with parsley. Pass remaining sauce in a separate bowl.

"With enough curry powder, even the pebbles of the Ganges will seem quite tasty!"—*old Indian saying.*

I acknowledge that truth from hearsay; I have never attempted any rock cookery. But Rock Cornish hens? Ah, that's another dish entirely—happily curried for your delectation!

CURRIED HENS

1 Heat oven to 450°. Rub hens well with garlic inside and out. Rub skins lightly with curry powder. Place ½ onion, 1 sprig parsley, and 1 sprig watercress in each cavity; truss. Rub well with butter.

2 Place hens in a shallow baking dish; sprinkle with salt and seasoned pepper. Cut bacon slice in half lengthwise; cut halves in half crosswise. Place 2 strips on each hen; pour chicken stock into dish. Bake 1 hour, basting every 15 minutes. (There should be enough pan juices to baste well each time; if not, add more chicken broth.) Reduce oven to 350°; bake 30 minutes, continuing to baste.

3 Remove trussing and place hens, whole or cut in half, on a serving platter. Place in oven; turn off heat.

4 Saute mushrooms in 1 tablespoon oil and 2 tablespoons butter in a small skillet over high heat until golden. Spoon over chicken.

5 Remove all but 1 tablespoon fat from skillet. Sprinkle flour into skillet; stir in cream and enough pan juices from hens to make a smooth sauce. Stir in ¼ teaspoon curry powder; cook over medium heat, stirring constantly, 5 minutes. Pour over hens. Garnish with chopped parsley.

2 Rock Cornish hens
1 clove garlic, bruised
Curry powder
1 small yellow onion, cut in half
2 sprigs parsley
2 sprigs watercress
Butter
Salt and seasoned pepper
1 slice bacon
½ cup chicken stock or broth (approximately)
1 cup sliced mushrooms
1 tablespoon olive or vegetable oil
2 tablespoons butter
1 tablespoon all-purpose flour
⅓ cup whipping cream
¼ teaspoon curry powder
Chopped parsley

Serves 2.

Cold curried salads are always a mainstay in my summer kitchen. Both the following are from my own collection but I didn't invent them. They are Victorian English supper adjuncts to a cold joint or a bird. More than likely these recipes returned from India a hundred years ago with some retired *pukka sahib* and his *memsahib,* but they are still very contemporary in savor. Pass the cold fried chicken, please!

COLD CURRIED VEGETABLES

1 Combine the broth and curry powder in a saucepan; boil until reduced by half. Cool slightly. Combine broth with mayonnaise, sour cream, lemon juice, hot pepper sauce, salt, and pepper in a medium bowl; whisk until smooth.

2 Stir in the vegetables and chopped mint; refrigerate until cold. Serve on lettuce leaves; top with mint leaves.

¼ cup chicken broth
1 tablespoon curry powder
¼ cup mayonnaise
1 cup sour cream
Juice of half a lemon
Dash of hot pepper sauce
Salt and freshly ground pepper to taste
¼ cup finely chopped celery
¼ cup finely chopped green pepper
1 cup cooked peas
½ cup diced cooked carrots
½ cup cooked corn kernels
1 teaspoon chopped fresh mint
Lettuce leaves
Mint leaves

Serves 4.

COLD CURRIED POTATO BALLS

8 large potatoes, pared
¾ cup finely chopped red onion
1 green pepper, minced
1 cup mayonnaise
1 cup sour cream
½ cup strong beef bouillon, cooled
2 tablespoons curry powder
Salt and freshly ground pepper to
    taste
¼ cup finely chopped parsley

Serves 6 to 8.

1 Scoop potatoes into balls with a melon baller. Cook in boiling salted water 5 to 6 minutes (they should be slightly crunchy). Drain.

2 Combine potato balls, onion, and green pepper in a large bowl.

3 Whisk mayonnaise, sour cream, beef bouillon, curry powder, salt, and pepper together in a medium bowl. Pour over potato balls; toss lightly. Sprinkle with parsley.

Dill

Is there an appetite so jaded it cannot be roused by some avenues of cookery?

Witches are said to be tempted by eye of newt and toe of frog, while those possessed are alleged to take the devil's humors for sustenance. But don't take my word as fact, for I have never officially been introduced to any of that stripe.

Leprechauns, I know, are vegetarian. They prefer to nibble the soft under-leaves of plants, or so an old Irish nurse once told me, because they are clever little people and know that whatever blooms directly over the root is the sweetest part of the flowering.

Dybbuks sup on soured wine and water. Vampires prefer blood. Parenthetically, I should note that all preternatural creatures are allergic to garlic; so *aioli* is automatically *de trop* at cocktail parties when one of Dracula's crowd is in residence.

When I was a tot, ladies with vapors swigged aromatic spirits of ammonia, sometimes laced with Coca-Cola. Somewhat before my time, adolescent males were spooned sulphur and molasses whenever they seemed "off their feed." And a good swallow of rhubarb and soda was kept waiting in the wings, in case the first prescription did not take.

My grandmother did not have much faith in those remedies for an appetite on the wane. She believed (and proved her theory on more than one occasion) that all a growing boy—or an invalid, for that matter—needed to be tempted back to vigor was a steaming bowl of soup. Chicken, or chicken with barley, was her formula, generously dusted with snippings of fresh dill.

Ah, you smile, shades of Philip Roth at the back burner. Not a bit of it—this lady was your untypical ethnic matriarch. Chicken fat was never substituted for butter in her skillet and shards of smoky bacon blanketed every turkey she ever roasted. *Dill,* you see, was her cure—not soup at all!

An herbalist when nobody had heard of the cognomen, my grandmother cooked in close conjunction with her green thumb. Fresh dill weed for her kitchen fringed her garden from spring to fall. In winter, Joe, the Italian green-grocer who came by horse-drawn wagon, made sure to stock a fresh supply of these soup greens for her—or he would hear about it for weeks afterward.

She preferred her own, however. And I clearly remember her, in the middle of a complex soup preparation, turning away from the stove and dashing outdoors to pick a *bouquet garni* on the spot. Fresh dill was not the only pot herb that grew in her garden; parsley, thyme, and tarragon bloomed in concert with the succulents of her rock garden and mint crowded the daffodils and narcissus right up to her back-porch steps. Sage and rosemary were sown in clay pots that she put into the ground when the seedlings flowered and dug up again before the first frost fell, for those lucky herbs wintered in her kitchen pantry.

What my grandmother produced with her herb garden was one wonderful dish after another, but none of them was ever overly redolent of the seasoning. The aforementioned chicken soup was a miracle of culinary handicraft; yet its flavoring was elusive. All trace of the vegetables (dill, of course, as well as carrots, onions, parsnip, and sometimes lettuce and peas) that enriched the stock was removed from the pot before serving; yet the brew was so full-bodied and gorgeously golden that it made the mouth water as it was ladled into the waiting bowls.

I still recall the scent of that soup and I have not tasted its like again since my grandmother took her leave of earthly cookery.

In her memory, however, I keep fresh dill in my refrigerator year round, so that I can, from time to time, palely approximate her prodigy.

The wonderful aftermath of my grandmother's chicken soup was the largesse of crisp-skinned chicken that immediately followed it to the table. Having removed the bird from the broth at precisely the right moment (when the soup was neither too bland nor the chicken overcooked), the knowing cook would carve up the meat, rub the skin with a mite of butter and a little soup stock, and broil it until the crust turned russet from the fire. Only then was it piled high with vegetables—feathered with more dill—and sent to pleasure the palate of her tribe.

I use dill in a multitude of ways that my grandmother might consider highly unorthodox, but she would never disapprove of this variation on her theme:

CHICKEN WITH DILL— WITH OR WITHOUT SAUCE

1 Rub chickens with garlic and place in a large heavy pot. Add water to cover, 2 teaspoons salt, the peppercorns, carrot, onion, celery, parsley, and lemon slice. Heat to boiling; reduce heat. Simmer just until tender, about 1 hour; remove scum with a spoon as it rises to surface.

2 Heat broiling unit. Remove chickens from broth; reserve broth. Cut chickens into serving pieces. Place pieces in baking dish; broil, skin side up, until crisp. At this point, sprinkle chicken with dill and serve or keep warm in low oven and proceed with recipe to make sauce.

3 Melt butter in a heavy saucepan; stir in the flour. Whisk over low heat 2 minutes; stir in 2 cups reserved chicken broth. Simmer 5 minutes. Add lemon juice, salt, and pepper. Remove from heat.

4 Beat cream and egg yolk in a small bowl until smooth; stir in ¼ cup sauce. Stir egg yolk mixture back into sauce. Cook over low heat 2 minutes; do not boil. Stir in dill. Transfer chicken to serving platter; pour sauce over.

Note: For an excellent chicken soup, remove chickens after Step 1 and boil broth until reduced by one third. Strain broth; add chicken pieces, noodles or whatever.

2 whole chickens (about 3 pounds each)
1 clove garlic, bruised
2 teaspoons salt
10 peppercorns
1 carrot, chopped
1 onion stuck with 2 cloves
1 rib celery with leaves, broken into pieces
2 sprigs parsley
1 slice lemon
2 tablespoons butter
2 tablespoons all-purpose flour
1 tablespoon lemon juice
Salt and freshly ground pepper to taste
3 tablespoons whipping cream
1 egg yolk
⅓ cup chopped fresh dill

Serves 6 to 8.

As I reported earlier on, I grew up next door to a family of healthy-appetited Swedes. Their kitchen was redolent of heady aromas and flavors too improbable for my untried palate to properly decode. Luckily for me, I never knew that the *gravlax* served there on holidays as part of a traditional *sillbricka* (a tray of assorted cold fish dishes) was made of raw salmon pickled with fresh dill. If I had, I never would have tried it—and might not have developed the fondness I have for this great Scandinavian hors d'oeuvre.

My good friend Dr. Bruce Scott (not a whit more Swedish than I) gave me the following formula after he produced a copious supply of the dish for starters one night. His recipe is one of the best I have ever seen on the subject. And, in passing, the mustard sauce is very, very salutary to hot broiled shrimp or cold cracked crab as well.

BRUCE SCOTT'S SCANDINAVIAN GRAVLAX

¼ cup olive oil
1 fresh salmon fillet (about 4 pounds) with skin on, but all bones removed
2 tablespoons granulated sugar
1 tablespoon salt
1 teaspoon crushed white pepper
1 cup finely chopped fresh dill
¼ cup dry white wine
Mustard Sauce (recipe follows)

Serves 16 to 20.
(Recipe can be cut in half.)

1 Dip a cloth in the olive oil and rub fish well on both sides. Combine sugar, salt, pepper, and 1 tablespoon dill; rub into fish on both sides.

2 Use a shallow dish in which salmon fits snugly and sprinkle bottom of dish with half the remaining dill. Place the fish over dill; pour wine over. Sprinkle with remaining dill.

3 Cover fish with a wood plank or other flat, heavy item; place a weight on top. Refrigerate 48 hours, turning fish several times.

4 To serve, remove skin from fish. Cut fish into ¼-inch slices. Serve with mustard sauce.

Note: You must use a good olive oil in this recipe. I prefer Olio Sasso or Plagniol brands.

1 tablespoon granulated sugar
2 tablespoons Dijon mustard
3 tablespoons white wine vinegar
¾ cup olive oil
1 teaspoon lemon juice
1 teaspoon chopped fresh dill
Salt and freshly ground pepper to taste

MUSTARD SAUCE

Combine sugar, mustard, and vinegar in a small bowl. Gradually whisk in oil, 1 tablespoon at a time, until thick. Season with lemon juice, dill, salt, and pepper.

Scandinavian (like Russian and German) cuisine has a natural affinity for the piquancy of fresh dill. The green always adds a pleasant element of surprise to stews and meatballs. The next recipe offers a classic example of that palatable association.

SWEDISH LAMB STEW

1 Place meat in a large pot; add cold water just to cover. Bring to a boil over high heat. Drain immediately; return meat to pot. Place pot under cold water; let water run over the meat until it runs clear. Drain meat.

2 Place meat in a Dutch oven. Add chicken broth and enough water to cover by 1 inch. Tie the coarsely chopped dill, the bay leaf, peppercorns, parsley, thyme, and white onion in cheesecloth; press into middle of meat. Sprinkle meat with salt and pepper. Heat to boiling; reduce heat. Simmer until meat is tender, 50 to 60 minutes.

3 Remove and discard cheesecloth. Drain meat, reserving liquid. Place meat in a bowl; cover with aluminum foil to keep warm.

4 Melt 3 tablespoons butter in a large, heavy saucepan. Add yellow onion; cook over low heat 5 minutes (do not brown). Whisk in allspice and flour; cook 2 minutes. Add reserved meat liquid; whisk until smooth. Simmer 5 minutes.

5 Meanwhile, combine vinegar and sugar in a small saucepan; stir over medium heat until sugar dissolves. Raise heat; boil until slightly syrupy, about 8 minutes.

6 Stir vinegar mixture into sauce. Add the meat, hot pepper sauce, and 3 tablespoons finely chopped dill; cook until heated through. Remove from heat.

7 Beat the cream with the egg yolk; stir into stew. Stir in remaining 2 tablespoons butter. Add salt and pepper, if necessary. Sprinkle with remaining dill. (Serve with rice or boiled new potatoes.)

Note: I use meat from leg of lamb in this stew.

2 pounds boneless lamb, cut into 2-inch cubes
1 cup chicken broth
⅓ cup coarsely chopped fresh dill
1 large bay leaf
12 peppercorns
3 sprigs parsley
2 sprigs fresh thyme or ½ teaspoon dried thyme
1 whole white onion, peeled
Salt and white pepper to taste
5 tablespoons butter
1 small yellow onion, finely chopped
Pinch of ground allspice
3 tablespoons all-purpose flour
5 tablespoons white distilled vinegar
2 tablespoons granulated sugar
Dash of hot pepper sauce
¼ cup finely chopped fresh dill
½ cup whipping cream
1 egg yolk

Serves 4 or 5.

Use of the dill plant (*Anethum graveolens*) for seasoning originated in central Europe. The dill seeds came from the East, but they were used there only in the manufacture of strong medicines— never in cooking. In fact, a blight in 600 B.C. ended all dill growth in Babylon and Assyria and the fragrant, peppery herb was forgotten until almost a thousand years later, when an army chef attached to a band of returning Crusaders discovered it

Dill   135

growing alongside the roads of Bavaria. He put it into a *salat*—and dill entered cuisine at last.

A very happy marriage of dill, cream cheese, and crabmeat provided The Store in Amagansett with one of its most intoxicating hors d'oeuvre. I cannot calculate how many gallons of crab dip we produced during the years that the little shop flourished by the sea—but it was probably enough to pave the gulf to Gardiner's Bay and back. The dip is designed for sloshing with cold, crisp, raw vegetaria. Never, never potato chips!

DILLED CRAB DIP

1 package (8 ounces) cream cheese, room temperature
1 package frozen king crabmeat (6 ounces), thawed, chopped
3 shallots, minced
1 teaspoon beef bouillon powder (optional)
¼ cup sour cream
1 cup mayonnaise
½ teaspoon hot pepper sauce
½ cup chopped fresh dill
Salt to taste

Makes about 2½ cups.

Beat cream cheese in a large bowl until fluffy. Add crabmeat, shallots, and bouillon powder. Stir until well mixed; add sour cream and mayonnaise. Beat until fairly smooth. (If too thick, thin with a little milk.) Add hot pepper sauce, dill, and salt. Refrigerate until well chilled.

Fresh dill is one of the joys of my table year-round. Theoretically, the herb should be as readily available as parsley at the supermarket. If it isn't there—demand it! If you cannot find fresh dill, however, chop dried dill weed (or seeds) with a mite of parsley. It's better than plain dried, but it's never more than a pale substitute for the flavor of the fresh stuff.

Canny gardeners (or window-box growers) with a mouth for dill should sow seeds continuously from April through June to ensure a constant supply of the herb. Seedlings should be thinned to eight inches apart, but they cannot be transplanted. Hardy dill matures in less than two months and the plants should be snipped for kitchen duty whenever yellow flowers (and seed heads) appear.

Try the following poor man's version of a potentate's fare whenever the dill needs thinning. It's a favorite eggplant dish that I concocted during my salad days.

EGGPLANT ORIENTAL

1 Heat oven to 450°. Place eggplant slices in a single layer on a generously buttered baking sheet or in a buttered, shallow baking pan. Cover with one layer of onion slices. Press mashed garlic into onions. Sprinkle with oil, salt, and pepper. (If necessary, use two pans.)

2 Bake until eggplant is soft, about 45 minutes. Cool slightly. Place eggplant mixture in a wooden bowl and coarsely chop. Stir in vinegar and 3½ tablespoons dill. Add more salt and pepper, if necessary.

3 Transfer to a serving bowl. Garnish with remaining dill. Refrigerate until cold.

3 medium eggplants, cut into ½-inch slices
2 large yellow onions, thinly sliced
2 cloves garlic, mashed
⅓ cup olive or vegetable oil
1 teaspoon coarse salt
¼ teaspoon freshly ground pepper
Dash of red wine vinegar (preferably Dessaux)
¼ cup coarsely chopped fresh dill

Serves 6 to 8.

Scandinavian mothers add dill weed to milk for children—and claim it acts as a natural sedative. The herb is said to have lulled babies to sleep for centuries—a fact not vouchsafed here. The word *dill,* however, which comes from Old English and Old Norse, does mean "to lull, soothe, or dull."

Certainly its amiable flavor soothes the savage stomach when a prescient host provides a crock of Potted Shrimp (also an Old English derivative) and a stack of good dark bread with rounds of icy martinis.

Cheers!

LONDON POTTED SHRIMP

1 Toss shrimp with lemon juice in a bowl. Refrigerate 1 hour. Drain.

2 Whip butter, using high speed of an electric mixer, until light. Add anchovies, dill, cayenne pepper, and salt; beat until mixed. Add shrimp; beat at high speed 1 minute.

3 Pack mixture into one or more crocks or bowls and smooth the surface. Sprinkle heavily with coarsely ground black pepper. Refrigerate until cold.

Note: I always serve potted shrimp with pumpernickel on the side. But warm toast fingers do equally well for spreading.

2 cups cooked, cleaned small shrimp
½ cup lemon juice
1 cup unsalted butter, softened
½ can anchovies, mashed
3 tablespoons chopped fresh dill
Pinch of cayenne pepper
¼ teaspoon salt
Coarsely ground black pepper
Thinly sliced dark bread

Serves 6 to 8.

The Russians have raised dill to culinary heights of splendor in several national dishes. Pelmeny with Sauce Kiev is one such triumph. I ate it in Kiev, Moscow, and Leningrad with nary a disappointment—but I never dined on the dish with more flourish than the time I shared it with the late, tempestuous owner of New York's Russian Tea Room, Sydney Kaye. The original kitchen tyrant, Sydney shrieked: "More dill! More dill!" at the waiter before his fork had even sliced into one of the delicious dumplings.

PELMENY WITH SAUCE KIEV

For the dough:
2 cups all-purpose flour (approximately)
1 teaspoon salt
1 egg, beaten
⅔ cup water

For the filling:
1 medium onion, minced
1 clove garlic, crushed
2 tablespoons butter
1 pound ground veal
Pinch of ground allspice
1 tablespoon finely chopped dill
½ teaspoon salt
¼ teaspoon pepper

For the Sauce Kiev:
2 tablespoons butter
1 tablespoon all-purpose flour
1½ cups whipping cream
1½ tablespoons Dijon mustard
1 tablespoon white horseradish
¼ cup strong chicken stock
1 tablespoon lemon juice
1 egg yolk, beaten
Salt and freshly ground pepper
Chopped fresh dill

Serves 4 as a main course; more as an appetizer.

1 To prepare the dough: Combine flour and salt in a bowl. Make a well in the center; add the egg and water. Gradually blend flour into egg and water with a wooden spoon; mix gently. (Dough will be very sticky; if it is too wet, add ¼ to ½ cup more flour.) Refrigerate covered 1½ hours.

2 To prepare the filling: Saute onion and garlic in butter in a small skillet over low heat until tender. Place in a bowl with remaining filling ingredients; mix thoroughly.

3 Roll out ⅓ of dough as thin as possible on a well-floured marble surface or a board. (Keep the surface and rolling pin coated with flour at all times; the dough tends to be very sticky.) Cut into 2-inch circles.

4 Place 1 heaping teaspoon of filling in center of each circle. Brush edges with cold water. Stretch dough over filling and press to form half-moons; seal edges with the tines of a fork. Place on a lightly floured surface. (Dough scraps can be rolled out again; patch them together and roll them as thin as possible. Dough will toughen if it is overworked.)

5 Bring 3 quarts salted water to a rolling boil. Drop pelmeny, 5 at a time, into boiling water. Cook until they float to the top or no longer than 4 minutes. Drain thoroughly in a colander.

6 To prepare the sauce: Melt butter in a heavy saucepan; stir in flour. Cook over low heat 2 minutes. Whisk in cream; stir until smooth. Cook 5 minutes. Add mustard, horseradish, chicken stock, and lemon juice; cook, stirring frequently, until sauce thickens slightly, about 10 to 12 minutes. Just before serving, stir ¼ cup sauce

into egg yolk; then stir mixture back into sauce. Cook over low heat 5 minutes; do not boil. Add salt and pepper to taste. Pour over warm pelmeny. Sprinkle generously with chopped dill.

Note: To reheat pelmeny, place them on a buttered serving platter and drizzle with melted butter. Place in 300° oven until warmed through, about 25 minutes. Pelmeny may be cooked, cooled, and frozen in airtight plastic bags; heat frozen pelmeny in boiling salted water until fork-tender, 4 to 5 minutes.

Pelmeny can also be served—without Sauce Kiev—in fresh, strong chicken soup. Pass a little horseradish on the side.

As far as I can determine from my food sleuthing, dill has absolutely no frame of reference in Chinese cuisine. But the following recipe for Crab Pancakes, like Chinese food, is easily put together and reminds me of egg foo yong—hence, the vague title. Eminently unvague in every other aspect, the pancakes make prodigious last-minute party food (they're also wonderful for Sunday night doldrums). So try to remember to keep a package of frozen crab in the freezer for such occasions.

VAGUELY CHINESE CRAB PANCAKES

1 Whisk egg yolks in a small bowl until light and lemon-colored. Place crabmeat in a large bowl; break up large pieces with a fork. Sprinkle with salt, pepper, and thyme. Add ham, pork, onion, dill, green pepper, parsley, melted butter, and baking powder; mix gently. (Ingredients should not lose their individual character.) Stir in egg yolks.

2 Beat egg whites with a pinch of salt until stiff but not dry. Stir half of egg whites into crabmeat mixture; fold in remainder.

3 Heat a heavy skillet or omelet pan; remove from heat. Place 1 tablespoon butter in pan and tilt pan to coat it. Place 1 heaping soupspoon of batter in skillet. Cook until golden brown on both sides, turning once with a metal spatula. (Pancake will not turn easily if it is not completely cooked on one side. Gently shape pancake with spatula if necessary.) Remove pancake to serving platter; keep warm in low oven. Repeat with remaining butter and batter.

Note: Serve pancakes as the Chinese would, with hot, hot mustard

4 eggs, separated
1 package (6 ounces) frozen crabmeat, thawed
Salt and freshly ground pepper
1 sprig fresh thyme, chopped, or ⅛ teaspoon dried thyme
¼ cup thinly slivered cooked ham
¼ cup thinly slivered cooked pork
1 medium onion, minced
¼ cup coarsely chopped dill
½ green pepper, finely chopped
2 tablespoons parsley, minced
1½ tablespoons unsalted butter, melted
¼ teaspoon baking powder
Pinch of salt
10 tablespoons butter (approximately)

Serves 4 to 6.

and duck sauce. Or serve them as I do with the following Shrimp Sauce and rice.

SHRIMP SAUCE

3 tablespoons unsalted butter
3 tablespoons sifted all-purpose flour
1 cup hot court bouillon or clam juice
1¼ cups whipping cream
1 cup cooked shrimp, shelled, deveined
2 tablespoons Madeira or dry sherry
Dash of hot pepper sauce
¼ teaspoon freshly grated nutmeg
Salt and white pepper to taste
2 egg yolks
⅛ teaspoon paprika
Chopped fresh dill for garnish

1 Melt butter in a saucepan. Add flour; whisk over low heat 2 minutes. Whisk in court bouillon or clam juice. Whisk until smooth; add cream. Cook over low heat, stirring frequently, until thick. Stir in shrimp, Madeira, hot pepper sauce, nutmeg, salt, and pepper; cook 3 minutes.

2 Beat egg yolks in a small bowl; add ¼ cup hot sauce. Gradually stir egg yolk mixture back into sauce. Cook over very low heat, stirring constantly, 3 minutes. Stir in paprika. Spoon some over each crab pancake. Serve remainder, garnished with dill, on the side.

Note: For court bouillon, see recipe for Cold Fillet of Sole Romanoff (see Index).

Eighteenth-century Quaker colonists called dill the "meeting-house herb" because the dried root and seeds of the strong-scented plant were nibbled as an appetite depressant during long hours spent at prayer.

Dill was one seasoning deemed common enough not to violate the Quaker dictum against "glorification of the fare at thy table." The herb was used in many guises in a plain-wife's kitchen—from pickled meat to herbal essences and jellies. One such dish, beef in broth, was always served with a sauce of crushed dill flower and "spoiled cider," or vinegar.

I have in my fond possession two receipts for beef with dill sauce. A Quaker prescription, written in a barely legible hand in a copy of Mrs. Beeton's cookbook, notes that "the raw chine be mauled and brawled well with herbs before it goes into a fiery soup." It also insists that the dish "be not made unless the weeds of dill are a foot off the ground."

The mint original of the same formula was laid down a hundred years earlier in another cookbook, which was privately printed by Queen Henriette Marie of England and published in 1668. That tome is called *The Queen's CLOSET Opened.* A subtitle notes that it holds "Incomparable Secrets in Physic, Surgery, Preserving, and Candying, etc.," which were presented to the queen by "most experienced persons of the times."

Here's her secret for Collared Beef with Dill Sauce:

COLLARED BEEF WITH DILL SAUCE

1 Sprinkle meat with salt and pepper. Roll up and tie with string in several places; wrap meat in cheesecloth to keep it moist.

2 Place meat in a large, heavy saucepan or Dutch oven. Add beef broth and enough water to cover. Add allspice, 1 tablespoon dill, the peppercorns, sage, and bay leaf. Heat to boiling; reduce heat. Simmer partially covered 3 to 4 hours (1 hour per pound of meat). One hour before meat is done, add garlic and 1 teaspoon salt. Skim fat from surface as meat cooks.

3 Remove meat from cooking liquid; keep warm in low oven. Strain cooking liquid; return to pan and boil until reduced to 1½ cups.

4 Melt butter in a saucepan; stir in flour. Cook over low heat 2 minutes. Whisk in cooking liquid. Add vinegar, sugar, and remaining 2 tablespoons dill; cook 3 minutes. Remove from heat; whisk in egg yolk.

5 Remove cheesecloth and string from meat. Slice meat very thin; serve with sauce.

Note: Meat can also be refrigerated and served cold with a sauce of whipped cream liberally seasoned with dill and grated fresh horse-radish.

1 large flank steak (3 to 4 pounds), all fat removed
Salt and freshly ground pepper
2 cups beef broth
½ teaspoon whole allspice
3 tablespoons chopped fresh dill
6 peppercorns
Pinch of sage
1 bay leaf
1 clove garlic
1 teaspoon salt
1½ tablespoons butter
1½ tablespoons all-purpose flour
1½ tablespoons cider vinegar
½ tablespoon granulated sugar
1 egg yolk

Serves 6 to 8.

Fresh dill is an unabashed confederate of seafood, and wise cooks snip a bit of this green over anything that swims, even lobster. One of my favored adjuncts to fried fish is the following Tartar Sauce. There are as many versions of this piquant relish as there were Tartars in the Caucasus; mine is picked up from a chef-friend who added a dribble of Pernod to the herby compound. Remember the formula when you have read on a bit and come upon the recipe for Battered-Up Fish and Shrimp (see Index).

1 cup mayonnaise
½ cup sour cream
½ teaspoon Dijon mustard
1 small shallot, minced
1 sour gherkin or cornichon, chopped
1 teaspoon finely chopped parsley
1 tablespoon finely chopped dill
¼ teaspoon lemon juice
Dash of Pernod
Salt and freshly ground pepper to taste

Makes about 1½ cups.

TARTAR SAUCE

Whisk the mayonnaise with the sour cream and mustard in a bowl. Stir in remaining ingredients; mix well. Refrigerate until cold.

The recipes people write me about most are my never-ending supply of meat loaves. There are several of merit in this book and one of them (from a country fair collection), composed of pork sausage, dill pickle, and chopped fresh dill, is fair game to try right now.

1 pound ground sirloin
½ pound ground spicy pork sausage
½ cup chopped cooked ham
1 medium onion, finely chopped
½ cup bread crumbs
2 eggs, beaten
½ cup chopped fresh dill
½ cup finely chopped dill pickles
½ cup pickle juice
½ teaspoon salt
½ teaspoon freshly ground pepper
¼ cup chili sauce
1 teaspoon Dijon mustard
1 teaspoon Worcestershire sauce
Dash of hot pepper sauce
Chopped fresh dill for garnish

Serves 6 to 8.

DILLED MEAT LOAF

1 Heat oven to 425°. Combine all ingredients through pepper in a bowl; mix thoroughly. Shape into a loaf in a shallow baking dish.

2 Whisk together remaining ingredients except dill for garnish. Spread over meat. Bake 30 minutes. Reduce oven heat to 350°; bake 45 minutes. Pour off fat. Garnish with freshly chopped dill.

Each of the four assorted vegetables seasoned with dill that follow is so independent of the others in taste and texture that one might almost be tempted to serve them all together—but don't!

Dilled carrots are of a Norwegian stripe. They are blanched and then sauteed in cream and chicken broth until tender. At the end, the cream is scorched to a fine thick sauce that turns the carrots pure gold. This dish is excellent with any broiled or sauteed fish.

Dilled beets with horseradish, a savory combination of flavors from Austria, provides rosy magic at a hearty dinner table. Consider placing this dish adjoining a roasted chicken or a goose. It is one side order that even confirmed beet-haters can become addicted to!

Dilled Cucumbers, a nouvelle cuisine approach from France, places the hot bland vegetable in a light, light butter sauce flecked with greens. It makes a nice accompaniment for roasts like lamb or duckling.

Rösti, from Switzerland, is a delectable potato cake seasoned with fragments of bacon and fresh dill. Sound good? It lives up to the promise. I eat Rösti with scrambled eggs or steak. It's an item for fast party food, too, and makes midnight supper worth staying up for!

OSLO DILLED CARROTS IN CREAM

1 Pare carrots; cut into thin sticks about ¼-inch wide and 3 inches long. Cook in boiling salted water 2 minutes. Rinse under cold running water and drain.

2 Melt butter in a large saucepan over medium heat. Add carrots and reduced broth; stir to coat carrots. Add 3 tablespoons cream. Cook over high heat, stirring constantly, until mixture begins to thicken. Reduce heat; add dill. Toss well; stir in remaining 1 tablespoon cream. Season to taste with salt and pepper.

4 large carrots
2 tablespoons butter
½ cup chicken broth, boiled down to about 3 tablespoons
¼ cup whipping cream
¼ cup chopped fresh dill
Salt and freshly ground pepper to taste

Serves 4 to 5.

DILLED BEETS IN HORSERADISH CREAM

1 Pare beets. Cook in boiling salted water until almost tender, about 30 minutes. Drain. Cool slightly and dice.

2 Melt butter in a skillet. Saute Canadian bacon until lightly browned. Add beets, horseradish, and cream; toss well. Cook over low heat until thickened, 5 to 6 minutes. Season to taste with salt and pepper. Serve garnished with dill.

1¼ pounds beets
2 tablespoons butter
4 slices Canadian bacon, coarsely chopped
2 tablespoons white horseradish
½ cup whipping cream
Salt and freshly ground pepper
3 tablespoons chopped fresh dill

Serves 4.

DILLED CUCUMBERS

3 medium cucumbers
4 tablespoons butter
Salt and freshly ground pepper
1 tablespoon good strong chicken
   broth or ½ teaspoon chicken
   bouillon powder
Chopped fresh dill

Serves 4.

1 Pare the cucumbers; cut in half lengthwise and scoop out seeds. Cut into ½-inch slices; rounding off edges of slices with a sharp knife.

2 Place cucumbers in a saucepan; cover with cold water. Heat slowly to boiling. Immediately remove from heat, rinse under cold water and drain.

3 Return cucumbers to saucepan. Add 3 tablespoons of butter and salt and pepper to taste. Cover pan with a piece of well-buttered waxed paper and a lid. Cook over medium heat, until crisp-tender, 8 to 10 minutes; shake pan vigorously several times during cooking. Remove from heat. Add remaining 1 tablespoon butter and the chicken broth; toss well. Sprinkle generously with dill. Serve at once.

RÖSTI

3 medium potatoes
2 tablespoons butter
2 tablespoons vegetable oil
Salt and seasoned pepper to taste
2 teaspoons chopped fresh dill
6 strips crisply fried bacon,
   crumbled

Serves 4.

1 Shred or coarsely grate potatoes with skins.

2 Melt butter with oil in a heavy skillet over medium heat. Spread potatoes evenly in skillet. Cook without stirring 20 minutes. Sprinkle with salt, pepper, 1 teaspoon dill, and the bacon.

3 Turn potatoes over; cook 15 minutes. (The easiest way to turn potatoes without breaking them apart is to butter a second skillet of approximately the same size, place it over potatoes, and invert.) Sprinkle potatoes with remaining 1 teaspoon dill.

Garlic

I was brought up in a strictly **WASP** tradition. Both my mother and father, having been born in this country, conspicuously denied themselves the pleasurable traditions of their Eastern European Jewish forbears—out of misguided allegiance to American blandness, I am afraid.

Ours was a home where (until the day the banks failed) all meals were eaten in the dining room rather than the kitchen; where Emily Post called the shots in matters of etiquette and Fanny Farmer absolutely ruled the kitchen roost; where an aromatic seasoning like garlic—always associated with swart racial types—was as forsaken as wolf's bane.

They say talent skips a generation; I'd like to believe that's true. My mother's mother (as I have said over and over) was a magnificent cook and a passionate gardener whose sensual endowments were denied to all of her four children. Some of my aunts fell heir to her house pride and love of flowers but none of them (and least of all my mother) displayed the consuming largesse of her culinary accomplishment.

"After I am gone, you will get the crystal," my grandmother would sometimes promise—waving at an array of smoky Belgian champagne glasses or a set of particularly noteworthy clam shell goblets. "Because you alone appreciate them."

I never ceased to admire those glasses, although only by peering through the locked glass doors of her china cabinet. For though I was a rapt connoisseur of her *objets d'art,* my grandparent knew my reputation for clumsiness.

"Don't touch. Just look. But remember!" she would admonish. "When the time comes, I want you to have them."

I remembered well but others in the family (who dispersed her small legacy when the time finally came) obviously did not.

What the hell! In the end I received a better gift by far—her blessed aptitude for living extravagantly. While all her other inheritors remained unendowed in that department.

My grandmother never peeled garlic when she cooked. She merely hit the purplish bulb lightly with the back of a large, flat kitchen knife until the cloves separated slightly. Then she slipped the papery shell off as many cloves as she wanted with her fingers.

She used garlic (like a fine perfumer I once observed selecting flower petals) with meticulous concern for all the other aromas in a creation. After bruising a kernel, she would rub it over the surface of a roasting chicken but never for a moment would she consider using more than that trace on the skin. I remember watching her rub a pan for a rib roast with garlic until it practically glistened; then she threw away the clove itself so that the seasoning would not overpower the beef's essential savor.

Pin-strips of garlic cloves, cut fine as copper wire, were always inserted beneath the skin of a spring leg of lamb in her kitchen. And sometimes she would rashly cut a sliver or two into a pan of half-cooked potatoes that would later be drained and sauteed to heavenly gold in butter with parsley. But she absolutely demurred at the idea of ever using garlic in salad dressing. Even rubbing the bowl was anathema to her:

"That's too much of a good thing, I think," she would shrug when I demanded to know why. "Garlic in everything is just as bad as garlic in nothing." A slant reference to my mother's celebrated benign cookery, I suppose.

When I began to cook seriously at home, I emulated my grandmother's style as best I could. But I had to make do with garlic salt because my parent resisted the purchase of the whole bulb vociferously.

"You don't need it. It will only go to waste because you don't use it up quickly enough!" she sighed. "Besides, garlic gives bad breath!"

There was no answer to that argument. My sister was almost of a marriageable age—and we lived in a time when radio advertising warned of halitosis every time the Philco was turned on. Even I (utter destroyer of icons) knew that bad breath could blight our lives forever!

After I had cooked with garlic salt for a while, however, my parents realized that the potency of dried seasoning (particularly in my profligate hand) far outreached any damage a sliver or two of fresh might occasion. So, having stocked up on Listerine, my mother presented me with a bulb of garlic.

"Go easy," was her only comment. And I accepted that mandate. Truth to tell, I restrain myself still.

Garlic was held in ill favor for centuries. Egyptians grew it as early as 2900 B.C. but absolutely none of their extant recipes feature it as a seasoning. The pharaohs only fed it to their slaves and horses as a source of energy. And Herodotus later wrote that Cheop's Great Pyramid at Giza never could have been built if it hadn't been for the laborers' diet of garlic and onions.

Upperclass Egyptians shunned the flavoring entirely, as did the people of the Indus Valley, who abhorred the scent of garlic so strenuously that the bulbs were forbidden planting space in their vegetable gardens. Anyone with a hankering for a clove of garlic had to go out of town to grow it—and to eat it as well. But since the fine for garlic on a citizen's breath often was the removal of that citizen's nose, most Indians made do on a blander diet.

You have complete license to take garlic or leave it—but I suggest your diet would be a dull thing without a mite.

A deceptively egregious-sounding dish, Avocados with Garlic Ice Cream, comes from a notebook of memorable meals kept by Alice B. Toklas—and she really ate well. If you, like me, are a confirmed avocado-lover and always looking out for new ways to stuff the fruit, stop searching this instant!

AVOCADOS WITH GARLIC ICE CREAM

1 cup mayonnaise
2 small ripe tomatoes, peeled, finely chopped
1 small clove garlic, minced
1 small shallot, finely grated
1 teaspoon soy sauce
⅛ teaspoon hot pepper sauce
½ teaspoon seasoned salt
Pinch of ground allspice
3 or 4 ripe avocados

Serves 6 to 8.

1 Beat all ingredients except avocados together until well mixed. Pour into a freezer tray. Freeze 1 hour.

2 Remove from freezer and beat until smooth. Return to freezer tray; freeze 1 hour.

3 Cut the avocados in half and remove the pits. Scoop ¼ to ⅓ cup garlic ice cream into each avocado half.

Note: I prefer Kikkoman brand soy sauce or the light soy sauce imported from China and available in Oriental markets.

The Chinese, even in early, early times, were generous partakers of garlic in all dishes—except soup. No one seems to know why!

I like a clove of garlic in chicken soup myself, but I always fish it out after the stock has simmered for a couple of hours. Garlic is to gazpacho, the great Spanish cold soup, what Nelson Eddy was to Jeanette MacDonald when I was a boy—an indispensable adjunct. Consider two splendid versions of that noble broth: both are garlicked and furbished with assorted fresh vegetables like more conventional gazpachos, but absent is the tomato that usually hues this soup. Consequently . . .

⅔ cup salted, blanched whole
    almonds
2 large cloves garlic
1 small yellow onion, chopped
2 cups water
½ cup cubed bread, crust removed,
    soaked in milk and squeezed dry
⅓ cup olive oil
2 tablespoons tarragon vinegar
¼ cup unflavored yogurt
Salt and ground white pepper to
    taste
1 large cucumber, peeled, seeded,
    finely chopped
1 cup seedless green grapes,
    peeled, cut in halves

Serves 6.

WHITE GAZPACHO

1 Place the almonds, garlic, and onion in a blender container; add 1 cup water. Blend 3 minutes. Add the bread and oil. Blend until smooth.

2 Transfer almond puree to a mixing bowl. Beat in 1 cup water, the vinegar, yogurt, salt, and pepper to taste. Stir in the cucumber. Chill thoroughly.

3 Just before serving, taste for seasoning and add half the grapes. Ladle soup into bowls; garnish with remaining grapes.

2 cloves garlic, cut into quarters
2 shallots, cut into quarters
1 green pepper, coarsely chopped
1 cucumber, peeled, seeded,
    chopped
1 cup watercress leaves
1 tablespoon chopped fresh dill
1 cup strong chicken broth
4 teaspoons red wine vinegar
½ cup mayonnaise
½ cup sour cream
Salt and ground white pepper to
    taste

Serves 4.

And if that color does not suit your palate, try this one (named for the author, of course!):

GREENE'S
GREEN GAZPACHO

1 Place the garlic, shallots, green pepper, cucumber, watercress, dill, chicken broth, and vinegar (in that order) in a blender container. Blend 5 minutes, until very smooth. Transfer to a large mixing bowl.

2 Whisk the mayonnaise with the sour cream; whisk into the vegetable mixture. Add salt and pepper to taste. Chill at least 4 hours.

Garlic is a lily of the field actually. Distantly related to the onion, garlic, or *Allium satvium,* as it is officially known, is as far removed from a scallion or a ripe Bermuda as it is from the tiger lily on the other side of its family tree.

Applied by the Romans about three thousand years ago, the cognomen, *allium,* was corrupted to *aglio* during the Dark Ages, around the same time the Italians banned its use as a sorcerer's potion. The French later shortened the name to *ail,* which the Middle English could not pronounce at all. Their compromise translation was *garly,* which became corrupted to *garlec* during Elizabethan times. There, for all practical purposes, it has remained ever since.

One great garlic invention is a dish from Provence, where, even today, workers often breakfast on just a piece of bread dipped in olive oil and rubbed with garlic. Culinary wizardry turned that simple diet into a brilliant cold mayonnaise called *aioli,* the inventor of which goes uncredited here only because his name has been lost to the ages.

However, the man who created a perfect foil for aioli—fresh vegetables cooked *al dente*—is a culinary wizard whose name I know well. Denis Vaughan, who co-owned The Store in Amagansett with me for a glorious decade, was the first man I ever met who could undercook a vegetable like string beans and make customers stand in line to bite into them!

Denis came to his culinary devise in rebellion against the washed out, vitamin-purged veggies his Irish mother served him at home in Chicago. But not many Francophile kitchens (in Paris or New York either) were doing much better with fresh produce twenty years ago.

Overcooking and, even worse, steaming to reheat vegetables, the maverick concluded, whittled down the essential nourishment in a green and irremediably wilted its flavor. So, taking a leaf from the naturalists, Denis merely blanched his vegetables, let them rest a bit, and then reheated or simply sauced them cold before serving. His official prescription:

Have a pot of boiling, salted water on your stove. Cut your vegetables into strips. If you are using string beans, take a pair of scissors, which you should always have handy in your kitchen, snip off both tips and cut the bean in two. Rinse in cold water; then plunge into the violently boiling water while you hum a few bars of your favorite song and count to eighty. Instantly upon arriving at the magic number, remove the vegetables from the flame, pour into a colander and douse with more cold water to retard further cooking. The vegetables will then be al dente!

I never make Green Beans in Aioli without following his advice. You won't either—once you've tried the crunch on for size.

4 to 6 tablespoons Aioli (recipe follows)
1 pound green beans
1 shallot, minced
1 tablespoon chopped fresh basil (optional)
Salt and freshly ground pepper to taste
2 tablespoons finely chopped parsley

Serves 4.

GREEN BEANS IN AIOLI

1 Make aioli. Prepare and blanch the beans in the Denis Vaughan manner outlined above.

2 Place the drained beans in a bowl and mix with the shallot, basil, aioli, salt, and pepper. Refrigerate until chilled. Toss and sprinkle with parsley before serving.

AIOLI

1 slice stale homemade white bread or 2 slices French bread, ½-inch thick
3 tablespoons milk
6 cloves garlic, crushed
1 egg yolk, room temperature
¼ teaspoon salt
1 cup vegetable oil
½ cup olive oil
3 tablespoons boiling water
2 to 3 tablespoons lemon juice

Makes 2 cups.

1 Trim the crusts from the bread and break the bread into pieces in a small bowl. Add the milk and let stand 10 minutes. Twist the bread into a ball in the corner of a towel and squeeze to extract all liquid.

2 Scrape the bread into a large heavy bowl or a large mortar and pound the garlic into it with the back of a heavy wooden spoon or a pestle until a *very* smooth paste is formed, about 5 minutes. Pound in the egg yolk and salt.

3 Pound in the oil, a drop at a time, until mixture thickens; then whisk in the remaining oil, 3 tablespoons at a time until smooth. Thin with boiling water and lemon juice. Taste and add salt if necessary. Keep refrigerated.

Besides being a prime kitchen inventor, Denis Vaughan is a remarkable chef, as Southerners discovered when he took over The Olde Towne Tavern in Petersburg, Virginia, a while back. He has since established an even larger following at The French Corner, a *boîte* of impeccable culinary exequatur in Sanibel, Florida. He also teaches cooking classes that are destined to put new savor into the region's cuisine.

Here's a Denis Vaughan formula for a dish (redolent of garlic in concert with bacon) from another part of the country as well:

DENIS VAUGHAN'S NEW ENGLAND CLAM CHOWDER

1 Scrub the clams well and place in a large pot with the water, 2 tablespoons butter, 2 sprigs parsley, the bay leaf, and onion. Cover and bring to a boil over high heat. Reduce heat; simmer 5 minutes. Remove the clams from their shells; if large, cut in half. (The clams will be open far enough to pry open with a knife if necessary. Do not overcook! Discard any clams that do not open.) Strain the liquid and keep warm.

2 Cook the bacon in boiling water 5 minutes. Drain; pat dry with paper toweling. Fry in a skillet until crisp and golden brown. Drain on paper toweling. Remove all but 1 tablespoon of fat from the pan and add 2 tablespoons butter. Saute the minced onion, garlic, celery, and green pepper over medium heat 5 minutes.

3 Transfer the onion mixture to a large pot. Add the bacon and potatoes. Add the scalded milk and bring to a boil. Add the warm clam liquid.

4 Combine 3 tablespoons butter with 2 tablespoons flour; stir into the soup. Bring to a boil; reduce heat. Stir in the cream; simmer 5 minutes. Season with hot pepper sauce, Worcestershire sauce, thyme, salt, and pepper. Add the corn and clams; simmer until thick, 5 to 10 minutes. Just before serving, add the remaining 1 tablespoon butter and sprinkle with parsley. Serve with crackers or crusty French bread.

1½ to 2 quarts clams or quahogs
1½ cups water (or 1 cup clam juice and ½ cup water)
½ cup unsalted butter, room temperature
2 sprigs parsley
1 bay leaf
1 small onion stuck with 1 clove
4 thick slices bacon, diced
1 large onion, minced
1 large clove garlic, minced
1 rib celery, finely chopped
2 tablespoons minced green pepper
6 or 7 potatoes, peeled, diced, parboiled for 3 minutes
2 cups milk, scalded
2 tablespoons all-purpose flour
2 cups whipping cream
Dash of hot pepper sauce
Dash of Worcestershire sauce
¼ teaspoon fresh thyme or a pinch of dried
Salt and freshly ground pepper to taste
1 cup uncooked corn kernels
Chopped fresh parsley
Crackers or French bread

Serves 6 to 8.

While garlic and clams play an irresistible duet, scallops wait in the wings. Another garlicky inspiration, from the south of France this time:

SCALLOPS D'AIL

1 Wash the scallops and dry between layers of paper toweling. If using sea scallops, cut them into quarters.

1¼ pounds bay or sea scallops
6 tablespoons butter
3 large cloves garlic, minced
1 tablespoon all-purpose flour
1 large ripe tomato, seeded, chopped
6 green onions with tops, chopped
Pinch of thyme
⅓ cup vermouth
2 tablespoons lemon juice
½ teaspoon salt
⅛ teaspoon freshly ground pepper
2 tablespoons finely chopped parsley

Serves 2 to 3.

2 In a large skillet, melt 2 tablespoons butter. Add ⅓ of the garlic; cook over medium heat 1 minute. Add ⅓ of the scallops; cook over high heat, stirring constantly, until golden, 5 to 6 minutes. Transfer to a warm serving platter. Repeat the process with remaining butter, garlic, and scallops. Keep warm in the oven.

3 Sprinkle the flour into the skillet and stir until all liquid is absorbed. Add the tomato, onions, and thyme; cook over medium heat until the tomato is soft. Gradually stir in the vermouth and lemon juice; cook until the sauce is syrupy. Stir in salt and pepper.

4 Pour the sauce over the scallops and sprinkle with the chopped parsley. Serve hot.

Note: Recipe may be doubled.

I was about fourteen or fifteen when I started to cook with garlic. Shortly afterward, I acquired my first garlic press. My grandmother never trusted that gadget because she was such an estimable chopper. My mother, who was not, heartily approved.

"Because our hands won't stink of garlic anymore," she stated flatly.

She was right, I suppose. Over the years I certainly have had a succession of these garlic mangles in my various kitchens and used them to signal advantage—but with a nagging doubt, of late, about their efficacy.

My misgiving stems, I know, from an article that appeared in *House Beautiful.* Back in 1974, that publication ran a story entitled "The Ultimate Utensil," in which fourteen enthusiastic chefs (myself included) were asked to name their prized kitchen tools. I brightly named a French enameled pan, a balloon whisk and copper bowl, *and* a garlic press.

In the same article, not two paragraphs away, Craig Claiborne's list appeared—with the garlic press conspicuously absent from his collection of steamers, woks, and a professional meat-slicing machine. Quizzed, he expressed his dislike of that bit of equipment vociferously.

"I wouldn't dare use a garlic press," he snapped, "because it transforms the flavor of garlic!"

A cooking pal of mine, perusing a copy of the article, noted the dissidence of our opinions guardedly.

"Does this make you feel foolish?" he inquired, pointing to Mr. Claiborne's smiling photograph.

"Not in the least," I replied indignantly. "He's just being posy. I always use a garlic press. Don't you?"

"Of course, of course," my slightly intimidated friend replied.

I cannot rightly state when this canker surfaced into a full-blown boil. But when I began to write about food for a living, my cooking techniques started to change. Gradually, they became more prudent, more carefully attuned. Bouillon powder, for instance (once my culinary panacea whenever a dish failed to measure up to my flavor expectation), was gradually replaced with a pinch of allspice or a teaspoon or two of boiled-down strong stock. Likewise, a sharp carbon chopping knife (from Japan) was substituted for my garlic press.

I can't precisely recall when I began to chop garlic instead of pressing it. Why, is an even touchier subject. I certainly hadn't recognized Mr. Claiborne's purported transformation of flavor, but I began to suspect that the master (along with James Beard, Jacques Pépin, and Marcella Hazan) knew his onions! And, indeed, I discovered that garlic minced with a knife does hold a more delicate bouquet and a subtler, less oily flavor than garlic mashed in a press.

So I have joined the great cooks' conspiracy—making more work for mother! For that, dear reader, forgive me.

In the following recipe for Lamb Chops Persille, however, the garlic should be *mashed*. I solve that dilemma equitably by chopping it very fine (first with vertical strokes, then by back-tracking horizontally) until it is the texture of sea salt. Then, using the flat side of my knife blade, I whack it a few times. *Et voilà!* Mashed!

LAMB CHOPS PERSILLE

1 Heat oven to 400°. Rub the chops well with the mashed garlic. Sprinkle with salt and pepper.

2 Rub a heavy skillet with 1 tablespoon butter and brown the chops on both sides over high heat. Remove chops.

3 Wipe out the skillet and add the remaining butter. Cook the minced garlic and the bread crumbs over medium heat 3 minutes; stir in the parsley. Pat the garlic mixture over the tops of the lamb chops.

4 Place the chops in a shallow baking dish. Bake 10 minutes for medium rare or longer if preferred. Place under the broiler 1 minute to brown.

4 thick rib lamb chops
1 clove garlic, mashed
Salt and freshly ground pepper
4 tablespoons butter
1 large clove garlic, minced
¼ cup fresh bread crumbs
⅓ cup finely chopped parsley

Serves 2.

No meat seems more unexpectedly delicious after a liberal seasoning with garlic than pork, unless it is ham—but that is the same thing, I suppose. This recipe is not truly unusual, but it is salutory in its celebration of homely flavors. It's the kind of dish I love best.

ROAST PORK WITH GARLIC

1 center cut pork roast (about 6 pounds)
3 large cloves garlic
Salt and freshly ground pepper
2 tablespoons vegetable oil
1 teaspoon chopped fresh thyme leaves or ½ teaspoon dried
1 onion, cut into quarters
1 cup chicken stock

Serves 6 to 8.

1 Heat oven to 400°. Cut each clove of garlic into 8 slivers. Cut small slits between the bones on the rib side of the roast and insert 3 of the slivers. Turn the meat over, cut small slits on the fat side of the roast, and insert remaining slivers.

2 Rub the meat well on both sides with salt and pepper. Rub with the oil. Place in a shallow roasting pan, fat side down; sprinkle with thyme. Add the onion quarters. Roast meat 1 hour; then turn fat side up. Baste with pan juices and ¼ cup chicken stock. Roast ½ hour.

3 Pour off all fat from the pan. Add remaining chicken stock, scraping loose any brown particles in the pan. Roast ¾ hour, basting occasionally. Serve pork with pan gravy on the side.

Note: Have your butcher crack the bone at the base of the ribs in the pork roast for easier carving.

Another peasanty dish for garlic aficionados is this Provençal recipe for chicken sauteed with small, tender potatoes. Easy to prepare, it nevertheless gives the impression of a great *cuisinier* when you are in need of such an ego boost.
    Consider serving it with a salad of raw tomatoes with basil (but no garlic) and oil and vinegar in generous amounts. Have plenty of crusty bread on the table—and damn the carbohydrates!

CHICKEN SAUTE

1 Heat oven to 325°. Peel the potatoes and cover with salted water. Bring to a boil. Reduce heat; simmer 5 minutes. Drain.

2 Sprinkle the chicken with salt and pepper. Saute in butter and oil in a large skillet over medium heat until golden, about 10 minutes on each side. Transfer to a baking dish and sprinkle with rosemary.

3 Add the potatoes to the skillet; cook over medium heat, turning occasionally, until light brown, about 5 minutes. Remove from skillet and arrange around the chicken.

4 Add the mushrooms to the skillet. Saute until golden. Remove from skillet and spoon over chicken.

5 Add the garlic to the skillet with the stock and cream. Bring to a boil; cook over high heat 3 minutes, scraping the sides and bottom of the pan. Add salt and pepper to taste. Pour over chicken; bake 25 to 30 minutes. Garnish with parsley.

12 small new potatoes
1 chicken (3½ to 4 pounds), cut into serving pieces
Salt and freshly ground pepper
3 tablespoons butter
1 tablespoon olive oil
1 teaspoon chopped fresh rosemary or ½ teaspoon dried
½ pound mushrooms, sliced
3 cloves garlic, minced
¼ cup chicken stock
2 tablespoons cream
Salt and freshly ground pepper
Chopped fresh parsley

Serves 4.

In Morocco, Kufte (garlic-scented meat patties) are sold on the street at every *souk*. The seller, usually at the very entrance to a *medina,* keeps a bowl of meat mixture near his charcoal brazier and marvelously blackened fry pan. The mixture is a target for green flies that he never bothers to swat but merely waves away when he has a customer (with an appetite) waiting.

I have known travelers (alive and still well) who insist that a Kufte sampled in Marrakesh is twice as tasty as one eaten in my kitchen. But you can't prove it by me! You'll love the savor— one way or t'other.

1½ pounds ground lamb
½ pound ground beef
¼ pound ground veal
2 cloves garlic, mashed
1 medium onion, finely chopped
½ cup bread crumbs
Pinch of ground allspice
1 tablespoon chopped fresh mint or 1 teaspoon dried
2 tablespoons chopped parsley
Dash of hot pepper sauce
1 egg
¼ cup water
½ teaspoon salt
⅛ teaspoon freshly ground pepper
2 tablespoons olive oil
3 tablespoons butter

KUFTE

1 Combine all ingredients except oil and butter. Mix thoroughly and form into sausages, each about 3 inches long and ¾ inch thick. (Kufte must not be too thin or they will break.)

2 Heat the oil in a heavy skillet until hot; stir in the butter until melted. Add the sausages and cook over medium heat until deep golden on all sides. Shake the pan back and forth to turn the sausages; do not use a fork as the uncooked meat tends to fall apart. Drain on paper toweling. Serve immediately or keep at room temperature until serving time and reheat in the oven at 300°.

Serves 4 to 6.

Back in the seventeenth century, Thomas Nashe said that "garlic makes a man wink, drink and stink." I do not agree. Garlic lovers, I have noted, share neither lechery nor venery in common and they keep their breath sweetened by eating parsley after dinner. Hence the garnish for the next dish. The mint formula for Garlic Mashed Potatoes, an eminently delectable vegetable, appeared in *Mastering the Art of French Cooking I.* And I hereby thank the authors, Mesdames Child, Beck, and Bertholle for their culinary triumph. I fiddled with it only slightly in the early days of The Store, when Denis Vaughan and I prepared hundreds of pounds of these potatoes for other people's Thanksgiving dinners. (We ate hamburgers and frozen French fries instead.)

Thirty cloves of garlic are the wonderful aspect of this recipe around which the flavors of potatoes, butter, and cream meld. I adore this dish with turkey, as you may have gathered, but it's dandy with any roast beef or (ungarlicked) roast pork of your acquaintance.

GARLIC MASHED POTATOES

2 bulbs garlic or about 30 cloves
½ cup unsalted butter, softened
2 tablespoons all-purpose flour
1 cup boiling milk
¼ teaspoon salt
Pinch of ground white pepper
2½ pounds baking potatoes
⅓ cup whipping cream
Salt and freshly ground pepper
1 tablespoon finely chopped
   parsley for garnish

Serves 6 to 8.

1 Separate the cloves of garlic. Drop into boiling water; cook 2 minutes. Drain, cool slightly, and peel.

2 Melt 4 tablespoons butter in a heavy saucepan. Add the garlic. Cook covered over low heat until tender, about 20 minutes. Do not allow to brown.

3 Stir in the flour. Cook 2 minutes and remove from heat. Whisk in the milk, salt, and pepper. Return to heat; boil 1 minute.

4 Transfer garlic mixture to a blender container; puree until smooth. Return to saucepan.

5 Peel the potatoes and cut into quarters. Drop into boiling salted water. Cook until tender, 15 to 20 minutes; drain. Rice potatoes with a potato ricer. Keep hot.

6 Cook garlic puree over medium heat, stirring constantly, until moisture is evaporated. Remove from heat. Beat in remaining butter and the potatoes. Beat in the cream and season to taste with salt and pepper. Sprinkle with parsley.

Montaigne said: "Give me a kitchen full of utensils and a stock of unprepared food and I would starve." I am more resourceful, thank God. A leftover loaf of bread and a package of frozen spinach plus a mite of cheese can provide any householder with a spectacular timbale/soufflé to nip malnutrition in the bud. The recipes for Tian Épinard, and for Broccoli d'Ail, the warmish broccoli salad that follows, were cajoled from a Provençal innkeeper's wife. Both are secrets worth their weight in garlic, if not gold.

TIAN ÉPINARD

1 Remove the crust from the bread (save for bread crumbs); break bread into chunks. Place in large bowl; cover with hot water. Soak 5 minutes; squeeze dry.

2 Chop the bread and place in a mixing bowl with the onion, garlic, parsley, egg, 1 teaspoon oil, and 1½ tablespoons cheese. Mix thoroughly.

3 Melt the butter in a heavy skillet. Add the shallot and ham; saute over medium heat 4 minutes. Stir in the spinach. Add the nutmeg, bouillon or stock, and Madeira. Season to taste with salt and pepper. Cook over high heat, stirring occasionally, until the liquid has been absorbed, about 5 minutes. Remove from heat.

4 Heat oven to 350°. Brush a baking sheet with 1 tablespoon oil. Divide the bread mixture into two portions. Shape one portion into a ball and press down on the baking sheet to form a 9-inch circle. Sprinkle with 1½ tablespoons oil and 1½ tablespoons cheese. Spread evenly with the spinach mixture.

5 Shape the remaining bread mixture into a ball and flatten with your hands as much as possible. Gently press flattened bread mixture over the spinach to cover; press edges inward to seal filling. Sprinkle with the remaining oil and cheese. Place in oven; increase heat to 425°. Bake 15 minutes. Reduce heat to 375°; bake until golden and crisp, 50 to 60 minutes. Transfer to a serving platter; let stand 10 minutes before cutting.

Note: To make a variation, Tian Mozzarella Aux Anchois, follow Steps 1, 2, and 4 of the recipe, substituting ¾ cup of mozzarella cheese, cut into ¼-inch cubes, and ½ can anchovy fillets, finely chopped, for the spinach mixture. Proceed with Step 5.

1 loaf (1 pound) French or Italian bread
1 onion, finely chopped
2 large cloves garlic, minced
½ cup chopped fresh parsley
1 egg
4 tablespoons plus 1 teaspoon olive oil
5 tablespoons grated Parmesan cheese
2 tablespoons butter
1 shallot, chopped
½ cup coarsely chopped ham
1 package frozen chopped spinach, thawed
⅛ teaspoon freshly grated nutmeg
1 packet chicken bouillon powder or 1 teaspoon reduced chicken stock
1 teaspoon Madeira wine
Salt and freshly ground pepper

Serves 8.

BROCCOLI D'AIL

1 bunch of broccoli, cut into 3-inch flowerets
¼ cup unsalted butter
2 tablespoons olive oil
6 cloves garlic, minced
1 tablespoon chopped fresh basil or 1 teaspoon dried
Salt
1 tablespoon tarragon vinegar
2 tablespoons red wine vinegar
½ cup finely chopped macadamia nuts
Freshly ground black pepper
Lemon wedges

Serves 8.

1 Drop the broccoli into boiling salted water; cook 2 minutes. Rinse under cold running water until cool; drain.

2 Melt the butter with the oil in a large skillet. Add the garlic and saute until golden. Add the basil and broccoli; cook and stir over high heat until the broccoli wilts slightly and is fork tender. Add salt to taste.

3 Add the tarragon vinegar and remove from heat; mix well. Add the wine vinegar; mix again. Place in a serving dish and sprinkle with the nuts. Season well with pepper. Garnish with lemon wedges. Serve hot or at room temperature.

The only hors d'oeuvre I ever serve before dinner at my house are the following wonderful Garlic Almonds. I made up the recipe while thinking of things to give friends for Christmas and, I must confess, the flavor changed slightly from batch to batch until a captious friend caught me in the act and wrote down the prescription. Now the Garlic Almonds are standardized—but I liked them better off the cuff!

GARLIC ALMONDS

1 tablespoon unsalted butter
2 teaspoons red pepper sauce
3 cloves garlic, mashed
2 tablespoons soy sauce
1 pound blanched whole almonds
¼ teaspoon crushed hot red peppers
1 tablespoon seasoned pepper
Salt

Makes 1 pound.

1 Heat oven to 350°. Grease a baking sheet with the butter and sprinkle with hot pepper sauce, garlic, and soy sauce. Spread the almonds over the sheet and stir with a fork until well coated with the seasonings. Sprinkle with crushed red peppers, 1½ teaspoons seasoned pepper, and salt.

2 Bake 10 minutes. Sprinkle almonds with remaining seasoned pepper and more salt; stir with fork. Bake 15 minutes longer. Cool before serving. Garlic Almonds can be stored in a jar with a tight-fitting lid for up to 3 months.

Good cooks are apt to experiment. I won't be offended in the least if you feel you must tamper with my almonds (or even turn them into pecans on occasion). That's how great garlic recipes came about in the first place!

Ginger

How do you feel about ZuZus?

You read it correctly the first time—and there is no slant reference to a carnivorous appetite in that query either. I practically grew up on ZuZus and find that, as with Animal Crackers, I still have—as they say down South—a passing mouth for those beloved childhood cookies.

I never chance upon a supermarket anywhere (even in the Soviet Union) without immediately casing its aisles in quest of this treat. And though I did find a pack once at a roadside greengrocer on the way to Pontpridd, Wales, I was fully aware of the anachronism. Elsewhere, the sweet tidbits have long been retired to a Mount Olympus marketplace where other delights of my youth are stored—sharing a shelf of memory with Nabs, LoveNests, and Frozen Malts (the drink you eat with a spoon!).

ZuZus were even more special than the others. A tangy treat to the tongue (as claimed on the label), they were what I, in my dotage now, would pronounce the perfect mini-gingersnap. A circle of crackled spice, they were round as a half dollar in the palm and a lot harder on the teeth. ZuZus took forever to chew and were, therefore, prime snack food for movie-going. A slender box (containing twenty cookies) usually lasted through an entire feature and well into the short subjects as well.

Best of all, they reminded me of the taste of gingerbread men, but were a good deal less difficult to come by after the yuletide passed. A yellow oblong box (emblazoned with a prancing impertinent monkey) cost only a nickel and stemmed the appetite for some while after purchase because the cookies were so zesty in flavor. The contents of a ZuZu box, moreover, were absolutely guaranteed to leave a kid's molars the color of taffy apples. Oh, I dearly loved them.

In my home, ZuZus were also a kitchen staple, called into service whenever sauerbraten or stuffed cabbage was on the family menu. The practice of tossing gingersnaps into the cookpot began with the first nursemaid I can remember, a pink-faced country girl, newly arrived from Hungary, who passed on more than one prized recipe from her country's heritage during her stay with us. Marion (that was her name) added the crumbled cookies to a pot roast along with a spare handful of raisins, apples, and a chopped onion. And long after pretty Marion returned to Budapest to marry, my mother's cooking retained that distinctive hue and tang.

Until I was fully grown, I associated ginger exclusively with Slavic cookery because of Marion's influence. So it came as something of a shock, years later, to discover Marco Polo's role. Returning to the Adriatic from China, the explorer carried a few corms of a golden ginger plant tucked inside his knapsack as a souvenir—a present to European cuisine from Ghengis Khan.

Ginger is definitely Orient born and bred. One of the classic five Chinese seasonings, it takes its name from the area where it was first discovered growing wild (centuries and centuries before the birth of Christ), the Gingi district of India.

Wild ginger was transplanted to China by roving bands of Mongolian *blamas* (monk-cooks), who moved from Asian city to city during the first century A.D.—promulgating religious and culinary wisdom from their rice bowls among landowners who had previously subsisted on raw meat and vegetables. Ginger rapidly became so well established that it is still known in China as "the favorite son of the kitchen god."

A cousin of the gladiola, ginger is a romantic plant. The beckoning perfume of a ginger blossom, which is always pure white, is said to lead all needy chefs to its root, where the flavor lies. According to more Chinese folklore, the flower is so compelling that it stuns a viewer on first sight, and a plain woman wearing a bloom will seem to have irresistible allure. Hence came the rumor of ginger as a potion of love.

The Romans first procured the phallic-shaped ginger roots from Egyptian traders who cruised into Asian waters and they treated the spice exclusively as an aphrodisiac—an item always in short supply in heady Rome, it seems. Pliny, the food and drink critic of the ancient world, attributed the tonic action of the root on a male's waning member to the fact that the rhizomes were first cultivated "in a land overrun by horny, yellow Troglodytes."

Today ginger is no longer considered a tumescent medication for man or beast—although a veterinarian I know reports that horse traders (the unscrupulous kind) now and then place a pinch of powdered ginger under a horse's tail to force the animal to hoist it higher when being shown for sale.

But that's obviously a different kind of gingersnap.

My fondly remembered nurse, Marion, insinuated her way into our hearts and bellies when I was young with a wondrous sweet and sour pot roast (exuberantly flavored with eight crushed ZuZus) that is like no other sauerbraten I have ever eaten.

GINGERED SAUERBRATEN

1 Place the meat in a ceramic or enamel dish wide enough so that the meat lies flat. Add the vinegar, water, cloves, parsley, bay leaves, celery, thyme, rosemary, basil, juniper berries, onion, and garlic. Cover tightly and refrigerate 3 to 4 days, turning meat twice daily.

2 Heat oven to 325°. Heat the oil or bacon drippings in a heavy skillet and sear the meat on all sides. Transfer the meat to a Dutch oven and pour the marinade over it. Add the pureed tomatoes, beef stock, brown sugar, lemon juice, lemon peel, gingersnaps, Worcestershire sauce, and bouillon. Cover and bake until tender, 3½ to 4 hours. Remove meat to serving platter. Strain the sauce and serve with the meat.

Another childhood dish I remember well is sweet and sour cabbage (courtesy of Marion too, I suppose). My mother's hand-inscribed cookbooks somehow became mislaid late in her life (after she had moved cross-country to California and then restlessly returned, a year or so later). So I have had to approximate the savory taste of this green and red farrago. But it's a mighty good approximation.

SWEET AND SOUR CABBAGE

1 Melt 3 tablespoons butter in a large saucepan. Saute the shallot and apple over medium heat until tender, about 5 minutes.

2 Add remaining ingredients, except the butter, and cook over medium-high heat until the cabbage is tender but still crunchy, 8 to 10 minutes. Taste for seasoning; cabbage may require additional ground ginger and salt to accent the flavors. Stir in remaining butter.

1 beef brisket (3½ to 4 pounds)
1 cup vinegar
1 cup water
8 cloves
6 sprigs parsley
2 bay leaves
2 celery ribs with leaves, coarsely chopped
1 teaspoon chopped fresh thyme or ½ teaspoon dried
1 teaspoon chopped fresh rosemary or ½ teaspoon dried
1 teaspoon chopped fresh basil or ½ teaspoon dried
2 crushed juniper berries
1 onion, sliced
2 cloves garlic, minced
2 tablespoons vegetable oil or bacon drippings
2 large tomatoes, peeled, pureed
1½ cups beef stock or broth
1 tablespoon brown sugar
1 tablespoon lemon juice
1 teaspoon slivered lemon peel
8 gingersnaps, crushed
1 tablespoon Worcestershire sauce
2 packets beef bouillon powder or 2 beef bouillon cubes

Serves 6 to 8.

4 tablespoons butter
1 shallot, finely chopped
1 apple, pared, cored, chopped
½ medium red cabbage, coarsely chopped
½ medium green cabbage, coarsely chopped
1 teaspoon ground ginger
2 tablespoons red wine vinegar
½ teaspoon salt
⅛ teaspoon freshly ground pepper

Serves 4.

Indian cuisine is highly dependent upon the pharmacy of ginger. A very special dish from Kashmir, Chicken Jasmine, combines the spice with yogurt and a scant touch of chili powder—and very little else—for absolutely propitious results. After being sauteed and lightly broiled, the meat is the color of pale fire but the taste is celestial bliss.

CHICKEN JASMINE

1 chicken (3 to 3½ pounds), cut into serving pieces
Salt and freshly ground pepper to taste
1 teaspoon ground ginger
5 tablespoons butter
1½ pints unflavored yogurt
Chili powder
Chopped parsley for garnish
4 cups cooked rice

Serves 4.

1 Heat oven to 275°. Rub the chicken well with salt, pepper, and ginger.

2 Melt the butter in a large skillet. Add the chicken and saute about 5 minutes on each side. Remove the chicken and whisk in the yogurt.

3 Return the chicken to the skillet and cook over medium heat 20 minutes, basting often. Turn the chicken; cook 20 minutes longer.

4 Remove the chicken to a shallow heatproof serving dish and sprinkle each piece with a pinch of chili powder. Keep warm in the oven. Cook the sauce over medium heat until very thick, about 5 minutes. Spoon the sauce over the chicken. Just before serving, place under the broiler to lightly brown the top, about 1 minute. Sprinkle with parsley and serve with rice. (And pass the chutney.)

Ginger as a spice is available to cooks in three forms:

Ground Jamaica ginger—for sweet dishes traditionally flavored with powdered spice, like cookies. Try a pinch in strong black coffee sometime soon.

Whole dried ginger root—from the Moluccas, grown between Sulawasi and New Guinea, this is sometimes known as gray ginger. Cognoscenti grind the dried root, like black peppercorns, as they cook. The French use bits of the dried bark in infusions for tea.

Whole fresh ginger root—a prerequisite in practically all Chinese, Japanese, and Indian cooking, this is also known as three finger ginger because of the configuration of its root stock. It is very tonic in the following Szechwan pork and rice dish, which is served in bright green wrappings of fresh lettuce.

PORK FRIED RICE IN LETTUCE LEAVES

1 Melt 1 tablespoon butter in a heavy skillet. Stir in the eggs and cook over very low heat, stirring frequently, until soft and creamy, about 15 minutes.

2 Melt remaining butter in a wok or heavy skillet and add the meat. Cook the meat over high heat, stirring to break up any lumps, until no longer pink.

3 Stir in the ginger and mix thoroughly. Add the rice, the shallot mixture, and the soy sauce; mix well. Stir in the eggs. Add salt and pepper to taste.

4 Place 1 tablespoonful of the Pork Fried Rice on each lettuce leaf and roll up—or allow guests to do it right at the table.

Note: Serves 4 as a first course. Recipe can be doubled.

2 tablespoons butter
2 eggs, lightly beaten
½ pound ground pork
1 teaspoon grated fresh ginger root or ½ teaspoon ground ginger
1 cup hot cooked rice
2 shallots minced with 2 large sprigs parsley
Dash of soy sauce
Salt and freshly ground pepper
Lettuce leaves

Serves 2 to 3.

Fresh ginger root spoils quickly. So some cooks freeze it. Others bury the root in a little pot of soil—like a window plant— watering it as they would a geranium. The ginger does stay fresh in its flower pot—and it may even send up new shoots. Mine did! When a recipe calls for fresh ginger, cavalier chefs merely dig up the root, snip off a bit, and bury it again. Gingerphiles I know claim to preserve their ginger in this manner for years.

I am an iconoclast in the matter and also bury a root in a small apothecary jar filled with sherry, which definitely retards growth. Vodka works in a pinch too. This marinating process produces a nice gingery essence that can be used from time to time—whenever a sauce needs a vitamin shot from the doctor at the stove. Keeping your ginger stewed, as it were, also manages to preserve the root in a fairly firm condition, especially if it is not exposed to too much air!

I find that freshly grated ginger imparts a flavor decidedly different from that of the ground spice. Taste the difference yourself in Cold Avocado Soup.

COLD AVOCADO SOUP

1 Melt the butter and stir in the flour. Cook over low heat, stirring constantly, 3 minutes. Gradually stir in the milk and cream. Cook until thick.

4 tablespoons butter
4 tablespoons all-purpose flour
2 cups milk, hot
2 cups light cream, hot
3 avocados
¼ teaspoon grated fresh ginger root
Grated peel of 1 orange
Salt

Serves 8.

2 Peel the avocados. Cut enough avocado into cubes to equal 1 cup; reserve.

3 Mash the remaining avocado and stir into the milk mixture. Add the ginger and orange peel. Transfer mixture to a blender container; blend until smooth. (If soup is too thick, thin with additional milk.) Add salt to taste. Chill.

4 Serve soup icy cold garnished with the avocado cubes.

A favorite summery dish of mine is a cold jellied meat loaf, the flavoring of which is dependent upon a mite of raw ginger. It seems simple-minded, I know, to warn you not to make it if that ingredient is missing, but something of the unusual flavor goes awry when the ginger is not fresh.

COLD JELLIED LOAF

1½ pounds veal shoulder with
    bones
1½ pounds lamb shoulder with
    bones
1 bay leaf
2 teaspoons salt
5 peppercorns
2 onions, sliced
½ teaspoon grated lemon peel
1 teaspoon freshly ground pepper
½ teaspoon minced fresh ginger
    root
½ teaspoon ground allspice
1 envelope unflavored gelatin
½ cup strong chicken stock or
    broth
Watercress leaves

Serves 6 to 8.

1 Place the meats, bay leaf, salt, peppercorns, and one sliced onion in a large pot with enough water to cover. Bring to a boil; reduce heat. Simmer covered until meat is tender, 1½ to 2 hours.

2 Remove the meat and discard bones. Strain the cooking liquid; discard seasonings. Bring liquid to a boil and cook over high heat until reduced to about 1 quart.

3 Grind the meat with the remaining onion. Stir in the lemon peel, pepper, ginger root, and allspice. Add the meat to the cooking liquid; cook over low heat 10 minutes. Remove from heat.

4 Soften the gelatin in the chicken stock in the top of a double boiler. Place over hot water; stir until dissolved. Stir into meat mixture; mix thoroughly. Pour meat mixture into a greased 9- × 5-inch loaf pan and cool. Chill in the refrigerator overnight. Unmold and garnish with watercress.

If all that palaver about fresh ginger makes your cannister of powdered feel unloved, console it with a bit of excessive usage

soon. Ground ginger is astounding when mashed to a paste with garlic and rubbed all over a pot roast before the meat is browned. It's also a wonder-worker for fish fillets. Sprinkle it on the ubiquitous flounder before the flouring up and I promise you a sensuous fish fry.

And if all the foregoing leaves you cold, try and make a pot of creamed chipped beef without ground ginger. I'd rather heat up my old hat for dinner!

CREAMED CHIPPED BEEF ON BAKED POTATOES

1 Heat oven to 400°. Bake potatoes until a fork easily pierces the skin, 50 to 55 minutes.

2 While the potatoes are baking, cover the chipped beef with boiling water; let stand 5 minutes. Drain and chop coarsely.

3 Melt 4 tablespoons butter in a large saucepan over medium heat. Add the minced onion; saute until barely golden, about 5 minutes. Add the flour and stir quickly until well blended. Whisk in the hot broth; cook, stirring constantly, until sauce begins to thicken. Stir in the beef, cream, mustard, ginger, and hot pepper sauce. Cook over low heat, stirring constantly, until smooth. Stir in the sherry. (The creamed beef should have a velvety consistency; if it is too thick, thin with a little milk.)

4 Cut the baked potatoes lengthwise in half; fluff the centers with a fork and dot each half with ½ tablespoon butter. Spoon creamed chipped beef onto each half. Sprinkle with chopped parsley.

4 large baking potatoes
6 ounces dried chipped beef
¾ cup boiling water
½ cup unsalted butter
2 tablespoons minced onion or shallot
4 tablespoons all-purpose flour
1 cup hot chicken broth
¾ cup whipping cream
½ teaspoon Dijon mustard
¼ teaspoon ground ginger
Dash of hot pepper sauce
Jigger of sherry
Chopped fresh parsley

Serves 4.

Gingerbread was created by the Egyptians, according to Apicius. It is still probably the most popular food made with the spice, and that includes a heck of a lot of gingered pork rice being stir-fried all over the Peoples Republic of China, too!

Gingerbread came to its full flower during the reign of Elizabeth I of England. That lady, often noted as the Virgin Queen, employed a court baker whose only job was to fashion gingerbread likenesses of all her court.

My mother, as I have implied, was not a particularly inspired cook, but somewhere in her cooking apprenticeship (perhaps even at Grandma's elbow) she learned how to make the best gingerbread I ever tasted. What's even more remarkable, to my way of thinking, is that my mother could just walk into the kitchen, start pulling a few ingredients together, and—without cracking Irma Rombauer or Fanny Farmer at all—produce in minutes a luscious, spicy, heart-warming dessert. In my mother's house we ate it most often with cream cheese and thick raspberry jam. Now I prefer whipped cream. This recipe is not my mother's—that was lost along with the sweet and sour cabbage—but it's every bit as good!

GINGERBREAD

½ cup unsalted butter
1 cup granulated sugar
2 eggs
1 cup buttermilk
2 teaspoons baking soda
1 cup molasses
2½ cups all-purpose flour
½ teaspoon ground cinnamon
½ teaspoon ground cloves
2 teaspoons ground ginger
½ cup dried currants
Sweetened whipped cream

Serves 6 to 8.

1 Heat oven to 375°. Cream the butter and sugar together until light and fluffy. Beat in the eggs, one at a time, beating well after each addition.

2 Mix the buttermilk with the baking soda. Stir into the molasses.

3 Sift the flour with the cinnamon, cloves, and ginger. Stir in the currants. Add the flour mixture to the butter mixture in three parts, alternating with thirds of the buttermilk mixture. Mix well.

4 Pour the batter into a buttered 9-inch square cake pan. Bake until a toothpick inserted in center comes out clean, 50 to 60 minutes. Cool and serve with sweetened whipped cream.

In France they call ginger *l'epice blanche,* the white spice. It was first used in a French kitchen in 1350 by Taillevent, who later became *chef extraordinaire* to King Charles VII. But although ginger was an integral part of *cuisine de la faire* for two centuries after—flavoring oceans of souffles and acres of tart pastry—it lost its popularity (along with powdered wigs) after the French Revolution. Historians and food snoops alike are cloudy on the reason for this lapse—except that one of Marie Antoinette's favorite indulgences, a ginger ice, may have damned the spice irredeemably for popular consumption!

Even today, the best French cooks are chary of ginger in their creations. One exception to this prejudice is *mousse gingembre,* a production served in the late, great Trocadero restaurant in Paris.

Here is my humble attempt to duplicate that shimmeringly fragile dessert. You'll note that the recipe calls for crystallized ginger, which is the scraping of the raw root cooked until it becomes completely transparent, then rolled in granulated sugar and dried. Preserved ginger is exactly the same stuff but boiled until barely tender and kept intact in a sweet, thickish syrup. Both are considered confections rather than spices—but both add gingery tang to sweet dishes.

GINGERED MOUSSE

1 Combine 1½ cups milk, the granulated sugar, nutmeg, 1 teaspoon ground ginger, and 2 tablespoons crystallized ginger in a small saucepan; bring to a boil.

2 Beat the egg yolks with the cornstarch and rum in the top of a double boiler. Gradually whisk in the milk mixture. Cook over simmering water, stirring constantly, until thick enough to coat a wooden spoon.

3 Soften the gelatin in ½ cup milk; let stand several minutes. Stir the gelatin into the thickened egg yolk mixture; cook 5 minutes. Cool; refrigerate until mixture begins to set, about 30 minutes.

4 Whip the cream with the confectioners' sugar and 1 teaspoon ground ginger until stiff. Fold into chilled custard. (If gelatin has already set, beat until smooth with a few drops of boiling water before folding in cream.)

5 Beat the egg whites until stiff but not dry; fold into the custard.

6 Spoon mixture into a 2-quart souffle dish or serving bowl. Refrigerate at least 4 hours before serving. Garnish with remaining crystallized ginger.

2 cups milk
1 cup granulated sugar
½ teaspoon ground nutmeg
2 teaspoons ground ginger
¼ cup finely chopped crystallized ginger
4 eggs, separated
4 teaspoons cornstarch, sifted
2 tablespoons dark rum
2 teaspoons unflavored gelatin
1 cup whipping cream
¼ cup confectioners' sugar

Serves 8 to 10.

An Italian I know gave me the following formula for what he claims is a very Siennese cheese tart. The recipe calls for a crust of crushed gingersnaps. How do you suppose they translate ZuZu in Italian?

The filling, which resembles a pudding, is dense and white and gingered to a fare-thee-well. You'll love it.

TORTA ZENZERO AL FORNO

Butter
1 cup crushed gingersnaps
¼ cup butter, melted
2 pounds cream cheese, room
  temperature
½ cup whipping cream
4 eggs
1½ cups granulated sugar
2 teaspoons ground ginger
Grated peel of 1 tangerine
½ cup finely chopped crystallized
  ginger
½ cup finely chopped dried or
  crystallized pineapple
Confectioners' sugar

Serves 12 to 14.

1 Heat oven to 325°. Wrap the outside of a 9-inch springform pan with a piece of aluminum foil measuring 16 × 18 inches. Fold over the rim to secure. Butter the inside of the pan. Combine the crushed gingersnaps with the melted butter and press over the bottom and halfway up the sides of the pan.

2 Beat the cream cheese with an electric mixer until fluffy. Add the cream, eggs, sugar, ground ginger, and tangerine peel. Beat until smooth. Stir in the chopped crystallized ginger and the pineapple. Pour into the prepared pan.

3 Place the pan in a large roasting pan and pour boiling water around it to a depth of 2 inches. Bake 1 hour and 30 minutes. Turn off heat and let cake stand in oven 1 hour longer.

4 Remove the cake from the oven and let it cool on a wire rack for 2 hours. Run a sharp knife around the edge and remove the side. Invert cake onto a serving platter. Chill at least 2 hours. Just before serving, dust with confectioners' sugar.

There is no sign of prejudice against ginger in Anglo-Saxon countries, thank God. The English and their breed add ginger to ale, beers, and brandies. They even have a special ginger wine that they drink on holidays. English cooks have produced some of the most notable sponges, flavored with ginger and cream, and entrancing fruit tarts, enriched with gingery caramel, that I have ever set my tongue upon. Two brilliant examples herewith:

GINGER-WALNUT CAKE ROLL

6 eggs, separated
¼ cup granulated sugar
2½ teaspoons ground ginger
2 teaspoons vanilla
3 tablespoons ground walnuts
6 tablespoons confectioners' sugar
2 cups whipping cream
1½ tablespoons coffee liqueur
¼ cup chopped toasted walnuts

Serves 10 to 12.

1 Heat oven to 350°. Butter a 10×15-inch baking pan and line with waxed paper extending one inch beyond both ends of the pan. Butter and flour the paper.

2 Beat the egg yolks with the granulated sugar until light and fluffy. Stir in 2 teaspoons ginger, 1 teaspoon vanilla, and the ground walnuts.

3 Beat the egg whites until stiff but not dry; fold into the egg yolk mixture. Spread batter in prepared pan. Bake until cake springs back when touched, 17 to 18 minutes. (Do not overbake.)

4 Soak two paper towels in cold water and wring dry. Place over the cake. Top with two dry paper towels. Let cake stand 20 minutes.

5 Carefully remove the paper towels and sift 1 tablespoon confectioners' sugar over the surface of the cake.

6 Soak a dish towel in cold water and wring dry. Stretch taut over the cake pan and quickly invert. Remove pan; carefully remove waxed paper, using a sharp knife if necessary.

7 Whip 1½ cups cream with 4 tablespoons confectioners' sugar and 1 teaspoon vanilla until stiff. Spread evenly over the cake. Carefully roll up cake, starting from one wide edge and rolling toward you. Lifting towel, flip cake roll onto a long, narrow board or flat serving platter. Chill 1 hour.

8 Whip remaining cream with ½ teaspoon ginger and 1 tablespoon confectioners' sugar until stiff. Beat in the coffee liqueur.

9 Spread cream over the entire top of the cake roll, being careful not to let it drip over the ends. Chill until ready to serve. Just before serving, sprinkle with chopped walnuts.

PEAR ON PEAR TART

1 Heat oven to 425°. To prepare the pastry: Place the flour, salt, sugar, and butter in a bowl. Blend with a pastry blender until the texture of coarse crumbs. Combine the egg yolk with the water and stir into the flour, adding more water if necessary to form a dough. Knead briefly until smooth. Butter a 10-inch quiche pan; pat dough in bottom and up sides of pan. Trim edges. Line the pastry with aluminum foil and fill with dried beans or rice. Bake 10 minutes. Remove foil and beans; bake until light brown, 5 to 10 minutes. Cool on a wire rack.

2 To prepare the caramel: Place the sugar and water in a small saucepan and boil until the mixture turns a light caramel color. Carefully brush the bottom and sides of the pastry shell with the caramel.

3 To prepare the filling: Peel six pears, cut in half, and remove cores. Cut each half into four slices. Place pears in a heavy skillet. Mix the sugar and ginger with the water and pour over the pears. Bring to a boil; reduce heat. Simmer covered until pears are soft but not mushy, 8 to 10 minutes. Cool.

For the pastry:
1¼ cups all-purpose flour
⅛ teaspoon salt
2 tablespoons granulated sugar
½ cup unsalted butter
1 egg yolk
2½ tablespoons water
    (approximately)

For the caramel:
⅓ cup granulated sugar
2 tablespoons water

For the filling:
8 ripe Comice or Anjou pears
    (about 3 pounds)
⅔ cup granulated sugar
1 teaspoon ground ginger
1 cup water
⅓ cup apricot preserves

Serves 8.

Ginger   169

4 Drain pears; reserve liquid. Arrange the cooked pear slices in the pastry shell.

5 Peel the remaining pears, cut into quarters, and remove cores. Cut quarters into thin slices. Arrange pear slices symmetrically over the cooked pears.

6 Combine the apricot preserves with 4 tablespoons reserved pear liquid (save remaining liquid to use as a syrup for fruit or ice cream). Bring to a boil and strain.

7 Brush the tart with half the apricot mixture. Bake 30 minutes. Remove from oven and brush with remaining apricot mixture. Serve warm with ice cream or whipped cream.

People always gift me with cookbooks and I dearly love the bequests. But my favorite recipes come from treasured notebooks of grandmothers and maiden aunts. Perhaps these recipes are more wondrous because the faded lavender ink invests them with historical importance for me. The following ginger ice cream (unlike Marie Antoinette's *glace*) came from such a trove. It was clipped from a yellowed newspaper in the early 1920s. Frozen Passion was its name then, as it is now. I fiddled with the recipe very little and produced a wonderful confection, I think.

FROZEN PASSION CIRCA 1920

5½ cups ginger ale
2 cans (14 ounces each) sweetened condensed milk
1 tablespoon ground ginger
3 cups whipping cream, whipped with 3 tablespoons vanilla
½ cup thinly slivered preserved ginger
½ cup thinly slivered preserved pineapple slices

Makes 3½ to 4 quarts.

1 Stir the ginger ale into the condensed milk in a large bowl until smooth. Stir in the ground ginger. Fold in the whipped cream. Stir in the preserved fruits. Mix well.

2 Pour into the canister of an ice cream maker. Freeze according to manufacturer's directions.

Lemon

Out in the world beyond the pantry, when I was growing up, a "lemon" almost always referred to some "extra-peccable" element in an already blemished universe. Lemons were always the duds.

During my childhood, our family cars were usually second-hand. And while they looked resplendent enough in the car lot and functioned with admirable grace on the test drive, all of these automobiles shared a common mechanical frailty—which never seemed to surface until after the first down payment had been made.

"Well, well," my mother would announce wryly to her dispirited brood, as a second or a third of these cars went dead on the highway and emergency tow-trucks were summoned.

"It seems as if your father bought another lemon!"

Another lemon! With such familiar precedence I probably should have acquired a fruit-grower's nose for all potentially motorized ravage early on. Truth to say, I never did. And in the mid-fifties, when everybody else's car was a real "cherry," the tiniest flaw hidden deep, deep beneath the fins and chrome of my first convertible inevitably qualified for a repeat of my mother's lament. A lemon? That Chevy was surely "the pits."

All in all, as you can plainly see, the lemon was a much maligned crop in my house. I know that I was certainly well into manhood before I discovered the multitudinous virtues the poor fruit possessed outside of a teacup!

For besides adding savor to oolong and bona fide divinity to mere water, sugar, and ice, the lemon alone has a rare taste factor that liberates every viand with which it is mated.

Consider if you will: lemon and chicken . . . lemon and beef . . . lemon and lamb! I must pause here to digress, because no piquancy addresses that highly spirited, last-named victual more (no, not even garlic) than the implacement of needle-sized slivers of lemon peel beneath its skin. Even the simplest broiled lamb chop is assured of new authority under a lattice of lemon. But the golden peel is positively a crowning achievement for a tender young roast—and a lemon juice bath before salt and peppering, plus a dab or two of mustard prior to the stake, will provide a gustatory experience mystical enough to convert the most prejudiced die-hard of the Anti-lamb Establishment.

The following lemon-inscribed roast was served to me by a beautiful part-Scandinavian lady of my acquaintance who claimed to have invented the recipe. More power to her paradigm! She served it mintless with an equally-lemony tart applesauce. So I follow her example:

LEMON ROASTED LAMB

2 lemons
1 leg of lamb (about 6 pounds)
1 large clove of garlic, cut into ½-inch slivers
1 tablespoon Dijon mustard
Pinch of ground ginger
2 tablespoons olive oil
Salt and freshly ground pepper

Serves 6 to 8.

1 Peel the lemons with a vegetable peeler, keeping the peel in one long strip. Reserve lemons. Cut each peel in thirds lengthwise with a scissors (you should have 3 long strips of peel from each lemon).

2 Without breaking the skin, lightly score the surface of the lamb diagonally at 1½-inch intervals. With a larding needle, make small incisions along the score marks at 1-inch intervals. Place one long strip of lemon rind into the eye of the larding needle; insert needle in one incision, bring it underneath one section of meat and over the next section as you pull it through. Continue to "weave" lemon peel along score marks; repeat with remaining strips of peel. (The finished surface of the lamb should resemble a half basket weave.)

3 Make rows of 10 small incisions with an ice pick or sharp knife between the rows of lemon peel. Insert garlic slivers in incisions. Place lamb in roasting pan.

4 Squeeze the juice of the lemons and combine with remaining ingredients. Spoon half the lemon juice mixture over the lamb and refrigerate 2 hours.

5 Heat oven to 450°. Roast lamb 15 minutes. Reduce heat to 325°. Roast lamb 60 to 70 minutes (10 to 12 minutes per pound for rare to medium-rare), basting with remaining lemon juice mixture every 30 minutes.

I dote on lemons because they are both economical and aesthetically pleasing—a rare combination in the kitchen or out! Neither attribute, however, explains why I and a hundred million other Americans cram our refrigerators with the citrus daily.

But the reason for that is as simple as lemonade. The fruit's uses are so unique and varied as to make it literally a culinary indispensable. The juice of the lemon can replace vinegar in salad dressing, its flesh will tenderize tough meat, and a scrap of its peel adds savor to the driest martini or steamiest espresso. And just consider the lemon in conjunction with some less assertive fare—like the aforementioned applesauce for starters.

LEMON APPLESAUCE

1 Pare, core, and cut apples into sixths. Place in a heavy saucepan with the water and lemon slices. Cook covered over medium-high heat until very tender, 12 to 15 minutes. Remove lemon slices.

2 Mash the apples with a vegetable masher. Sweeten to taste, beginning with ½ cup sugar and adding more if necessary. Stir in cinnamon, nutmeg, and lemon juice. Cook uncovered over medium heat 3 minutes. Serve warm or cold. Store tightly covered in refrigerator.

6 to 8 apples (about 3 pounds)
¼ cup water
2 lemon slices, each ½-inch thick
½ to 1 cup granulated sugar
½ teaspoon ground cinnamon
⅛ teaspoon freshly grated nutmeg
Juice of 1 lemon

Makes about 2½ pints.

Citrophiles suspect that all rue plants—lemons, oranges, and limes, too—were cultivated on a single root stock by a tribe of gardeners in the warm climate of the Tigris and Euphrates valley eight thousand years ago. Cross-breeding divided the crops and the crop-growers as well. An unstable band, they argued interminably about the merits of one citrus versus another until they neglected their groves entirely—and, in time, developed cabbages and cucumbers instead!

It's a miracle that lemons survived. Early travelers may have stolen them as souvenirs from this "cradle of civilization." Or perhaps the sirocco blew the seeds north.

Egyptians used lemons for embalming. Babylonians grew them merely for decoration—as we do petunias. No one knows how lemon entered the Greek diet. (For centuries that hardy people considered lemon juice merely an emetic for sick live-stock and an antidote to snake bite.) But here is one legend, anyway:

The famous Greek dish, Soupa Avgolemono (Egg Lemon Soup), is said to have originated on the island of Delos after a remarkably temperate winter. The harvest was larger than usual that year and the growers, wishing to praise the sun god Apollo for this yield, amended their meals to include a little bit of "sun fruit," or lemon, in every dish.

Fact or fiction? Who cares! Whoever invented the beautiful matrix of chicken broth, rice, eggs, and a mite of lemon juice was certainly a Delphian oracle.

A word of caution: The trick in making this soup is to be certain that the beaten egg does not curdle. A sure, steady hand (much like the one you used for lemon mayonnaise) will insure a velvety smoothness. So, be steady!

SOUPA AVGOLEMONO

½ cup rice
6 cups chicken stock (or 3 cups chicken stock mixed with 3 cups lamb or veal stock)
2 egg yolks
Juice of 1 large lemon
1 cup whipped cream flavored with 2 tablespoons grated lemon peel and 1 tablespoon grated Parmesan cheese (optional)

Serves 6.

1 Rinse the rice under cold running water to remove excess starch. Drain thoroughly.

2 Bring the stock to a boil and add the rice. Reduce heat; simmer uncovered until the rice is soft, about 15 minutes. Remove from heat.

3 Beat the egg yolks with the lemon juice until very light in color. Gradually add 1 cup of stock, beating continuously so that the eggs do not curdle.

4 Slowly stir the egg yolk mixture into the stock. Cook over low heat, stirring continuously, 3 minutes. Serve immediately. Pass the whipped cream.

Note: This soup is excellent cold as well. Allow soup to cool. Refrigerate at least 5 hours. Garnish with paper-thin, peeled lemon slices and chopped chives.

Another Hellenic national dish, this one is sauced with essentially the same ingredients as those combined in Soupa Avgolemono. But the garlic-scented cinnamon meatballs make a world of difference to the ductile sauce.

GREEK MEATBALLS
IN AVGOLEMONO SAUCE

1 Soak the bread in milk for 5 minutes; crumble the bread. Combine the bread, milk, onion, garlic, shallot, allspice, cinnamon, parsley, lemon juice, and lemon peel in a large bowl. Beat until smooth.

2 Add the meats, kosher salt, ½ teaspoon pepper, the bread crumbs, eggs, and egg white to the bread mixture. Mix well with your hands and shape into small meatballs, about 1 inch in diameter. (If the mixture seems too wet, add more bread crumbs.)

3 Melt ¼ cup butter in a large skillet. Brown the meatballs on all sides, ⅓ at a time, over high heat, adding more butter as needed. Keep warm.

4 Heat ¼ cup butter in a large saucepan over high heat until it foams. Reduce heat. Whisk in the flour; cook, stirring constantly, until smooth, about 3 minutes. Add the broth; cook, stirring constantly, 5 minutes longer.

5 Add the meatballs to the sauce. Simmer 15 minutes. Remove from heat.

6 Combine the cream and egg yolk in a small bowl. Stir into the sauce. Cook over low heat 3 minutes (do not let mixture boil). Stir in the lemon juice and salt and pepper to taste; sprinkle with parsley.

2 slices white bread
¼ cup milk
1 small onion, minced
1 clove garlic, finely chopped
1 large shallot, finely chopped
¼ teaspoon ground allspice
⅛ teaspoon ground cinnamon
¼ cup chopped fresh parsley
2 tablespoons lemon juice
1 teaspoon slivered lemon peel
½ pound cooked ham, finely chopped
1 pound ground round steak or a mixture of ½ pound ground lamb and ½ pound ground beef
1 teaspoon kosher salt
½ teaspoon freshly ground pepper
½ cup dry bread crumbs
2 eggs
1 egg, separated
¾ cup unsalted butter (approximately)
2 tablespoons all-purpose flour
1½ cups strong chicken broth, hot
1 cup whipping cream
⅓ cup lemon juice
Salt and freshly ground pepper
Chopped fresh parsley

Serves 4 to 6.

Definitely, lemon is a food evangelist. But it was not always so. The "sun citrus," as recorded in kitchen folklore for over five thousand years, had a vastly checkered history. In medieval times, for instance, the juices were considered to be mildly poisonous, while earlier on they were reputed to contain flagrant aphrodisiac properties—but then, what flavoring did not share that reputation?

Some rather intrepid biblical interpreters even believe that the apple in the Garden of Eden was actually a culpable citrus but that point remains manifestly moot here.

Even without sexual implications, the history of the lemon (or *citrus medica* as Apicius referred to an early Roman variety that was used to keep moths from woolen togas in the summertime) is sufficiently zesty to stand on its own merits.

Thoughts of the Romans conjure an elegant Italian amalgam of soft lemony mayonnaise and thinly shaved raw beef served at Orsini's. The delectable dish is known as Carpaccio, though no one seems to know why. Certainly the eminent Renaissance painter (1450-1522) seems worthy of the salutation!

CARPACCIO WITH LEMON MAYONNAISE

1½ pounds boneless shell steak
2 tablespoons finely chopped shallots
1 egg yolk*
2 teaspoons Dijon mustard
2 tablespoons lemon juice
1 cup olive oil
Salt
12 lemon wedges, seeded
Freshly ground pepper

Serves 6 to 8.

1 Cut the meat into 12 slices, each about ¼-inch thick. Place slices, one at a time, between two sheets of plastic wrap. Pound with a flat mallet until paper thin. Refrigerate until serving time.

2 Wrap the shallots in cheesecloth and hold under cold running water. Squeeze to extract moisture; reserve.

3 Combine the egg yolk, mustard, and lemon juice in a mixing bowl. Slowly beat in the oil, a few drops at a time, until mixture begins to thicken; then rapidly beat in the remaining oil, one third at a time. Stir in the shallots and salt to taste. Chill.

4 To serve, arrange the chilled meat on a serving platter and spread 1 tablespoon of mayonnaise over each slice. Garnish with lemon wedges and pepper.

Note: Egg yolk, mustard, lemon juice, and oil must be at room temperature. Instead of pounding the meat, you can partially freeze it and cut it into paper-thin slices with a knife or meat slicer.

Lemon is an indispensable adjunct in a kitchen precisely because of its elusive identity. A lemon's taste can be strong and still reinforce lesser flavors on our tongue—even when the other essence is as alien as the malt spirits in Scotch whiskey.

Speaking of which, I am not at all certain of the Highland authenticity of the next dish. But the union of crunchy meat and mushrooms enveloped in a spirituous and creamy sauce makes it one of my starred preferences. The lemon is barely tasted but its presence is felt mightily, all the same.

SCOTCH WHISKEY CHICKEN

1 Marinate the chicken pieces in the juice of 1 lemon for at least 1 hour.

2 Cook the bacon in boiling water 1 minute. Drain and pat dry on paper toweling.

3 Melt 7 tablespoons butter in a heavy skillet and saute the bacon and shallots until golden. Remove with a slotted spoon.

4 Combine the flour, salt, and pepper. Remove the chicken from the marinade; reserve marinade. Dust each piece of chicken with the flour mixture. Saute in the butter until golden on all sides.

5 Warm the whiskey and pour over the chicken. Using a long match, ignite the whiskey; when the flame subsides, add the cooked shallots and bacon, sugar, wine, and reserved marinade. Cook covered over medium-high heat, turning occasionally, until tender, 40 to 50 minutes. (If chicken begins to get too brown, lower the flame.)

6 Meanwhile, melt the remaining 1 tablespoon butter in a small skillet and saute the mushrooms over high heat until golden.

7 Remove cooked chicken to a heatproof serving platter. Cover with the mushrooms. Keep warm in the oven while making the sauce.

8 Remove all but 1 tablespoon of the pan drippings from the skillet. Add the chicken broth. Cook over high heat 1 minute, scraping the sides and bottom of the pan. Stir in the cream and lemon juice; cook 2 minutes. Remove from heat. Whisk ¼ cup sauce into the egg yolks and slowly beat this mixture into the rest of the sauce. Cook over low heat, stirring constantly, 2 minutes (do not boil). Pour sauce over chicken. Garnish with parsley.

1 chicken (about 3 pounds), cut into serving pieces
Juice of 1 lemon
3 thick slices bacon, diced
½ cup butter
3 large shallots, finely chopped
½ cup all-purpose flour
1 teaspoon salt
½ teaspoon freshly ground pepper
½ cup Scotch whiskey
½ teaspoon granulated sugar
½ cup white wine or vermouth
1 cup sliced mushrooms
½ cup chicken broth
½ cup whipping cream
2 tablespoons fresh lemon juice
2 egg yolks
Chopped fresh parsley

Serves 4.

Tyrants frequently turn up as lemon lovers. Between exiles, Napoleon enjoyed a glass of lemonade. The Persian king Darius very often dined on a dish of dried pottage (lentils) cooked in lemon juice when he was off on maneuvers slaughtering Greeks.

A dish I have made for years is a slightly less astringent version of Darius's salad. Use a good oil in the dressing and lots of fresh parsley for garnish—and you'll be "hailed Caesar" in your own kitchen.

LENTIL AND LEMON SALAD

1 pound dried lentils
1 onion stuck with 2 cloves
½ bay leaf
5 cups water
1 clove garlic, minced
3 or 4 green onions, finely chopped
Vinaigrette Dressing (see Index)
Salt and freshly ground pepper
1 small lemon, peeled, cut in half, seeded, sliced paper thin
Chopped fresh parsley

Serves 4 to 6.

1 Rinse the lentils under cold water; sort to remove any bits of gravel or shriveled lentils. Put the lentils, onion, and bay leaf in a large heavy saucepan. Cover with 5 cups water and bring slowly to a boil. Reduce heat; simmer until tender, about 30 to 40 minutes. Drain thoroughly and chill.

2 Place lentils in serving bowl. Add the garlic, green onions, and Vinaigrette Dressing. Season to taste with salt and pepper. Gently stir in the lemon slices. Chill well. Garnish with chopped parsley.

Speaking of tyrants—lemon and sugar baked in a pie literally took Nero's breath away. Indeed, the terrible-tempered emperor reputedly swooned over custards and meringues of every description. It was from Persian slaves in the kitchen that the Romans learned to concoct the sweet appeasements. And the fragrance of their output was often so tantalizing that foot soldiers had to be called upon to protect royal bakers from over-zealous mobs! Think of Nero's reaction to the following pie—and to hell with the mob!

LEMON MERINGUE PIE

For the crust:
1¼ cups all-purpose flour
¼ teaspoon salt
¼ cup cold unsalted butter
¼ cup cold vegetable shortening
Grated peel of 1 lemon
2 tablespoons cold orange juice

1 Place the flour, salt, butter, shortening, and lemon peel in a bowl. Blend with a pastry blender until the texture of coarse crumbs. Stir in the orange juice with a fork just until a dough is formed. (Do not overwork.) Chill 1 hour.

2 Heat oven to 350°. Roll out pastry to an 11-inch circle. Line a 9-inch pie plate; trim and flute edge. Line pastry with aluminum foil; weight with dried beans or rice. Bake until the edges start to brown, about 10 minutes. Remove foil and beans; bake 5 minutes. Cool.

3 Lightly beat the egg yolks with 2 cups sugar and the salt. Stir in the lemon juice. Transfer mixture to the top of a double boiler. Cook over hot water until thick, about 20 minutes. Remove from heat. Beat in the lemon peel. Cool.

4 Heat oven to 550° or broil. Beat the egg whites until almost stiff. Add the remaining ½ cup sugar, 1 tablespoon at a time, beating until mixture becomes stiff and glossy. Fold half the meringue into the egg yolk mixture and pour into crust. Spread the remaining meringue over the pie; sprinkle with lemon drops. Place pie under broiler until top is brown, about 1 minute.

Note: Since there is no thickening agent used in this pie, the custard is creamier than usual. Pie may be served at room temperature but it will get firmer when chilled.

For the filling:
10 eggs, separated
2½ cups granulated sugar
¼ teaspoon salt
1 cup fresh lemon juice
Grated peel of 1 lemon
3 lemon drops or sour balls, crushed to a fine powder

Serves 8.

Two wonderful desserts anyone might swoon over are a lemony pound cake, drenched with sugar and fruit juice as it cools, and an icebox tart that's as moist as a field of yellow daisies, enhanced by a crust of cloudlike meringue and topped with drifts of whipped cream.

GLAZED LEMON LOAF

1 Heat oven to 325°. Sift together the flour, baking powder, and salt.

2 Cream the butter with 1 cup sugar and the lemon peel in a large bowl. Add the eggs one at a time, mixing well after each addition. Stir in the flour mixture in three parts, alternating with thirds of the milk. Mix well.

3 Pour into a well-greased 9×5×3-inch loaf pan. Bake until a toothpick inserted in the center comes out clean, 60 to 70 minutes.

4 Just before removing cake from oven, heat the lemon juice with the remaining ¼ cup sugar in a small saucepan until the sugar dissolves.

5 As soon as the cake is done, pierce the top all over with a long thin needle. Pour lemon juice mixture over. Cool on a wire rack 1 hour. Remove from pan; cool on rack 2 hours longer before serving.

2½ cups sifted all-purpose flour
1 tablespoon baking powder
1 teaspoon salt
⅓ cup butter
1¼ cups granulated sugar
2 tablespoons finely grated lemon peel
2 eggs
1 cup milk
⅓ cup lemon juice

Serves 6 to 8.

LEMON ICE BOX TART

For the meringue shell:
4 egg whites
⅛ teaspoon salt
¼ teaspoon cream of tartar
¾ cup granulated sugar
½ teaspoon vanilla

For the filling:
4 egg yolks
1 cup granulated sugar
½ cup lemon juice
Grated peel of 1 lemon
1½ cups whipping cream
½ cup confectioners' sugar

Serves 8.

1 Heat oven to 275°. Thoroughly grease bottom and sides of a 9-inch pie pan. Beat egg whites, salt, and cream of tartar in a mixing bowl until soft peaks form. Beat in the sugar, 1 tablespoon at a time; beat until stiff. Stir in vanilla. Spread meringue over the bottom and sides of the pie pan, building up the sides. Bake 1 hour. Cool in the oven.

2 Beat the egg yolks, sugar, lemon juice, and peel until light and fluffy. Place in the top of a double boiler. Cook over simmering water, stirring often, until mixture thickens. Cool.

3 Whip the cream with the confectioners' sugar until stiff. Spread ½ of the cream over the bottom of meringue. Cover with the egg yolk mixture. Spread with remaining cream. Refrigerate 24 hours.

During the Middle Ages, the concord of lemon and sugar advanced to a state far beyond even Nero's vivid imaginings. Egg yolks and wine were subtly fused to create a drink (or dessert) called frumenty, an antecedent of the greatest combination of egg, lemon, and sugar yet conceived, Lemon Souffle.

Later, by some kitchen miscalculation that managed to come up roses, the same essential ingredients were combined in a slightly cooler oven. A souffle did not rise but the best Lemon Sponge Cake did. Take your pick of winners!

LEMON SOUFFLE

2½ tablespoons butter, softened
3 tablespoons granulated sugar
2 lemons
3 tablespoons sifted all-purpose flour
¾ cup milk
⅓ cup granulated sugar
5 eggs, separated

Serves 4.

1 Heat oven to 400°. Using ½ tablespoon butter, grease the entire inner surface of a 6-cup souffle dish. Combine thoroughly 3 tablespoons sugar and the grated peel of 1 lemon. Coat the sides and bottom of the dish evenly with the sugar mixture. Shake out excess and reserve.

2 Sift the flour into a 2-quart saucepan. Add ¼ cup milk and beat until smooth. Stir in the remaining milk and ⅓ cup sugar. Bring to a boil over medium-high heat. Boil, stirring constantly, 30 seconds. Remove from heat; beat 2 minutes. Beat in the egg yolks, one at a time, beating thoroughly after each addition. Stir in 1 tablespoon butter; dot the top of the sauce with remaining butter.

3 Beat the egg whites until stiff but not dry.

4 Beat the juice of 1½ lemons and the grated peel of 1 lemon into the egg yolk mixture. Stir in ¼ of the egg whites; gently fold in the rest.

5 Place the dish in the oven and reduce heat to 375°. Bake 20 minutes. Sprinkle the top of the souffle with the reserved sugar mixture. Bake until puffed and golden, 10 to 15 minutes longer.

LEMON SPONGE CAKE

1 Heat oven to 325°. Rinse a large mixing bowl with very hot water and wrap a hot towel around the base of the bowl. Beat the egg yolks in the warm bowl, adding the sugar, 1 tablespoon at a time. Add the peel of ½ lemon, the lemon juice, and vanilla. Continue beating until mixture has doubled in volume.

2 Beat the egg whites until stiff but not dry.

3 Sprinkle the cake flour over the egg yolk mixture and fold in, lifting the batter with a mixing spoon to incorporate as much air as possible. Fold in the beaten egg whites until thoroughly blended.

4 Butter a 9-inch tube pan and sprinkle with sugar. Pour the batter into the pan. Bake until cake is golden and springs back when touched, about 1 hour. Cool. Just before serving, sprinkle top of cake with confectioners' sugar and the grated peel of 1 lemon.

5 eggs, separated
1½ cups granulated sugar
Grated peel of 1½ lemons
1 teaspoon lemon juice
1 teaspoon vanilla
1 cup cake flour, sifted twice
Confectioners' sugar

Serves 8.

Another grand alliance is the confederation of lemon, butter, and egg yolk known as *sauce hollandaise*.

Though purely French in origin, this velutinous concoction was inspired by the shortage of Dutch butter from Delft (the only kind a Parisian *saucier* worthy of his sauce considered melting over crisp *légumes*). To disguise the butter that was available—it was Irish—some freethinker added a spoonful or two of Portuguese lemon juice and a beaten egg yolk. And it is only out of reverse snobbery that the dressing we spoon over our tender asparagus every June is not known as *sauce portugaise!*

Everybody has a trick with hollandaise sauce—making it off the stove, adding cold water, using a double-boiler or not. But the following is one of the best methods that I have ever encountered; so the recipe enters the fold. The "Fail-Proof" proposition offered by Virginia Ward (whose devise I have

irreverently modified with mustard and Tabasco) is that the
butter be absolutely frozen stiff prior to the operation.

It never fails. Can your hollandaise make that claim?

VIRGINIA WARD'S "FAIL-PROOF" HOLLANDAISE SAUCE

2 egg yolks
2 tablespoons lemon juice
¼ teaspoon Dijon mustard
½ cup unsalted butter, frozen
Dash of hot pepper sauce
Pinch of white pepper
Salt to taste

Makes about 1 cup.

1 Beat the egg yolks with the lemon juice. Place in the top of a double boiler over boiling water, being careful that bottom of pan does not touch the water. Stir in the mustard.

2 Divide the butter into eight pieces. Using a fork, stir the butter into the egg yolk mixture, one piece at a time. Stir well after each addition. Stir in hot pepper sauce, white pepper, and salt.

From hollandaise sauce to Tarte Tartin Normande is a two-century culinary leap. The country French dessert (Pie? Cake? You name it!) from Normandy is amazingly similar to an early American apple upside-down cake. Unfortunately, I have no receipt to offer you for comparison—so you must take my word for it.

Tartin (literally, "a slice") postdated the French Revolution by a decade or so. It was invented when public dining came into fashion in France and a lot of small country farmers' wives decided that running a dining place for travelers was a more tonic form of enterprise than harvesting apples.

This dish is a jewel in anyone's dessert repertoire—and a prime example of the beneficence lemon bestows on other flavors.

TARTE TARTIN NORMANDE

1 Make Short Crust Pastry.

2 Heat oven to 450°. Blend 12 tablespoons butter with ⅓ cup granulated sugar, 4 tablespoons brown sugar, and the bread crumbs. Pat the mixture over bottom and up the sides of a 10-inch glass or ceramic baking dish or pie plate. Refrigerate until ready to use.

3 Pare and core the apples. Cut into ⅛-inch slices; sprinkle slices with lemon juice as they are cut. Toss with the lemon peel, liqueur, and orange peel. Arrange the mixture in overlapping layers in the baking dish.

4 Melt the remaining 2 tablespoons butter and 4 tablespoons brown sugar together; mix well. Spread over apples. Roll out the pastry to a 12-inch circle. Place over baking dish; press over rim to seal. Cut a small slit in the center to allow steam to escape.

5 Place baking dish on a foil-lined baking sheet. Bake 30 minutes. Increase heat to 550°; bake 10 minutes.

6 Loosen tart by running knife around rim of dish. Place a large heatproof serving plate over baking dish; invert tart onto plate. Let stand to cool at least 1 hour.

7 Just before serving, warm tart in oven heated to 350°, 10 to 15 minutes. Melt ⅓ cup granulated sugar with 2 tablespoons water over medium heat until sugar turns dark amber in color. Quickly, but *carefully,* pour melted sugar over tart in a small stream, making a criss-cross pattern over the entire crust. Let stand 5 minutes. Serve with sweetened whipped cream.

Short Crust Pastry (recipe follows)
14 tablespoons unsalted butter
⅔ cup granulated sugar
8 tablespoons brown sugar
½ cup homemade bread crumbs
6 medium Macintosh apples
Grated peel and juice of 1 small lemon
1½ tablespoons Grand Marnier liqueur
Pinch of grated orange peel
2 tablespoons water
Sweetened whipped cream

Serves 6 to 8.

SHORT CRUST PASTRY

1 Sift the flour and salt into a bowl. Add the shortening and butter; blend with a pastry blender until texture of coarse crumbs.

2 Sprinkle water over flour mixture, 1 tablespoon at a time, until all flour is moistened and mixture forms a dough. (Be careful not to overwork.)

1 cup all-purpose flour
½ teaspoon salt
2 tablespoons cold vegetable shortening
1 tablespoon cold unsalted butter
3 to 4 tablespoons cold water

Makes one 10-inch crust.

One last tribute to the lemon: Think of bananas and cream; then add a touch of almond liqueur and sugar, sour cream to cut the sweetness, and lemon juice to temper the bouquet. Combine all these flavors in one frothy mixture that is whisked and chilled to icy perfection. Neither kings nor philosophers have ever dreamed of such a tenuous substance as this Banana Ice Cream softly melting off a spoon!

BANANA ICE CREAM

2½ cups granulated sugar
⅛ teaspoon salt
2 cups light cream
1 piece of vanilla bean, 1-inch long
½ cup lemon juice
1 cup sour cream
6 ripe bananas, mashed through a
   sieve or in a food processor
4 cups whipping cream
2 tablespoons Amaretto liqueur

Makes about 3½ to 4 quarts.

1 Mix the sugar, salt, and light cream in the top of a double boiler. Add the vanilla bean. Cook over hot water only until the sugar dissolves. Remove the vanilla bean, slit the husk, and scrape the seeds into the cream mixture; discard husk. Cool.

2 Stir the lemon juice and sour cream into the bananas in a large bowl. Add the sugar mixture and the whipping cream. Beat until well blended. Stir in the Amaretto.

3 Pour into the canister of an ice cream maker and freeze according to manufacturer's directions.

Madeira and Port, too!

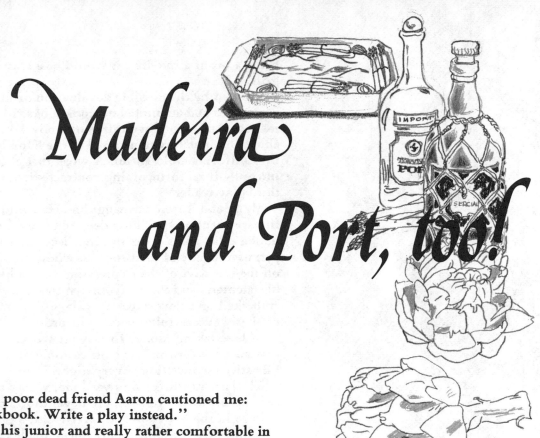

Long, long ago, my poor dead friend Aaron cautioned me: "Never write a cookbook. Write a play instead."

Being eight years his junior and really rather comfortable in the role of acolyte, I took his advice. But this was sheer politesse. We both knew that playwriting was my mentor's exclusive prerogative in our relationship. Was it not he who had two musicals optioned and, alas, dropped for Broadway? Was it his name or mine that led the roll of lapsed (non-paying) members of the Dramatists Guild?

Gauntlets. *Schmauntlets.* I chose not to accept the suede.

"OK, then write a novel or a novella even. A real short one." Aaron was an inveterate lip-sniffer. And a good deal of very pertinent lip-sniffing and nose-twitching accompanied this last statement.

"I mean, why not give it a whirl? If you feel you've got something to say. The novel's not exactly dead y'know—just under heavy sedation. Who knows? You might even be the one to revive it. Mailer can't or won't—and you're in better form. You're still *untried.*"

Aaron pondered his own wisdom.

"Just remember. No cookbooks!"

If I ventured a *why,* he had a barrage of ammunition to support his point of view.

"Because they're precious for one thing and inconsequential for another. Good cooks don't really use recipes anyway. All they need is fresh ingredients. Also, if you'll forgive me for being a bit of a *buttinsky,* it would be a waste of your valuable gifts.''

Blinded by the possible devaluation of my pound of talent, I acquiesced and attempted no cookbooks. I kept a recipe file instead. And wrote two thirds of a novel and a ridiculous play about Oedipus Rex transposed to the Klondike (or perhaps it was the California Gold Rush). A work that elicited enormous interest—if no forthcoming contract—from the Theatre Guild's third play reader.

My friend Aaron was sanguine. He could afford to be. My literary mentor was elbow deep in his own three-part science fiction salad and a series of reminiscences concerning a sexually permissive lady of the Bronx in whose company he had polished off the last days of the Depression. When his stories did not sell, his talented hand turned from pen to scissors and he immediately embarked on a new career as collage-illustrator—becoming surprisingly successful in very short order.

''I hate taking money for my art work,'' he would complain, ''because it's turning my stuff commercial. But I gotta eat—and I do still keep writing. Every night!''

The last was directed toward me, who wavered from time to time on my literary safari. He never did. This was Greenwich Village in the late 1940s and early 1950s, a place where we thrived on a diet of wish fulfillment. Aaron made certain that I had at least five pages per day logged on my Smith-Corona before he allowed me to invite him over for dinner. And though he was unstinting in his praise for my culinary performance, his demeanor at the table was decidedly wary, like a missionary with a native chieftan—always watchful lest the gleam in an eye betray an over-serious purpose.

My friend Aaron was rather short, fat, and owlish—almost solemn in appearance—and indulgence was his secret vice. Not for himself, but for everyone else in his orbit. He pampered me shamelessly. Aries to Libra, he was my best friend, dearest critic, and a long believer in excessive encouragement of all my talents—except in the area of cookery:

''Listen! You've got to produce . . . write more! Your trouble is you have no discipline. Look at Maugham. Only an hour a day he works . . . but day after day after day! Look at Proust . . . Joyce . . . all the big ones. Think they cooked? They probably lived on yogurt. Screw the Cordon Bleu—and the cooking lessons. Your output . . . (lots of sniffing and a fast wad of spit for stunning punctuation) is diminishing, kiddo.''

Under his excessive tutelage, I began to equate my literary gifts with a dwindling flow of gold. With misspent energy, I quickly attempted a rambling travel book about South American countries I had never visited.

No publisher seemed interested, but Aaron, always the fatherly, big-brotherly, Jewish P. A. L. representative, never wavered. Instead of rueing my literary extravagances, he was the soul of forbearing.

"You're out on a limb with this fluke South of the Border opus—so what? Get it out of your system. I and you already know that you're just walking down Prokosch's footsteps. So maybe it won't be another *Asiatics*—at least it's not a lousy cookbook!"

And the recipe files grew to bulging.

When Aaron began to write one-act plays ("They're more saleable—if only there was a market out there to sell to!"), I became involved in a writer's workshop and produced a near-novel. A contract was dangled and my friend became ecstatic for me. And though we still wrote our separate ways, he began to toy with communal success.

"Maybe you should come over to my place twice a week," he ventured after a bit. "I'll cook simple food for us—like quiche and omelets—and we'll read each other's stuff. OK?"

I agreed. But my talent ebbs under a spotlight; so in the end he wrote while I merely read (or listened) and cooked. Eventually we both stopped writing and merely gained weight. For the first time in our long friendship, we had become competitive—not over our literary merits but over our cooking skills.

"You cook purer than I do," he would grudgingly allow. "Not better. Just purer! Your palate is very light—that's interesting. But you *care* too much. And you use too many pots! You'll forgive me if I say this . . . but you make an absolute pigsty out of the kitchen." He sniffed more than ever. "But, undeniably, you've got the talent!"

My dear friend loved to (lived to) eat. He would reflect on my haute cuisine with rhapsodic near-gluttony—but not without reservations.

"This crab soufflé—exceptional, a triumph texturally, but too much talent going to waste. It's draining your work. Cook less . . . write more. Or else, cook the way I do. Less scruples and less wash-ups later. I've got to be free!"

Eventually we ate together so often that it seemed logical to collaborate literally. We worked on a play, an adaptation of Kafka, that was finally produced Off-Broadway. As collaborators, we would take equal turns at the typewriter—but we never cooked in concert. Either I cooked and he ate. Or he cooked and I concurred. Undeniably, he had talent, too.

The Trial ran an unconscionably long time, breaking all contemporary records. But no one made much money—there was a fare-thee-well of red accountants' tallies in the final statements.

Aaron was never bitter about the lack of adequate financial remuneration.

"We learned a lot from this one," he would say idly. "So what if Walter Kerr didn't like it? They loved us in *Cue, The New York Post,* and *The Newark News.* . . . " (He hummed under his breath.) "So Brooks Atkinson goes off to Tibet for the summer and we're stuck with *The Times'* second stringer—a Kafka hater! We were at the mercy of *grand forces,* kid. But, we ate well!"

Passive-activist, opti-pessimist, he thrived on activity and abhored the results.

"Essentially, the theatre bores me. But you must admit we cooked a lot of interesting dishes . . . writing this number," he reflected. "So? It turns out to be a turkey in the final analysis! So what? We came up with a lot of excellent . . . *souffles* while writing the second act."

My friend Aaron never wanted me to write recipes but a lot of time has passed. And if I cook as much as I write nowadays, who is left to separate the golden yolks of genius that go into producing a masterpiece omelet from the latest egg laid on the Great White Way? Certainly not my friend Aaron, who was pure pragmatist right to the end—and even beyond.

A while back, from a Ouija board, he still remonstrated me.

DNT COOK. OK COOK IF U MUST. BUT LESS. BIG HIT BROADWY SOON. IF YOU WORK WOK WK! GOODBYE.

While cooking with Aaron, I first indulged in fortified wines in the kitchen. He loved to cook with vermouth and tended to over-use the elixir from time to time—in excessive appreciation of the body it could add to a characterless dish. In self defense, I countered with Madeira and port as flavoring agents for his saute pan.

He totally disapproved of my largesse—but only because of the expense. Being the kind of man who denied himself small luxuries while being profligate to the world-at-large, he resented having to become used to extravagance.

"Rainwater Madeira. What's wrong with tapwater Madeira for Chrissakes?" he upbraided. "As a matter of fact, since we're on the subject, what's wrong with vermouth?"

Nothing at all. But Aaron's nose knew the difference. And it pleasured me after a while to notice that the chef had begun to replenish his stock of port whenever it was depleted.

The one bit of classic cuisine my friend prized most was the following rendering of Alice B. Toklas's creamy summer veal. For him, it summed up the best of all possible worlds, being at once sexy, intellectual, French, and fattening.

I wish I could make it for him again. Since I cannot, you make it for yourself, instead.

VEAU D'ÉTÉ ALICE B. TOKLAS

1 Melt butter in a heavy skillet. Place veal scallops in skillet without overlapping pieces (two skillets may be necessary). Cover and shake the skillet. Cook veal over medium heat for 20 minutes, making sure it does not brown.

2 Add the port, salt, and pepper to the skillet. Turn the veal over; add the cream. Simmer uncovered, basting frequently with the juices, until sauce is very thick and creamy, about 20 minutes. Remove veal to a serving dish, arranging pieces so that they overlap. Pour sauce over veal.

3 If using fresh artichokes, remove thorny chokes; cook in boiling salted water until tender, 12 to 15 minutes. Discard leaves and stems; reserve hearts. If using frozen, cook in boiling salted water with a few drops of lemon juice for 3 minutes. Drain well.

4 Peel asparagus stalks with a vegetable peeler. Cook asparagus in boiling salted water 4 minutes. Rinse under cold running water; drain. Tie asparagus spears into four bunches with green onion tops that have been blanched in boiling water for a minute.

5 Arrange asparagus bunches and artichoke hearts alternately around veal. Garnish veal with snipped chives; garnish artichoke hearts with pimiento strips. Serve at room temperature.

½ cup butter
12 veal scallops
½ cup port wine
¾ teaspoon salt
¼ teaspoon freshly ground pepper
¾ cup whipping cream
8 fresh artichokes or 8 frozen artichoke hearts
16 asparagus spears
4 limp green onion tops
Chives
Pimiento strips

Serves 4.

My friend Aaron was incredibly erudite but I doubt if even he knew why Madeira and port are considered fortified wines. I only happened on that intelligence myself a short while back— but I'll pass on the scoop.

Until the mid-eighteenth century, wine produced in Portugal was considered to be every bit as good as wine produced in France. Both vintages were co-equally drunk by the middle classes all over Europe and shipped in large quantities across the Atlantic, where the American colonists' tastes were notoriously uncultivated.

Oddly enough, the popularity of Portuguese wines ebbed when oenophilia came to full flower. After the American Revolution (with business flourishing and taxes on spirits excised), wine connoisseurism began in earnest. And as more wine was consumed, the American palate perceived that French bottlings had a decided edge over the competition.

The Portuguese market faltered and might have disappeared entirely if it had not been for a British wine agent who consid-

ered the canny notion of adding fine brandy (in small doses, to be sure) to the pressings of Portuguese wines before they were casked.

That was the beginning of *fortified* wine.

At first the beefed-up Madeira and port was harsh to the tongue. And it was said in France (with some smugness) that the brandy lion and the grape lamb would never lie down together.

They were wrong—as vintners in Portugal discovered, inadvertently, when casks of Madeira were left out on the docks in the sun too long and the wine's strongish taste softened appreciably. And later, during a difficult storm at sea, when bad weather kept a shipment of wine on the rough Atlantic for twice the time of a normal voyage, it was found upon decanting a bottle that not only had the vintage greatly improved but also that the very taste had altered. The constant shaking and swaying of the barrels in the hold had produced a different wine—one that was clearer in color and actually velvety to the tongue!

Shortly thereafter, the best and most expensive Madeiras were labeled "East India"—to indicate to prospective buyers that bottles had been carried to Java and back (in the hot sun) before being considered worthy of sale!

Madeira has an unmistakable savor—in a glass or a saute pan! Like my friend Aaron, I find it most salubrious in a dish when the alcohol has been burned away completely and only the merest hint of heady vapor remains to color the viand to which it was added. Beef Fillets with Madeira is an Italian recipe from a very grand household in Florence that proves my point *in excelsior!*

BEEF FILLETS WITH MADEIRA

8 small new potatoes
2 teaspoons butter
2 slices bacon, chopped
1 white onion, thinly sliced
4 beef tenderloin fillets, each 1-inch thick
1 small clove garlic, bruised
Salt and freshly ground pepper
1½ tablespoons butter, melted
¼ cup hot beef stock
¼ cup Madeira
Chopped parsley

Serves 4.

1 Heat oven to 350°. Cook the new potatoes in boiling salted water for 15 minutes. Drain.

2 Heat 2 teaspoons butter in a heavy skillet. Stir in the bacon and onion. Add the potatoes and cook over moderate heat until brown on all sides.

3 Transfer the potatoes to a baking dish; bake until tender, 35 to 45 minutes depending on size. Baste once with pan drippings from the skillet. Keep warm in oven.

4 Remove bacon and onion from the skillet and discard. Heat pan drippings. Rub beef fillets lightly with garlic. Cook fillets in pan drippings over high heat for 2 minutes on each side.

5 Sprinkle fillets with salt and pepper to taste. Add melted butter to

skillet. Pour beef stock and Madeira into skillet around (not over) fillets. Cook fillets over medium heat for 2 minutes on each side.

6 Immediately transfer fillets to a platter; pour sauce over. Sprinkle with parsley. Arrange potatoes around fillets.

Madeira is a natural ally of ham in almost any guise. I once compiled 108 ham recipes and found that a dram of the spirituous liquor was included in all but eight!

The ''Flauf'' from Budapest's Hotel Metropole is one of the collection. It makes a remarkable brunch or luncheon focal point. High and light as a souffle, crustless, yet baked like a pie, it seems a natural alternative to the over-quiched appetite. Best of all, the cooking time is a mere forty-five minutes from start to finish!

HUNGARIAN FLAUF

1 Heat oven to 400°. Make a 2-inch high aluminum foil collar and tape around a 10-inch glass or ceramic quiche pan. Grease collar lightly with butter.

2 Melt 2 tablespoons butter in a heavy skillet. Add the shallots and ham; cook over low heat 3 minutes. Add the Madeira; cook over high heat, stirring constantly, until most of the liquid has evaporated, about 5 minutes. Cool slightly.

3 Beat the egg yolks until slightly thickened. Beat in the sour cream, bread crumbs, cheese, and caraway. Stir in the ham, salt, and pepper.

4 Beat the egg whites until stiff peaks form; fold into the egg yolk mixture.

5 Place the remaining 1 tablespoon butter in the bottom of the prepared quiche pan. Place in oven until butter foams. Swirl butter around pan to coat bottom and sides. Pour in egg mixture. Bake until puffy and golden, 30 to 35 minutes. Carefully remove collar and serve immediately.

3 tablespoons butter
2 large shallots, minced
1½ cups chopped cooked ham
¼ cup Madeira
6 eggs, separated
1 cup sour cream
¼ cup bread crumbs
¼ cup finely grated Jarlsberg cheese
2 teaspoons caraway seeds
1 teaspoon salt
½ teaspoon freshly ground pepper

Serves 4 as a luncheon entrée or 8 as an appetizer.

Over the years, port has gained a considerable reputation as being the only felicitous companion to Stilton cheese. And

rightly so, for the post-prandial quaff is invariably an aged port that was carefully chosen to match the savor and aroma of the cheese. Such perfect ports often have been kept corked for as long as fifty years before being considered ripe enough for the marriage.

Irreverently, I must note that port is also one of my favored cooking allies. But I never use the truly prime stuff in my veal stew. Third grade does quite nicely there.

There are three major types of port. *Vintage* is absolutely the best. But vintage port is quite rare, since it's made only when the weather is perfect *during an entire growing season*. The label inscription "A Vintage Year" implies that the port within has been aged in the cask no longer that twenty four months but that its stay in the bottle is of a longer duration—never less than ten years and often upwards of fifty! Great vintage ports are very dark and purpley in color—the exact shade to suit a royal palate. *Tawny port* is reddish in color, as the name suggests, and made of blended wines. These wines are aged in the cask longer than vintage ports (thus they lose their deep rich color) but are not aged in the bottle as long. They are still excellent considering the price, which is less than half the vintage tariff. *Ruby port* (the one I buy for cooking) is neither left in the cask long enough to fade tawny nor adjudged pure enough to mature in the bottle. A compromise wine, it is of weaker character than tawny but far more affordable—and excellent in a kitchen!

Port is a Slavic acquisition. The wine appears in lots of Russian and Polish cuisine, perhaps because those countries produce a makeshift (non-Portuguese) port of their own. I suggest you use the mint original in this nationalist rendering, however.

6 tablespoons unsalted butter
1 teaspoon vegetable oil
2 pounds boneless veal, cut into 1-inch cubes
2 tablespoons all-purpose flour
4 large green onions with tops, finely chopped
2 cups pitted morello or other sour cherries
⅓ cup seedless golden raisins
⅔ cup hot chicken stock or broth
¾ cup port wine
1 cardamom pod
Salt and freshly ground pepper
8 to 10 small white onions
Pinch of sugar
3 tablespoons kirschwasser
5 cups cooked rice

Serves 4 to 5.

RUSSIAN VEAL AND CHERRY STEW

1 Melt 4 tablespoons butter with the oil in a heavy skillet. Brown the meat on all sides, a few pieces at a time, over high heat. Transfer to a Dutch oven.

2 Sprinkle the meat with flour; cook over low heat 1 minute. Stir in the green onions, cherries, raisins, stock, and ½ cup port.

3 Open the cardamom pod with a sharp knife; remove and crush the seeds. Add to the meat. Season to taste with salt and pepper. Bring to a boil; reduce heat. Cook covered over very low heat, stirring occasionally, until meat is tender, 1½ to 2 hours.

4 Peel onions and cut a cross in root end of each. Melt remaining 2 tablespoons butter in skillet; brown the onions on all sides. Sprinkle with sugar and remaining ¼ cup port. Cook covered over medium heat 5 minutes, shaking the pan occasionally. Remove cover, raise heat and cook until any liquid evaporates. Add to meat during last ½ hour of cooking time.

5 Just before serving, stir in the kirschwasser. Serve with rice.

Note: If using fresh cherries, you might wish to add a drop of red wine vinegar before serving; stew should be sweet and sour. If using canned cherries, make sure you use the unsweetened kind.

Madeira's conjunction with ham, I have observed, is often duplicated with port and pork. The following roast is remarkably tasty cold, as it is limned below, or hot. If a sizzling roast is what you have in mind, be sure to refer to the recipe for Heavenly Mashed Potatoes (see Index) for a most propitious coupling of flavors. The Horseradish and Apple Sauce, however, is brilliant regardless.

COLD BARBECUED LOIN OF PORK

1 Rub the pork well with the mustard, thyme, salt, and pepper.

2 Combine ½ cup port, the soy sauce, garlic, and ginger. Pour over the pork. Refrigerate covered 24 hours, turning pork several times.

3 Heat oven to 325°. Place pork in a roasting pan; pour marinade over. Bake 45 minutes per pound, basting every 20 minutes.

4 Melt the jelly in a small saucepan. Stir in 2 tablespoons port and 1 tablespoon pan juices from the pork. Heat to boiling; boil 5 minutes. Stir in lemon juice.

5 Transfer pork to a shallow pan; remove strings. Pour jelly mixture over top; let stand at room temperature (room should be cool) at least 1 hour. Baste with jelly mixture every 5 minutes.

6 Transfer pork to serving platter. Arrange sliced tomatoes, onions, and watercress around pork. Serve with Horseradish and Apple Sauce (recipe follows).

1 **boneless pork roast (4 to 5 pounds), rolled and tied in 2 or 3 places**
1 **tablespoon Dijon mustard**
¼ **teaspoon dried thyme**
Salt and freshly ground pepper
½ **cup plus 2 tablespoons port wine**
¼ **cup soy sauce**
3 **cloves garlic, crushed**
2 **teaspoons ground ginger**
1 **jar (10 ounces) currant jelly**
Juice of ½ lemon
Sliced tomatoes
Thinly sliced onions
Watercress leaves

Serves 8 to 10.

HORSERADISH AND APPLE SAUCE

3 Granny Smith apples
1 cup water
Juice of ½ lemon
1 piece vanilla bean, 3 inches long
1 cinnamon stick
½ cup granulated sugar
2 to 3 tablespoons horseradish

Makes about 2 cups.

1 Pare, core, and cut each apple into eight pieces. Place in a saucepan with the water and lemon juice.

2 Slit vanilla bean and scrape out seeds; add seeds, bean, and cinnamon stick to apples. Heat to boiling; reduce heat. Simmer covered until apples are soft, about 8 minutes.

3 Stir and break up the apples with a wooden spoon, leaving some small chunks. Add the sugar; cook over medium heat, stirring constantly, until sugar dissolves. Let stand at room temperature 1 hour. Remove cinnamon stick and vanilla bean. Refrigerate until cold.

4 Just before serving, stir in 2 to 3 tablespoons horseradish, according to taste.

Sherry is also a fortified wine, but out of a purely personal cook's idiosyncracy, I find it more pleasant in a glass than in my measuring cup. In a pinch, however, a mite of Bristol Cream might be substituted for Rainwater Madeira in a dish as eloquent as the following Rolled Shrimp and Crab Souffle. But *this* chef would notice the difference!

Homemade Tomato Sauce (see Index)
1 package (6 ounces) frozen King Crabmeat
½ cup plus 2 tablespoons all-purpose flour
2 cups cold milk
4 egg yolks
¼ teaspoon salt
⅛ teaspoon freshly ground pepper
¼ teaspoon freshly grated nutmeg
Dash of hot pepper sauce
½ cup grated Jarlsberg cheese
6 egg whites
2 tablespoons butter
¾ cup whipping cream
2 tablespoons Madeira
½ pound raw shrimp, cleaned and coarsely chopped
Salt and freshly ground pepper to taste
Pinch of cayenne pepper

Serves 4 to 6 as a main course, 8 to 10 as an appetizer.

ROLLED SHRIMP AND CRAB SOUFFLE

1 Make tomato sauce; reserve.

2 Place the package of crabmeat in a saucepan of boiling water until thawed. Drain crabmeat; reserve liquid.

3 Line a 10×15×1-inch baking pan with aluminum foil. Butter and flour the foil. Heat oven to 400°.

4 Place ½ cup flour in a heavy 1-quart saucepan. Gradually whisk in enough milk to form a smooth paste; then whisk in remaining milk. Cook and stir over medium heat until mixture thickens. Remove from heat. Beat in the egg yolks, one at a time, beating thoroughly after each addition. Stir in the salt, pepper, a pinch of nutmeg, and the hot pepper sauce. Stir in the cheese.

5 Beat egg whites until stiff peaks form. Stir ¼ of egg whites into

egg yolk mixture; fold in remainder. Spread mixture in prepared pan. Bake until toothpick inserted comes out clean, 18 to 20 minutes.

6 Meanwhile, melt 2 tablespoons butter in a heavy saucepan. Add 2 tablespoons flour, stirring until smooth; cook 2 minutes over low heat. Whisk in ½ cup cream and ¼ cup reserved crab liquid. Stir in the Madeira and shrimp. Cook over low heat, stirring constantly, until the shrimp turn pink, about 5 minutes. Break up the crabmeat and add to saucepan. Stir in salt, pepper, cayenne pepper, and remaining nutmeg.

7 Soak a dish towel in water and wring dry. Stretch over baking pan; invert pan on towel. Remove aluminum foil. Spread crabmeat mixture evenly over souffle and roll up. Place on a serving dish; cover with aluminum foil. Keep warm in oven. Roll will keep this way up to 1 hour.

8 Heat the tomato sauce with ¼ cup cream. Spread hot sauce over top of the roll; pass remaining sauce.

The major difference between port and Madeira is a touch of sweetness. All ports are saporously dulcet while Madeira (like sherry) can be either sweet or dry.
    You'll find various types of Madeira, several of them named for the grapes from which they are pressed. *Sercial,* **made of grapes cultivated on the highest ground, is the dryest. Most chefs prefer Sercial because its aromatic savor is said to outstay all other comers in a chafing dish. No comment. I prefer Rainwater Madeira (not named for a grape, but for the part of the island of Madeira that depends on natural rainfall for its moisture). Rainwater Madeira is light and dry—and I enjoy a nip now and then between flambées. Slightly sweeter** *Verdehlo,* **a more accepted drink, is imbibed as an aperitif all over Portugal. The best Verdehlo, as its name would imply, is greenish in color and slightly abrasive to the untried tongue.**
    There are two famous dessert Madeiras, *Boal* **which is creamy light (and ideal in eggnog because it is so notably fragrant) and** *Malmsey.* **Malmsey, its name a distortion of the grape called** *malvoisie,* **is the deepest, richest Madeira of them all—and much favored by the British who see the wine as a culinary equivalent of vintage port. But Malmsey is served with coffee and walnuts—and never with cheese!**
    A thoroughly Anglophile tradition is a cold Veal and Ham Pie. Thick-crusted and crammed with goodies like herbed ham,

snowy hunks of veal, and golden hard-boiled eggs, it makes the best picnic (or buffet table) fare I can think of. And Madeira plus brandy produces the classic perfume that arises when the knife cuts the first slice.

VEAL AND HAM PIE

For the hot water pastry:
4 cups sifted all-purpose flour
¾ teaspoon salt
½ cup plus 2 tablespoons water
½ pound lard

For the meat filling:
1 pound smoked ham, diced
3 shallots, finely chopped
3 tablespoons Madeira
2 tablespoons butter
1½ pounds boneless veal, diced
6 tablespoons brandy
6 tablespoons chicken stock
2 tablespoons lemon juice
Grated peel of 1 whole lemon
¼ cup finely chopped parsley
½ teaspoon dried tarragon
½ teaspoon dried marjoram
Pinch of dried thyme
2 teaspoons salt
½ teaspoon freshly ground pepper
4 hard-cooked eggs
1 egg yolk
1 tablespoon whipping cream
1 envelope unflavored gelatin
1 cup chicken stock

Serves 6 to 8.

1 To prepare the pastry: Place the flour in a medium bowl and stir in the salt. Place the water and lard in a small saucepan; bring to a boil and cook until lard is completely melted. Pour lard mixture over the flour; mix well. Gather pastry into a ball; knead on a lightly floured board 5 minutes. Cover with a damp cloth; let rest for ½ hour.

2 Heat oven to 350°. Saute the ham and shallots in the Madeira and butter until liquid is absorbed, about 3 minutes. Transfer to a mixing bowl; add the veal, brandy, 6 tablespoons chicken stock, the lemon juice, lemon peel, herbs, salt, and pepper. Mix well.

3 Generously butter a 9×5×2½-inch loaf pan. Roll out two-thirds of the pastry ¼-inch thick. Ease into the pan and gently press into place to line sides and bottom; trim excess with rolling pin.

4 Spoon slightly less than half the meat mixture into the pan. Arrange hard-cooked eggs lengthwise in a row in center of pan, trimming ends to fit tightly. Spoon remaining meat mixture over eggs.

5 Roll out remaining pastry ¼-inch thick. Drape over pan. Trim edges with a knife; reserve scraps. Crimp edges. Cut a hole in the center large enough for a funnel to fit in.

6 Roll out pastry scraps; cut into decorative shapes. Combine egg yolk and whipping cream. Moisten shapes with the egg yolk mixture and arrange on the pie. (You may wish to cut flower and leaf shapes to surround hole in center and diamond shapes for each corner.) Brush the entire surface with the egg yolk mixture.

7 Bake 2 hours. (If the crust begins to get too dark, cover loosely with aluminum foil.) Cool on a wire rack 15 minutes.

8 Soften the gelatin in 1 cup chicken stock in a small bowl; place bowl in a pan of hot water. Stir until gelatin dissolves. Insert a funnel in hole in top of pie; pour gelatin mixture into pie, tilting back and forth to distribute evenly. Cool completely. Refrigerate several hours or overnight.

9 To unmold pie, run a sharp knife around the edges; dip the bottom of the pan into boiling water for about 10 seconds. Cover pan tightly with a dish towel and invert. Tap the bottom of the pan, if necessary, and remove. Turn upright onto serving platter. Cut into ½-inch slices to serve.

My friend Aaron Fine was a good cook under normal circumstances but his talent turned to genius whenever a vegetable crossed his path. He had crotchets of course: Spinach must always be ameliorated with some spirit " . . . to kill the taste of iron" was one of his dictums. I never argued the point—and the following crustless tart of spinach, ham, and Madeira will surely demonstrate why.

COTTAGE TART

1 Heat oven to 350°. Heat 2 quarts of water to boiling. Add spinach and return to boiling. Drain immediately in a wire sieve, pressing out all liquid with the back of a wooden spoon. Reserve.

2 Combine ½ cup bread crumbs with ½ cup Parmesan cheese and the allspice in a medium bowl. Add melted butter and 1 teaspoon Madeira. Mix well with a fork. Press mixture over bottom and sides of a lightly buttered 9-inch glass pie plate.

3 Beat the cottage cheese with sour cream and remaining ½ cup Parmesan cheese until smooth, about 5 minutes. Sift in the flour and beat in the eggs, one at a time. Add bouillon powder and salt. Beat at high speed 3 minutes longer. Divide mixture in half and reserve.

4 Cook the ham with remaining ½ cup Madeira in a small saucepan over medium-high heat until all liquid is absorbed, about 5 minutes.

5 Mix the spinach with half the cheese mixture and spread over the bottom of the prepared pie plate.

6 Mix the ham with the remaining cheese mixture and spread evenly over the spinach.

7 Sprinkle the top of the tart with seasoned pepper and remaining 3 tablespoons bread crumbs. Bake 40 minutes. Serve immediately.

1 package (10 ounces) frozen chopped spinach, thawed
½ cup plus 3 tablespoons bread crumbs
1 cup freshly grated Parmesan cheese
⅛ teaspoon ground allspice
2 tablespoons butter, melted
¼ cup plus 1 teaspoon Madeira
1 pound cottage cheese
2 tablespoons sour cream
2 tablespoons all-purpose flour
2 eggs
½ teaspoon bouillon powder
1 teaspoon salt
¾ cup diced cooked ham
½ teaspoon seasoned pepper

Serves 6.

Aaron Fine always called me "Greene." It was his prerogative in our relationship. When we cooked together, he would caution me, "Greene, you're over-chopping" or "Greene, put down that salt shaker" whenever he sensed my will to embroider at work. He was a perfect kitchen collaborator because his ego (as a chef at least) was inviolable.

Aaron was, as I hope I have imparted, a supreme artist to the tips of his stubby fingers. Once we compared our handprints with published photos of Picasso's palms. Aaron's came closest to the master's for all-round talent but lacked the thick thumb joint that indicated a ruthlessness essential for super-stardom. He labored this physical betrayal morosely for a bit and then produced a wonderful children's book and the following kitchen culling of Carrots with Port. A dish of sheer and indisputable vegetable genius!

CARROTS WITH PORT

1½ pounds carrots
¼ cup olive oil
2 large cloves garlic, mashed
1 yellow onion, cut into ¼-inch-thick slices
Salt and freshly ground pepper
¼ cup strong beef stock
¾ cup port wine
Chopped parsley for garnish

Serves 4 to 5.

1 Pare the carrots and cut into thin strips, 2 inches long and ¼-inch thick.

2 Heat the oil in a heavy skillet. Add the garlic and onion; cook over low heat 5 minutes. Add the carrots; sprinkle with salt and pepper to taste. Mix well.

3 Combine the beef stock and port in a small saucepan. Bring to a boil; pour over the carrots. Cook covered over medium heat until carrots are almost tender, about 5 minutes. Remove cover; cook over high heat, stirring frequently, until most of liquid has evaporated. Sprinkle with parsley.

Some of my late friend Aaron's best dishes were very simple—something he could stew or pot or fricasee all the while he sat hunched over his typewriter "getting ideas." Some recipes were lost because I was confident he would produce them forever, but several I hoarded out of outrageous emulation.

He loved to cook fowl. "The wilder the duck, the better the performance," he often declared, aligning himself with Ibsen on the subject. But goose was, without a doubt, his major culinary

accomplishment. And since he was his own man in the kitchen, he thought nothing at all of seizing a poor bird at mid-roast and placing it (still warm) in the freezer until all excess fat could be scrupulously removed from the carcass and the pan. Then he would calmly set the bird back into a fiery oven to let it roast, undisturbed for a change (while he composed a sonnet or two), to a crisp and golden mean.

My own methods are hardly so unorthodox. But the fruit and nut stuffing is all Aaron's devise, recaptured lovingly.

ROAST GOOSE WITH FRUIT STUFFING

1 Soak the prunes in hot water 5 minutes; drain. Pit and slice in half.

2 Place prunes and wine in a saucepan; cook covered over low heat until prunes are just tender, about 10 minutes. Drain; reserve fruit and liquid.

3 Place apricots, orange juice, orange peel, and sugar in a saucepan; simmer 15 minutes. Drain; reserve fruit and syrup. Cut orange peel into slivers. Add the syrup to the prune liquid.

4 Place apples in a large bowl; add lemon juice, lemon peel, and dates. Let stand 10 minutes. Add reserved prunes, apricots, and orange peel. Add the butter, walnuts, allspice, cinnamon, and port; mix thoroughly. (If the mixture seems too wet, add a tablespoon or two of bread crumbs.)

5 Heat oven to 425°. Remove liver, giblets, neck, and all loose fat from goose. Rub the skin with ½ lemon. Wipe interior cavity; stuff loosely with fruit mixture. Using a trussing needle and twine, sew up cavity; secure legs, wings, and neck skin to body. Prick skin of thighs, back, and lower breast with a fork. (This is to allow fat to dribble out during roasting.) Set goose breast side up in a roasting pan; roast 15 minutes.

6 Reduce heat to 350°. Turn goose on its side; roast 1 hour, basting every 15 minutes with 2 tablespoons boiling water. (With a bulb baster, remove all excess fat that accumulates in the roasting pan.) Turn goose on its other side; roast 1 hour, basting every 15 minutes with 2 tablespoons boiling water.

7 Increase heat to 425°. Turn goose on its back. Roast until skin is crisp, about 15 minutes.

1 pound prunes
1 cup white wine
1 cup dried apricots, cut into halves
½ cup orange juice
1 piece orange peel, 3 inches long
2 tablespoons granulated sugar
2 tart apples, pared, cored, and coarsely chopped
Juice of ½ lemon
2 teaspoons slivered lemon peel
1 cup chopped dates
1 tablespoon unsalted butter, cut into small pieces
1½ cups ground walnuts
Pinch of ground allspice
Pinch of ground cinnamon
⅓ cup port wine
Bread crumbs (optional)
1 goose (9 to 10 pounds)
½ lemon
Boiling water
Kosher salt
Freshly ground pepper
2 tablespoons cognac
2 tablespoons unsalted butter

Serves 6.

8 Remove goose to serving platter; remove trussing. (Keep warm in turned-off oven, with door ajar, for up to 30 minutes before serving, if desired.)

9 Skim fat from roasting pan. Add reserved fruit liquid and season to taste with kosher salt and pepper. Bring to a boil; boil until liquid is reduced slightly. Add the cognac; cook 1 minute. Remove from heat. Stir in 2 tablespoons butter.

10 To serve, carve goose and spoon some sauce over each serving; pass remaining sauce.

Note: Goose fat can be strained through several layers of cheesecloth and stored in a tightly covered jar in the refrigerator for weeks. Use it to saute cabbage or for frying sliced potatoes in the Danish manner—with caraway seeds and lots of fresh dill added at the end.

My friend Aaron's love affair with France and the French was long and unrequited. The ultimate Francophile, he embarked on French lessons and embraced French novels, French philosophers, and French cooking. That he never arrived on French shores was only because his flesh was weak—he was afraid to fly there—which is odd and sad to me, because of all his witty drawings and posters the most famous exhorted Americans to Paris via Pan Am.

His recipes for Vol-Au-Vent Renoir (Parisian as the Eiffel Tower) and Plum Croquant (as provincial as his French teacher's home in Aix) attest to my friend's utter Gallic veneration.

VOL-AU-VENT RENOIR

1 Make Puff Pastry.

2 Heat oven to 425°. Sprinkle the chicken with salt, pepper, and allspice. Melt 4 tablespoons butter in a heavy skillet over medium-high heat. Add chicken; saute until golden brown, about 2 minutes on each side. Drain on paper toweling. Place in a shallow, approximately 7×12-inch, baking dish.

3 Add the veal to the skillet; saute 5 minutes on each side. Remove and cut into strips. Add 1 tablespoon butter and the mushrooms to the skillet. Saute mushrooms 5 minutes; remove from pan with a slotted spoon. Add the ham to the skillet; cook and stir 4 minutes. Add the cognac; stir and ignite. When flame subsides, add the Madeira; stir and ignite once more. When flame subsides, remove ham with a slotted spoon.

4 Add 1½ tablespoons butter to skillet; cook and stir until liquid becomes syrupy. Sprinkle with flour; cook over low heat, stirring constantly, 2 minutes.

5 Whisk in the cream. Stir in the nutmeg, hot pepper sauce, and lemon juice; cook over low heat, stirring constantly, 5 minutes. Add the veal, mushrooms, and ham; cook until very thick, about 3 minutes. Season with salt and pepper to taste; pour over chicken. Let stand 20 minutes.

6 Roll out puff pastry; cut to fit baking dish, leaving 1-inch margin on all sides. Place over chicken; seal edges by folding pastry into sides of dish and pressing gently. Cut a steam hole in the center; brush with egg. Bake until crust is crisp and brown, about 30 minutes.

Puff Pastry (recipe follows)
2 whole boneless chicken breasts, skin removed, cut into halves
Salt and freshly ground pepper
½ teaspoon ground allspice
6½ tablespoons butter
4 veal scallops, pounded thin
1 cup sliced mushrooms
1 cup diced ham
2 tablespoons cognac
3 tablespoons Madeira
1 tablespoon all-purpose flour
1½ cups whipping cream, hot
Dash of freshly grated nutmeg
Dash of hot pepper sauce
1 teaspoon lemon juice
1 egg beaten with 1 teaspoon water

Serves 4 to 6.

PUFF PASTRY

1 Combine the flours; remove ½ cup and reserve. Stir the oil into the flour mixture, using a rubber spatula. Stir in the salt and water. Press dough firmly into a mass and place in a plastic bag. Refrigerate 45 minutes.

2 Soften butter by beating it gently with a rolling pin. Knead with the heel of your hand until butter is soft and smooth but not oily. Work in the reserved flour; scrape into a bowl. Refrigerate 5 minutes.

3 Remove dough from refrigerator and place on lightly floured surface. Shape into a 16×8-inch rectangle with your hands so that narrow edge is parallel to you. Spread the butter over the upper two-thirds of the dough with a spatula, leaving a ⅛-inch border all around. Fold the unbuttered third over the middle third; fold the top third down to cover it. (Don't worry if there are a few holes; simply pinch dough together.)

4 Turn the dough 90 degrees. Roll it with a rolling pin into a 16-×8-inch rectangle. (Keep the sides as even as possible; gently press them in if they become uneven.) Fold in the narrow edges so that they meet in the middle. Fold the bottom half over the top half. Place dough in a plastic bag; refrigerate 1 hour.

2¾ cups all-purpose flour
¾ cup cake flour
¼ cup vegetable oil
2 teaspoons salt
1 cup ice-cold water
1½ cups unsalted butter

5 Place dough on floured surface and beat lightly with a rolling pin until it begins to soften. Roll into a 16×8-inch rectangle with narrow edge parallel to you. Fold bottom third over middle third; fold the top third down to cover it. Turn the dough 90 degrees; repeat rolling and folding procedure. Place dough in a plastic bag; refrigerate at least 2 hours.

6 When ready to use, place dough on a floured surface and beat lightly with a rolling pin. Roll out to a 15-inch square. Cut as directed in recipe. (Leftover dough can be cut and used for croissants. Bake in 450° oven 10 minutes.)

Note: Preparation of the butter and the dough should be done on a piece of marble or a pastry board chilled for at least ½ hour. Room should be cool.

PLUM CROQUANT

2 pounds plums
1½ cups granulated sugar
½ cup port wine
Juice of ½ lemon
½ cup blanched almonds, finely
    chopped
½ cup granulated sugar
½ cup all-purpose flour
Pinch of salt
4 tablespoons cold unsalted butter
1 teaspoon vanilla
Vanilla ice cream

Serves 4 to 6.

1 Place the plums in boiling water 1 minute to loosen skins. Peel and remove pits.

2 Place the plums, sugar, port, and lemon juice in a large pot; let stand 1 hour. Heat oven to 400°.

3 Bring the plums to a boil; reduce heat. Simmer until tender, about 20 minutes. Remove plums from the liquid with a slotted spoon; place in buttered 1-quart souffle dish. Cook the liquid over high heat until thick, about 35 to 40 minutes. Stir into the plums. Cool.

4 Combine the remaining ingredients, except ice cream, in a medium bowl; blend with a pastry blender until the texture of coarse crumbs. Sprinkle half of mixture over the plums; bake 10 minutes. Sprinkle remaining mixture over plums, mounding it slightly in the center; bake 10 minutes. Serve Plum Croquant warm with vanilla ice cream.

My poor friend Aaron would never have approved of this book, no less to being relegated to public scrutiny betwixt the welter of Madeira and port (no matter how often he used those spirited flavorings in his kitchen output). His own full-blown style and

aromatic persona obviously deserve a freer-formed tribute, covering his every cooking crotchet. Better still, an entire tome.

I dreamed of him quite often while going through the business of electing and rejecting recipes for this book from his small file. In my dreams, he is always uneasy—probably because of the culinary association.

I beg him to accept the homage. Like the last recipe in this chapter, it is only a trifle of what I feel.

RASPBERRY AND CURRANT TRIFLE

1 Make sponge cake; let stand 24 hours.

2 Make creme patissiere.

3 Cut the sponge cake into 1-inch cubes. Line the bottom of a glass bowl with cake cubes; sprinkle with Madeira and Amaretto. (Use more Amaretto to moisten if cake is very dry.) Spread currant jelly evenly over the cake; top with the raspberries, reserving 12 berries for garnish.

4 Reserve 1 cup creme patissiere; spread remainder over raspberries.

5 Whip the cream; stir in enough sugar to sweeten slightly. Fold in the reserved creme patissiere.

6 Spread cream mixture evenly in bowl with a rubber spatula. Garnish with ring of reserved raspberries; place one berry in center and surround with mint leaves. Refrigerate until well chilled.

Sponge Cake (recipe follows)
Crème Pâtissière (recipe follows)
¼ cup Madeira (approximately)
4 tablespoons Amaretto liqueur
1 jar (10 ounces) currant jelly
½ pint raspberries
1¼ cups whipping cream
Confectioners' sugar
Fresh mint leaves for garnish (optional)
Serves 6 to 8.

SPONGE CAKE

1 Heat oven to 325°. Rinse a large mixing bowl with very hot water and wrap a hot towel around the base of the bowl. Beat the egg yolks in the bowl, gradually adding 1¼ cups sugar, until doubled in volume. Stir in the lemon peel and Amaretto. Fold in the flour; then fold in the egg whites.

2 Butter a 9-inch tube pan; sprinkle with sugar. Pour in batter. Bake until golden and firm, about 1 hour. Cool on wire rack.

5 egg yolks
1¼ cups granulated sugar
Grated peel of ½ lemon
1½ teaspoons Amaretto liqueur
1 cup cake flour, sifted twice
5 egg whites, beaten until stiff
Sugar

Serves 8.

CRÈME PÂTISSIÈRE

1 cup milk
1 cup whipping cream
5 egg yolks
1 cup granulated sugar
7 tablespoons sifted cornstarch
1 piece vanilla bean, 1 inch long
1 tablespoon unsalted butter

1 Combine the milk and cream in a saucepan; bring to a boil. Remove from heat.

2 Place the egg yolks in a medium bowl; gradually beat in the sugar.

3 Sift the cornstarch over the egg yolk mixture; mix thoroughly. Stir in the milk and cream. Add the vanilla bean.

4 Transfer mixture to the top of a double boiler. Cook over boiling water, stirring constantly, until thick. Dot with butter and allow to cool. Mix well and chill.

Mint

Mint is an aggressive herb—no doubt about it. Outspoken in all its culinary collaborations, the aromatic plant is also hell on a garden—and the gardener!

The first herbs I ever planted were bordered by a tall hedge of this odiferous green foliage: peppermint, spearmint, mountain mint, pineapple balm, even catnip—I had them all. Their collective aroma scented the air for miles around and turned the garden into an air-strip for the fattest kamikaze bumblebees I have ever seen. I am not particularly nervous in the company of bees but this task force was so combative that merely reaching over the mint patch to weed the tarragon became a death-defying act—especially if one happened to hoe in shorts!

A seasoned East Hampton horticulturist I know took a very dim view of my mint cultivation. Staring hard (over a very dry martini) at the band of variegated greenery that stretched around the other herbs like a scented rope, he shook his head dourly.

"You'll regret all that *Mentha spicata,* chum," he said, sipping the icy cold gin and shuddering. "That stuff is like crab grass. It sends out runners—root hairs actually—that go on forever. By August your pretty sylvan glade of mint will have choked the life out of every other plant you put in. Take my advice: dig it *all* up now!

Dig? Now! When *all* looked as provincial as a French print? I'd rather uproot my peonies and poppies. Thank you for the sage advice but this gardener (armed with spade and trowel) would take his chances with the wily mint. And so I did.

The garden was a jungle of disorder by mid-July. No matter

205

how hard I snipped and hacked at the encroachment, the mint border insisted on becoming wall-to-wall vegetation. By the end of summer, I was lucky even to find the scrapings for a bouquet garni.

The next year I routed the entire spread. The mint was confined to three pots imbedded near a pipe that fed the oil burner. Within two years, however, even that slim harvest managed to invade the empty areas of the garden where the annuals, like basil and chervil, are planted—fully six or seven feet away from its original root stock.

Now when I place a pot on the window sill I watch out for my geraniums' safety.

Why plant mint at all? Pliny tells us that the leaves whet the appetite for meat. Ancient Persian chefs (and their descendants, who today produce the wonderful cookery of Morocco and the Middle East) claimed that crushed mint is a stimulant for the tongue, that the stinging irritant opens the tastebuds to receive differences of flavor.

In Mexico, oddly enough, mint is referred to as the "good herb," *yerba buena.*

Mint's origins are vague. The plant has never been found growing in a purely natural state; it has been a domesticated perennial down through the ages—despite its wandering roots. Even wild mint grows best in tilled soil. The plant thrives in gravelly, damp places margined by shorelines and streams. The flowering period is from July to September and the lavenderish-pink flowers, whorled in the axils of the leaves, produce the most succulent honey in the world.

According to Greek mythology, the slim stalk was the product of Olympian marital discord. The dainty nymph Menthe is said to have been turned into a bit of greenery by an envious rival, Persephone (a demi-goddess), who found that the much younger girl's charms were a mite too beguiling for her husband Pluto, the king of the underworld, to resist.

There are disparate tales about Menthe and Pluto's liaison—both fairly minty. In one version, the girl craved Pluto but he managed to withstand her blandishments until she made her physical aroma so tantalizing that the poor man could no longer hold out; then Persephone punished Menthe for her provocation. Another bit of lore alleges that Pluto was so smitten with Menthe that he grieved for months after her transfiguration. According to this tale, Pluto repined with longing and could no longer perform his husbandly obligations at home; so a deprived Persephone was forced to further endow her former rival with aphrodisiac powers. Then she fed her grieving husband a few mint leaves and turned him in her own direction.

Of course, if you have been following this text with any

vigilance at all, you will have observed that practically every other aromatic also was once thought to be an aphrodisiac—so mint is hardly worth getting steamed up about. In the sixteenth century, however, Culpeper, the physician, warned of the herb's love-inducing propensities thus: "Generally full of virtue as an anodyne—and helpful indeed for many of those loathsome and debilitating side effects of venerous connections—the herb must *never* be consumed by a wounded man because it will stimulate his organs to such lengths as there can never be a cure."

South Americans drink great quantities of *yerba maté* (minted tea) as a nerve tonic. Chinese believe mint added to oolong or jasmine will contain the appetite. And Moroccan tea, which is brewed exclusively from fresh crushed mint leaves, is said to be a sure cure for the traveler's affliction, "tourist tummy."

I like my mint with fresh peas. The herb also forms an unholy alliance with lamb—unholy, per se, because churchmen in the Middle Ages considered the coupling of wild mint with the holy and blessed lamb to be Satan's handiwork.

Try this Roman recipe for mint-flavored cold fish for starters. Its devise is over five hundred years old; yet (if you'll forgive the pun) it tastes absolutely newly minted.

COLD HADDOCK WITH CUCUMBER AND MINT

1 Cut fish in half lengthwise; cut halves in half crosswise. Place onion, lemon slice, wine, water, thyme, parsley, bay leaf, 1 teaspoon salt, and the peppercorns in a large heavy skillet. Heat to boiling; then immediately reduce heat until liquid barely simmers. Add fish; cook, basting fillets constantly, until fish flakes easily when pierced with a fork, about 5 minutes. Drain. Place on a serving dish; sprinkle with lemon juice and paprika. Let stand until cool; drain again and refrigerate.

2 Pare cucumber. Cut into quarters lengthwise; cut each quarter into four pieces. Sprinkle with salt; let stand in a colander 30 minutes. Brush off salt; finely chop cucumber. Press out all excess liquid.

3 Whip cream with white pepper in a small bowl until slightly thickened; stir in sour cream. Stir in cucumbers, shallot, mint, and parsley.

4 Remove fish from the refrigerator; pour off any juices. Spoon sauce over and around fish. Refrigerate until very cold. Just before serving, sprinkle with vinegar.

1 large haddock fillet (about 1½ pounds)
1 onion, cut in half and studded with 2 cloves
1 slice lemon
1 cup dry white wine
1½ cups water
Pinch of thyme
2 sprigs parsley
1 bay leaf
1 teaspoon salt
5 peppercorns
Juice of 1 lemon
Paprika
1 large cucumber
Salt
½ cup whipping cream
Pinch of ground white pepper
2 tablespoons sour cream
1 small shallot, minced
1 tablespoon chopped fresh mint or 2 teaspoons dried
1 tablespoon chopped parsley
1 tablespoon tarragon vinegar

Serves 4.

Where to grow mint in your garden?

Beneath a sunshade of hollyhocks is claimed to be the optimum garden territory for this good green; yet my sowings, as I have confessed, run wild anywhere. Late March or early April is the best time to stake out the perennial plants; the roots should be dug up, divided, and replanted every three years for greenest herb consumption.

There are true and false mints blooming side by side in my patch. Peppermint is the strongest and truest of the species in any aromatic hoedown; so be wary of its tang in your saute pan, for a little goes a long way. Spearmint is a milder aromatic and I add its fringed green leaves to iced tea, diet drinks, and even lemonade. Apple, orange, and pineapple mint are fruitier cousins, which I grow for agricultural aesthetics. Showy plants, they keep the bees busy, in the main, but crop up to decorate punch bowls and fruit compotes from time to time, too. Sherbet? Never!

False mints are those flowering greens like catnip and tansy, that smell good but whet only the feline appetite. My favorite mint of all (false or true, I do not know) is crème de menthe—no, not the cordial but a tiny cresslike plant, no higher than my thumb, that grows in mossy clumps like the best Kentucky bluegrass. I wait impatiently for its return every season, for it is a remarkable adjunct to a cold summer soup that I make when the tomatoes start to ripen. And before you smile at that alliance, remember that mint is a second cousin to basil.

3 tablespoons butter

½ cup minced onion

1 clove garlic, minced

½ teaspoon ground allspice

3 tablespoons all-purpose flour

3 cups hot strong chicken broth or stock

2 pounds ripe tomatoes, each cut into eighths

Pinch of sugar

Salt and freshly ground pepper to taste

½ cup sour cream

2 tablespoons fresh mint leaves or 1 teaspoon dried chopped with ½ cup chopped, seeded cucumbers

Sour cream

Serves 4 to 6.

CHILLED TOMATO SOUP WITH MINT

1 Melt butter in a saucepan. Saute onion, garlic, and allspice over medium heat 3 minutes. Stir in flour; cook, stirring constantly, 2 minutes. Whisk in hot broth. Add tomatoes; sprinkle with sugar, salt, and pepper. Heat to boiling; reduce heat and simmer 20 minutes. Let cool.

2 Transfer cooled soup, one half at a time, to a blender container; blend until smooth. Pour through a fine strainer into a large bowl; beat in ½ cup sour cream. Refrigerate until cold.

3 Just before serving, sprinkle with mint. Ladle into serving bowls; add a dollop of sour cream to each bowl.

Salads seasoned with mint are a Middle Eastern tradition and there are hundreds of such dishes. But one of these, Tabbouleh, is a particular indulgence of mine. I have collected tabbouleh recipes for years: some are made with cooked eggplant; some are laced with roasted peppers, and others with tomatoes; some are even mated with poached eggs and sprinkled with sesame seeds. All are tonic appetite stimulants, whether served as a first course or in conjuction with cold meats (like garlicky broiled chicken). The version I have chosen to represent the definitive tabbouleh was given me by a charming lady who grows her own mint in her Chappaqua garden—far, far from Istanbul or Baghdad. But the dish seems mighty authentic for all its geographic displacement!

LOUVERA RAYMOND'S TABBOULEH

1 Soak wheat in cold water to cover until softened, 2 to 2½ hours. Line a strainer with a dish towel; pour in the wheat. Twist towel around wheat and squeeze until all moisture is extracted.

2 Place wheat in a large bowl; knead in the onions with your hands. Add salt, pepper, parsley, mint, and oil; mix well. Add lemon juice and the tomato, if desired. Taste for seasoning; add more lemon juice, salt, or pepper, if necessary. Refrigerate until serving time.

3 Mound wheat mixture in a shallow bowl or on a platter. Surround with lettuce or fresh grape leaves. Garnish with any of the following: whole cherry tomatoes, marinated artichoke hearts, olives, hard-cooked eggs, and nasturtium leaves and/or flowers. Sprinkle toasted pine nuts over salad. (Tabbouleh is excellent served with fried chicken or broiled fish and meats.)

Note: Use a good oil—Olio Sasso or Plagniol brand, if possible.

1 cup cracked bulgur wheat
1 cup finely chopped onions (yellow and green, mixed)
1 teaspoon salt (approximately)
¼ teaspoon freshly ground pepper (approximately)
1½ cups finely chopped parsley
½ cup finely chopped fresh mint leaves
¼ cup olive oil
¼ cup lemon juice (approximately)
1 or 2 chopped seeded tomatoes (optional)
Lettuce or fresh grape leaves and additional garnishes (see Step 3)
Toasted pine nuts

Serves 6 to 8.

Mint is a summertime thing. Garden manuals claim that the herb may be forced indoors as a winter plant but never on my window sill, I can tell you! I used to chop dried mint leaves (like basil) with equal amounts of fresh parsley after the last bloom had withered. Recently, however, I discovered a better way. I now collect bunches of fresh mint at summer's end, strip the leaves from the stems, wipe them clean, and layer them in a deep glass jar. Then I add three-quarters of a cup of green crème de menthe plus one tablespoon of tarragon vinegar to each cup of mint leaves. I keep the jar tightly covered in a kitchen cabinet and drain the preserved leaves on paper toweling before chopping them whenever the taste of chopped fresh mint is required. Sometimes the top leaves turn grayish from the light; if that occurs, I merely weed past the discolored layer for the verdant supply below.

Lamb and mint are old and wise culinary partners. Consider mint-roasted Greek pascal lamb or North African *mechoui* or any of the countless kebabs and shashliks that dot Turkish or Persian menus; they offer vivid proof that even a whisper of mint on a slice of lamb can be enough to color the entire dish.

In the following recipe from an Italian kitchen, lamb is first studded with garlic, then anointed with mint and mustardy herbs. The meat must sit at least an hour before it roasts to allow the flavors to coalesce. But the result is a kitchen triumph in any language. With the lamb, instead of the usual accompaniment of oven-roasted potatoes, I offer *risotta pomidoro,* or Tomato Rice. *Bravissimo!*

LEG OF LAMB CASTELLET WITH TOMATO RICE

1 leg of lamb (about 4 pounds)
Salt and freshly ground pepper
2 to 3 cloves garlic, cut into slivers
1½ tablespoons chopped fresh mint leaves or 2 teaspoons dried
1 teaspoon chopped fresh basil or ½ teaspoon dried
½ teaspoon chopped fresh thyme or ¼ teaspoon dried
2 tablespoons Dijon mustard
Juice of ½ lemon
½ cup olive oil
Tomato Rice (recipe follows)

Serves 6 to 8.

1 Rub lamb with salt and pepper. Lightly score surface with a lattice pattern. Make a 1-inch incision, using an ice pick or the point of a sharp knife, at each intersection; insert 1 garlic sliver in each. Let stand 30 minutes.

2 Combine mint, basil, thyme, mustard, and lemon juice in a small bowl; whisk in oil, 1 tablespoon at a time, until thick. Rub mixture over top and sides of lamb. Let stand 30 minutes.

3 Heat oven to 450°. Place lamb on a rack in a roasting pan. Roast 15 minutes. Reduce oven heat to 350°; roast 12 to 15 minutes per pound for medium rare.

4 Meanwhile, make Tomato Rice. Let lamb stand 15 minutes before slicing. Serve with Tomato Rice.

TOMATO RICE

1 Melt 2 tablespoons butter in a Dutch oven. Saute shallots until golden. Add rice; stir until rice turns milky in color.

2 Add tomatoes, sugar, chicken broth, and hot pepper sauce. Heat to boiling; add bouquet garni. Cover and bake in 350° oven 18 minutes. (If rice is still wet after 18 minutes, remove cover and bake until liquid is evaporated.)

3 Discard bouquet garni; stir in remaining 1 tablespoon butter. Sprinkle with mint.

3 tablespoons butter
½ cup finely chopped shallots or onions
1 cup rice
1½ cups chopped, seeded tomatoes
½ teaspoon brown sugar
2 cups hot strong chicken broth
Dash of hot pepper sauce
Bouquet garni composed of 1 sprig parsley, 1 sprig thyme, 1 bay leaf, 1 clove garlic
2 tablespoons chopped fresh mint for garnish

Serves 6 to 8.

In Cajun patois, *lagniappe* means "a little something extra." The following recipe for Very Special Lamb Hash turns leftovers into largesse with flecks of mint and a golden crust of Parmesan cheese. Now, that's *lagniappe!*

VERY SPECIAL LAMB HASH

1 Place potatoes in a medium saucepan; add cold water to cover. Heat to boiling; reduce heat. Simmer 15 minutes; drain. Cut potatoes into ½-inch cubes.

2 Heat butter and oil in a large, heavy ovenproof skillet. Saute onion and garlic until golden; push to edge of skillet. Place meat in center of skillet; cook and stir over medium heat until light brown.

3 Heat broiling unit. Add potatoes, olives, green pepper, red pepper, mint, salt, pepper, and soy sauce to skillet; stir until well mixed and gently flatten against bottom of skillet. Cook over medium heat, stirring occasionally, until potatoes are brown but still slightly crunchy, about 10 minutes. Add beef broth as mixture begins to dry out.

4 Raise heat under skillet; cook, without stirring, 5 minutes. Sprinkle Parmesan cheese over potato mixture. Place under broiler until top is brown and crisp. Serve with chili sauce, if desired.

3 large potatoes
3 tablespoons butter
1 tablespoon olive or vegetable oil
1 large onion, finely chopped
2 cloves garlic, minced
2 cups diced cooked lamb
¼ cup chopped black olives
1 small green bell pepper, coarsely chopped
1 small Jalapeño pepper, chopped, or 2 teaspoons crushed dried chili peppers
2 tablespoons chopped fresh mint leaves or 2 teaspoons dried
Salt and freshly ground pepper to taste
2 tablespoons soy sauce
¼ cup beef broth
3 tablespoons freshly grated Parmesan cheese
Chili sauce (optional)

Serves 4.

The coolness of garden mint misleads many a fledgling cook into thinking of this herb as a tranquilizer in a saute pan. Far from it! South of the border, mint is considered a powerful seasoner. A Mexican stew that I dote on for its curious amalgam of flavors unites pork and fresh pineapple with crushed red peppers and mint. It tastes vaguely Oriental to my enthusiastic tongue; so invariably I serve it over snowy white rice. But after a little kitchenly rumination on the subject, I would deem brown rice equally acceptable—or tiny *spätzle,* or noodles, or *nockerln*. Be my guest!

PORK WITH PINEAPPLE

2 tablespoons butter
1 tablespoon vegetable oil
2½ pounds boneless pork, cut into 1-inch cubes
Salt and freshly ground pepper
2 large onions, thinly sliced
1 small clove garlic, minced
¼ cup dry sherry
1 cup chicken broth
1 jar (4 ounces) pimientos, drained, chopped
½ teaspoon crushed dried hot peppers
1 small pineapple, pared, cut into chunks
2 teaspoons chopped fresh mint leaves or 1 teaspoon dried mint chopped with 1 teaspoon parsley
4 cups cooked rice

Serves 6.

1 Heat butter and oil in a heavy skillet. Add meat, ½ pound at a time; cook until brown on all sides. Transfer browned meat to a Dutch oven; sprinkle with salt and pepper.

2 Add onions and garlic to skillet; saute until golden. Transfer to Dutch oven with a slotted spoon. Remove excess grease from skillet; stir in sherry over medium-high heat, scraping bottom and sides of skillet until smooth. Pour sherry over meat.

3 Add chicken broth, pimientos, hot peppers, pineapple, and 1 teaspoon mint to Dutch oven. Heat to boiling; reduce heat. Simmer covered until meat is tender, about 2 hours. Sprinkle with remaining mint. Serve with rice.

Since it has no logical national antecedence, mint pops up in every cuisine imaginable. A vegetable farrago, dubbed Gypsy Eggplant, from Transylvania, depends as much on the sharp flavor of the herb as a French farm-kitchen stew, Veau Provençale, does. Mint is a culinary citizen of the world—and a welcome addition in whatever pot it appears!

GYPSY EGGPLANT

2 medium eggplants
Salt
3 tablespoons butter
2 large shallots, minced
2 cloves garlic, minced
3 tomatoes, seeded, chopped
1 rib celery, finely chopped
3 sprigs parsley, finely chopped
1 sprig thyme, finely chopped
1 basil leaf, finely chopped
1 bay leaf, crumbled
1 tablespoon chopped fresh mint leaves or 1 teaspoon dried chopped with 2 teaspoons parsley

1 Cut eggplants into ½-inch-thick slices. Sprinkle well with salt; let stand in a colander 30 minutes.

2 Meanwhile, melt butter in a heavy saucepan. Saute shallots and garlic until golden. Add tomatoes, celery, parsley, thyme, basil, bay leaf, mint, and allspice. Cook over low heat, stirring occasionally, 20 minutes. Add red pepper, salt, and freshly ground pepper; cook 10 minutes longer.

3 Heat oven to 400°. Heat ¼ cup oil in a heavy skillet. Fry eggplant slices, a few at a time, until golden brown on both sides, adding remaining oil as needed. Drain on paper toweling.

4 Beat eggs until frothy in a large bowl. Gradually stir in tomato mixture. Add eggplant; toss to coat. Scrape mixture into a buttered casserole; sprinkle with Parmesan cheese. Bake 20 minutes. Dust with parsley.

Pinch of ground allspice
1 **large sweet red pepper, seeded, cut into thin strips**
Salt and freshly ground pepper to taste
½ **cup olive or vegetable oil (approximately)**
3 **eggs**
¼ **cup freshly grated Parmesan cheese**
1 **teaspoon chopped parsley**

Serves 4.

VEAU PROVENÇALE

1 Melt 3 tablespoons butter in a heavy skillet over medium-high heat. Saute meat, ¼ pound at a time, until light brown on all sides. Return all meat to skillet; pour vermouth over. Stir over medium-high heat 2 to 3 minutes, scraping bottom and sides of skillet. Transfer to a Dutch oven.

2 Add 3 tablespoons butter to skillet. Saute onion and garlic over medium heat until soft. Transfer half of mixture to Dutch oven with a slotted spoon. Add mushrooms to remaining half in skillet; saute until brown. Add rice; stir over medium heat until rice turns milky in color. Scrape mixture into a bowl; reserve.

3 Stir tomato paste, chicken stock, tomatoes, salt, pepper, and bouquet garni into Dutch oven over low heat. Heat to boiling; reduce heat. Simmer covered until meat is tender, about 1 hour and 20 minutes.

4 Meanwhile, trim ends of zucchini; cut each zucchini into eighths. Cook in boiling salted water 2 minutes; rinse under cold running water until cool and drain on paper toweling. Dice zucchini; reserve.

5 When meat is fork-tender, stir reserved rice mixture into Dutch oven. Heat to boiling; reduce heat. Simmer covered until rice is tender and has absorbed all liquid, about 20 minutes.

6 Remove bouquet garni from Dutch oven. Stir in reserved zucchini; cook 2 minutes. Stir in cheese; sprinkle with mint and parsley. Serve immediately.

7 **tablespoons butter**
2 **pounds boneless veal, cut into 1-inch cubes**
¼ **cup dry vermouth**
1 **large yellow onion, minced**
1 **large clove garlic, minced**
3 **large mushrooms, thinly sliced**
1 **cup rice**
1 **teaspoon tomato paste**
2 **cups hot chicken stock**
3 **tomatoes, seeded, chopped**
½ **teaspoon salt**
¼ **teaspoon freshly ground pepper**
Bouquet garni composed of 1 bay leaf, 1 sprig thyme, 2 sprigs parsley tied in cheesecloth
2 **small zucchini**
¼ **cup freshly grated Parmesan cheese**
2 **tablespoons chopped fresh mint leaves or 2 teaspoons dried**
1 **tablespoon parsley**

Serves 6.

Baked Stuffed Cucumbers (*Gurken mit Fleischfüllung*) is a Saxon dish that I first ate when a child as a guest of our German next-door neighbors. The lady who stuffed the cucumbers then was Danish but such a great cook that her repertoire covered all of *mittle-Europa*. I remember that she picked the mint from a patch growing in her backyard near the wash-line and she always gave us a bit to chew at the same time, "to make a fine appetite, later!"

It certainly seemed to work.

She insisted that the dish could not be made at all times of the year. It was a spring recipe, she declared, that required new baby cucumbers and tender green mint leaves. But I must confess that I have made the dish admirably—with minor deviations from her dictum—in January as well as June throughout the intervening years. And I advise you to do the same. But do scrub the wax off the cucumbers before you pare them—truly, it makes a difference.

STUFFED CUCUMBERS

6 medium cucumbers
Salt
Lemon juice
1 pound ground pork
1 potato, pared, parboiled, grated
1 onion, finely chopped
1 tablespoon finely chopped fresh mint leaves or 1 teaspoon dried chopped with 1 tablespoon parsley
2 slices Canadian bacon, finely chopped
1 teaspoon salt
Freshly ground pepper to taste
¼ cup butter
1 cup beef stock
1 teaspoon all-purpose flour
1 tablespoon tomato paste
2 tablespoons whipping cream
⅓ cup sour cream
Freshly chopped mint leaves

Serves 6 as an appetizer.

1 Pare cucumbers; cut in half lengthwise. Scoop out seeds and watery pulp; sprinkle with salt and lemon juice. Invert halves in pairs on paper toweling. Let stand to drain 30 minutes.

2 Combine pork, potato, onion, mint, Canadian bacon, 1 teaspoon salt, and pepper in a bowl; mix thoroughly. Wipe cucumbers with paper toweling. Fill each half with pork mixture. Tie each pair together with kitchen string.

3 Heat oven to 375°. Melt 3 tablespoons butter in a large Dutch oven. Saute cucumbers, three at a time, over medium heat until golden on all sides. Arrange cucumbers in Dutch oven; add beef stock. Bake covered 15 minutes. Turn cucumbers over; bake 15 minutes longer.

4 Reduce oven heat to 275°. Carefully remove cucumbers and arrange in one snug-fitting layer in a serving dish. Remove strings. Keep warm in oven.

5 Combine flour and tomato paste; stir into beef stock in Dutch oven. Add cream; cook over low heat until thickened, about 10 minutes. Add remaining 1 tablespoon butter; whisk in sour cream until smooth. Pour sauce over the cucumbers; sprinkle with mint.

Tongue and Vegetable Salad, spiced with mint, comes from Switzerland. I have never crossed an Alp but a charming Swiss once crossed my path when I was giving cooking lessons. He observed all my rules dutifully for an entire season and, at the last class, produced the following salad (and a bottle of cool Swiss wine) for a celebration. It is the nicest apple a teacher ever received!

TONGUE AND VEGETABLE SALAD

1 Place tongue, cheese,* and vegetables in a large bowl; toss lightly.

2 Combine remaining ingredients in a bowl; whisk until smooth. Add to tongue mixture; mix well. Refrigerate until cold.

*Note: I prefer Emmenthal or Gruyère.

2 cups julienne cooked tongue
1 cup julienne Swiss cheese
1½ cups julienne raw potatoes, parboiled 1 minute
1 cup French-cut wax beans, parboiled 1 minute
1 cup thawed frozen peas
½ cup fresh bean sprouts
¼ cup chopped sweet red pepper
1 red onion, minced
1½ cups mayonnaise
½ cup sour cream
1½ teaspoons Dijon mustard
1 tablespoon lemon juice
½ teaspoon olive oil
1 teaspoon tarragon vinegar
1 teaspoon caraway seeds
1 tablespoon freshly chopped mint leaves or ½ teaspoon dried chopped with 1 tablespoon parsley
Salt and freshly ground pepper to taste

Serves 4 to 6.

As I have said before, I was a deep-dyed movie fan in my youth. I started going to picture shows regularly before I was out of short pants and all my earliest (and misconceived) notions of high and low society alike were acquired Saturday afternoons and evenings in those darkened pleasure domes.

As a matter of fact, the first drink (one that could truly be designated an adult libation) that I coveted was a mint julep—because I had seen so many fastidious movie Southerners (like Leslie Howard, George Brent, and Henry Fonda) quaff that beverage in sagas of plantation life at the Loew's Plaza and the Fox Granada. To emulate the conceit of juleps at home, I even packed ice tea with mint until it turned viridian, but somehow the effect lacked authority. So I could not wait until I was old enough to order the genuine item at a bar.

The occasion came, as I recall, on my eighteenth birthday. My newly married sister had taken me to a play to celebrate; after the theatre, as a fillip to the evening, she allowed me to escort her to a particularly glossy cocktail lounge.

I do not remember her order at all but mine is imprinted in memory forever. Without pause, I sidled onto the bar stool and requested a mint julep, please—to the bartender's distress, it occurs to me now, for it always has been a troublesome drink to prepare. I was a rapt audience as he crushed the leaves and muddled sugar and ice together. And I could hardly wait as he covered the mug with a layer of white frost before he poured in the bourbon.

It looked absolutely wonderful. It tasted dreadful! The sweetest, strongest, most sickening concoction I ever swallowed. But swallow it I certainly did, in the tradition of trusty Howard, Brent, Fonda, et al. The movies, you see, had provided a prime model for my behavior (comparable to those famous playing fields of Oxford) and I would never let my alma mater down— even if it meant throwing up in the men's room later. Which it did. But I never regretted the experience. Bourbon, I learned, should never be mixed with anything, except water perhaps. Mint and ice, I later deduced, are best combined in tart unions, such as the following:

LEMON-MINT SHERBET IN LEMON SHELLS

1 dozen large lemons
4 cups water
3 cups granulated sugar
2 tablespoons finely grated lemon peel
2 tablespoons minced fresh mint leaves
Fresh mint leaves for garnish

Serves 12.

1 Cut a ½-inch-thick slice from stem end of each lemon; reserve slices. Cut a very thin slice from opposite end of each lemon, so that lemons will stand on end; discard thin slices.

2 Carefully cut around insides of lemon shells and remove pulp. Discard seeds; place lemon shells and reserved slices in a plastic bag; freeze at least 3 hours or until ready to serve.

3 Place lemon pulp in a blender container or food processor; blend until pureed. (If any large pieces of membrane remain, pick them out by hand.) There should be about 2 cups of lemon puree; if there is less, add freshly squeezed lemon juice to make 2 cups.

4 Combine water and sugar in a saucepan; heat to boiling. Boil 5 minutes; remove from heat. Stir in lemon puree; let stand until cool.

5 Strain lemon mixture. Stir in grated lemon peel and minced mint leaves. Pour into the canister of an ice cream maker; freeze according to manufacturer's directions.

6 Place sherbet in freezer until ready to serve. At serving time, spoon sherbet into frozen lemon shells. Cover with the lemon slice "tops"; garnish with fresh mint leaves.

Note: Recipe can be cut in half. Extra sherbet can be stored in freezer.

Mustard

There are a host of seasonings I suppose I could make do *without*.
Sustaining only some slight culinary deprivation, I might get
along sans celery seed, for instance, and cardamom, too, in a
pinch. Giving up marjoram and savory entirely would be
another matter, although neither of those are active-duty herbs
in my kitchen. And though I do not think my Thanksgiving
turkey would cotton to the idea of a sageless dressing, I rarely
dip into the sage canister the rest of the year.

Why belabor the point further? What I am trying to state is
that some aromatic adjuncts, while they most decidedly enhance
the dishes in which they're used, are an occasional thing in this
cook's life. On the other hand, there are seasonings to which I
am so helplessly addicted that I cannot manage to slip on an
apron unless I know they are within easy reach. Mustard is one
such staunch ally.

How it came to be a substance of such authority in my life, I
cannot tell. Like the rest of middle-America during the 1930s and
1940s, I grew up on sandwiches polarized by Gulden's mustard
on one slice of soft white bread and Hellmann's mayonnaise on
the other. The formula was absolutely unchanged whether the
filling was ham, cheese, or roast beef. The taste? Bland enough
to disguise any hint of relish in the final assemblage.

I know full well that I never tasted any mustard that bore a
true savor (or that wasn't, for that matter, made in America)
until a thoughtful friend, knowing I relished the prose of
M. F. K. Fisher, brought me an enormous crock of the *real thing*
from Dijon, France, one of the author's early literary landscapes.

I remember that I was so impressed with the packaging—the seals and embossments—that I let at least a month pass before I scraped the red sealing wax from the cork and inserted a finger into the contents. But what a glorious surprise awaited my tongue once I did! That this pungent flavor and heady perfume (compounded of crushed seeds and Burgundian white wine) could be even distantly related to the muddy dressing in my family's refrigerator was an anathema to which I am still unreconciled.

Good fortune brought M. F. K. Fisher herself into my life not too long afterward. We met in Amagansett shortly before I was to embark on my very first trip to Europe and she on her umpteenth return. In a moment of instant, mutual admiration over a dinner I had cooked, we agreed to meet in France, in the foothills of the Alpes Maritimes, later that year.

The planned rendezvous colored my entire travel itinerary. Instead of leisurably enjoying my role as an American in Paris, I felt impelled to repair to every French provincial town and inn that the remarkable writer had lovingly described in *The Gastronomical Me*. Having exchanged the good smells of Left Bank bistros for gas-polluted autoroutes, I soon found myself on the way to Dijon in a rented Renault with an unfamiliar transmission and an Avis manual printed in a language that I barely understood.

I left Paris in late afternoon without a road map or any knowledge of my destination, except that it was smack in the center of Burgundy. More pertinently, I neglected to request any pre-tour rundown of the automobile's working parts; consequently, I was to discover after sundown that I could not fathom how to turn on the headlights.

After being hopelessly lost for hours—and driving on the shoulder of the road to avoid being hit by clearly hostile Gallic motorists—I finally eased off the superhighway onto a small dirt towpath apparently traveled only by oxen, sheep, and geese. Trailing a particularly torpid flock for some miles, I made my way to a very primitive garage where a puzzled mechanic listened to my tale of woe in disbelief. Blinking hard, he opened my car door and flicked on the lights at once. Since the connection was affixed to the base of the steering wheel, where, it seemed to me, only windshield wipers belonged, I had neglected its presence pointedly.

Embarrassed, but much relieved to be on my way, I was about to ask the young Frenchman one additional favor—directions to Dijon—when I sneezed. And then promptly sneezed again.

I could not help myself, for the air was thick with such a heady aroma that it had a galvanic effect on my sinuses.

"Mustard," I cried, sniffing like a bloodhound. "We must be very close to Dijon!"

We were in fact a mere quarter mile from that fabulous city where unwary tourists awaken with eyes smarting from the gingery condiment in the wind.

The narrow, crooked streets of Dijon are rich with *moutardiers,* shops as grand as Victorian apothocaries, that sell china crocks (plain or incised with ornate tracery) crammed with spirited and odorous emollients. These containers come in every size imaginable, from six to sixty inches high. I bought three the very next morning.

That first mustard pot brought to me from Dijon now holds a bouquet of yellow daisies in my kitchen. Although I have made many pilgrimages to the city of its manufacture since I first sampled its contents, no other mustard I have ever tasted can compare with the initial lick from my forefinger way back when.

Some food authority recently noted that mustard is probably the world's favorite condiment. As I have not traversed the entire globe, I cannot verify his statement but I can aver with certainty that it is the best known in history.

Hippocrates, the original Greek physician, first praised medicinal powers of mustard in 460 B.C. Some time later, when Darius of Persia sent Alexander the Great a bag of sesame seeds, apparently to symbolize the size of his army, canny Alexander replied with a sack of a like-number of mustard seeds—to reflect not only equal legions of troops but also their ferocity!

Curiously enough, despite its tang mustard was said by the ancient oracle at Delphi to signify indifference. (Not in my salad dressing, however!)

A proper cosmopolite among seasonings, the spicy sauce is known by a multitude of aliases: *moutarde* in France; *seuf* and *mostrick* in Germany; *mostarda* or *senape,* depending upon region, in Italy. It is *mostaza* all over Spain and Latin America and *senap* or *sennep* in the Scandinavian countries.

All these names reveal a twin etymology. The Latin *sinapis* comes from a Celtic root; it was the Gauls of Brennus who first imported black mustard seeds into northern Italy. The French *moutarde* undoubtedly stems from *moût,* meaning "must," which is unfermented grape juice. The city of Dijon claims that its motto, *Moult me tarde,* gave the condiment its name but food scholars disparage that belief as a chauvinistic fiction—one probably bruited about by the town fathers in the fourteenth century as advertisement for the local produce.

Mustard, you understand, is not exclusively a European prerogative. The Chinese cultivated beds of the diminutive seeds over 3,000 years ago. The following recipe for an eastern vegetable dish, Mallum, was passed down through generations of Asian cooks. I have eaten this exotic cabbage, mustard seed, and coconut fusion as a curry side dish at a proper Ceylonese dinner party. And I have also whipped it up at home when the fare was merely broiled fish.

A friend of the recipe-giver (who begs anonymity here) claims that she makes up a batch of Mallum during the "Late, Late Show" whenever the interminable commercials drive her into the kitchen!

CEYLONESE MALLUM

1 small cabbage, shredded
1 tablespoon water
1 teaspoon ground turmeric
3 tablespoons olive oil
1 tablespoon brown mustard seeds
1 large onion, finely chopped
3 large dried red chili peppers, crushed
Salt and freshly ground pepper
½ coconut, pared, shredded (2 cups, loosely packed)
2 teaspoons lemon juice

Serves 4 to 6.

1 Place cabbage in a bowl; sprinkle with 1 tablespoon water and ½ teaspoon turmeric and toss until well mixed.

2 Heat oil in a large saucepan over high heat. Add mustard seeds; cover immediately, as seeds will pop. Cook until popping stops, 5 to 10 seconds.

3 Reduce heat to medium; stir in onion and chili peppers. Cook, stirring constantly, until light brown.

4 Add cabbage; cook, stirring constantly, until tender, 8 to 10 minutes. Sprinkle with salt and pepper. Stir in coconut until mixed; cook covered 4 to 5 minutes.

5 Stir in lemon juice. Taste for seasoning; add salt and pepper, if necessary (cabbage loves salt). Cook uncovered over medium heat 5 minutes.

To describe table mustard as a condiment made of crushed yellow or white seeds of *Brassica hirta* or brown and black seeds of *Brassica nigra* is essentially correct. But that statement is as misleading as labeling wine "fermented grape juice"!

Just as there are wines and *wines,* so there are mustards and, oh well, *mustards!* Of all those ochery pastes, the product of Dijon is obviously the winner for me. Pale and creamy, with a clean, sharp taste that enhances other flavors admirably, it may be hot but it is never bitter, salty, or (heaven forfend!) sweet. It is so special that it is singled out for *haute cuisine* appearances in recipes printed the world over. I think Dijon mustard is best, however, in the savory devises of Burgundian housewives— dishes like the following, which absolutely depend on a touch of the native elixir.

ÉMINCÉ DE BOEUF DIJONNAISE

1 Boil potatoes in salted water 15 minutes. Rinse under cold running water until cool and drain. Cut into ¼-inch slices.

2 Melt butter in a heavy skillet. Stir in mustard. Add onions; saute over medium heat until tender. Stir in potatoes until well coated; cook, stirring frequently, 5 minutes.

3 Add meat; sprinkle with garlic and allspice, rubbing the seasoning into the meat with a knife. Cook, tossing gently, for 10 minutes. Season with salt and pepper.

4 Sprinkle with vinegar and beef broth; cook over medium heat until most of moisture is evaporated, 3 to 4 minutes. Sprinkle with parsley.

5 **medium baking potatoes**
3 **tablespoons butter**
2 **tablespoons Dijon mustard**
2 **cups minced onions**
1 **pound leftover cooked pot roast, thinly sliced (about 2 cups)**
1 **clove garlic, minced**
Pinch of ground allspice
Salt and freshly ground pepper to taste
1½ **tablespoons red wine vinegar**
¼ **cup beef broth, white wine, or water**
Chopped parsley for garnish

Serves 6.

Burgundians showed a serious dedication to the business of mustard-making as far back as 1336, when the Duke of Burgundy invited his cousin, King Phillip the Fair, to a picnic in Dijon to sample the local produce. According to stalwart collectors of such trivia, Phillip was so overwhelmed by Dijon's mustard that he ignored most of the other viands and consumed a *poinçon* (about sixty gallons) during his week of gourmandising al fresco!

Only slightly more circumspect, Pope John XXII of Avignon was so enamored of the Dijon mustard that he insisted it be used to spice every dish he ate—loaves and fishes alike.

Since mustard and seafood make such zesty confederates, it is no wonder the Pope's appetite flourished. Reckon the stunning possibilities of a Crab Souffle dependent upon ripe eggplant for body and Dijon mustard for temperament.

CRAB SOUFFLE WITH EGGPLANT

Homemade Tomato Sauce (see
Index)
1   eggplant (about ¾ pound)
¼   cup unsalted butter
2   tablespoons grated Jarlsberg or
    Gruyère cheese
3   tablespoons all-purpose flour
1½ cups milk, hot
⅓   cup whipping cream
1   tablespoon cornstarch
1½ tablespoons water
½   teaspoon salt
¼   teaspoon freshly ground
    pepper
Pinch of cayenne pepper
⅛   teaspoon freshly grated
    nutmeg
4   eggs, separated
⅓   cup grated Parmesan cheese
⅓   cup grated Jarlsberg or
    Gruyère cheese
1   large shallot, minced
1   clove garlic, minced
¼   teaspoon chopped fresh
    thyme, or a pinch of dried
1   package (6 ounces) frozen
    crabmeat
1½ tablespoons Dijon mustard

Serves 4 to 6.

1   Make tomato sauce.

2   Heat oven to 400°. Wrap the eggplant in aluminum foil; bake until tender, about 40 minutes. Let stand to cool; cut in half. Scrape pulp into a small bowl. Reserve.

3   Grease a 1½- to 2-quart souffle dish with ½ tablespoon butter; sprinkle with 1 tablespoon grated Jarlsberg (or Gruyère) cheese. Place in refrigerator to chill.

4   Melt 2½ tablespoons of the butter in a saucepan. Add flour; whisk until smooth. Cook over low heat, stirring constantly, 2 minutes. Quickly add hot milk; cook, stirring constantly, 5 minutes. Blend in half the cream.

5   Combine cornstarch and water; stir into the sauce. Add salt, pepper, cayenne, and nutmeg and cook 5 minutes. Remove from heat. Beat in egg yolks, one at a time, beating well after each addition. Return saucepan to low heat (Do not boil!); stir in the ⅓ cup each of the Parmesan and Jarlsberg cheeses. Scrape into a bowl; cover and let stand to cool. (This mixture is called a *panade*.)

6   Melt the remainder of the butter in a saucepan. Add shallot, garlic, thyme, and reserved eggplant. Cook covered over medium heat 5 minutes.

7   Meanwhile, thaw crabmeat in a pan of boiling water. Drain and coarsely chop. Stir into eggplant with mustard and remaining cream. Spoon into souffle dish.

8   Beat egg whites until stiff but not dry. Stir ¼ of egg whites into the panade; fold in remainder. Pour over the eggplant mixture in souffle dish. Sprinkle with remaining 1 tablespoon Jarlsberg (or Gruyère) cheese. Place in oven; reduce heat to 375°. Bake until golden, about 40 minutes. Serve at once with warm tomato sauce.

English mustard is usually sold as a powder. Colman's is the optimum mustard on British shores; though it is composed of a

mixture of black and yellow mustard seeds (an alliance never even conceded as a possibility in Dijon), the flavor of this powder affords a razor-sharp zest that suits seafood remarkably well on occasion.

A bastardized fish 'n chips recipe that I admire hugely is doubly tasty because it combines both English and Dijon produce in its aromatic composition.

BATTERED-UP FISH AND SHRIMP

1 Combine 1 cup flour, the dry mustard, nutmeg, and ½ teaspoon salt in a medium bowl. Combine egg yolks, Dijon mustard, and beer; whisk into flour mixture until smooth. Refrigerate covered 8 hours.

2 Place flounder and shrimp in a bowl. Whisk together 1 cup oil, the lemon juice, vinegar, 2 teaspoons salt, and the pepper. Pour over fish; refrigerate covered 4 hours.

3 Make tartar sauce.

4 Beat egg whites until stiff but not dry; fold into cold batter. Remove seafood from marinade; pat dry with paper toweling. Dust seafood with flour.

5 Heat oven to 275°. Heat 1 inch of oil in a large heavy skillet over medium-high heat. Dip seafood into batter with a slotted spoon; fry, a few pieces at a time, in the hot oil until golden brown on both sides. Drain on paper toweling. Keep warm in oven while frying remainder. Serve at once with tartar sauce.

Note: A touch of Dijon mustard (about 1 teaspoon to each cup of sauce) will turn the tartar sauce into a genuine Tartar!

1 cup all-purpose flour
2 teaspoons dry mustard
1 teaspoon freshly grated nutmeg
½ teaspoon salt
4 eggs, separated
2 teaspoons Dijon mustard
1 cup beer
1½ pounds flounder fillets, cut into 3-inch-long strips
1 pound uncooked shrimp, shelled, deveined
1 cup vegetable oil
½ cup lemon juice
½ cup white wine vinegar
2 teaspoons salt
¼ teaspoon freshly ground pepper
Tartar Sauce (see Index)
Flour
Vegetable oil

Serves 4 to 6.

A very French specialty, spicy Shrimp à la Moutarde, makes a welcome first course when the mustard is Dijon and the Burgundy is white. Each portion of shrimp fits neatly into a scallop shell (like Coquilles St. Jacques) but little ramekins will do just as nicely. The salient feature of this appetizer is that it may be prepared without baking hours before serving, then doused with Parmesan and sent to the oven while guests gulp down the last of their aperitifs!

SHRIMP
A LA MOUTARDE

3 tablespoons butter

2 tablespoons all-purpose flour

1 cup warm milk

⅛ teaspoon freshly grated nutmeg

Pinch of cayenne pepper

½ teaspoon salt

¼ teaspoon freshly ground pepper

1½ tablespoons minced shallot

2 tablespoons chopped parsley

¼ cup dry white wine

2 tablespoons Dijon mustard

1 small egg yolk

1 pound small uncooked shrimp, shelled, deveined

2 tablespoons freshly grated Parmesan cheese

Serves 4.

1 Heat oven to 450°. Melt 2 tablespoons butter in a heavy saucepan over low heat. Stir in flour; cook, stirring constantly, 2 minutes. Whisk in milk; add nutmeg, cayenne, salt, and pepper. Cook, stirring occasionally, 10 minutes longer.

2 Melt ½ tablespoon butter in a skillet. Add shallot; saute 1 minute. Add parsley and wine; cook over high heat until almost all wine is evaporated.

3 Add shallot mixture to sauce and cook 5 minutes. Remove from heat. Stir in 1½ tablespoons mustard and the egg yolk; set aside. Wipe out the skillet the shallots were sauteed in; add ½ tablespoon butter. Saute shrimp over medium heat, stirring constantly, until shrimp turn pink, about 4 minutes. Stir in remaining 1½ tablespoons mustard. Remove from heat and add ⅓ of the sauce.

4 Divide shrimp mixture among 4 ramekins or scallop shells; spoon equal amounts of sauce over shrimp. Sprinkle ½ tablespoon Parmesan cheese over each ramekin. Bake until bubbly and light brown, 12 to 15 minutes. Let stand 5 minutes before serving.

12 small (or 6 medium, cut in half) sole or flounder fillets

Court bouillon composed of 4 cups water, 1 cup dry white wine, 1 small onion stuck with 1 clove, ½ rib celery with leaves, 1 small bay leaf, ½ lemon, 6 peppercorns, 1 teaspoon salt

¾ cup sour cream

¾ cup mayonnaise

4 teaspoons Dijon mustard

1½ teaspoons lemon juice

1 clove garlic, crushed

1 shallot, minced

¼ teaspoon salt

¼ teaspoon white pepper

¼ cup Russian vodka

1 small jar (2 ounces) red caviar

Serves 6.

I went to the Soviet Union in 1971—with an open culinary mind and an insatiable appetite for caviar. The latter was never slaked, I might add, since Black Sea sturgeon was in short supply that year. And the rest of the cuisine was so uninspired I lost five pounds. Russian mustard is dark and sweet—and really awful, as I can report first hand. So it's not surprising that a Czarist recipe for cold mustardy fillet of sole, flecked with red caviar, called for Dijon mustard in its original notation. And that's the way I have passed it on to you. A very elegant summery dish, it makes do nicely for brunch, luncheon, dinner, or midnight supper. Breakfast? *Nyet!*

COLD FILLET OF SOLE
ROMANOFF

1 Roll fish fillets; secure with toothpicks. Heat court bouillon to boiling in a heavy saucepan (not aluminum). Reduce heat and simmer

BERT GREENE'S *Kitchen Bouquets*

5 minutes. Add fish; poach gently until fish flakes when pierced with a fork, 4 to 5 minutes. Drain well; refrigerate covered at least 6 hours.

2 Whisk together sour cream, mayonnaise, mustard, lemon juice, garlic, shallot, salt, white pepper, and vodka. Refrigerate covered 6 hours.

3 Place rolled fillets on a serving platter; spoon sauce over each. Spoon some caviar on top of each fillet.

All French mustards are preparations of black and white mustard seeds which have been very finely ground, then boiled and steeped with vinegar, sour *must,* and a variety of regional seasonings for local color. Most of the famous ones boast the names of established wine-producing areas: Dijon, Meaux, Bordeaux, Rouen, Rheims, to name-drop just a few.

One of my favorite homemade mustards depends on a mite of dark rum for its flavor. I acquired the recipe in Haiti, but it is called Bahai for some reason unknown to me.

BAHAI MUSTARD

1 Place dry mustard in a bowl; add vinegar and rum. Do not stir. Cover and let stand 5 to 6 hours or overnight.

2 Place mustard mixture in the top of a double boiler over hot (not boiling) water; whisk until well blended. Add eggs, one at a time, whisking vigorously after each addition.

3 Gradually whisk in sugar until smooth. Beat in butter, salt, and pepper and cook until thick, about 5 minutes. *Do not overcook or eggs will curdle.*

4 Spoon mustard into sterilized jars and seal. Store in the refrigerator until ready to use.

Note: Bahai Mustard keeps very well and makes quite a delicious addition to a picnic basket—to say nothing of a mustard recipe file!

¼ cup English dry mustard
½ cup tarragon vinegar
1½ tablespoons dark rum
3 eggs
6 tablespoons granulated sugar
4 tablespoons unsalted butter
½ teaspoon salt
Pinch of freshly ground pepper

Makes 1 pint.

My favorite mustard story took place at The Store in Amagansett a short while before it was sold. By then, accounts of The Store's remarkable output and honored cuisine had made it almost legendary and *The Store Cookbook* had given its owners a kind of unsought "supper-stardom" that was hard to live down.

"Those fellahs can do anything!" I once overheard an old grand dame of East Hampton say, pointing out The Store to a visitor from her limousine. "They are Escoffiers returned to this earth! I know, for remember dear, *I knew Auguste, well!*"

Be that as it may. The mustard story concerns a less matriarchal type—a lady of what we referred to as "the eccentric stripe." Neither arty nor famous and perhaps not even rich, she enjoyed the atmosphere of The Store the way others take satisfaction in garden clubs or literary societies.

She was a customer who really loved to chat. We knew by then that talking about food arouses certain individuals the way talking about sex does others! This lady was addicted to vocal gourmetry in extreme. Each Friday, upon arriving from the city, she would appear early in the afternoon to discuss her menu for the following two days—in depth!

She invariably ordered three portions of everything. "One for Mother. One for me. And," punctuating the sentence with much laughter, she would add, "one just on the odd chance. . . ." The phrase was always left mysteriously dangling. If she was single, widowed, or divorced, we never knew, but her appetite was healthy and her options obviously were open.

One day she came into The Store, when I was not present, quite distraught. An unexpected guest was due to arrive on the 7:50 train—and the food must be *very, very* special that night. Three portions, as usual, but something different.

She perused our menu carefully (though she must have known it by heart) before ordering a poached fish. "But I don't want it the way it's listed here," she announced as she put down the bill of fare. "It must be stuffed with shrimp in a mustard sauce. The way they used to do it at The Algonquin. For The Round Table!" she insisted. "Bert will know!"

Bert had no clue. And three volumes of *Gourmet* cookbooks offered no assist.

After an agonizing dusk spent in serious soul searching and not a little whining, I decided to resist the impulse to telephone the Hotel Algonquin for help. Instead, I placed a few familiar ingredients in a pan and, after enriching the sauce with golden egg yolks and a healthy dab of Dijon mustard, prayed.

After inspecting her supper, the lady in question took it away without demurral. Was it truly the fish they served in halcyon days at the Algonquin? I never found out. But by summer's end, Fillet of Sole Pseudo-Algonquin, as we had come to call it, had become a standard item on the lady's diet. So (to return to an oft-sullied phrase), we must have been doing something right!

Consider the dish yourself. This formula serves four.

FILLET OF SOLE PSEUDO-ALGONQUIN

1 Place wine, water, parsley sprigs, onion, salt, peppercorns, bay leaf, and lemon slice in a heavy saucepan (not aluminum). Heat court bouillon to boiling. Reduce heat and simmer 5 minutes. Add shrimp; cook until barely pink, about 3 minutes. Remove shrimp with a slotted spoon; shell and devein. Reserve 8 shrimp. Wrap 1 fish fillet around each remaining shrimp; secure with toothpicks.

2 Heat oven to 250°. Strain court bouillon; return to skillet. Heat to simmering. Add fillets and cook until fish barely flakes when pierced with a fork, 3 to 4 minutes. Remove with a slotted spoon, draining fish well; place on a serving dish. Surround with reserved shrimp. Keep warm in oven.

3 Add shallot to cooking liquid; boil until reduced by half. Stir in 1 tablespoon butter; remove from heat. Beat egg yolks with cream; stir into liquid. Return to low heat (do not allow to boil); stir in mustard, hot pepper sauce, salt, pepper, and remaining 1 teaspoon butter. Pour sauce over fish; garnish with parsley.

Note: As with wine, I never add prepared mustard to an aluminum saucepan or, indeed, any pot not equipped with an enamel surface. It seems to me that the wine in good mustard is sullied by contact with such vessels.

1 cup dry white wine
3 cups water
2 sprigs parsley
1 onion stuck with 2 cloves
1 teaspoon salt
4 peppercorns
½ bay leaf
1 lemon slice
16 uncooked shrimp
8 small sole or flounder fillets
1 large shallot, minced
1 tablespoon plus 1 teaspoon butter
2 egg yolks
¼ cup whipping cream
2 tablespoons mustard
Dash of hot pepper sauce
½ teaspoon salt
¼ teaspoon pepper
2 tablespoons chopped parsley

Serves 4.

In 1978, according to the French Census Bureau, each citizen of France consumed .74 kilos (1.63 pounds) of mustard. More than 47,000 tons were produced in Dijon. That's a powerfully spicy plenitude, considering that none of it was spread on my favorite liaison of mustard, beef, and vegetables. Pot au feu? Well, in a manner of speaking. Bert Greene's very own New England boiled version!

NEW ENGLAND
POT AU FEU

1 corned beef brisket (about 3
   pounds)
2 carrots, each cut in half
1 turnip, cut in half
1 parsnip, cut in half
2 onions, each stuck with 2 cloves
1 bay leaf
2 sprigs parsley
1 teaspoon mustard seeds
12 peppercorns
2 cloves garlic
2 tablespoons red wine vinegar
2½ pounds smoked pork butt or
   picnic shoulder
1 large saucisson a l'ail (French
   garlic sausage) or 1 Polish
   Kielbasi about 12 inches long
½ cup unsalted butter
2 medium tomatoes, seeded,
   chopped
1 tablespoon chopped shallot or
   green onion
1 small cabbage (about 2 pounds),
   coarsely chopped
6 large carrots, cut into sticks ¼-
   inch thick and 3 inches long
1½ tablespoons all-purpose flour
1½ tablespoons Dijon mustard
2 tablespoons grated horseradish
¼ cup sour cream
¼ cup whipping cream
1 teaspoon lemon juice
¼ cup chopped fresh dill

Serves 6 to 8.

1 Place corned beef, 2 carrots, the turnip, parsnip, onions, bay leaf, parsley, mustard seeds, peppercorns, garlic, and vinegar in a large (5 quart or larger) pot. Add enough water to cover meat. Heat to boiling; remove scum from surface. Reduce heat to very low; cook partially covered 1½ hours. Add pork butt; cook 1 hour longer. Add whole sausage; cook ½ hour or until all meat is tender.

2 Heat oven to 300°. Remove meats from cooking liquid; drain in a colander. Place meats on a serving platter; keep warm in oven. Reserve cooking liquid.

3 Melt 4 tablespoons butter in a skillet. Saute tomatoes and shallot until tender. Add chopped cabbage and ½ cup reserved cooking liquid; cook over medium heat, stirring frequently, just until tender, about 10 minutes.

4 Meanwhile, tie carrot sticks in cheesecloth. Add to cooking liquid in pot. Heat to boiling and cook until crisp-tender, about 10 minutes. Drain; remove cheesecloth.

5 Heat remaining 4 tablespoons butter in a small saucepan over low heat until foamy. Stir in flour until smooth. Stir in ½ cup cooking liquid; whisk in Dijon mustard and horseradish. (Mixture will be fairly thick.) Remove from heat; stir in sour cream and whipping cream. Add lemon juice; return to low heat. (Do not allow sauce to boil or it will curdle.)

6 Arrange carrots around meats on serving platter; spoon sauce over and sprinkle with dill. Place cabbage in separate serving dish. (Serve pot au feu with potatoes whipped with cream, lots of butter, and salt and pepper, if desired. Pass additional Dijon mustard with meats.)

Cabbage plus mustard in quite another form made The Store in Amagansett's cole slaw famous. That piquant salad originated in my grandmother's kitchen but the formula below is a culinary amendment that was dreamed up by a former Store employee (who is now a caterer herself). With some imagination, this lady

increased the mustard and added dill to *red* cabbage. So, with a bow to her:

DIRTY RED SLAW

1 Fry the bacon in a heavy skillet until crisp. Crumble and set aside. Reserve bacon drippings.

2 Combine the cabbage, carrots, pepper, onion, and shallots in a large mixing bowl.

3 Beat the mayonnaise with the reserved bacon drippings in a large bowl until smooth. Add the sour cream, whipping cream, mustard, bouillon powder, allspice, chili powder, salt, pepper, and dill. Pour over the vegetables and mix well. Sprinkle with crumbled bacon and parsley. Serve at room temperature.

The French believe—and more and more of the world seems to concur—that nothing can replace the clean piquancy of mustard in cookery. The devil-may-care tang of Chicken Diable, for instance, and the subtle aroma of a cheese-tossed, buttery platter of Parisian-style dumplings result from the essential speck of Burgundy's best in each of these creations. Naturally, the Dijonnais extol the credo—as they lave more hot mustard on yet another regional specialty, lamb stewed with beans.

Bon Appetit, mustard-lovers!

BROILED CHICKEN DIABLE

1 Heat broiling unit. Place chicken in shallow baking dish. Combine butter and oil; brush chicken with some of mixture. Broil chicken 6 inches from heat source, 10 minutes on each side, basting often with butter mixture. Sprinkle with salt and pepper.

2 Combine mustard, shallots, thyme, basil, and cayenne; gradually whisk in half of remaining butter mixture until thick and creamy. Spread mixture over chicken; roll in bread crumbs. Broil chicken, basting with butter mixture every 5 minutes, until chicken is brown and crispy, about 10 minutes on each side.

6 slices bacon
1 small red cabbage (3 pounds), shredded
2 large carrots, shredded
1 green pepper, seeded, finely chopped
1 yellow onion, finely chopped
2 small shallots, minced
2 cups mayonnaise
½ cup sour cream
¼ cup whipping cream
1½ tablespoons Dijon mustard
1 teaspoon bouillon powder
½ teaspoon allspice
½ teaspoon chili powder
½ teaspoon salt
½ teaspoon freshly ground pepper
2 tablespoons chopped fresh dill
1 tablespoon chopped parsley

Serves 8.

2 broiling chickens (2½ to 3 pounds each), cut into serving pieces
6 tablespoons butter, melted
2 tablespoons olive oil
Salt and freshly ground pepper
6 tablespoons Dijon mustard
3 large shallots, minced
½ teaspoon chopped fresh thyme or ¼ teaspoon dried
½ teaspoon chopped fresh basil or ¼ teaspoon dried
Pinch of cayenne pepper
4 cups white bread crumbs

Serves 4 to 6.

GNOCCHI PARISIENNE

1½ cups cold water
3 tablespoons butter, softened
1½ cups all-purpose flour
3 large eggs
1 teaspoon Dijon mustard
½ teaspoon dry mustard
1 teaspoon salt
Pinch of cayenne
⅓ cup grated Parmesan cheese

Serves 4.

1 Place water and butter in a heavy saucepan; heat to boiling. Remove from heat. Immediately add flour all at once; beat with a wooden spoon until smooth. Beat in eggs, one at a time, beating well after each addition. Stir in mustards, salt, cayenne, and Parmesan cheese. Spoon mixture into a pastry bag fitted with a large plain tip.

2 Heat a large pot of salted water to boiling; reduce heat so that water barely simmers. Pipe out dough in 1-inch lengths and let fall into water. Cover pot with paper toweling; let stand until gnocchi float to surface, about 15 to 20 minutes. (Remove one and see if it has set.) Drain gnocchi. (Serve with tomato sauce or with melted butter and Parmesan cheese.)

LAMB DIJONNAISE

2 pounds boneless lamb shoulder
  or breast, cut into 1½-inch cubes
1 tablespoon soy sauce
Salt and freshly ground pepper
2 tablespoons vegetable or olive
  oil
2 tablespoons all-purpose flour
1 large carrot, finely chopped
1 cup finely chopped onion
1 tablespoon minced shallot
2 cloves garlic, minced
Pinch of dried rosemary, crushed
¼ cup dry white wine or vermouth
½ cup Dijon mustard
¾ cup strong chicken broth
  (approximately)
2 large tomatoes, seeded, chopped
1 tablespoon cognac
1¾ cups dried flageolets or white
  pea beans, cooked in boiling
  salted water until almost tender
1 tablespoon unsalted butter
½ cup finely chopped parsley

Serves 6.

1 Heat oven to 375°. Sprinkle lamb with soy sauce, salt, and pepper.

2 Heat oil in a large Dutch oven. Saute lamb over medium heat until well browned, 20 to 25 minutes. (Do not crowd pieces; cook in two batches, if necessary.)

3 Sprinkle lamb with flour; mix well. Add carrot, onion, shallot, garlic, and rosemary. Cook, stirring occasionally, 7 minutes. Stir in wine, mustard, chicken broth, and tomatoes. Cover and bake 1 hour.

4 Skim excess fat from cooking liquid. Heat cognac in a small saucepan; ignite. Pour over lamb and let flame subside. Add cooked beans and more chicken stock if mixture seems dry. Bake covered until the lamb is fork tender, about 20 minutes. Gently stir in butter and parsley. Season to taste with salt and pepper.

Belgian mustard is thickened with cream on occasion, and it has a silky texture on the tongue—and an even silkier one in a saute

pan, I would presume. But I have no idea where one would buy the tincture in the United States. I substitute Dijon in a recipe for Belgian Pork Chops—but obviously I am as prejudiced as a Dijonnais on the subject.

This recipe was originally tested for me by my associate Phillip Schulz's mother, who lives in Golden, Colorado. Have Mrs. Schulz's comment on the formula: "It's a once-in-a-while dish because it's rich. And one chop per person is enough!"

BELGIAN PORK CHOPS

1 Sprinkle chops with salt and pepper. Slash any fat around the meat with a knife.

2 Heat oil and butter in a heavy skillet. Add chops; cook over medium heat until brown on one side, about 10 minutes. Turn chops over; cook until brown and cooked through.

3 Meanwhile, combine cheese, mustard, cream, garlic, shallot, and egg yolk in a small bowl; mix well. Heat broiling unit.

4 Spread tops and sides of chops with cheese mixture. Place in a shallow baking dish. Broil until tops are golden, about 2 minutes.

5 Pour off fat from skillet. Add wine and water. Heat to boiling, scraping bottom and sides of pan. Add allspice; pour over chops. Sprinkle with parsley.

4 loin pork chops, 1½ inches thick
Salt and freshly ground pepper
1 tablespoon vegetable oil
1 tablespoon butter
¼ pound finely grated Gruyère or Jarlsburg cheese (about 1 cup)
1 tablespoon Dijon mustard
2 tablespoons whipping cream
½ teaspoon finely chopped garlic
1½ tablespoons finely chopped shallot
1 egg yolk
¼ cup dry white wine
2 tablespoons water
Pinch of ground allspice
Chopped parsley for garnish

Serves 2 to 4.

Speaking of national mustards, Italians cook ripe Lombardy fruits into a mustardy, chutneylike relish they call *mostarda*. They import regular mustard from France. Tyrolians season their mustard with beer; Mexicans flavor theirs with hot, red chili peppers.

One mustard dish that I love dearly comes from Germany. It is called Rouladen and I think it is absolutely best made with Dusseldorf mustard. I keep a jar of that white-wine flavored condiment on the pantry shelf just for such occasions. But I am a notoriously profligate cook! You can exercise discretion in the choice of lubricous seasoning.

ROULADEN

4 beef cube steaks, flattened
Salt and freshly ground pepper
Paprika
Dijon or Dusseldorf mustard
⅔ cup diced slab bacon
1 cup finely chopped onion
¼ cup finely chopped parsley
1 tablespoon finely chopped chives
4 sour gherkins or cornichons
3 tablespoons butter
2 carrots, diced
1¼ cups dry red wine
1 cup beef stock
1 teaspoon all-purpose flour
2 teaspoons water
1 teaspoon Dijon or Dusseldorf
   mustard
½ cup whipping cream

Serves 4.

1 Sprinkle steaks with salt, pepper, and paprika on one side only. Spread each one with mustard to taste.

2 Combine two-thirds of the bacon with ⅔ cup onion, 3 tablespoons parsley, and the chives. Divide mixture equally and press onto steaks. Place 1 pickle on each steak. Roll up steaks; tie with string in several places.

3 Melt butter in a Dutch oven. Saute remaining bacon and onion and the carrots until golden, about 10 minutes. Remove with a slotted spoon. Add steak rolls; brown over high heat on all sides. Remove meat; stir in wine, scraping the bottom and sides of pot. Add the beef stock.

4 Whisk flour and water together until smooth; stir into pot. Return meat and vegetables to pot. Heat to boiling; reduce heat. Simmer covered until meat is tender, about 1 hour and 10 minutes.

5 Heat oven to 250°. Transfer meat to a shallow baking dish and remove strings. Keep warm in oven. Boil cooking liquid until reduced by half, about 8 minutes.

6 Combine 1 teaspoon mustard with the cream; whisk into sauce. Heat to boiling and cook until slightly thickened. Spoon sauce over meat. Sprinkle with remaining 1 tablespoon parsley.

Nutmeg

When asked what is my favorite type of cooking, invariably I reply, "American regional." Pressed to name a specific dish, I shame the devil and admit to an unsophisticated appetite for southern-style fried chicken.

The *real* fried chicken, that is. No store bought (or frozen) versions at my table. Nor that miscreant rendering that poor, old, declining Colonel Sanders proclaims so "finger-lickin' good!" My digits deserve better than that, sir!

Real fried—the kind I am thinking of—is skinned first, then floured and hailed with salt, pepper, allspice, and a grind (the *merest* grind makes all the difference) of whole nutmeg.

The trick inherent in a great American fry is the slow saute (best in a black iron skillet) that turns each piece of chicken the color of dark honey. Then the ductile parts must rest in a warm oven for about an hour—or until a fork pressed into the fattest drumstick emits only a buttery yellow juice. And only then may the cream gravy be stirred up happily in the pan.

The revelation that there was an American cooking style that I might conceivably emulate came upon me when I left home for college. At seventeen, I went to William and Mary in Virginia. And the snowy day that I boarded the Pennsylvania Railroad for its ivied enclave was the first time in my life that I had ever been totally on my own.

My mother, noting a night's stopover in Richmond, gave me an injunction on how to spend the interval.

"Get into a taxi cab and ask the driver to take you to a clean, *moderately priced* hotel," she counseled. "One where salesmen stay! And eat in your room or in a cafeteria if there is one—because they're generally cleaner!''

Well, though I was immature for my age and certainly intimidated by everything untried, I had no intention of doing *that!* Instead, I bid the driver take me to the best hotel in town, please!

It was then (back in the 1940s) The John Marshall. A splendid hostelry with large dun-colored rooms plus bathtubs sinfully built for two. With an exorbitant tariff—ten dollars a night.

Under the same mad impulse that took me on this downward trek from wisdom, I also ventured to Richmond's bustling Main Street and partook, for the very first time, of the joys of southern fried chicken! The restaurant, called Aunt Somebody-or-other's Kitchen (Fannie? Flossie?) is now gone. I searched for it in vain for years before admitting to myself that it could pass away so unheralded—for it was truly a miracle of excellence.

Slightly more than half a chicken was cut up and fried gold and served in a wicker basket with a little jug of honey and a mess of beaten bisquits. But the chicken was the prodigious ingredient of the meal—moist and *so* flavorous, with a coating that seemed to be composed of buttery shavings that melted on contact with the tongue. Altogether a culinary wonder, the like of which I had never sampled before and which I cannot cease to praise—even after a lifetime of good eating.

SOUTHERN FRIED CHICKEN

1 chicken (about 4 pounds), cut into 10 pieces (legs cut at joint; breast cut into 4 pieces)
1 cup plus 2 tablespoons all-purpose flour
½ teaspoon salt
¼ teaspoon freshly ground pepper
Pinch of ground allspice
⅛ teaspoon freshly grated nutmeg
¾ to 1 cup unsalted butter
2 tablespoons vegetable oil
1 cup strong chicken stock, hot
1¼ cups whipping cream
Salt and freshly ground pepper
1 teaspoon cognac or bourbon

Serves 4.

1 Remove skin from chicken. Combine 1 cup flour, salt, pepper, allspice, and nutmeg in a large paper bag. Place chicken, a few pieces at a time, in bag; shake to coat evenly with flour mixture.

2 Heat oven to 275°. Melt ½ cup butter plus 1 tablespoon oil in a large, heavy skillet over medium heat. (Be careful not to let butter burn.) Place chicken gently in skillet (do not crowd pieces; use 2 skillets, if necessary); saute over medium-low heat until golden brown, about 10 minutes on each side. Add butter and oil as needed. Remove chicken; drain on paper toweling. Place chicken in a baking dish; place in oven for at least ½ hour and up to 1 hour.

3 Remove all but 2 tablespoons fat from skillet. Stir in 2 tablespoons flour over low heat; cook 2 minutes. Whisk in hot chicken stock, scraping bottom and sides of pan. Stir in cream; cook over low heat 20 minutes. Season with salt and pepper to taste.

4 Just before serving, add the cognac or bourbon. Spoon some sauce over chicken; pass the rest.

BERT GREENE'S *Kitchen Bouquets*

It took place over thirty-six years ago, but I remember that Richmond menu as if I had dined on it last night. First there was scuppernong shrub—an amalgam of sweet grapes, freshly squeezed somehow and anointed with a scoop of sour, lemony sherbet. Then a creamy corn soup—and *that chicken,* served with a salad of greens and beet tops bathed in a mustard sauce that stung the roof of the mouth until one ached for the palliative of dessert. And what a restorative that was! Warm peach pie. The crust a lacing of butter, brown sugar, and crumbs; the peaches redolent of nutmeg and blanketed in drifts of orange-scented whipped cream. Paradise!

RICHMOND PEACH PIE

1 Prepare pastry; chill 1 hour.

2 Heat oven to 350°. Roll out half of pastry; refrigerate remainder. Line a 9-inch pie pan with pastry; line pastry with aluminum foil; fill with dried rice or beans. Bake 10 minutes. Remove foil and rice; allow pastry to cool.

3 Place peaches in a large bowl; add almond extract, granulated sugar, 1 cup brown sugar, 4 tablespoons flour, the salt, and lemon juice. Mix well; let stand 5 minutes.

4 Layer peach slices in pastry with 3 tablespoons butter, cut into bits, 1 teaspoon cinnamon, the nutmeg, and orange peel. (Fruit should be piled high, about 3½ inches, because it will shrink as it bakes.) Sprinkle with 1 tablespoon of the peach juices and Grand Marnier.

5 Roll out remaining pastry. Cut into ¾-inch-wide strips. Arrange strips in a lattice pattern over filling; trim ends and press them into edge of lower crust.

6 Heat oven to 400°. Place remaining ⅓ cup brown sugar, 2 tablespoons flour, 2 tablespoons butter, and ½ teaspoon cinnamon in a bowl; blend with a fork to crumblike texture. Spoon mixture into spaces between lattice pastry so that pie is almost covered.

7 Place pie on foil-lined baking sheet. Bake, basting occasionally with juices that run over, until fruit is tender and top is crusty, 35 to 40 minutes. Cool. To serve, reheat slightly, if desired; serve with whipped cream.

Grandma Rose's Favorite Pie Crust (see Index)
5 cups ½-inch-thick, ripe peach slices (about 8 peaches)
1 teaspoon almond extract
1 cup granulated sugar
1⅓ cups dark brown sugar
6 tablespoons all-purpose flour
¼ teaspoon salt
2 tablespoons lemon juice
5 tablespoons butter
1½ teaspoons ground cinnamon
1 teaspoon freshly grated nutmeg
1 tablespoon finely slivered orange peel
1 tablespoon Grand Marnier liqueur
Sweetened whipped cream

Serves 6 to 8.

My time in the South offered a storehouse of treasured cookery. More importantly, it seems now, it awakened my taste buds to the seasonings and extracts that sat above the kitchen stove at home, previously ignored in all my cooking endeavors.

As a sprat-cook, I had no use for any boxed or powdered flavorings. With the same early mistrust I held for cinnamon and clove, I adjudged nutmeg as merely something brown and acrid that had ruined the frothy sweetness of the eggnog prescribed for me after a siege of chicken pox.

I rather suspect it was my first invitation to call on a classmate's family (at one of the great houses on Monument Avenue in Richmond) that gave me new respect for the spice. The occasion was a New Year's Day open house, and I remember being struck by the heady scent of nutmeg in the air from the first moment I entered the vast hall.

There, under imposing family portraits, a small army of even more imposing black servants (in what I can only describe as livery) passed among the throng, distributing sandwiches and thin slices of fruit cake along with antebellum courtesies that I had doubted ever existed outside of *Gone with the Wind*.

The source of the nutmeg soon became apparent. For every guest, as if by ritual, sooner or later approached a table in the center of the dining room. There, under branches of glittering candelabra, a silver-haired aristocrat (also black, and obviously the oldest family retainer of all) ladled eggnog from a shiny, grand silver punch bowl that reflected the four corners of the room.

This attendant (improbably dubbed "Uncle Cato") was a personage of note in the household. Everyone who made their way to his table called him by name. Most of the men shook his hand as well, before they allowed him to pour.

Uncle Cato did not merely ladle the velvety libation. He stirred it long and lovingly before he lifted a cup. And he paused over each serving to grind a freshet of nutmeg over the peaks of whipped cream.

"To your health, gentlemen," was his eulogy. "And to the health of the commonwealth of Virginia!"

That toast (quite like the taste), I have never ever forgotten!

Soon after, the spice seriously entered my kitchen. But I insisted then (and do now) that the nutmeg be freshly grated. This is *my* personal crotchet on the subject. I keep a glass apothecary jar full of whole nutmeg at all times, and merely opening the stopper expands my culinary repertoire. Have you ever sprinkled fresh nutmeg on hash-brown potatoes? Or grated a speck into the creamy contents of a clam pie? If not, quickly repair the omission—for an instant appetite restorative!

The nutmeg-scented potato turns up in the following recipes for Cape Cod Clam Pie and Rapée Alsace. The former receipt comes from Buzzard's Bay, Massachusetts; the latter hails from the French region of Alsace-Lorraine, home of the ubiquitous quiche. Either will appear like manna from heaven on a brisk Sunday morning when the Bloody Marys are apour! But do not let me twist your arm about the brunch business. The clam pie also makes a very respectable dinner with a salad, and the grated potato dish (even with its egg and cream enrichment) takes very kindly to a grilled steak straight from the barbecue. Just be prudent about the size of the portions!

CAPE COD CLAM PIE

1 Place the flour, salt, sugar, butter, and shortening in a large mixing bowl. Blend, using a pastry blender, until the texture of coarse crumbs. Add the water and continue blending until dough is formed. Knead briefly on a floured surface. Refrigerate 1 hour.

2 Heat oven to 400°. Roll out half the dough (keep remaining dough refrigerated). Line a 9-inch pie plate; trim edges. Line pastry with aluminum foil; weight with dried rice or beans. Bake 12 minutes.

3 Fry bacon in a skillet until crisp. Drain on paper toweling; crumble bacon. Remove bacon drippings. Add 2 tablespoons butter; saute onion until golden. Add the celery, potato, carrot, parsley, clams, and bacon; cook and stir over medium heat 5 minutes. Remove to a bowl; reserve.

4 Melt the remaining 2 tablespoons butter in a small saucepan. Whisk in the flour; cook and stir 2 minutes. Whisk in the hot clam liquid and the vermouth; cook, stirring constantly, over low heat until mixture is smooth. Gradually add the cream; cook, stirring constantly, until mixture is very smooth and thick, about 2 minutes.

5 Heat oven to 400°. Add reserved clam mixture to sauce; stir in hot pepper sauce, nutmeg, and salt and pepper to taste. Spoon into baked pastry. Roll out remaining pastry dough to 10-inch circle; place over clam mixture. Press overhanging pastry under rim of plate to seal; flute edge. Cut a slit in top to allow steam to escape. Bake 10 minutes. Reduce oven temperature to 350°; bake until golden brown, 35 to 40 minutes.

For the pastry:
1½ cups all-purpose flour
¼ teaspoon salt
Pinch of sugar
6 tablespoons cold butter
2¼ tablespoons cold vegetable shortening
4 to 4½ tablespoons cold water

For the filling:
1½-inch-thick slice of bacon, diced
4 tablespoons butter
1 large onion, finely chopped
1 rib celery, finely chopped
1 large baking potato, pared, diced
1 medium carrot, diced
1 tablespoon finely chopped parsley
24 large clams, shucked, finely chopped
3 tablespoons all-purpose flour
½ cup clam liquid, hot
1 tablespoon dry vermouth
⅓ cup whipping cream
Dash of hot pepper sauce
Good grating of fresh nutmeg
Salt and freshly ground pepper

Serves 4 to 6.

RAPÉE ALSACE

6 slices bacon
4 tablespoons butter
1 small yellow onion, minced
4 eggs
½ clove garlic, crushed
2 tablespoons minced parsley
1¼ cups grated Jarlsberg cheese
¾ cup whipping cream
Good grating fresh nutmeg
½ teaspoon salt
¼ teaspoon freshly ground pepper
3 large potatoes
Chopped parsley for garnish

Serves 6.

1 Heat oven to 400°. Fry bacon in a skillet until very crisp; drain on paper toweling. Crumble bacon; reserve.

2 Remove all but 2 tablespoons bacon fat from the skillet; add 2 tablespoons butter. Add the onion; saute over low heat until soft, but not brown.

3 Beat the eggs in a bowl; add the garlic, parsley, 1 cup cheese, the cream, nutmeg, salt, and pepper. Stir in the onion.

4 Peel and shred the potatoes one at a time; squeeze out as much moisture as possible. Stir into the egg mixture. (Handle the potatoes quickly to prevent them from turning brown.)

5 Grease an 11- or 12-inch baking dish with 2 tablespoons butter; place in the oven until the butter foams. Spread half the potato mixture in the dish; sprinkle with half the reserved bacon. Repeat layers; sprinkle with remaining cheese. Bake until golden brown and puffed, about 35 minutes. Garnish with parsley.

Nutmeg is the oval-shaped seed of an evergreen tree, the *Myristica fragrans,* which is a native to the islands of Molucca—and only bears fruit for fifty years *exactly* before it abruptly stops the cycle of its parturition.

No one seems to know why it suddenly quits. But a young mother of my acquaintance (with four children at varying stages from infancy to adolescence) advanced a personal theory on the subject.

"Boredom," was her rationale.

Maybe so. But the nutmeg tree leads a fairly heady life while it is fertile. The blossoms are said to be so beguilingly fragrant that a flock of birds flying over a grove of nutmeg trees will become intoxicated by the scent, lose their sense of direction, fly out over the sea, and often drown.

I have a like reaction stove-side. Grating the stuff into bechamel sauce, I quite lose my sensibility to the spice's perfume, often use too much and am forced to add cream like crazy just to tone down the volume. This kitchen offense is trifling when one is stuffing an eggplant but it certainly cuts into the cook's reputation when chicken or turkey tetrazzini is the *plat du jour.*

The eggplant I stuff most often is a dish I call Aubergines Farcies. But for all its French pretension, it is my own culinary caper. Gifted with a mountain of purple vegetables from an overripe garden, I made moussaka one night, ratatouille the next, and eggplant oriental the day after—until I went berserk (or creative, depending upon how you look at it) and produced the following. It is a supper dish that's never refused at my table, which is all the self praise modesty allows!

AUBERGINES FARCIES

1 Make tomato sauce.

2 Trim eggplants; cut in half lengthwise. Slash pulp in several places with a sharp knife; sprinkle with salt. Let stand at least ½ hour. Brush off salt; squeeze eggplants to remove moisture. Scoop out pulp; chop fine.

3 Melt 2 tablespoons butter with 1 tablespoon oil in a heavy saucepan. Add the eggplant pulp, the shallots, and garlic; saute over medium heat until eggplant is tender. Remove from pan with a slotted spoon. Place in a large bowl with the ground veal or pork, ham, nutmeg, parsley, basil, and lemon peel; mix well. Heat oven to 350°.

4 Add 2 tablespoons butter and the remaining oil to saucepan. Add the eggplant shells, skin sides up. Cook over medium-high heat, pressing down on shells with the back of a spoon, until insides are brown; turn shells over and cook until skins are tender, 15 to 20 minutes in all. Eggplants should appear roasted when done.

5 Melt remaining 2 tablespoons butter; stir in the flour. Whisk in the hot broth; cook over medium heat, stirring constantly, until smooth, about 2 minutes. Add the cream and cook over low heat until thick, about 2 minutes. Stir in hot pepper sauce. Add cream sauce to meat mixture and blend thoroughly. Season to taste with salt and pepper.

6 Spoon meat mixture into eggplant shells, mounding tops. Place shells on baking sheet. Sprinkle with bread crumbs and Parmesan cheese. Bake eggplant 20 minutes. Place under broiler 2 minutes to brown. Serve with tomato sauce and rice.

Homemade Tomato Sauce (see Index)
6 small eggplants (about 4 inches in length)
Salt
6 tablespoons butter
3 tablespoons olive or vegetable oil
3 shallots, finely chopped
1 clove garlic, minced
1 cup cooked ground veal or pork (turkey or chicken can be substituted)
1 cup cooked ham, ground or finely chopped
Half a whole nutmeg, grated
2 tablespoons chopped parsley
1 basil leaf, finely chopped, or ¼ teaspoon dried basil
1 teaspoon grated lemon peel
2 tablespoons all-purpose flour
¾ cup chicken broth, hot
½ cup whipping cream
Dash of hot pepper sauce
Salt and freshly ground pepper
⅔ cup buttered bread crumbs
Parmesan cheese, freshly grated
6 cups cooked rice

Serves 6.

I did not invent chicken tetrazzini. That bit of culinary master-work was concocted a hundred years ago by some unknown San Francisco chef, who whipped it up in honor of Luisa Tetrazzini, the fabled Italian coloratura. I did borrow the notion, however, for turkey—and Turkey Tetrazzini is one dish that outshines the original *plat du jour*. I could not face Thanksgiving without this recipe in my apron pocket.

TURKEY TETRAZZINI

½ pound mushrooms, sliced
6 tablespoons butter
½ pound thin spaghetti
2 tablespoons all-purpose flour
2 cups hot chicken broth or stock
1 cup whipping cream
3 tablespoons dry sherry
¼ teaspoon freshly grated nutmeg
Salt and freshly ground pepper
2 cups cooked turkey, cut into strips
½ cup grated Parmesan cheese

Serves 4 to 6.

1 Saute mushrooms in 3 tablespoons of butter in a skillet until golden; reserve. Cook spaghetti in boiling salted water just until tender. Rinse under cold running water and drain.

2 Heat oven to 350°. Melt the remaining butter in a saucepan over medium heat. Stir in the flour until smooth. Gradually add the hot broth; cook, stirring constantly, until smooth, about 2 minutes. Add the cream and sherry; cook over low heat until thick, about 8 minutes. Add nutmeg and salt and pepper to taste.

3 Combine the sauce with the spaghetti in a large saucepan. Toss over low heat 2 minutes. Add the turkey and reserved mushrooms; mix well.

4 Transfer the turkey mixture to a buttered ovenproof casserole. Spoon Parmesan cheese over top. Bake 20 minutes.

In a wonderful book called *Herbal Delights,* Mrs. C. F. Leyely (a grand dame of all manner of culinary trivia) relates the fact that "the sterling silver graters our great grandmothers wore on their chatelaines were for one purpose only—to scrape a little nutmeg powder into the air when the room became musty or overheated with human presence."

If that's a euphemism for lust, Mrs. Leyely is far too discreet to say. In Queen Victoria's time, I know for a fact, ladies often carried a few scented nutmeg "marbles" on their person for a fast curative—should the occasion arise when they felt faint or vaporish in public.

Marie Antoinette, who was reportedly small breasted as a young queen, had whole nutmegs sewn into all the decolletage of her gowns to enhance the shape and size of her endowments.

According to the letters of the Duchess de Lambal (her confidante in these matters), this always gave the queen's person and quarters a curiously refreshing scent, night and day.

My kitchen in Manhattan is small and the smell of onions cooking often infects the entire apartment—but never unpleasantly, if I thoughtfully add a pinch of nutmeg as they saute.

Consider the following Italian onion-nutmeg entente—it's quite cordial.

SAUSAGE-STUFFED ONIONS

1 Heat oven to 350°. Peel the onions and cut a ½-inch slice from the top of each one. Remove centers of onions, leaving shells about ¼-inch thick. Cut a thin slice off each root end so that onions will stand upright; cut a cross in root end to prevent onions from separating. Cook onions in boiling water 5 minutes. Drain upside down on paper toweling.

2 Remove sausage from casing. Saute in a heavy skillet until no longer pink, breaking up lumps with a wooden spoon. Drain on paper toweling. Wipe out skillet.

3 Melt butter in skillet. Add the cooked sausage, parsley, nutmeg, bread crumbs, cream, and 1 tablespoon Parmesan cheese; stir well to combine. Spoon sausage mixture into onions, mounding tops.

4 Place onions in a small baking pan. Pour chicken stock into pan to depth halfway up sides of onions. Bake 40 minutes.

5 Remove onions from pan; pour out stock. Return onions to pan; sprinkle with Parmesan cheese. Place under broiler until light brown.

8 small white onions
1 sweet Italian sausage
1 tablespoon butter
1 tablespoon parsley
¼ teaspoon freshly grated nutmeg
1 tablespoon bread crumbs
2 teaspoons whipping cream
Freshly grated Parmesan cheese
Chicken stock

Serves 4.

As a flavoring, nutmeg barely came into its own during the last two hundred years. The ancients thought it was poisonous and avoided all contact with it and mace as well. "Nutmeg is a lethal cherry, while mace is the bark of an unknown tree that kills any bird unlucky enough to light on its branches," wrote Pliny the Elder.

Nutmeg did appear in Europe at the end of the first millennium, but mainly as a cure for sick oxen. Later it came to be included in the medicine cabinets of the Byzantines. But by some quirk of bad luck it was deemed lethal again once the Romans sacked Byzantium.

Nero is said to have attempted to murder his wife, Poppaea, by mixing her wine with dog urine, nutmeg, and mustard. She merely became testier after the dosage—and Nero had to find better means of mayhem.

It was the early Germans who first discovered the flavoring possibilities of nutmeg. They pulverized the seed with potatoes and allowed it to ferment for beer—a blend quite different from the following tonic combination, I assure you.

HEAVENLY MASHED POTATOES

2 pounds (7 to 8 medium) potatoes
1 teaspoon salt
¼ teaspoon pepper
Good grating of fresh nutmeg
¾ cup unsalted butter, softened
4 egg yolks
½ cup whipped cream
4 tablespoons butter, melted

Serves 4 to 6.

1 Heat oven to 350°. Bake potatoes until tender, about 1 hour. Remove the skins; rice the potatoes or mash through a strainer.

2 Place the potatoes in a large bowl with the salt, pepper, nutmeg, and ¾ cup butter; mix thoroughly. Add the egg yolks, one at a time, mixing well after each addition. Stir in the whipped cream. Transfer to a buttered serving dish; pour melted butter over.

3 Increase oven temperature to 450°. Bake potatoes until tops are brown, about 5 minutes.

Potatoes and nutmeg are co-partnered in two other recipes I treasure. One is a regional American canon for airy dumplings that has a certain tie to Italian *gnocci* but calls for much less cheese and no tomato sauce. The other formula, Dusty Potatoes, was found in a German cookbook printed around the turn of the century. The precept was discovered and translated for me by my partner and good-cooking associate Phillip Schulz. Happily for me, he makes this dish every time he roasts a chicken or broils a steak!

3 cups cold mashed potatoes
1 cup all-purpose flour
   (approximately)
2 egg yolks
½ cup grated Parmesan or Swiss
   cheese
½ teaspoon freshly grated nutmeg
¼ cup butter, melted
Salt and freshly ground pepper
Grated Parmesan cheese

Serves 4 to 6.

PENNSYLVANIA DUTCH POTATO DUMPLINGS

1 Heat oven to 300°. Place potatoes on a floured surface; work in the flour, egg yolks, cheese, and nutmeg by hand, adding flour if necessary to make a soft dough. Roll into ropes about 1 inch in diameter. Slice into 1-inch lengths. Press ends of dumplings with the tines of a fork.

2 Drop dumplings, 8 to 10 at a time, into a kettle of boiling salted water; cook until they float to the top, about 5 minutes. Remove with a slotted spoon; drain on paper toweling. Keep warm in oven.

3 Just before serving, pour melted butter over dumplings; sprinkle with salt, pepper, and Parmesan cheese. Serve extra cheese on the side.

DUSTY POTATOES

1 Heat oven to 400°. Peel potatoes and cut each into eight long wedges. Combine bread crumbs and nutmeg. Dip potatoes in butter; roll in bread crumb mixture.

2 Arrange potatoes in a single layer in a greased baking dish; pour any remaining butter over. Sprinkle with salt and pepper. Bake until crisp and brown, about 1 hour. Let stand 5 minutes before serving.

4 baking potatoes
1½ cups fine bread crumbs
½ teaspoon freshly grated nutmeg
½ cup butter, melted
Salt and freshly ground pepper

Serves 4.

The Chinese discovered practically every green and seasoning in our Western vocabulary. Early mandarins cultivated carrots, spinach, and rice—but they seem to have lost the advantage when it came to nutmeg. For it is one of the few Eastern-grown flavorings not included in the "perfume powders of the Orient."

More's the pity, for nutmeg brings a vital culinary grace note to each of the above-named vegetables. Regard the liaison of carrot and nutmeg in a propitious golden version of Louis Diat's noble Vichyssoise:

CARROT VICHYSSOISE

1 Place the potatoes, chopped carrots, the green onions, and chicken stock in a saucepan; bring to a boil. Reduce heat; simmer until vegetables are tender, 20 to 25 minutes.

2 Transfer vegetable mixture to a blender container, half at a time; blend until smooth. (Begin at low speed, taking care not to overfill container as the hot liquid will expand.) Pour into a large bowl.

3 Whisk white pepper, nutmeg, cream, and salt to taste into soup. Cool; refrigerate 3 hours. To serve, sprinkle each portion with grated carrot.

2 cups pared, chopped potatoes (about 2 medium)
1¼ cups chopped carrots (about 3 medium)
6 chopped green onions (white part only)
3 cups chicken stock
⅛ teaspoon white pepper
½ teaspoon freshly grated nutmeg
1¼ cups whipping cream
Salt
1 small carrot, grated

Serves 4 to 6.

My good friend Gail Firestone combines spinach, rice, cream, and nutmeg, of course, into a sublime green mélange that she has generously shared with me. Now, I happily pass it on to you under her imprimateur.

It makes a salubrious side dish when steak or chops are on the menu. And I would be tempted to stuff the leftovers into a fluffy omelet for lunch the next day—if ever there were leftovers when it is served at my house!

GAIL FIRESTONE'S HOT SPINACH AND RICE

⅔ cup rice
1 pound spinach, stems trimmed
4 tablespoons butter
2 tablespoons all-purpose flour
1 cup hot milk
½ cup whipping cream
¼ teaspoon freshly ground pepper
Pinch of cayenne pepper
1 teaspoon sugar
Good grating of fresh nutmeg

Serves 4.

1 Add rice to a large pot of boiling salted water; stir once. Boil until just tender, 12 to 15 minutes. Drain in a colander. Place colander over boiling water; steam rice in colander, covered with one layer of paper toweling, for 15 minutes.

2 Meanwhile, cook the spinach in boiling salted water just until wilted, about 3 minutes; drain. Place spinach in blender container; puree until smooth.

3 Melt 2 tablespoons butter in a saucepan over medium heat. Add flour; cook, stirring constantly, 2 minutes. Reduce heat; whisk in the milk. Cook until smooth, about 2 minutes longer. Stir in the cream, pepper, cayenne pepper, sugar, and nutmeg; simmer until slightly thickened, about 5 minutes. Add the spinach; cook 3 minutes.

4 Combine the spinach mixture with the rice; cut in the remaining butter.

The leaves of the nutmeg tree (which looks like a peach tree, incidentally) are green on one side and rather whitish underneath. When rubbed between the fingers they give off a smell far sweeter than jasmine.

In the Philippine Islands, they are used to flavor more stews and soups than the equally fragrant bay leaves, but unfortunately they cannot be found west of the Celebes.

Cooks here must make do as best they can with the nutmeg seed—as in the following, remarkably tasty, Zucchini Soufflé. The scent of it will perfume your house for hours, with any luck at all!

ZUCCHINI SOUFFLE

1 Heat oven to 400°. Grease a 1½- or 2-quart souffle dish with 1 teaspoon butter. Sprinkle with 1 tablespoon Parmesan cheese, turning dish to coat bottom and sides.

2 Melt 2 tablespoons butter in a heavy skillet. Add the onion, zucchini, basil, parsley, nutmeg, and salt and pepper to taste; mix well. Cook covered over medium heat 5 minutes; then cook uncovered over high heat, stirring frequently, until all liquid is evaporated. Remove from heat.

3 Melt 3 tablespoons butter in a heavy saucepan. Stir in the flour; cook over low heat, stirring constantly, 2 minutes. Remove from heat. Whisk in the milk; beat until smooth. Return to heat; boil 1 minute. (Mixture will be quite thick.) Remove from heat. Beat in the egg yolks, one at a time. Stir in the cayenne, allspice, and 6 tablespoons Parmesan cheese. Fold in the zucchini mixture.

4 Beat the egg whites until stiff but not dry. Fold into the egg yolk mixture. Pour into the prepared dish. Sprinkle with remaining 1 tablespoon Parmesan cheese and nutmeg. Place in the oven and immediately reduce heat to 375°. Bake until puffed, 30 to 35 minutes.

5 tablespoons plus 1 teaspoon unsalted butter
½ cup freshly grated Parmesan cheese
1 small onion, minced
½ pound zucchini, coarsely grated
2 to 3 fresh basil leaves, chopped, or a pinch of dried basil
1 tablespoon finely chopped parsley
½ teaspoon freshly grated nutmeg
Salt and freshly ground pepper
3 tablespoons all-purpose flour
1 cup boiling milk
4 egg yolks
Pinch of cayenne pepper
¼ teaspoon ground allspice
5 egg whites
Freshly grated nutmeg

Serves 2 to 4.

Neither crêpe, souffle, nor omelet, this next-to-last nutmeg celebration retains an arresting Gallic relationship to all three. Invented by Frank Sanabria, the Spanish/Swiss owner of Vermonti, a well-traveled gourmet shop on Jane Street in New York's Greenwich Village, the concoction is decidedly forenoon or post-midnight fare. However, since it takes but eighteen minutes to prepare, I have often whipped it up whenever the mood (and the mouth for nutmeg) strikes me.

FRANK SANABRIA'S PARIS BREAKFAST

1 Heat oven to 400°. Place a 10-inch glass pie plate in the oven until hot. Add the butter to the plate and brush sides and bottom well. Keep plate in oven until ready to use.

2 Place the eggs, milk, Grand Marnier or kirsch, lemon juice, nutmeg, and sugar in a blender container; blend on low speed until combined. Add the flour; blend at high speed until light and frothy. Scrape down sides and blend a few seconds longer.

2 tablespoons unsalted butter
2 eggs
½ cup milk, at room temperature
1 tablespoon Grand Marnier or kirsch liqueur
Juice of 1 lemon
¼ teaspoon freshly grated nutmeg
2 tablespoons granulated sugar
½ cup all-purpose flour
Confectioners' sugar
Maple syrup or jam

Serves 2.

3 Pour the mixture into the hot pie plate. Bake 15 minutes. Dust with confectioners' sugar. Serve hot with maple syrup or jam.

The monumental eggnog of Monument Avenue, Virginia, was well apportioned with bourbon, rum, and cognac before any dusting of nutmeg hit the foam. Yet the spice alone filled the air—for blocks around, I would wager now.

In fond memory of that magical elixir and the mystical aroma, here is a most intoxicating dessert: Cold Eggnog Pie. It's *not* for kids or the W. C. T. U.!

COLD EGGNOG PIE

1½ cups ground gingersnaps
¼ cup granulated sugar
⅓ cup unsalted butter, melted
3 eggs, separated
2 tablespoons superfine sugar
1 cup bourbon
1 cup milk
¼ cup light rum
¼ teaspoon freshly grated nutmeg
1 tablespoon unflavored gelatin
¼ cup cold water
⅓ cup granulated sugar
2 tablespoons cornstarch
Pinch of salt
1½ ounces unsweetened chocolate, broken into pieces
1 teaspoon vanilla
2 cups whipping cream
¼ cup confectioners' sugar
¼ cup cognac
Grated nutmeg for garnish
Chocolate curls for garnish

Serves 6.

1 Heat oven to 450°. Combine the gingersnaps, ¼ cup sugar, and the melted butter in a bowl; blend with a fork. Pat mixture over bottom and sides of a buttered 9-inch pie plate. Bake 5 minutes. Let cool; refrigerate.

2 To make eggnog base, beat the egg yolks until fluffy; stir in the superfine sugar, bourbon, milk, light rum, and nutmeg. Beat the egg whites until stiff but not dry; fold into the egg yolk mixture.

3 Soften the gelatin in the cold water.

4 Combine ⅓ cup sugar, the cornstarch, and salt in the top of a double boiler over simmering water. Add ½ cup eggnog base; whisk until smooth. Gradually add remaining eggnog base; cook, stirring constantly, until thick. Stir in the softened gelatin; cook 1 minute longer. Divide mixture in half; chill one half in refrigerator.

5 Cook the chocolate with the vanilla in a small saucepan over low heat, stirring constantly, until melted. Beat into unchilled half of eggnog mixture. Let stand at room temperature.

6 Whip 1 cup cream; fold into chilled half of eggnog mixture. Spread evenly over the bottom of gingersnap crust. Refrigerate until partially set, about 15 minutes.

7 Spread chocolate mixture evenly over eggnog-cream mixture. Refrigerate 15 minutes.

8 Whip remaining 1 cup cream with the confectioners' sugar and cognac. Spread over top of pie. Garnish with grated nutmeg and chocolate curls, if desired. Refrigerate until ready to serve.

Orange

It might seem strange to you that the one thing that I, whom the world might unkindly label "a housewares junkie," have never possessed is a proper orange juice maker. *Never* is a mite imprecise, for I did own a glamorous citrus squeezer once. And therein lies a tale.

My mother, after a brief period of widowhood, decided that she must marry again—for security reasons. She was still a vital and remarkably attractive woman and her target for monied matrimony turned out to be an eccentric former beau who not only had pined after her for thirty years but also had accumulated some very solid capital during the interval.

She was re-wed shortly before I turned twenty-three; so when she asked, "What would you like for your birthday, dear?" she felt she could safely add, "It may be fairly extravagant this year!"

My mother's notion of extravagance, I knew, differed sharply from my own. To her, largesse meant a wristwatch with a Swiss movement; my own version was somewhat more solid—like a foreign sports car. But, having recently acquired a bachelor apartment of my very own, I compromised with a request for an orange juice squeezer.

"Why in heaven's name would you want a thing like that?" my mother asked, her voice registering dismay. "Particularly since the new frozen stuff is supposed to be so good. Who wants to squeeze oranges at twenty-three, anyway? You should be out *skylarking*—having the time of your life, you dope!"

Noting the fixed demeanor of my eye, she matched it perfectly. "Besides, be realistic. You have no space for large contraptions in that dinky little kitchenette!"

This last remark, while not kind, was undisputably true. It was only a one room apartment. But I had already observed in my young life that there was no space so small that it could not be stretched for out-and-out indulgence.

What I desired, in any event, was no electrical mammoth, but merely one of those functional gadgets, beloved by bartenders, that effortlessly turn base fruit into streaming freshets of liquid with the flick of a wrist. I even took my mother to a posh cocktail lounge on Madison Avenue so that she might observe at close range the appliance I coveted.

As I recall, she noted its arrangement of chrome and black plastic critically.

"That won't fit under your kitchen cabinets."

"I'll have them lifted then!"

"You're really being ridiculous, but it is entirely up to you. If that's what you want for your birthday, you shall have it!"

My mother, I noted warily, had never acquiesced so gracefully before.

As my birthday approached, she and my stepfather impulsively flew south for a short vacation. So when the present (boxed and crated and swathed in excelsior) duly arrived from Hammacher Schlemmer, I was happily able to unwrap it out of familial scrutiny.

Knowing my parent to be an expedient lady, I did not expect to find an exact duplicate of the object I had requested, but never, never could I have foreseen the weird contrivance she had selected.

It was low enough, of course, to fit under the kitchen cabinets! Indeed, it was so shallow that I was forced to bend at the waist to manipulate its crank. And while an orange half might, with some difficulty, be inserted into the press, no tumbler I owned (except perhaps a shot-glass) was small enough to fit beneath the spout. The juices could flow into a very small bowl or a saucer, but I had no desire to lap up breakfast!

Besides being a lime-squeezer, I am sure, the mechanism was also downright flimsy. Its chrome parts bowed the very first time minimal pressure was applied to an orange and its strainer shot clear across the room whenever the crank was depressed— causing more orange juice to be sopped up than sipped.

My parent called me long distance to reassure herself.

"Well? Did the *thing* come?" she shouted happily. "Are you pleased with it?" Not waiting for me to answer, she added, "I know it's a bit smaller than the one you wanted but I'll bet a nickle it really fit in your kitchen. Because I'll tell you a little secret—I measured the height when you weren't looking!"

My thank-you's must have seemed sufficiently effusive. And I never disabused my mother of the notion that her jerrybuilt juice squeezer kept me hale and hearty during the winter that followed. I merely popped vitamin capsules instead.

Later, when I moved from one part of New York City to another, the virtually unused appliance disappeared in the chaos of transplantation. My mother grieved its loss far more than I, but as her husband's fortune had been tempered by financial reverses, she didn't volunteer to duplicate the gift.

I was not particularly regretful.

While oranges are a favorite fruit, I must confess I imbibe the juice most frequently nowadays well-laced with vodka and topped with vanilla ice cream. They call this drink a "Golden Screw" and the cognomen, I venture to say, sullies the orange's Biblical reputation for purity a trifle.

I frequently grate orange peel into sweets and there's a literary tradition behind this usage. The author of the first cookbook ever written by a woman (published anonymously in London, in 1747) bids the reader: "Regard the curl of a bright orange skin with care. For beside parfuming a cheek it will also emit a happy flavour when pressed hard onto a biggin of sugar or a cake of sweet butter, freshly churned."

The book, entitled *The Art of Cookery Made Plain and Easy, Which Far Exceeds Any Thing of the Kind Ever Yet Published,* is credited only to "A Lady." The reason for such anonymity? Have the sentiment expressed by Dr. Samuel Johnson when the publication first appeared: "Women," the good doctor observed, " . . . can spin very well. But they cannot yet make a good book of cookery."

Times change. Flavors stay constant. Like the aforementioned lady cookbook-writer, I find the delicate skin of a bright orange totally imperative in all manner of sweet desserts. But it is the surprise of the pungent flavor in a beef stew or a farrago of seafood and vegetables that sets my taste buds abloom. As a point of reference, here's a prized egg dish—a version of the great Basque concoction, *piperade.*

A versatile, vegetarian scramble (rather than an omelet), *piperade* is definitely Hispanic in character though Frenchified somewhat by the substitution of sweet butter for olive oil. It definitely deserves a place on your luncheon agenda— particularly when the creamy eggs are fortuitously spliced with tiny, supple shrimp, as on the next page.

PIPERADE

2 small green peppers, seeded, cut
  into thin strips
1 onion, thinly sliced
3 tablespoons unsalted butter
4 tomatoes, peeled, seeded,
  chopped
1 clove garlic, minced
1 teaspoon finely grated orange
  peel
Salt and freshly ground pepper
1 pound shrimp, shelled, deveined
10 eggs
¼ cup whipping cream
Buttered toast

Serves 6 amply.

1 Saute peppers and onion in butter in a large, heavy skillet until tender but not brown. Add tomatoes, garlic, orange peel, salt, and pepper; cook over low heat, stirring occasionally, 20 minutes.

2 Add shrimp and cook until shrimp turn pink, 4 to 5 minutes.

3 Beat eggs with cream in a bowl. Stir into shrimp mixture. Cook, stirring constantly, over low heat until eggs become velvety in texture, 15 to 20 minutes. Serve immediately with buttered toast.

Orange is one of the seven fruits most often mentioned in the Bible. A symbol of virtue, as opposed to the sinful apple, oranges are said to have bloomed wildly in the Garden of Eden, which dogged historians insist must have flowered in the heart of the Indus Valley.

It was in the Orient, however, that canny Mandarin farmers first realized the potential of the fruit as food. Previously, although much admired for their beauty, oranges were not eaten but grown only for oil to perfume the body. But traveling merchant bands brought seeds from the Indus to northern Asia, where the fruit's nutrition was recognized. The earliest recorded dish naming orange as one of its ingredients was a Chinese soup served in 2200 B.C. In fact, the botanical name for the modern sweet orange is *Citrus sinenis,* the latter word meaning Chinese in Latin.

Speaking of soups, the following is based on an unusual Arabian combination of oranges, lemons, and vegetables called *naranj* (which means "sour orange"). I make Naranj in a blender, serve it well-chilled, and proclaim it a perfect tart beginning for dinner when a rich viand (like goose or duckling) will follow.

3 tablespoons butter
1 onion, finely chopped
8 medium carrots, coarsely
  chopped
1½ cups chicken broth
1½ cups water
½ teaspoon ground cloves
½ teaspoon salt
½ teaspoon freshly ground pepper
1½ tablespoons all-purpose flour
Juice of 1 lemon
2 cups orange juice
Chopped fresh mint leaves

Serves 6 to 8.

NARANJ

1 Melt butter in a heavy saucepan. Saute onion over medium heat until golden. Add carrots, chicken broth, water, cloves, salt, and pepper. Heat to boiling. Reduce heat and simmer 10 minutes.

2 Whisk flour with 3 tablespoons hot soup in a small bowl. Stir into soup and cook 2 minutes. Transfer soup, one half at a time, to a blender container; blend until smooth. Pour into large mixing bowl.

3 Stir lemon juice and orange juice into soup. Refrigerate at least 4 hours before serving. Garnish with mint.

Oranges were not even heard of in Europe until the end of the Middle Ages, when crusaders returning from the Holy Land reported "lang grene hedgerovs of oranjus schrubbes abloom out on the Salem's planus. Flors senten the ayrs for mils and mils."

During the centuries that followed, the citrus was introduced to the Mediterranean from Persia by India-bound trade ships. But the bitter orange was the only variety known until a Portuguese expedition to Ceylon returned with sweet fruit in 1529. As a matter of fact, *portugal* is still the generic term for a juice orange in most of Greece and Albania and all of the Middle East.

Chinese oranges (much sweeter and more heavily seeded than *portugals*) reached Lisbon a hundred years afterward—causing a greater uproar about the fruit than Anita Bryant! These dulcet oranges became so popular that the Portuguese government, fearing competitive foreign plantations, refused trade with any country having a temperate climate and forced all outward-bound vessels to be searched for smugglers.

However, a wily Spanish ambassador circumvented this "orange curtain." Obviously imbued with more regard for king and country than for his own colon, this knavish fellow swallowed over a hundred orange pits at a royal dinner and then hurried (by horse and carriage) across the border to Spain before he evacuated. Following his windfall, Spain became the largest orange-producing country in the world. And that country still grows (and exports) the exquisitely flavored Seville orange, which is my favorite for cooking.

Two tantalizing orange-flavored additions to this tome also come from Spain. The first, a rack-roasted pork loin, is marinated in orange juice overnight and then tenderly basted with the liquid (and certain essential seasonings) until it roasts to the color of well-aged mahogany. It is superlative eating— particularly when the meat is garnished with the spirituous, glazed orange rounds that you will find prescribed in the "Vinegar" chapter.

Another Seville-inspiration is a chicken stuffed with oranges and roasted and sauced with a wondrous compound of meat juices, a mite of vinegar, and a generous shredding of some golden peel. *Delicioso!*

SPANISH PORK WITH GLAZED ORANGES

1 pork loin roast (3½ to 4 pounds)
1 cup orange juice
3 tablespoons brown sugar
1 onion, cut into quarters
1 bay leaf, crumbled
1 tablespoon Dijon mustard
1 clove garlic, minced
Finely grated peel of ½ orange
⅛ teaspoon dried thyme
Salt
Seasoned pepper
1 tablespoon butter
Betsy Cooper's Baked Orange Slices (see Index)

Serves 6 to 8.

1 Place pork in a shallow dish. Whisk orange juice with 2 tablespoons brown sugar in a small bowl; add onion and bay leaf. Pour marinade over pork. Refrigerate at least 6 hours or overnight.

2 Heat oven to 475°. Remove pork from marinade; pat dry. Strain marinade; reserve. Combine mustard, remaining 1 tablespoon brown sugar, the garlic, orange peel, thyme, and salt and seasoned pepper to taste. Rub over surface of pork.

3 Place pork, fat side up, on a rack in a roasting pan. Roast 20 minutes. Reduce oven heat to 350°; roast 40 minutes longer, basting several times with pan juices.

4 Pour off grease from pan. Spoon reserved marinade over meat. Continue to roast 1 hour and 30 minutes, basting frequently.

5 Remove pork to serving platter; keep warm. Remove any excess fat from pan juices; pour juices into a saucepan. Boil until thick and syrupy, about 3 minutes; stir in butter. Pour sauce over pork. Surround with Baked Orange Slices.

ROAST CHICKEN WITH ORANGES

1 roasting chicken (about 3½ pounds)
Salt
1 clove garlic, bruised
2 small oranges
1 cup toasted bread cubes
½ cup thinly sliced celery
¼ cup butter, melted
½ teaspoon salt
¼ teaspoon freshly ground pepper
2 sprigs fresh tarragon, chopped, or ¼ teaspoon dried
2 sprigs fresh rosemary, chopped, or ¼ teaspoon dried
6 tablespoons chicken stock
¼ cup white wine vinegar
3 tablespoons sugar
1½ cups chicken stock
1 tablespoon cornstarch
Salt and freshly ground pepper to taste
Watercress sprigs or chopped parsley for garnish

Serves 3 to 4.

1 Heat oven to 375°. Sprinkle chicken cavity and skin with salt and rub thoroughly, inside and out, with garlic.

2 Using a vegetable peeler, remove outer peel of 1 orange in 1 long strip. (Strip should be very thin; do not cut into white part.) Cut peel into slivers; reserve. Squeeze juice from orange; reserve. Remove peel and white membrane from second orange; remove orange segments and seed if necessary.

3 Combine bread cubes, celery, butter, ½ teaspoon salt, the pepper, and half of the tarragon and rosemary in a bowl. Stir in the orange segments. Spoon mixture into chicken; truss. Roast chicken 1 hour and 45 minutes, basting every 30 minutes with 2 tablespoons stock.

4 Meanwhile, combine vinegar and sugar in a heavy saucepan; boil until sugar dissolves. Add 1½ cups chicken stock; boil until reduced by half. Reduce heat; stir in reserved orange juice and remaining tarragon and rosemary. Simmer 10 minutes.

5 Remove chicken to serving platter; keep warm. Stir pan juices into cornstarch; gradually whisk mixture into sauce. Cook over medium

heat, stirring constantly, until thick. Strain the sauce and add the reserved slivered orange peel; season to taste with salt and pepper. Spoon some sauce over chicken; serve remainder in a gravy boat. Garnish chicken with watercress or parsley.

In 1493 Columbus discovered Hispaniola (now Haiti) and planted sweet-orange seeds on the island. Approximately 480 years later, I discovered orange-scented Haitian French Toast. I encountered this treat on the spacious veranda of the Hotel Oloffson in Port-au-Prince. Having arrived too late for the regular breakfast fare, I wheedled the surrogate for bacon and eggs from a very ancient black waiter, after he had announced quaveringly that "le tranche de larde et les oeufs—c'est tout finis, m'sieur!"

Unfortunately, I admired the "make-do" breakfast so hugely that the poor lady chef was forced to prepare it every day of my stay. With a wreath of Franco-Haitian curses and much grumbling in my direction, she would shake her head and her smoking black frying pan in the air—and proceed to create the culinary masterpiece morning after blissful morning.

It took some careful sleuthing (at a discreet distance from the chef's kitchen stove) and a measure of cursing and grumbling on my own part before I was able to duplicate the magical invention at home but the result was well worth any travail. Like no other French toast, this dish is best made when the bread is at least two days old and so crusty that it splinters under a knife!

HAITIAN FRENCH TOAST

1 Whisk together orange juice, cream, eggs, cinnamon, nutmeg, and granulated sugar in a large bowl. Place bread slices in mixture until they are soaked but not mushy.

2 Heat oven to 250°. Heat 4 tablespoons butter in a heavy saucepan until foamy. Saute bread, 3 or 4 slices at a time, on both sides until golden brown, adding more butter as needed. (Bread will puff up slightly.) Remove slices to a platter and dust with confectioners' sugar; keep warm in oven until all bread is sauteed. Dust once more with confectioners' sugar and serve with maple syrup.

1 cup orange juice
⅓ cup whipping cream
2 eggs
1 teaspoon ground cinnamon
⅛ teaspoon freshly grated nutmeg
¼ cup granulated sugar
1 loaf (1 pound) stale French bread, cut into 1½-inch slices
½ cup unsalted butter (approximately)
Confectioners' sugar
Maple syrup

Serves 4.

Spanish orange seeds took hold well in the New World. The fruit was introduced to California (then part of Baja Mexico)

when the first Franciscan mission was founded in San Diego in 1769. About five years later, the first orange grove of any consequence (400 seedlings on six acres of land) was planted at the same San Gravid Mission. Obviously, it proliferated.

Baja Mexican cookery displays many classic Hispanic seasonings. Consider the following recipe for Chiles Rellenos, which, like no other formula for this dish I have encountered, is subtly accented with a touch of grated orange peel in the cheese filling.

I always use fresh *chiles poblanos* to make this dish and buy them at a Mexican grocery; some lazy cooks I know use canned. Sweet Italian peppers are a mild stand-in.

In any case, the trick is to roast the peppers over a gas flame until they blister. Then place them in a plastic bag for half an hour and the skins will peel off easily.

CHILES RELLENOS

Jalapeño Sauce (recipe follows)
8 poblano chilies (or sweet Italian peppers for milder flavor)
¾ pound Monterey Jack cheese, grated
¾ pound Cheddar cheese, grated
½ teaspoon grated orange peel
Flour
4 eggs, separated
4 tablespoons all-purpose flour
Vegetable oil

Serves 4.

1 Make jalapeno sauce.

2 Roast chilies over a gas flame until well seared on all sides. Place in a paper bag; place paper bag inside a plastic bag and seal. Let stand 20 minutes. Remove from bag and rub off skins. Using a sharp knife, make a slit in one side of each chili; remove seeds and membranes.

3 Combine cheeses with 2 teaspoons jalapeno sauce and the orange peel. Fill chilies with mixture and roll in flour.

4 Beat egg yolks with 4 tablespoons flour in a medium bowl. Beat egg whites until stiff but not dry; fold into egg yolk mixture.

5 Heat 1½ to 2 inches oil in a heavy saucepan. Dip chilies into egg batter. Fry until golden on both sides. Serve hot with jalapeno sauce.

Note: Do not touch eyes while handling chilies; wear rubber gloves to avoid irritating skin.

1 small onion, chopped
1 large clove garlic, minced
4 tablespoons olive oil
4 cups peeled, seeded, chopped tomatoes
1 cup chicken stock
Grated peel of ½ orange
2 tablespoons chopped canned jalapeño chilies or to taste
1 teaspoon crushed dried oregano
¼ teaspoon salt
¼ teaspoon freshly ground pepper

Makes 3½ to 4 cups.

JALAPEÑO SAUCE

Saute onion and garlic in olive oil in a saucepan until soft. Stir in remaining ingredients. Cook over medium-high heat, stirring occasionally, until thick, about ½ hour.

The original precept for the following stew calls for the true *narang* of Persia, which is a small and slightly bitter red-fleshed orange. I have never been able to find any bitter oranges that I could stomach. (I tasted a canned variety once in France and they were terrible!) So I have fiddled with this recipe over the years and have discovered, after messing around with tangerines and Jaffa oranges, that the dish is at its most delicious when the orange is as sweet and juicy as possible.

Don't be put off by the strange mélange of components. Beef, scallions, garlic, pea beans, and oranges do indeed seem like odd companions in any dish, but the total effect is quite tasty.

PERSIAN STEW

1 Heat oven to 350°. Heat butter with oil in a Dutch oven. Add meat, a few pieces at a time; saute until quite brown on all sides.

2 Return all meat to pot with any juices. Add green onions, garlic, 1 cup parsley, and salt and pepper to taste. Cook and stir over medium-high heat 3 minutes. Stir in orange juice, scraping bottom and sides of pot. Stir in lemon juice, orange slices, and beef stock; heat to boiling. Cover and bake until meat is tender, about 1½ hours.

3 Stir beans into Dutch oven. Bake covered 20 minutes. Serve sprinkled with remaining ¼ cup parsley.

4 tablespoons butter
1 tablespoon olive or vegetable oil
3 pounds boneless beef chuck, cut into 1½-inch cubes
½ cup chopped green onions with tops
1 large clove garlic, minced
1¼ cups chopped parsley
Salt and freshly ground pepper
¼ cup orange juice
1 tablespoon lemon juice
½ orange, thinly sliced, slices cut in half
1 cup beef stock
2 cups cooked white pea beans

Serves 6.

Oranges come from a prodigiously thrifty tree. The bark may be stripped and used for fine rattan caning. And besides being a plentiful source of daily vitamins, the fruit supplies many manufactures: the skin flavors candy, marmalade, flower water, and lots of spirited brandies; oil from the pith (oddly enough) is a prerequisite for milling fine French hand soap; and essences extracted from the pits are used to produce the highest-grade cooking oil and oleomargarine one can buy! The leaf oils and twigs of the orange tree are used for sachet and bath salts. The delicate orange blossoms are used in the finest perfumes.

My grandmother knew none of this but invariably placed a curl of orange peel on her coal stove and left it there until it turned to fine white ash. I can't remember a house that smelled quite so good, either!

Wise Italian *signorini* know another orange secret. They grate tangerine peel into the sauce for Ossobuco and it is that remarkable ingredient that gives the dish its ultimate bouquet.

OSSOBUCO

4 tablespoons unsalted butter

1 cup minced onion

2 cloves garlic, minced

½ cup minced shallots

½ cup chopped carrot

½ cup chopped celery

6 to 7 pounds veal shanks, cut into 2½-inch-long pieces, tied with string around the exposed marrow

Salt and freshly ground pepper

½ cup all-purpose flour (approximately)

½ cup olive oil

1 cup dry white wine or vermouth

1 cup strong chicken stock

1 teaspoon chopped fresh basil or ½ teaspoon dried

½ teaspoon chopped fresh thyme or a pinch of dried

3 cups chopped ripe tomatoes

1 tablespoon sugar

7 parsley sprigs and 2 bay leaves, tied in cheesecloth

Northern Italian Risotto (see Index)

1 tablespoon grated lemon peel

1½ tablespoons grated tangerine peel

1 tablespoon minced garlic

3 tablespoons finely chopped parsley

Salt and freshly ground pepper to taste

Serves 6 to 8.

1 Heat oven to 350°. Melt butter in a large Dutch oven. Add onion, 2 cloves garlic, the shallots, carrot, and celery; cook and stir over low heat until golden, about 10 minutes. Remove from heat.

2 Sprinkle veal with salt and pepper; coat with flour, shaking off excess. Heat 6 tablespoons oil in a heavy skillet. Brown veal, 4 pieces at a time, on all sides over medium-high heat. Transfer to Dutch oven, standing pieces on end on top of the vegetables.

3 Remove excess fat from skillet. Add remaining 2 tablespoons oil and the wine; cook over high heat, scraping bottom and sides of skillet until smooth. Boil until reduced by half. Add chicken stock, basil, thyme, and tomatoes; sprinkle with sugar. Heat to boiling. Reduce heat and simmer 15 minutes.

4 Pour sauce over the veal; add parsley and bay leaves. Bake covered until meat is tender, about 1 hour and 15 minutes, basting every 20 minutes.

5 Make risotto.

6 Remove veal from Dutch oven; reserve sauce. Place veal on an ovenproof serving platter; return to oven and raise heat to 450°. Bake until veal is deep brown and glazed, 5 to 10 minutes.

7 Meanwhile, strain sauce through a fine sieve into a saucepan, pressing vegetables with a wooden spoon. Heat to boiling; add lemon peel, tangerine peel, 1 tablespoon garlic, and the chopped parsley. Boil until reduced by half. Season with salt and pepper to taste. Pour over veal. Serve with risotto.

Note: Have your butcher saw the veal shanks and tie exposed marrow sides.

Oranges are steadfast seasoners all over Italy. In Calabria, every sensible married woman gathers a peck of *pallini* (those succulent

Bolzano plums that turn an orchard blue with their yield in September), sprinkles some generously with orange peel, sugar, and a goodly portion of strong orange brandy, and bakes them into a delectable cake that is guaranteed to keep an errant husband from straying (at least while the plums last)!

BOLZANO PLUM CAKE

1 Heat oven to 375°. Butter and flour a 9-inch springform pan. Sprinkle plums with ¼ cup granulated sugar; reserve.

2 Cream butter with 1 cup granulated sugar until light and fluffy in a large mixing bowl. Beat in egg yolks, one at a time. Stir in orange peel, lemon peel, and vanilla.

3 Sift together flour, cornstarch, and baking powder. Beat egg whites until stiff but not dry. Fold flour mixture into egg yolk mixture in three parts, alternating with thirds of the egg whites.

4 Spread half of batter in the prepared pan. Bake 10 minutes. Arrange plum halves, cut sides up, on top of pre-baked batter. Sprinkle with Grand Marnier. Carefully spread remaining batter over plums. Bake until light brown on top, 50 to 55 minutes.

5 Cool cake on wire rack 5 minutes. Loosen the edge with a sharp knife. Cool on rack 45 minutes longer; remove sides of pan. Serve while still slightly warm, sprinkled with confectioners' sugar.

1 pound Italian plums, cut in half, pitted
1¼ cups granulated sugar
14 tablespoons butter, softened
4 eggs, separated
Finely grated peel of 1 orange
Finely grated peel of ½ lemon
1 teaspoon vanilla
1½ cups all-purpose flour
½ cup cornstarch
2 teaspoons baking powder
2 tablespoons Grand Marnier liqueur
Confectioners' sugar

Serves 8 to 10.

All orange liqueurs stem from a single fiery libation distilled in Dutch Curaçao in 1634 when a clever Hollander, having discovered a small, greenish orange growing wild in the islands, determined that the oil in the fruit's skin would make a remarkable base for *genever,* the sweet Dutch gin. Somehow the distiller went wrong in his calculations but the pungent essence he produced (and called Curaçao) has captured the fancy of the world's palate for over 300 years.

During this spate of time, the seeds of the Curaçao orange have been scattered to the four corners of the globe and orange liqueurs are now as numerous as orange varieties. The island of Curaçao still maintains one remarkable distillery, Senior's Curaçao of Curaçao, that produces Triple Sec, the treble-strength dry infusion without which a *margarita* would be merely tequila and lime!

Oddly enough, my favorite orange liqueur, Grand Marnier, uses no Curaçao fruit in its distillation. But the golden liquid is so heady that I have been inspired to invent two very salutory recipes based on its unparalleled bouquet.

The first is an orange-scented flan, which is somewhat more velvety than *crème renversée* and a hundred times more fragrant!

BERT GREENE'S GRAND MARNIER FLAN

½ cup granulated sugar
1½ cups milk
1 cup whipping cream
1 tablespoon vanilla or 1-inch piece of vanilla bean
3 eggs
3 egg yolks
¾ cup granulated sugar
6 tablespoons Grand Marnier liqueur
½ cup water
2 tablespoons granulated sugar

Serves 6.

1 Heat oven to 350°. Warm a 1-quart souffle dish by placing it in oven 5 to 6 minutes.

2 Meanwhile, heat ½ cup granulated sugar in a saucepan over high heat until sugar starts to melt; cook, stirring constantly with a wooden spoon, until sugar liquifies. Reduce heat; cook, stirring constantly, until caramel turns deep golden. Remove from heat.

3 Pour caramel into the warm souffle dish, turning dish to coat bottom and sides; reserve saucepan. Invert souffle dish on a buttered piece of waxed paper (to prevent drippings from hardening on any work surfaces); let stand until cool. (Do not worry if caramel does not look smooth.)

4 Heat milk, cream, and vanilla or vanilla bean in a medium saucepan until hot; do not boil. Remove from heat.

5 Beat eggs with egg yolks in a bowl. Beat in ¾ cup sugar until light and lemon-colored. Stir in 3 tablespoons Grand Marnier. If using vanilla bean, remove it from milk mixture, slit, and scrape seeds into egg mixture; discard pod. Gradually pour milk mixture into egg mixture, stirring constantly.

6 Pour custard into caramel-coated souffle dish. Place dish in a roasting pan on middle rack in oven. Pour boiling water into roasting pan to ½ depth of souffle dish. Bake until a knife inserted in center comes out fairly clean, about 1 hour. (Do not let water in pan boil; if it begins to boil, add cold water.) Cool flan on a wire rack; refrigerate at least 6 hours or overnight.

7 To make sauce for flan: Add ½ cup water to reserved saucepan used to make caramel. Heat to boiling, scraping remaining caramel bits from bottom and sides of pan. Boil, stirring constantly, until mixture forms a thick syrup; stir in 2 tablespoons sugar until smooth.

Remove from heat; stir in remaining 3 tablespoons Grand Marnier. Let stand to cool; refrigerate until cold.

8 To unmold flan: Heat 1 inch of water in a skillet to boiling; turn off heat. Dip a sharp knife in water; run it around the sides of the flan. Dip bottom of souffle dish in skillet for a few seconds. Place a serving dish over the souffle dish and invert; remove souffle dish. Pass sauce in pitcher with flan.

Note: Flan may be prepared through Step 3 and left standing 4 to 5 hours before you proceed with next step.

The following condiment is one for which you can give thanks every Thanksgiving! I made up this recipe by inadvertence when I was a much, much younger cook. Having allowed my ripe cranberries to stew far too long—while I was busily talking on the kitchen telephone—I realized that they were about to jell unless I tossed the nearest handy liquid into the pan. The nearest liquid was Grand Marnier. And the result was a runny, under-sweetened sauce that scrupulously respects the sovereignty of a turkey's seasoning.

CRANBERRIES IN GRAND MARNIER

1 Pick over cranberries and wash in a colander under cold running water.

2 Place the orange juice and sugar in a large saucepan; cook and stir over medium heat until sugar dissolves.

3 Add cranberries, orange pulp, and orange peel. Heat to boiling; reduce heat. Simmer until skins pop and cranberries are tender, 10 to 15 minutes. Add Grand Marnier and simmer 2 minutes longer. Refrigerate. (Sauce will be runny rather than jellied. Serve with goose or turkey.)

1 **pound (about 4 cups) cranberries**
1 **cup orange juice**
2 **cups granulated sugar**
Pulp of 1 orange, membranes removed, seeded, chopped
2 **tablespoons finely slivered orange peel**
½ **cup Grand Marnier liqueur**

Serves 8.

Thoughts of the holidays bring me to one of the best orange recipes in my entire collection. A sunny, yellow fruitcake (*sans*

gooky candied fruits), it depends on orange and bits of crystal-ized pineapple for its extraordinary tincture.

For this yuletide offering, we must all give thanks to a charming southern friend of mine who snatched the recipe from her mother's heirloom anthology and presented it to me as a Christmas-stocking stuffer a few years back. I thank her (and you will too) every time the first snows fall.

GOLDEN CHRISTMAS CAKE

1 cup unsalted butter, softened
1 cup superfine sugar
4 eggs
3⅔ cups sifted all-purpose flour
1 teaspoon baking powder
½ teaspoon salt
1½ cups buttermilk
1 teaspoon baking soda
Grated peel of 2 oranges
2 teaspoons vanilla
1 cup coarsely chopped pecans
½ cup shelled whole pistachio nuts
1 cup chopped dates
½ cup chopped crystallized
    pineapple
½ cup orange juice
1 cup granulated sugar
¾ cup confectioners' sugar
3 tablespoons Grand Marnier
    liqueur
1½ tablespoons orange juice

Serves 10 to 12.

1 Heat oven to 325°. Beat butter until light and fluffy in a large bowl; gradually beat in superfine sugar. Beat in eggs, one at a time, beating well after each addition.

2 Sift flour, baking powder, and salt together. Combine buttermilk and baking soda. Using a wooden spoon, stir flour mixture into egg mixture in six parts alternating with sixths of the buttermilk mixture; stir until thoroughly mixed (do not use an electric mixer; batter might curdle). Stir in orange peel, vanilla, pecans, pistachio nuts, dates, and pineapple.

3 Grease a 10-inch tube pan. Spread batter evenly in pan. Bake until toothpick inserted comes out clean, 1 hour and 25 to 30 minutes.

4 Heat ½ cup orange juice and granulated sugar in a saucepan to boiling. Pierce top of cake with a fork all over; spoon orange juice mixture over cake. Let stand in pan on a wire rack 2 hours; tilt pan occasionally to distribute orange juice.

5 Unmold cake and turn right side up on serving plate. Combine confectioners' sugar, Grand Marnier, and 1½ tablespoons orange juice in a small bowl; drizzle over cake.

Every reasonable cook's kitchen bouquet depends on the be-quests of cooking friends: something old, something new, some things definitely borrowed, and—here and there—something blue.

My late friend Edith Macaulay was a rare person: she read three books at a time, knew the answer to everything down and across in *The New York Times* crossword puzzle, and was one of the best and most effortless cooks I ever met. She could write a

quatrain and compose a souffle at the same time, and she maintained a marvelous 200-year-old farmhouse (where, she proudly proclaimed, Major André once slept) because, she said, it gave her a connection with the past.

Dear Edith suffered one terrible blow—at my hands. She was never able to settle me properly into matrimony with any of the eligible girls she had in mind.

"It's a shame you're not married," she wrote me in one of her last letters, "for you are far too precious to waste!" So was she.

I prepare her favorite (Grand Marnier-soused) blueberry pie in the only pie crust worthy of the legacy—Grandma Rose Naftalin's super, orange-spiked pastry. The only "fooling-around" I do with the latter recipe is to add a little grated orange peel from time to time. For this, Grandma dear, forgive me!

EDITH MACAULAY'S FAVORITE BLUEBERRY PIE

½ recipe Grandma Rose's Favorite Pie Crust (recipe follows)
¾ cup granulated sugar
2½ tablespoons cornstarch
¼ teaspoon salt
⅔ cup water
3 cups fresh blueberries, cleaned
2 tablespoons butter
1½ tablespoons lemon juice
1½ tablespoons Grand Marnier liqueur
Sweetened whipped cream for garnish (optional)

Serves 6 to 8.

1 Make pie crust pastry and refrigerate. Heat oven to 425°. Roll out pastry to an 11-inch circle. Line a 9-inch pie pan with pastry; trim and flute edges. Line pastry with aluminum foil and dried beans or rice. Bake 10 minutes; remove foil and beans. Bake 5 minutes longer. Let stand to cool.

2 Combine sugar, cornstarch, and salt in a saucepan. Add the water and 1 cup blueberries. Heat to boiling, stirring constantly; boil until very thick, about 15 minutes. Remove from heat; stir in butter, lemon juice, and Grand Marnier. Cool.

3 Fold in remaining 2 cups blueberries; refrigerate 1 hour. Spoon into pie shell. Refrigerate at least 1 hour before serving. Garnish with whipped cream, if desired.

GRANDMA ROSE'S FAVORITE PIE CRUST

2½ cups all-purpose flour
½ teaspoon salt
½ cup cold unsalted butter
½ cup vegetable shortening
1 teaspoon grated orange peel
4 tablespoons cold orange juice

Makes enough for two 9- or 10-inch single crusts or one 9- or 10-inch, double-crust pie.

1 Sift flour with salt into a large bowl. Cut in butter and shortening; add orange peel. Blend with a pastry blender until the texture of coarse crumbs.

2 Using a fork or knife, cut orange juice into flour mixture to form a soft dough. (Do not overwork!) Refrigerate 1 hour before using.

My oldest buddy in this world is someone I met in college when we were both in our late teens.

George Klauber is a brilliant designer who never cared a fig about cooking until he bought an awesome mansion in Brooklyn Heights a brace of years ago. His kitchen is six flights above ground and small but so charmingly contrived that the culinary habit overtook him there.

A few years after the first purchase, he bought another house on the bay side of Fire Island. However, the following paradigm improvisation for beach plums does not stem from that habitation; George has been making the same exotic concoction (jam or conserve—name it as you will!) since the days when he shared a summer house with me in Amagansett two decades ago. Now he simply has more beach front in which to search for the elusive fruit.

Klauber cautions the reader that seeking out the beach plum is truly a picker's art. This delicate berry (inedible raw) grows in sandy bogs along the shore and must he hard-hunted. Although some beach plum plants (in uninhabited areas) grow to shrubby-tree size, most are small, twisted brush plants that grow between the beach-pea and the dusty-miller.

George is an old hand at routing out a truly hard-to-find crop and he usually makes several quarts of his marvelous concoction every fall. His most awesome production resulted from a discovery of apricot-colored beach plums—several years ago—that yielded a score of jars to his lucky friends' cupboards. Unfortunately, the glittering beach plum, like gold itself, is illusive stuff: the following summer the fruit was nowhere to be found!

When picking the golden (or silvery blue) fruit, my friend advises, collectors should lift the sand around the lowest branches, as beach plums sometimes grow underground and "those are the fattest and sweetest ones you will ever find!"

Incidentally, I must confess that the following formula is the only one in this book that has *not* been tested by me. It was a bad year for beach plums, according to George; so nary a cup was able to be picked for experimentation. Since my friend makes his "Beach Plum Madness" by eye (and tongue), there was no formal prescription and we had to reconstruct his method by memory.

George Klauber is not a man to give up, however. The very last weekend before Fire Island shuttered up for the season, he made one more fruit-searching safari into the underbrush—and produced a single quart of plums, so that he might verify his recipe. His gleaning was terrific. I know, because I claimed the first jar!

GEORGE KLAUBER'S
BEACH PLUM MADNESS

1 Rent a house near the shore.

2 In late September, take a pail and nose around the beach grass for tiny red, purple, or yellow fruit growing there.

3 Place the plums in your sink and wash well under cold running water to remove all sand.

4 Squeeze the pits from the beach plums. Place the pulp in one heavy pot, the pits in another, including any water that clings.

5 Heat pits to boiling; cook over medium-high heat ½ hour. Using a wire sieve, strain pits over the pot with the pulp, stirring and mashing with a wooden spoon until pits are clean and excess pulp is forced through.

6 Heat pulp to boiling; add the orange peel. Reduce heat; cook over medium-low heat 1 hour, stirring occasionally. Skim off foam as it rises to the surface.

7 When jam is fairly thick, stir in sugar to taste. Cook until sugar is dissolved. Add the Grand Marnier. Ladle into sterilized jars and seal.

1 quart beach plums plus a few unripe ones (they contain more natural pectin)
Finely grated peel of 1 orange
4 cups granulated sugar (or to taste)
¼ cup Grand Marnier liqueur

Makes about 4 half-pints.

Orange and chocolate is the most stunning culinary coalition I know. So I saved for very last the most special recipe in this chapter—a luscious chocolate-mousselike ring enhanced by an inner circle of orange-scented berries and whipped cream.

The devise for this monumental confection came from a most talented and beautiful young woman, my best friend in the whole wide world, Margo Henderson.

She was a remarkable singer and a sensitive cook who once called me long-distance from California and spent two hours reciting back my instructions for Boeuf à La Bourguignonne— just to be sure my reputation would be upheld in her translation.

Margo loved to eat and, best of all, she loved to have friends eating beside her in her own home. Her kitchen repertoire was not large but it was choice. And many a recipe that she was pressed into testing for me became annexed for her own table. My friend was not always sanguine about the results, however. "It's not nearly as good as when you make it," she would complain, shaking her head at any praise. That was Margo.

Unfortunately, she never lived to see this collection published nor her wonderful chocolate dessert immortalized—and that is the saddest liner note I have ever had to write.

GÂTEAU MARGO

20 fresh strawberries or raspberries, washed
3 tablespoons granulated sugar
6 tablespoons Grand Marnier liqueur
Bakers' Secret (see note)
8 ounces semisweet chocolate, broken into pieces
4 large eggs
1¼ cups granulated sugar
1 cup unsalted butter, softened
6 tablespoons cornstarch
1 cup whipping cream
¼ cup confectioners' sugar

Serves 10.

1 Sprinkle berries with 3 tablespoons granulated sugar and 2 tablespoons Grand Marnier; toss to coat. Refrigerate.

2 Heat oven to 350°F. Grease a 1-quart savarin ring mold with Bakers' Secret. (See note.)

3 Melt chocolate in the top of a double boiler over hot water; remove from heat.

4 Beat eggs in a large mixing bowl until foamy; gradually beat in 1¼ cups granulated sugar. Continue to beat until mixture is pale yellow in color and forms a ribbon when beater is lifted.

5 Cream butter in a bowl until light and fluffy. Beat in melted chocolate. Add chocolate mixture to egg mixture; beat until fluffy. Fold in cornstarch, 2 tablespoons at a time. Stir in 2 tablespoons Grand Marnier. Pour into prepared mold.

6 Place mold in a large roasting pan on the middle rack of the oven. Pour boiling water into the roasting pan to ½ depth of mold. Bake until toothpick inserted comes out clean, about 50 minutes.

7 Run a knife around edges of mold. Cool cake completely on wire rack. Unmold onto a serving plate.

8 Whip cream with confectioners' sugar and remaining 2 tablespoons Grand Marnier until stiff.

9 Place berries in center of cake, reserving some for garnish. Mound whipped cream in center over berries. Dry berries for garnish; arrange over cream.

Note: To make Bakers' Secret, combine ¼ cup shortening, ¼ cup vegetable oil, and ¼ cup all-purpose flour. Beat until creamy. Store in a jar in the refrigerator. Use Bakers' Secret or any similar nonstick commercial product to grease cake pans, bread pans, etc. Also, I use a good, imported chocolate, like Maillard's, Tobler, Lindt, or Lanvin.

Pepper

Collectors are an insatiable breed. I know, because I am one myself—a *rabid* recipe compiler. As a group, we hobbyists suffer a common plaint: "pack-rat passion" (which is a kinder way of putting it than *greed*). And the manic urge to possess more—and then still more—is every collector's downfall.

Psychiatrists hold that the hoarding fetish usually surfaces in middle age when sex and other athletic impulses diminish. Mine became apparent much earlier on, slightly before puberty—when I found myself channeled into light cookery by the working parents (about whom I have already told you), who determined that schoolwork, done early enough in the afternoon, left considerable time for light housework.

Bedmaking, like algebra, I failed from the start. (And I still cannot properly trisect a hospital corner in percale any better than I can calculate the square root of pi.) Thus the kitchen became my province, the flaming gas range being better suited to my temperament in any case!

There I first ventured into serious collocation. Merely lighting blue flames under the various pots and pans my diligent mother had partially cooked the night before left much to be desired in this budding chef's bosom; so I improvised on her cookery. I won't say that I improved it, but I did change things considerably. Flavoring the hardy comestibles with every herb and spice I could find in our kitchen cupboard, I often produced less than mouth-watering results. But I yearned, you see, for prolific gastronomy.

To my tongue, our family fare was singularly bland. My

father (although on the surface a hale and hearty fellow) had an appetite that might be characterized as ranging from diehard to downright dull. Gray, overcooked meats, boiled chicken, and fried smelts were the only viands he found acceptable. Meat balls and casseroles would be tolerated sometimes (it was, after all, the middle of the Depression) but spaghetti and macaroni were out of the question.

Although the other three members of his family doted on hash, my father rejected it—because, as he stated so often with dogged righteousness, "One never knows what *they* put into it!"

I knew. "They" put in leftover beef, potatoes, and onions. Oh yes, and seasonings! The whole gamut was employed when I made the dish—paprika, cayenne pepper, Tabasco, Worcestershire sauce, and chili powder from a can, when that was handy. I used the stinging adjuncts with such verve and gusto that my mother and sister, whose palates were a good deal more sophisticated than my father's, begged for surcease.

"Enough with the pepper shaker!" my mother cried out in dismay on one occasion. "You are beginning to cook like an *Irishman,* for God's sake!"

That was my mother's culinary prejudice showing.

At mealtime, my parents (first-generation Jews) abandoned their own heritage and attempted to emulate the demeanor of Yankee Americans. Salt was the only condiment (aside from ubiquitous ketchup) allowed on the table. And no racy seasoning, like garlic or pepper, had ever contaminated our menu until the day I began to cook.

Indeed, pepper was to prove the test of my sister's husband-to-be. This young man of Czech background courted my sister assiduously (and most often at mealtimes, it seemed). But my parents decided that any alliance would be doomed the first time he requested cayenne pepper at our dinner table. This breach of taste caused severe familial reverberations:

"I do not trust anyone who uses that much seasoning on decent American food," my father stated unequivocally.

"He probably drinks too," my mother agreed.

Truth to tell, he did. And more than his penchant for spice caused matrimonial discord in the end. But the middle-European appetite for *capsicum* certainly foreshadowed it in our household!

There are over forty different formulas for chili con carne (with varying degrees of fire) in my hoard of recipes. Here is the best one. Serve it to strong friends and proceed with some caution when it comes to the *chiles serranos,* please!

PEPPERED CHILI

1 Heat oven to 300°. Melt 3 tablespoons butter in a heavy skillet. Add half the garlic, half the onions, and the green pepper; saute over medium heat 5 minutes. Make a large well in center of vegetables; place ground beef in center. Cook over high heat, stirring and scraping bottom of pan with a metal spatula, until the meat is brown. Gradually stir vegetables into meat as it browns. Transfer mixture to a Dutch oven.

2 Add 2 tablespoons butter and the oil to the skillet; saute steak over high heat, a few strips at a time, until well browned on all sides. Transfer cooked strips to a plate. Remove all fat from skillet. Return steak to skillet; stir in chili powder. Cook over low heat 3 minutes. Transfer to Dutch oven.

3 Add 2 tablespoons butter and remaining onions and garlic to skillet. Cook over medium heat, stirring and scraping bottom of pan, 3 minutes. Add tomatoes; sprinkle with sugar, basil, and bay leaf. Cook 10 minutes. Transfer to Dutch oven.

4 Stir remaining ingredients, except beans, rice, and sour cream into Dutch oven. Bake covered 3 hours. Stir in beans; bake ½ hour longer. Serve over rice; pass sour cream in a bowl, if desired.

For pepper lovers, here's the first recorded recipe for an aphrodisiac, from Ovid.

> *Pepper, with biting nettle seed, first bruise,*
> *Then with yellow pillatory wine infuse.*

Naturally the results are not vouched for here, but the ingredients would seem to ensure a heck of a blast!

Equally inflammatory to the tongue is the following prescription for Rouille. A provincial French mayonnaise-type (minus the eggs) preparation, Rouille is a fiery emollient that the good people of the Mediterranean always spoon into fish soups like *bourride* or *bouillabaisse*. From time to time, I enflame my guests at the cocktail hour by having a bowl of the tangerine-colored blend handy for dipping raw vegetables and shrimp. Very potent with the potables!

Rouille also makes an exotic dressing for cold meats, like leftover turkey or lamb, and is unusually bracing spread on toast for sandwiches when the filling is a bland one. Stir some into bouillon too! Simple to make, rouille can be kept for weeks and weeks in a cold refrigerator as emergency rations.

7 tablespoons butter
2 cloves garlic, minced
4 onions, finely chopped
1 large green pepper, finely chopped
1¼ pounds ground beef round
1 tablespoon vegetable oil
1 beef shoulder steak (1½ pounds), fat removed, cut into strips 2-inches long and ½-inch wide
3 tablespoons chili powder (or more to taste)
3 large tomatoes, chopped
1 teaspoon granulated sugar
4 basil leaves, chopped, or a pinch of dried basil
1 bay leaf, crumbled
Pinch of dried thyme
½ teaspoon paprika
½ teaspoon cayenne pepper
½ teaspoon ground allspice
1 dried red chili pepper, crushed
1 teaspoon soy sauce
½ teaspoon hot pepper sauce
6 canned serrano chilies, chopped
½ cup dry red wine
¾ cup beef broth
1 teaspoon salt
½ teaspoon freshly ground pepper
3 cups cooked red kidney beans
6 cups cooked rice
Sour cream (optional)

Serves 4 to 6.

ROUILLE

2 medium potatoes, pared, cut into eighths
1½ cups chicken broth
½ jar (12 ounces) sweet red peppers
¼ cup chopped red bell pepper, simmered 3 minutes in salted water, drained
½ jar (10 ounces) hot cherry peppers, well drained
1 jar (4 ounces) pimientos, well drained
Dash of hot pepper sauce
6 cloves garlic, mashed
1 teaspoon fresh basil leaves or a pinch of dried
Pinch of dried thyme
Dash of red wine vinegar
8 to 10 tablespoons olive oil
Salt and freshly ground pepper to taste

Makes about 2 cups.

1 Place potatoes and chicken broth in a saucepan. Heat to boiling; reduce heat. Simmer until potatoes are tender. Drain; reserve chicken broth.

2 Place potatoes, peppers, pimientos, hot pepper sauce, garlic, basil, thyme, and vinegar in a blender container. Blend at low speed 1 minute; then blend at high speed until smooth. Transfer to a mixing bowl.

3 Whisk in the olive oil, a few drops at a time, until mixture thickens. Add 4 tablespoons reserved hot chicken broth. Season to taste with salt and pepper. Store tightly covered in a glass jar in the refrigerator.

Red pepper is native to the New World, both chili and cayenne being products of *Capsicum annuum,* a bush plant grown in Mexico, South America, and the West Indies. Paprika, grown and processed in Hungary these days, was also an American native; it is made by crushing the dried ripe fruit of *Capsicum tetragonum.*

Paprika and cayenne have twin but disparate roles on a kitchen shelf. Either sweet or hot paprika may be used to accent and color a dish without overwhelming it, while cayenne will season the fare volcanically. A great chef I once met claimed that cayenne should be added to the pan in the early stages of cooking, so that its fine stinging dust can be dispersed in the cooking steam. Paprika, on the other hand, may be sprinkled on at the last moment as a decorative accent. Cayenne is available everywhere, but good, fresh paprika is hard to come by. Most supermarket canned varieties have too long a shelf-life to retain any potency. Fine-quality paprika may be ordered by mail, however, from Paprikas Weiss, Importers, 1546 Second Avenue, New York, New York 10028.

Neither paprika nor cayenne is any kin to *Piper nigrum,* the source of the elusive fruit peppercorns that Columbus sought when he set forth for India in 1492.

A wondrous peppery meatloaf I know calls for one-quarter cup of crushed peppercorns in its bracing prescription. A great dish to clear the sinuses, it is probably my favorite meatloaf at the moment. So throw caution to the winds and make it while you have the courage! It's delightful served hot and even better stuffed cold into crusty bread the following day.

PEPPER LOAF

1 Heat oven to 350°. Place meat in a large mixing bowl. Place celery, parsley, and chicken stock in a blender container; blend until pureed.

2 Add vegetable puree, peppercorns, bread crumbs, egg, and salt to meat. Mix thoroughly.

3 Shape mixture into a loaf in a shallow baking dish. Lay bacon strips on top. Bake 1½ hours.

2 pounds ground veal
3 ribs celery, chopped
½ cup chopped parsley
½ cup chicken stock or strong broth
¼ cup peppercorns, crushed
½ cup bread crumbs
1 egg, lightly beaten
½ teaspoon salt
2 strips bacon

Serves 4 to 6.

In the Middle Ages, dowries, kings' ransoms, and taxes were often paid in bags of peppercorns in lieu of gold. That should give you some idea of the spice's value back then! Even today, the pepper trade generates much piracy and more crimes are said to be committed in Asia over pepper than heroin.

All the black and white peppercorns in the world originally stemmed from the Malabar Coast of southwest India. The names of Malabar pepper varieties trip off the tongue like the drumbeats in a Kipling ode: Mangalore, Calicut, Tellicherry, Alleppey, Sarawak. These are still said to be the very best.

The world consumes about 175 million pounds of this *Piper nigrum* a year. And while black pepper outsells white in the United States, white is the preferred seasoning in Europe. Both are made from the red berries of the same perennial vine: white pepper is the ripened berry stripped of its outer bark and then dried; black pepper (somewhat stronger than white) is picked earlier than white, sun dried and then allowed to age for proper bite.

The world's largest pepper-consumer (50 million pounds of black pepper annually) is the United States; the Soviet Union places second. The smallest pepper-user is Switzerland, which seems anomalous to me, for one of the best pepper recipes I possess comes from Zurich. It uses green, or unripe, peppercorns—and can turn Thanksgiving leftovers into prime feasting.

SWISS TURKEY SALAD

1 egg yolk*
1 teaspoon Dijon mustard
Juice of ½ lemon
½ teaspoon salt
1 tablespoon green peppercorns
⅛ teaspoon hot pepper sauce
½ cup vegetable oil
½ cup olive oil
4 cups cubed cooked turkey
1 cup diced celery
1½ cups diced, pared apples
⅔ cup chopped walnuts
Finely chopped parsley
Watercress leaves

Serves 6 to 8.

1 Place egg yolk in a medium bowl; whisk in mustard, lemon juice, salt, peppercorns, and hot pepper sauce. Whisk in oil, 1 teaspoon at a time, until thick; whisk in remaining oil until smooth.

2 Stir turkey, celery, and apples into dressing. Mound on a serving dish; sprinkle with walnuts and parsley. Surround with watercress leaves.

Note: Egg, mustard, lemon juice, and oil must be at room temperature.

Haitian cuisine manages to juggle several strong seasonings in a single dish without leaving battle scars in unfortunate diners' mouths. The following chicken broil is a distillation of hell's hottest fires—chili powder, cayenne, freshly ground black pepper, and mustard. Nevertheless, it is surprisingly temperate to the tongue; in fact, it's benign enough to please even those cousins from Duluth who show up for a visit from time to time. Serve it with rice, a salad, and one of the creamy desserts you will uncover in the "Vanilla" chapter.

2 frying chickens (about 2½ pounds each), cut up
Juice of 4 limes
2½ tablespoons honey
1 teaspoon mustard
1½ tablespoons chili powder
Pinch of cayenne pepper
1 large clove garlic, minced
2 tablespoons olive oil
1 teaspoon salt
½ teaspoon freshly ground pepper
¼ teaspoon paprika
2 tablespoons chopped fresh basil or 1 teaspoon dried
Bread crumbs
Chopped parsley

Serves 4 to 6.

HAITIAN CHICKEN

1 Arrange chicken pieces, skin side down, in a shallow baking dish. Combine all ingredients except bread crumbs and parsley in a small bowl. Pour over chicken. Refrigerate covered at least 4 hours.

2 Heat oven to 350°. Bake chicken uncovered 30 minutes, basting often. Turn chicken over; bake 30 minutes, continuing to baste.

3 Heat broiler unit. Transfer chicken, skin side down, to an oven-proof serving dish. Broil until brown. Turn the chicken over; sprinkle generously with bread crumbs. Spoon pan juices over crumbs; broil until crisp and brown. Sprinkle with parsley. Serve hot or cold.

Pepper is said to be a "masculine" seasoning—a no-nonsense spice. According to Escoffier, that is why women regard it so highly. "Like the ideal hero of the kitchen," the great chef wrote, "fresh pepper is stimulating and sometimes abrasive but always tender at the heart!"

Doctors agree. Strong pepper may sting the body's "hot" receptors but it also massages and soothes the tastebuds at the same time; then the fiery condiment goes about its true business—chivying the alimentary canal into action to convert food into energy.

The next prescription, for old-fashioned chicken stew, is heavily seasoned with freshly ground pepper—but each grind of the peppermill falls upon a cushion of soft and delectable dumplings that are simmered right in the pot.

PEPPER CHICKEN WITH DUMPLINGS

1 Melt 8 tablespoons butter in a Dutch oven. Saute chicken and onion over medium heat until chicken is light brown. Do not let the butter burn.

2 Add wine and chicken stock to cover. Add celery, peppercorns, and 1 teaspoon salt. Heat to boiling; reduce heat. Simmer covered until tender, 1 hour and 20 to 30 minutes. Meanwhile, sift 2 cups flour with the baking powder, brown sugar, cayenne pepper, ½ teaspoon black pepper, and ¼ teaspoon salt. Cut in 2 tablespoons butter; blend well with a pastry blender. Stir in milk with a fork. Roll out dough ½-inch thick on a lightly floured board; cut into 2-inch circles.

4 Heat oven to 275°. Remove chicken to a shallow baking dish; cover with aluminum foil. Keep warm in oven.

5 Strain cooking liquid and return to Dutch oven. Combine 1 tablespoon flour with 2 tablespoons cream; whisk into liquid. Heat to simmering; place dumplings on top, without overlapping. Cook covered 18 to 20 minutes.

6 Remove dumplings with a slotted spoon. Stir remaining 2 tablespoons cream into cooking liquid. Heat to boiling; boil 1 minute. Spoon half of sauce over chicken; top with dumplings. Spoon remaining sauce over all. Sprinkle with parsley and pepper.

10 tablespoons butter
2 small chickens (2½ pounds each), cut into serving pieces
1 onion, grated
1 cup dry white wine or vermouth
Chicken stock
2 ribs celery with leaves
16 peppercorns
1¼ teaspoons salt
2 cups plus 1 tablespoon sifted all-purpose flour
2½ teaspoons baking powder
1 teaspoon brown sugar
Pinch of cayenne pepper
½ teaspoon freshly ground black pepper
⅔ cup milk
¼ cup whipping cream
Chopped parsley for garnish
Freshly ground pepper

Serves 6 to 8.

In France, pepper is *poivre*; in Germany, *pfeffer*; in Italy, *pepe*; and in the Middle East, *felfel*. All these similar cognomens stem from the Sanskrit term, *pippala,* which was inscribed in the ancient Vedas and has been in common usage for over 2500 years.

The Romans considered *piperaecae* a drug/spice of great value; it was used not only to make barren women fertile and to cure baldness, but also to pickle fish and cure meat.

The spice's meat-curing properties inspired a fifteenth-century French chef to make a less-than-fresh shoat fit to eat by impregnating it with peppercorns—literally hammering them into the skin—before cooking it over an open fire. Thus the first steak *au poivre* was created.

Later the dish took on certain refinements: the meat was no rancid hog but fillet of beef and the peppers were only lightly pressed around the seasoned flesh before the meat was grilled. The diner was the King of France. *Vive le roi!*

My favorite *au poivre* recipes are for a sirloin steak, a ham steak, and a pair of lamb chops—all prepared with green (undried) peppercorns. In honor of that roast prepared back in the 1400s, I offer the ham first.

HAM AU POIVRE VERT

1 ham steak, about 1-inch thick
1½ tablespoons green peppercorns
1 small shallot, minced
1 small clove garlic, minced
1 teaspoon Dijon mustard
1 tablespoon butter, softened
¼ cup dry white wine
1 tablespoon water
1 tablespoon very strong beef stock or 1 teaspoon beef bouillon powder

Serves 2.

1 Heat oven to 350°. Wipe ham steak with paper toweling. Combine peppercorns, shallot, garlic, mustard, and 1 teaspoon butter in a mortar; mash with a pestle. Spread over both sides of ham. Let stand 30 minutes.

2 Melt 1 teaspoon butter in a heavy skillet. Saute ham over high heat on both sides. Transfer to a shallow baking dish.

3 Stir wine into skillet over high heat, scraping bottom and sides of pan. Add water and beef stock or bouillon; boil 3 minutes. Stir in remaining 1 teaspoon butter. Pour over ham. Bake 15 minutes.

STEAK AU POIVRE VERT

1 Heat oven to 400°. Rub steaks well with garlic. Heat oil in a heavy skillet over high heat; sear steaks quickly on both sides. Place steaks

in a shallow baking dish; bake 7 minutes for rare, 10 minutes for medium-rare.

2 Meanwhile, remove excess grease from skillet. Stir in wine over high heat, scraping bottom and sides of pan with a wooden spoon. Stir in mustard, tomato paste, soy sauce, peppercorns, pepper, and salt. Boil down until thick. Spoon sauce over steaks. Serve immediately.

Note: Recipe can easily be doubled for four servings, but do not increase the wine to more than ½ cup.

2 shell steaks, about 1¼ inches thick
1 clove garlic, bruised
1 tablespoon vegetable or olive oil
⅓ cup dry red wine
½ teaspoon Dijon mustard
¼ teaspoon tomato paste
Dash of soy sauce
2 teaspoons green peppercorns
¼ teaspoon freshly ground pepper
¼ teaspoon salt

Serves 2.

LAMB CHOPS WITH PEPPER SAUCE

1 Heat oven to 400°. Wipe chops with paper toweling. Mash butter with peppercorns; rub into chops.

2 Brown chops on both sides in a heavy skillet over high heat. Place in a shallow baking dish.

3 Add chicken broth and wine to skillet; boil, stirring constantly, until reduced by half. Stir in whole peppercorns, cream, and salt. Spoon over the chops. Bake 10 minutes for medium-rare.

4 thick rib lamb chops
1 tablespoon butter
1 teaspoon crushed green peppercorns
¼ cup strong chicken broth
¼ cup dry red wine
½ teaspoon whole green peppercorns
1 tablespoon whipping cream
Salt to taste

Serves 2.

Another green peppercorn-cum-beef entrée comes from Su Casa, which is, I believe, one of the world's great restaurants—despite the fact that it is located smack in the middle of a Rockefeller garden of Eden, the super-lush Dorado Beach Hotel, in Puerto Rico.

What makes a restaurant great? In my opinion it is a combination of utterly felicitous essentials: graceful surroundings and an efficient staff, plus inspired cookery, of course.

No one knows how long a restaurant will remain great. My assessment of Su Casa is based on a recent visit made under optimum conditions—you must make further evaluations for yourself.

Although Su Casa is Spanish in character, the head chef is Swiss and the menu (limited to only four entrées each night) is international. The following dish was created by chef Walter Hunziker for the restaurant (and adapted for my own tiny kitchen). The green-peppered Wellington is upholstered in an airy, golden brioche dough that makes it very special. Beef is certainly expensive these days—and even green peppercorns run high—but this recipe is well worth the investment (both financially and emotionally!), I assure you.

BOUEF EN BRIOCHE SU CASA

The day before:

1 package dry yeast
¼ cup lukewarm water
2⅔ cups all-purpose flour
2 teaspoons granulated sugar
2 teaspoons salt
¾ cup unsalted butter, melted
3 eggs

The next day:

3 to 3½ pounds beef tenderloin, barded with pork fat
Salt and freshly ground pepper
3 tablespoons vegetable oil
3 tablespoons butter
3 large shallots, minced
½ pound mushrooms, finely chopped
1 can (1¾ ounces) green peppercorns, drained, crushed
¼ cup bread crumbs
2 egg yolks
Salt
1 tablespoon milk
1 tablespoon cognac
¼ cup strong beef broth or stock
2 tablespoons whipping cream
1 teaspoon finely chopped parsley

Serves 4.

To make the brioche dough: Combine yeast, water, and 1 cup flour in a bowl; stir until smooth. Let stand covered 1 hour. Combine remaining ingredients in a large bowl; stir in yeast "sponge." Mix well. Refrigerate covered overnight. Remove from refrigerator 2½ hours before using.

1 Carefully remove barding fat from meat; reserve. Rub meat with salt and pepper. Heat oil in a skillet over high heat; sear meat on all sides. Remove meat from skillet; let stand to cool.

2 Remove fat from skillet. Melt 2 tablespoons butter; add 2 minced shallots. Cook over low heat until soft. Raise heat to medium-high; stir in mushrooms. Cook until all moisture is evaporated. Reserve 1 teaspoon peppercorns; stir remainder into mushrooms with the bread crumbs. Remove from heat; stir in 1 egg yolk and salt to taste. Spread mixture evenly over meat; replace barding fat. Refrigerate covered.

3 Heat oven to 425°. Roll out brioche dough ¼-inch thick on a floured surface. Place meat, top side down, in center; wrap dough around meat. Trim excess dough. Place meat, right side up, on a large, buttered baking sheet. Let stand 30 minutes.

4 Whisk remaining egg yolk with milk; brush over dough. Bake 30 to 35 minutes for medium-rare, brushing with egg mixture twice during baking. (To test for doneness, insert an ice pick in center of meat; if pick comes out lukewarm to the touch, the meat is ready.) Let meat stand 15 minutes.

5 Meanwhile, melt 1 tablespoon butter in a heavy saucepan; add remaining shallot and cook until soft. Add cognac; heat to boiling. Stir in beef broth, cream, and reserved peppercorns. Cook until slightly thickened, about 5 minutes. Add parsley. Serve sauce with meat.

Note: Recipe easily can be doubled.

Though pepper is a universal seasoning, not everyone knows how to use it properly. Those poor unfortunates whose only knowledge of the spice comes from a little tin container of irritating black dust are more to be pitied than censured by me.

If you haven't done so already, buy yourself a pepper mill, for heaven's sake, and get to know the taste of the freshly ground seasoning at once. The mill doesn't have to be elaborate. I avoid those five-foot-tall jobs and recommend a small, easy-to-handle grinder with a removable top for convenient filling. Have one of these in hand before you attempt the best luncheon dish (or dinner first course) I know, Peppered Lima Beans and Mushroom Salad. It mates exquisitely with a cold, dry white wine and a very crusty loaf of bread. And that's all it requires!

PEPPERED LIMA BEANS AND MUSHROOM SALAD

1 Combine mushrooms, oil, vinegar, pepper, and garlic in a medium bowl.

2 Cook lima beans in boiling salted water until just barely tender, 2 to 3 minutes. Rinse under cold running water and drain.

3 Fry bacon in a skillet until crisp; drain on paper toweling. Crumble bacon. Toss beans, bacon, and cheese with mushroom mixture. Season to taste with salt and more pepper if desired.

¼ pound mushrooms, sliced
½ cup olive oil
3 tablespoons wine vinegar
½ teaspoon freshly ground pepper
1 small clove garlic, crushed
1 package (10 ounces) frozen baby lima beans, thawed
4 strips bacon
4 ounces Gruyère cheese, chopped
Salt

Serves 4 to 6.

A word of caution: Now that you are in command of a pepper grinder, be discreet. Used over-generously, any seasoning can mask a dish's flavor. And pepper is meant to add piquancy—never physical pain!

Having said all that, I commend to your kitchen a unique recipe for a salubrious rendering of old-fashioned pot roast. Cooked in an oven roasting bag, the meat is seasoned with twenty-five (count 'em) peppercorns! I am not a physicist, only a cookbook writer; so I can't explain the mystery but the meat does not taste peppery at all. Believe me!

POT ROAST IN A BAG

1 teaspoon all-purpose flour
1 beef brisket (3 to 3½ pounds)
1 clove garlic, crushed
1 teaspoon anchovy paste
3 tablespoons red wine vinegar
1½ tablespoons honey
2 bay leaves, crumbled
½ teaspoon ground allspice
½ teaspoon salt
25 black peppercorns
1 onion, cut into quarters
4 to 6 medium baking potatoes, pared
Chopped parsley (optional)

Serves 4 to 6.

1 Heat oven to 350°. Sprinkle flour in an oven-roasting bag; shake the bag. Rub meat with garlic; discard garlic. Place meat in bag; shake until flour is distributed evenly.

2 Combine anchovy paste, vinegar, honey, bay leaves, allspice, salt, and peppercorns; spoon over meat. Place onion quarters around meat. Seal bag and place it in a roasting pan. Make four or five 2-inch-long slits in top of bag. Bake 1½ hours.

3 Untie bag. Carefully place potatoes around meat. Close bag; bake 30 minutes. Then cut open top of bag with a scissors to allow meat to brown; bake until meat is tender, about 30 minutes longer.

4 Remove meat from bag; place on a serving platter. Surround with potatoes. Strain meat juices; spoon some over meat. Garnish meat with parsley, if desired. Pass remaining meat juices on the side.

In America, southern cookery seems to have a peculiar penchant for pepper—apart from the obvious meat-and-potato alignments. I am most addicted to a Virginian ritual of "hotting up" cornmeal with bacon drippings and pepper. And a Carolina Sugar and Pepper Pie (from Charleston) is the most uncommon dessert you'll find on either side of the Mason-Dixon line. So proceed to the pepper mill posthaste!

1 cup cornmeal
¾ cup all-purpose flour
2 tablespoons granulated sugar
½ teaspoon baking soda
2 teaspoons baking powder
½ teaspoon salt
½ teaspoon freshly ground pepper
1 cup sour milk
⅛ teaspoon hot pepper sauce
1 egg, beaten
2 tablespoons bacon fat, melted

Serves 6 to 8.

OLD-FASHIONED CORNBREAD

1 Heat oven to 425°. Grease an 8-inch-square glass baking dish.

2 Sift together cornmeal, flour, sugar, baking soda, baking powder, salt, and pepper into a medium bowl. Add milk, hot pepper sauce, egg, and bacon fat. Mix well, but do not beat. Pour into baking dish. Bake 20 minutes.

CAROLINA SUGAR AND PEPPER PIE

1 Make pastry and refrigerate.

2 Heat oven to 425°. Roll out pastry to an 11-inch circle. Line a 9-inch pie pan with pastry; trim and flute. Line pastry with aluminum foil; fill with dried beans or rice. Bake 10 to 12 minutes. Remove foil and beans.

3 Combine sugar, salt, and flour in a large bowl. Stir in eggs, butter, corn syrup, pepper, vanilla, and whipping cream; mix well. Pour into pie shell.

4 Bake 10 minutes. Reduce oven heat to 325°; bake 40 minutes longer. Cool completely on wire rack. Just before serving, spread pie with whipped cream.

Some classicists insist that pepper doesn't play a role in sweets—which shows how wrong formal education can be!

Apart from Peter the Great, who spiked his black coffee with pepper and then had to cut the flavor with champagne and sugar, great cooks have created a multitude of felicitous matings of pepper with honey, brown sugar, and maple syrup.

Except for references to pfeffernüsse, however, most cookbooks avoid the issue. Mine does not. Two of the most mouthwatering temptations in this volume are possessed of generous amounts of pepper—and they are much easier on the choppers than pfeffernüsse, which I have hated since childhood, when I broke several teeth on them.

The Peanut and Pepper Pie is a marvel of crunchy, penuche-like indulgence that is quite worth the few cavities it may cause. The recipe comes from Georgia (where else?) and it gives the peanut quite a fresh slant. The Brown Sugar and Pepper Bundt is a German slice of legerdemain—and a far, far cry from pepper cookies.

PEANUT AND PEPPER PIE

1 Make pie crust pastry and refrigerate. Roll out pastry to an 11-inch circle. Line a 9-inch pie pan with pastry; trim and flute edge.

2 Heat oven to 350°. Combine peanut butter, maple syrup, sugar, butter, salt, and pepper in a medium bowl.

3 Beat in eggs, one at a time; add the cream and beat until smooth. Stir in peanuts. Pour into pie shell. Bake until set, 50 to 55 minutes. Cool on wire rack. Serve with whipped cream.

½ recipe Grandma Rose's Favorite
  Pie Crust (see Index)
2 cups dark brown sugar
Pinch of salt
1 tablespoon sifted all-purpose
  flour
2 eggs
2 tablespoons butter, melted
¼ cup dark corn syrup
¼ teaspoon freshly ground pepper
2 teaspoons vanilla
1 cup whipping cream, at room
  temperature
1 cup whipping cream, whipped

Serves 8.

½ recipe Grandma Rose's Favorite
  Pie Crust (see Index)
½ cup crunchy peanut butter
1½ cups maple syrup
½ cup superfine sugar
6 tablespoons butter, melted
Pinch of salt
¼ teaspoon freshly ground pepper
3 eggs
¼ cup whipping cream
¾ cup coarsely chopped unsalted
  peanuts
Whipped cream

Serves 8.

BROWN SUGAR AND PEPPER BUNDT

¾ cup unsalted butter, softened
1½ cups dark brown sugar
1 package (3 ounces) cream cheese
4 eggs
1 teaspoon vanilla
¼ cup whipping cream
1 tablespoon orange juice
¼ teaspoon ground allspice
Pinch of salt
¾ teaspoon finely ground black
   pepper
1½ cups sifted cake flour
Confectioners' sugar

Serves 8.

1 Heat oven to 350°. Cream butter with sugar in a large electric mixer bowl until light and fluffy. Add cream cheese; beat 3 minutes.

2 Beat in eggs, one at a time, beating well after each addition. Stir in vanilla, cream, and orange juice.

3 Sift together allspice, salt, pepper, and flour. Stir into egg mixture.

4 Butter and flour an 8 to 10 cup Bundt pan. Pour in batter. Bake until toothpick inserted in cake comes out clean, about 1 hour. Cool completely in pan on wire rack. Unmold onto serving plate; just before serving, dust with confectioners' sugar.

Poppy Seed

My mother's father was an imposing man. Very tall, as I am, but slim and narrow waisted, with thick black hair and a mustache like a Prussian general. For most of his long life, he was a designer in the fur trade. And although he was fairly successful, it seems to me now that he always hankered after a more fashionable and socially oriented profession.

Family tales were often told of how he coerced my sensible grandmother into the business (cottage industry, really) of bottling soda water when they were both young and newly exposed to the American craving for sweet elixirs like sarsaparilla and orange phosphate. Quizzed many years later about the consequence of this seductive enterprise, my grandfather left the room while his wife merely shrugged.

My mother told me the story afterward. "Your grandfather was a bit of a dreamer. Mama made the syrups for him and they were truly wonderful but he never got the formula for the fizz right. He claimed to know all about yeast and how it fermented—but, he didn't. All the bottles of soda pop they manufactured blew up in the cellar one night!"

Much later, after another sojourn in the fur business to recoup his losses, my grandfather bought a grand hotel in Saratoga Springs.

His partners in this venture were my "Uncle" Mike—whose gaudy reputation in our family was based on the fact that he had been the first Jew to be hired as the conductor of a horse-drawn trolley in what was, then, the largely Irish-Catholic borough of Queens—and his wife, "Aunt" Rosie. Both Mike and Rosie (being cousins to each other) were my grandmother's third cousins and that blood tie along with Rosie's superior culinary achievements made them, in my grandfather's view, an ideal choice to run a resort hotel.

Rosie and Mike were as different from my grandparents as they were from one another. Mike was short-fused—a wiry man with a terrible temper but a smile so winning it could disarm the devil. More to the point, he was a complete American dandy. Handsome and without a trace of accent (or Yiddish intonation), he bore a dashing resemblance to "Gentleman" Jimmy Walker, who was then the mayor of New York City.

None of the married ladies who rocked themselves silly on the verandah outside his hotel office every afternoon and evening could resist Mike's roving blue eyes or the tilt of his turned-up nose. Always dressed to the nines, Mike gave the hotel a rakish air that made it popular with the sporting crowd that only visited Saratoga in August for the racing season as well as with the more settled clientele that came to soak their unlovely bodies in geyser water all summer long.

His wife was his complete emotional opposite. A Polish farm girl, Rosie spent her childhood in an unloving home before being shipped off to Germany and apprenticed to a master chef at a tender age. Obviously she learned the craft well, because she cooked like an angel for the rest of her life.

And though her husband (with my grandparents) managed a splendid hostelry, Rosie never aspired to be more than a dogged worker in its behalf. With foreign ways and an accent that she never attempted to lose, wearing thick gold-rimmed glasses that she would look over mistily from time to time, she stayed out of sight of the guests. She slaved in the hotel's kitchen from morning till night—sometimes as long as twenty hours a day!

Not conventionally pretty, as her husband was handsome, Rosie was, in my mother's words, "good-hearted as the day is long!" She was a large, motherly earth goddess, whose apron always held something sugary and good to eat and whose ample bosom smelled of poppy seeds when she held me close.

What I remember best about Rosie was her laughter—and the way she tottered in ceaseless motion between the hotel kitchen's mammoth shining stoves. Her poor feet, usually encased in black leather shoes that laced halfway up her calves, were crippled from standing all day. And her legs were crisscrossed with varicose veins—but that physical trial never kept her from the hundred and one tasks she set for herself each day.

Arms dusty with flour, she would giggle to herself like a young girl as she coaxed sheets of strudel dough to the texture of tissue paper before they satisfied her critical eye.

"*Leicht. Mehr Leicht jetzt!*" she would murmur as she pulled the tenuous pastry thinner still, before laying it out to dry like bed linen. "Now . . . ," she would laugh with pride as the dough became translucent with sweet butter, "now it will be OK. *Leicht genug!*"

Rosie was an absolute genius in the kitchen. Her strudel was composed of sheer sunlit air. The herring fillets she deep-fried for breakfast were so crisp and frangible that the tender fish flaked on the fork before a mouth could ever reach it! The little filled cakes and golden yeasty horns that she sprinkled with sugar and cinnamon destroyed any dietary willpower at first bite and left a buttery perfume on the tongue long afterward.

In short, if I haven't already made it clear, this lady's culinary abilities were so formidable and various that they rivaled (and threatened to eclipse) even my grandmother's awesome kitchen performances.

It was a contest between titans who were destined to clash!

For ten short years, The Hotel Lafayette (on Circular Street, off Filer) had the best cuisine in Saratoga Springs—and most probably in the whole of the United States. Not Jewish cooking at all, it was a glorious mix of German, Hungarian, and Viennese dishes, meticulously prepared and served with great pampering style. Patrons from all over the resort town flocked nightly to the handsome Victorian dining room like so many pilgrims to Mecca. But my grandmother was not happy.

Though the hotel's managerial chores were divided by four, Rosie was the sole acknowledged chef. This rankled my grandmother, who was relegated to being the dining room watchdog. While she (being small and not that strong) couldn't possibly have attempted Rosie's feats in the kitchen, she was a very proud woman and tenaciously eager for a share of the approbation. When it did not come her way, she chafed and resented her status in the Lafayette organization.

To be fair, my grandmother often praised her third cousin's cooking achievements, but her heart was never in the commendation.

"Rosie uses too many pots and pans for me," she would say, with a sweet, if slightly off-center, smile. "And her apron! Always so messy. *Schmutzig!* Everything that woman cooks ends up on her apron!"

I turned out to be the same kind of cook. Perhaps that's why I always empathized with poor Rosie. And that apron held, for me, the most heavenly scent of crushed poppy seed. I can still smell it as I write.

Eventually my grandmother nagged her husband out of the hotel business and back to fur designing, where she felt he properly belonged. The official reason given for the split in my grandparents' very successful partnership with Mike and Rosie was the projected impact of the stock-market crash on resort traffic, although business actually remained brisk at the Lafayette until World War II, when gasoline rationing hampered all travel. In fact, however, it was my grandmother's ego that split up the golden alliance.

Overly loyal to her family, my mother dissuaded my father (who doted on Rosie's cooking) from bringing us back to the Lafayette after her parents decamped—although the Depression probably also had something to do with that decision.

Whatever the reason they ended, I missed the long sunny days of being shepherded through Congress Park by Jeanette and Melvin (Rosie and Mike's children) and the daily trip, sometimes by horse and carriage, to Red Springs to take the waters before dinner.

Moreover, the whole texture of our lives seemed to change when my grandparents left the hotel. My mother and older sister went to work, for one thing, and vacations became a time when the chief topic of conversation centered around whether or not I would get a summer job, myself. I didn't—out of inanition or fear, I cannot say—until I was in college. But the subject was discussed endlessly.

One August, in the late 1930s, when I was fifteen or so, my father, in a flush moment, resolved to dine on Rosie's fried herring once more. So, without advance warning, he packed our bags and loaded down the old Hudson for a return to the wondrous Lafayette Hotel on Circular Street.

Nothing had changed by then. There were still no throughways or turnpikes to Albany and the piney route to Saratoga required a journey of seven long hours.

Seven hours until the familiar white gingerbread facade came into sight! But there it was, lighted by lanterns at every portico—familiar, reassuring, and unchanged.

I wish I could say that it is there still, yet I cannot. The Lafayette lives only in memory. But I have never forgotten the shouts, the surprise, the unbelievable rush of love I felt that cool Saratoga night as we were embraced in turn by all my cousins. A haze of poppy seed still hangs over the recollection—like a magical aroma that would unlock the secrets of the past if only I could properly conjure it.

Unfortunately most of the Saratoga treasury of recipes seem to have been lost. I even wrote my cousin Jan in Connecticut, hoping to find some tangible remnant of her mother's largesse. No luck! Like most great cooks, Rosie never bothered to write down the formulas she stored in her head.

Therefore, the following is only a half-remembered and reconstructed version of a goulash that tastes like hers.

A goulash (or *gulyas*) is a Hungarian herdsman's stew. Most often it is composed of beef or veal and vegetables amply seasoned with sweet paprika. Mine is said to be a "Triple-Threat" rendition simply because beef, veal, and pork all enter the stew pot in equal proportions. Rosie would not, I know, approve of the last victual a jot, but poppy seeds give the dish her imprimatur.

TRIPLE-THREAT GOULASH

1 Melt the butter in a large heavy saucepan. Stir in the onions. Cook covered over very low heat 15 minutes.

2 Push the onions to one side of the pan. Add the beef; saute over medium heat until light brown. Combine with onions. Cover and cook over low heat ½ hour.

3 Stir pork into beef mixture; cook covered ½ hour. Stir veal into beef mixture; cook covered 1 hour.

4 Stir the paprika, poppy seeds, salt, and beef stock into meats. Cook covered ½ hour longer.

5 Add peppers to saucepan; cook until wilted and soft, about 10 minutes. Stir in the sour cream; cook 3 minutes. Sprinkle with parsley. Serve with buttered noodles.

Note: Hot paprika can be used instead of the sweet for a spicier flavor.

¾ cup butter
6 large onions, coarsely chopped
1 pound sirloin, cut into 1-inch cubes
1 pound lean pork, cut into 1-inch cubes
1 pound veal, cut into 1-inch cubes
3 tablespoons imported sweet paprika
2 teaspoons poppy seeds
1 teaspoon salt
1 cup strong beef stock
2 large green peppers, cut into thin rings
2 cups sour cream
Chopped parsley for garnish
6 to 8 cups buttered cooked noodles

Serves 6 to 8.

Although the poppy seed is known in Latin as *Papaver somniferum* (sleep-inducing poppy), none of the following recipes will have any narcotic effect on your appetite whatsoever—nor will they put you to sleep.

Although opium is cultivated from the same plant, it is the sap that flows from the Oriental poppy's green pod that affords the high time in all those dens of iniquity—and never the blue seeds. So cook away, without care.

Poppy seeds are often assumed to be native to the Orient but they are not. According to food historians, they were first cultivated in the Mediterranean area and brought to the Far East by Islamic missionaries. Actually, the poppy seed has been considered a health food staple for thousands of years. Mixed with equal portions of wine and honey, the seeds were a regular ingredient in the training diet of competitors in the earliest Olympic games.

Poppy seeds, either whole or ground, mixed with honey still make a salubrious filling for cakes and sweet pastries, but I find the taste utterly bracing in meat and fish dishes as well.

A geographically off-course formula from Glasgow for a fish and potato pie amply proves my point. I think this dish, combined with a cold gazpacho (with or without the vodka embellishment) and a salad, makes the best brunch-lunch-supper menu I can think of.

SCOTCH FISH PIE

2 cups mashed potatoes
2 cups cooked non-oily, white fish, flaked
1 tablespoon chopped parsley
¼ cup butter, melted
½ cup milk
1 teaspoon dry English mustard
1 cup bread crumbs
1 teaspoon salt
1 teaspoon poppy seeds
¼ teaspoon freshly ground pepper

Serves 4.

1 Heat oven to 300°. Spread half the potatoes over the bottom of a buttered casserole. Spread the fish over the potatoes; sprinkle with parsley.

2 Spoon half the butter over the fish and parsley; add the milk. Cover with remaining potatoes. Combine the mustard, bread crumbs, salt, poppy seeds, and pepper. Sprinkle over the potatoes; spoon remaining butter over top. Bake 1 hour. Place under broiler to brown top.

I am certain that someone will resent the assumption, but I tend to think of Eastern Europe as the true poppy seed terrain. And while I know that most of the seeds we eat in this country are from The Netherlands (and that the Dutch ''blues'' are considered to be of the highest quality) I cannot properly disabuse myself of the notion.

I have eaten delicious poppy seed dishes in Holland but it seems to me that Hungarians, Czechs, Serbs, Croats, and Austrians have a more knowing way with the flavoring. For one thing, they always cook the seasoning slightly before they add it to a dish. Heating poppy seeds in butter over a low fire invariably improves their flavor.

Toast the seeds before you use them in any of the recipes in this chapter (except for the sweet, cooked fillings) and you'll discover what I mean.

HUNGARIAN CHICKEN

1 Wipe the chicken with paper toweling. Sprinkle with salt and pepper.

2 Heat the oil and 2 tablespoons butter in a large heavy skillet over medium heat until butter melts. Add the chicken; saute on both sides until golden. Remove chicken from skillet. Pour off cooking fat.

3 Melt 1 tablespoon butter in skillet; add onion and pepper. Cook and stir over medium heat 3 minutes. Stir in the tomato. Place chicken in skillet skin-side-down; cook uncovered over medium heat ½ hour, turning once.

4 Remove chicken from skillet. Stir in paprika, tomato paste, and chicken broth. Return chicken to skillet. Simmer gently for 15 minutes, basting frequently.

5 Transfer chicken to a serving dish; keep warm. Stir the sour cream into the skillet until thoroughly blended; stir in the poppy seeds. Pour sauce over chicken; sprinkle with parsley. Serve with the buttered noodles.

2 small chickens (about 2½ pounds each), cut into serving pieces
Salt and freshly ground pepper
2 tablespoons vegetable oil
3 tablespoons butter
1 large yellow onion, finely chopped
1 green pepper, seeded, finely chopped
1 firm ripe tomato, chopped
2 tablespoons paprika
1 tablespoon tomato paste
1 cup hot chicken broth
1 cup sour cream
2 teaspoons poppy seeds, toasted
Chopped parsley for garnish
6 to 8 cups buttered cooked noodles

Serves 6 to 8.

Poppy seed is often pounded with yogurt to a thick racy paste (not unlike a chutney) in India. The same sweetish oily compound is aligned with sugar and honey in a poppy nougat that is popular in Turkey. Egyptian cooks make a sort of mayonnaise of poppy seeds and oil that is curiously analeptic—if you have a mouth for dark sauces that are as muddy as the Nile.

My favorite poppy seed prescriptions are from Austria, where some imaginative Viennese combined the stuff with grated raw potato, strips of ham, and ground meat in a distinctive *hackbraten*. This is a meatloaf dish that you will remember happily whenever the larder needs a lift and the pocketbook is low.

WIENER HACKBRATEN

1½ pounds meatloaf mixture (½ ground beef, ¼ each ground pork and veal)
1 medium potato, pared
1 medium onion, grated
2 eggs, lightly beaten
1½ teaspoons poppy seeds
2 teaspoons Dijon mustard
Pinch of ground allspice
Pinch of dried thyme
1 tablespoon finely chopped parsley
¼ cup bread crumbs
5 strips of hamsteak, 5 inches long × ½ inch wide
2 tablespoons catsup
2 slices bacon
1 tablespoon all-purpose flour
1 tablespoon imported sweet paprika
½ cup strong beef broth, hot
¾ cup sour cream

Serves 4 to 6.

1 Heat oven to 425°. Place the meat in a large bowl. Grate the potato; combine with meat. Add onion, eggs, poppy seeds, 1 teaspoon Dijon mustard, the allspice, thyme, parsley, and bread crumbs. Mix thoroughly.

2 Place half the mixture in the bottom of a shallow baking dish and shape into a 7½- × 4½-inch loaf. Arrange 3 ham strips lengthwise on loaf in 2 parallel rows, 2 inches apart. (Each row will require 1½ strips.) Cover with remaining meat; press to seal layers. Arrange 2 ham strips lengthwise down center of loaf; press ends into sides of loaf.

3 Combine 1 teaspoon mustard with the catsup; spread over meat. Cut bacon slices in half lengthwise. Place 2 bacon strips diagonally over loaf, about 3 inches apart; then arrange 2 strips diagonally over them to form a lattice. Bake 30 minutes. Reduce heat to 350°; bake 1 hour.

4 Pour all pan drippings into a saucepan; discard all but 1 tablespoon fat. Whisk in the flour until smooth. Stir in the paprika; gradually whisk in the beef broth. Cook over medium heat until thickened, 4 to 5 minutes. Stir in the sour cream. Place meatloaf in serving dish. Pour sauce around, not over, the meat.

German Spätzle (little arrows) hit the target whenever an accompanying stew is bubbling away on *der Ofen*. The tiny, glistening sliced dumplings are thicker and more substantial than noodles and not a particular trial to prepare. I always make them in advance and heat them just before I salt the stewpot!

2¼ cups all-purpose flour
1 teaspoon salt
3 teaspoons poppy seeds
1 egg, beaten
½ to ¾ cup water
4 tablespoons butter
¼ cup sour cream
2 tablespoons freshly grated Parmesan cheese

Serves 6.

SPÄTZLE

1 Sift the flour with the salt into a bowl. Stir in 2 teaspoons poppy seeds. Make a well in the center; place the egg and ¼ cup water in the well. Blend with a fork, adding only enough water to form a smooth but stiff dough.

2 Turn the dough onto a floured surface; flatten with hands. Cut thin strips, about 2-inches long and ¼-inch wide, off the dough with a very sharp knife.

3 Drop dough strips into boiling salted water, about 12 at a time; cook 5 minutes. Drain.

4 Just before serving, melt the butter in a large heavy saucepan. Add the sour cream; cook and stir over low heat until smooth. Add the spatzle, cheese, and 1 teaspoon poppy seeds; toss to combine. Cook over low heat, stirring frequently, until hot, about 5 minutes.

The best noodles I have been lucky enough to sample came from a contest of culinary wills between my maternal grandmother and cousin Rosie. The encounter took place in the Hotel Lafayette kitchen one summer day long, long ago.

My grandparent, perhaps overly critical of the quality of the noodles being served in *her* dining room, insisted on taking a hand in her third cousin's weekly rolling and flouring operation.

Together, dressed like midwives, the women worked side by side at the long zinc tables, stretching the dough between them until the raw stuff became so flimsy that you could read the headlines of *The Saratogan* through it.

"Now, that's what I call a *luxen!*" My grandmother stated with some superiority after the product had been poached and served to her.

Until I was much older, I thought the term she used was "luxury," which was a point of view I shared.

The following noodle dish (when composed with homemade noodles) is extravagant enough to tempt the world's most tarnished palate. Truly a luxury!

NOODLE CASSEROLE

1 Heat oven to 400°. Cook the noodles in boiling salted water just until tender. Drain.

2 Melt the butter in a heavy skillet. Add the mushrooms and saute until golden. Add the ham; cook over high heat 2 minutes. Transfer mixture to a large bowl; add the noodles.

3 Whisk the sour cream, whipping cream, and eggs together in a small bowl. Stir into the noodle mixture. Add the nutmeg, 2 tablespoons poppy seeds, and salt and pepper to taste. Toss well. Place in a buttered casserole dish; sprinkle with bread crumbs, Parmesan cheese, and remaining poppy seeds. Bake until golden, 15 to 20 minutes.

1 pound broad egg noodles
2 tablespoons butter
½ pound mushrooms, sliced
½ pound cooked ham, diced
¾ cup sour cream
¼ cup whipping cream
2 eggs, beaten
¼ teaspoon freshly grated nutmeg
2½ tablespoons poppy seeds
Salt and freshly ground pepper
3 tablespoons buttered bread crumbs
¼ cup grated Parmesan cheese

Serves 4.

In German, poppy seed is called *mohnsamen*. I can only presume that Rosie called her rich, black poppy seed tart a *mohnkuchen* to honor the tradition of the German baker under whose tutelage she had mastered the art.

A lustrous, unusual dessert, it best suits an adventuresome appetite. Lovers of the bland should skip this recipe right off the bat! But cooks should note in any case: when poppy seeds are used for dessert fillings they are most often cooked in milk and mashed into a velvety-smooth paste. To save time, I use a blender for the maceration and it produces an equally respectable pastry—whether you call it a tart or a torte!

POPPY SEED TORTE

Grandma Rose's Favorite Pie Crust
  (see Index)
1 cup pitted prunes
2 cups poppy seeds
½ cup orange juice
½ cup honey
1 cup sugar
2 teaspoons vanilla
Grated peel of ½ orange
½ cup chopped walnuts
3 tablespoons milk
Sweetened whipped cream or
  vanilla ice cream

Serves 8.

1 Prepare pastry; refrigerate 1 hour. Roll out half the dough and line a lightly buttered 10-inch quiche pan. Refrigerate remaining dough and pastry shell 1 hour.

2 Heat oven to 350°. Place the prunes in a bowl and cover with boiling water. Let stand 10 minutes; drain. Coarsely chop the prunes.

3 Place the poppy seeds, orange juice, honey, and ½ cup sugar in a blender container; blend until smooth. (This will require numerous starts and stops as the mixture will be quite thick. Scrape down the sides frequently.)

4 Scrape the poppy seed mixture into a bowl. Add the prunes, remaining ½ cup sugar, the vanilla, orange peel, and walnuts; mix well. Spoon into pastry shell.

5 Roll out remaining dough to an 11-inch circle and cut into ¾-inch-wide strips. Weave strips in lattice pattern over filling (strips should be quite close together); fold edges into pan and press to seal. Brush pastry with milk. Bake until light brown, 70 to 75 minutes. Serve with sweetened whipped cream or vanilla ice cream.

As I tried to point out earlier on, I am a very lackluster Jew. I was baptized at an early age at the hands of an overzealous Catholic nursemaid, an old woman who loved me dearly and took me to mass with her every day of her employment in our household (from the time I was first born until I was seven or eight years old). My parents knew about my churchgoing but never seemed to object, and Grandma Burke, as I always called her, saw me as a chosen convert. She lifted me to the font, the priest blessed me, and the first seeds of religious confusion were planted in my head.

Later, given the option of a ritual confirmation (a bar mitzvah) at age thirteen, I vociferously rejected the idea. My parents, I suspect, were secretly relieved—those affairs being costly ventures even then. But they never admitted it. My mother was sanguine about her role in my religious ambivalence until the day she died.

"You were a crazy kid with a mind of your own!" she would say with some annoyance whenever I brought up the subject. "Who could ever tell you what to do?"

No one, perhaps. I don't know. But as I grow older the Jewish heritage persists—for all of the Christian ethic I espouse.

The memory of my cousin Rosie rolling out Hamantaschen, the fruit-filled triangles of sweet dough that celebrate at Purim the Jews' deliverance from the tyrant Haman, fills my mouth with the taste of religious martyrdom as much as *mohn*, I think.

HAMANTASCHEN

1 Place the poppy seeds and milk in a blender container; blend until machine stops. Stir in the honey; blend until mixture is as smooth as possible.

2 Place poppy seed mixture in the top of a double boiler over hot water; cook, stirring occasionally, 10 minutes. Stir in the pecans, sugar, and cinnamon. Cook 5 minutes. Let mixture cool slightly; stir in the vanilla. Refrigerate at least 6 hours or overnight.

3 Sift the flour with the salt and baking powder into a bowl. Add butter; blend with a pastry blender until the texture of coarse crumbs. Make a well in the center; place eggs and ½ cup honey in well. Mix thoroughly until a soft dough is formed. (Add more flour if dough seems too sticky.) Place dough in freezer for ½ hour.

4 Heat oven to 375°. Divide dough in half. Roll out one half as thin as possible on a well-floured surface; cut into 3-inch squares. Repeat with remaining dough.

5 Combine egg yolk and cream; brush edges of squares with mixture. Place a scant tablespoon of poppy seed filling in center of each square; fold each square in half into a triangle. Seal edges by pressing with the tines of a fork. Place triangles on ungreased cookie sheets; brush with egg yolk mixture. Bake 20 minutes. Cool on a wire rack.

For the poppy seed filling:
1 cup poppy seeds
1 cup milk
½ cup honey
½ cup pecans, chopped
¼ cup sugar
Pinch of cinnamon
1 teaspoon vanilla

For the honey dough:
2½ cups sifted all-purpose flour (approximately)
¼ teaspoon salt
¾ teaspoon baking powder
¼ cup unsalted butter
2 eggs
½ cup honey
1 egg yolk
2 tablespoons cream

Makes about 40.

No explanation was given when our summer dalliance at the Hotel Lafayette abruptly ended. And for me, as a child, the Depression itself was hard enough to comprehend but my parents' defection from what I considered paradise seemed heartless and unfeeling.

My sister and I discussed it often, attempting to perceive some logic behind our exile. And only when my grandparents spent a second summer quietly at home did we truly understand why Saratoga was off limits to my family.

What my sister missed most acutely (aside from cousin Jeanette, who had always been her closest friend) was a special treat made every Friday night. Rosie would cut up thin sweet dough like noodles, deep fry the slices until they puffed into parabolas the color of fall leaves, and bury the twists under a snowfall of powdered sugar.

She called these pastry triumphs *ausshen blasen* (blown air) and I have never tasted the like outside her kitchen in all my life. Although years later I discovered that Italians (from the North) make a similar confection they call *Bugi'a* (tapers), which are excellent but not quite as delicate as Rosie's airborne treat.

The last poppy seed recipe is not for *ausshen blasen,* although I dearly wish it were. It features, instead, deep-fried cakes from South America. Pressed to the size of saucers before they hit the oil, the wafers of dough must be so light that the hot bath causes them to swell in the center like a blow fish!

COLOMBIAN BUNUELOS

2 cups all-purpose flour
½ teaspoon salt
2 teaspoons baking powder
Grated peel of ½ lemon
Grated peel of ½ orange
½ cup unsalted butter, cold
1 tablespoon poppy seeds
2 eggs
1 teaspoon cider vinegar
Vegetable oil
Confectioners' sugar
Cinnamon
Honey (optional)

Serves 8 to 10.

1 Combine the flour, salt, and baking powder in a large mixing bowl. Stir in the grated lemon and orange peels. Cut in butter. Blend with a pastry blender until the texture of coarse crumbs. Stir in poppy seeds.

2 Beat the eggs with the vinegar; stir into the flour mixture with a fork to form a soft dough.

3 Pat the dough into a rectangle on a well-floured surface. Divide into 16 pieces. Shape each piece into a ball and roll with a rolling pin into a paper-thin circle, about 7 inches in diameter.

4 Heat 1½ inches of oil to 370° in a heavy saucepan. Fry dough circles, one at a time, until golden on both sides. Drain on a layer of paper toweling. Sprinkle with a mixture of confectioners' sugar and cinnamon while still hot. Continue until all are done. Serve with honey, if desired.

Rum

I was a kid who predated "The Pepsi Generation" by thirty-five years. My contemporaries and I grew up during the war years and were virtually nameless as a group. But if anyone had sought a collective tag for us, a most appropriate designation would have been "The Rum 'n' Coke Contingent"!

Lord, how much of that demon brew we drank during those halcyon days! Though why, I will never understand—unless it was a massive nutritional deficiency due to sugar rationing. More likely our predilection for overly saccharine mixed drinks (flushed with maraschino cherries) was a reaction to our parents' earlier consumption of such rank potables as bathtub gin and bootleg whiskey.

In retrospect it seems as if rum and Coke dominated all our entertainments. In New York City, people night-clubbed (or in my own case, "prommed") at exotic *boîtes* named after rum-soaked ports of call—The Copacabana, The Riobamba, and Le Martinique—all heavy on the palms and bongo drums. My favorite of these south-of-the-border establishments was a mite more theatrical than the rest. Dubbed "Monte Proser's Beachcomber," it flourished like a giant artificial hibiscus on the corner of Broadway and Fiftieth Street for years and disappeared only when the generation after my own eschewed the rum culture for more temperate vodka-and-tonic diversions.

Monte Proser's Beachcomber was a very dark, sultry emporium, obviously designed to cater to the wish fulfillment of landlocked civilians and military types who were bent on having the time of their lives at home! Exotic, sloe-eyed waitresses, wearing only scanty sarongs and lots of flowers, served the rum concoctions while a transported rhumba band shook maracas in a lanai offstage. It was very, very Hollywood, let me tell you. There was even a mild typhoon—complete with thunder, lightning, and very real rain—that pounded the room's thatched roof between dance sets.

What is more, amidst the Planter's Punches, the Piña Coladas, and the Zombies, which should have anesthetized the crowd, everyone regularly jammed the dance floor (stopping conversation in mid-sentence) whenever the magical phrase "La Conga!" was pronounced.

Oh, the Conga! How does one explain that phenomenon to an uninitiate? It could be described as a dance, I guess, but snake-line is a more apt characterization. A single-file formation of revelers is what it really was. A squadron of mild exhibitionists kicked their heels in unison as they punished the parquet and sometimes overflowed into the city streets when the rhythms became too frenzied to contain them. The Conga was choreographed spoon-fashion: each dancer clasped his or her forearms tightly around an apparent stranger's waist as the line twisted from side to side. All the participants, twirling shoulders and flinging hips madly, shrieked "One, two, three, kick! *Conga!*" To the heavens!

The Conga line at the Beachcomber was reputed to be the most uninhibited in the city and it was never less than forty-persons long. But there was a snare to this eccentric gambol. One never, *never* allowed himself to be positioned as end-man of the column. For, like a musical version of "Crack the Whip," the Conga line swung about mercilessly when the band really began to percolate. And the unlucky stepper at the rear, who twirled and kicked his ankle into the air as he shouted "Cong-AH!," often received a case of whiplash—which, I warrant, still occasions a visit to the chiropractor thirty-odd years later!

My very first hangover was the result of much-too-much rum too soon. I was, at the tender age of twenty, a pretend-sophisticate who had acquired a taste for tall, tan Planter's Punches (composed of icy orange juice darkened with rum and sugar), which were usually so sweet that every tooth in my mouth ached after two such libations. At the time of the hangover, I had been bet that I could not drink five of these potions and still stand up! The proposition did not seem too outrageous, since I had long proclaimed that because of my size I was totally immune to the effects of alcohol! The site of this terrible wager was the most glamorous dining place (to my youthful knowledge) on Long Island, the then ultra-chic Canoe Place Inn in Hampton Bays.

After having consumed three largish Planter's Punches, I knew I was feeling somewhat unsteady. Two more and I was still standing, though feeling violently ill. And perhaps I was immune—for I did manage to stagger out of the restaurant (abandoning the dinner party I was with) and drive a friend's car back to a beach-house five miles away, without incident. Although, truth to tell, I had never sat behind the wheel of a car before!

Needless to say, a hangover of staggering proportions showed up the morning after (and driving lessons soon followed).

Now I take my rum in smaller doses.

The sweet liquor (distilled from fermented sugar cane) is always on duty in my kitchen, where it is often used to flame a roast chicken or to scent the flavor of this lovingly devised soup of dried and fresh mushrooms!

SIENNA MUSHROOM SOUP

1 Place dried mushrooms in a small bowl with 1½ cups boiling water. Let stand until soft. Drain, reserving 1 cup liquid.

2 Melt butter in a heavy saucepan. Saute onion over low heat until soft. Add fresh mushrooms; saute until tender.

3 Sprinkle flour, salt, and pepper into saucepan; cook and stir 2 minutes. Add beef broth and rum; cook and stir until smooth. Add the reserved mushroom liquid and the dried mushrooms; simmer 15 minutes.

4 Transfer soup to a blender container; blend until smooth. Return to saucepan. Heat to boiling; reduce heat. Stir in cream and cook 1 minute. Garnish soup with chives.

Note: I use Bruschi Borgotaro brand dried mushrooms imported from Italy.

1 package (20 grams or about .7 ounce) imported dried mushrooms
1½ cups boiling water
1 tablespoon butter
½ cup chopped onion
½ pound fresh mushrooms, sliced
2 tablespoons all-purpose flour
½ teaspoon salt
½ teaspoon freshly ground pepper
1 cup beef broth
1 tablespoon dark rum
½ cup whipping cream
Chopped chives for garnish

Serves 4.

Rum's forebear, sugar cane, the tall green grass with sweet-running sap, is said to have been one of Alexander the Great's discoveries. During an overland campaign to conquer India in the fourth century B.C., Alexander wrote in his diary: "Today I have found a sweet-tasting plant growing wild that natives chop for kindling because of the pleasant aroma it lends a cooking fire. Tasting it, the flavor stings the teeth on prolonged chewing—yet the breath sweetens as if by draughts of jasmine honey."

For all of that, Alexander was not sufficiently impressed with raw sugar (*Saccharum officinarum*) to make it part and parcel of his conqueror's booty. A thousand years elapsed before it was carried to the Mediterranean by the prescient Moors who invaded Spain. The first sugar cane was planted in the Canary Islands in 711 A.D. by an intrepid Saracen sea captain.

Another seafaring man, Columbus, brought sugar-cane cuttings from the Canaries to the New World on his second voyage in 1493. The thick-stemmed plants took root in Hispaniola (Haiti), where the ideal climate, soil, and rainfall nurtured fields of green cane from the shoreline to the mountains.

Haitian field workers invented rum from the raw sugar. Having discovered that the sweet juices that exuded from the cane when it was cut would ferment in the sun, they gathered the youngest stalks they could find, pressed them in great earthenware crocks, and stewed the pulp until it gave off "white steam and black viscous syrup." They strained this syrup, which was molasses, and allowed it to age for a month or so. The result? A potent libation that was described in a seventeenth-century report on Barbados (where sugar cane had by then proliferated) as "a kill devil. A hot, hellish, and terrible liquor."

Early rum was said to turn sighted men blind and to cause "enormous sexual swelling to the members of men; patriarchs and babes as well." Strong stuff, no doubt.

Later, rum was refined to the degree that a man could sip a dram without fear of losing his eyesight or his respectability! And as soon as enterprising European distillers got wind of the drink's potential, they set up factories in the West Indies to process the thick, aged molasses into "rumbullion"—a beverage that was advertised on early handbills as "a drink more palatable than coffee and less taxing to the nervous system than spirituous wines"!

A bracing kitchen combination of ground meats seasoned with rum comes from the early-American cookbook, *Art of Dressing Viands, Fish, Poultry and Vegetables,* written by Amelia Simmons in 1796. Nothing much is known about the author except her name and the fact, stated in the book, that she was an orphan. Lusty eating was her dominion and she will forgive, I hope, a measure of license in the retelling of her pioneer efforts.

MEATBALLS WITH RUM AND SOUR CREAM

1 Place meat in a large mixing bowl; add egg, shallot, bread crumbs, milk, nutmeg, soy sauce, hot pepper sauce, 1 teaspoon salt, and ½ teaspoon pepper. Mix thoroughly. Shape into small meatballs.

2 Melt 1 tablespoon butter in a large, heavy skillet. Saute onion until soft.

3 Melt 2 tablespoons butter in another heavy skillet. Brown the meatballs, about 10 at a time, over high heat. Transfer browned meatballs to skillet with the onion. Remove fat from skillet; add 2 tablespoons butter. Saute mushrooms over high heat until golden. Reserve.

4 Heat meatballs over medium-low heat. Add rum, broth, and cream, stirring well to coat meatballs. Cook partially covered for 20 minutes, turning meatballs occasionally. Remove cover; stir in reserved mushrooms. Cook uncovered 5 minutes longer. (Add more beef broth if mixture is too dry.)

5 Stir sour cream into meatballs until thoroughly blended. Cook, without boiling, until hot. Season to taste with salt and pepper; sprinkle with parsley. Serve with buttered noodles.

1½ pounds meatloaf mixture consisting of ¾ pound ground beef round, ½ pound ground veal, ¼ pound ground pork
1 egg, lightly beaten
1 small shallot, minced
½ cup fine bread crumbs
⅓ cup milk
⅛ teaspoon freshly grated nutmeg
1 teaspoon soy sauce
Dash of hot pepper sauce
1 teaspoon salt
½ teaspoon freshly ground pepper
5 tablespoons butter
1 small yellow onion, minced
¼ pound mushrooms, sliced
⅓ cup dark rum
½ cup beef broth (approximately)
⅓ cup whipping cream
1¼ cups sour cream
Salt and freshly ground pepper to taste
¼ cup finely chopped parsley
4 to 6 cups buttered cooked noodles

Serves 4 to 6.

The first rum distillery in the North American colonies was set up by the British on Staten Island in 1664—after the Dutch had been routed from Nieu Amsterdam. Before the British renamed the city, they held a referendum to choose an appellation. And historians report that "New Rum" was a strong contender before "New York" was finally chosen!

Pot-roasted pork with rummed applesauce is my favorite meal come late November—when I cannot face another turkey drumstick. Both the meat and sauce recipes are excellent and may be served either together or apart. They stem from a small but perfect treasury of handwritten French formulas passed down to me from a friend whose mother and grandmother were both born in Provence; both dishes prove without a doubt how inventive family cooks can be in that marvelous region.

Incidentally, the applesauce makes a wonderful dessert when it is heavily spread on thin rounds of trimmed French bread that have been buttered, lightly sugared, and toasted under a broiler. Whipped cream flavored with a speck of vanilla is the obligatory accompaniment.

POT ROASTED PORK

2 tablespoons butter
1 tablespoon vegetable oil
1 pork loin roast (3½ to 4 pounds)
3 small carrots, chopped
4 small onions, sliced
3 cloves garlic
½ teaspoon dried thyme
Salt and freshly ground pepper to taste
1 cup chicken broth
1 jigger dark rum
Chopped parsley

Serves 4 to 6.

1 Heat the butter and oil in a Dutch oven over medium-high heat. Brown meat well on all sides. Turn meat fat side up; add carrots, onions, garlic, thyme, salt, and pepper. Reduce heat and cook covered for 1 hour. Turn meat over and cook until done, about 35 to 40 minutes a pound.

2 Transfer meat to serving platter; keep warm. Add chicken broth and rum to Dutch oven; boil until reduced by half. Strain sauce. Pour some over meat; pass remainder on the side. Sprinkle meat with parsley.

Note: Have your butcher crack the chine bone and tie the pork roast with string for convenient cooking and carving.

APPLESAUCE WITH RUM

3 pounds green apples
½ teaspoon finely grated lemon peel
½ cup apricot preserves
1 cup dark brown sugar
2 teaspoons lemon juice
¼ cup dark rum
3 tablespoons butter

Makes 2 pints.

1 Pare, core, and cut apples into ⅛-inch-thick slices. Place in a heavy saucepan with lemon peel. Cook covered over low heat, stirring occasionally, until very tender, about 30 minutes.

2 Mash apples with a wooden spoon. Strain apricot preserves; stir into apples with the sugar, lemon juice, rum, and butter. Cook partially covered over low heat, stirring occasionally, 10 minutes. Raise heat slightly if mixture seems too thin. Press applesauce through a strainer; refrigerate until cold.

Another New World recipe heavily dependent upon the flavor of rum is a Mexican canon, Pollo Evinado, which combines the

flaming spirit with chicken, peas, and white wine. I serve this truly delicious dish with rice and a salad—that's all, except for more white wine, of course!

POLLO EVINADO

1 Heat oven to 350°. Combine garlic, thyme, marjoram, rosemary, vinegar, salt, and pepper. Rub chicken pieces well with mixture. Coat chicken with flour, shaking off excess.

2 Saute chicken in butter and 1 tablespoon oil in a large skillet until golden on all sides. Transfer chicken to a casserole.

3 Remove excess fat from skillet. Pour in wine. Cook over high heat 3 minutes, scraping bottom and sides of skillet. Pour over chicken.

4 Heat 2 tablespoons oil in skillet. Saute onions over medium-high heat until golden on all sides; sprinkle with sugar. Reduce heat; cook covered until onions begin to soften, about 5 minutes. Remove cover and raise heat; cook, stirring constantly, until all moisture evaporates. Add to chicken.

5 Heat rum in a small saucepan; ignite. Pour over chicken, tilting casserole back and forth until flames subside. Bake until juices run yellow when chicken is pierced with a fork, about 45 minutes. Stir in peas; bake 5 minutes longer. Sprinkle with parsley.

2 cloves garlic, crushed
Pinch each of dried thyme, marjoram, and rosemary
3 tablespoons red wine vinegar
½ teaspoon salt
½ teaspoon pepper
1 large frying chicken (3½ to 4 pounds), cut into serving pieces
Flour
2 tablespoons butter
3 tablespoons vegetable oil
½ cup dry white wine
8 small white onions
1 teaspoon sugar
½ cup light rum
1 package (10 ounces) frozen peas, thawed
1 tablespoon chopped parsley

Serves 4.

At the end of the American Revolution, in 1789, the rum industry was centered in New England, and it became the new democracy's most unsavory enterprise. The huge profits derived from distilling West Indian sugar cane were used to finance over seventy percent of all the slave ships that mercilessly raided the African coast.

By 1812, the rum trade in the United States was staggering: the average citizen was said to consume almost four gallons of the liquor annually. Considered a medicinal aid, low-alcohol rum was sold as a home remedy for constipation, baldness, wind, chilblains, and milk fever, to name just a few. Rum also ruled the taverns and taprooms of the early states because beer spoiled easily and British whiskey was considered an unpatriotic drink. Actually, Americans drank little else but rum until the mid-nineteenth century, when a cheaper form of spirits was invented by a Baptist clergyman in Bourbon County, Kentucky.

Three of my most favored vegetable dishes follow—all made extraordinary by the judicious dispensation of rum. The Celery Puree is another French notion; it was served to me once at the fabled Trocadero in Paris—and hijacked on the spot. Rummed Onions and Apricots is a Florentine wedding-feast dish that is a most salubrious adjunct to such fowl as duck, goose, or turkey. The last of the trio is a prescription for the best baked beans I have ever eaten. The precept comes from Haiti, where the first rum was made. Some claim the best rum is still produced on that island. Not me, however; I prefer Demerara every time.

CELERY PUREE

3 large ribs celery, chopped
1 inner heart of celery with leaves, chopped
2 baking potatoes, pared, cut into 1-inch cubes
Salt and freshly ground pepper
2 tablespoons strong chicken stock
1 tablespoon butter
1 tablespoon light rum
⅓ cup whipping cream
Chopped parsley for garnish

Serves 4 to 6.

1 Place celery, celery heart, and potatoes in a saucepan of boiling water seasoned with salt and pepper. Cook until tender, about 20 minutes. Drain.

2 Place vegetables in a food processor or blender container; add chicken stock. Puree until smooth. (If using a blender, add some of the cream, if necessary.)

3 Place puree in a saucepan over low heat; stir in butter, rum, and cream. Cook, stirring frequently, 5 minutes. Taste for seasoning; add salt and pepper, if necessary. Sprinkle with parsley.

RUMMED ONIONS AND APRICOTS

⅓ cup dried apricots, coarsely chopped
12 to 16 small white onions
1½ tablespoons vegetable oil
2 tablespoons butter
2 tablespoons red wine vinegar
3 tablespoons dark rum
2 tablespoons dark brown sugar
1 tablespoon chopped parsley

Serves 4.

1 Cover apricots with hot water; reserve.

2 Pare onions; cut a cross in root end of each to prevent onions from falling apart during cooking. Heat oil with 1 tablespoon butter in a skillet. Saute onions over medium-high heat until partially brown. Reduce heat slightly; stir in the vinegar and 2 tablespoons rum, scraping bottom and sides of skillet. Add remaining 1 tablespoon butter and the brown sugar; stir until onions are well coated.

3 Drain apricots; stir into onions. Cook covered over medium-low heat until tender, 20 to 25 minutes. Just before serving, add remaining 1 tablespoon rum; cook over high heat 1 to 2 minutes. Serve garnished with parsley.

HAITIAN BAKED BEANS

1 Place beans in a large pot of boiling water and return to boiling. Turn off heat; let stand 1 hour. Heat oven to 275°.

2 Grease a bean pot or casserole with butter; rub with garlic. Drain beans; place in a mixing bowl. Add all ingredients through rum; mix well. Add ¼ cup tomato juice; transfer to bean pot. Place uncooked bacon on top. Bake covered 7 or more hours, adding tomato juice as beans dry out.

An authority on the subject once stated unequivocally that the rums with the greatest character speak neither Spanish nor French but have lilting British accents instead. Indeed, for more than 200 years the finest rums have been shipped from the West Indies to be aged in casks (sometimes for as long as twenty years) in English warehouses. These rums become luxury drinks, like Plantation St. James from Martinique, Barbancourt from Haiti, and Eldorado from Puerto Rico. Too subtle for mixed drinks or cookery, such libations are best taken after dinner in warmed brandy snifters.

The ideal rum to use in the sauce for the Caribbean fish dish that follows is a light, dry Bacardi Silver Label, never more than 80 proof—to give the flavor a fighting chance!

ESTOUFFADE OF SEAFOOD

1 Heat oven to 450°. Melt 3 tablespoons butter in a heavy saucepan. Add onion, celery, and green pepper; cook over medium-low heat, stirring constantly, 5 minutes. Sprinkle with ½ teaspoon paprika, salt, and pepper; stir in shrimp. Cook ½ minute; remove from heat. Stir in bread crumbs until well mixed.

1 pound dry white beans
2 teaspoons butter
1 clove garlic, bruised
1 large onion, finely chopped
3 strips crisply fried bacon, crumbled
2 tablespoons dark brown sugar
2 teaspoons Worcestershire sauce
4 tablespoons molasses
5 tablespoons chili sauce
1 tablespoon dry English mustard
1 teaspoon curry powder
1½ teaspoons salt
½ cup dark rum
1½ cups tomato juice (approximately)
3 strips uncooked bacon

Serves 6 to 8.

5 tablespoons butter
½ cup finely chopped onion
½ cup finely chopped celery
½ green pepper, seeded, finely chopped
½ teaspoon paprika
Salt and freshly ground pepper to taste
¼ pound uncooked shrimp, shelled, deveined, coarsely chopped
½ cup bread crumbs
8 small flounder fillets
Chopped parsley for garnish

Serves 4.

2 Butter a baking dish in which four flounder fillets will fit snugly without overlapping. Arrange four fillets in dish; mound each fillet with shrimp mixture, spooning any excess into spaces between fish. Place remaining fillets on top, covering bottom fillets. Melt 2 tablespoons butter; spoon over fish. Bake 15 minutes.

3 Meanwhile, make Sauce Caribe. When fish is done, spoon sauce over it and sprinkle with parsley.

2 tablespoons butter
½ tablespoon finely chopped
   shallot
1 tablespoon all-purpose flour
½ teaspoon tomato paste
1½ cups whipping cream, hot
Salt and freshly ground pepper
¼ teaspoon paprika
1 tablespoon dry sherry
1½ tablespoons light rum

Makes about 2 cups.

SAUCE CARIBE

Melt the butter in a heavy saucepan. Saute shallot until soft. Add flour; stir over low heat 2 minutes. Whisk in tomato paste and cream; season with salt, pepper, and paprika. Cook until thick, about 5 minutes; stir in sherry and rum.

To stay within rum's latitudinal boundaries, I next offer a native Colombian dish. The formula is said to have been invented by the Tunja Indians, who prepared it on feast days for over a thousand years. In its purest form, it is an unsweetened tortilla filled with roasted plaintain and a mite of rum. I prefer the version wrought by culinary license: a fluffy, golden omelet filled with vanilla-scented bananas and covered with sour cream. Best made with ripe fruit and dark rum, this concoction (ideally served at room temperature) does not resemble a breakfast dish in the least!

TORTILLA DE BANANA

1 Melt 3 tablespoons butter in a skillet. Add bananas; stir over medium heat until well coated. Add sugar and vanilla; cook until sugar starts to caramelize, about 3 minutes. Remove from heat.

2 Whisk 2 eggs with a pinch of salt and 1 tablespoon water in a small bowl.

3 Place an omelet pan or small skillet over high heat for several seconds. (Pan is hot enough when a drop of water sprinkled in the center sizzles.) Place 1 tablespoon butter in center of the pan; as butter melts, tilt pan to coat sides. When the butter foam subsides slightly, but before it turns brown, pour in beaten eggs.

4 Holding pan handle with left hand, slide pan rapidly back and forth over heat while stirring and spreading eggs with wooden spatula or fork. Vigorously scramble eggs until they thicken to a custardlike consistency.

5 Place half of banana mixture on one side of omelet. Tilt pan handle at a forty-five-degree angle and run a fork around edge of omelet to keep it from sticking. Loosen omelet; fold it over bananas. Hold tilted pan over heat 1 to 2 seconds, to brown bottom lightly. Slide and invert omelet onto a serving dish.

6 Repeat Steps 2 through 5, using the remaining eggs, salt, cold water, and butter.

7 To serve omelets warm, place in a low oven. Whip sour cream with rum and confectioners' sugar; spread over the omelets. Serve warm or at room temperature.

5 **tablespoons butter**
2 **ripe bananas, peeled, sliced, sprinkled with lime juice**
2 **tablespoons sugar**
1 **teaspoon vanilla**
4 **eggs**
2 **pinches salt**
2 **tablespoons cold water**
¼ **cup sour cream**
2 **tablespoons dark rum**
1 **tablespoon confectioners' sugar**

Serves 4.

Rum cognoscenti are a snobby lot. The decision of what to blend into your daiquiri or what to take neat should be purely a matter of personal preference. Nevertheless, I offer some small wisdom on the subject:

White Rums: **These colorless infusions are least satisfactory if flavor is demanded, whether in a dish or a glass of soda. I suspect the rum industry has been blanching its product of late to attract vodka and tequila devotees to rum. Many drinkers, I have observed, do take rum in their gimlets and screwdrivers these days. But I would skip white rum in anything other than a daiquiri or a bacardi. The most aromatic whites come from Barbados and Jamaica. Check the labels before you buy!**

Golden (Light) Rums: **Always the cook's standby for their heady aroma, these can be doused with tonic or soda when a rum fancier comes to call. Golden rums range from very pale to rich, full-bodied blends. Jamaican and Puerto Rican Bacardi have the slight edge in my book.**

Dark Demerara Rums: **The most aromatic and powerful rum flavor is that of the dark Demeraras. They have a honey smoothness to the tongue that comes from long, careful aging in the barrel. The color of these should be that of strong coffee without cream. Puerto Rican Ron del Barrilto is excellent but Jamaican Lemon Hart is the one that seasons all my chocolate desserts.**

Luxury Rums: **Very expensive brews made for sipping straight-up (possibly in a brandy snifter), these may be aged fifteen years or longer.**

A curious Russian confection, made of chocolate, pumpernickel crumbs, dark rum, whipped cream, and raspberry preserves, requires no cooking. Its taste is most exotic and it looks as super-festive as a birthday cake. Not a dessert for those with lackluster palates, this is an after-dinner reward of some spirit!

4 ounces stale dark pumpernickel bread (about 3⅔ slices), crushed to fine crumbs

½ cup dark rum (or 6 tablespoons rum and 2 tablespoons strong coffee)

1½ cups whipping cream

¾ cup confectioners' sugar

½ teaspoon vanilla

4 ounces semisweet chocolate, grated

½ cup strained raspberry preserves

1 tablespoon grated semisweet chocolate for garnish

Serves 6 to 8.

KATCHKA

1 Place bread crumbs and rum in a bowl. Mix well.

2 Whip cream with sugar and vanilla until stiff.

3 Spread ¼ of the cream in bottom of a glass serving bowl. Sprinkle with ⅓ of bread crumbs, ⅓ of chocolate, and ⅓ of preserves. Repeat layers twice; spread with remaining ¼ of cream. Sprinkle top with 1 tablespoon grated chocolate. Refrigerate covered 8 hours or overnight.

Note: Bread may be grated or crushed in an electric blender. If bread is not stale and dry, toast it in a low oven for at least 15 minutes.

Two more rummed desserts to bolster a cook's reputation, these delicate fancies will suit even fragile palates.

Coconut Macaroon Torte is a food I doted on as a child. The chewy golden shell (which falls slightly in the center, forming a cup) provides pure bliss when filled with a mixture of raspberries and cherries and blizzarded with whipped cream. Wow!

Rum Savarin is a dish with a most noble lineage. Brillat-Savarin is said to have lent his name to the original rum-drenched devise. Here it is bastardized (done quickly, without yeast or risings) but light as air. Serve it with fresh fruit or ice cream on the side. And make sure the dark rum is truly dark!

COCONUT MACAROON TORTE

1 Heat oven to 350°. Beat egg whites with salt until soft peaks form. Gradually add the sugar; beat until stiff and shiny. Beat in rum.

2 Combine coconut, almonds, flour, and lemon peel. Fold into egg white mixture.

3 Butter and flour a 9-inch round cake pan. Spread mixture evenly over bottom. Bake until top is light brown, about 20 minutes. Cool in pan on a wire rack. Unmold and mound top with berries and cream.

4 egg whites
Pinch of salt
¾ cup sugar
3 tablespoons light rum
1½ cups sweetened shredded
   coconut
¼ cup ground blanched almonds
2 tablespoons all-purpose flour
½ teaspoon grated lemon peel
Fresh berries or pitted sweet
   cherries
Whipped cream

Serves 6.

A QUICK RUM SAVARIN

1 Heat oven to 325°. Rinse the bowl of an electric mixer with hot water; pat dry with paper toweling. Add eggs and sugar; beat until doubled in volume. Combine flour, baking powder, and salt; fold into eggs.

2 Pour batter into a buttered savarin ring mold. Bake 20 minutes. Raise oven heat to 400°; bake 10 minutes longer. Place on a wire rack; cover with a dry towel. Let stand 5 minutes.

3 Unmold cake. Pierce top all over with a fork. Heat rum, water, and sugar in a saucepan until sugar dissolves. Spoon over cake. Serve warm or cold with sweetened whipped cream if desired.

2 eggs
½ cup sugar
½ cup sifted all-purpose flour
1 teaspoon baking powder
⅛ teaspoon salt
¼ cup dark rum
2 tablespoons hot water
4 tablespoons sugar
Sweetened whipped cream
   (optional)

Serves 4 to 6.

The last recipe in this chapter yields a towering fantasy cake. The combination of light and dark rums in the cake, filling, cream, and icing gives it something no other dessert in this book can claim—double-whammy flavoring! Cut me a slice and let me dream of the Cuba Libres of yesteryear!

RUMMED BOSTON CREAM CAKE

For the cake:
½ cup unsalted butter
1¼ cups sugar
2 eggs, separated
1 teaspoon vanilla
¼ teaspoon almond extract
2 cups sifted cake flour
2 teaspoons baking powder
¼ teaspoon baking soda
¼ teaspoon salt
½ cup orange juice
4 tablespoons dark rum combined
   with 1 teaspoon light rum

For the pastry cream filling:
2 egg yolks
¼ cup sugar
¼ teaspoon vanilla
1 tablespoon cornstarch
½ cup milk, scalded
1 teaspoon light rum

For the rum cream filling:
1½ teaspoons unflavored gelatin
1½ tablespoons water
¼ cup light rum
1½ cups whipping cream
⅓ cup confectioners' sugar
½ teaspoon vanilla

For the icing:
3 ounces unsweetened chocolate
1 can (14 ounces) condensed milk
1 teaspoon dark rum
4 tablespoons unsalted butter
1 egg yolk

Serves 8 to 10.

1 To make the cake: Heat oven to 350°. Cream butter with 1 cup sugar in a large bowl. Beat in egg yolks, one at a time; beat until light and fluffy. Stir in vanilla and almond extract.

2 Sift flour with baking powder, baking soda, and salt. Combine orange juice with 3 tablespoons rum. Stir flour mixture into butter mixture in three parts, alternating with thirds of the orange juice.

3 Beat egg whites until soft peaks form, gradually adding remaining ¼ cup sugar. Beat until stiff. Fold into batter.

4 Butter and flour two 9-inch round cake pans. Line with waxed paper; butter and flour the paper. Spoon batter into pans. Bake until toothpick inserted in center comes out clean, 25 to 30 minutes. Cool in pans on a wire rack.

5 Unmold layers; cut each in half horizontally to make four layers. Sprinkle each layer with 1 teaspoon rum.

6 To make the pastry cream filling: Combine egg yolks, sugar, vanilla, and cornstarch in a bowl; beat until smooth. Whisk in milk. Place mixture in the top of a double boiler; cook over simmering water, stirring constantly, until thick. Stir in rum. Refrigerate until cold.

7 To make the rum cream filling: Soften gelatin in water and 2 tablespoons rum in a small bowl. Place bowl in pan of hot water; stir until gelatin is dissolved. Beat cream with confectioners' sugar until stiff; add the vanilla, remaining 2 tablespoons rum, and the gelatin.

8 Place one cake layer on serving plate; spread with half the rum filling. Place second cake layer on top; spread with pastry cream filling. Place third layer on top; spread with remaining rum filling. Top with fourth layer. Refrigerate 2 hours.

9 To make the icing: Melt the chocolate with condensed milk in the top of a double boiler over hot water. Add rum and butter; beat until smooth. Add the egg yolk and stir until slightly thickened. Cool slightly.

10 Scrape any excess filling from sides of cake. Spread icing over sides and top of cake. Refrigerate at least 1 hour more before serving.

Saffron

My personal cooking history is really not too dissimilar from the kitchen experience of most of my peers. Depression striplings all, we chopped, peeled, and hashed only because we were too young or too green to work at anything more financially rewarding. And our tour of duty at the range was seen as a responsibility in those days—rather than the diversion it has since become.

I suppose I cooked well from the start. I know that I grew up sensible to the fact that only diligence to my task would produce palatable fare for the family dinner. And because I enjoyed eating well myself, the effort turned into its own reward.

But, truth to tell, I never sensed that culinary skill could produce bona fide joy until I was in my late teens and met an ex-opera singer (a refugee from war-torn Paris, and Stuttgart before that) whose artistic animus actually seemed to be fulfilled at her own kitchen stove. And she prepared, I might add, the best meals I have ever tasted in my life!

Hedwig (for that was the name of my inductor into the burgeoning world of haute cuisine) was neither young nor even a very imposing female at the time we met, although from all evidence she had certainly once been a glamorous creature. Foster-mother to a girl I was unaccountably infatuated with at the time, she was a very, very short European woman who obviously held my enormous size in great esteem.

"*Himmel!* What a giant is here, Margaret!" she laughed, greeting me at her apartment door for the very first time.

Puffing clouds of blue smoke from a Gauloise that dangled from her lips, and furrowing a beetle brow under a crop of mannish-cut gray hair (curiously out of style then, in the 1940s), she shepherded me through a long corridor hung heavy with German and French paintings (all Fauves) to her daughter's bedroom.

"We must feed this fellow Greene well, I think, *Margele,*" she announced, winking mysteriously at me before closing the door, " . . . or he will never come back!"

The occasion of my first visit to this utterly alien household on Central Park West was a birthday party—my own! An impromptu celebration that had been determined by daughter Margaret the day before (between our anatomy class and history of art).

"It will be *such* fun!" the fair and sexy Margaret had promised in her best lilting Franco-Prussian accent when I demurred at the suggestion. "Dar-ling . . . it will be the best birthday party you have ever had. I promise."

The warrant implied secret (and, I hoped, fleshly) favors that were never forthcoming. Instead, my hostess unseasonably developed tonsilitis overnight. So though festivities dwindled to a party for two they were held most unseductively in the convalescent's bedroom—with a menthol vaporizer blowing clouds of antiseptic steam between the two of us. No, actually I lie. Another friend of Margaret's attended my wilted birthday celebration as well. A long-nosed British girl named Betty Cook, who looked remarkably like a Modigliani painting and, what is odder still, painted and drew everything she saw in *his* (or her own) image!

If I tend to dismiss her presence, it is only because this English girl and I were an ill-matched pair in a bedroom. She was a war refugee too, but several years older than Margaret— and decidedly plainer. An early survivor of the London blitz, she had been sequestered with relatives in Canada for the duration but had recently journeyed to New York to study painting at the same art school I had transferred to from college in Virginia.

Betty Cook was very militant about her country's role in the war effort. And though I wore a glittering "Bundles for Britain" emblem in my lapel, she obviously mistrusted any male who was six feet four inches tall and over two hundred pounds—yet not in uniform.

We had never spoken to each other formally in any of our mutual classes and even on this meeting we eyed each other with strongly shared suspicion. While the invalid Margaret (palely elegant in a violet-sprigged featherbed) openly courted one and then the other of us by turns—only to reject our responses, when they were forthcoming, for her pillow or throat spray.

"Why don't you two just ignore me and talk to each other, *sweetie!*" she whispered plaintively, face turned to the wall.

But we would not acquiesce in that final indignity. Instead, Cook (as she was almost always called by the slightly autocratic Margaret) and I sat side by side on the adored one's narrow bed, avoiding any eye contact and listening fixedly to Hildegarde singing Cole Porter songs on our hostess's portable phonograph.

After hours of abstinence and *Argyrol* fumes, we indulged in glasses of birthday champagne and the dryest single layer cake I had ever swallowed. When Margaret's mother presented me with the first slice, it tasted like straw.

"Delicious," I murmured, hoping to bury the plate under the bed.

"Mommy made it in your honor, Bert darling," Margaret recovered long enough to coo seductively. "So you must eat it all."

I hated it. But being Libran to the teeth (and never about to hurt anyone intentionally), I chewed on. After a second or third helping, the dusty sweet texture assailed my untried palate with a vengeance. And I developed my first craving for that prodigious French confection, *le génoise*.

It may have been the wine that stimulated my appetite, but who cared? In those halcyon days no young man ever drank champagne in a bedroom unless it was his wedding night. So even with one girl too many, the experience was quite invigorating for a boy from Jackson Heights—let me tell you!

My birthday party ended on a champagne-inspired note of aspirin the next morning but the episode presaged many other visits to that wondrous lair overlooking "the rambles" in the park. And the end results were invariably physical joy.

Margaret's mother, Hedwig, sensed in me from the beginning a kindred gourmand spirit, I suspect, and for my sojourns at her table she plied kitchen art with the same verve and gusto she had once reserved for Mozart and Verdi.

My appearance at the family apartment became a weekly occurrence. And though the soignée daughter of the house never actively discouraged the attention, it soon became apparent to both wooer and wooed that it was her parent's most remarkable ability to cook that truly kept my suit at the sticking point.

I was eighteen or nineteen at the very most and Margaret's mother and father (the first exiles I had ever met) were taken not only with my admiration for their cuisine but also with my absolute and unquestioning emulation of their Continental way of life. It gave them hope that they would survive the transplanting from Old World to New.

They were the first family I had ever encountered who drank wine with dinner nightly. This was often vintage champagne and it was drunk from straight-up tumblers rather than stem-ware because, as Hedwig's dapper spouse Leo (pronounced Lay-oh) informed me on one occasion:

"There is nothing *déclassé* about drinking fine wine out of a jelly glass, Be-ert. But drinking it in Baccarat crystal in our kitchen would be very pretentious indeed!"

Did the logic escape me? They were wonderful, witty person-ages, citizens of an unfamiliar world that I adored sight unseen—whose manner and mode I attempted to imitate out-rageously. Despite a sickening awareness that my conversion to *savoir faire* made me deeply ashamed of my own background whenever I left their enchanted territory for home.

"Be-ert," they always called me. Two syllables where one usually sufficed. "Be-ert is a most unusual person," Hedwig would aver and Leo would concur. Not only to each other but to the unbelieving coterie of glamorous foreigners (mostly French or German refugees) who questioned my presence beneath the Chagall drawings and the Dürer etchings.

"This fellow is not like an American at all," they would assert with some patronizing—over tumblers of Moët et Chan-don or bone china tea cups so translucent that one's thumb was plainly visible on the golden handle as the jasmine elixir was swallowed.

"He not only likes to eat but do you believe, he cooks too!"

Did I really feel complimented? Probably. It was a shallow period of my life. Fortunately, I grew out of it.

My love suit with the daughter of the household went on somewhat longer—in and out of disquieting bedrooms and sad cafés. Only to end on a slightly sourish note when I grew out of *that* as well!

Margaret lives in Paris now (after an impetuous love-marriage and a recriminatory divorce) amid the splendor that her indul-gent parents collected to please her.

There are Picassos on her walls but the aroma of her *rive gauche* kitchen is not the same as the one where we ate so joyously, facing blacked-out Central Park during the war. A rich and glamorous woman, she has a retinue of cook and housekeeper now. And though the family recipes have been handed down by rote for domestic interpretation, the alchemy has somehow gone out of them.

In her small New York kitchen, Hedwig kept all her spices and herbs in tiny phials and ornamental glass containers. Though she cooked with all the aromatics at her command, saffron is the one scent I most associate with her output. The sharp smell of that dried crocus stamen, extracted from a small ruby-glass flask and quickly crushed, strand by strand, into a saute pan of chopped onions and rice still suffuses my recollec-

tion of the miracles Hedwig worked in that apartment baili-
wick.

Like my own grandmother, she sometimes dried orange peel
over the pilot light of her gas range. But not to perfume her
house. No, Hedwig dried the fragrant rind so that she might add
a curl to her saffrony rice before the chicken broth or white wine
was poured in. She made risotto fit for a king—even when it was
to be consumed merely by her voracious American admirer. I
learned many, many of her cooking tricks and kitchen counsels
because she was truly a generous woman. Sometimes I attempt
to cook exactly as she did, but, I must confess, with far less
mastery and surety than the brilliant innovator who tutored me.

One grace note gives Hedwig and me a kitchen continuity,
however. In my own arrangement of spices and herbs (all in
apothecary jars), there sits the same ruby-red glass flacon that
Hedwig once used. Still filled, to this very day, with ductile
strands of saffron.

My bequest from a great cook's daughter, in the end!

Saffron, at times, has been called "edible gold." Not really a
far-fetched notion, since it is a kind of culinary currency.

They say that saffron was the essential seasoning Columbus's
patrons at the Spanish Court were most anxious to procure from
an alternate route to the East. Rare and precious then, it still has
an anomalous market value among the spice traders of the
world. For while the source of saffron, *Crocus sativus,* is easily
grown, the processing of the flower's stigma into the dried spice
is both difficult and costly. To harvest a pound of saffron fila-
ments, a plantation must reap over seventy-five thousand blossoms. Even more dreadful, a laborer in the fields must remove
each crocus plant's three hairlike stigmata—225,000 of which
make up a pound (more or less) of unprocessed saffron.

Saffron is cultivated in southern France, Spain, Italy, Greece,
and, recently, South America as well. And while the Mediterranean product is the most highly bid for, even third-rated saffron
sells for about $750 a pound these days.

No wonder that dealers who trafficked in spurious saffron
mixtures (adulterated by goose feathers and strands of turmeric)
were promptly burned at the stake in the Middle Ages!

To my palate, saffron is an utterly indispensible adjunct of
rice—and no goose plumage (no matter how grand) will convert
that tender grain into such succulent and aromatic bounty. The
paradigm confederation of saffron and rice is, of course, Spain's
pungent national dish, *paella,* of which more anon.

The following Italian fabrication, from Milan, combines the redolent seasoning with rice, strips of ham, and shrimp. The citizens of Milano love their risotto dearly and the international fame of this local dish attests to its gastronomic delights. For a richer bouquet, try adding a mite of dry white wine (two or three tablespoons at most) while the rice and saffron saute until golden with the onions and butter.

MILANESE SAFFRON RISOTTO WITH SHRIMP AND HAM

3 tablespoons butter
1 yellow onion, finely chopped
1 teaspoon loosely packed saffron threads
2 cups Italian rice (such as Arborio brand)
1 cup diced ham
1 pound shrimp, shelled and deveined
1 cup chopped mixed red and green sweet peppers
Salt to taste
Pinch of cayenne pepper
1 quart boiling chicken broth
Bouquet garni composed of 3 parsley sprigs, 1 bay leaf, and ½ teaspoon dried thyme tied in cheesecloth
1 cup fresh young peas or 1 package frozen peas, thawed

Serves 6 to 8.

1 Melt 2 tablespoons butter in a Dutch oven. Stir in the onion; cook over medium heat until tender. Crumble the saffron over the onions; add the rice. Cook and stir over medium heat until rice turns milky in color.

2 Stir in the ham, shrimp, peppers, salt, cayenne pepper, and 1 cup of broth. Add the bouquet garni and bring to a boil. Continue to cook over medium heat, stirring the mixture constantly and adding more broth (½ cup at a time) until all liquid is absorbed. This should take about 30 minutes.

3 Stir peas and remaining 1 tablespoon butter into rice with a fork. Serve immediately.

It is worth noting that saffron has an infinite variety of graces other than those it bestows on rice. Long ago, the Babylonians, Romans, and Greeks used infusions of saffron as a perfume. Egyptian women tinted their hair with it. An extract of saffron was sprinkled on the streets of Pompeii and Herculaneum, because its brilliance implied virtue. And the flag of India was originally banded in saffrony gold for the same reason. Even today, in the Orient, Hindu monks wear saffron-dyed robes because the color is still said to signify courage, sacrifice, and the spirit of renunciation.

In the Bible, the Song of Solomon praises the golden virtues of doves roasted with *karkhom*, which food scholars presume to be the earliest reference to saffron as a seasoning for fowl.

There is an almost endless number of Spanish and Mexican poultry dishes that call for saffron as part of their seasoning alloy. The Spanish classic, Paella Valenciana, is prepared in all parts of the world where Hispanic culture flourishes. But the devise of this dish is so varied by national quirk that its contents are different everywhere—even among the localities of Valencia!

There is a persistent legend concerning the origin of paella: A warrior returning home to Spain after the Moorish wars had not eaten or slept for days. Forced to swim when his ship was attacked and sunk, he caught a vicious lobster in his boot.

"Do not bite off my toe," the soldier supplicated, "and I will promise you greatness beyond belief!" When the foolish crustacean complied, however, the soldier broke its claws.

Later, trudging through the sandy shore, he began to sink into quicksand. "Do not let me die," he begged the rice plants that grew along the marshy edge, "and I will promise you greatness beyond belief." The tender rice bent their long stems toward him so that he was able to climb to safety—and he tore off their ripest kernels by way of thanks.

On the road to his native village a wild goshawk suddenly swooped over the soldier's head. "Do not pluck out my eyes," shouted the warrior, "and I will promise you greatness beyond belief!"

"The way you promised the lobster and the rice?" replied the hawk. "Never!" But because the bird foolishly flew low enough to respond, the soldier was able to reach up, catch its tail, and bag it.

"Greatness, greatness," the soldier sang to himself as he arrived home. "Just see, wife," he cried, emptying his knapsack of its various ingredients. "I want you to give all these greatness beyond belief!"

His wife, being a sensible woman, ordinarily would have prepared three dishes to honor each viand separately. But her husband was starving and could not wait. The result? The first paella. A dish of greatness—beyond belief!

In the Catalan language, the term *paella* refers to the pan in which the food is prepared and served. Made of wrought iron with twin handles, the large shallow pan is designed to allow the various liquids in the seafood mixture to evaporate easily and leave the saffrony rice at exactly the precise degree of flavorsome dryness.

PAELLA VALENCIANA

1 Remove lobster claws; crack and reserve. Remove meat from rest of lobster; reserve. Shell and devein shrimp; reserve. Scrub mussels and clams; let stand in cold salted water to cover.

1 lobster (2 pounds), cooked
1½ pounds uncooked shrimp
1 quart mussels (optional)
24 small clams

1 teaspoon dried oregano
¼ teaspoon dried thyme
2 peppercorns, crushed
2 cloves garlic
1½ teaspoons salt
9 tablespoons olive or vegetable oil
1 teaspoon white wine vinegar
1 chicken (2½ to 3 pounds), cut into 10 pieces (legs cut at joint; breast cut into 4 pieces)
1 cup unsalted butter
1½ cups chopped yellow onions
4 large shallots, finely chopped
1½ ounces salt pork, chopped
1 green pepper, cut into strips
½ teaspoon ground coriander
2 teaspoons capers
5 chorizos (Spanish sausage), sliced
3 slices ham, ½-inch thick, cut into strips
4 large ripe tomatoes, seeded
2 tablespoons chopped fresh basil leaves or 1 teaspoon dried
3 cups rice
½ teaspoon crushed saffron
4 cups chicken broth enriched with chicken bouillon powder
1 white onion, chopped
4 parsley sprigs
½ lemon, sliced
1 bay leaf
1½ cups white wine
2 pounds fish fillets (flounder, cod, pike, or any white fish, cut into pieces, tied in cheesecloth)
1 jar (2 ounces) pimientos
1 can (6 ounces) black olives, drained
1 package (10 ounces) frozen peas, thawed
2 jiggers Pernod liqueur
White wine
Butter
Chopped parsley for garnish

Serves 10 to 12.

2 Combine the oregano, thyme, peppercorns, garlic, salt, 2 tablespoons oil, and the vinegar in a mortar or heavy bowl. Mash with a pestle to the consistency of a paste. Coat chicken pieces with paste. Let stand at room temperature ½ hour.

3 Melt ¼ cup butter with 4 tablespoons oil in a large skillet. Add half the onions and shallots; saute until golden. Add the salt pork and green pepper; cook and stir over medium heat 2 minutes. Add the reserved shrimp, the coriander, and capers. Cook, stirring constantly, until shrimp turn bright pink. Remove shrimp mixture. Wipe out skillet with paper toweling.

4 Add chorizos; saute until brown. Remove sausage; wipe out skillet. Melt ¼ cup butter with 3 tablespoons oil in skillet; add chicken and saute until golden on all sides, 15 to 20 minutes. Add the ham strips; stir until well-coated with pan drippings. Add tomatoes and basil and cook for an additional 10 minutes. Remove mixture from skillet.

5 Melt ½ cup butter in skillet; saute remaining onions and shallots until golden. Add rice and saffron; cook and stir over medium heat until rice becomes translucent and then milky in color.

6 Heat chicken broth to boiling. Add to rice and stir once; cook covered over low heat 20 minutes without stirring. If rice has not absorbed all liquid, cook uncovered over medium heat 3 to 5 minutes.

7 Place the white onion, parsley sprigs, lemon, and bay leaf in a large pot. Add 1½ cups white wine; heat to simmering. Add the mussels and clams; cook 5 minutes. Add the fish fillets; cook 8 minutes longer. Meanwhile, heat oven to 350°.

8 Spread about ⅔ of the rice mixture in a large ovenproof serving dish. Arrange the chicken, lobster, shrimp, fish, and meats over the rice. Spoon additional rice over, reserving enough to stuff the clams and mussel shells. Arrange stuffed clams and mussels over rice. Decorate with pimientos, black olives, and peas. Pour Pernod over entire dish to bring out the fusion of flavors.

9 Dip a large piece of cheesecloth in white wine; stretch over the Paella. Dot cheesecloth with butter. Bake until piping hot, 20 to 25 minutes. Remove cheesecloth. Garnish Paella with chopped parsley.

Note: This recipe can be cut in half, but it seems like a lot of trouble for so few servings.

Pollo Jitomate is a Mexican conceit that can be considered either a casualty or a happy accident of the Spanish conquest—depending upon your point of view. This dish requires only a good heavy skillet and a few hot *serrano* chilies for its "greatness beyond belief." If you are an incendiary type, you may add more than the three chilies specified—but at your own risk!

POLLO JITOMATE

1 Sprinkle the chicken with salt and pepper. Heat the oil in a heavy skillet; saute the chicken on both sides until crisp and golden. Remove from skillet.

2 Add the garlic and onion to skillet; saute until light brown. Remove with a slotted spoon. Add the bread; saute until golden on both sides. Drain on paper toweling; break into pieces.

3 Place ⅓ of the tomatoes, the garlic, onion, and bread in a blender container; blend until very smooth. Add remaining tomatoes; blend until smooth. Add the chilies, ¼ cup chicken stock, the cloves, and cinnamon; blend until smooth. Pour into a large heavy saucepan. Add remaining chicken stock.

4 Bring the sauce to a boil; add the saffron. Reduce heat to a simmer; add the chicken. Cook uncovered over low heat 1 hour and 15 minutes. Stir and baste chicken often.

5 Sprinkle chicken with parsley and serve with barley.

1 large chicken (4 to 4½ pounds), cut into serving pieces
Salt and freshly ground pepper to taste
4 tablespoons vegetable oil
2 cloves garlic
1 onion, chopped
1 slice white bread
3 large tomatoes, chopped
3 canned serrano chilies
1 cup chicken stock
⅛ teaspoon ground cloves
⅛ teaspoon ground cinnamon
⅛ teaspoon crumbled saffron
Chopped parsley for garnish
4 cups buttered cooked barley

Serves 4.

The Spanish are very particular about the ways in which they use saffron. They eschew the tradition favored elsewhere around the Mediterranean of eating saffron-flavored breads and cakes during Lent and employ the spice only for its palate-reviving flavor.

A remarkable fried fish dish from a farm kitchen near Toledo features a sauce of saffron, pecans, and hot peppers. The original recipe instructions advise the cook to saute the fish (which can be any white-fleshed catch you come upon in the market) until "it turns the color of bricks drying in the sun!" *Nice!* Nice dish, too.

PESCADO INSÓLITO

1½ pounds flounder (or other white fish) fillets
½ cup all-purpose flour
Pinch of paprika
Salt and freshly ground pepper to taste
5 tablespoons butter (approximately)
1 teaspoon vegetable oil
1 small onion, finely chopped
1 clove garlic, minced
2 tablespoons white wine or vermouth
Pinch of saffron
Pinch of crushed hot red peppers
½ teaspoon chopped fresh basil or a pinch of dried
½ cup chopped pecans
¼ cup finely chopped parsley
Lemon wedges

Serves 4.

1 Pat fish dry; cut large fillets in half. Combine the flour, paprika, salt, and pepper. Roll fish in flour mixture; shake off any excess.

2 Heat oven to 275°. Melt 3 tablespoons butter with 1 teaspoon oil in a large, heavy skillet. Saute fish over high heat until golden on both sides, adding more butter if necessary. Transfer to serving platter; keep warm in oven.

3 Add 2 tablespoons butter to skillet. Cook onion and garlic over low heat 2 minutes. Add the wine, saffron, hot pepper, basil, and pecans. Cook over medium heat, stirring constantly, until pecans are toasted. Stir in parsley. Spoon over fish. Garnish with lemon wedges.

Saffron has had its ups and downs in the kitchen. It was highly valued as a seasoning until the end of the Renaissance, but its popularity abruptly diminished and remained so for the next two centuries. No one seems to know why. By the 1800s saffron was adjudged to be toxic stuff. Dumas, as a matter of fact, had such an opinionated view of the herb's dark powers that he noted in his *Dictionaire de Gastronomie* that "its penetrating odor can cause violent fever, piteous headaches and even death!"

No evidence was submitted.

Oddly enough, at the end of the same century saffron began its comeback when Auguste Escoffier created a brilliant luncheon dish called Oeufs Brouillés au Saffron. Pretty opinionated himself, the great chef specified that this velvety concoction be served only as a luncheon hors d'oeuvre. Dictums to the contrary, it makes a fine Sunday night supper in my house—along with a salad, some cheese, and crusty loaf of bread.

OEUFS BROUILLÉS AU SAFFRON

8 eggs
¼ cup whipping cream
1½ tablespoons butter
¼ teaspoon strong beef stock
⅛ teaspoon saffron
Dash of hot pepper sauce
Salt and freshly ground pepper

Serves 4.

1 Beat the eggs lightly with the cream.

2 Melt the butter in a heavy skillet over low heat. Add the beef stock and saffron; stir until blended. Stir in the eggs.

3 Cook the eggs over very low heat, stirring constantly with a wooden spoon, until smooth and creamy, about ½ hour. Sprinkle with hot pepper sauce, salt, and pepper.

Most of the memorable saffron dishes in my cook's repertoire come from Nice, a city that I lived only twenty minutes away from for a short but intensely glorious period of my life.

The delicious vitality of the bouillabaisse I cooked there had much to do with being able to select the correct-size mullet, the perfect "blue-eyed" mussels, and the silvery crayfish for the soup from the fishmongers who lined the quay each morning.

I have eschewed a pale imitation bouillabaisse in favor of a frankly Americanized devise that can be collected in any decent fish store or supermarket.

It's not authentic in the least—just very, very good!

BOUILLABAISSE AMERICAN-STYLE

1 Heat the oil in a large heavy saucepan. Add minced garlic, the onion, green onions, and celery; cook over low heat 5 minutes.

2 Add the thyme, bay leaf, tomatoes, clam juice, wine, fennel seeds, saffron, parsley, sugar, salt, and pepper. Tie the fish head in cheesecloth; add to pan. Simmer uncovered 30 minutes. Discard head.

3 Meanwhile, wash the lobster and cut its spinal cord by inserting a very sharp knife where the tail and body meet. Turn the lobster over on its back and slit the undershell lengthwise with a scissors. Remove the dark vein, the sac near the head, and any spongy tissue. Cut into pieces, cutting the tail into three pieces. Cut off the claws; crack them and any other piece that may require it.

4 Add the seafood to the tomato mixture. Simmer covered, stirring occasionally, 10 minutes. Mash 1 clove garlic with the anchovy paste and 1 teaspoon of the cooking liquid. Stir into saucepan; simmer 5 minutes longer.

Note: After scrubbing the mussels, place them in a pot of cold water to which you have added 1 tablespoon cornstarch. Let stand ½ hour; drain and rinse under cold water. This procedure cleans the mussels quite effectively.

¼ cup olive oil
1 clove garlic, minced
1 onion, finely chopped
3 green onions with tops, finely chopped
1 rib celery, finely chopped
½ teaspoon thyme
1 small bay leaf, crumbled
1 cup finely chopped, peeled, and seeded fresh tomatoes
1 can (8 ounces) imported Italian tomatoes
1½ cups clam juice
1 cup dry white wine
½ teaspoon fennel seeds, crushed
Pinch of saffron
2 tablespoons finely chopped parsley
Pinch of sugar
Salt and freshly ground pepper to taste
1 pound red snapper or cod with head, cut into pieces
1 small lobster
12 mussels, scrubbed well, beards removed
16 small shrimp, shelled, deveined
1 small clove garlic
½ teaspoon anchovy paste

Serves 4.

The Muslim invaders are said to have introduced the stigma of the dried crocus into Spain during their sorties on the Iberian continent in the eighth century A.D. From there, saffron's sphere of influence spread to the rest of the Mediterranean and back again to the Middle East—where the seasoning was born.

In Morocco, like most of North Africa, saffron-scented dishes are a staple of the national diet. Couscous (tiny dumplings made of semolina and water and steamed over a stew) is a native Moroccan dish whose time has come for American cooks. It takes one and a half hours, from start to finish, to make couscous—and it is worth every precious minute. In lieu of a Moroccan couscousiére, an adequate steamer may be concocted of a large colander fitted neatly into the top of a saucepan. Line the colander with a double layer of cheesecloth before you place the semolina in it. The important thing to remember is that all steam escaping from the *tagine* (the stew that cooks in the pot below) must pass through the couscous to flavor the dish. So keep the colander and the saucepan (or the two parts of the couscousiére) sealed together—even if you have to use masking tape!

Harissa (recipe follows)
1 leg of lamb (about 5½ pounds)
2 tablespoons olive oil
1 whole yellow onion, peeled
6 peppercorns
2 cloves garlic
1 carrot
9 sprigs parsley
1½ quarts chicken broth
1½ quarts water
Salt and freshly ground pepper
5 tablespoons vegetable oil
¾ cup butter, at room temperature
5 large yellow onions, coarsely chopped
½ teaspoon ground ginger
⅛ teaspoon saffron (or to taste)
½ teaspoon ground cinnamon
½ teaspoon ground turmeric
½ teaspoon freshly grated nutmeg
3 sprigs fresh coriander
1 pound couscous (semolina grains)
3 medium turnips, cut into 1½-inch pieces
5 carrots, cut into 2-inch strips
3 medium zucchini, cut into 2-inch strips
Salt
4 tomatoes, seeded and coarsely chopped
¼ cup dark honey
½ cup raisins
1 can (6 ounces) chick peas, drained, skins removed
1 can (6 ounces) whole blanched almonds, lightly sauteed in oil and drained on paper toweling
Chopped parsley and coriander for garnish

Serves 6 to 8.

MOROCCAN COUSCOUS

1 Make Harissa; reserve.

2 Remove the meat from the leg of lamb; cut into 1½-inch cubes. (If you have the butcher do it, ask for the bones.) Place 2 tablespoons olive oil in a Dutch oven. Add lamb bones; cook over high heat until brown. Add the onion, peppercorns, garlic, carrot, 4 sprigs parsley, chicken broth, and water; bring to a boil. Cook until reduced to 7 cups, about 30 minutes.

3 Sprinkle lamb cubes with salt and pepper; saute in 3 tablespoons vegetable oil in a heavy skillet until brown. Transfer to the bottom of a couscousiere; add ½ cup butter, 2 chopped onions, the ginger, saffron, ¼ teaspoon cinnamon, the turmeric, and nutmeg. Tie remaining parsley and the coriander in cheesecloth; add to pot. Pour in the lamb stock; cover and bring to a boil. Reduce heat; simmer 20 minutes.

4 Meanwhile, spread couscous in a roasting pan; cover with 9 cups cold water. Drain in a fine sieve; return to roasting pan, spreading evenly. Let stand 10 minutes. Using wet, cupped hands, lift up the grain and rub it together, letting it fall back into the pan. When all lumps are broken up, gently rake grains with fingers.

5 Remove cover from couscousiere. Cut strip of cheesecloth to match the circumference of pot. Dampen cloth and dust with flour;

place over rim of pot. Place steamer over pot, making sure no steam escapes. Sprinkle ¼ of couscous into steamer; steam 5 minutes over medium heat. Gradually add remaining couscous; steam uncovered until lamb is tender, 20 to 35 minutes longer.

6 Remove steamer and cheesecloth. Add turnips to pot, cover, and turn off heat. Place couscous in roasting pan; sprinkle with 1 cup lightly salted cold water. With lightly oiled hands, break up lumps; rake grains with fingers until smooth. Cover pan with damp towel.

7 Sprinkle carrots and zucchini lightly with salt; reserve. Heat 2 tablespoons vegetable oil in a heavy skillet; saute remaining 3 chopped onions until golden. Stir in ¼ teaspoon cinnamon, the tomatoes, honey, and raisins. Cook over high heat until all liquid is absorbed.

8 Rinse and drain zucchini; add to stew with carrots and tomato mixture. Bring to a boil; reduce heat.

9 Place dry strip of cheesecloth over the rim of pot; place steamer over pot. Rake couscous with fingers; place in steamer. Steam over medium heat 25 minutes.

10 Remove steamer. Add 2 tablespoons Harissa, the chick peas, and almonds to stew. Place couscous in center of a large serving dish; stir in remaining ¼ cup butter. Form into a mound in the center. Drain stew, reserving the broth. Arrange lamb and vegetables around couscous. Sprinkle with chopped parsley and coriander. Serve with bowl of broth and the remaining Harissa on the side.

Note: Use regular couscous if possible. Precooked couscous is available in 1-pound packages; it requires only one steaming but is not as flavorful. Couscous can be prepared through Step 6 several hours in advance. If semolina grain is not available for making a classic couscous, you might consider substituting dried barley instead. To make this substitution, merely replace the semolina grains with an equal quantity of barley and proceed with the recipe as directed. It is imperative, however, that the barley be parboiled for 15 minutes, in a large quantity of water, prior to Step 4.

HARISSA

Pound the garlic and chili peppers together. Place in a blender container or an electric spice mill. Grind as fine as possible. Add caraway, cumin, and coriander; grind until fine. Combine with salt and hot pepper sauce. Place in a small jar; add olive oil to cover. Harissa will keep tightly covered in refrigerator for months.

2 cloves garlic, minced
2 ounces dried red chili peppers, crushed
4 teaspoons caraway seeds
1 teaspoon ground cumin
1 teaspoon ground coriander
1 teaspoon salt
1 tablespoon hot pepper sauce
Olive oil

Makes about ½ cup.

Ancient Phoenicians baked saffron into crescent-shaped cakes that they ate to honor Ashtoreth, goddess of the moon and fertility.

In the fourteenth century, the great chef Taillevent produced a saffron wafer to end a royal meal that King Charles VI "enjoyed so hugely" that the royal plate was filled ten times over.

Taillevent's association with saffron was so lasting that his tomb is emblazoned with a coat of arms—three tiny cooking pots over a crocus bulb in flower.

A Medieval conceit, the last saffron recipe is for a cake that had been passed down from family cookbook to family cookbook (for several hundred years) before it came into my hot hands. Antique though the formula may be, the end result is utterly satisfying: a yellow cake more strongly redolent of grated citrus than of saffron—although that seasoning's presence can be felt unmistakably after every single bite.

I admire the formula for several reasons. It gives me a sense of the past to recreate history in a baking dish. And to cook what others ate centuries ago and still be delighted by the end result is no small thing, I think. On a more personal level, the old-time saffron cake is a legacy—the gift of a great cook who inspired this chapter in the first place!

1 cup unsalted butter
2 cups granulated sugar
2 eggs plus 3 egg yolks
1 teaspoon vanilla
1 tablespoon caraway seeds, ground in a blender
⅛ teaspoon saffron, crushed
3 cups sifted all-purpose flour
2 teaspoons baking powder
½ teaspoon salt
½ teaspoon each of ground nutmeg, cloves, mace, and cinnamon
1 cup milk
Peel of 1 large lemon, finely grated
Peel of 1 orange, finely grated
1¼ cups sifted confectioners' sugar
1 tablespoon orange juice
1 tablespoon lemon juice
1 tablespoon boiling water

Serves 10.

OLD-TIME SAFFRON CAKE

1 Heat oven to 350°. Cream the butter with the sugar until light and fluffy. Add the eggs and egg yolks, one at a time, beating well after each addition. Stir in the vanilla, caraway seeds, and saffron.

2 Sift the flour with the baking powder, salt, nutmeg, cloves, mace, and cinnamon. Add to butter mixture in three parts, alternating with thirds of the milk. Mix well; stir in lemon and orange peels.

3 Turn the batter into a greased and floured 10×3½-inch tube pan. Bake until toothpick inserted comes out clean, 1 hour and 20 to 25 minutes. Cool in pan 10 minutes; invert on wire rack. Let stand while preparing glaze.

4 To prepare glaze: Combine the confectioners' sugar, orange juice, lemon juice, and boiling water. Stir until smooth. Spoon over top of cake, allowing some to run down sides. Cut into thin slices to serve.

Note: Cake gets softer and improves with age.

Tomato

My very first vegetable garden was cultivated on a mossy strip of lawn behind the family garage. It was a well-shaded area, as I recall, entirely protected by high hedges on its sun side and shielded against fauna by an enormous, unpruned wild rose bush that outrageously took over the garage walls as its own occupied territory (and sent out yards and yards of thorny nettles calculated to resist a meddlesome gardener's fingers at weeding time).

Though I was a mere eight years old at the occasion of this foray into agriculture, I had a shining example. My grandmother was a remarkable gardener; any alien cutting she casually snipped with a thumbnail took root in her home soil. What is even more astounding is that these woodland flowers (lady's slipper or jack-in-the-pulpit) always bloomed to staggering proportion under her watchful eye. My mother did not inherit her parent's gift—around our house she planted spikey irises and hardy perennials that she perennially ignored. Being influenced by neither matriarch, but held in thrall by tales of Peter Rabbit and Farmer MacGregor instead, I only planted greens. Nothing but rows of carrots and radishes grew in my garden. Why? I cannot remember. We certainly did not have bunnies in residence; so perhaps wishful thinking on my part reasoned that a bumper crop of rabbit food might occasion a migration. (No such luck, however!)

The vegetables grew well enough in their sunless trap—and my poor family dutifully ate as many carrots and radishes as I produced (until blight overtook one and the other went to seed)—but the glamour of plantation never took hold.

The next time I took to the soil, twenty-five years had elapsed. And the emergence of Greene's thumb (if one may pander to that terrible pun) only came with the rental of a small beach house close by the shore, at the very end of Long Island, in 1958.

With three erstwhile chums, I impulsively drove to the fringe of East Hampton one February day and, at first sight, pledged my unearned vacation pay as down payment for a summer house—a woebegone gray clapboard dwelling (more Kansas than South Fork in anyone's Baedeker) with no close neighbors to speak of and a hundred acres of dune nudging the porch.

On a freezing, unheated March weekend, we painted the house's interior snow white. And shortly thereafter, armed with staple-guns, we reupholstered all the rickety rattan in brilliant hues of burlap. Next came curtains for every window—and pots and pans to make the kitchen habitable.

The owner of the house was so astounded at our dervish decorating efforts that she made several unannounced (and unwelcome) landlordly tours of inspection before she pronounced our mutual efforts eminently *houseworthy* (her term). And promptly doubled the rent for the following year—"If you fellas are interested in coming back to these parts next summer, of course!"

Of course.

But enough of house—garden awaits.

One of the other shareholders was my oldest friend in the world, George. We had met, as I said before, at college. Even then, at age seventeen, George knew everything about anything you could mention—philosophy, religion, politics, sex (well, possibly less about sex, but time repaired the lack!). Point of fact, George also knew all there was to know about gardening. And I became his acolyte in matters of mulch and bonemeal, hoe, and hose.

Together we spent a cold spring visiting every respectable greenhouse and seedsman in the territory. Our plot of gardening land was not large (about nine feet by twelve feet), but it was carefully planned for produce. Shortly I learned to know the difference between a Big Girl tomato, which blooms in mid-July, and a Better Boy, which likes a hardy, chalky soil (with which we were happily endowed) and blooms red as a bull's eye August first on the dot!

Tomatoes we planted, as well as eggplant, zucchini, peppers, and tender yellow onions by the bushel—ratatouille on the vine, if you will. Parsley and tarragon, dill and basil bordered the rows. George was a designer to the teeth; so his plan was measured and calculated for decorative balance as well as good eating after the harvest was reaped.

He was, also, an absolute tartar with a trowel!

From him, I learned the basics: that tomatoes are likely to ripen faster if the plants are grown along a sheltered south wall (which again by luck we possessed); that seedlings planted in hillocks of earth are less likely to be washed out in late-spring rains; and, most important of all, that cow manure is best when it is well rotted. None of those powdered, deodorized fertilizers for our garden, George decreed. Instead, a trip to the local dairy with burlap bag and rubber gloves, so that we could pick our compost fresh!

Our garden began as a four man enterprise. It took two hands to turn over the soil and two more to rake up the broken rocks and clear the land. Two hands accomplished the dreadful task of manure-spreading. And it certainly took two hands, at least, to cultivate and stake. We could have used an army of hundreds just for weeding—though the garden was no larger than a living-room rug.

If the tomatoes flourished (and they did), weeds prospered with them—the more robust I think for mulch and Malthion 'round the clock.

As the kitchen greenery flowered, a dearly-paid-for summer approached as well. But while the other members of the household turned into dedicated sun-worshipers as soon as the temperature hit seventy-five, I did not.

My friend George (the original agronomist) deserted me only when the Atlantic's waves proved too beguiling to resist, for he is also part porpoise, as all his friends knew in advance. What happened to our garden then is what has happened to every communal garden since Eden: the meek merely inherited the earth!

I stayed at that beach house all of the long summer, ostensibly to write a play, while my companions buzzed in from the city on Friday night (usually with guests) and waved farewell on Sunday. But the true reason for my tenure was not artistic freedom at all. It was, rather, an obsession with chickweed, aphids, and whiteflies! The garden, you see, had become my inheritance and my unbelievable passion at one and the same time.

If I live to be a hundred, I will never forget the bliss of smelling a tomato as it first appears, dwarf-green, pale, and slightly fuzzy, from its petallike cocoon. Fragrant of dry leaves and rich dark loam. The gardener's joy is watching this globe grow daily. Fighting the beetle and borer, he knows that his table will be more sumptuous soon with the addition of this majestic juicy fruit—simply cut and dusted with salt and pepper. For a vine-ripened tomato requires nothing more. But don't tell basil I said so!

Though the tomato is definitely a native American product (predating Columbus by a couple of thousand years), it was not consumed with any relish in this country until the end of the nineteenth century. Before that, it was always assumed to be as venomous as snakebite!

Funnily enough, the tomato, *Lycopersicon esculentum* (also translated to "love apple" at times), is indeed a cousin, albeit a distant one, of deadly nightshade. But so are the potato and the eggplant—so no sweat!

The notion that tomatoes are dangerous stems from their having been listed among the narcotic plants of the *Solanum* family (nightshade again!) by Pierandrea Mattioli, the Italian herbalist, in 1544. In his *Commentaries on the Six Books of Dioscorides,* Mattioli called the tomato *mala surea* (the golden evil) because all early tomatoes were of a yellowish hue. And he grouped it with belladonna, henbane, mandrake root, and arsenic—all considerably stronger stuff in a spaghetti sauce!

The tomato's revenge on Mattioli's countrymen was sweet. Ever since the early 1800s, when the fruit's status as a deadly poison was officially reversed, more tomatoes have been consumed annually in southern Italy—mostly in confederation with pasta and cheese—than anywhere else on the face of the globe, and the tradition shows no sign of abatement.

One excellent reason for this flavoring's popularity is immediately apparent when one inhales the felicitous vapor of the following Italian classic.

1 chicken (about 3 pounds)
2 cans (13¾ ounces each) chicken broth
1 onion stuck with 2 cloves
1 rib celery with leaves, chopped
2 sprigs parsley
1 bay leaf
½ teaspoon salt
½ teaspoon freshly ground pepper
5 tablespoons butter
1 yellow onion, chopped
1 can (8 ounces) imported Italian tomatoes
3 large ripe fresh tomatoes, seeded, chopped
½ teaspoon sugar
½ pound mushrooms, sliced
1 teaspoon chopped fresh tarragon or ½ teaspoon dried
1 teaspoon chopped fresh basil or ½ teaspoon dried
3 tablespoons all-purpose flour
1 cup whipping cream
⅓ cup dry white wine
Salt and freshly ground pepper
2 cups grated Mozzarella cheese
1 cup Ricotta cheese
½ pound wide lasagne noodles, cooked *al dente,* rinsed in cold water
⅓ cup freshly grated Parmesan cheese

Serves 6.

CHICKEN LASAGNE

1 Place the chicken in a large pot. Add the chicken broth, the onion stuck with cloves, celery, parsley, bay leaf, ½ teaspoon salt, ½ teaspoon pepper, and enough water to cover chicken. Bring to a boil. Reduce heat; simmer until chicken is tender, about 50 minutes.

2 Remove chicken from broth; cool slightly. Remove skin and meat from bones; return skin and bones to broth. Heat broth to boiling. Reduce heat; simmer ½ hour. Cut chicken into 1-inch pieces.

3 Melt 2 tablespoons butter in a skillet; saute chopped onion until golden. Add the tomatoes; sprinkle with sugar. Add the mushrooms, tarragon, basil, and salt and pepper to taste. Simmer 20 minutes; raise heat and cook until most of the liquid is evaporated. Stir in the chicken.

4 Melt remaining butter in a medium saucepan; stir in the flour. Cook over medium heat 3 minutes. Whisk in 1 cup of hot broth and the cream. Heat to boiling; cook, stirring constantly, until thickened. Add the wine and salt and pepper to taste.

5 Heat oven to 350°. Butter an 8×8-inch Pyrex baking dish. Spread ⅓ of the tomato mixture over the bottom; spoon ⅓ of the white sauce over. Sprinkle with 1 cup Mozzarella cheese; dot with ½ cup Ricotta cheese. Cover with layer of noodles. Repeat layers. Top with remaining tomato mixture and white sauce. Sprinkle with Parmesan cheese. Bake until hot and bubbly, about 35 minutes.

Peruvians have an old tradition of combining tomatoes with citrus juice to cure and season meat and fish. One of the more bracing of their innovations is the following recipe for Shrimp Seviche. A delectable hors d'oeuvre or refreshingly tart first course, it would also make a fine picnic lunch with some French or Italian bread, cheese, and a thermos of chilled white sangria.

SHRIMP SEVICHE

Combine all ingredients except parsley for garnish in order listed. Cover and refrigerate for at least 12 hours. Sprinkle heavily with chopped parsley before serving.

How did the tomato come to be known as a "love apple"? Theories proliferate on the subject. The one I choose for credence claims that the Spanish (who first brought this tart fruit back from the New World) called it *manzana,* or apple, because at first sight that's what they thought it was. The Italians, who liked the look of this plant in their gardens, if not in their saucepans, translated *manzana* into *pomo.* And since the early tomatoes were yellow, *pomo d'oro,* or apple of gold, became its cognomen. According to speculation, when Italian chefs first began flavoring foods with tomatoes, they feared a negative response to their using what had long been considered a noxious ingredient; so they changed the name to *pomo d'Moro,* or Moor's apple, to emphasize the fruit's Spanish antecedence. Later, a Frenchman visited Naples, tasted the local cookery, and inquired about the odd sauce ingredient. When told its name, he misun-

1 pound uncooked shrimp, shelled and deveined
1 cup fresh lime juice
¼ cup chopped shallots
1 clove garlic, minced
¼ cup chopped parsley
1 small tomato, peeled, seeded, cut into strips
3 tablespoons finely chopped green chili peppers
1½ teaspoons salt
1 teaspoon freshly ground pepper
Dash of hot pepper sauce
¼ cup chopped fresh coriander
½ cup olive oil
Chopped parsley for garnish

Serves 4.

derstood and assumed that *pomo d'Moro* was *pomme d'amour,* or apple of love.

The highly erroneous notion that tomatoes are aphrodisiac stems from this mix-up. However, there is no mistake about the Italian practice of tossing tomatoes and thin pieces of asparagus into a marvelous pasta dish, Pasta con Asparago e Pomidori—or *fettuccine meraviglioso!*

PASTA CON ASPARAGO E POMIDORI

5 tablespoons butter
2 teaspoons olive or vegetable oil
1 clove garlic, minced
1 shallot, minced
1 medium fresh tomato, seeded, finely chopped
1 can (6 ounces) Italian tomatoes, drained, mashed
Pinch of sugar
2 teaspoons chopped fresh basil
2 teaspoons chopped parsley
Salt and freshly ground pepper to taste
¾ pound thin asparagus
½ pound fettuccine noodles (homemade, if possible)
1 egg
1 egg yolk
3 tablespoons whipping cream
1 cup grated Parmesan cheese

Serves 4.

1 Melt 2 tablespoons butter in a heavy skillet; add 1 teaspoon oil. Add the garlic and shallot; cook over low heat until soft, about 5 minutes. Add the tomatoes, sugar, basil, parsley, salt, and pepper. Cook over low heat until fairly smooth, about 20 minutes.

2 Break off the ends of the asparagus; peel stems with a vegetable peeler. Cut into 1½- to 2-inch pieces. (If asparagus is not very thin, cut pieces in half lengthwise.) Cook in boiling salted water 1 minute; rinse under cold running water and drain.

3 Heat 4 quarts of water to boiling; add 1 teaspoon oil. Add pasta; cook in boiling water just until tender, 3 to 4 minutes. (Packaged pasta will take longer.) Drain. Return to pot; stir in 2 tablespoons butter.

4 Melt 1 tablespoon butter in a small skillet; add asparagus. Cook just until hot; add to pasta. Add tomato mixture to pasta. Toss over low heat until well mixed. Taste for seasoning; add salt if necessary.

5 Whisk the egg, egg yolk, and cream together until smooth. Stir into pasta over low heat. Stir in half the Parmesan cheese. Serve with remaining cheese on the side.

Tomatoes were eaten in Italy and Spain (in cooked form only) by the beginning of the sixteenth century. England and France, however, resisted the idea for another hundred years. And while Shakespeare noted that Othello (as a Moor) ate tomatoes prodigiously, the playwright himself never touched one, since Elizabethans generally viewed "the giant *ugli escarlate globus*" with ill-concealed horror.

Early Frenchmen shared this intense distaste until Catherine de Medici (1519-1589) began to change their point of view. When this Italian princess came to France to wed Henry II, she is said to have brought the following dowry: charm, cheese, and tomato sauce, as well as cooks to put the last two together.

One noble French usage of fresh tomatoes and cheese blends them with cream in a sauce for oven-poached fish fillets. This is the very subtly flavored and splendid dish, Fillet of Sole Duglère.

I have made this wonderful recipe for years—and even printed its devise before. It remains the single quintessential mating of fish and tomato I know; so please forgive the repetition.

FILLET OF SOLE DUGLÈRE

1 Heat oven to 350°. Soak fillets in the juice of ½ lemon and water to cover for 10 minutes. Drain; pat dry with paper toweling. Melt 1 tablespoon butter; place in a baking dish and turn dish to coat bottom and sides. Lightly sprinkle skinned sides of fillets with salt and pepper. Fold fillets lengthwise and arrange in dish.

2 Melt 4 tablespoons butter in a saucepan; add mushrooms. Shake the pan to coat mushrooms with butter; add 1 tablespoon lemon juice and a pinch each of salt and pepper. Cook 2 minutes over medium heat. Add wine and water; bring to a boil. Spoon mixture over fish. Cover baking dish with buttered waxed or brown paper. Bake 15 minutes (this is actually oven-poaching). Pour off cooking liquid; strain and reserve. Cover fish to keep warm.

3 Gently squeeze tomatoes to remove juice. Shred 1 tomato. Cut remaining 3 tomatoes into pieces and place in a blender container; blend until pureed.

4 Melt 6 tablespoons butter in a saucepan; remove from heat. Stir in the flour, ½ teaspoon salt, and the cayenne; whisk until smooth. Stir in the reserved cooking liquid and pureed tomatoes. Cook and stir over low heat until mixture thickens and begins to boil. Reduce heat; stir in the cream and ½ cup grated cheese. Simmer 5 minutes. Cut 1 tablespoon butter into small pieces; stir in, one piece at a time, until melted.

5 Stir in the shredded tomato and parsley. Pour sauce over fish. Sprinkle with bread crumbs and remaining cheese. Place under broiler until browned.

8 sole (or flounder) fillets
Juice of ½ lemon
¾ cup unsalted butter
Salt and freshly ground pepper
⅓ cup sliced mushrooms
1 tablespoon fresh lemon juice
1 cup dry white wine
⅓ cup water
4 tomatoes, seeded
4½ tablespoons all-purpose flour
½ teaspoon salt
Pinch of cayenne pepper
1 cup whipping cream
½ cup plus 2 tablespoons grated Swiss or Parmesan cheese
1 tablespoon chopped parsley
1½ tablespoons buttered bread crumbs

Serves 4.

While most of the rest of France admitted tomatoes into its cookpots during the seventeenth century, Parisians (and particularly the *haute cuisine chefs de Paris*) resisted Catherine de Medici's bequest until Napoleon III's wife, Empress Eugènie (of the famed hats), introduced a buttery tomato sauce at a state dinner in the mid-1800s. But then, Paris adored everything Eugènie did!

The Mediterranean regions of France, Italy, Spain, and Greece had made the tomato a dietary staple long before Paris conceded the point. A letter from an American traveler to Naples (written directly after the close of the War of 1812) noted with astonishment that "grown men would pick love apples off a vine in public view . . . and after slicing them in two like melons stuff the half bulbs to their lips and squeeze the rosy juices down their throats!"

That libation preceded the Bloody Mary, you may note, by a hundred and fifty years!

One remarkable tomato amalgam, from Naples, is veal scallops, rolled around Mozzarella cheese and simmered in a delicate tomato sauce. This dish is one that even diehard "tomatophobes" have eaten with relish at my table.

3 tablespoons butter
2 shallots, finely chopped
2 cloves garlic, minced
2 teaspoons all-purpose flour
2 fresh tomatoes, peeled, seeded, chopped
1 can (17 ounces) imported Italian tomatoes
1 teaspoon tomato paste
½ teaspoon sugar
Pinch of dried rosemary
Pinch of ground allspice
3 tablespoons chopped parsley
Salt and freshly ground pepper
8 veal scallops, pounded thin
¼ pound whole-milk Mozzarella cheese (approximately)
2 tablespoons olive oil
¼ cup dry white wine
Grated Parmesan cheese

Serves 4.

ROLLED SCALLOPINE PARMIGIANA

1 Melt the butter in a heavy skillet. Add the shallots and garlic. Cook over low heat 3 minutes; sprinkle with flour. Stir to combine. Add the tomatoes, tomato paste, sugar, rosemary, allspice, parsley, and salt and pepper to taste. Cook over medium heat 10 minutes. Reduce heat; cook until very thick, about 20 minutes.

2 Heat oven to 400°. Sprinkle veal scallops with salt and pepper. Cut cheese into eight strips. Place one strip of cheese in center of each scallop; roll up lengthwise. Tie with string in two or three places.

3 Heat the oil in a large heavy skillet. Add veal and cook over high heat until brown on all sides. Transfer veal to an ovenproof serving dish; remove strings. Pour the wine into the skillet; stir, scraping sides and bottom of pan. Stir in the tomato sauce; cook over low heat 5 minutes. Spoon sauce over veal; sprinkle with ¼ cup grated Parmesan cheese. Bake 15 minutes. Serve with additional grated Parmesan.

Strictly speaking, tomatoes are a fruit. But since we eat them as a vegetable, they are classified as such.

However, a wonderful French dessert blows that fiction entirely. I first encountered this treat at a small inn in a town along the Loire. Since we arrived there too late for lunch and well before dinner time, the proprietor "made do"—with a bit of pâté, an omelet, and a slice of tart. The tart was half tomato and half Normandy apple, caramelized with sugar and covered with runny cream—a dessert to dream over.

TARTE NORMANDE AUX POMMES D'AMOUR

1 To make the pâte sucrée, place the flour, salt, sugar, and butter in a bowl; blend with a pastry blender until the texture of coarse crumbs. Combine the egg yolk and water; stir into the flour to form a soft dough. Knead briefly on a lightly floured board. Refrigerate ½ hour.

2 Heat oven to 400°. Butter a 9-inch loose-bottom tart pan. Pat pastry about ¼-inch thick over bottom and sides of pan. Line pastry with aluminum foil; fill with dried rice or beans. Bake 10 minutes; Remove rice and foil; bake 5 minutes. Cool.

3 To make the filling, combine the tomatoes, 4 tablespoons butter, the sugar, orange juice, lemon juice, cloves, orange peel, and lemon peel in a saucepan. Bring to a boil; cook, stirring frequently, until reduced to 1 cup, about 30 minutes.

4 Heat oven to 375°. Arrange apple slices, overlapping, in a circle in the bottom of the pastry; fill center with extra apples. Spoon tomato mixture over apples. Sprinkle with brown sugar; dot with 1 teaspoon butter. Place tart pan on a foil-lined baking sheet. Bake until apples are tender and pastry is light brown, 30 to 35 minutes. Serve warm with whipped cream.

Note: Tart apples are imperative in this recipe; don't make it with anything else.

For the pâte sucrée:
1¼ cups all-purpose flour
⅛ teaspoon salt
2 tablespoons granulated sugar
½ cup cold unsalted butter, cut into 8 pieces
1 egg yolk
2½ tablespoons cold water

For the filling:
2 large ripe tomatoes, peeled, seeded, coarsely chopped (about 1¼ cups)
4 tablespoons plus 1 teaspoon unsalted butter
1½ cups granulated sugar
¼ cup orange juice
1 tablespoon lemon juice
Pinch of ground cloves
½ teaspoon slivered orange peel
½ teaspoon slivered lemon peel
3 Granny Smith apples, pared, cored, cut lengthwise into ¼-inch-thick slices
¼ cup light brown sugar
Whipping cream, whipped with confectioners' sugar and Grand Marnier liqueur, for topping

Serves 8.

Early American farm cooks made their reputations on green tomato pie. I happened on a formula for the celebrated sweet once and tried it. No contest for the ripe French concoction I have just described, it turned out to be a sour, flavorless composition—as appetizing to the eye as a mess of boiled wash and no more of a treat for the tongue. So now I set my green tomatoes in a dark place (instead of a pie crust) and let them ripen to sweetness on their own.

American cuisine has contributed two quite remarkable tomato dishes to my recipe files, however. One is a hearty beefsteak stew lovingly transplanted from under Colorado skies—a wondrous and economical (a wonder in itself) meal for all seasons. The other is chicken fried and smothered in tomatoes and cream (what better way to go?)—and is absolutely staggering eating! Both are native dishes I think we may be rightfully proud to claim as part of our tomato heritage.

COLORADO-STYLE STEAK

½ cup all-purpose flour
1 teaspoon salt
½ teaspoon seasoned pepper
2 pounds beefsteak (round or chuck), about 1-inch thick, cut into 4 pieces
5 tablespoons butter
3 tablespoons vegetable oil
1 large onion, chopped
1 clove garlic, minced
⅓ cup dry red wine, warmed
1 can (17 ounces) Italian tomatoes, undrained
3 large fresh tomatoes, chopped
⅓ cup chopped carrots
⅓ cup chopped celery
1 tablespoon Worcestershire sauce
Freshly chopped parsley

Serves 4.

1 Heat oven to 325°. Combine ½ cup flour, salt, and pepper. Coat steak with flour mixture, pounding it into both sides of steak with a wooden mallet. Reserve excess flour.

2 Heat 3 tablespoons butter with the oil in a large heavy skillet; add meat and brown well on both sides. Transfer to an ovenproof casserole.

3 Saute onion and garlic in remaining 2 tablespoons butter over medium heat until onions are transparent, about 5 minutes. Remove with a slotted spoon; add to meat. Whisk 2 tablespoons excess flour into skillet; gradually stir in the wine. Whisk until smooth. Stir in the tomatoes, carrots, celery, and Worcestershire sauce. Simmer 5 minutes. Pour over meat.

4 Bake covered until meat is tender, 1½ to 2 hours depending on the cut of meat. Remove cover; bake 30 minutes. Garnish with a generous sprinkling of parsley.

SMOTHERED CHICKEN NEW ORLEANS-STYLE

1 Heat oven to 300°. Combine flour, salt, and pepper. Coat chicken pieces with flour mixture. Heat 7 tablespoons butter in a large skillet until foamy; add the oil. Add the chicken; saute over medium heat, turning frequently, until golden brown. Transfer chicken to a baking dish; bake 10 minutes.

2 Add the garlic, onion, thyme, and ham to skillet. Saute over medium heat until onions are transparent. Add mixture to chicken; bake 10 minutes.

3 Add mushrooms to skillet; saute over medium heat until lightly browned (you may have to add more oil). Stir in the tomatoes and sprinkle with sugar; cook until tomatoes are tender. Add mixture to chicken; bake 10 minutes.

4 Meanwhile, mix remaining 1 tablespoon butter and 1 tablespoon flour in a small bowl. Stir in bouillon powder. Place mixture in skillet; cook and stir over low heat, scraping bottom and sides of pan, until smooth. Gradually stir in the wine and ½ cup cream; cook, stirring constantly, until mixture is thick. Stir in remaining ½ cup cream. Pour over chicken. Bake 15 minutes. Chop parsley with tarragon; sprinkle over chicken. Serve with rice (or dumplings).

Since I love growing tomatoes almost as much as I enjoy eating them, I'll offer some garden wisdom on the subject. (The disinterested should feel free to skip all this!)

Early in spring, but well before planting time, a sensible tomato grower turns the soil and adds a measure of humus (and lime, if needed). I like to poke compost and well-rotted manure into the soil as well—if you figure about one quart to every ten yards of garden you won't overdo.

Tomato seedlings are best raised indoors in peat pots, which do not require transplanting. I buy mine, I confess, at a reliable nursery, but I never put them into the ground until all fear of frost is completely gone from my mind. It's a good idea (but not essential) to water the plants before you set them out in the garden. Do it the night before to spare the seedlings any trauma. I like to mark out the row where I'll put the plants and make the holes with my trowel in advance—so I don't start trying to do everything at once.

When you set the seedlings, make sure to mound the earth around each plant. A well-made tomato garden should look like a series of giant anthills, each with a tomato plant in dead center.

Not all tomatoes require stakes, but I take no chances. I start putting in supports a week or ten days after the plants are set and

¼ cup all-purpose flour
1 teaspoon salt
¼ teaspoon pepper
1 frying chicken (about 3 pounds), cut up into serving pieces
½ cup unsalted butter
2 tablespoons vegetable oil
1 clove garlic, minced
1 tablespoon chopped onion
1 teaspoon chopped fresh thyme or ½ teaspoon dried
½ cup diced ham
1 cup sliced mushrooms
3 medium tomatoes, seeded, cut into small wedges
1 teaspoon sugar
1 tablespoon flour
1 packet chicken bouillon powder
½ cup white wine
1 cup whipping cream
2 sprigs parsley
1 teaspoon fresh tarragon or ½ teaspoon dried
4 cups cooked rice

Serves 4.

use the poles as loose underpinnings until the plants are tall enough to be tied loosely to them. I use those flexible ties you get in packages of plastic bags, but nurseries (and hardware stores) stock an endless variety of garden twines.

The good gardener is fearless and pinches back the tops of his tomato plants as soon as they have sprouted to about two inches. Don't be timid about this. The plants will be grateful to you, in the final analysis, because their energies can be concentrated on a healthy harvest rather than a showy growth.

I water my tomatoes often in warm weather. It's best to do this before sunrise or after sundown and to water generously. Spray pesticides at your own good judgment. I never do, because frankly I prefer having a patch of rust on my tomatoes, or a cutworm, to including any more chemical warfare in my life.

Having said all that, I am reminded that the best use a tomato can be put to is the dining room table.

Consider the following spareribs—better than any you have *ever* eaten in your life! They are tomatoey, peppered, and sugared to a fare-thee-well, and a treat on the barbecue or off. I make them in the broiler of my stove and they are marvelous. Oh yes, the recipe is from a wonderful pamphlet published by the Baptist Church of Alexandria, Virginia, forty years ago.

4½ to 5 pounds spareribs
1   onion stuck with 2 cloves
¼ cup soy sauce
2   teaspoons dried marjoram
1   teaspoon salt
½ teaspoon freshly ground pepper
2   tablespoons olive oil
2   yellow onions, finely chopped
2   cloves garlic, minced
½ tablespoon finely chopped fresh ginger
1   can (17 ounces) imported Italian tomatoes with juice, mashed
1   cup chili sauce
¼ cup dark brown sugar
5   tablespoons honey
⅓ cup soy sauce
¼ cup dry sherry
Pinch of cayenne pepper
1   tablespoon chili powder
⅛ teaspoon dried oregano

Serves 4 to 6.

FREETOWN SPARERIBS

1 Cut the ribs into 3-inch sections. Place in a large saucepan with water to cover. Add the onion with cloves, ¼ cup soy sauce, marjoram, salt, and pepper. Bring to a boil; reduce heat. Simmer 1 hour, turning ribs once. Drain.

2 Meanwhile, heat the oil in a medium saucepan. Add the chopped onions, garlic, and ginger. Cook over low heat, stirring constantly, 5 minutes. Add remaining ingredients; bring to a boil. Reduce heat; simmer, stirring occasionally, 30 minutes.

3 Heat oven to 350°. Using a sharp knife, cut rib sections into single portions and arrange in a single layer in a roasting pan or baking dish (pan must fit under broiler). Spoon sauce over and around the ribs.

4 Bake 30 minutes, turning once and basting well with sauce. Place ribs under broiler until crisp; turn and broil other side until equally crisp.

Note: Spareribs may be prepared in advance through Step 3 and refrigerated before baking.

The finest tomatoes in the world are grown along the eastern seaboard of the United States—most of them in the middle of big cities, like New York. City folk without the luxury of a terrace garden seem to make do admirably with window boxes and office ledge arboretums. And a local landscape gardener informs me that Ramapos and Ultra-Fantastics bloom on the highest towers of the World Trade Center these days!

Yeoman agriculture—lofty or otherwise—produces at least a summer remedy for the appalling supermarket selection. The packaged tomatoes one finds nowadays are grim! Those baseball-hard orbs, packed green and shipped to ripen prematurely, never come to a harvest at all. And, what is worse, most of them are sprayed with ethylene gas, which anesthetizes whatever lingering flavor they might have accumulated in a normal shelf life.

Buy tomatoes only when you are absolutely desperate! I combine the least dreadful Florida yield with cans of imported Italian *pomidoro* and pray for an early spring!

One robust recipe that makes do with such kitchen subterfuge is a pork stew that mixes the tomatoes with sauerkraut, herbs, and assorted spices. There's no denying that it is best made when the fruit is heavy on the vine—but beggars, obviously, cannot be choosers!

SAUERKRAUT WITH PORK

1 Heat oven to 375°. Sprinkle meat with salt and pepper. Heat oil in a Dutch oven; saute the meat until brown on all sides. Cook covered over medium-high heat 15 minutes. Stir in the onion, bay leaf, thyme, caraway seeds, tomatoes, and sugar. Bake covered until tender, 1½ to 2 hours.

2 Meanwhile, saute the salt pork in a heavy skillet over medium heat until golden. Transfer pork with ½ teaspoon pan drippings to a baking dish. Sprinkle with crushed juniper berries.

3 Wash and drain sauerkraut, if desired; squeeze out all liquid. Place over the salt pork; make a well in the center. Tie the garlic, peppercorns, and parsley in cheesecloth and place in the well. Pour the stock, wine, and water over the sauerkraut. Bake covered ½ hour. Drain.

4 Stir sauerkraut mixture into meat. Cook over medium heat until hot, about 5 minutes. (Serve with boiled potatoes.)

2½ pounds boneless pork, cut into
 1½- to 2-inch cubes
Salt and freshly ground pepper
2 tablespoons vegetable oil
1 large onion, chopped
1 bay leaf, crumbled
Pinch of dried thyme
1 teaspoon caraway seeds
1 can (8 ounces) imported Italian
 tomatoes
2 large ripe fresh tomatoes,
 chopped
Pinch of sugar
⅓ cup diced salt pork or bacon
6 juniper berries, crushed
1 package (2 pounds) sauerkraut
1 small clove garlic
6 peppercorns
1 sprig parsley
1 cup chicken stock
1 cup white wine or vermouth
½ cup water

Serves 4 to 6.

Mexico's link to the tomato is pre-Colombian. The fruit first grew wild there and the Aztec name, *xitomate,* is still applied. According to Diana Kennedy, Mexican tomatoes are among the very best in the world. Picked ripe and brought to the market at peak color, they are fat, juicy, and sweet.

Unfortunately, not much Mexican produce is imported into the United States. So when you do see a basket of tomatoes (or bell peppers) from Mexico, stock up. Their unparalleled quality shows up especially well in dishes dependent upon the flavor of a really prime tomato—like this south-of-the-border stew studded with nuggets of yellow corn.

MEXICAN PORK STEW WITH CORN

½ cup butter (approximately)
1 large onion, chopped
1 tablespoon minced garlic
⅓ cup flour (approximately)
Salt and freshly ground pepper
3 pounds boneless pork, cut into 1-inch cubes
3 tablespoons vegetable oil
3 cups strong beef broth
2 tablespoons chili powder
1 tablespoon ground cumin
2 teaspoons chopped fresh oregano or 1 teaspoon dried
1 large tomato, peeled, seeded, chopped
3 green or red sweet peppers, seeded, cut into thin strips
3 ears of corn
10 pimiento-stuffed olives, cut in half
6 to 8 cups cooked rice

Serves 6 to 8.

1 Melt 2 tablespoons butter in skillet; saute onion and garlic until transparent, about 5 minutes. Transfer to a Dutch oven.

2 Season flour with salt and pepper. Coat meat with flour mixture (using more flour if necessary). Heat oil and 4 tablespoons butter in a large, heavy skillet. Add meat, about ⅓ at a time, and brown on all sides, adding more butter to the pan if necessary. Transfer meat to the Dutch oven.

3 Stir broth into the skillet over high heat; cook 3 minutes, scraping bottom and sides of pan. Pour into Dutch oven. Add the chili powder, cumin, oregano, and tomato. Simmer covered over low heat until meat is very tender, about 2½ hours.

4 Melt 2 tablespoons butter in skillet. Add peppers; cook covered over medium heat until crisp-tender, about 5 minutes. Remove from heat.

5 Cut corn off cobs. Add to Dutch oven and cook over medium heat 5 minutes. Stir in peppers and olives. Serve with rice.

The French cooks of Provence, past masters at anything and everything that concerns the *pomme d'amour,* invariably dip their

tomatoes in boiling water before they peel and seed them—even for a simple *salade Niçoise*.

I am less dogmatic on the subject. I usually split a tomato in half (like an orange) and merely squeeze the halves over a sink until the seeds run free. I don't peel the skin unless it's rubbery tough—but you will notice exceptions to this rule.

One of my best tomato prescriptions is the following sauce of my own invention. It's a quick and satisfying emollient for pasta that can be made within one hour. The secrets are butter (don't be skimpy) and fresh basil. If the basil is dried, sprinkle it over a few sprigs of fresh parsley and chop the herbs together.

HOMEMADE TOMATO SAUCE

Melt the butter over low heat. Add remaining ingredients. Cook over medium heat, stirring frequently, until thick.

½ cup unsalted butter
4 large ripe tomatoes, peeled, seeded, chopped
1 medium yellow onion, chopped
1 clove garlic, mashed
1 rib celery, finely chopped
1 teaspoon fresh basil leaves or ½ teaspoon dried
1 teaspoon fresh oregano leaves or ½ teaspoon dried
Pinch of thyme
1 tablespoon sugar
¼ teaspoon grated orange peel

Makes about 1 to 1½ cups.

Ripe tomatoes are truly one of my favored foods—a fact that has always amazed my mother, for I detested them with ill-concealed passion as a child. My aversion was so pronounced that I once faced restriction to summer-camp barracks for 24 hours, rather than swallow a mouthful. Time, obviously, amends quirks of palate. My pet recipe for the tomato season follows:

TOMATO HEAVEN

Split the tomato and spread each half lightly with honey. Salt and pepper them well. Add a dab of sour cream, if desired. *Delicious!*

1 ripe tomato
2 teaspoons honey
Salt and freshly ground pepper
1 tablespoon sour cream (optional)

When my friend George and I were in college, back in the days of frat hops and slumber parties, coeds had you up to their dormitory rooms for one reason alone—cake sent from home! These delights were usually spooned up on squares of Kleenex and eaten in bright light—with the door to the room open as wide as possible.

I am a Neanderthal man, obviously, but my memory still retains a special letch for a particular dormitory cake that I was permitted to taste but once (like forbidden fruit). It was the gift of a girl who admired me because I was six feet four inches tall. She was six-foot one. Her cake was a family specialty, a thick fudgy chocolate layer made, strangely enough, of tomato sauce and other ingredients.

I never logged more than a kiss with Edythe Laws. But here is what I have recreated of her largesse—which was generously apportioned thirty-six years ago. Only yesterday, it seems!

TOMATO DEVIL'S FOOD CAKE

4 ounces sweet chocolate
½ cup milk
1 cup dark brown sugar
1 egg yolk
2 cups sifted cake flour
1 teaspoon baking soda
½ teaspoon salt
½ cup unsalted butter
1 cup granulated sugar
2 eggs, separated
1 can (8 ounces) tomato sauce
1 tablespoon whipping cream
1 teaspoon vanilla

Serves 8 to 10.

1 Heat oven to 350°. Place the chocolate, milk, brown sugar, and 1 egg yolk in the top of a double boiler. Cook over hot water, stirring occasionally, until smooth and thickened.

2 Sift the flour with the soda and salt.

3 Cream the butter in a large mixing bowl. Add the granulated sugar; beat until light. Add 2 egg yolks, one at a time, mixing well after each addition. Combine tomato sauce with cream and vanilla. Add the tomato sauce mixture to the butter mixture in three parts, alternating with thirds of the flour mixture. Stir in the chocolate.

4 Beat the egg whites until stiff but not dry. Fold into the batter. Pour into two buttered and floured 9-inch round cake pans. Bake 25 minutes. Cool on a wire rack. Frost cake with My Mother's Chocolate Icing (see Index) or, for a more classic rendition, the following:

BOILED WHITE ICING

½ cup water
⅓ cup light corn syrup
2½ cups granulated sugar
2 egg whites
⅛ teaspoon salt
1 teaspoon orange juice
1½ teaspoons vanilla

Frosts a 2-layer, 9-inch cake.

1 Boil the water, corn syrup, and sugar together until mixture thickens. Test for doneness by dropping ½ teaspoon of mixture into a bowl of ice cold water; mixture should form a ball.

2 Beat the egg whites with the salt in a mixing bowl until stiff but not dry. Continue to beat, gradually adding the hot syrup mixture in a fine stream. Continue to beat until of spreading consistency. Beat in the orange juice and vanilla. (If the icing thickens before it is done, beat in a few drops of boiling water.)

Vanilla

I grew up in a family of ice cream lovers. And the delectable frozen food, I have always believed, was our sole reward for surviving the Great Depression. Even in the face of bank failures and mortgage foreclosures, my father maintained a connoisseurism about the subject of ice cream that was positively tonic.

Vanilla was unvaryingly his choice of flavor. While my mother's selection often wavered among coffee, strawberry, and peach, depending upon the season and her mood, my father always ate vanilla. And he became such a discerning critic of the golden elixir that he would suggest expeditions miles and miles away from our family turf just to test the quality of some newly touted Greek or German ice cream parlor's offerings.

My mother, somewhat more of a realist than my father, would tactlessly point out the arthritic condition of our antique Hudson automobile whenever her spouse proposed these quests. But his ice cream passion was so contagious that she rarely lagged behind when he suggested another "little evening spin." And yet another soda shoppe along the way!

Saturday nights, our family treat was never so much the different movie palaces in which we inevitably found ourselves (my father, you see, also had a circuit rider's zeal for discovering cinematic outposts), as the prospect of a frappé or a banana split after the show—eaten at some creamery my father had just gotten wind of from "one of the boys," a place that reputedly made its own stuff in the back!

While it was the thought of a tantalizing and uncommercial

vanilla confection that always sent my parent on these odysseys, the technicolor memory of honest-to-goodness homemade ice cream, cranked on a back porch, never belonged to him. That was my mother's preserve. But her tales of a bucolic girlhood, with four sisters taking turns arm-wrestling the ice and rock salt, produced such ambrosial fantasies that he (and I still) vicariously hankered after them.

As I have implied before, my father was a man of prejudiced appetite. All vanilla ice creams did not please him. And even when some did, he resented the intrusion of other flavors cheek-by-jowl in the carton.

"I don't care what you buy for yourself," he would counsel me before my nightly trip to the drug store where we bought our ice cream in bulk. "Just make sure he packs the vanilla last! On the top. So it doesn't get mixed up with anything else!"

I admired the taste of vanilla too, but in moderation. I liked it best allied with chocolate—with both substances stirred with a spoon into a runny, dun-colored soup.

My father had no tolerance at all for this predilection.

"That's a disgusting way to eat . . . " he would snort loftily each time he discovered me stirring away at my dessert plate, "and a perfect waste of vanilla cream in the bargain!"

Aside from ice cream, this man admitted few pleasures in his life and fewer vices, if I am any judge. He never looked at another woman because he thought my mother was perfect— even when plainly she was not. He drank infrequently; a glass of beer turned him instantly torpid and he stayed continent of any other alcoholic beverages.

He did like to gamble, however. During the Depression he wagered only on the horses—and often earned enough to pay our rent in a single afternoon (or so I learned after his death). Before the Depression, he had maintained a penny-ante pinochle game in the back of his electrical shop. The diversion started in late afternoon (when he returned from "the job") and often went on until well past midnight. Like a true benedict, my father would excuse himself from the game to come home for supper (a mile or so away from the action), eat his meal, fold his napkin, and, kissing his wife as he went out the door, return to the cards again.

His gambler's blood grew thin when his money ran out, which was really rather a shame because winning made him very cheerful around the house. And losing kept him equally amenable out of contrition.

He had been a very rich man at a young age and he married my mother in a flush of victory—after the county had awarded him a contract to install all the power lines in the borough of Queens.

I cannot truly remember him in those palmy days. He lost his fortune in bank failures and ill-conceived land development schemes when I was about eight or nine years old. My earliest memories of my father were of his absences. An appointed alderman, he was always off on political sorties: Turkish baths with the mayor; to Albany to see the governor; or away on inspection tours of prison and postal facilities upstate while we waited patiently at home for his return.

During the dark days of the mid-1930s, after his business faltered and my mother was forced to work to support the household, my father's absences ended. He was always either around the house during the day or at the movies.

If I spent the Depression in the kitchen, my parent spent his time at picture shows. Waiting for illusive projects to materialize, houses to be built and wired, he occupied himself with endless rounds of matinees. What he really wanted, I suppose, was a place to hibernate until the promised prosperity came around the corner. And their low, ten-cent admission made movie houses more attractive than sleeping at home.

There was a quasi-mystery film called *Blessed Event* that featured Lee Tracy, the noted stage actor and long-time favorite of my father, making his screen debut. It played the local theater in our town for quite a long time and, while my father admitted to me (in private) that he had seen it on at least a dozen occasions, he didn't know the denouement.

"I never find out which guy turns out to be the murderer," he complained, "because I fall asleep half an hour after the movie begins!"

My father always believed his fortune would change.

"I'll be a rich man again, yet!" he would promise me as we drove across the darkened Queensborough Bridge to Manhattan on Thursdays to collect my mother after her late-night employments.

"You'll see!"

I wanted to. Truth to tell, my father was somewhat of an embarrassment to me as an adolescent—sleeping at the movies. He was so ashamed of the fact that my mother worked that he often pretended to old cronies that she was away or visiting, when she was actually waiting on tables at Schrafft's or demonstrating Hartz Mountain bird food with an army of trained canaries (which she detested) in a New York Woolworth's. Eventually she became a successful saleslady at Macy's fur department (working on a commission plus salary) and her employment could no longer be denied. By then, my father grudgingly admitted that his wife's income paid for many of our household expenses, but all luxuries, he insisted, were still exclusively his prerogative.

When we went out to dinner, he chauvinistically called for the check. And those Saturday-night movies were always his dispensation as well, no matter how grand the picture palace he had found for us to visit. He was a generous man who truly enjoyed largesse and it is a pity that beneficence was ever denied him. But he was not above arguing with the managers of those same movie theaters about his inalienable rights—to my eternal mortification, let it be said.

I was a boy who grew tall fast and by age eleven I matched my father's height; so a problem invariably arose when my parent purchased a half-price admission in my behalf.

"That kid is fourteen at least," ticket-takers would snarl as they inspected me charily from head to toe before calling the manager for arbitration. "He's a big boy," the executives would usually concur.

"You're damned right," my father would rage, "but he's under twelve! Under twelve, *half-price,* is what your sign says. Right?"

The managers never looked into my father's eye.

"How old *are* you, son?" they would quiz me instead.

I never wished to answer that question but my father stood at my shoulder, prodding me to it. "Tell this guy your birthday before we miss the start of the show!"

I always did, of course (flushed with shame at the imposition), but I spoke the date with extreme reluctance. My father, to his credit, understood the wound inflicted on my pride, but he was adamant about the issue.

"It's not the extra quarter damn it! It's the principle of the thing," he would maintain, pounding the marble counter of the ice cream parlor we visited after the show.

"I hate it," I muttered, scraping at my sundae.

"I don't blame you. But you're not twelve yet, are you?" He didn't wait for my answer. "And they have no right to say that you are! If they want to charge tickets by size, let them change their damned policy!"

I remember staring down at the silver ice cream dish before me, hoping he would stop talking about it. Other patrons had begun to listen, too. But my father needed reinforcement for his argument and my mother and sister were determinedly noncommittal on the subject.

"Look at the way you eat your ice cream, for Chrissakes! Stirring it up like that! When you're twelve, I hope you'll eat your vanilla (he always pronounced it "van-ella") like a man!"

Like *me,* he meant!

A jingoist to the teeth, my father certainly would have chafed at the information that vanilla was an essence of Mexican origin.

More irksome still would have been the knowledge that the Spanish conquistadors only brought it to European kitchens because they considered it a satisfactory adjunct to *chocolate!* Indeed, vanilla and chocolate seemed such perfect taste-mates to Cortez that the two flavors remained inseparable until an English chef advised Elizabeth I that the flavor of vanilla was quite delicious alone. (And that, my friends, really shook up the ice cream trade!)

Cortez also divined that *vainilla* (meaning "little scabbards") enhanced coffee as well as chocolate. He sent letters to the royal chefs of Spain advising that equal parts of vanilla pods and coffee beans be roasted together for the king's late night beverage, as this mixture would "provide a deep night's sleep for his Majesty without horrid dreams." The suggestion was not taken—but only because vanilla was too rare a commodity to be used to indulge even such an elevated slumberer.

Vanilla (*Vanilla planifolia*) is a member of the orchid family, but it grows on high, treacherous mountains and comes to bloom a mere day each year. The fragile, yellowish-green flower makes way for a cluster of longish green pods (not unlike garden-variety lima beans on the vine) which, when dried, become the flavoring agent.

Vanilla is the only New World gift, incidentally, for which history may be grateful to Cortez. More precious by far than the gold he plundered from Montezuma or the kingdoms he claimed for God and taxed mercilessly for the realm, this delicate flavoring seems to make all sweets sweeter. Yet it also tames the passionate sting of acid on the tongue!

I am thinking particularly of a dulcet raspberry custard that gains its majesty from a soupçon of vanilla in the cream. But no other culinary seasoning can lend more authority to lemon tarts, orange mousse, or even pineapple Bavarian cream! And where would the wonderful world of home baking (butter, flour, sugar, and eggs) be without vanilla?

The first recipe I offer from an enormous personal vanilla collection comes, appropriately, from Guadalajara, but I have eaten versions of it in Haiti and Puerto Rico, too. A touch of native vanilla gives the golden kernels of this splendid, crustless pie a benign but not sugary taste. Needless to say, Fresh Corn Tart is best prepared with fresh-picked corn but frozen kernels (or, better yet, whole frozen corn sliced off the cob) makes a very tolerable substitution.

I relish this dish served in confederation with golden, crusty fried chicken but it also makes a very splendid centerpiece for a country-style breakfast—with a rasher of grilled ham alongside and a healthy pitcher of honest-to-gosh maple syrup to smooth the rough edges off a Bloody Mary!

FRESH CORN TART

2 tablespoons bread crumbs
1½ cups fresh corn (about 3 large
    ears cut from the cob)
1 teaspoon salt
¼ cup granulated sugar
2 tablespoons butter, melted
3 eggs, separated
2 tablespoons all-purpose flour
½ cup whipping cream
¾ cup milk
1 teaspoon vanilla
Freshly ground pepper

Serves 4.

1 Heat oven to 400°. Grease a 1-quart souffle dish and dust with bread crumbs.

2 Combine the corn, salt, sugar, and butter; mix well. Beat the egg yolks with the flour in a large bowl until smooth; stir in the cream, milk, and vanilla. Add the corn to the egg yolk mixture.

3 Beat the egg whites until stiff, but not dry; fold into the egg yolk mixture. Pour into the prepared souffle dish. Sprinkle with fresh pepper.

4 Bake 20 minutes. Reduce heat to 375°; bake until a toothpick inserted in center of tart comes out fairly clean, 35 to 40 minutes.

A particular childhood association imprinted my every taste bud with an impossible craving for soft, vanilla sponge cake. Or better yet, ladyfingers—those ductile confections that seem to melt on my tongue *sans* any mastication whatsoever.

I love ladyfingers best with a bowl of heavily sugared fruit and a pitcher of cream as thick as a spring thaw. With this treat, I prefer only a glass of milk and a napkin tied around my chin to catch the juices when the raspberries or blackberries go wild (but, let it be noted, I usually partake of the exercise in more accepted garb).

There are several winning desserts in this tome (like Norman Giguere's Coffee Refrigerator Cake) that are absolutely dependent upon ladyfingers for their substance—but I suggest you make your first batch for sheer indulgence.

LADYFINGERS

3 eggs, separated
½ cup plus 1 tablespoon granulated
    sugar
1 teaspoon vanilla
⅔ cup sifted cake flour
Confectioners' sugar

Makes about 2 dozen.

1 Heat oven to 325°. Butter and flour two baking sheets.

2 Beat the egg yolks with ½ cup sugar. Add the vanilla and continue beating until light and fluffy.

3 Beat the whites until stiff but not dry. Beat in 1 tablespoon sugar; continue beating several minutes. Fold egg whites gently into egg yolks in three parts, alternating with thirds of the flour. (Do this carefully, as batter *must* remain light.)

4 Spoon batter into a pastry bag fitted with a medium-sized tube. Pipe batter onto baking sheets in even 3-inch lines about 1 inch apart. Sift confectioners' sugar over tops. Bake until cake springs back when touched, about 20 minutes.

Vanilla beans were born in Mexico and that country still produces the best crop—for my money. But most vanilla is now harvested in the islands of Madagascar. Most of the orchids imported into the United States are nurtured in Madagascar's semi-temperate climate as well, but it is the vanilla trade that made the plantations rich. The multi-million dollar industry that has developed in Madagascar over the past two decades has even spawned bootleg vanilla pods, which are smuggled out of the country to be processed. So most legal vanilla beans are now branded with a bizarre series of pin-prick markings to discourage vanilla bean hijacking by miscreant spice mongers.

Like orchids, vanilla beans require special climactic conditions for the initial phase of their growth. And the flowers must be painstakingly pollinated by hand and scrupulously tended until the pods are ripe enough to be picked. Then the individual beans must be hand-gathered, graded, and dried, in a slow tedious process; months may elapse before they are ready for shipment. The mature pods will look like nothing more than shriveled twigs but their aroma and delicate body make them comparable to fine vintage wines.

The vanilla bean's definitive seasoning is trapped in the thousands of tiny specklike seeds inside the dried brown pod. And while many excellent commercial extracts combine these grains with fermented essences (in liquid vanilla pressings), there is nothing in the world, for this cook at least, like the original pod for flavoring.

I keep my vanilla bean in an old apothecary bottle with a tight, ground-glass stopper. More to the point, after I place the vanilla bean inside the glass container, I pour in enough cognac or 100-proof vodka to immerse the pod completely in liquid. Within a month or so, the alcohol takes on a deep amberlike hue and its aroma can knock your hat off. It is the purest infusion of golden vanilla you have ever sniffed!

This kind of distilled flavoring is most desirable when recipes call for large measures of liquid vanilla. When the alcohol starts to run low, I merely add a few drams to the original concoction and keep pouring away. Be advised *not* to keep this tincture on a windowsill or in direct sunlight; alcohol quickly loses its potency (unless it is in a dark-colored bottle) outside a whiskey cabinet!

The foregone conclusion (as I am sure you have gathered by now) is that a home-brewed vanilla works best in dishes that require body rather than illusive seasoning—like a wonderful blighty devise, Vanilla Treacle Tart, that takes a "quarter cuppa" vanilla in its canon. It's a dessert that men, women, and children adore universally, especially when the sweet is amended with a blob of (what else?) vanilla-flavored whipped cream!

VANILLA TREACLE TART

½ recipe Grandma Rose's Favorite
   Pie Crust (see Index)
1 egg
½ cup condensed milk
½ cup light corn syrup
¼ cup vanilla
½ cup ground almonds
Pinch of salt

Serves 8.

1 Prepare the pastry and chill 1 hour.

2 Heat oven to 400°. Roll out the dough as thin as possible. Line a 9-inch quiche pan; trim edges and flute. Line pastry with aluminum foil; weight with dried beans or rice. Bake 5 minutes. Remove foil and rice; bake 5 minutes. Cool slightly.

3 Beat the egg in a mixing bowl. Whisk in the remaining ingredients. Pour into pastry shell. Bake 15 minutes. Reduce oven heat to 350°; bake 20 minutes longer. Cool on a wire rack.

Vanilla is reported to be the world's most universally accepted flavor. The Chinese take exception, of course, but they have managed to resist the blandishments of chocolate as well for over six centuries. And even the worldly Maoists show little sign of cranking up the bamboo flavoring curtain—after all this time!

The odd thing about vanilla, unlike chocolate, is that you are barely aware of the seasoning when it is giving its best performance. That small brackish bottle of extract in most kitchen pantries—destined to be measured out (like T. S. Eliot's life-line) in teaspoons—usually turns anonymity into a virtue.

Once neophyte cooks understand the part that a scant teaspoon and a half of vanilla plays in a frangible shortbread recipe from Scotland, their whole world of kitchen perceptions will expand. For vanilla not only smooths the raw taste of the flour and tones down the egginess of the golden yolk, but it also turns the very sugar sweeter and the orange peel zestier. Most important of all, it makes the cup of unsalted butter yield all the richness it possesses—and it unifies all the peculiar and unique tastes into one remarkable and harmonious layer in the bargain!

ST. BRIDE SHORTBREAD

1 Heat oven to 325°. Cream the butter with the sugar in a mixing bowl. Beat in the egg yolk. Add the cream, vanilla, and orange peel; mix well.

2 Combine the flours and work them into the butter mixture with your fingers. Knead lightly and form into a ball.

3 Invert a 9-inch round cake pan; butter and flour the underside of the pan. Press the dough ball onto the surface to form a smooth 9-inch circle. Sprinkle a baking sheet with cornmeal; invert the dough onto the sheet, loosening it from the cake pan with a metal spatula if necessary. Smooth the top and press the edges with the tines of a fork.

4 Bake 10 minutes. Remove from oven and press shortbread lightly in the center with a shortbread mold. (A decorative cutter or butter mold will work as well.) Score the shortbread into 8 to 12 wedges around the pattern, using a pastry wheel or serrated knife. Return to oven and bake until edges begin to brown, about 40 minutes. Remove to a wire rack and cool completely.

1 cup unsalted butter, softened
½ cup granulated sugar
1 egg yolk
2 tablespoons whipping cream
1½ teaspoons vanilla
½ teaspoon grated orange peel
2½ cups all-purpose flour
½ cup rice flour
Cornmeal

Serves 8 to 12.

I never buy anything labeled "artificial vanilla" or "ethyl vanillin." Besides being weak sisters in the flavoring department, these substitute extracts are not substantially cheaper than the 100% pure essence.

The best and most economical way to enhance your flavoring palette is to buy vanilla beans. Most supermarkets across the country carry the Spice Island brand of vanilla beans. Many specialty food shops or gourmet departments of major stores sell them too. If you are in a sticky wicket of the country that can't supply reliable pods, you may order them from Aphrodisia, 28 Carmine Street, New York, N.Y. 10014. Mexican vanilla beans are available by mail from Casa Moneo, 210 West 15th Street, New York, N.Y. 10014.

Those of you who didn't learn how to use vanilla beans at grandma's knee, please take note of some small wisdom on the subject:

—Even if you don't want to get your vanilla bean "soused," keep it in an airtight container. Glass is best for this.

—Vanilla may be buried in sugar to produce a delicately scented sweetening. But it's difficult to figure the amount to use in

recipes that specify sugar and vanilla quantities separately! I keep a very small jar of powdered sugar with a third of a vanilla bean in it just for sweet shakings. But be my guest on the subject.

—Do realize that no matter where you store your vanilla the bean retains its bouquet even after months of use. Don't throw away a snippet of vanilla after you've boiled it with milk or in a sugar syrup—it can be re-used. The dried pod is delicious grated into hundreds of sweet dishes. Only if the vanilla bean has been split to extract a more pungent flavor would I not bother to use it again!

The Marquis de Frangipani was an Italian perfume-maker who flavored everything he created (from ice creams to gloves and silk scarves) with a combination of vanilla essence and bitter almonds—which sounds awful to me! But Italians also use vanilla and a mite of almond in a curious milky extract that they mix with fizzy water or serve over shaved ice. It is called *oregata*—and it's not awful at all!

In the Caribbean, vanilla often is blended with rum and coconut milk in a lethal drink they call a "Rum Koka" and served in an enormous green coconut shell. I say it's lethal on the world's best authority—my own!

In Denmark, where cooks are fearless, they roast geese with a basting of rhubarb and apple sauce well-flavored with vanilla. In Provence they prepare *quenelles de brochet* of ground pike, orange peel, and a hint of vanilla at Eastertime. I've never tried this dish—but I shall when next I am asked, I promise.

Salzburg Nockerl is a lovely German froth (I guess you might call it baked meringues) that is remarkably dependent upon the bit of vanilla bean scraped into its exquisite devise. I present it to you with my compliments as well as a beauty of a vanilla sauce that should be made in advance of the nockerl and chilled before serving.

SALZBURG NOCKERL

½ recipe Classic Vanilla Sauce
  (recipe follows)
3 egg yolks
1 teaspoon all-purpose flour
Grated peel of ½ lemon
1 teaspoon vanilla plus (optional) some seeds scraped from vanilla bean
1 tablespoon butter
5 egg whites
1 tablespoon granulated sugar
3 tablespoons superfine sugar

Serves 2 to 4.

1 Make vanilla sauce.

2 Heat oven to 425°. Beat egg yolks lightly; whisk in the flour, lemon peel, and vanilla.

3 Place 1 tablespoon butter in a glass pie plate or ceramic quiche pan; place in oven for 5 minutes.

4 Beat egg whites until soft peaks form. Sprinkle with the granulated sugar; beat until stiff. Fold into the egg yolk mixture.

5 Remove pie plate from oven; swirl butter to coat bottom and sides. Spoon the batter onto plate in four high mounds. Bake 10 minutes. Sprinkle with superfine sugar and serve with vanilla sauce.

Note: This dessert is also wonderful served with maple syrup for breakfast. Omit the vanilla, add a good grating of fresh nutmeg, and substitute confectioners' sugar for the superfine sugar.

CLASSIC VANILLA SAUCE

1 Beat the egg yolks with the sugar in the top of a double boiler. Whisk in the milk. Cook over hot water, stirring constantly, until thick, about 30 minutes. Remove from heat.

2 Whisk in the vanilla. Cool to room temperature.

3 Stir the kirsch into the sauce. Fold in the cream. Refrigerate until chilled.

Note: Recipe may be cut in half.

6 egg yolks
1 cup granulated sugar
2¼ cups milk, scalded
1 teaspoon vanilla
1 tablespoon kirsch liqueur
½ cup whipping cream, whipped

Makes 3½ to 4 cups.

From France (where clever cooks add a speck of vanilla to fruit dishes and jams to accent their natural sweetness) comes Alice B. Toklas's recipe for a Rice Pudding *nonpareil.*

If you have ever wondered where all the great flavors and remarkable tastes of yesterday went, stop the rumination at once! They are all still at your fingertips, collected by dedicated cooks and devoted food-lovers like the late Miss Toklas. Look up her books in libraries—they are gems of cuisine, every one!

Her prodigal dessert is best made early in the day (or even the day before), as the delicate custard and the sauce, too, seem to ripen magnificently in a cold refrigerator.

I have my own conceit for eating this dish. I love it exactly as limned below, but with an extravagant bit of overkill—a spoonful or two of freshly stewed raspberries to top the creamy sauce.

Like the canny French I was speaking of, I suggest you stew your fruit in the following manner: Bring 1 cup of berries, ½ cup of water, and ¼ cup of sugar to the boil. Add 1 teaspoon of essence of vanilla. Do not stir; turn off the heat and allow the mixture to cool.

AN UNEXCELLED
RICE PUDDING

¼ pound rice
1 quart milk
Pinch of salt
8 egg yolks
1 cup granulated sugar
5 tablespoons all-purpose flour
2 cups milk, scalded
1 teaspoon vanilla
3 egg whites
Classic Vanilla Sauce (see preceding
   recipe)

Serves 6 to 8.

1 Heat oven to 350°. Combine the rice, 1 quart milk, and salt in the top of a double boiler. Cook over hot water, stirring occasionally, until rice is tender, about 1 hour. Transfer to a bowl and let stand while proceeding with the next two steps.

2 Beat the egg yolks with an electric mixer at medium speed until light and lemon-colored. Sift the sugar with the flour; gradually beat into the yolks. Beat 10 minutes. Add the scalded milk.

3 Cook egg yolk mixture in the top of a double boiler over hot water, stirring constantly, until thick enough to coat a wooden spoon.

4 Strain egg yolk mixture into a large bowl. Beat in the vanilla. Drain rice; stir into egg yolk mixture.

5 Beat egg whites until stiff but not dry; fold into rice mixture. Pour into a buttered 2-quart souffle dish. Bake 25 to 30 minutes; center should be slightly wet. Serve Rice Pudding slightly warm, at room temperature, or chilled, with vanilla sauce.

Note: Don't use parboiled rice.

Yet another raspberry and vanilla alignment? I must confess that I love the confederation of flavors—and in my emotional state (unaided by French chefs) devised the following variant on a classic crème renversée.
   I hate to brag—but it's *delicious!*

1¼ cups granulated sugar
2 packages (10 ounces each) frozen
   raspberries, thawed
1½ cups whipping cream
3 eggs
3 egg yolks
1½ teaspoons vanilla
½ teaspoon dark rum

Serves 6.

RASPBERRY FLAN

1 Heat oven to 250°. Place a 1-quart souffle dish in the oven until warm, about 10 minutes.

2 Place ½ cup sugar in a small, heavy saucepan. Cook over medium-high heat, stirring constantly with a wooden spoon, until sugar caramelizes. (The color of the caramel depends on how long it is cooked; so do not allow syrup to burn.)

3 Pour the hot syrup into the warm souffle dish. Hold dish with potholders and quickly swirl the syrup, tilting dish to coat bottom and sides. (The syrup will harden as it cools; so work quickly.) When syrup has ceased to run, invert the souffle dish on a plate. When dish is cool to the touch, turn it upright. (This caramelized mold may be prepared well in advance.)

4 Increase oven heat to 350°. Using a wooden spoon, press 1½ packages thawed raspberries through a fine sieve into a bowl. Crush pulp so that nothing is left but the seeds; discard seeds. (You should have 1 cup of liquid.)

5 Mix the raspberry liquid with the cream in a saucepan; heat to just below a simmer.

6 In a large bowl, beat remaining ¾ cup sugar with the eggs and egg yolks until light and foamy. Beat in the vanilla, rum, and hot raspberry mixture.

7 Pour mixture into prepared souffle dish. Place dish in a deep roasting pan; pour boiling water into the pan to depth halfway up sides of souffle dish. Place in bottom half of oven; immediately reduce heat to 325°. Bake until a knife inserted in the center comes out clean, 45 to 50 minutes. (*Make sure the water in the roasting pan does not boil at any time. Add a little cold water to the pan if it does.*)

8 Remove souffle dish from water; allow to cool. Refrigerate covered until well chilled, 3 to 4 hours.

9 To unmold flan: Place serving dish in the freezer 10 minutes. Meanwhile, fill a large saucepan with 1 inch of water; bring to a boil and remove from heat. Dip a sharp knife into the water; run it around the edges of the flan. Set the souffle dish in the water 5 seconds to heat bottom. Immediately place the serving dish over the souffle dish and invert it. The flan will come free easily. Decorate with remaining raspberries. (Serve with whipped cream flavored with 1 teaspoon kirsch liqueur, if desired.)

Note: This tip bears repetition: *Make sure the water in the roasting pan does not boil at any time!* If it does, the custard will turn grainy and all will be lost—well, maybe not all, but the lovely texture certainly will be destroyed. If the oven heat is not *à point,* as they say, the custard will take longer to set. But don't be afraid if the darn thing seems runny and has to remain in the oven for an hour; as long as the water remains still, the custard will set well!

The following Vanilla Blanc Mange is a custard-mousse-*bavaroise* of an entirely different stripe. The trick here is adding vanilla ice cream to cool your custard quickly. Need I really add that the better the quality of the "vanilla cream," as my father liked to call it, the better the quality of your blanc mange! I am not suggesting that you necessarily whip up a batch of homemade vanilla before you start the next prescription—but by some strange coincidence, there does happen to be the most mirific recipe at the very end of this chapter. Just something to bear in mind!

VANILLA BLANC MANGE

3 egg yolks
⅓ cup granulated sugar
¼ teaspoon vanilla or 1-inch piece of vanilla bean
1½ tablespoons cornstarch
½ cup milk combined with ¼ cup whipping cream, scalded
3 heaping tablespoons vanilla ice cream
1 tablespoon unflavored gelatin
¼ cup white crème de cacao
¾ cup whipping cream, whipped stiff
3 egg whites, beaten stiff

Serves 6 to 8.

1 Beat the egg yolks with the sugar until light. Add the vanilla, if using extract. Whisk in the cornstarch; then add the hot milk mixture. Beat until smooth. Add the vanilla bean, if using the bean. Cook in the top of a double boiler over hot water, stirring constantly, until thick. Remove vanilla bean. Cool slightly.

2 Add the vanilla ice cream and allow to melt without stirring. Refrigerate custard 1 hour.

3 Combine the gelatin and creme de cacao in a small bowl; place bowl in pan of hot water. Stir mixture until gelatin is dissolved. Cool.

4 Combine the cold custard with the gelatin mixture in a large bowl. Fold in the whipped cream; then fold in the egg whites. Pour into a serving bowl. Refrigerate at least 6 hours or overnight. (This dessert is of a soft texture—unlike a mousse or a bavarian—and is quite delicious with a fruit sauce, such as pureed raspberries, or a delicate chocolate sauce.)

Michel Guerard, the guru of *nouvelle cuisine*, is said to have admitted to a hankering to add a drop of vanilla to hollandaise and béarnaise sauces—to enhance the tone of those emollients while softening the acidity of the lemon juice and vinegar. I pass the thought on to you *untried*.

I prefer vanilla in tradition-bound formulas that maximize

my sense of emotional comfort when I lick the spoon. Like broiled cream, which is French, most certainly. Or is it? I was recently informed that my sovereign rendering of Crème Brûlée—despite its froggish cognomen—was invented by a chef at Trinity college in Cambridge, England, around the century's turn. Whoever was truly the designer is unimportant here. The classic dessert could not be improved—in any language.

CRÈME BRÛLÉE

1 Heat oven to 325°. Heat the cream and granulated sugar in the top of a double boiler over hot water until sugar is dissolved.

2 Beat the egg yolks in a medium bowl until light and lemon-colored. Gradually pour in the hot cream. Add the vanilla. Strain mixture into a 1½- to 2-quart ovenproof serving dish.

3 Place the serving dish in a roasting pan; pour boiling water into the pan to a depth of 1 to 1½ inches. Place pan in the oven. Bake until a sharp knife inserted in the center comes out fairly clean, about 1½ hours. (Time varies with the weather.) Remove dish from water; allow to cool. Refrigerate at least 6 hours or overnight.

4 About 15 minutes before serving, heat broiling unit. Sprinkle light brown sugar over custard. Place dish in a pan and surround with ice. Place under broiler until the sugar topping is melted and brown. Serve immediately.

3 cups whipping cream
6 tablespoons granulated sugar
6 egg yolks
2 teaspoons vanilla
½ cup light brown sugar

Serves 6 to 8.

More vanilla—excelsior! The following confections are of the same old-time swag as Miss Toklas's memorable rice pudding, but these are purely American in character. Both recipes are long on family tradition, but the formula in each case has been appended somewhat by generations of good cooks who knew when to be expedient and when to hold fast!

Lavinia Mumphard was a dearly-beloved black lady who *did* for me for years and years until she died. Her forebears were Gullah people and though she cooked plainly, in the southern style, odd conceits of flavoring (like combining lemon juice and vanilla) betrayed African antecedents. Her Vanilla Caramel Layer Cake was one of a trio of great cakes—all utterly delicious—that she would produce if prompted sufficiently. (The others were a carrot loaf and a tenderly moist three-layer affair of crushed hazelnuts and pecans.) I made her write down the caramel ingredients on the back of a brown paper sack one morning between vacuum and broom. And though I mostly had to reconstruct the flavor, since Ms. Mumphard never remembered how to cook anything exactly the same way twice, this recipe is a remarkable stab in the right direction!

LAVINIA MUMPHARD'S VANILLA CARAMEL LAYER CAKE

For the cake:
½ cup unsalted butter, softened
1 cup granulated sugar
3 eggs
1 tablespoon vanilla
1 teaspoon lemon juice
2 cups sifted all-purpose flour
¼ teaspoon salt
4 teaspoons baking powder
⅔ cup milk

For the icing:
1 cup whipping cream
2¼ cups light brown sugar
2 tablespoons butter
2 teaspoons vanilla

Serves 8.

1 Heat oven to 375°. Cream the butter with the sugar until light and fluffy. Add the eggs, one at a time, beating well after each addition. Add the vanilla and lemon juice.

2 Sift the flour with the salt and baking powder. Stir flour mixture into the butter mixture in three parts, alternating with thirds of the milk. Pour into two buttered and floured 9-inch cake pans. Bake until a toothpick inserted in center comes out clean, about 25 minutes. Cool on a wire rack.

3 To make the icing, combine the cream and sugar in a saucepan. Boil over low heat until ½ teaspoon of mixture forms a ball when dropped into cold water, about 20 minutes. Place the pan in a bowl of cold water; stir in the butter and vanilla until thick enough to spread.

4 Ice cake immediately. If icing becomes too thick to spread, beat in a few drops of boiling water.

Barbara Knowles's pound cake prescription is quite a different cup of tea. Ms. Knowles is another old chum (long in companionability if not in actual years), who manages to combine a splendid career as a book designer with raising four children and keeping a watchful eye on home and hearth.

I suspect that "No sweat!" is Barbara's maxim for all cookery, although she has never spoken it to me. Her excellent rendition of a family receipt (passed down from her husband's mother's mother) is tempered with dispatch and good judgment as well. But here is a direct quote from Barbara on the subject: "I started making this cake with an electric mixer but was forced to make it by hand one non-electrified summer at Fire

Island—and was more pleased with the coarser but lighter texture. The secret of doing it by hand is very, very soft butter. The less beating . . . the better!''

BARBARA KNOWLES'S POUND CAKE

1 Heat oven to 350°. Grease a 13-inch loaf pan and line the bottom with buttered wax paper. (Barbara uses trimmed butter wrappers.)

2 Combine the butter and sugar. Sift flour and baking powder together; stir into butter mixture until blended. Stir in the milk. Add the eggs, one at a time, mixing well after each addition. Add the vanilla; mix thoroughly. Pour into pan.

3 Bake on center rack of oven until a toothpick inserted in the center comes out clean, about 55 minutes. Cool in the pan 15 minutes. Remove from pan and cool completely on a wire rack.

Note: Pound cake can be wrapped and frozen or kept in the refrigerator indefinitely. If it hardens, toast slices and serve with ice cream.

½ cup plus 6 tablespoons butter, room temperature
1½ cups granulated sugar
1½ cups all-purpose flour
1½ teaspoons baking powder
¼ cup milk
4 eggs
2 teaspoons vanilla

Serves 10.

In the end, it is easier to write about flavors and recipes than people, because the emotions are less cloudy. What more truth is there to tell about my father—aside from his passion for vanilla ice cream and a religious devotion to the movies? I who knew him slightly (by mutual consent) can only recall the uneasy trivialities that passed between us to cloak the deeper feelings we denied each other.

A last vanilla tale, then, concerning my parent:

From time to time my mother was given to deploring the multitude of good things her generation enjoyed that mine was categorically denied (like magic lantern shows in the barn and torchlight parades on the Fourth of July). Homemade ice cream inevitably made this list.

Her own mother had been a legendary cook, of course. So the lore of that lady's art with a freezer blanched the taste of any ice cream that came after it. "The taste . . . the creaminess!" my mother would rhapsodize. "You won't believe this, but people would literally come from miles away when they knew Ma was planning to make us a batch of ice cream."

A working woman with no time, less money, and a small talent for culinary expression at best, my mother nevertheless wanted her husband and children to share her commemoration of the natural wonders that enriched her girlhood. So she made ice cream for us.

Not quite from scratch, however, as her forebear had done, because the concept of such rigid scripture seemed hopelessly out of date (and dogmatic) to the liberated woman of the late 1930s that my mother had become. Instead, her version of "homemade" was updated. Concocted of powdered mixes advertised in women's magazines, it was laved with canned milk (for economy's sake most likely—certainly not for flavor!). And, as hand-cranked freezers were as passé as hand-cranked Gramophones by then, she froze her offering in the ice trays of our refrigerator—where it turned to unbreakable Venetian glass overnight.

No amount of flagellation with a hand beater—or the last minute addition of heavy cream (as a desperation measure)—could salvage that glacial congealment. Truth to tell, the flaky memory of rough ice and that terrible tinned flavor haunts my tongue to this very day!

As we had an exceptionally high level of tolerance in my family, my father, sister, and I stoically ate my mother's frozen disaster without comment. But my father waylaid me in the hall afterward.

"Wait a bit . . . until it doesn't seem too obvious," he said, throwing me a dollar bill as he made his way toward the bathroom to read the paper. "Then run down to the corner and buy us a quart of *real* cream for Chrissakes! Any flavors—as long as there's some *van-ella!*"

FRENCH VANILLA ICE CREAM

4 cups whipping cream
1 piece of vanilla bean, 3 inches long
2½ cups granulated sugar
2 teaspoons vanilla
8 egg yolks
½ cup hot milk or light cream
1 tablespoon cognac
1 teaspoon Grand Marnier liqueur

Makes about 2 quarts.

1 Place 2 cups cream in a bowl with the vanilla bean; refrigerate 1 hour. Whip remaining 2 cups cream until soft peaks form; refrigerate until ready to use.

2 Beat the sugar, vanilla, and egg yolks in a mixing bowl until light and lemon-colored. Gradually add the hot milk, beating well to dissolve the sugar. (If sugar does not dissolve completely, place bowl in pan of hot water and stir just until sugar dissolves—no longer. Then remove bowl from water and beat mixture several minutes.)

3 Remove vanilla bean from cream. Split bean and scrape seeds into cream; discard pod. Stir cream into egg yolk mixture; fold in the whipped cream. Add the cognac and Grand Marnier. Pour mixture into the canister of an ice cream maker. Freeze according to manufacturer's directions.

Vinegar

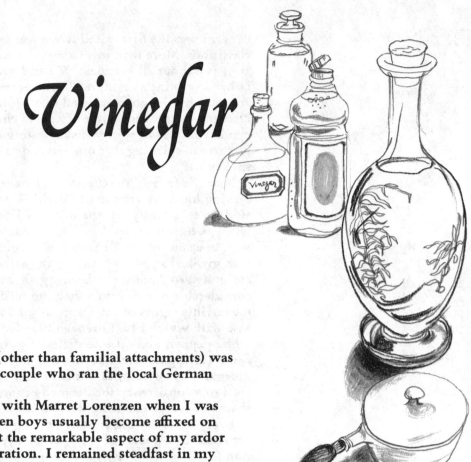

The first love of my life (other than familial attachments) was the daughter of a foreign couple who ran the local German delicatessen.

I suppose I fell in love with Marret Lorenzen when I was about five—at the age when boys usually become affixed on some outside female—but the remarkable aspect of my ardor was its overwhelming duration. I remained steadfast in my feelings for this golden girl well into adolescence and long, long after our entire neighborhood became convinced that the involvement was not entirely innocent—which it was, regardless of the street gossip.

I have always maintained that real feeling never dies. Relationships are aborted and wild excitation palls but the original response (that chemical attraction that causes warmth, inspiration, and, let's face it, even pain) never truly abates. It is merely an emotion submerged while a lover suspends disbelief—and seeks out enchanting similarities in all the other sexual partners he acquires. To emphasize that point, I will admit that all whom I loved afterward had something of Marret in them!

An only child, my first love was a closely guarded treasure in her parents' store. And why not? She was pretty, slim, and long-legged; the best tree climber on our block, she had hair bobbed like a dandelion and skin so fair her nose peeled all summer long. She loved me for our differences it seems. I couldn't climb anything, not even a low fence, unless she helped me over it. And my body turned dark as effortlessly as chocolate melts in the sun. I was shy of everything, but she was so extroverted that her arm was the first raised to answer any question posed in our classroom. More than just smart, she was very definite and assertive about all her ideas. When I grew diffident under her father's scrutiny (I assumed he never truly liked me hanging around), his daughter insisted that I join her in the delicatessen kitchen—where the clatter of knives chopping and the great cymbal crashes of wire whisks beating cream and salad dressing was so ear-splitting that one learned to speak up smartly when spoken to.

Marret's father, Marcus, was a martinet with a Solingen carving knife. A veteran of World War I, but from the enemy side, he reluctantly left the military life for culinary enterprise when *zweinhunerste marks* were devaluated and he met his future wife one summer in Denmark. Recognizing that the Scandinavian girl had a golden touch in the kitchen, he married her and emigrated to America, where together they proliferated her considerable talents into a thriving business that withstood all the terrible rigors of the Depression. I still recall the extreme ease with which Etta Lorenzen blended egg yolks, lemon juice, white pepper, and oil into drifts of golden mayonnaise with a fork. Testing the sauce on her finger, she would judiciously add vinegar, and sometimes salt or sugar, until the airy froth whitened to a consistency she deemed proper to grace the silvery shards of barely cooked potato in her spectacular *kartoffelsalat*.

Every Saturday night of my young life, supper at home consisted of a pound of sugar-crusted Virginia ham (sliced extra thin to please my father) and two boat-shaped cardboard containers filled with Mrs. Lorenzen's best potato salad and cole slaw. The latter was vinegary with a sauce of soured cream, mustard, and celery seed and liberally anointed with diced green pepper and scarlet spikes of ripe tomato.

Fridays, we ate Mrs. Lorenzen's fish cakes. Like no other croquette so named before or after her invention, these pale patties were formed only of ground cod, minced onion, and buttery mashed potatoes. Yet the consistency of each was so light, so airy, that they seemed to float from the frying pan to the plate.

We ate them with lots of ketchup at home, but in the back of the delicatessen they were always swallowed unadorned—exactly as they came from the shiny black frying pan in which they browned on the stove. With a long silver spatula, Mrs. Lorenzen would choose a perfect circle for a snack and, without dropping a speck of grease, place it directly in the middle of the zinc work table where Marret and I played cards on rainy days. We were far less impatient about winning at rummy or Old Maid, I might add, than about waiting for the toothsome cake to cool enough to be split apart and devoured on the spot. Was there ever again such ambrosial food?

A mist of slightly intoxicating vinegar enveloped that kitchen always. Even when creamy tapioca was being folded into billows of freshly whipped meringue or trays of dusty almond cakes (flat and pale as cloth-covered buttons) were set out to cool, the scent of pickles aging in brine lent savor to the sweetness.

Marret was my best friend, my closest confidante. Not a day passed that we did not share some newly acquired information or some intimate secrets. We were a club and a union at one and the same time. Even being absolutely quiet together, drawing or reading, both of us were so intensely aware of the other's need that we merely had to stretch a hand or move a leg slightly and touch for happiness to suffuse our beings.

To know that the universe was in its rightful place, we would lie flat on our backs in the grass and stare as hard as we could at the clouds moving above us. Secure in the knowledge that nothing could separate our amity.

It is odd to write of these feelings in a more sexually permissive light for though Marret and I saw each other naked many times, we never for a moment considered further intimacy. Like natural lovers, perhaps we eschewed the complication that sex would bring to Eden.

I mix the reasons why we slipped away from each other, Marret and I. There was the rise of Nazi Germany and the persecution of the Jews. Mr. Lorenzen, partially hidden behind the yellow pages of the *Journal American,* discussed the subjects endlessly, which made me very uncomfortable.

Marcus Lorenzen had enormous pride in the accomplishments of the *Wehrmacht;* he was the only man who clapped for Hitler during a newsreel at the Loew's Plaza Movie Theatre, or so they said. I was not there at the time.

More painfully, I recall the other stories—ugly neighborhood tales concerning his daughter and myself. My sister initiated the brouhaha at our house. She told my parents something nasty overheard at school, which I denied with heat and some tears. My mother, too self-concerned at the time to give credence to small talk, dismissed the rumors.

"He and Marret have been playing together for years," she said, shrugging her shoulders.

"Well! Maybe he should play with boys for a change!" was my father's reaction.

Later, some well-intentioned customer passed the same scurrilous information on to the Lorenzens (between the liverwurst and the cervelat, as it were). My being nominally Jewish made this gossip appear even more vile in Marret's righteous Aryan household, I imagined.

By mutual agreement, Marret and I met in our secret place, a high-weeded lot that completely screened us from sight, to discuss all this.

"Who cares what they say," I declared virtuously. "It's not true."

"My father and mother know that," Marret assented. "But they care anyway."

"Do you care?"

"I don't know."

"Well . . . I think it is too stupid even to think about," I said, very high-minded.

"You really mean that?"

"Of course," I replied. But it was a patent lie.

Marret must have known, for, as if by design, we began to see less of each other immediately afterward. She transferred to junior high school at precisely the same time that my father lost his substantial real estate holdings, including our house. We moved to a small apartment building only a few miles away, but it might just as well have been to China—for I did not see her (or the wondrous delicatessen where she lived) for years afterward.

When we met once more, it was inadvertently. Marret and I next encountered each other in the great hall of the Hayden Planetarium on a science field trip attended by second year students in all five boroughs. She wore lipstick and a matronly red coat with an impossibly large fur collar; in high heels, she was as tall as I. Her appearance had altered and ripened, but her eyes were unchanged. And that remarkable glow behind the blueness (like the gas flame in her father's kitchen) still flickered so brightly that I picked her out of a crowd of five hundred noisy teenagers.

She had a friend linked to her arm, a girl who was, in contrast, very plain and drab. This young woman was plainly not too pleased at the prospect of being intercepted by me.

"We have to go," she said, as soon as she had looked me over, "or there won't be any seats left."

"Maybe we can sit together," Marret suggested.

"No. It's too crowded already."

"I can find seats," I volunteered, unconvincingly—such intrepid acts always having been beyond my reach.

"Never mind." The girl pulled Marret away in a most proprietary manner. "We will be OK."

I followed at a discreet distance and, when they finally settled in, managed to find a single place for myself just behind Marret's fur collar—much to the annoyance of her friend, who knew I was anxious for intimacy (under the stars) and resented the presumption, although I received no encouragement from Marret.

I bought them both hot chocolate later at a frowzy old coffee shop on Amsterdam Avenue and held Marret's hand over-long at the subway station before they departed. But the curious blue blade of separation had left us both uneasy and slightly incompatible. At the last possible moment we made a commitment—a date to meet the following Saturday, same time and place. When that day arrived, Marret was not there.

Only after I had returned home did my sister Myra remember that Marret had telephoned during the week to say she would not be able to come. "She sounded very different on the phone," my sister reported airily, "very grown up."

"At fifteen? I'm almost fifteen; yet you never say I'm grown up!"

"Girls mature faster than boys," was my sibling's last word on the subject.

I did not forgive either of them readily. Women were totally undependable, I concluded. Having just read *You Can't Go Home Again,* I believed implicitly in Thomas Wolfe's dictum. Now, forty years after the fact, I have some reasonable doubt.

In a small town a domestic tragedy can never run its course discreetly. Ex-neighbors barely contained their spleen when the delicatessen owner abruptly closed his shop for the summer and took his family to Germany. This was back in 1939, when gossip about Nazis in America was rife with invention. The rumor-mongers even hinted that the holiday was actually an abduction, that Marret had traveled to the Third Reich to ransom her father from the *herrenvolk.* Very Helen MacIness—but was there a shred of truth in all that prattle? I pretended utter indifference to the stories (lovingly chewed over by Lorenzen's Jewish clientele) but why I can no longer say.

What happened to my childhood love?

She grew up, I suppose, even as I. Years after the war I was told that her family's business decamped from Queens to the Bronx but I never found a listing for a like-named delicatessen in that borough's telephone directory. In time, all news of the Lorenzens ceased entirely.

A year ago I thought I stood behind her on a supermarket check-out line. The open face (blurred by time, as my own), the tilt of the chin, even the blonde hair turning gray, seemed familiar. And my heart beat very fast at the idea of yet another meeting. But when I stared into the stranger's face (causing her needless confusion, I am certain), I realized that the blue flame was missing in her eyes. It was not my friend at all.

I must confess I was relieved. Once, not a week passed that I did not cast about in memory for some clue in our relationship that would explain why we were not together, as clearly we had been meant to be. But no longer. Time darkens those feelings somewhere along the way.

I am a happy man now and quite content with my life. Still

sometimes, with no apparent provocation, I am assailed with secret longing for persons and times long gone. Like those afternoons spent in the back of the warm and steamy delicatessen where I learned to play "Fish" and Old Maid amid the sweet, vinegary airs.

Though the fragrant vinegars I always associated with the Lorenzen kitchen were invariably clear alcohol or yellow apple-cider distillates, the kind I use in mine is made from wine, either white or red.

Vinegar is an ancient invention. It's much older, in fact, than the Old Testament description of Boaz bidding Ruth, "Eat of the bread and dip your morsel into vinegar." Probably the first vinegar used in a kitchen was fermented seven or eight thousand years ago, for the artifacts of the Indus valley include several interesting cruets that could only have held oil and vinegar in their cavities.

The name we apply, however, comes from the French *vin aigre,* meaning "soured wine." Actually a fungus, *Mycoderma aceti,* ferments wine left exposed to air, dissipating the alcoholic content and leaving the mixture of acetic acid and water that adds such a tonic zing to salad dressings.

The most economical vinegar is produced at home simply by leaving an open carafe of wine exposed to the air. It takes about six weeks for a vinegar environment to develop. A skin forms on the surface of the liquid in about two or three weeks; in another two weeks a gelatinous mass, known as "the mother" of the vinegar, takes shape beneath it. After another week or so, you can pour in additional wine and the mother will turn it into more vinegar.

A single mother can ferment about three hundred gallons of liquid before being depleted. To name drop here, I must add that the mother of my vinegar originated in the East Hampton kitchen of Craig Claiborne. He gave some to a friend, who gave some to a friend, who gave some to me.

If you cannot tarry at the wine cask long enough to produce home fermentation, I recommend Dessaux Fils (4500 Orleans) brand from France as the choicest vinegar for your kitchen. Dessaux makes both a white and red wine vinegar and I keep a bottle of each on my kitchen shelf. The rule for usage is very basic: use white wine vinegar for any dishes that you would serve with white wine (veal, fish, fruit, etc.) and red wine vinegar for beef, lamb, and all vegetable dishes. Chicken presents an option: use red or white as your taste dictates.

Terituan, a prime hors d'oeuvre I make whenever forced to the wall these days, is of Persian design. Arabians eat this mix of chopped cucumber, walnuts, herbs, garlic, yogurt, and vinegar as a light lunch or supper. I serve it with drinks, spooned onto lettuce leaves instead of dreary crackers or chips. But be advised that vinegar does not compliment all alcoholic beverages. Eschew sweet drinks and tonic and lime mixtures when Terituan is passed. Stick with grain spirits like vodka, scotch, gin, and bourbon instead.

Incidentally, Terituan does not keep. Make the sauce early and refrigerate it. Then add the chilled chopped cucumbers and herbs just before you bring out the bowlful and each time you refill it. Its flavor won't spoil if the dish is made ahead of time, but its appearance will suffer.

TERITUAN

1 Pare the cucumbers; cut in half lengthwise. Scoop out the seeds and discard. Finely chop the cucumbers; refrigerate covered.

2 Place the garlic, walnuts, salt, basil, vinegar, and oil in a blender container. Blend until smooth. Transfer to a serving bowl; refrigerate until thoroughly chilled.

3 To serve, stir the cucumbers into the sauce; sprinkle with parsley and mint. Pass with lettuce leaves and cherry tomatoes. (The correct way to eat Terituan is to place a spoonful on a lettuce leaf and fold it over like a crepe. Dip the tomatoes.)

2 small cucumbers
2 cloves garlic
1 cup walnuts
1 tablespoon salt
2 fresh basil leaves or a pinch of dried
2 tablespoons red wine vinegar
½ cup olive oil
2 teaspoons chopped fresh parsley
1 teaspoon chopped fresh mint
Romaine lettuce leaves
Cherry tomatoes

Makes about 2 cups.

There is a French kitchen expression that translates roughly thus: "Like the character of a good woman, a good dish requires a touch of vinegar from time to time!"

It's a sound culinary rule of thumb—even though described, obviously, from a chauvinistic point of view. Scientists claim that the fermenting agent in vinegar excites the taste buds, forcing them to respond to a variety of seasonings, while the acid stimulates digestion.

In my own saute pan, a spot of vinegar seems to bond seemingly irreconcilable ingredients—like fried fish, red onion, white wine, and olive oil. For one such divine kitchen formula, reflect on Pesco Fritto, please. It's an Italian first course or luncheon dish collected from the city of Venice.

PESCO FRITTO

1½ pounds flounder fillets, cut into
    1½- × ½-inch strips
Flour
Salt and freshly ground pepper to
    taste
¼ cup vegetable oil
3 tablespoons butter
2 medium red onions, sliced paper
    thin
1½ cups olive oil
⅓ cup dry white wine
½ cup white wine vinegar
¼ cup chopped parsley

Serves 6 to 8.

1 Lightly coat fish with flour seasoned with salt and pepper. Saute in the oil and butter until golden brown on both sides.

2 Place one layer of fish in a 2-inch-deep serving dish; cover with one layer of onion slices. Repeat layers. Combine olive oil, wine, and vinegar; pour over top. Sprinkle with salt, pepper, and parsley. Refrigerate several hours or overnight.

Note: Soaking onion slices in cold water for several hours prior to using will make them more digestible. Drain well before using.

In France, vinegar was a by-product of winemaking until the mid-seventeenth century, when the canny vintners determined that the manufacture of bottled *verjus* (the fermented leftovers of unripened grapes) would make a healthy enterprise of its own—since many chefs deliberately left wine to spoil to use for flavoring.

No self-respecting French vinegar is made from anything but grapes. In England, however, leavings from the hops, from which that country's beer and ale are produced, are turned into a pale liquid that pickles many an egg served pub-side from Cornwall to Hampshire. Americans (as early as the Pilgrim fathers) made a tart, spicy vinegar from fermented apples, which was taken as a tonic every spring and fall. Cider vinegar also seasons the best state fair offerings of piccalilli and cole slaw.

A French fish dish from Toulon is so simple that it barely requires notation here. But it is such a classic example of vinegar's remarkable ability to align other flavors that it's imperative that I include it—just to prove a point!

HADDOCK SAUTE AU VINAIGRE

3 large haddock fillets, cut in half
½ cup all-purpose flour
½ cup milk
1¼ cups soft bread crumbs
½ cup butter
2 tablespoons vegetable or olive
    oil
1 tablespoon red wine vinegar
Lemon slices
Chopped parsley

Serves 4 amply.

1 Heat oven to 350°. Roll fillets in flour; shake off excess. Dip in milk and roll in bread crumbs.

2 Melt 4 tablespoons butter with 1 tablespoon oil in a large, heavy skillet. Saute fish until golden, about 3 to 4 minutes on each side. (Add remaining butter and oil as you need it.) Transfer fish to heatproof serving platter.

3 Sprinkle vinegar over the fish. Bake until fish flakes easily when pierced with fork, 8 to 10 minutes. Garnish with lemon slices and chopped parsley.

The culinary inspiration of vinegar makers is seemingly endless. The Chinese, for instance, have practiced the art of fermenting rice and strawberry tree spirits for almost 5,000 years. In India, they pickle tamarind seeds for their vinegar extract; Canadians prefer maple syrup. In Spain, a fine sherry vinegar is fermented from Manzanilla elixirs, while the Japanese make do with a colorless compound leavened with sake. Russians and Poles produce a fiery distillation of vodka and red peppers that will singe a tongue irrevocably in a green salad—but a few drops added to a pot of borscht produces a fragrance that is absolutely ennobling to the sinuses.

The following canon for Russian borscht *extraordinaire* is from a remedy book of my late friend Margo Henderson, whose kitchen abilities have been described earlier. Margo snatched this recipe from her good friend, Liza Redfield (the musical conductor), who was rumored to have purloined it from an ex-mother-in-law. And so the lore of the pottage multiplies.

It is a wonderful one-dish dinner, I might add, coupled with a loaf of bread and a tub of sweet butter. Mrs. Henderson, however, always served her borscht in two acts: first, the steaming soup in man-size trenchers with potatoes and sour cream; then the sliced beef with a bowl of string beans, more potatoes, and horseradish. Her husband, Luther, invariably insisted on another bowl of soup even as the beef was brought out—and everyone else at the table followed suit. Why? I will never know. But it was a delectable tradition, nonetheless!

RUSSIAN CABBAGE BORSCHT

1 Arrange half the onion and half the cabbage in a large Dutch oven. Place the meat on top; cover with remaining onion and cabbage. Add the beef broth and enough water to barely cover the meat. Add the tomatoes, sugar, apple, raisins, lemon juice, vinegar, salt, pepper, and allspice. Bring to a boil; reduce heat. Simmer covered until meat is tender, 3½ to 4 hours.

2 To serve as two courses, place one or two boiled potatoes into each soup bowl; ladle soup over potatoes. Pass the sour cream. (Keep remaining borscht warm.) When the soup course is finished, remove the meat from the hot liquid to a platter; slice. Serve with additional boiled potatoes; ladle some more soup over each portion. (Meat is excellent served with string beans.)

1 yellow onion, finely chopped
1 small head cabbage, shredded
1 beef brisket (3 to 4 pounds), trimmed of all fat
1 can (13¾ ounces) beef broth
2 cans (17 ounces each) imported Italian tomatoes, mashed
1½ tablespoons sugar
1 green apple, cored, chopped
¼ cup white raisins
3 tablespoons lemon juice
1 tablespoon tarragon vinegar
2 teaspoons salt
1 teaspoon freshly ground pepper
Pinch of allspice
Boiled potatoes
Sour cream

Serves 6 to 8.

Perhaps because the French gave vinegar its name, they remain proprietors of its best kitchen usage. I wish now to add two of the best French formulas for sauteing a bird that I have ever encountered. Both are curiously similar as to ingredients and cooking procedures but the first husbands tomato to its breast, while the second is bathed in sweet cream. Experience the differences for yourself!

SAUTEED CHICKEN WITH VINEGAR I

2 small chickens (2½ pounds each), cut into serving pieces
1 clove garlic, bruised
Salt and freshly ground pepper
4 tablespoons butter
1 tablespoon vegetable or olive oil
3 large shallots, minced
3 tablespoons red wine vinegar
4 large tomatoes, seeded, chopped
1 tablespoon mixed chopped fresh tarragon and parsley
4 to 6 cups cooked rice

Serves 4 to 6.

1 Rub the chicken pieces lightly with garlic; sprinkle with salt and pepper.

2 Melt the butter with the oil in a large, heavy skillet. Saute the chicken pieces until golden brown, about 10 minutes on each side.

3 Add the shallots to the skillet, placing them between the chicken pieces. Add the vinegar. Cook over high heat until vinegar is almost evaporated. Reduce heat. Add tomatoes; cook covered until chicken is tender, 15 to 20 minutes. If necessary, raise heat and cook uncovered until sauce is slightly thickened.

4 Sprinkle chicken with herbs. Serve with rice.

SAUTEED CHICKEN WITH VINEGAR II

2 small chickens (2½ pounds each), cut into serving pieces
1 clove garlic, bruised
Salt and freshly ground pepper
5 tablespoons butter
1 tablespoon vegetable or olive oil
2 large shallots, minced
⅓ cup red wine vinegar
2½ cups whipping cream
Freshly chopped parsley
4 to 6 cups cooked rice

Serves 4 to 6.

1 Heat oven to 250°. Rub the chicken pieces lightly with garlic; sprinkle with salt and pepper.

2 Melt 4 tablespoons butter with the oil in a large, heavy skillet. Saute chicken over low heat, 20 minutes on each side. Remove chicken to baking dish; keep warm in oven. Remove grease from skillet.

3 Melt 1 tablespoon butter in skillet. Add the shallots; cook and stir over medium heat until soft, 3 to 5 minutes. Add vinegar; cook over high heat, scraping bottom and sides of pan, until most of the vinegar

is evaporated. Add the cream; boil rapidly 5 minutes. Reduce heat; return chicken to skillet with pan juices. Simmer over low heat 5 minutes, basting chicken frequently.

4 Sprinkle chicken with parsley. Serve with rice.

A few vinegar hints:

—A mite of vinegar stirred into jams or jellies after they have been boiled will help them jell.

—A speck of vinegar added to rapidly boiling rice or potatoes will keep them white and fluffy.

—Vinegar is a mild bleach; so a bit of it in water will keep artichokes from turning color and a small amount brushed over mushrooms will keep them from rusting as well. A tiny portion of vinegar mixed with water will keep apples and pears nice and white-fleshed, too.

—A judicious teaspoon of white vinegar will keep your white fish firm (and whiter) in a poaching liquid.

—A drop of white vinegar sprinkled on dried fruit will send it through a food chopper or processor with nary a bit of clogging—if that's ever a kitchen problem.

—The drops of vinegar that Slavic chefs always add to zesty dishes like borscht and goulash make such fare more digestible!

—Two teaspoons of white vinegar will transform a half pint of cream into thick sour cream—if you find you're out of that ingredient at a crucial stage of cookery. Likewise, two table-spoons will sour a cup of milk. A mere drop will help thicken chilled cream into whipped cream when your stirring arm falters.

—A spot of vinegar added to a day-old salad dressing always seems to revive it!

Consider now a definitive German formula for beef stew simmered long in dark beer and vinegar. This is an excellent *inexpensive* party dish that's best made a day or two in advance. The recipe was given me by a German lady who always insisted on Lowenbrau as one of her ingredients. But that was when the brew was still made in Munich and not Milwaukee!

CARBONNADE MÜNCHEN

3½ pounds boneless beef chuck, cut
    into 1-inch cubes
Salt and freshly ground pepper
5 tablespoons butter
1 tablespoon vegetable oil
1 large onion, finely chopped
1 clove garlic, minced
2 tablespoons all-purpose flour
1 cup hot chicken stock
1½ cups dark beer
1½ tablespoons sugar
3 tablespoons plus 2 teaspoons red
    wine vinegar
⅛ teaspoon dried thyme
1½ tablespoons chopped parsley

Serves 4 to 6.

1 Heat oven to 350°. Sprinkle meat heavily with salt and pepper. Melt 2 tablespoons butter with the oil in a large, heavy skillet. Add the meat and brown well on all sides. Transfer to a Dutch oven.

2 Add 1 tablespoon butter to the skillet. Saute the onion and garlic over high heat until brown. Reduce heat; add 2 tablespoons butter. Stir in the flour and cook 2 minutes. Whisk in the chicken stock; then stir in the beer. Add the sugar, 3 tablespoons vinegar, the thyme, and 1 tablespoon parsley. Pour over meat.

3 Bake meat covered 1½ hours. Let stand to cool; refrigerate overnight.

4 To reheat meat, simmer over low heat 30 minutes. Add salt and pepper, if necessary. Just before serving, stir in 2 teaspoons vinegar; simmer 3 minutes. Sprinkle with remaining parsley.

Vinegar was once used as a medication to ward off the plague. As a matter of fact, Vinegar of Four Thieves, as this preparation was called, remained in stock in British pharmacies until the end of the eighteenth century.

    A canon for tartly dressed roast beef salad (particularly restorative to the palate if there is a left-over joint in the larder) provides traditional English boating fare and serves up equally well at landlocked picnics.

¾ cup Vinaigrette Sauce (recipe
    follows)
3 cups cooked roast beef (the rarer
    the better), fat trimmed, cut into
    ¼-inch-wide strips
1 can (8 ounces) cooked beets,
    drained, cut into thin strips
4 large shallots, minced
1 package (6 ounces) frozen pea
    pods or ½ pound fresh
¼ cup finely chopped parsley
Salt and freshly ground pepper to
    taste

Serves 6 to 8.

ROAST BEEF SALAD

1 Make vinaigrette sauce.

2 Combine roast beef, beets, shallots, and vinaigrette; toss lightly.

3 If using frozen pea pods, cook in boiling salted water just until separated and thawed; rinse under cold water. If using fresh pea pods, cook in boiling salted water 2 minutes; rinse under cold running water and drain. (Cooked pea pods should be crisp.)

4 Reserve eight pea pods for garnish. Add remainder to meat; toss well. Arrange in serving bowl. Sprinkle with parsley, salt, and pepper. Garnish with reserved pea pods. Refrigerate; serve chilled.

VINAIGRETTE SAUCE

1 Place garlic and salt in a small bowl. Mash together with the back of a spoon until the mixture forms a paste.

2 Stir in the mustard and lemon juice. Whisk in the oil, vinegar, and pepper.

1 **small clove garlic, crushed**
½ **teaspoon kosher salt**
1 **teaspoon Dijon mustard**
Juice of ½ lemon
½ **cup vegetable or olive oil**
2 **teaspoons red wine vinegar**
½ **teaspoon freshly ground pepper**

Makes about ¾ cup.

Historians claim that Cleopatra once dissolved a perfect pearl in a goblet of vinegar to demonstrate to Marc Antony that even perfection may be destroyed by a matching degree of proficiency. It was a perfect vinegar, you see!

Cleopatra had a mind of her own about everything. Her beauty shelf held a variety of sweet and sour essences for every occasion. Vinegar was one she prized so highly that, they say, she very often bathed in it!

Orlèans, the French city renowned for producing Joan of Arc among other rarities, yields the finest wine vinegars in the world. Made from the ripest *blanc de blancs* harvested along the Loire, only Orlèans vinegar is acetified in oak barrels (*poinçons*, as they are called), which give the extract a flavor comparable to that of great cognac.

A French devise for utterly mouth-watering calves' liver—quickly seared and deglazed with garlic and red wine vinegar—demonstrates, contrary to the queen of the Nile's theory, that dual perfections can exist in happy confederation.

SAUTEED CALVES' LIVER

1 Cut liver into thin slices. Season the flour with salt and pepper; coat liver with flour mixture. Melt 4 tablespoons butter in a skillet over medium-high heat. Saute the liver, about 2 minutes on each side, adding up to 3 tablespoons butter as needed to cook all liver. Remove to a platter; keep warm.

2 Add garlic and 4 tablespoons butter to skillet; saute garlic over high heat. Stir in half the parsley. Pour over liver.

3 Add vinegar to skillet. Bring to a rapid boil, scraping sides and bottom of pan; boil 3 minutes. Pour over liver. Sprinkle with remaining parsley.

1½ **pounds calves' liver, skin and**
   veins removed
½ **cup all-purpose flour**
Salt and freshly ground pepper
11 **tablespoons unsalted butter**
   (approximately)
1 **small clove garlic, minced**
¼ **cup finely chopped parsley**
¼ **cup red wine vinegar**

Serves 4.

Vinegar 365

¼ cup olive oil
2 cloves garlic, minced
1 medium yellow onion, minced
2 pounds shrimp, shelled and
  deveined
¼ cup vegetable oil
2 tablespoons wine vinegar
6 green onions, minced
1 teaspoon chopped fresh basil
  leaves
2 teaspoons chopped parsley
1 dried red chili pepper, crushed
1 teaspoon salt
¼ teaspoon freshly ground pepper
¼ teaspoon cayenne pepper

Serves 8.

1½ cups rice
1 cup diced cooked ham
½ cup chopped parsley
4 green onions, minced
2 teaspoon capers
2 egg yolks*
Juice of 1 lemon
1 tablespoon Dijon mustard
⅔ cup olive or vegetable oil
¼ cup red wine vinegar
1 teaspoon salt
½ teaspoon freshly ground pepper

Serves 8.

The American Deep South has a healthy regard for vinegar at the table. Two prime Dixie bequests, both served cold, reflect that tartness precisely.

LOUISIANA "SWIMPS"

1 Heat olive oil in a heavy skillet and add garlic and yellow onion. Cook over medium-low heat, stirring occasionally, 10 minutes. Add shrimp and cook, stirring constantly, until shrimp turn pink, about 4 to 5 minutes. Allow to cool.

2 Combine the vegetable oil, vinegar, green onions, basil, parsley, red chili pepper, salt and freshly ground pepper, and cayenne. Beat until smooth and pour over the shrimp. Mix thoroughly; transfer to a serving dish and refrigerate covered for at least 12 hours or overnight.

RICELING

1 Heat a large pot of water to boiling. Add rice and stir once with a wooden spoon; cook until tender, about 15 minutes.

2 Drain rice in a colander. Place colander over a pot of boiling water and steam rice, covered with paper toweling, 15 minutes. Remove from heat; cool and then refrigerate for 2 hours.

3 Place rice in a large mixing bowl and add the ham, parsley, onions, and capers. Mix well.

4 Beat the egg yolks with the lemon juice and mustard until slightly thickened. Beat in the oil, a few tablespoons at a time. Add the vinegar, salt, and pepper.

5 Pour the dressing over the rice mixture and toss with two forks until well mixed. Chill for 3 hours before serving.

Note: Eggs, lemon juice, mustard, and oil must be at room temperature.

Tarragon is the ingredient most commonly used to flavor vinegar, but other seasonings abound. I have put up basil and mint

vinegars, even raspberry on occasion. But rose petal, pear, cumin, champagne, mustard seed, and corn vinegars still await my fickle palate.

The most utilitarian vinegar I ever espied was manufactured in Parma, Italy, where decanters of a local brew (for tourists only, one assumes) were labeled "flavored with Parmesan cheese." Its taste, however, left something to be desired.

For the following Milanese stuffed tomato conception (an amalgam of every possible Italian import, it seems), I would suggest a good, old-fashioned red wine vinegar, please. This dish is perfect for lunch and excellent, too, as a dinner first course if the second one is light. And it is absolute bliss when one is foraging in the refrigerator late at night.

POMODORI RIPIENI

1 Heat oven to 375°. Cut tops off tomatoes and discard. Gently squeeze tomatoes over a bowl; reserve juice and pulp. (Use a spoon to scoop out pulp, if necessary.) Sprinkle tomatoes with salt and pepper; drain inverted on paper toweling.

2 Remove sausage meat from casings; chop coarsely.

3 Heat oil and butter in a heavy skillet. Add onion and garlic; cook over medium heat 2 minutes. Add sausage; cook until sausage is no longer pink, breaking up any lumps with a wooden spoon. Add the tomato juice and pulp; sprinkle with sugar and bouillon powder. Cook over medium-high heat, stirring frequently, until all liquid evaporates. Sprinkle mixture with the vinegar as it cooks.

4 Reduce heat; stir in the rice, parsley, basil, pine nuts, half the Parmesan cheese, and the egg. Mix well. Remove from heat; let stand to cool.

5 Spoon sausage mixture into tomatoes, mounding tops. Place on a greased baking dish. (They should fit snugly.) Sprinkle remaining Parmesan cheese over tomatoes. Bake 30 minutes. Serve hot or cold.

6 small or 4 large, firm, ripe
  tomatoes
Salt and freshly ground pepper
3 mild Italian sausages
½ tablespoon olive oil
1 tablespoon butter
¼ cup finely chopped yellow onion
1 clove garlic, minced
½ teaspoon sugar
½ teaspoon bouillon powder
2 teaspoons wine vinegar
1 cup cooked rice
2 tablespoons chopped parsley
1 tablespoon chopped fresh basil
3 tablespoons pine nuts
¼ cup freshly grated Parmesan
  cheese
1 egg, lightly beaten

Serves 4 to 6.

Vinegar is unmistakably versatile.
Italians even make a sweet version of the stuff that their chefs find quite salubrious in fruit tarts and ices. They call it *aceto dolce*

to distinguish it from the *sotto aceti* that they sprinkle on antipasto.

However, to my mind, the French provincial kitchen understands the acid best of all. There it is diluted on occasion with water to poach fish or with wine to baste a roasting chicken. In its most modest usage, it's mixed with various fragrant herbs as the base for a quintessential pork stew, which is called Routissons and is worth its weight in gold, I think.

ROUTISSONS

3 pounds lean boneless pork, cut into 2-inch cubes

2 teaspoons chopped fresh marjoram or 1 teaspoon dried

2 teaspoons chopped fresh thyme or 1 teaspoon dried

1 whole sage leaf, slivered, or a pinch of dried

1 clove garlic, minced

4 tablespoons vegetable or olive oil

Salt and freshly ground pepper

½ cup red wine vinegar

½ teaspoon slivered lemon peel

1 cup finely chopped parsley

2 tablespoons chopped fresh basil or 1½ teaspoons dried

2 tablespoons finely chopped chives or green onion tops

4 to 6 cups cooked rice

Serves 4 to 6.

1 Sprinkle meat with marjoram, thyme, sage, and garlic. Let stand 1 hour.

2 Heat oil in a large, heavy skillet or Dutch oven. Add all the meat; sprinkle with salt and pepper. Cook, stirring occasionally, over medium heat until meat is very brown and crisp, about 30 minutes.

3 Drain fat from skillet. Stir in the vinegar, scraping bottom and sides of pan. Cook covered over low heat until meat is tender, 35 to 40 minutes. (If the meat begins to dry out during cooking, add a few tablespoons water or dry red wine.)

4 Just before serving, skim any excess fat from sauce with a chilled soup ladle. Add the lemon peel and chopped herbs. Add salt and pepper to taste. Serve with rice.

Betsy Cooper, my letter-writing friend from Bristol, Tennessee, has graciously provided this vinegar compilation with its most unusual invention—a tasty glazed orange compound that is both sweet and sour. It makes a brilliant addition to the various condiments I feel compelled to serve whenever curry is on the menu.

But Betsy's delicious orange slices are more than an occasional visitor to the dining room table. I find their taste salutary with all manner of roast fowl and baked ham too. Best of all, they make a wonderful dessert (the last moment variety) with a dollop of whipped cream or homemade lemon sherbet. I suggest you put up a jar or two for the refrigerator posthaste. The oranges keep splendidly—thanks to that half cup of vinegar, I imagine.

BETSY COOPER'S BAKED ORANGE SLICES

1 Place the whole oranges in a saucepan; add water to cover and the salt. Boil 30 minutes. Drain well. Cover oranges with cold water; let stand 30 minutes. Drain. Let stand to cool completely.

2 Heat oven to 325°. Combine ¾ cup water with the sugar, corn syrup, and vinegar in a large saucepan. Bring to a boil; reduce heat. Simmer 5 minutes.

3 Cut each orange into 6 slices. Add to the syrup; boil 15 minutes.

4 Pour oranges and syrup into a shallow baking dish. Bake 1 hour. Cool. Store in a tightly covered jar in the refrigerator. Use as a garnish with roast duck or chicken or curry. Or serve as a dessert with whipped cream.

4 **large navel oranges**
1 **tablespoon salt**
¾ **cup water**
2 **cups granulated sugar**
½ **cup light corn syrup**
½ **cup tarragon vinegar**

Makes 24 slices.

Since I had spent much time during my formative years in the back of a delicatessen, it was rather like a prodigal return to find myself at the kitchen stoves of The Store in Amagansett.

The remarkable elder Lorenzens, as I recall, invariably wrapped themselves in long white aprons that tied across the middle but hung well below the knee like surgical gowns. They never stirred a pot or attacked a pile of potatoes with a peeler until they were fully outfitted.

My style was somewhat more laissez-faire: I wore blue denim carpenter's aprons at my trade. And though Marcus and Etta's garb was as clean and pristine when they took it off at night as it had been twelve hours earlier, mine usually rivaled a Jackson Pollock painting (spatter for spatter) an hour after I tied myself into it.

Cherry pie makes a messy kitchen worker messier. Particularly when the fruit is ripe, sweet, and crimson with summer juices, as in the very last of this long vinegar bouquet. The formula inside is my own inspiration but the tantalizing, ivory-pale crust comes from Darlene Schulz's family treasury. Purely South Dakota born, this pastry is such a brilliant addition to any pie maker's manual that you will want to use it repeatedly with other fillings as well.

Darlene is the sister-in-law of my closest friend (and cooking/writing collaborator), Phillip Schulz. I first tasted her prodigious handiwork at a soul-satisfying dinner she made for us both in Brownsville, Wisconsin. After one bite of her pie crust, I tabbed her for instant immortality!

"LAST OF THE CHERRIES" PIE

½ recipe Darlene Schulz's Pie
  Pastry (recipe follows)
4 cups pitted fresh sweet cherries
1 cup granulated sugar
1 tablespoon red wine vinegar
5 tablespoons all-purpose flour
1½ tablespoons butter

Serves 6 to 8.

1 Prepare the pastry and chill.

2 Heat oven to 450°. Combine the cherries, sugar, and vinegar. Sift in the flour 1 tablespoon at a time; stir gently after each addition.

3 Roll out half the pastry and line a 9-inch pie pan. Fill with the cherry mixture; dot with butter.

4 Roll out remaining pastry. Place over cherry filling. Trim edges; seal and flute. Make several slashes in the top of the pastry to allow steam to escape. Place pie in oven on a baking sheet. Bake 15 minutes. Reduce heat to 350°; bake until crust is light brown, 30 to 35 minutes. Cool on a wire rack.

DARLENE SCHULZ'S PIE PASTRY

4 cups all-purpose flour
1 tablespoon granulated sugar
2 teaspoons salt
1¾ cups lard or vegetable
  shortening
1 tablespoon wine or cider vinegar
1 egg, beaten
½ cup cold water

Makes enough for two 9- to 11-inch pies.

1 Combine flour, sugar, and salt in a bowl. Add the shortening; blend with a pastry blender until the texture of coarse crumbs.

2 Add the vinegar, egg, and ¼ cup water. Stir into the flour with a fork, adding more water as needed to form a soft dough. Knead briefly on a lightly floured surface. Chill 1 hour before using.

Wine

As a man of some integrity in the kitchen, I would like to acknowledge my debt to the peerless culinary instructors who stirred my senses as well as my saute pans along the way.

I never would have learned to make an omelet correctly, for instance, if the majestically British Dione Lucas (approving and admonishing by turns) had not once slapped my wrist hard with a wooden spatula in cooking class, commanding me to "Stop scrambling for heaven's sake and let the lovely thing rest before you turn it out!" And, in an impeccable aside, she added, "Impatient cooks inevitably make simp-ply dread-ful omelets, my dear."

I must have watched that unflappable lady slide a hundred perfect eggs from buttery pan to waiting plate before I was able to master a smidgen of her finesse. But once I acquired it, I never forgot the trick she taught.

My apprenticeship in Alice B. Toklas's ménage (by second-hand sensibility, it must be made clear) developed my first glimmering of the classic French cook's attitude toward food. I, who wanted to improve virtually every recipe I tried, learned from this mistress of *cuillere et couteau* that fidelity to classic dishes can be truly gratifying. And, moreover, that a dedicated and careful rendering of a peasant stew like *boeuf à la Bourguignonne* can demonstrate just as much creativity as some pyrotechnical display from the tomes of Raymond Olivier.

Julia Child (and cohorts, Mesdames Beck and Bertholle) reinforced the idea that one could truly enjoy the labor of cookery and still produce something wonderful to eat. The indomitable

Julia, on television at least, made all the techniques that had seemed awesome when performed by other great chefs appear quite do-able. She made them a part of my *everyday* kitchen expertise.

The books of James Beard (particularly in the 1950s) brought clarity and enormous wisdom to my cooking. My grandmother, as I have already stated, left me the legacy of her garden and pot herbs. And good kitchen companions awakened my senses to most of the bouquets of seasonings I have chronicled here.

But it was a fairly recently found friend, now my closest partner in all the enterprise of food (the long hours of research to come up with interesting recipes, the wearisome shopping, and the endless testing of dishes), who brought the glorious aroma of good French wine to my table and my stoveside.

Why? I shall never be able adequately to explain. But Phillip Schulz, green and untried to the world of *haute cuisine,* no less degustation, hailed from Golden, Colorado, with a perfectly golden nose for the grape.

We met about eight years ago, while The Store in Amagansett was still flourishing under its original authority. And although Schulz joined The Store's crew as a diffident, if not downright unwilling, chef (having had less than tonic experience with mass feeding in the kitchens of the U.S. Army), he soon brought a sense of tacit order to what had always been tatterdemalion entrepreneurism.

Determining that each pot rightfully belonged on a pot latch and that every spoon would more easily be found if it were returned to an accustomed place, he tricked us all into an elaborate yet gentle game of Follow the Leader.

He would never say, "Look, I am putting away the dough hook for the electric mixer," as I might righteously proclaim; or state as boldly as my sister Myra did that "these stainless steel mixing bowls belong on the top of the refrigerator, so why the hell aren't they there?" Phillip said nothing. He was a very shy fellow in those days and merely performed the essential tasks in silence, allowing himself to be observed, mind you—and even emulated in the act of tidying.

Unfortunately, Schulz was only a summer weekend worker at the time. And though his discreet stewardship wrought change as long as he was on the premises, chaos usually reigned during his absence. Even the weeds in the kitchen garden seemed to grow half a head taller from Sunday night to Friday morning! So no one blamed him much when he shifted gears after the first summer from scullery surveillance to bakery.

The Store had never before had a proper pastry chef in its employ. I doubled in brass from time to time and made most of the cakes in our small repertoire reasonably well—but only when the panic of our peak summer catering business did not completely unglue me! More often, my highest hopes for fragile and towering confections (like wedding cakes) sank under stress or on a draughty cooling shelf. But not Phillip's creations! And if they did, his sangfroid was so indestructible at the time that he would not be confounded. Instead, using a razor-sharp French carving knife, he would merely trim any lopsided layers to level proportions and frost them over-lavishly—so no customer was ever the wiser! I guess he must have suffered inwardly, but being the only Spartan in that kitchen (amid the daily outbursts of temperament) gave him unique distinction and Phillip seemed to thrive on his own derring-do.

Nowadays, Phillip is in charge of testing every recipe that I dig up from my considerable storehouse. And he attacks each toothsome new find with faint heart.

"You think this recipe sounds good, Phillip?" I will query him.

"How in the world would *I* know?"

He never knows but launches nevertheless, time and again, into the disaster area of my small kitchen. Flailing spoons and forks, measuring cups and balloon whisks, he curses and howls above the clatter—sending his terrible epithets into the world at-large and frightening his cats half to death. He is no longer shy, you see. Indeed, he complains at the very top of his lungs; "This sonofabitch thing simply isn't working! It is going to be terrible. Awful! A complete disaster!" But it never is. From the oven ashes, Schulz inevitably plucks a golden phoenix.

Phillip Schulz, as I said earlier on, brought his love of wine to my cooking vocabulary. Lord knows where or why he acquired his discerning tongue and his sensitive nose for the subject, but his opinion on matters of the grape are remarkably on target. When we traveled through France a while back, he honed in on all the wines the Loire had to offer, proclaiming this Montrachet too young and that Mâcon Rouge too acetous, until he found the one vintage whose body and bouquet absolutely suited his palate and persistence.

"We must remember the name of this wine," he admonished me, "because it is so absolutely perfect."

Several days later, when I asked him why we weren't still drinking it, he merely shrugged.

"I can't recall the name." And then, sensing that some criticism might be forthcoming, he ended the subject succinctly.

"Just because I appreciate good wine doesn't mean that I am going to memorize the names of all of them! Besides . . . you know me!"

I do.

Before I worked so closely with this quixotic young man, I

often used less than prime vintage in my stew pot—and the final result usually pleased my expedient appetite. But since Schulz entered my kitchen door, I don't dare.

Someone once sent me a complimentary case of German wines, with Blue Nun accounting for most of the selection. When I suggested to Schulz (who would not think of drinking the stuff) that it be used for fish poaching, he exploded, "And ruin a perfectly fine fresh salmon? Throw it out!" he commanded. "Or use it to poach pears." When I did, Phillip tasted the end product very warily. "Not bad. But you can still taste that wine, of course!"

If I consider the substitution of Madeira for port in the Alice B. Toklas veal dish I truly love to prepare—merely because I have an ampler supply of the former wine on hand and the liquor shop is half a block away—Phillip is openly dismayed. His mouth narrows and his eyebrows furrow into a censoring margin of reproof, from which there is no exculpation.

"Do whatever you wish," he begins mildly. "But why you bother to invest in veal that costs five dollars a pound when you plan to muck up the dish is something I simply cannot understand!"

How do I explain? He knows that I am not addicted to kitchen subterfuge. I will have just walked a mile across town to find the exactly right, thin, grassy, end-of-June asparagus to complement the flavor of the veal. Perhaps I have grown overly confident in the kitchen domain—unjustifiably certain that every sauce will survive, no matter which wine enriches it.

A good cook needs a kitchen conscience. Schulz is mine. It is not an easy relationship for either party, however. Sometimes my associate is so demanding that I begin to believe he assumes I can do anything—climb Mount Everest, if pressed.

We take no excursions to the Himalayas as of the moment, but it is his wild faith—in the kitchen and out—that keeps my rope and pick-axe at the ready!

According to the nineteenth-century gastronome, Alexander Dumas, "Wine is the intellectual part of any meal . . . and food is the material underpinnings." Dumas devoted the longest article in his *Grand Dictionaire de Cuisine* to a treatise on wine as food but completely forgot or dismissed the idea of wine cookery. That was obviously his loss!

The mixture of viands with spirituous elixirs is a very, very old notion. Archestratus of Syracuse (who is generally acknowledged to have been the first food critic) celebrated the virtues of early vine-based recipes in pentameters!

At Photolivos, archaeologists have unearthed small portions of tiny black seeds, which bear a very strong resemblance to grape pits, in early kitchen artifacts. These indicate that wine cookery was known to the Indus civilization 4,000 years before Christ was born. The very first grape-producing vine (*Vitis vinifera*) probably predated this usage by 2,000 years. We know from the Bible that no crop was attended with more ritual and care than the grape—and its subsequent yield.

Wine is the end-product of naturally fermented grape juices. It is composed of alcohols, aldehydes, fixed and volatile acids, carbon dioxides, tannins, esters, sugars, pectins, vitamins, and aromatic substances.

All this goes into your pot when you splash a half cup of red Burgundy into a simmering beef stew! What flavors the *Bour-guignonne* in the end, however, is merely the "ash" of the wine, the residue of organic matter that remains after the liquid has evaporated. The amount of ash in a dish determines its bouquet and savor in the end. Since most fine (aged vintage) wines leave a higher percentage of ash than lesser (newer) ones, the argument is put forth that "the better the wine, the better the dish!" Some oenophiles may disagree with that principle. But let me state it loud and clear: this cook does not!

Some counsel on wine in the kitchen:

—I prefer French wine for all my cooking, but I know I am prejudiced. An excellent American vintage will produce an equally robust French stew, but it should be poured more judiciously. Spanish wines are too harsh for most cookery but, like Italian wines, they stand up admirably in their native cuisine.

—White wine is a seasoning imperative for many sauces. Add a mite of Pouilly-fuissé to your next Bechamel, before you pour the cream, for a more velvety texture and extra zest.

—White wine used to flavor broiled or quickly sauteed fish should be sprinkled on with discretion. Since the fast cooking that is best for seafood does not always allow enough time for the alcohol to evaporate, an overly anointed dish can taste harsh. French cooks always boil down their wine slightly before adding it to the *matelote* or flounder.

—Red wines have a regional authority in my kitchen: I try to use Bordeaux wines in dishes that are seasoned with mushrooms, truffles, garlic, and onions, and Burgundy in hearty stews and for basting pot roast or lamb. But either red will sauce a brace of pheasant admirably.

—The color of sauces made with red wines is sometimes too grape-hued to be appetizing. I often add a teaspoon of tomato sauce or paste to enrich the crimson of a *coq au vin*. The aforementioned Dione Lucas always insisted that a bit of burnt sugar (caramelized with an onion or two) did the same trick in Provençal kitchens.

—Instead of flouring a gravy for your next roast of beef, skim as much fat as possible from the juices and add a cup of wine. Boil the mixture until reduced by half and scrape the delicious burnt bits from the pan into it as it cooks. If it reduces too much, add a little beef broth. I usually pour in some heavy cream (or add a lump of sweet butter) at that point. A spritz of cognac won't hurt either.

—Wine is an excellent tenderizer for less than prime meat. The toughest slice of beef will become succulent if bathed in a marinade of wine, oil, onions, herbs, and spices for several days. Boil down the marinade afterward and use it to baste the meat and make the sauce.

—I never throw away any leftover wine. It goes directly into the "mother" in my vinegar bottle on the kitchen shelf.

The following fragrant Northern Italian Risotto best retains its integrity with imported rice and Parmesan cheese as well as a white Soave in the cookpot.

NORTHERN ITALIAN RISOTTO

3½ tablespoons butter
2 large shallots, minced
¼ pound mushrooms, thinly sliced
Salt and freshly ground pepper
¼ cup dry white wine
1 cup Italian rice (I prefer Arbori or Tesori Ambra)
2½ to 3 cups simmering chicken stock
⅓ cup freshly grated Parmesan cheese (optional)

Serves 4 to 6.

1 Melt 2½ tablespoons butter in a heavy skillet; saute shallots 1 minute. Add the mushrooms; cook and stir just until slightly wilted. Sprinkle with salt and pepper; add wine. Cook over medium-high heat until almost all liquid evaporates.

2 Reduce heat to medium-low. Stir in rice until well coated with shallot mixture. Pour 1 cup simmering stock over rice and, without stirring, let the rice absorb it. Add a second cup of stock; when it is absorbed, add ½ cup more. If rice is dry but not fully cooked, repeat with the remaining ½ cup of stock. When rice is fully cooked, but not mushy, raise heat slightly and cook until any excess liquid evaporates. (This entire step should take about 15 minutes.) Stir in remaining butter.

3 Serve rice without cheese to accompany strongly flavored dishes. Stir in cheese if serving with blander foods.

In 1970 I was lucky enough to live in the south of France for a spate of time. The small town where I stayed (and cooked) was Eze—a tiny speck of *moyen âge* stone and red tile tucked well below the traffic of *le grande corniche* on the autoroute between Nice and Monaco.

Eze is a restaurant (very famous and respected), twenty stone houses on a mountainside, and a gas station. The nearest village of any size, with an open air vegetable market for an inveterate shopper (like me), is Beaulieu—a doll-sized resort for the rich perched right at the edge of the blue Mediterranean.

Beaulieu has a remarkable baker, a tonic *confiseur* and the best *charcuterie* in all of France, I warrant. So I traveled there at least two or three times a day for all manner of supplies. The region also produces an excellent local red wine, which may be purchased as *vin ordinaire* at either of the two street cafés that face the market square. Five francs a glass. A hundred francs for the six bottles (stoppered litres) that were delivered to my little white villa twice a week—just like the milk of my youth.

More importantly, the *charcuterie* at Beaulieu produced (in addition to inspiring pâtés and terrines) an absolutely divine cold onion salad. Slightly Middle Eastern in character, the dish was redolent of red wine and tomatoes, black currants, and tiny white cooked onions the size of large beads. I never went into Beaulieu for a packet of sugar or a loaf of bread that I did not return with a portion of that prodigious hors d'oeuvre.

When I returned home, I reconstructed an Amagansett version for The Store's salad counter. But I must confess that the bloom was off the rose, for me, after I had peeled the first 500 white onions! You will be more prudent, I am certain.

OIGNONS BEAULIEU

1 Place all ingredients through cayenne pepper in a large, heavy saucepan. Bring to a boil over medium heat.

2 Meanwhile, heat the butter and 1 tablespoon oil in a heavy skillet. Brown the onions on all sides over high heat, shaking the pan frequently. Transfer onions to saucepan with a slotted spoon. Boil over high heat 15 minutes, stirring frequently.

3 Reduce heat; add mushrooms. Simmer until mushrooms are soft and the mixture has the texture of a slightly runny chutney, about 5 to 10 minutes. (Do not overcook, as the mixture will become too thick.) Transfer to serving dish; sprinkle heavily with parsley. Serve at room temperature.

1 cup dry white wine
½ cup white wine vinegar
2½ cups water
¾ cup currants
1 cup granulated sugar
⅓ cup olive oil
½ cup chopped tomatoes
3 small bay leaves, crumbled
3 sprigs fresh thyme, chopped, or ⅛ teaspoon dried
1 teaspoon salt
½ teaspoon freshly ground pepper
¼ teaspoon cayenne pepper
1 tablespoon butter
1 tablespoon vegetable or olive oil
2½ pounds tiny white onions, peeled, with a cross cut in each root end
6 ounces white button mushrooms
Chopped parsley

Serves 6 to 8 as a first course.

Cooking with wine has taken on the mystique of disparate mores. The Chinese, for instance, "fry" their wine—set it wildly sizzling in a pan—before adding it to the other ingredients in a dish. The Swiss, on the other hand, simply pour raw wine into a fondue and stir the liquid quickly over high heat for the best-known rendering of that dish.

The original epicure, Apicius, described the ancient Roman kitchen doctrine for seasoning with *vino* this way:

Brown the fowl. Add the vegetables first. Then sprinkle on the spices and the herbs. Finally, add the wine and let it boil down until it is syrupy. Later a measure of water may be added. And at the end other emollients such as butter and cream to charm the other flavorings.

That could be an early rendering of the next formula at hand—a homely dish of chicken stewed with carrots. Although provincial French in character, the recipe was passed along to me by the autocratic Dione Lucas when I was a student at her elbow.

1 chicken (3½ to 4 pounds)
1 clove garlic, bruised
Salt and freshly ground pepper
7 tablespoons butter
1 bunch young carrots (about 1 pound), trimmed, thinly sliced
1 onion, thinly sliced
½ teaspoon tomato paste
3 tablespoons all-purpose flour
1 cup hot chicken stock
½ cup plus 2 tablespoons dry white wine
¼ teaspoon ground allspice
Dash of hot pepper sauce
1 bay leaf
1 sprig tarragon
2 sprigs parsley
Juice of ½ lemon
3 tablespoons sour cream
Chopped parsley for garnish
4 cups cooked rice

Serves 4.

PROVINCIAL CHICKEN WITH CARROTS

1 Rub chicken inside and out with garlic; reserve garlic. Rub with salt and pepper. Truss chicken.

2 Melt 3 tablespoons butter in a Dutch oven. Brown chicken well on all sides over high heat.

3 Remove chicken; reduce heat. Add 1 tablespoon butter, 1 sliced carrot, the onion, and the reserved garlic. Cook over medium heat 5 minutes; discard garlic.

4 Add 1 tablespoon butter to Dutch oven. Stir in the tomato paste and flour; cook 2 minutes. Stir in the stock, ½ cup wine, the allspice, hot pepper sauce, bay leaf, tarragon, and parsley. Place chicken in Dutch oven breast side up. Cook covered over low heat until tender, 1¼ to 1½ hours.

5 Meanwhile, add remaining carrots to a large pot of boiling salted water. Return to boiling; then immediately rinse under cold running water and drain.

6 When chicken is cooked, melt 2 tablespoons butter in a saucepan; add carrots. Sprinkle with 2 tablespoons wine, the lemon juice, and

salt and pepper to taste. Cook covered over medium heat 5 minutes. Remove from heat; stir in sour cream. Transfer mixture to a shallow baking dish. Keep warm.

7 Remove the chicken from Dutch oven; cut into serving pieces. Place pieces over carrots. Remove sauce from Dutch oven and strain. Spoon half of sauce over chicken. Sprinkle with parsley. Serve with rice; pass remaining sauce.

My other transcendent cooking mentor, Alice B. Toklas, provided the next hatching, this one of white wine, veal, and leafy spinach.

I have chivied about with this recipe somewhat from the original canon because it has been in my own repertoire so long that I have grown to feel proprietary about it! Miss Toklas used well-cooked spinach to crown her dish—a touch that never pleased my palate as much as barely blanched greens. So I have amended the *maître* (or mistress, if you will). The dish is marvelous served following a tart tomato salad or the stuffed Pomidoro Ripieni limned a chapter ago. I'd accept a slice of rhubarb cake for dessert, too! And a bottle or two of chilled white wine to accompany the feast.

VEAL IN A SAUCE AS GREEN AS A FIELD

1 Melt the butter in a Dutch oven; add the meat. Cook meat over medium heat, stirring constantly with a wooden spoon, until all pieces are coated with butter and slightly golden in color. Sprinkle with flour; cook and stir 3 minutes longer. Add the hot stock, the wine, and bouquet garni. Cook over medium-low heat 45 minutes, turning meat frequently. Stir in salt and pepper.

2 Cook spinach in boiling salted water 1 minute. Rinse immediately under cold running water and drain. Press out all liquid through a fine mesh sieve and chop roughly.

3 Remove bouquet garni from Dutch oven. Stir spinach into the meat. Beat the egg yolks with the cream; gradually stir into Dutch oven over very low heat. Do not allow mixture to boil. Cook and stir until sauce is thick enough to coat a spoon. (Serve with rice, noodles, or toasted croutons.)

4½ tablespoons unsalted butter
3½ pounds boneless stewing veal, cut into 2-inch cubes
2 tablespoons all-purpose flour
¾ cup chicken or veal stock, hot
¾ cup dry white wine
Bouquet garni composed of 1 bay leaf, a pinch of thyme, 3 sprigs parsley, 1 green onion, 1 crushed clove garlic tied up in cheesecloth
1 teaspoon salt
½ teaspoon freshly ground pepper
1½ pounds spinach, washed
4 egg yolks
⅓ cup whipping cream

Serves 6.

Bavette Farcie is made of economical flank steak stuffed with veal and all manner of delectable vegetaria and simmered in wine. It's wonderful cold, with a platter of the cold scalloped potatoes nearby. But hot is not bad either!

5 tablespoons butter
¼ cup plus 1 tablespoon vegetable or olive oil
2 cups ½-inch bread cubes without crusts
1 pound ground veal
2 eggs, lightly beaten
1½ cups chopped onions
½ rib celery, chopped
1 tablespoon chopped parsley
Salt and freshly ground pepper
1¼ teaspoons fresh chopped thyme or ½ teaspoon dried
1 flank steak (about 2½ pounds), trimmed of all fat, with a pocket for stuffing
¾ cup chopped carrots
2 bay leaves
1 large ripe tomato, chopped
½ cup beef broth
½ cup dry red wine
Chopped fresh parsley (optional)

Serves 6 to 8.

BAVETTE FARCIE

1 Heat 3 tablespoons butter and ¼ cup oil in a skillet. Add the bread cubes; saute until golden on all sides. Drain on paper toweling.

2 Combine the veal, eggs, ¾ cup onion, the celery, parsley, 1½ teaspoons salt, ½ teaspoon pepper, and ¼ teaspoon thyme in a large bowl. Add the bread; mix thoroughly.

3 Stuff meat pocket loosely with bread mixture. Bring up bottom edge of pocket and press against stuffing; press top edge of pocket over bottom edge. Tie meat roll with string at 2- to 3-inch intervals. Sprinkle with salt and pepper.

4 Heat remaining 2 tablespoons butter and 1 tablespoon oil in a large, deep baking dish. Brown the meat on all sides. Add the carrots, remaining ¾ cup onions, the bay leaves, remaining 1 teaspoon thyme, and the tomato. Cook over medium heat 5 minutes. Add the broth and wine. Bring to a boil; reduce heat. Simmer covered 1¼ hours.

5 To serve hot, remove meat from cooking liquid; keep warm. Strain liquid and serve with the meat. To serve cold, remove meat from liquid and refrigerate until chilled. Garnish with parsley.

The Burgundians (who ought to know) have a saying: "With enough good wine, good bread, and good meat, a cook can send the doctor into retreat!"

The denizens of Lombardy have their own wine proverb: "In a country without wine, the citizens never laugh and the meat is without flavor!"

No such complaint can be bruited about the following dish of Italian ancestry—the inestimable Vitello Tonnato.

There was a time, long, long ago, before I had made this recipe, when I experienced a kitchen pang at the conceit of tuna fish, pickles, anchovies, and garlic partnered in a stewpan with veal and white wine. But I have had no second thoughts since the moment I first placed a cold forkful of the tender white veal in my mouth. This confederation of opposites is one of the great culinary alignments of the world!

VITELLO TONNATO

1 Heat oil in a large Dutch oven. Lightly brown meat on all sides. Remove meat.

2 Add onion, carrots, celery, and garlic to Dutch oven; saute over low heat 5 minutes.

3 Return meat to pot; add the anchovies, tuna, pickle, half the capers, the wine, parsley, bay leaves, thyme, salt, and pepper. Cook covered over low heat 2 hours. Remove meat; let stand to cool. Refrigerate meat until cold.

4 Boil sauce in Dutch oven until reduced by half; cool slightly. Transfer to a blender container; blend until smooth. Refrigerate until cold.

5 Just before serving, combine the sauce with the mayonnaise in a bowl; whisk until smooth. Season to taste with lemon juice. Slice the veal as thinly as possible; arrange on a serving platter. Spoon sauce over each slice. Garnish with chopped parsley and chives. Sprinkle with remaining capers. Serve remaining sauce on the side.

2 tablespoons olive oil
3½ pounds boneless leg of veal, rolled and tied
1 large onion, thinly sliced
2 medium carrots, chopped
2 ribs celery, chopped
2 large cloves garlic, minced
1 can (2 ounces) anchovy fillets
1 can (6 ounces) tuna
1 large dill pickle, cut into quarters
¼ cup capers
1 cup dry white wine
3 sprigs parsley
2 small bay leaves
1 sprig fresh thyme or a pinch of dried
½ teaspoon salt
¼ teaspoon freshly ground pepper
1 cup mayonnaise (preferably homemade, see Index)
Lemon juice to taste
Parsley chopped with chives for garnish

Serves 6.

The art of cooking with wine has rigid strictures—which good cooks seem to delight in breaking!

Red wine *only* is an accepted dictum for beef or pork dishes. Yet an astonishingly delicious creation from Provence combines those two viands with veal and pot-roasts them together in *white* wine.

The taste of this dish is indescribable. The intermingling of three distinctive meat juices gives it a kind of kitchen majesty. And white wine, oddly enough, is the sole liquid delicate enough to bond all the flavors.

The original recipe for Trois Viandes de Provence was passed down to me (untried) by my late friend Aaron Fine, who hadn't the patience, he said, to perform such culinary labors in his small kitchen.

The prescription came into his possession from his French teacher, Madame Françoise Brulot, who was born in Aix-en-Provence and shared all the linguistic and gastronomic derring-do of her native birthplace with her students. I am sorry I never traded intransitive verbs with her!

Madame Brulot proclaimed, on occasion, that dishes like Trois Viandes were most often prepared for very important family occasions, such as weddings and funerals, because one potful fed an awful lot of people.

TROIS VIANDES DE PROVENCE

3 large cloves garlic
1 beef brisket (about 3 pounds), tied with string
1 pork shoulder roast (about 3 pounds), tied with string
10 tablespoons butter
2 tablespoons vegetable or olive oil
1 veal shoulder roast (about 3 pounds), tied with string
2 cups onions, minced
1 sprig fresh thyme, chopped, or a pinch of dried
2½ cups chopped, seeded tomatoes
1 teaspoon sugar
½ teaspoon chopped fresh rosemary or a pinch of dried
½ cup strong chicken stock or broth
2½ cups dry white wine
1 teaspoon salt
½ teaspoon freshly ground pepper
3 tablespoons cognac
½ tablespoon finely slivered orange peel
Chopped parsley for garnish

Serves 8 to 10.

1 Bruise 1 clove garlic; rub over beef and pork. Mince all garlic; reserve.

2 Melt 4 tablespoons butter with the oil in a heavy skillet. Brown beef well on all sides; transfer to a large, heavy pot or Dutch oven. Repeat with pork and veal.

3 Remove all grease from skillet; add 4 tablespoons butter. Melt butter over medium heat, scraping bottom and sides of pan. Add reserved garlic and the onions; saute until golden. Add mixture to meat.

4 Cook meat covered over medium-low heat 30 minutes. Add the thyme and tomatoes. Sprinkle the tomatoes with sugar; stir in the rosemary, chicken stock, wine, salt, and pepper. Bring to a boil; reduce heat. Simmer covered until meat is tender, 2½ to 3 hours.

5 Heat oven to 250°. Remove meat to a large serving platter; keep warm in oven. Skim all grease from sauce. Boil sauce until thickened, about 10 minutes.

6 Heat cognac in a small saucepan; ignite. Pour over sauce; stir in orange peel. Spoon some of the sauce over the meat; sprinkle with parsley and serve with remaining sauce.

Burgundians are as full of wine aphorisms as their province is full of wine.

"Good wine revives the heart of man," they are given to murmuring, the way other Frenchmen might say "Good night!" or "Good morning!"

Here is a full-bodied Burgundian prescription for pork chops baked in red wine, which, if not guaranteed to revive the old aorta, will surely lighten it!

PORK CHOPS IN BURGUNDY

1 Trim all fat from pork chops. Sprinkle with salt and pepper. Coat with flour; shake off excess.

2 Heat butter and oil in a heavy skillet. Cook the chops over medium heat until very crisp and golden, about 12 to 15 minutes.

3 Heat oven to 350°. Transfer chops to a baking dish. Add shallots and garlic to the skillet; cook over medium-low heat 5 minutes. Add the wine and cook over high heat until sauce is reduced by half. Pour sauce over meat. Bake 40 to 45 minutes, depending on size of chops, basting several times. Sprinkle with parsley.

4 thick pork chops
Salt and freshly ground pepper
Flour
3 tablespoons butter
2 tablespoons vegetable oil
¼ cup finely chopped shallots
1 large clove garlic, minced
1 cup red Burgundy wine
4 tablespoons chopped parsley

Serves 4.

All provincial French cooks are opinionated on the subject of wine cookery. No amount of the vintage grape, they insist, should ever be added to a sauce unless it has been boiled down first.

Out of the wine country of Burgundy comes an unusually tasty vegetable dish. A puree of kidney beans flavored with red wine, this devise makes a palatable difference when the menu calls for a Christmas goose or a Thanksgiving turkey.

I must confess that I uncovered this recipe in a very old and thumb-worn cooking manual published in Beaune, which I found while browsing in a book stall along the Seine. I translated this prescription first (and so far exclusively) simply because it is the only one in the book without complex grammatical structure. But it's a prodigious bit of cookery, nonetheless!

PUREED KIDNEY BEANS

1 pound dried kidney beans
6 quarts water
2 teaspoons salt
1½ cups dry red wine
1 small carrot, chopped
1 onion, chopped
1 bay leaf
1 sprig parsley
Pinch of thyme
3 slices bacon
2 teaspoons all-purpose flour
Pinch of ground allspice
Salt and freshly ground pepper
1½ tablespoons butter, cut into
    pieces

Serves 6 to 8.

1 Wash the beans and soak overnight in 6 quarts water in a large pot.

2 Bring beans and water to a boil over medium heat. Reduce heat; add 2 teaspoons salt and simmer until tender, about 1¾ hours. Drain; set aside 1 cup cooking liquid.

3 Combine wine, carrot, onion, bay leaf, parsley, and thyme in a saucepan. Bring to a boil and reduce by half. Strain mixture and reserve.

4 Puree beans in a food processor or mash through a sieve. Add some cooking liquid if puree is too thick.

5 Fry bacon in a skillet until crisp; drain on paper toweling. Remove all but 2 tablespoons bacon fat from skillet. Add flour; cook and stir over medium heat for 2 minutes. Whisk reserved, boiled wine into skillet; simmer until thickened, about 3 minutes. Stir in the beans and season with allspice, and salt and pepper to taste. Add the butter, one piece at a time.

For geographical variety, try next the best hamburger recipe I know. A veritable Burgundyburger, if you will!

BURGUNDYBURGERS

8 large mushrooms
4 tablespoons butter
1 small shallot, minced
2 pounds ground beef chuck
1 tablespoon Dijon mustard
¼ teaspoon Worcestershire sauce
¼ teaspoon beef bouillon powder
Pinch of allspice
Salt and freshly ground pepper to
    taste
3 tablespoons finely chopped
    parsley
⅓ cup red Burgundy wine

Serves 4.

1 Remove mushroom caps and chop the stems. Saute caps and stems in 1 tablespoon butter in a skillet over high heat until golden. Remove with a slotted spoon; reserve. Add remaining butter and the shallot to skillet; saute until tender. Remove with a slotted spoon.

2 Place meat, shallot, mustard, Worcestershire sauce, bouillon powder, allspice, salt, pepper, and 2 tablespoons parsley in a bowl; mix well. Shape mixture into four hamburgers. Add to skillet; cook over high heat, about 3 minutes on each side for rare.

3 Transfer hamburgers to a serving dish. Remove all but about 3 tablespoons fat from skillet. Add the wine and reserved mushrooms; cook over high heat until sauce is reduced and thickened. Pour over hamburgers; sprinkle with remaining parsley.

The last two precepts in this chapter are for desserts that combine the tincture of white wine with fresh fruit.

The first, a pear gratin from the Anjou country of France, is included for its ease of preparation as well as its mirific aroma. Serve these pears warm for fruitiest flavor and grate a bit of fresh orange peel into the whipped cream garnish for overkill.

If you feel very rich, serve a sweet dessert wine (like German Piesporter Treppchen) as a heady companion to end the meal. If not, make it strong black coffee!

POIRES AU GRATIN

1 Heat oven to 400°. Peel, quarter, and core the pears. Cut lengthwise into ½-inch-thick slices. Grease a 9×13-inch baking dish with 1 tablespoon butter and set aside.

2 Combine the wine, orange juice, preserves, and 2 tablespoons orange peel in a small bowl; mix thoroughly.

3 Layer the pears in the baking dish, sprinkling with half the macaroon crumbs and dotting with 3 tablespoons butter as you go. When finished, pour the wine mixture over pears. Sprinkle with remaining crumbs; dot with remaining 1 tablespoon butter. Bake until top is golden brown, 25 to 30 minutes. Serve hot or cold with the whipped cream.

2 pounds ripe pears
5 tablespoons butter
4 tablespoons dry white wine or vermouth
4 tablespoons orange juice
¼ cup apricot preserves
2 tablespoons grated orange peel
2 cup crumbled macaroons, lightly toasted
Whipping cream, whipped with grated orange peel

Serves 6.

Just desserts, eh?

This one is a heavenly concoction, let me tell you. It was first served to me at Paris's glamorous Étoile restaurant—and later reconstructed on a wing and a prayer. The secret ingredient, I discovered after much trial and even more error, is dry champagne. You must soak *firm* strawberries in this elixir for a few hours before making the dessert. But *firm* means firm; over-ripe berries should be bathed only long enough to absorb a mite of the wine's flavor or they will turn mushy. A whipped cream-enriched custard and a lacing of crunchy caramel give the fruit a setting worthy of Van Cleef and Arpels.

I think of this dish as a holiday event—like eggnog. But you may feel free to partake of it during any season at all—with or without a magnum of iced dry champagne (Dom Perignon instantly comes to mind).

FRAISES DE L'ÉTOILE

1½ pints strawberries, washed, hulled
3 tablespoons confectioners' sugar
1 split (6.5 ounces) champagne
4 egg yolks
⅔ cup granulated sugar
2 tablespoons cornstarch
1½ teaspoons vanilla
1 cup milk, scalded
¾ cup whipping cream

Serves 4.

1 Combine strawberries and confectioners' sugar in a bowl; mix well. Pour champagne over strawberries. Refrigerate covered at least 2 hours.

2 Beat the egg yolks with ⅓ cup granulated sugar and the cornstarch until light and fluffy. Beat in vanilla and gradually add milk. Cook in the top of a double boiler over hot water until thick. Remove from heat; let stand to cool.

3 Whip the cream until thick; fold into the custard. Spoon ⅔ of the custard into an ovenproof glass serving bowl or a souffle dish. Drain the strawberries. Press strawberries, one at a time, into the custard. Spread remaining custard over top. Refrigerate at least 2 hours; then place bowl in freezer while proceeding with Step 4.

4 Melt ⅓ cup granulated sugar in a heavy saucepan over low heat; cook until syrup turns into a rich brown caramel. Immediately remove custard from the freezer and drizzle caramel over top in a thin lattice. (This must be done as quickly as possible or caramel will harden.) Refrigerate until ready to serve.

Yeast

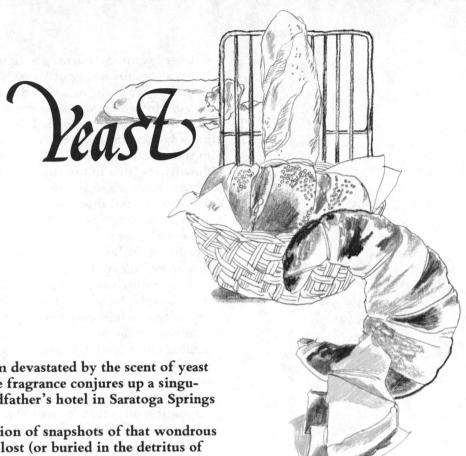

Proust had his madeleines; I am devastated by the scent of yeast bread rising, myself. That pure fragrance conjures up a singularly strong image of my grandfather's hotel in Saratoga Springs as it was when I was young.

I used to have a large collection of snapshots of that wondrous hostelry but in time they were lost (or buried in the detritus of my sister's attic crawl space); so now my evidence of its existence lies solely in memory.

My favorite portrait of The Lafayette Hotel was printed on three-by-five-inch postal cards in the late 1920s. Hundreds of these pasteboard lithographs filled my closets and desk drawers once, but I have not seen one in almost forty years. And I think I would pay any ransom just to glimpse that gaudy rendering once more. The photo probably was taken on a late summer's day just before a rain shower swept in from the Adirondacks, for although the sky appeared bright Cerulean blue, winy shadows below the building seemed menacingly dark and the gingerbread railings and fluted columns were too sharply white—like a stage set placed against the wrong backdrop. What I remember best about this picture, though, is the people. The front porch of the hotel (beneath an overhang of ivy and boxed geraniums) was filled with anonymous, orange-faced guests—all of them settled in rocking chairs and blissfully unaware that their moment of immortality was at hand.

The porch crowd is gone now. On the leveled ground where the majestic white elephant once stood, butterfly weed and crab grass hold sway today. But bake me a bread and the scent of it will make the whole place come alive again!

Every summer morning at dawn, before the first guest stirred in his sleep, dreaming of Rosie's fried herrings, the bread baker would arrive at the hotel's dairy kitchen. I discovered this fact because my room was over the vast pantry (near my grandparents' quarters) and I smelled the bread rising in the dark. It was not a far descent from my room to the bakery and I soon began to wake before anyone else in the family, so that I could slip downstairs (still in my pajamas) to watch the baker begin his labors. Red-haired and red-bearded, like a drawing of the god Thor in my childhood book of myths, this handsome giant had arms the size of a bear's. He could pick up a fifty-pound sack of flour with ease and toss it across the room as lightly as if it were a bedroom pillow. The only flaw in his godliness, for me, was that he neither spoke nor smiled as he worked.

A recent arrival from some small village bake shop in Latvia or Lithuania, he understood none of what was spoken to him in any of the dialects mustered by my "Uncle" Mike and other members of the hotel's staff. A recruit fresh off the boat, sent to Saratoga by a Slavic employment agency in New York City, this man kept counsel only with the loaves he turned out daily. He produced an aromatic bouquet of rye, white, pumpernickel, and golden egg challah breads with utter dedication from dawn until early afternoon; then he would abruptly dust himself free of flour and leave as wordlessly as he had arrived.

As the baker spoke no English and I knew nothing of his language, we communicated only by a series of shy nods or grunts when I would retrieve a spoon or dishcloth that had fallen to the floor during his labors. I would make certain that the path to the brick ovens was completely unobstructed before he loaded his pans of unbaked loaves in his arms—and for this he would sometimes shake his head in a silent "thank you."

Once in a while, he would select a random curl of raw dough from his floured board after all the loaves were formed and, with a single motion of his steel blade, slice it in two. One piece to go into his mouth—and the other for mine.

Perhaps it was then that I first came to love the slightly sourish flavor of uncooked dough. I do not rightly know where else the predilection for yeasty flavors could have come from, but, even today, I never send a bread into the oven without first chomping a bit of it raw.

My days in the bakery were numbered, however. One summer morning, my mother, having awakened earlier than usual, noted my absence in the bedroom and went to ferret me out. "*Bertram*," come upstairs and brush your teeth," she ordered sweetly but firmly. Then, having waited until we had gotten out of earshot of my friend the baker (who could not understand in any event): "Where do you get these weird ideas?" she queried. "Hanging around for hours with that strange foreign man, in that stifling room. You'll be lucky if you don't come down with a fever!''

My health never was better; so I can only assume that my mother felt there was something perverse in my attentions to the fiery-haired giant.

After that morning, whenever I attempted to slip down the back stairs to join him, I was waylaid by some hotel employee (like Zinnia, the chambermaid, or Mack, the porter) who, obviously on instruction from my parent, found some means of diverting me to outdoor activities—like fetching the morning editions of the New York papers from a newsdealer's shop across town. I was only a little kid at the time and my attention span was short; so I soon forgot the long hours spent watching my friend's bread magically rise in the steamy kitchen.

The next summer, there was a different baker at work: a short dark man who unaccountably spit whenever he spoke. Though he understood my language perfectly, I never visited the bakery at dawn again.

But, as Proust said so much better than I ever could, '' . . . when from a long-distant past nothing subsists, after the people are dead, after the things are broken and scattered, still . . . the smell and taste of things remain. . . .''

Cereal grains have been a part and parcel of man's diet since the first cave dweller chewed the seeds of wild grasses to survive. When early hunters failed to provide an adequate supply of meat, the women of the tribe learned to crush millet, barley, and wheat and mix the powders with water into a rough gruel that would extend the family diet until another kill was organized.

Subsequently, some intrepid cave-lady-cook ground the grains finer than her predecessors and came up with proper flour, which in turn lead to proper bakery. We know this because flat, bread-like cakes were found in the caves of Choukoutien, China, among the artifacts of Peking man. These cakes, probably made of rice flour, were either dried in the sun or cooked on flat rocks over wood fires.

Millenniums later, the Egyptians developed a similar kind of unleavened bread into a thriving industry. Three thousand years before the birth of Christ, professional millers were grinding barley into flour for Egyptian farmers. For a surcharge, they added water to some of this flour and turned it into a dough that the farmers could either add to their stewpots (like a steamed dumpling) or bake in the public ovens, which were hollowed out of the ground and lined with clay to retain heat.

Early Egyptian bread was coarse and rough-grained and hell on the stomach. It contained no leavening agent to make the dough rise; so the end result was less than a treat to the palate or the gums. And it is generally agreed that it was eaten more for survival than pleasure!

That all changed, however, when the first migratory Hebrews wandered into the Nile Valley and brought sourdough with them! No one seems to know how or when sourdough evolved but it most likely originated among the Semite tribes of the Tigris-Euphrates valley who cultivated grapes early on and may have agitated the juices into wine. One theory that sounds plausible is that some foxy baker's assistant added grape juice to the stone-ground meal instead of water and thus caused the mess to ferment.

The Egyptians, in turn, discovered that sourdough contained yeast and they became the first people to isolate the bacterial spores and develop separate yeast cultures. Though the Hebrews used their sourdough to leaven sweet cakes and such, the Egyptians became the first people to bake bread with it. And their yeast-baked creations (made with at least forty different varieties of grain, from lotus seeds to almonds) became the astonishment and envy of the ancient world!

Bread *aficionados* insist that no other slice on earth has the special taste and texture of that old-time favorite, sourdough bread. In our heritage, sourdough is usually traced back to the gold rush of 1848, when prospectors carried lumps of fermenting flour with them on their westward trek, so that they could bake bread between grizzlies and shootouts.

Today the cult of sourdough breadmakers is divided into two factions: those who stick with the pioneer's natural fermentation method and those who cheat by adding yeast. The common complaint with the naturalists' way is that their formula does not always work. Spontaneous fermentation is finicky; changes in temperature affect it as do humidity and pollutants in the air. Educated breadophiles do not recommend making sourdough in big cities at all. I suggest you try yours with yeast!

If you plan to use Sourdough Starter often, there is really no need to refrigerate it. Simply renew it by adding water and flour in equal parts every time you deplete the original batch. If you do not expect to use the starter frequently, allow it to stand tightly covered (plastic-wrap with a rubber band is best) for two days; then store it in a cold place. Remember to allow the starter to return to room temperature before you use it!

SOURDOUGH STARTER

1 package yeast
2 cups warm water
2 cups all-purpose flour

Dissolve the yeast in the water in a 2-quart ceramic bowl. Stir in the flour; mix well. Cover tightly; let stand at room temperature 2 days. Stir well before using, because mixture will have separated somewhat.

Note: This recipe makes enough starter for both the Sourdough White Bread and the Sourdough Rye Bread recipes that follow.

SOURDOUGH WHITE BREAD

1 Combine ingredients in a large bowl. Cover tightly; let stand at room temperature overnight. This will be the sponge needed for the next day's baking.

2 Dissolve the yeast in the water in a small bowl. Let stand 5 minutes. Stir the yeast, water, and salt into the sponge; mix in 4 cups flour. Transfer to a lightly floured board. Knead until smooth, about 10 minutes. Place in an ungreased bowl, sprinkle with flour and cover. Let rise until doubled in volume, about 2½ to 3 hours.

3 Punch down dough; knead briefly. Shape into 2 loaves. Let rise for 1 hour. (If using a baking sheet, sprinkle it with cornmeal and let dough rise on sheet.) Heat oven to 450°.

4 If using tile baking surface, sprinkle it with cornmeal; transfer bread to surface. Brush loaves with egg wash, if desired. Bake until loaves sound hollow when tapped, about 25 minutes.

Note: See "About Bread and Its Baking," page 393, before proceeding with recipe.

The night before:
1 cup Sourdough Starter
1 cup warm water
2 cups all-purpose flour

The next day:
1 package dry yeast
1 cup warm water
1 tablespoon salt
4 cups all-purpose flour
Cornmeal
1 egg yolk mixed with 1 tablespoon water (optional)

Makes 2 loaves.

SOURDOUGH RYE BREAD

1 Combine ingredients in a large bowl. Cover tightly; let stand at room temperature overnight. This will be the sponge needed for the next day's baking.

2 Dissolve the yeast in the water in a small bowl. Let stand 5 minutes. Stir the yeast, water, and salt into the sponge. Add the seeds and mix in 4 cups flour. Transfer to a lightly floured board. Knead until smooth, about 10 minutes. Place in an ungreased bowl, sprinkle with flour, and cover. Let rise until doubled in volume, about 2½ to 3 hours.

3 Punch down dough; knead briefly. Shape into 2 loaves. Let rise 1 hour. (If using a baking sheet, sprinkle it with cornmeal and let dough rise on sheet.) Heat oven to 450°.

4 If using tile baking surface, sprinkle it with cornmeal; transfer bread to surface. Brush loaves with egg wash, if desired. Bake until loaves sound hollow when tapped, about 25 minutes.

Note: See "About Bread and Its Baking," page 393, before proceeding with recipe.

The night before:
1 cup Sourdough Starter
1 cup warm water
2 cups rye flour

The next day:
1 package dry yeast
1 cup warm water
1 tablespoon salt
1 tablespoon caraway seeds
1½ teaspoons poppy seeds
4 cups all-purpose flour
Cornmeal
1 egg yolk mixed with 1 tablespoon water (optional)

Makes 2 loaves.

Home bakery did not come into my life until I was a grown man and already secure in the ways of gastronomy. I decided to bake bread because I had a splendid country kitchen at my disposal, a whole month to "loaf" and a growing appetite for a taste of the past.

Some cookbook writers must share responsibility for my interest in this homely undertaking. Adelle Davis and James Beard were spiritual seconds in all my early duels with dough!

Nutrition-minded Ms. Davis, particularly, was my mentor because her dark augury of contamination in *Let's Cook It Right* forced me to consider carefully what I put into my bread. I learned from her that the "biblical" seven grains—wheat, oats, corn, rye, barley, rice, and soybeans—produce the most natural flavors by far. So they became my basic ingredients—*stone-ground,* of course. What Ms. Davis neglected to add and what I did not ascertain until after some notably sodden slices had been chewed is that stone-ground flour also produces the heaviest bread. Therefore, a wise baker usually doubles the yeast when making loaves exclusively with these flours.

Beard, on quite the other hand, dismissed the matter of grain but figuratively seduced me into the oven with his rhapsody on golden crumbs in a small but replete paperback (*The James Beard Cookbook*) that was my first culinary guide. The prophet of the palate described the rich, yeasty smells of baking with such lyricism that I half expected brown, crusty loaves to fall unassisted from my oven door like manna from the heavens!

Sad to say, my initial batch of homemade white bread was pallidly disappointing—wan as an invalid in need of summer sun! Nothing in Mr. Beard's instruction suggested how to deepen the tan, either. When I left the bread pans in the oven longer, the crust freckled slightly but the inside turned dry as dust. If I raised the heat, my loaf scorched. I am not declaring that the bread was a total disaster; it wasn't. Each loaf had a tonic aroma and an agreeable taste but the texture was disappointingly dense. And no matter at what temperature I affixed the oven, the outer crust never achieved that distinctive crackling quality I remembered from the Saratoga hotel kitchen of my childhood.

While visiting a bread shop in France some time after my first baking attempts, I was struck with envy by the professionalism of the *boulanger,* who every morning tapped his crusty loaves for the correct hollow sound. My loaves had been made of sterner stuff: when thumped they echoed not at all! This same baker also aroused my admiration by transporting a dozen unbaked loaves on one arm and depositing them all onto the white-hot stones of his oven merely by flexing his muscles; then, after dipping a cloth into a bucket of water he managed effortlessly to wring it dry inside the blazing interior. Smiling with gratification as the scattering drops of water produced clouds of steam over his rising loaves, he turned to me and announced with more than a touch of Gallic pride: *"C'est le meilleur pain du monde, monsieur!"*

He was probably right. But trying his technique for "the best bread in the world" in my apartment kitchen was another cup of tea! The freshets of steam produced a ductile loaf of bread that certainly was resonant when tapped, but a slight accident marred my victory celebration: the dish towel that I, too, dutifully squeezed and shook into the oven somehow became lodged irretrievably between the stove wall and the hot metal rack. So, while the crusts were definitely darker and crispier than those of any previous output, the bread was distinguished by a most unusual flavor—smoked linen! And my kitchen, far from conjuring up the scent of a French bake shop, smelled exactly like a Chinese laundry.

In a *götterdämmerung* of bake-offs, and with a deep bow to Mr. Beard's splendid volume, *Beard on Bread,* I have managed to compile a clutch of admonitions about bread and its baking that just might serve to leaven your loaf somewhat.

About Bread and Its Baking:

—*Temperature:* Most bread-making manuals suggest that the baker work in a warm room (80-85°F); I do not. My instruction is that bread be made in a decidedly cooler atmosphere (70°F is perfect) and on a dry day, if possible. The reason? Yeast gains in flavor the longer it takes to ferment. If the yeast works too quickly or is forced to rise by artificial heating, the finished bread will have an unpleasant "beery" flavor. Also, there is a noticeable improvement in the texture of slow-risen bread.

—*Yeast:* The most readily available is a dry granular variety that comes in handy packets. I use Red Star or Fleischmann's brand. If you are lucky enough to find compressed yeast cakes, note that they are sold in different amounts. The best size for translation into recipes that call for one package of dry yeast is the baker's half-ounce size (which is actually .6 ounces, maddeningly enough).

—*Flour:* As I have said before, natural flour (from health food stores) is usually my first option. If commercial flour is the only kind available, be sure to use an unbleached all-purpose brand, like Hecker's.

—*Kneading:* While not exactly the serendipity that some cookbook writers promise, throwing dough can be fun for the bread-maker once he gets the hang of it. Dough is often somewhat tacky when it is first scraped onto a floured board. Let it rest a bit before you pummel. Start with a pastry scraper or a spatula and flip the dough over on itself until it begins to stiffen. Then, using the heel of your hand, push the dough forward and continue the flipping process. If it seems overly sticky, add a bit more flour. Doing this for about ten minutes should produce a smooth and elastic dough—and a pacific personality change in you!

—*Rising of the dough:* This sounds like a religious experience but it isn't. Rising means that the fermenting yeast is producing gas bubbles that in turn expand the gluten in the flour and leaven the loaf. Always be sure to grease or lightly flour the bowl in which a dough is to rise according to the recipe's instruction. It is best to place the dough in a bowl large enough to accommodate its doubling in size. Cover the bowl tightly with plastic wrap, lay a folded bath towel or blanket over the top, and definitely keep it out of drafts. A cool oven is a nice place for the rising action to take place. Once the dough has risen and been formed into a loaf it must rise again. I like to place my loaves on the edge of a tea towel that has been well rubbed with flour. I cover them with another towel until they double in size and then simply roll them off onto my baking surface.

—*Baking:* All breads may be made in pans or on baking sheets but, as I reported earlier, only bread baked in a true brick oven will approximate an old-fashioned crusty loaf. There are several ways to simulate the brick oven's combination of intense heat and steam. One possibility is to bake bread directly on unglazed quarry tiles. Six of these terra cotta slabs, each 5½-inches square, will fit compactly onto an oven rack; they can be sprayed with water from a common indoor-plant sprayer to achieve the degree of steamy heat that guarantees an authentic crust. Another method is to bake on a commercially available oblong sheet of glazed pottery (a Grateful Bread Plate) on a rack in the lower third of the oven and liberally spritz it with water from time to time.

The Apple Butter and Honey Whole-Wheat Bread that follows, like all the other yeast loaves in my canon, should be sprayed with a mist of cold water the moment it goes into the oven and sprayed again after three minutes of baking to ensure a splendidly crusty loaf. This formula produces an unusual, delicately fruity flavor. I make it with homemade apple butter—a real plus if you have some lurking about.

APPLE BUTTER AND HONEY WHOLE-WHEAT BREAD

1 Dissolve yeast and sugar in ½ cup warm water in a large bowl; let stand 10 minutes. Stir in remaining water, the butter, apple butter, honey, and salt. Beat in flour, 1 cup at a time. Turn out onto a floured board; knead until smooth, about 10 minutes. Shape into a ball and place in a well-buttered bowl; turn dough to coat with butter. Cover tightly; let rise until doubled in volume, about 1½ hours.

2 Punch down dough; knead briefly. Shape dough into two loaves. Cover and let rise 1 hour. (If using a baking sheet, sprinkle it with cornmeal and let dough rise on the sheet.) Heat oven to 425°.

3 If using tile baking surface, sprinkle it with cornmeal; transfer bread to surface. Brush loaves with egg wash. Bake 10 minutes; reduce oven heat to 375°; bake until loaves sound hollow when tapped, 20 to 25 minutes longer.

2 packages dry yeast
1 tablespoon granulated sugar
2 cups warm water
¼ cup butter, melted
½ cup apple butter
2 tablespoons honey
1½ tablespoons salt
3½ cups whole-wheat flour
2 to 2½ cups all-purpose flour
Cornmeal
1 egg beaten with 1 teaspoon water

Makes 2 medium-size loaves.

When I was a small child (and we were still rich), I had a nursemaid named Marion who had just arrived from Hungary. She talked endlessly in broken English about "the vunderful breasts of Budapesh" every time we sat down to dinner. No wonder, since we Greenes ate only flaccid, packaged white bread at the time! The fennel seeds on the following loaf could convert even a dedicated rye man (like me) to Marion's cause.

HUNGARIAN FENNEL BREAD

1 Dissolve yeast with sugar in ½ cup water in a large bowl; let stand 10 minutes. Stir in remaining water, the salt, 2 teaspoons fennel seeds, the butter, and enough flour to make a stiff dough. Knead on a floured board, about 10 minutes, adding more flour if needed. Shape dough into a ball. Place in a buttered bowl; turn dough to coat with butter. Cover and let rise until doubled in volume, about 1½ to 2 hours.

2 Punch down dough; knead briefly. Shape into a round loaf. Cover and let rise 1 hour. (If using a baking sheet, sprinkle it with cornmeal and let dough rise on sheet.) Heat oven to 375°.

1 package dry yeast
1 teaspoon granulated sugar
1 cup warm water
2 teaspoons salt
4 teaspoons fennel seeds
2 tablespoons butter, melted
4 cups all-purpose flour
1 egg beaten with 1 teaspoon water

Makes 1 loaf.

3 If using tile baking surface, sprinkle it with cornmeal; transfer bread to surface. Using a sharp knife, slash a cross in the top of the loaf; brush loaf with egg wash. Sprinkle remaining fennel seeds over top. Bake 30 minutes.

Note: See "About Bread and Its Baking," page 393, before proceeding with recipe.

Aside from golden loaves of French bread, the finest baking achievement of France, in my opinion at least, is the buttery and utterly frangible pastry known as a *croissant*.

I confess that I have never eaten a less-than-perfect rendering of this airy crescent anywhere on the continent. But I have rarely found its counterpart at home—even in the most snobbish French bakeries on New York's Upper East Side.

The art of the croissant is considerably difficult to master. I should amend that to *was,* for food processors have turned the dough-making into short work for a cool baker. Mine is a non-fail method and may be prepared with or without the bacon fillip at the cook's discretion. It is undoubtedly *yeast's finest hour!*

BACON-FILLED CROISSANTS

8 strips bacon
2 tablespoons dry yeast
2 tablespoons granulated sugar
½ cup scalded milk, cooled to lukewarm
1 cup water
2 tablespoons unsalted butter
2 cups unbleached all-purpose flour
1 teaspoon salt
¾ cup unsalted butter, at room temperature
Chive Butter (recipe follows)
1 egg yolk beaten with 2 tablespoons water

Makes 12 to 16.

1 Fry bacon in a heavy skillet until very crisp. Drain between two layers of paper toweling. Crumble bacon and reserve.

2 Dissolve yeast and 1 tablespoon sugar in the lukewarm milk. Let stand 10 minutes.

3 Heat 1 cup water with 1 tablespoon sugar and 2 tablespoons butter in a small saucepan until sugar dissolves and butter melts. Cool to lukewarm.

4 Combine flour and salt; place in the bowl of a food processor. Add yeast mixture and water mixture. Process until the dough forms into a ball.

5 Lightly butter a mixing bowl. Place dough in bowl and turn it to lightly coat with butter. Cover tightly; let stand in a warm place (free of drafts) until doubled in volume, about 1 hour.

6 Turn dough onto a lightly floured board (or a piece of marble or

formica) and pat into a rectangle. Using a floured rolling pin, press dough into an 8×12-inch rectangle. Transfer dough to a floured baking sheet; cover with a dish towel. Refrigerate 1 hour and 15 minutes.

7 Place chilled dough on a lightly floured board; roll out to a 13-×17-inch rectangle. Spread two-thirds of dough with ¾ cup butter, leaving ¼-inch border unbuttered. (The butter should be at room temperature exactly and in no danger of melting.)

8 Fold the unbuttered third of the rectangle over half of the buttered portion; fold remaining half of the buttered portion over unbuttered third. (Dough will resemble an envelope.) Place dough on baking sheet; cover and refrigerate 20 minutes.

9 Place chilled dough on surface with layers facing you; roll out to a 14×16-inch rectangle. Fold down top third of dough; fold bottom third over it. Lightly sprinkle folded dough with flour on both sides; place on baking sheet. Cut folded dough in half. Cover with dish towel; refrigerate 1 hour.

10 Remove one half of dough from refrigerator. Roll out to a 9-×16-inch rectangle (dough should not be more than ¼-inch thick). Fold up bottom third of dough; fold top third over it. Return folded dough to the refrigerator; chill 30 minutes. Repeat step with remaining half of dough.

11 Roll out one half of dough to a 9×16-inch rectangle. Using a sharp knife, cut rectangle in half crosswise (you should have two 4½×16-inch strips). Cut each strip into 3 or 4 triangles. Repeat step with remaining half of dough.

12 Place 1 teaspoon of the reserved bacon in middle of each triangle. Roll up triangles, starting from edge and rolling toward point. With floured fingers, gently shape triangles into crescents.

13 Brush two baking sheets with butter. Place croissants on sheets. Cover and let rise in a warm place until doubled in volume, about 30 minutes. Heat oven to 475°.

14 Meanwhile, make chive butter.

15 Brush croissants with egg wash. Place baking sheets in oven on middle rack. Bake until croissants are puffed and brown, 12 to 15 minutes. Cool on wire racks 10 to 15 minutes before serving. Serve with chive butter.

Notes: If using a wooden board, make sure it is well-chilled before you roll out the dough. If at all possible, use a chilled marble or formica surface.

Filled and shaped croissants can be frozen before baking. Bake frozen croissants 2 or 3 minutes longer.

½ cup unsalted butter, at room temperature
¼ cup minced chives or green onion tops
Dash of hot pepper sauce

CHIVE BUTTER

Beat butter until fluffy. Stir in chives and hot pepper sauce. Pack into a small crock or serving dish. Refrigerate until 30 minutes before serving.

It is a far cry from a French croissant to a New England raised biscuit but geography, I discovered long ago, has nothing at all to do with culinary goodness. These excellent dinner companions have a texture and a flavor distinctively their own— courtesy of yellow butternut squash mated with yeast and pure maple syrup. The recipe is from a Methodist church bulletin printed in New Hampshire around the turn of the century— when everything in America still had natural savor. And when we still believed that *that* was an inalienable right!

1½ teaspoons (½ package) dry yeast
¼ cup lukewarm water
3 to 3¼ cups sifted unbleached all-purpose flour (approximately)
¼ cup plus 2 tablespoons granulated sugar
¼ teaspoon salt
2 tablespoons butter, melted
2 eggs, lightly beaten
¾ cup pureed boiled butternut squash
¼ cup maple syrup
¼ teaspoon freshly grated nutmeg
½ cup scalded milk, cooled to lukewarm
Melted butter

Makes 1½ to 2 dozen.

RAISED SQUASH BISCUITS

1 Dissolve yeast in lukewarm water in a large bowl. Stir in ¼ cup flour and 1 tablespoon sugar. Cover and let rise 1 hour.

2 Stir remaining sugar, the salt, 2 tablespoons melted butter, the eggs, squash, maple syrup, and nutmeg into yeast mixture; beat thoroughly. Beat in the milk and enough of the remaining flour to form a sticky dough. Sprinkle dough with flour. Cover tightly; let rise 2 hours.

3 Punch down dough; turn out onto a well floured board. Sprinkle lightly with flour; knead, incorporating flour as required, until dough is smooth, 5 to 8 minutes. (Use a pastry scraper to begin kneading sticky dough.)

4 Divide dough in half. Roll each half ½-inch thick with a floured rolling pin; cut into 2-inch circles. Place ½-inch apart on ungreased

baking sheets. Cover with flour-rubbed towels; let rise 45 minutes. Heat oven to 425°.

5 Bake biscuits until lightly browned on top, about 15 minutes. Brush biscuits with melted butter as soon as they come out of the oven.

Note: Do not use frozen pureed squash in this recipe.

The Centennial State has provided my kitchen with more than its share of wonderful native dishes because I am lucky enough to have a Coloradan, Phillip Schulz, in my kitchen. Every time the May breezes blow and the tender rhubarb shows darkly pink, I give thanks to Schulz's mother Mildred for her prodigious wonderworks—rhubarb pie and cake.

Now, from Mrs. Schulz's good neighbor (Irma Wehausen, also of Golden, Colorado) comes Sun Rise Bread. The memory of this sunny white loaf has plagued young Schulz in Manhattan for years. Periodically he will recall its tender crumbs and light-as-air texture and write his mother for the recipe—only to report later, after yet another formula has been dutifully forwarded from Colorado and tested in New York, "Funny, it's just not as good as I remembered it!"

When his younger sister Becky was visiting Manhattan a short while back, Phillip pursued the phantom loaf further.

"Whatever happened to Mom's recipe for that great white bread we used to eat—with only cream and sugar spread on it—when we were kids?" he quizzed his sibling. "That was the best bread she ever made."

"That wasn't Mom's bread at all, you dope!" quoth Becky Schulz. "It was Mrs. Wehausen's."

And thus it came to be immortalized.

Mrs. Wehausen should be permitted a final word on the subject:

"I call it my Sun Rise Bread as it turns out best when we have a sunshiny day and I set the dough by a window where the sun streams in. That is, in cooler weather, of course. I don't need to do this on hot summer days. It takes most of a day to get the bread ready as it is slow to rise. Also I like it best fresh; so I freeze most of it right away. Then I just get a loaf out and slice as much as I'll eat that day—and the rest goes back into the freezer. I usually slice my fresh bread with an electric knife, so that it won't 'squish' together as it might do with a dull knife. Another secret to making my bread turn out good is the amount of kneading. It takes more of it than some fast-rising recipes—but it is worth it!''

IRMA WEHAUSEN'S SUN RISE BREAD

2 packages dry yeast
3 cups warm water
2 teaspoons granulated sugar
1½ tablespoons cold vegetable shortening
7 cups unbleached all-purpose white flour (approximately)
1½ tablespoons salt

Makes 3 loaves.

1 Dissolve yeast in warm water in a large bowl; stir in 2 teaspoons sugar. Let stand 5 minutes.

2 Blend shortening with 1½ cups flour and the salt, using a pastry blender, until smooth. Stir into yeast mixture. Stir in enough flour, about 4½ to 5 cups, for dough to begin losing its stickiness.

3 Scrape dough onto a lightly floured board. Knead, incorporating flour as required, until dough is smooth, 15 to 20 minutes. (Use a pastry scraper to begin kneading sticky dough.) Cover with a small tea towel and plastic wrap; let rise until doubled in volume, about 1½ hours.

4 Punch down dough; knead briefly. Cover and let rise until doubled in volume.

5 Punch down dough once more. Divide dough into thirds and place in three loaf pans. Cover pans loosely with a towel; let dough rise until high (over rims of pans), 2 to 3 hours.

6 Heat oven to 375°. Bake loaves 1 hour.

Sicilian *sciocco* (pronounced Scotch-oh!), redolent of cheese, tomato, and sausage—all familiarly Italian, was pried from an ancient family recipe log of a friend of mine. The donor is Joe de Rosa (the well-known fashion photographer), who attended Newtown High School in Queens along with this writer back in the fourth century.

Joe claims that this devise has been in his sister's cooking repertoire for years. She learned it from her mother-in-law, Mrs. Gurriere, who acquired it from her own mother, who obviously acquired it from hers, who more than likely inherited it from some relative in Pompeii or Herculaneum.

According to Gurriere family lore, Sciocco was originally a picnic loaf, made to be eaten cold on holidays, when the religious did not cook. Lukewarm, however, it makes an incredible Sunday night supper or a great luncheon. Remember to slice it neither too thick nor too thin—three-fourths inch is just right.

MR. AND MRS. GAETANO GURRIERE'S "SCIOCCO"

1 Dissolve yeast with sugar in ¼ cup warm water in a large bowl; let stand 10 minutes. Stir in remaining water, 2 cups flour, and ½ teaspoon salt. Scrape onto a floured board; knead in ½ to 1 cup flour until smooth and elastic, about 10 minutes. Place dough in a greased bowl; turn greased side up. Cover tightly; let rise until doubled in volume, 1½ to 2 hours.

2 Meanwhile, rub a large, heavy skillet with olive oil. Brown sausage on all sides over medium heat. Cook covered 5 minutes. Remove sausage and cool slightly; cut into ¼-inch slices.

3 Wipe out skillet. Saute onion and garlic in butter in skillet until translucent. Add tomato sauce, cream, oregano, and basil. Cook over low heat 30 minutes. Season to taste with salt and pepper.

4 Scrape dough onto a floured board; knead 3 minutes. Roll out to 12×18-inch rectangle; brush lightly with olive oil.

5 Stir parsley into the tomato sauce; spread sauce over dough. Arrange sausage slices over sauce in a single layer. Dot with ricotta cheese; sprinkle with Caciocavallo cheese and salt and pepper.

6 Turn in the edges of the dough. Then, beginning at a long edge and using a long spatula, a shirt cardboard, or your hands, fold a 3-inch section toward the center; fold over again and continue until dough is rolled up.

7 Sprinkle a baking sheet with cornmeal. Place dough on sheet, seam side down; cover with a flour-dusted towel. Let rise 1 hour. Heat oven to 350°.

8 Brush dough lightly with oil; pierce in several places with a fork. Bake until loaf sounds hollow when tapped, 30 to 40 minutes. Cool on wire rack; serve at room temperature. Cut into ¾-inch slices.

For the dough:
1 package dry yeast
Pinch of granulated sugar
1¼ cups warm water
2½ to 3 cups all-purpose flour
½ teaspoon salt

For the filling:
Olive oil
1 pound mild Italian sausage
1 onion, finely chopped
1 large clove garlic, minced
3 tablespoons butter
1 jar (15½ ounces) tomato sauce
2 tablespoons whipping cream
Pinch of oregano
Pinch of basil
Salt and freshly ground pepper
1½ bunches Italian parsley (leaves only), finely chopped
4 ounces (½ cup) ricotta cheese
¾ cup grated Caciocavallo cheese or aged Provolone
Cornmeal

Serves 8.

From half a continent away from Italy's boot comes a prescription for English muffins—the *authentic* variety. Now if you are about to groan "Why bother?" bite your tongue. The genuine article is so far superior to any other muffin you have ever buttered that making it from scratch is truly worth the effort. The best I have ever tasted (or toasted for that matter), this muffin also freezes sensationally.

A mixture of yeast, potato, and grain, the English muffin has a long, long history. A version of this delectable stuff (called hearth- or hoe-cake) was chomped back in Shakespeare's time and its lineage is said to go back even further than that—to the Roman invasion of Britain, when a leavened bread was pounded and kneaded in the field during war maneuvers and baked on hot stones in a bonfire.

ENGLISH MUFFINS

1 small boiling potato
1 package dry yeast
Pinch of granulated sugar
1¼ cups warm water
1 teaspoon salt
2½ cups all-purpose flour
Cornmeal

Makes 10 muffins.

1 Cook potato in boiling, salted water until tender, 15 to 20 minutes. Drain, peel, and mash it by putting it through a food mill or potato ricer. Reserve.

2 Dissolve yeast with sugar in ¼ cup warm water in a large bowl; let stand 10 minutes. Stir in remaining water and the salt. Stir 5 tablespoons of the reserved potato into the yeast mixture until blended; stir in 2 cups flour.

3 Scrape dough onto a floured board; knead in remaining flour to make a smooth dough but do not overwork. Shape dough into a ball; place in a lightly floured bowl. Cover tightly; let rise until doubled in volume, about 1 hour.

4 Turn dough onto a floured board and flatten it with your hands. Divide into 10 pieces; roll each piece into a ball. Press balls into 4-inch circles. Let rise covered on the floured board 1 hour. (If using a baking sheet, sprinkle it with cornmeal and let muffins rise on the sheet.) Heat oven to 425°.

5 If using a tile baking surface, sprinkle it with cornmeal; place muffins on surface. Bake until muffins sound hollow when tapped, 12 to 15 minutes. Cool on wire racks. Split muffins with a fork and toast under the broiler before serving.

''Man does not live by bread alone'' was first noted in Deuteronomy 8:4 in the Old Testament. And rightly so!

The conceit that ''Bread is the staff of life'' comes from a seventeenth-century English homily but the sentiment is probably older. In recent times, the chief wage earner in a family has been dubbed ''the breadwinner.'' During the Depression, ''breadlines'' were set up on every corner. And in the hippie culture of the 1960s, the word "bread" became synonymous with dollars.

I am very old-fashioned in my bread loyalties. I prefer that my yeast be leavened traditionally, by and large. But one happy exception to this rule is an early-American prescription for Bubble Bread. I calculate that this cake is so named because the finished product resembles so many tiny buns interlaced with black currants and stuck together with a butter-and-brown sugar adhesive. Tear it apart with your fingers if you must!

OLD-TIME BUBBLE BREAD

1 Combine yeast, sugar, and water in a large bowl; let stand 10 minutes.

2 Melt ½ cup butter; combine butter with the salt and warm milk. Stir into the yeast mixture. Stir in the eggs and egg yolks.

3 Using a wooden spoon, stir in 5½ to 6 cups flour, 1 cup at a time, until dough becomes fairly stiff. Scrape onto a well floured board; knead with a pastry scraper 5 minutes, incorporating more flour as required to make a workable dough. Knead by hand 10 minutes. Shape into a ball; place in a buttered bowl. Cover with plastic wrap and a towel; let rise until doubled in volume, about 1½ to 2 hours.

4 Punch down the dough; scrape onto a lightly floured board. Let rest 10 minutes.

5 Meanwhile, melt remaining ½ cup butter with the brown sugar. Add currants. Butter a 10-inch tube pan.

6 Tear off pieces of dough and roll into 1½-inch balls. Roll each ball in the melted butter mixture and place in pan; layer dough balls loosely in pan. Place the pan on a baking sheet; pour excess melted butter mixture over top layer of dough. Cover the pan with a tent-shaped piece of aluminum foil. Let rise until dough just reaches the top of the pan. (Do not allow it to rise any higher or it will spill over during baking.) Heat oven to 375°.

7 Place the pan on the baking sheet in the oven. Bake until top of loaf sounds hollow when tapped, about 1 hour. Unmold onto a wire rack.

8 Whisk together the confectioners' sugar, vanilla, and cold milk. Spoon lightly over top and sides of hot bread. Serve while still warm or let cool.

2 packages dry yeast
1 cup granulated sugar
½ cup warm water
1 cup unsalted butter
1 tablespoon salt
1 cup warm milk
3 eggs plus 2 egg yolks, lightly beaten
6½ cups all-purpose flour (approximately)
½ cup brown sugar
½ cup dry currants, soaked in boiling water 10 minutes and drained
½ cup confectioners' sugar
¼ teaspoon vanilla
5 teaspoons cold milk

Makes 1 loaf.

My grandmother (who, I suppose, was responsible for this book in the first place) made a bread that was sort of a cake—or was it the other way around? The original formula for that ring of delights, glistening with cinnamon, melted sugar, and tantalizing bits of almonds and pecans, has been lost to the ages. Here is my reproduction—nevertheless a spectacular closing act.

I dedicate the recipe to my grandmother's kitchen bouquet, which gave mine so much color and potency.

MY GRANDMOTHER'S OLD-FASHIONED CINNAMON RING

1 package dry yeast
Pinch of granulated sugar
¼ cup warm water
1 cup warm milk
½ cup butter, melted
1¼ cups granulated sugar
1 teaspoon salt
3½ to 4 cups all-purpose flour
½ cup ground almonds
½ cup coarsely chopped pecans
¼ cup cookie crumbs
⅓ cup dry currants, soaked in cognac 1 hour
Ground cinnamon
Cornmeal
1 egg, lightly beaten
1 cup confectioners' sugar
2 tablespoons water
1 teaspoon rye whiskey

Serves 8.

1 Dissolve yeast with pinch of sugar in warm water in a large bowl; let stand 10 minutes. Stir in milk, ¼ cup melted butter, ¼ cup sugar, the salt, and 3 cups flour. Turn onto a lightly floured board. Knead, incorporating flour as required, until smooth and elastic, about 10 minutes. Shape into a ball; place in a lightly floured bowl. Cover tightly; let rise until doubled in volume, about 2 hours.

2 Punch down dough; scrape onto a lightly floured board. Let rest 3 minutes. Roll out to an 18- × 12-inch rectangle. Spread remaining ¼ cup melted butter evenly over surface. Combine 1 cup sugar with the almonds, pecans, and cookie crumbs; spread mixture evenly over the butter. Drain currants; sprinkle over the entire surface. Sprinkle with cinnamon to taste. (I prefer a lot of cinnamon, but not everyone does.) Beginning with a long edge, roll up dough.

3 Sprinkle a baking sheet with cornmeal; place dough on sheet, seam side down. Join ends to form a ring; pinch ends together to seal. Using a sharp knife, slice two-thirds of the way into the ring at 1½-inch intervals. Using two knives, gently press top of each slice into a ridge, allowing interior surfaces of slices to show. Cover with a flour-rubbed towel; let rise 1 hour. Heat oven to 350°.

4 Brush entire surface of ring with beaten egg. Bake until brown, 30 to 35 minutes.

5 Meanwhile, make icing by whisking together 1 cup confectioners' sugar, 2 tablespoons water, and 1 teaspoon rye whiskey until smooth. Spoon icing over warm cinnamon ring.

Index